PERSPECTIVES ON CONTEMPORARY ISSUES

READINGS ACROSS THE DISCIPLINES

PERSPECTIVES ON CONTEMPORARY ISSUES
READINGS ACROSS THE DISCIPLINES

KATHERINE ANNE ACKLEY
UNIVERSITY OF WISCONSIN
AT STEVENS POINT

Harcourt Brace College Publishers

Fort Worth   Philadelphia   San Diego   New York   Orlando   Austin   San Antonio
Toronto   Montreal   London   Sydney   Tokyo

Publisher	Christopher P. Klein
Executive Editor	Michael A. Rosenberg
Acquisitions Editor	John Meyers
Developmental Editor	Michell Phifer
Project Editor	Jeff Beckham
Production Manager	Diane Gray
Art Director	Vicki Whistler

Cover image by Kevin Tolman.

ISBN: 0-15-502480-9

Library of Congress Catalog Card Number: 96-76367

Address for Editorial Correspondence: Harcourt Brace College Publishers, 301 Commerce Street, Suite 3700, Fort Worth, TX 76102.

Address for Orders: Harcourt Brace & Company, 6277 Sea Harbor Drive, Orlando, FL 32887-6777. 1-800-782-4479, or 1-800-433-0001 (in Florida).

Harcourt Brace College Publishers may provide complimentary instructional aids and supplements or supplement packages to those adopters qualified under our adoption policy. Please contact your sales representative for more information. If as an adopter or potential user you receive supplements you do not need, please return them to your sales representative or send them to:

  Attn: Returns Department
  Troy Warehouse
  465 South Lincoln Drive
  Troy, MO 63379

THIS BOOK WAS PRINTED ON RECYCLED PAPER
MADE FROM 10% POST-CONSUMER WASTE AND
40% PRE-CONSUMER WASTE.
THE TOTAL RECYCLED FIBER CONTENT
IS 50% BY FIBER WEIGHT.

Printed in the United States of America

8 9 0 1 2 3 4 5 066 10 9 8 7 6 5 4 3

—

For my granddaughter Elizabeth Anne

PREFACE

Traditional curricula and course materials are typically composed of discrete, narrowly focused disciplines which give students little opportunity to see the relationship of their classes to one another. However, this textbook presents an approach to thinking, writing, and learning that views knowledge as the interconnectedness of ideas and disciplinary perspectives. It also assumes that contemporary issues engage student interest and that readings on such issues will provide rich material for both class discussion and writing topics. Hence, essays in this collection focus on individual, national, and global issues as they are treated by writers from a variety of disciplines and professions. These subjects are representative of the topics students are likely to read about and discuss across the disciplines. Likewise, writing assignments are designed to enhance writing skills that students will use no matter what their majors.

The goals of the book are to sharpen students' thinking skills by presenting them with a variety of perspectives on current issues; to give students practice in both oral and verbal expression by providing questions for discussion and writing after each selection; to provide students with a variety of writing assignments representing the kinds of writing they will be asked to do in courses across the curriculum; and to encourage students to view issues and ideas in terms of connections with other people, other disciplines, and other contexts. The questions for discussion and writing encourage critical thinking by asking students to go well beyond simple recall of the readings to use higher-order skills, such as integration, synthesis, or analysis of what they have read. Most of the discussion questions are suitable for work in small groups, a classroom strategy that can be highly engaging, challenging, and stimulating to students.

The textbook begins with a section devoted to reading and writing critically, acknowledging sources, and conducting research. It includes explanations and illustrations of summaries, paraphrases, quotations, and documentation of the materials in this book. It also provides directions for writing a synthesis. Finally, it devotes a lengthy chapter to the subject of writing a research paper. That chapter includes guidelines for taking notes, avoiding plagiarism, and documenting sources using either MLA or APA documentation styles.

The rest of the textbook is divided into four sections representing four broad disciplinary areas:

- humanities and the arts
- social sciences

- science and technology
- business and economics.

Within each broad division are chapters on specific topics related to the larger subject. "Arts and the Media" contains chapters with readings on visual arts, advertising, music, television, movies, and the role of the artist. In "Social and Behavioral Sciences," chapters address such matters as criminal behavior, multiculturalism, poverty, gender and sex roles, and international relations. In "Science and Technology," writers from a variety of disciplines explore such subjects as the relationships among science, technology and society, public health issues, the ethical implications of technology, human genetic experiments, and science and the imagination. Finally, in "Business and Economics," essays address marketing and the American consumer, the workplace, the American image abroad, and the United States in a global market.

The selections in each chapter encourage students to consider issues from different perspectives because their authors come from a wide range of disciplinary backgrounds and training. Often the writers cross disciplinary lines in their essays. For example, a psychiatrist argues for ways to combat homelessness, a chemist explores the metaphor of discovery, and a historian examines public responses to warnings about sexually transmitted diseases. The individual perspectives of the writers may differ markedly from students' own perspectives, thus generating discussion and writing topics.

The large areas and their subdivision are by no means exhaustive in their coverage of contemporary issues, nor are they meant to be restricted to their disciplinary labels. Rather, the unit headings and chapter subjects are representative of the variety of issues, topics, and concerns of individuals, of American society, or of the global population as a whole. The groups of readings in this collection are meant to reflect the truly interdisciplinary nature of our knowledge of ourselves and of society and to indicate the complexity of that interrelationship. The subject matter will generate questions, promote discussion, and enhance student understanding of issues and problems that cross disciplinary boundaries. Students may read a sociological inquiry, a scientific exploration, an examination of moral dilemmas, and an analysis of economic implications, perhaps all for the same day's assignment or within a class period or two of one another.

Following each selection, students will have an opportunity to respond on a personal level to some aspect of the reading. You may ask students to keep a journal or a special notebook for these private responses, or you may want to ask them to write for five or ten minutes at the beginning of class discussion of the essays. Each reading is also followed by questions appropriate for either small group or class discussion. These questions ask students to do more than recall facts or locate specifics of the reading. Instead, they invite students to think of larger implications, to discuss related issues, or to make connections between the readings and their own experiences. Many of these questions are appropriate for writing topics as well, and many others will prompt students and instructors to discover related topics on which to write. Finally, each chapter is followed by writing topics based on ideas generated by the collected readings in that chapter. These topics are arranged in three lists: suggestions for synthesis; additional writing topics suitable for argumentative and other modes of writing, such as the report, the letter, the personal essay, and the comparison and contrast essay; and research paper topics.

Given the title of this textbook, a definition of "issues" is in order. An issue is usually taken to mean a topic that is controversial, that prompts differences of opinion, or that can be seen from different perspectives. It often raises questions or requires taking a close look at a problem. While this is not primarily an argument textbook, the inclusion of topics and essays guaranteed to spark controversy is deliberate. Many of the readings will almost surely prompt students to take opposing positions. Some of the readings are provocative; others may anger students. Such differences of opinion will not only generate lively class discussions, but they will also result in writing opportunities that engage students.

ACKNOWLEDGMENTS

I would like to thank the following reviewers whose insights and suggestions helped to create this textbook: Diana Bowling, Arizona State U; Karen Patty-Graham, Southern Illinois U. at Edwardsville; Sarah Dye, Elgin CC; Alma Bryant, U of South Florida; Tom Hurley, Diablo Valley College; Susan Norton Stark, Boise State U; Michel de Benedictis, Miami Dade CC.

My family has been supportive in many ways during the production of this textbook. My heartfelt thanks go especially to my daughters Heather Anne Schilling and Laurel Leigh Yahi, who provided editorial assistance with the manuscript. Heather teaches English at Whitko High School, South Whitley, Indiana, and Laurel is a graphic artist for a design firm in Fort Wayne, Indiana. Both are also students. From their perspectives as both professionals and students, they provided valuable help on the selections and the questions for discussion. I am also grateful to my husband Rich Ackley, my son Jeremy White, and my sons-in-law Brian Schilling and Mourad Yahi for their encouragement during the project.

I am grateful to my colleagues in the English Department at the University of Wisconsin at Stevens Point. In particular, Tom Bloom and Ann Bloom shared their suggestions on writing an opinion paper, which I have incorporated into the discussion of the research paper, and Don Pattow, Director of Freshman English, gave me materials on writing across the curriculum. I also want to thank the following students in my English classes who gave me permission to use material from their research papers: Missy Heiman, Linda Kay Jeske, Steph Niedermair, Jennifer Sturm, and Cory L. Vandertie.

Finally, I thank Stephen T. Jordan, John Meyers, and especially Michell Phifer at Harcourt Brace College Publishers, who helped shape the project into this final form and whose assistance I greatly appreciate. They were a pleasure to work with.

CONTENTS

PART ONE

WRITING CRITICALLY AND CONDUCTING RESEARCH

CHAPTER 1

Participating in Classroom Activities

CHAPTER 2

Summarizing, Paraphrasing, and Quoting

CHAPTER 3

Documenting Sources and Writing a Synthesis

CHAPTER 4

Writing a Research Paper

CHAPTER I

PARTICIPATING IN CLASSROOM ACTIVITIES

OVERVIEW OF THE TEXTBOOK

This textbook is divided into four units representing the broad disciplinary areas of the arts and the media, social sciences, the "hard" sciences, and business and economics. Within each broad area, individual chapters present a cluster of readings on fairly specific topics or issues relevant to the broad subject area. These chapter subjects are similar to those you might take in college courses, either in your major or as general degree requirements. For example, in the unit on the arts and the media, you will find chapters on art, music, film and popular culture, advertising, and television. Obviously, a textbook cannot possibly cover all subject areas because such a text would be enormous in both size and cost, so this one is by necessity simply representative of typical courses offered at a college or university.

The readings in each chapter have been selected to represent differing perspectives on the same issue and are by no means all-inclusive or definitive. Chapter topics cover some of the most pressing concerns and issues of contemporary society, so you will already be familiar with many of them. Thus, you will bring your own understanding of the topics to bear as you read, discuss, and write about them. While few of the topics included in this textbook will be new to you, the readings will almost certainly add to and enhance your understanding. They will also in many cases provide perspectives different from your own. These differing perspectives will give you something to think about, to discuss in class, and to write about.

CHAPTER INTRODUCTIONS AND HEADNOTES

Each chapter introduction provides a context for the readings collected in the chapter and gives you a preliminary idea of the content of the readings. It also suggests questions to think about both before and while you are reading the essays. Thus, you should read the introduction to each chapter not only to gain an understanding of the nature of the subject the chapter covers but also to begin your thinking about that subject.

Each reading is preceded by a headnote giving brief biographical information about the author. These headnotes will add to your understanding of the context of the reading within the chapter by telling you something of what the author does for a living and what the author has published or worked on already. This information helps you gain a sense of the perspective from which the essay was written. Additionally, the headnote tells you where the essay was first published, again adding to your understanding of the context and perspective of the piece.

READING CRITICALLY

After reading the preparatory material, read the essay carefully, keeping an open mind. You may already have some idea of the perspective from which the author is writing, on the basis of the title and information in the headnote. But try to be as receptive and open to the author's viewpoint as possible until you have read all the way through. When you have finished reading the essay, write your response to the "Personal Response" question. Then go back through the essay once again, this time reading critically.

To be "critical" does not necessarily mean to be picky or to make objections to what someone has written. Rather, it means to be careful, thoughtful, and thorough in your consideration of the author's ideas and the evidence the author has supplied in support of those ideas. Reading critically means that you try to recognize the difference between reasonable, sensible ideas and those that are unreasonable or lack credibility. It requires you to distinguish between fact and opinion, and it requires you to sort out the evidence an author uses and to evaluate that evidence in terms of its relevance, accuracy, and importance. Thus, reading critically involves actively thinking about what you are reading.

Too often students read hastily, just to get an assignment done, without actually reflecting very long or very deeply about what they have read. However, if you want to be an active participant in the classroom, you must allow yourself some reflective time, time in which to assess the strength of an argument, the skill with which evidence is used, the degree to which you are persuaded by the author's reasoning, or other aspects of the piece that move you, anger you, or mystify you.

One important tool for an active, critical reader is a pen or pencil. On your first reading, underline, star, highlight, or make notes of words, phrases, or entire passages you think are important to the piece and that will bear looking at again when you review the essay critically. Look especially for its central idea or thesis and locate the major points of development and evidence or details that support these major points. If you have a question about something the author says, write it down. If you are struck by the beauty or logic or peculiarity of a particular passage, note it. Once you have done these things, you are ready for class discussion. Whether you agree or disagree with some or all of what the writer says, you will be prepared to explain why.

PERSONAL RESPONSE QUESTIONS

The first question after each selection asks you to respond on a personal level to some aspect of the reading because we usually react to what we read on some subjective level before we respond to it objectively. If the piece speaks to us emotionally, we react to it on that level. If it reminds us of someone else's experiences, we contextualize it accordingly. If we disagree with the essay, we respond angrily or indignantly; and if we agree, we nod approvingly or feel reassured that our views are correct. In any case, before we analyze what we read intellectually or objectively, we usually respond on this emotional plane. The personal response questions try to tap into certain aspects of the readings that you may feel more comfortable writing about than discussing or sharing with your classmates.

Your instructor may ask you to keep a journal or a special notebook for these private responses, or she or he may ask you to write in response for five or ten minutes at the beginning of the class period. Perhaps your instructor will ask students to share their personal responses with classmates, but such sharing will usually be voluntary.

CLASS AND SMALL GROUP DISCUSSIONS

The questions for class or small group discussion following each reading are designed to promote critical thinking by asking you to analyze or question what you have read. Often these questions ask you to work collaboratively in pairs or small groups, making the classroom a center for shared inquiry. Most questions are also appropriate for writing, either individually or in groups. Your instructor may assign all of the questions for discussion or select a few of them. In any event, get in the habit of reading the questions for discussion after you have read an essay the first time and responded to the personal response question. These questions will prompt your thinking on the piece, give direction to your rereading, and suggest ways in which your small group or class might handle the reading.

During the actual class period, try to participate as much as possible. Most students are shy about speaking out in class, so you may have to overcome some initial reluctance to volunteer. Keep in mind that your classmates are in the same situation and are probably feeling the same sort of apprehension you are. Pair and small group activities may make it easier for you to express your opinions. If you get to know your classmates early in the term and understand that the success of the course in some part depends on your own willingness to participate, then the small group and class discussions can be fun, stimulating, and exciting.

WRITING ASSIGNMENTS

Following each chapter is a list of writing assignments that direct you to make connections between two or among several of the pieces in that chapter or to articulate your own critical thinking on the topic. There are three categories of writing assignments: suggestions for synthesis, additional writing topics, and research topics. All of the discussion and writing topics are worded in terms that reflect a variety of approaches to intellectual inquiry that transcend disciplinary boundaries. For a quick reference, consult the glossary of terms at the end of the book. This glossary briefly defines terms used frequently in discussion questions and writing topics.

No matter what course you are writing for, you should approach all writing assignments by asking a few questions to clarify what you are expected to do. Knowing the exact nature of what is expected of you and who your audience is will be enormously helpful in writing your essay.

First, determine the nature and scope of your topic. What exactly does the assignment ask you to do? That is, what is your purpose for writing? Are you to argue, define, compare, synthesize, describe, or narrate something? Are there any terms in the assignment that you are unfamiliar with or that are open to interpretation? If so, clarify their meaning by either asking your instructor or working out from the context in which the words are used exactly what they mean. How long should your essay be? Is it to be brief or lengthy? Are you to write one page, several pages, or more? Also, what kinds of details or development are you expected to provide? Should you gather statistics, provide personal anecdotes, interview people, or incorporate the ideas of other writers into your own work?

Next, determine who your audience is. Are you writing to an audience sympathetic to your position or opposed to it? Are you writing for your peers, for your instructor, or for both? Are you to assume an audience familiar with what you are writing about or an audience who has never heard of your topic before? Is your audience specialized or general? If you are not clear who your audience is from the assignment itself, ask your instructor. Knowing who your audience is helps determine what kinds of evidence to use, what methods of development to use, what tone to take in the essay, and even what level of diction to use. It gives you direction for how much and what kinds of details you need to provide.

Directions for writing a synthesis are discussed and illustrated in Chapter 3, while the research process is discussed and illustrated in Chapter 4. The following pages briefly describe some of the common methods of developing ideas. These include argument and persuasion, cause and effect analysis, comparison and contrast, definition, exemplification, narration, and description. While these are by no means all of the ways in which writers develop their ideas, they are most likely the ones you will rely on for many of the writing assignments you do for this and other courses. You are probably familiar with them from previous courses for which you have written papers, so let this section serve as a refresher for you. Following the review of methods of development, you will find formatting guidelines for course papers, followed by a reading, complete with headnote, a personal response question, small group and class discussion questions, and writing topics.

Argument/Persuasion. Argument is a mode of persuasion in which your goal is either to convince your readers of the validity of your position (argument) or move your readers to accept your view and even act on it (persuasion). In argument, you set forth an assertion (often called *proposition*) and offer proof that will convince your readers that your position is valid or true. In persuasion, you go a step further and offer a course of action, with the ultimate goal of making your readers take action. Your evidence or proof must be so convincing that readers cannot help but agree that your position is valid. Your reasoning process must be so logical that readers inevitably draw the same conclusions that you do from the evidence.

These are not easy tasks. To set forth what you believe and provide supporting proofs that will convince readers, you will very likely rely on various modes of writing with which you are familiar and which are defined in the following sections: narration, description, cause and effect analysis, comparison/contrast, and/or exemplification. While you will be appealing primarily to readers' intellect, you may want to include an appeal to their emotions as well. Successful arguments often combine appeals to both thought and feeling.

Your primary concern in argument is to maintain an assertion you believe strongly in. To write a successful argument, state your position or assertion clearly at the beginning of your essay. State why you believe as you do, for example, that your position is worth upholding or endorsing because it has some bearing on the lives of your readers or the general common good of a community or a society. Organize your essay so that you present your least convincing or least important point first and then build to your strongest point. This pattern lends emphasis to the most important points and engages your readers in the unfolding process of your argument as you move through increasingly more compelling proofs.

For every point you make, give evidence of some sort, such as statistics, observations of authorities, personal narratives, or other supporting proof. You want to convince your readers by taking them from where they are on an issue to where you are—and where you want them to be. The only way to do this is to provide evidence that convinces readers that your position is right or true.

An excellent strategy in argument/persuasion is to address the opposition directly. Mention what those opposed to your position say, and state clearly and incontrovertibly what is wrong with their position. If you agree in part with the arguments of those opposed to you, say so. Admitting that you agree in part with the opposition is a show of strength because it suggests that you are willing to meet your opposition halfway, that is, that you do not believe as you do out of sheer stubbornness. Acknowledging what those opposed to you believe also demonstrates that you are thoroughly familiar with all aspects of an issue, that you have weighed the evidence and may even be willing to make certain concessions, but that you are sticking to your own position because of the overwhelmingly convincing nature of your evidence. If you fail to recognize or acknowledge what those opposed to you argue, then your readers are likely to think that you are careless or, worse, ignorant of all important aspects of an issue.

Many of the essays in this textbook are arguments. In fact, from time to time, arguments are paired so that you can read opposing views on an issue and determine which position, if either, you side with. See the following pairs of essays for opposing views on the same topic:

- William Lutz's "With These Words I Can Sell You Anything" and John O'Toole's "What Advertising Isn't" (Chapter 8)
- Either Newton N. Minow's "Making Television Safe for Kids" or Susan R. Lamson's "TV Violence: Does it Cause Real-Life Mayhem?" and William F. Buckley Jr.'s "Don't Blame Violence on the Tube" (Chapter 9)
- Robert Bly's "Iron John" and Alan Buczynski's "Iron Bonding" (Chapter 12)
- Charles Krauthammer's "Must America Slay All the Dragons?" and Paul Johnson's "Colonialism's Back—And Not a Moment Too Soon" (Chapter 14)
- Michael Fumento's "The AIDS Lobby: Are We Giving It Too Much Money?" and Naomi Freundlich's "No, Spending More on AIDS Isn't Unfair" (Chapter 18)

In addition, the *Time* magazine forum "Tough Talk on Entertainment" (Chapter 7) provides an excellent example of a wide variety of positions on a single issue, and Wallace S. Broecker's "Global Warming on Trial" (Chapter 19) presents the arguments of opposing sides on an issue.

Most of the writing assignments in this textbook, including suggestions for synthesis, additional writing topics, and research topics, ask you to argue a particular position on a subject. To argue convincingly and in detail, you will employ a variety of methods for developing and supporting your ideas. Some of the most common ones include cause and effect analysis, comparison and contrast, definition, exemplification, narration, and description.

Cause and Effect Analysis. Among the most common forms of inquiry are causal analysis, or determining reasons why things happen, and analysis of effects, determining what happened as a result of something. In causal analysis, a writer often wants both to determine the factors that brought something about and examine its effects. You may not always know what caused a particular event or situation nor what its long-term effects will be. There may be no readily apparent causes nor discernible effects. In that case, you must conjecture about reasons or possible effects. You will need to hypothesize what the probable causes were or, just as interesting, what might happen if something were to occur, assuming your conjecture is reasonable, given available facts.

Cause and effect analysis is used frequently in news broadcasts and magazine and newspaper articles to explain things, such as the chain of events that led to a particular action, the effects of a particular event or crisis, or both causes and effects of a specific situation. Cause and effect analysis is also used frequently to argue. If you argue that offering sex education in schools or making contraceptives readily available to high school students would be more effective in reducing the number of teenage pregnancies than a policy against showing explicit sex scenes on prime-time television, you are using the strategy of causal analysis. You will have to sort out possible causes to explain the phenomenon of the high rate of teenage pregnancies, determine which are likely most responsible and which are contributing factors, and then conjecture likely results if your recommendation were followed.

When sorting out all the data surrounding a particular event or incident, writers distinguish between immediate and remote causes and effects. An immediate cause is one that happens just before an event or phenomenon, but often other causes happen before an immediate one. You will need to decide whether the immediate cause is the most important one or if other, more remote, reasons account for the effect. If a friend drops out of college after failing a history exam, it is safe to assume that other things besides the failing grade were responsible: your friend's performance in other classes, your friend's personal problems, or your friend's financial situation. Similarly, an immediate effect happens just after an event or phenomenon, while long-term effects happen later. The pollution of air results in a depletion of the ozone layer, which in turn leads to health problems like emphysema and asthma.

Be aware of some dangers in cause and effect analysis. For instance, be careful not to assume that A caused B simply because it happened immediately before it. Another mistake is to assume that only one thing caused or was produced by something. Most of what happens to us is the result of many complex factors. Determine as many as you can when you are exploring causes, or effects, and try to determine which are most important.

Comparison/Contrast. Strictly speaking, to compare means to show how things (subjects, people, or events) are alike, while to contrast means to show how things are different. But often each term includes the other. When you want to show similarities, you may need to show differences as well, and vice versa. Comparison and contrast can be useful in an argument in which you support one of two possible choices and need to explain your reasons for the choice you made. In an expository essay—that is, one in which you explain something—comparison and contrast can be useful to demonstrate that you understand your subject thoroughly.

When comparing or contrasting, your purpose will usually be one of two things: to show each of two subjects distinctly by considering both side by side, or to evaluate or judge two things. Typically, comparisons and contrasts are organized in one of two ways: a subject by subject approach or a point by point approach. In the subject by subject approach, set forth all of the facts about subject A and then all of the facts about subject B. Then summarize the similarities or differences and state in your conclusion what you have shown. This organizational method works well for short papers or when comparison or contrast is only part of your purpose for writing because it requires readers to remember all of the points about A while reading about B. In a point by point approach, discuss each of the two things being compared or contrasted on the basis of each point. Thus, you compare or contrast as you go, a method that works better for longer papers or when the subjects are being compared or contrasted on the basis of many points.

While almost any two things can be compared and contrasted, it is often interesting to take two things that are apparently similar and show how they are different or to take two things that are apparently different and show how they are alike. As with other modes of writing, be selective in the details you choose to show similarities or differences. You cannot possibly include all points in which two things are alike or different, so choose only the most important features.

Definition. Definition is the process of making the precise meaning or significance of a thing clear. In definition, a writer conveys the essential characteristics of something by distinguishing it from all other things in its class. You are familiar with dictionary definitions of words. Writers employ a similar technique to clarify or to explain, but usually in more detail than dictionaries give. While your topic may call for a few brief definitions of terms, often you will also be called upon to provide an extended definition of something.

An extended definition takes the meaning of a word beyond its dictionary definition or beyond the limits of a simple definition. An extended definition may go for a paragraph or two or even for the length of an entire essay. If you use abstract terms or concepts unfamiliar to your audience, you will find the extended definition a useful tool. You might begin your definition with a statement of the class to which the term belongs and its chief characteristics—that is, the ways in which it differs from other members of its class—but then you will move to specific examples or illustrations of the thing. For example, you could begin a definition of poverty by saying that it is the state of being poor or the lack of the means for providing material comforts (dictionary definition). But then, to thoroughly explain what poverty is, you could provide an illustration in the form of a narrative about the experiences of a person or family you know, you could describe the squalid living conditions and inadequate meals of a particular person or family, or you could explain the effects of poverty on the health and well-being of a specific individual or group of individuals. One dramatic example or illustration often is more effective than an arsenal of statistics in an extended definition.

Exemplification. An example is an instance that reveals a whole type. When you give an example, you show the nature or character of the group from which it is taken. The example often serves to illustrate a general statement as well. Examples and illustrations are crucial to your writing, no matter what your primary purpose is. Without examples, writing will stay at the general or abstract level and leave your reader only vaguely understanding what you mean. Examples make your meaning clear and help make your writing more interesting, more lively, and more engaging than an essay without such details. Get in the habit of automatically giving examples, illustrations, or details for every general statement you make. Learn to routinely use such phrases as "for example," "for instance," "to illustrate," and other phrases that move your ideas from the general to the specific.

Examples may be brief and numerous or extended and limited in number. Whatever their length and however many there are, your purpose in exemplification is to bring some general concept, idea, or image down to a vivid, concrete, specific concept, idea, or image. There is no magic number of examples necessary to achieve this goal. You need to give as many examples or illustrations as it takes to make your point clear. When giving examples, you will find the methods of narration and description particularly useful. Sometimes an example takes the form of a narrative, that is, a brief anecdote, story, or case history. Sometimes it involves giving a vivid description of a person, place, or thing. Another useful method is comparison, whereby you use a familiar, simple example to illustrate an unfamiliar or complicated idea.

Narration. Narration is storytelling. When you narrate something, you re-create an experience for a specific purpose. Your purpose may be to explain something, to illustrate a particular point, to report information, or to argue or persuade. Often a narrative is just part of your essay, but occasionally it may be your entire means of development. A good narrative needs to have a point or specific purpose, and it holds the reader's interest by providing vivid, clear, specific details. Journalists are accustomed to asking a series of questions when they write their stories. Try answering all of them to make your narrative complete: What happened? Whom did it happen to? When did it happen? Where did it happen? Why did it happen? How did it happen, that is, under what circumstances or in what way did it happen?

The simplest method of narrating is to set down the events in chronological order, keeping in mind the importance of transition markers to make the sequence of events clear to your reader. Do not try to include every single detail of what happened. Rather, be selective. Include only important details, always keeping in mind your main purpose for telling your story. Narration often is combined with description.

Description. Description is depicting in words a person, place, or thing by appealing to the senses, that is, by evoking through words certain sights, smells, sounds, or tactile sensations. Description is an almost indispensable part of writing, certainly inextricably linked with narration. The purpose of description may be objective, to convey information without bias; or it may be subjective, to express yourself by explaining how you feel about a person, place, or thing.

As with narration and all other kinds of writing, you need to establish a purpose for your description—to be objective, subjective, or a combination of both for a particular end—and then arrange the details so that readers can see what is most important. Your purpose will be to create a definite impression for your readers, which you can achieve by using concrete, specific words to make your subject come alive. Description occurs frequently in arguments.

FORMATTING GUIDELINES FOR COURSE PAPERS

Margins, Spacing, and Page Numbers. Leave a one-inch margin on both sides and at the top and bottom of each page, except for the page number. Double space everything throughout the paper. Number pages consecutively throughout the paper except for the first page, which you need not number. Place page numbers on the right-hand side, one-half inch from the top of the paper, flush with the right margin. Some instructors request that you include your last name with each page number after the first.

Heading and Title on First Page. If your instructor tells you to put the endorsement on the first page of your paper rather than on a separate title page, drop down one inch from the top of the first page and write all of the information your instructor requires flush with the left margin. Then write your title, centered on the page. Double space between all lines, including between the date and the title and between the title and the first line of the paper. Do not underline your own title or put it in quotation marks.

```
Heather Anne Schilling

Professor Lee

English 102

November 28, 1996

          The Place of Spirituality in the College Curriculum

     Education today is more complicated than ever before.
The rapid rate at which knowledge increases and the almost
constantly changing nature of our society and the jobs
required to sustain it put great pressure on both institutions
of higher education and students alike. Colleges consider how
```

Title Page. If your instructor requires a title page, center your title about halfway down the page. Do not underline your title or use quotation marks around it. Underneath the title, write your name. Then drop down the page and put your instructor's name, the course, and the date:

The Place of Spirituality in the College Curriculum

by

Heather Anne Schilling

Professor Lee

English 102

November 28, 1996

THE HOLLOW CURRICULUM
Robert N. Sollod

Robert Sollod teaches clinical psychology at Cleveland State University. He was a member of the Task Force on Religious Issues in Graduate Education and Training for the American Psychological Association when he wrote this essay for the March 18, 1992, issue of The Chronicle of Higher Education, *a professional publication for faculty, staff, and administrators in colleges and universities.*

The past decade in academe has seen widespread controversy over curricular reform. We have explored many of the deeply rooted, core assumptions that have guided past decisions about which subjects should be emphasized in the curriculum and how they should be approached. Yet I have found myself repeatedly disappointed by the lack of significant discussion concerning the place of religion and spirituality in colleges' curricula and in the lives of educated persons.

I do not mean to suggest that universities should indoctrinate students with specific viewpoints or approaches to life; that is not their proper function. But American universities now largely ignore religion and spirituality, rather than considering what aspects of religious and spiritual teachings should enter the curriculum and how those subjects should be taught. The curricula that most undergraduates study do little to rectify the fact that many Americans are ignorant of religious and spiritual teachings, of their significance in the history of this and other civilizations, and of their significance in contemporary society. Omitting this major facet of human experience and thought contributes to a continuing shallowness and imbalance in much of university life today.

Let us take the current discussions of multiculturalism as one example. It is hardly arguable that an educated person should approach life with knowledge of several cultures or patterns of experience. Appreciation and understanding of human diversity are worthy educational ideals. Should such an appreciation exclude the religious and spiritually based concepts of reality that are the backbone upon which entire cultures have been based?

4   Multiculturalism that does not include appreciation of the deepest visions of reality reminds me of the travelogues that I saw in the cinema as a child—full of details of quaint and somewhat mysterious behavior that evoked some superficial empathy but no real, in-depth understanding. Implicit in a multicultural approach that ignores spiritual factors is a kind of critical and patronizing attitude. It assumes that we can understand and evaluate the experiences of other cultures without comprehension of their deepest beliefs.

Incomprehensibly, traditionalists who oppose adding multicultural content to the curriculum also ignore the religious and theological bases of the Western civilization that they seek to defend. Today's advocates of Western traditionalism focus, for the most part, on conveying a type of rationalism that is only a single strain in Western thought. Their approach does not demonstrate sufficient awareness of the contributions of Western religions and spirituality to philosophy and literature, to moral and legal codes, to the development of governmental and political institutions, and to the mores of our society.

Nor is the lack of attention to religion and spirituality new. I recall taking undergraduate philosophy classes in the 1960's in which Plato and Socrates were taught without reference to the fact that they were contemplative mystics who believed in immortality and reincarnation. Everything that I learned in my formal undergraduate education about Christianity came through studying a little Thomas Aquinas in a philosophy course, and even there we focused more on the logical sequence of his arguments than on the fundamentals of the Christian doctrine that he espoused.

I recall that Dostoyevsky was presented as an existentialist, with hardly a nod given to the fervent Christian beliefs so clearly apparent in his writings. I even recall my professors referring to their Christian colleagues, somewhat disparagingly, as "Christers." I learned about mystical and spiritual interpretations of Shakespeare's sonnets and plays many years after taking college English courses.

8   We can see the significance of omitting teaching about religion and spirituality in the discipline of psychology and, in particular, in my own field of clinical psychology. I am a member of the Task Force on Religious Issues in Graduate Education and Training in Division 36 of the American Psychological Association, a panel chaired by Edward Shafranske of Pepperdine University. In this work, I have discovered that graduate programs generally do not require students to learn anything about the role of religion in people's lives.

Almost no courses are available to teach psychologists how to deal with the religious values or concerns expressed by their clients. Nor are such courses required or generally available at the undergraduate level for psychology majors. Allusions to religion and spirituality often are completely missing in textbooks on introductory psychology, personality theory, concepts of psychotherapy, and developmental psychology.

Recent attempts to add a multicultural perspective to clinical training almost completely ignore the role of religion and spirituality as core elements of many racial, ethnic, and national identities. Prayer is widely practiced, yet poorly understood and rarely studied by psychologists. When presented, religious ideas are usually found in case histories of patients manifesting severe psychopathology.

Yet spiritual and mystical experiences are not unusual in our culture. And research has shown that religion is an important factor in the lives of many Americans; some studies have suggested that a client's religious identification may affect the psychotherapeutic relationship, as well as the course and outcome of therapy. Some patterns of religious commitment have been found to be associated with high levels of mental health and ego strength. A small number of psychologists are beginning to actively challenge the field's inertia and indifference by researching and writing on topics related to religion and spirituality. Their efforts have not as yet, however, markedly affected the climate or curricula in most psychology departments.

12   Is it any wonder that religion for the typical psychotherapist is a mysterious and taboo topic? It should not be surprising that therapists are not equipped even to ask the appropriate questions regarding a person's religious or spiritual life—much less deal with psychological aspects of spiritual crises.

Or consider the field of political science. Our scholars and policy makers have been unable to predict or understand the major social and political movements that produced upheavals around the world during the last decade. That is at least partly because many significant events—the remarkable rise of Islamic fundamentalism, the victory of Afghanistan over the Soviet Union, the unanticipated velvet revolutions in Eastern Europe and in the Soviet Union, and the continuing conflicts in Cyprus, Israel, Lebanon, Northern Ireland, Pakistan, Sri Lanka, Tibet, and Yugoslavia—can hardly be appreciated without a deep understanding of the religious views of those involved. The tender wisdom of our contemporary political scientists cannot seem to comprehend the deep spirituality inherent in many of today's important social movements.

Far from being an anachronism, religious conviction has proved to be a more potent contemporary force than most, if not all, secular ideologies. Too often, however, people with strong religious sentiments are simply dismissed as "zealots" or "fanatics"—whether they be Jewish settlers on the West Bank, Iranian demonstrators, Russian Baptists, Shiite leaders, anti-abortion activists, or evangelical Christians.

Most sadly, the continuing neglect of spirituality and religion by colleges and universities also results in a kind of segregation of the life of the spirit from the life of the mind in American culture. This situation is far from the ideals of Thoreau, Emerson, or William James. Spirituality in our society too often represents a retreat from the world of intellectual discourse, and spiritual pursuits are often cloaked in a reflexive anti-intellectualism, which mirrors the view in academe of spirituality as an irrational cultural residue. Students with spiritual interests and concerns learn that the university will not validate or feed their interests. They learn either to suppress their spiritual life or to split their spiritual life apart from their formal education.

16   Much has been written about the loss of ethics, a sense of decency, moderation, and fair play in American society. I would submit that much of

this loss is a result of the increasing ignorance, in circles of presumably educated people, of religious and spiritual world views. It is difficult to imagine, for example, how ethical issues can be intelligently approached and discussed or how wise ethical decisions can be reached without either knowledge or reference to those religious and spiritual principles that underlie our legal system and moral codes.

Our colleges and universities should reclaim one of their earliest purposes—to educate and inform students concerning the spiritual and religious underpinnings of thought and society. To the extent that such education is lacking, our colleges and universities are presenting a narrow and fragmented view of human experience.

Both core curricula and more advanced courses in the humanities and social sciences should be evaluated for their coverage of religious topics. Active leadership at the university, college, and departmental levels is needed to encourage and carry out needed additions and changes in course content. Campus organizations should develop forums and committees to examine the issue, exchange information, and develop specific proposals.

National debate and discussion about the best way to educate students concerning religion and spirituality are long overdue.

Personal Response

Describe the degree to which you are spiritual or religious. How important is religion in your life?

Questions for Class or Small Group Discussion

1. Sollod gives examples of how an understanding of religion and spirituality would help someone trained in his field, psychology, and how it would help political scientists. In what other disciplines or fields do you think such training would be important? Explain how it would enhance the understanding of persons trained in those fields.

2. Discuss whether you agree with Sollod that religion and spirituality have a place in the college curriculum.

3. Sollod calls for campus organizations to develop forums and committees to examine the issue of the place of religion and spirituality on the college campus and to develop specific proposals on the issue (paragraph 18). Conduct your own class forum or create a class committee to consider the issues Sollod raises. Where do people learn about spirituality? How do you think a person could benefit from learning about religion and spirituality in college courses?

Writing Topics

1. Argue in support of or against Sollod's contention that too little attention is paid to spirituality and religion at America's colleges and universities.

2. Write an editorial to your school paper in which you argue for or against the inclusion of courses on spirituality or religion in your school's curriculum.

3. Write a personal essay explaining the importance of religion in your life.

4. Sollod complains that neither traditionalists nor revisionists see a need for adding religion and spirituality to the college curriculum. Explain what is meant by the terms *traditionalist* and *revisionist* when used in the context of education. Then explain which label better describes your own views toward education and why.

CHAPTER 2

SUMMARIZING, PARAPHRASING, AND QUOTING

In many of your writing assignments for the course using this textbook, you will find frequent use for some of the information or ideas in the readings. Your instructor may ask you to write a brief summary of an entire essay or a passage from a reading. For formal writing assignments, you may choose to argue in favor of or against a position an author takes, or you may want to quote from one of the readings. You may decide to compare and contrast two or more essays, or you may want to use some of the readings in combination with library research and interviews in a research paper. No matter what your purpose, whenever you use any of the material from your textbook in writing assignments, you must be fair to the author of the material you are borrowing by accurately summarizing or paraphrasing the author's words or quoting them exactly as they appear in the text, and you must give credit to the author by naming the title of the reading, giving the page number(s) where the information is located, and stating where the work is published.

While this chapter and the next explain how to work with the materials in this textbook, the discussions of summarizing, paraphrasing, quoting, documenting sources, and synthesizing will also be of tremendous help to you when you write research papers. If you can master those skills in shorter writing assignments on the essays in this textbook, you will be ideally prepared for incorporating library materials into longer, more complex research papers. Some of the information in this and the next chapter will be repeated in the chapter on writing the research paper, but it is important information that bears repeating.

SUMMARIZING

Summarizing is the restatement of a passage or an entire essay in your own words in a much shorter version than the original. The purpose of a summary is to highlight the central idea(s) and major points of a work. Summaries do not attempt to restate the entire reading. It is possible to summarize an entire book in the space of a paragraph, for instance, though you will not be able to do full justice to a lengthy work that way. Reviewers of books or articles will summarize as they discuss and critique works, and both student and professional researchers alike find it useful to summarize an entire work as they report the results of their research. You will have occasion to summarize when you do your own research paper for this class or any other course requiring such a paper.

Some of the questions for small group and class discussion following selections in this textbook ask you to summarize major points or portions of a reading. Doing so will not only refresh your own memory, but in group work, it will

> **Guidelines for Summarizing**
> - Make notes about key points as you read, either in the margin, by high-lighting, or on a separate piece of paper.
> - Locate the thesis of the work or central idea of the passage you are summarizing.
> - Write in your own words a one-sentence statement of the thesis or central idea.
> - Locate major points the author has used to develop, illustrate, or support the thesis or central idea.
> - For each major point, write in your own words a one-sentence statement of the point and then briefly state essential details related to it.
> - Do not include minor points unless you believe their omission would not give a fair representation of what you are summarizing.
> - Keep your summary short, succinct, and focused on the central idea and major points of the piece you are summarizing.

help everyone understand the basis for discussion. Summarizing also helps impose order on your discussion or clarify any confusion people may have about the meaning of a selection. Your instructor may also ask you to summarize a piece you have read in order to gauge your understanding of it. This is a good strategy for your own study habits, too. After reading your assignment for any of your courses, try to write a summary of it. If you cannot put into your own words the major ideas of what you have just read, you may have to go back and reread it.

ILLUSTRATION: MAKING MARGINAL NOTES AND SUMMARIZING

Arthur Levine's report on his recent survey of college students is reprinted here, along with examples of the kinds of marginal notes a student might make when reading the piece. The notes simply highlight the central idea and major points of the report, so that when the student is ready to write a summary, he or she will already have marked the important points to include. Following the essay are questions for discussion and topics for writing.

THE MAKING OF A GENERATION

Arthur Levine

Arthur Levine is chair of the Institute for Educational Management and a member of the senior faculty of the Harvard Graduate School of Education. This essay appeared in the September/October 1993 issue of Change magazine.

Levine states his thesis in his first sentence.

Every college generation is defined by the social events of its age. The momentous occurrences of an era—from war and economics to politics and inventions—give meaning to lives of the individuals who live through them. They also serve to knit those individuals together by creating a collective memory and a common historic or generational identity. In 1979, I went to 26 college and university campuses, selected to represent the diversity of American higher education, and asked students what social or political events most influenced their generation. I told them that the children who came of age in the decade after World War I might have answered the Great Depression. The bombing of Pearl Harbor, World War II, or perhaps the death of Franklin Roosevelt might have stood out for those born a few years later. For my generation, born after World War II, the key event was the assassination of John F. Kennedy. We remember where we were when we heard the news. The whole world seemingly changed in its aftermath.

Introduction provides background. Levine explains a previous survey he took and what he told students then that generations of college students before them were likely to have named as the most influential social or political event in their lives.

THE ME GENERATION

For students in the 1979 survey, Vietnam and Watergate were the most influential events.

I asked what stood out for that generation of undergraduates on the eve of the 1980s. They said Vietnam and Watergate. These events had defined their world. Few could remember a time in their lives when there had been no war, and Watergate seemed a confirmation about the way the world worked in business, government, and all sectors of society. On Watergate, students' comments echoed one another:

> *"Government doesn't give a damn."*
> *"All politicians are crooks."*
> *"Nixon was like all of us, only he got caught."*
> *"It happens all the time."*
> *"I don't trust government as far as I can throw the Capitol building."*
> *"Nixon was a victim, that's all."*
> *"The whole thing was out of proportion."*

For three out of four students, the effects of Watergate and Vietnam had been distinctly negative, causing undergraduates to turn away from politics, politicians, and government. Most said they had no heroes.

Effects of those events included distrust of government, politics, and all social institutions.

Trust in all social institutions had declined among college students. A plurality of undergraduates described the major social institutions of society—Congress, corporations, labor unions, and the rest as dishonest and immoral. They expressed a belief that there was nothing left to hold onto: "Everything is bad."

This distrust led to an emphasis on the self, hence the label "the me generation."

In response, the students had turned inward, and the refuge they had chosen was "me." They described the mood on campus this way:

"*People only care about me, me, me.*"

"*We're just interested in staying alive.*"

"*We're part of the me generation.*"

"*Concerns today are not about social issues, but about me.*"

"*People are looking out for number one.*"

"*The me generation is not concerned with the good of society, but with what's good for themselves.*"

Students in the earlier survey felt optimistic about their personal futures but much less optimistic about their collective future.

Ninety-one percent of the undergraduates interviewed were optimistic about their personal futures, but only 41 percent expressed hope about their collective future together. Student interests focused increasingly on being well-off financially. At the same time they had become more and more vocationally oriented, seeking careers in the platinum professions: law, medicine, and business. They had adopted what might be called a Titanic ethic: a sense that they were riding on a doomed ship called the United States or the world, and as long as it remained afloat, they would go first class.

THE CURRENT GENERATION

Levine explains the selection criteria and numbers involved in his recent survey of college undergraduates.

The findings of the 1979 study were so telling that I decided to repeat it this academic year. Once again I, along with several colleagues, visited a diverse selection of colleges and universities across the country. We followed the same approach as the original study, meeting with intentionally heterogeneous groups consisting of 8 to 10 students on each campus. The number of institutions was raised to 28 to reflect the changing character of higher education since 1979. (This was part of a larger study including a survey of 10,000 undergraduates, a survey of 300 chief student affairs officers, and interviews with undergraduate student body presidents, newspaper editors, vice presidents and deans of students, and others.) Again we asked the undergrad-

Levine highlights each of the five commonly cited answers and discusses each in turn.

uate groups what social and political events had most influenced their generation. They gave five common answers.

Students cited the Challenger explosion most often.

Challenger.   The most frequent answer was the *Challenger* explosion. Once a student mentioned it, members of the group commonly nodded in affirmation or said "yes." It was the equivalent of the Kennedy assassination for this generation. The students all knew where they had been when they heard the news. Many had watched it on television in school. Those who had not, saw it "on the news over and over and over again." Some had been scheduled to have teacher–astronaut Christa McAuliffe teach them from space. For a number it was the first time they had ever seen an adult, their own teacher, break down and cry. It was a first brush with death for quite a few.

That students answered the *Challenger* explosion surprised me. When I thought about the responses students might give to my question, the Shuttle disaster was not on the list. My generation had witnessed other fatalities in the space program, and while the *Challenger* explosion was a very sad occurrence, it did not seem to me to be a defining moment for the nation.

Students explained that the explosion destroyed both their idealism and their sense of safety.

I asked them why they had selected the *Challenger*. Beyond the fact that it was the first shared generational tragedy, students talked of a shattering of both their idealism and their sense of safety:

"*I always thought NASA was perfect.*"

"*There were smashed dreams because of it.*"

"*My hopes were in it. There was an Asian, a black, and a woman.*"

"*Thought America invincible.*"

"*Burst my bubble.*"

"*It was something good and then it blew up.*"

"*NASA fell off its pedestal.*"

Students also said the *Challenger* explosion had marked a "wake-up call" or "reality check" for them and the nation. For some it was "a sign of a lot of things wrong" with the United States, such as in manufacturing, and for others it highlighted the decline of America due to its inability to compete economically and technologically. As one student put it, until then "I thought we were the best; we're really only second class."

The second most common answer was the fall of communism.

End of the Cold War.   The fall of communism was a second event students cited. They spoke in terms of "pride," "hope," "drama," "energy," and "a closer world." The symbol that stood out for them was the razing of the Berlin Wall.

Today's undergraduates are the last Cold War generation. They had studied Russia in school as an evil power to be feared. Although none of the 18-to-24-year-old undergraduates had seen Khrushchev bang his shoe at the U.N. or lived through the Cuban Missile Crisis, and only a small minority had engaged in duck-and-cover exercises in school, most had seen films like *The Day After,* which warned of the danger of a nuclear war. As a group, the students interviewed had been scared of the Soviet Union and afraid of the prospect of nuclear holocaust. In this sense the fall of communism was an extremely positive event.

The fall of communism has left many students worried about the instability of Central and Eastern Europe and about the Soviet nuclear arsenal.

However, the students were quite somber about the results. They regularly talked of the instability of Central and Eastern Europe, but in recent months, their focus shifted to U.S. involvement in a potential Vietnam-like ground war in Bosnia. They noted almost as frequently the danger of a now uncontrolled Soviet nuclear arsenal. They often worried whether the world was, in retrospect, a better place because of the demise of communism. One student put it this way: "For my generation, every silver lining brings a cloud."

Persian Gulf War.   The third event students mentioned was the 1991 Gulf War, which they described as "our first war"—"Every generation has a war: this was ours." Like the *Challenger* explosion, they had watched it on television. TVs in student lounges, which were usually tuned to soap operas, had stayed fixed on the war. With the rise of CNN, students joked that friends would drop by and say, "You want to watch the war for a while?" and off they would go.

Mentioned third most often by students was the Gulf War.

Despite fear of a draft and another potential Vietnam, students said the Gulf War had pulled them together. Many knew people who had been called up to serve in the Gulf. On their campuses, demonstrations against the war had tended to be tiny or absent in comparison to those in favor. The initial student reaction was pride: "We're still number one"; and "We can get things done." This seemed to be generally true among both liberal and conservative undergraduates. Students talked of flags and yellow ribbons appearing in profusion on many campuses.

By the 1992–93 academic year, undergraduate re-actions had changed, with students becoming much more critical:

"It's still a mess."

"We didn't finish the job."

"We botched another one."

"No reason to be there."

"Only a political show."

"Bush just wanted to be a hero."

"People were risking their lives and then had to return and not get jobs."

"We were in there to keep our oil prices down."

"Did it for economic interest only."

Many students were critical of the U.S. involvement in the Gulf War.

Few students were willing to speak out in favor of the Gulf War in spring of 1993 or to offer non-economic rationales for it. In conversation after conversation, students disavowed the U.S. role as world peace officer. They rejected the notion that when "anything goes wrong, we have to straighten it out."

AIDS.   A fourth event the students cited was the AIDS epidemic. AIDS has been a fact of life for this generation as long as sexuality has been a possibility for them. Many reported lectures, pamphlets, films, and condom demonstrations in school. They commonly lamented, "I hear about it all the time"; "I'm tired of it."

The AIDS epidemic has angered many young people, yet they act as if they could never get the disease. Some report that they are simply tired of hearing about it.

But more than being tired, the students were often angry. They frequently compared their situation with that of the baby boomers, complaining, "When the boomers had sex, they got laid. When we have sex, we get AIDS." One student said it this way: "Free love is more expensive [now]."

Nonetheless, even though undergraduates resented a sword dangling over their heads, they acted as if it were not there. Though most said they knew what constituted safe sex, only a minority said they prac-ticed it consistently. Students interviewed felt AIDS could not happen to them. They felt immortal. Very few knew anyone who had been diagnosed as HIV positive. Women undergraduates regularly expressed a greater fear of rape and pregnancy than AIDS.

Rodney King.   The final event students mentioned was the verdict in the Rodney King beating trial and the riots that followed. Minorities—African-Americans, Hispanics, and Asian-Americans—cited it most frequently, but by no means exclusively. Students expressed polar opinions; some had been appalled by the verdict, and others repulsed by the subsequent violence. The only commonality was the strong negative reaction:

The fifth most commonly cited event was the Rodney King beating trials and the riots that followed the verdict. Those events left students bitter and hostile about the judicial system and the police.

"I lost faith in the judicial system."

"I lost faith in the police."

"I lost confidence in people."

"It was a lesson in how to buy off a jury."

"Everything is politics."

"I used to believe the civil rights movement made a difference."

"Racism lives."

"Laws were created, but minds were not changed."

"Another shock to the system."

"Rioting inexcusable."

"Lawless."

"Verdict really disturbed me."

"I was glad. It's the only way to get people to see."

"It reminded me that society treats me differently."

"Police jobs are stressful."

WHAT DO THESE EVENTS MEAN?

Levine concludes that the five events that are significant to this generation of college undergraduates are all quite recent, and most are viewed negatively.

That the events are so recent suggests to Levine that the events their parents found significant have little or no meaning to today's students.

What stands out about the five events the students cited is first how recent they were. Most of today's freshmen were born in 1975—after John F. Kennedy's death, the end of the Great Society, the assassinations of Martin Luther King, Jr., and Robert Kennedy, the moon landing, the Watergate break-in and Richard Nixon's resignation, and the end of the war in Vietnam. They were a year old when Jimmy Carter was elected president, four when the hostages were taken in Iran, five when Ronald Reagan entered the White House, 10 when Gorbachev came to power, and 13 when George Bush became president. More than 40 percent have never heard of Hubert Humphrey, Ralph Nader, or Barry Goldwater.

As a consequence, the events that stand out to their parents and faculty have little meaning to current undergraduates. Those events do not stir the same anger, elation, frustration, or vivid emotions in students that they do in older adults. They are at best history to contemporary undergraduates.

Today's students really know only two presidents of the United States, Ronald Reagan and George Bush. They have lived through three wars, Granada, Panama, and Iraq. The longest war in their lives lasted six weeks. They are living through a period of profound demographic, economic, global, and technological change.

In addition to being recent, the five events the students cited were at least in part negative. They described three—the *Challenger* explosion, AIDS, and the Rodney King affair—in wholly negative terms, and their initial optimism about the fall of communism and the Gulf War has faded significantly. In general, students thought they were living in a deeply troubled nation in which intractable problems were multiplying and solutions were growing more distant:

Today's students are bothered by the nation's problems and believe, somewhat resentfully, that they will have to fix them.

"Our experience is of flaws, problems, decline. We're not number one in anything. Our generation grew up with that."

"The world seems to be falling apart."

"We don't have anything that stable to hold onto."

The students interviewed shared a sense that their "generation would be called on to fix everything." As a group, they rejected the likelihood of broadscale solutions. For them the five events they cited showed that such solutions are unlikely to occur and unlikely to work. They also dismissed the possibility that answers would come from government. They saw Congress as bankrupt, but held out hope for the Clinton presidency in its earliest days.

AN INCREASED, IF GUARDED, OPTIMISM

Despite their negativity, today's students feel optimistic about their personal futures and have replaced superheroes with local heroes.

Yet the students I interviewed expressed some optimism about the future. Again, more than nine out of 10 were optimistic about their personal fates, but the level of optimism about our collective future shot up to 55 percent. This is in large measure because students have shifted their focus. While they were rather negative about the future of the country, they were remarkably optimistic about the future of their communities. Today's students emphasize the local in their thinking and their action.

Heroes are back too. More than three out of four students had heroes, but those heroes were local—Mom and Dad, my teacher, my neighbor, the person leading the community clean-up campaign.

Participation in service activities increased dramatically as well. Prior to coming to college about half of all current undergraduates had been engaged in some form of community service. Such programs are booming on college campuses today as well, particularly in the area of environmentalism, a common interest among today's undergraduates. Even on some campuses in which political action was low or absent, recycling bins have appeared at the behest of students.

Although they have some optimism, students also are afraid and angry about the job market, the economy, and possible environmental disasters, among other things.

Nonetheless, fear and anger were a part of the conversation with every student group I interviewed. Current undergraduates were afraid of being unable to find jobs, of living in an economy in which they will do less well than their parents, of facing a mounting national debt, of having to contend with environmental disasters, and much, much more. They felt put upon, cheated, and robbed of the opportunity that had been given to previous generations. They especially resented the baby boomers for their advantages. They criticized the students of the 1980s for their "me-ism."

In conclusion, this generation seems torn between looking out for themselves and working for the common good.

For most of the students interviewed, the real struggle was choosing between making money and performing good deeds. Six out of eight undergraduates said it was essential or very important to be very well-off financially, but five out of eight said it was essential or very important to have a career that would make a meaningful social contribution. The big issue facing students I interviewed was how to choose. Most didn't want to be Donald Trump, but the prospect of Mother Teresa was not all that appealing either. Above all, this is a generation torn between doing good and doing well.

Personal Response

What motivates you when thinking about choosing a career? Do you think you will be driven by financial desires or by other reasons?

Questions for Class or Small Group Discussion

1. Discuss the five events that Levine discovered have had the most impact on today's generation of undergraduate students. Are they events you would have named? If not, what other events would you name? How have these events affected you personally? Share your answer with your classmates.

2. Respond to the remark that students feel that "their 'generation would be called on to fix everything'" (paragraph 25). Do you believe that your generation can fix the problems created by previous generations? Do you think you should have to? If your generation does not do it, then who will?

3. Discuss to what degree you and your classmates feel optimistic about the future. Are you more or less hopeful about the future of the global community than you are about your own personal future and that of your community?

4. Discuss to what extent you fear the future. What problems do you foresee? What makes you fearful?

5. Three-fourths of the students Levine interviewed said they had heroes. If you have heroes, who are they? Do you and your classmates have the same heroes?

Writing Topics

1. Using Levine's essay as a starting point, explain what social or political event has had the most influence on your life. Argue for its importance as a key influence by explaining the impact the event has had on you personally and how you believe it has affected society in general.

2. Explain the degree to which you feel optimistic about either your personal future or the future of your country and why.

3. Argue for or against taking an optimistic viewpoint about the future of your community by identifying those aspects or characteristics of it that support your position.

4. If you have a hero or heroes, state who they are and defend your reasons for regarding them as heroes. Include a definition of "hero" in your argument.

SUMMARY OF ARTHUR LEVINE'S
"THE MAKING OF A GENERATION"

In "The Making of a Generation," Arthur Levine reports the results of his 1993 survey of undergraduates at 28 American colleges and universities to support his thesis that college students are defined by the key social and political events of their age. To provide background for the report and comparative analysis that follows, Levine first explains the results of his 1979 survey of college students, who cited the Vietnam War and the Watergate scandal as most significantly affecting them. Those events produced a generation of people preoccupied with themselves rather than with the larger society.

The event cited most frequently by students in Levine's 1993 survey was the *Challenger* explosion. When asked why that event had had such a profound effect on them, most reported that the tragedy had both disillusioned them and shaken their sense of safety. The second event cited was the fall of communism, which students viewed positively, though their enthusiasm had been dampened somewhat by the instabilities in many Central and Eastern European countries that erupted as a result of that fall. In third, fourth, and fifth places, respectively, were the Persian Gulf War, which many viewed critically; the AIDS epidemic, which both terrifies and angers many young people; and the verdict in the Rodney King beating trial and the riots that followed, which left many students feeling disillusioned about the police, the judicial system, and humanity in general.

According to Levine, his survey reveals that while many of today's generation of college undergraduates feel as if their personal success is manageable, they are uncertain about the future of their society and find themselves torn between choosing a career that provides personal financial security and one that makes some meaningful contribution to society.

PARAPHRASING

Paraphrasing is similar to summarizing in that you state in your own words what someone else has written, but a paraphrase restates everything in the passage rather than highlights just the key points. Whereas summaries are useful for presenting the major points or ideas of long passages or entire works, paraphrases are most useful for clarifying or emphasizing the main point of a short passage. To paraphrase, put the ideas of the author in your own words, being careful not to use phrases or key words of the original. Paraphrases are sometimes as long as the original passage, though often they are slightly shorter. The purpose of paraphrasing is to convey the essence of a sentence or passage in an accurate, fair manner and without the distraction of quotation marks. If in your paraphrase you use the exact words of the original, then you are quoting and must put quotation marks around those words. Your paper will be more interesting and readable if you paraphrase more often than you quote. Think of your own reaction when you come across long quotations in your reading. If you are like most people, you probably tend to skip over or skim quickly long quoted passages. Readers are usually more interested in the ideas of the author, not in his or her skill at quoting others.

Guidelines for Paraphrasing
- Put the essential idea of the passage in your own words.
- Never repeat word for word any part of the original.
- If you must use a phrase, clause, or sentence exactly as it is in the original, put quotation marks around those words.
- Keep the paraphrase about the same length as the original.
- Give the source of the paraphrased information either in your text or immediately after the paraphrase, parenthetically.

QUOTING

For quoting directly, write the words exactly as they appear in the material you are borrowing from, using quotation marks before and after the words. Copy the words *exactly* as they appear in the text. Do not omit words or insert your own words when you quote directly. Be selective in the material you choose to quote. It is usually better to paraphrase the words of another, putting them into your own words, rather than copy the words exactly. You should quote only those passages that are especially well written or that you believe you cannot rephrase fairly without changing their meaning or effect. As with paraphrases, provide the source of the material you have quoted by either mentioning it in your text as you introduce the quotation or in a parenthetical note following the quotation.

Guidelines for Quoting
- Be selective in what you quote directly.
- Put quotation marks before and after the words you have quoted.
- Do not change one word of the material you quote without indicating that you have done so by using brackets, ellipses, or other conventions (see Chapter 4).
- Provide the source of the quoted material either in your text or in parentheses following the material.

ILLUSTRATION: PARAPHRASING AND QUOTING

Here are some examples of paraphrases and quotations from Gerald Graff's "Ships in the Night," which is reprinted following this section. For more discussion and examples of paraphrasing and quoting, see the sample synthesis in Chapter 3 and the discussion of incorporating sources into your research paper, as well as the excerpts from student papers in Chapter 4. Following Graff's essay are a personal response question, questions for small groups or class discussion, and writing topics. First, here is a brief summary of Graff's essay:

> In an excerpt from his book *Beyond the Culture Wars: How Teaching the Conflicts Can Revitalize American Education*, Gerald Graff argues that classrooms are essentially "ships passing in the night" because most of the courses students take seem completely unrelated to one another. Graff contends that too often individual instructors make their classrooms isolated communities and, by doing so, prevent open conversations across the disciplines.

Direct quotation (from paragraph 3)

> Gerald Graff suggests that college students have become "cynical relativists who care less about convictions than about grades and careers" (34).

Note: Direct quotations must always be introduced in some manner. One common method is to simply name the authority who is being quoted, in this case the author of the essay. The parenthetical citation after the quotation gives the page number in the source where the quotation is located. This example contains only the page number because the author's name has already been mentioned. If the author's name had not been given in the text, it would be included in the parenthetical citation.

Paraphrase (from paragraph 5)

> In discussing the factors that confuse people about college curricula today, Gerald Graff points out that both traditionalists and revisionists are angry over the canon debate (34).

Note: Even when you paraphrase, you need to indicate that you are borrowing material and give a page number where the paraphrased material is located in the source. One way of signaling that you are borrowing material is to name your authority. Here is an alternative way of identifying the source or authority, based on information supplied in the headnote to the Graff essay:

> In discussing the factors that confuse people about college curricula to-day, a professor at the University of Chicago points out that both traditionalists and revisionists are angry over the canon debate (Graff 34).

Note: Graff's name must be given in the parenthetical citation because it is not mentioned in the text, as it is in this example:

> In his 1992 book *Beyond the Culture Wars: How Teaching the Conflicts Can Revitalize American Education,* Gerald Graff points out that both traditionalists and revisionists are angry over the canon debate (34).

Paraphrase and direct quotations (from paragraph 8)

> In illustrating his point that students often have to readjust their thinking to conform to the approaches of different disciplines, Graff refers to one study of a bright student who did quite well in her freshman humanities course but earned a C in a social science course. "Imagine," he remarks, "trying to write an academic paper when you sense that . . . the intellectual moves that got you an A in existentialist philosophy may get you a C minus and a dirty look in Skinnerian behaviorism" (36).

Note: The three spaced periods (ellipsis points) indicate that words have been omitted from the original.

Paraphrase and direct quotation (from paragraph 20)

> College catalog covers provide "the most familiar representation of the sentimental image of the course as a scene of conflict-free community" when they portray students sitting outside on a sunny day, mesmerized by the instructor who stands before them, reading someone's words of insight or wisdom. The classroom becomes "a garden occupying a redemptive space inside the bureaucratic and professional machine" (Graff 39–40).

SHIPS IN THE NIGHT

Gerald Graff

Gerald Graff is a professor of English and education at the University of Chicago. He has published a number of books, including Literature Against Itself *(1981),* Professing Literature *(1989),* The Myth of Cultural Decline *(1992),* The Struggle for the University *(1992), and* Beyond the Culture Wars: How Teaching the Conflicts Can Revitalize American Education *(1992), from which this reading is excerpted.*

An undergraduate tells of an art history course in which the instructor observed one day, "As we now know, the idea that knowledge can be objective is a positivist myth that has been exploded by postmodern thought." It so happens the student is concurrently enrolled in a political science course in which the instructor speaks confidently about the objectivity of his discipline as if it had not been "exploded" at all. What do you do? the student is asked. "What else can I do?" he says. "I trash objectivity in art history, and I presuppose it in political science."

A second undergraduate describes a history teacher who makes a point of stressing the superiority of Western culture in developing the ideas of freedom, democracy, and free market capitalism that the rest of the world is now rushing to imitate. She also has a literature teacher who describes such claims of Western supremacy as an example of the hegemonic ideology by which the United States arrogates the right to police the world. When asked which course she prefers, she replies, "Well, I'm getting an A in both."

To some of us these days, the moral of these stories would be that students have become cynical relativists who care less about convictions than about grades and careers. In fact, if anything is surprising, it is that more students do not behave in this cynical fashion, for the established curriculum encourages it. The disjunction of the curriculum is a far more powerful source of relativism than any doctrine preached by the faculty.

4   One of the oddest things about the university is that it calls itself a community of scholars yet organizes its curriculum in a way that conceals the links of the community from those who are not already aware of them. The courses being given at any moment on a campus represent any number of rich potential conversations within and across the disciplines. But since students experience these conversations only as a series of monologues, the conversations become actual only for the minority who can reconstruct them on their own. No self-respecting educator would deliberately design a system guaranteed to keep students dependent on the whim of the individual instructor. Yet this is precisely the effect of a curriculum composed of courses that are not in dialogue with one another. . . .

Among the factors that make academic culture more confusing today than in the past is not only that there is more controversy but that there is even controversy about what can legitimately be considered controversial. Traditionalists are often angry that there should even *be* a debate over the canon, while revisionists are often angry that there should even be a debate over "political correctness," or the relevance of ideology and politics to their subjects. A recent feminist critic says she finds it "astonishing" that it still needs repeating at this late date that "the perspective assumed to be 'universal' which has dominated knowledge . . . has actually been male and culture-bound."[1] Since the feminist argument, however, is that

---

[1] Gayle Green, "The Myth of Neutrality, Again?" in *Shakespeare Left and Right,* ed. Ivo Kamps (New York: Routledge, 1991), p. 24.

we still fail to see how culture-bound our thinking is, it is hard to see why this critic should be astonished that she still needs to make the point. Another political critic writes that "we are perhaps already weary of the avalanche of papers, books, and conferences entitled 'The Politics of X,' and we have recently begun to question that most hallowed of all political slogans on the left, 'everything is political.'"[2] Yet the idea of politics that this critic and her audience are already "weary of" is one that most people have not yet encountered and might well find incomprehensible. The "advanced" academic and the layperson (or the traditional academic) are so far apart that what is already old news to one has not yet become intelligible to the other.

Imagine how this affects students who, at the moment they are negotiating the difficult transition from the lay culture to the academic culture, must also negotiate the unpredictable and unfathomable discrepancies between academic departments and factions. When there is no correlation of the different discourses to which students are exposed, it becomes especially difficult for them to infer which assumptions are safe and which are likely to be challenged. The problem is that knowledge of what is and is not considered potentially or legitimately controversial cannot be learned a priori; you cannot get it out of E. D. Hirsch's *Dictionary of Cultural Literacy.* Such knowledge comes only through interaction with a community, and that interaction is precisely what is prevented by a disconnected system of courses. Then, too, assumptions about what is and is not potentially controversial tend to change from one moment to the next and one subcommunity to the next, and they are changing at a faster rate today than in the past.

Thomas S. Kuhn in *The Structure of Scientific Revolutions* describes moments of crisis or "paradigm shift" in the sciences, when "a law that cannot even be demonstrated to one group of scientists may . . . seem intuitively obvious to another."[3] The fate of Kuhn's own book is an interesting case in point. Even as his sociological account of scientific paradigm change has been treated as virtual holy writ by many literary theorists (for a while it seemed almost obligatory to begin every book or essay with a respectful bow to Kuhn), his work has often been ignored or dismissed by scientists and philosophers of science, who accuse him of subverting the concept of objective truth in reducing scientific discovery to "mob psychology." As the controversy over Kuhn has revealed, both the literati and the scientists have remained largely walled up within their clashing assumptions about objectivity, the smugness of which might have been punctured had these parties been forced to argue with each other in their teaching. This mutual smugness has persisted in the sniper fire that continues to be

---

[2] Diana Fuss, *Essentially Speaking: Feminism, Nature and Difference* (New York: Routledge, 1989), p. 105.

[3] Thomas S. Kuhn, *The Structure of Scientific Revolutions,* 2d ed. (Chicago: University of Chicago Press, 1970), p. 150.

exchanged over the concept of objectivity and the extent to which knowledge is independent of the social situation of the knower; revisionists sneer at the concept and traditionalists sneer at the very idea of questioning it.

8   The question neither group seems to ask is what it must be like to be a student caught in the crossfire between these conflicting views of objectivity, each one prone to present itself as "intuitively obvious" and uncontroversial. A rhetoric scholar, Gregory Colomb, has studied the disorientation experienced by a bright high school graduate who, after doing well in a humanities course as a freshman at the University of Chicago, tried to apply her mastery to a social science course, only to come up with a grade of C.[4] Imagine trying to write an academic paper when you sense that almost anything you say can be used against you and that the intellectual moves that got you an A in existentialist philosophy may get you a C minus and a dirty look in Skinnerian behaviorism.

Consider the fact that the passive voice that is so standard in sociology writing ("it will be contended in this paper . . .") has been perennially rebuked in English courses.[5] Or consider something so apparently trivial as the convention of using the present tense to describe actions in literature and philosophy and the past tense to describe them in history. Plato *says* things in literary and philosophical accounts while in historical accounts he *said* them. Experienced writers become so accustomed to such tense shifting that it seems a simple matter, but it reflects deep-rooted and potentially controversial differences between disciplines. Presumably, Plato speaks in the present in literary and philosophical contexts because ideas there are considered timeless; only when we move over to history does it start to matter that the writer is dead.[6] We English teachers write "tense shift" in the margin when student writers betray uncertainty about this convention, but how do we expect them to "get" it when they pass from the very different time zones of history and philosophy/English with no engagement of the underlying issues?

One of the most frequent comments teachers make on student papers is "What's your evidence?" But nobody would ever finish a piece of writing if it were necessary to supply evidence for everything being said, so in order to write, one must acquire a sense of which statements have to be supported by evidence (or further argument) and which ones a writer can get away with because they are already taken for granted by the imagined audience. What happens, then, when a writer has no way of knowing whether an assumption that he or she got away with with audience A will

---

[4] Gregory Colomb, *Disciplinary "Secrets" and the Apprentice Writer: The Lessons for Critical Thinking* (Upper Montclair, N.J.: Montclair State College, Institute for Critical Thinking, 1988), pp. 2–3.

[5] For this point I am indebted to an unpublished talk by Susan Lowry.

[6] I am indebted for this point to Susan H. McLeod, "Writing across the Curriculum: An Introduction," forthcoming in *Writing across the Curriculum: A Guide to Developing Programs,* eds. McLeod and Margot Soven (Newberry Park, Calif.: Sage, 1992).

also be conceded by audience B? It is no wonder that students protect themselves from the insecurity of such a situation by "psyching out" each course as it comes—and then forgetting about it as soon as possible after the final exam in order to clear their minds for the seemingly unrelated demands of the next set of courses.

It is not only ideas and reasoning processes but the recall of basic information as well that figure to be impaired by disjunctive curricular organization. To use the jargon of information theory, an information system that is experienced as an unrelated series of signals will be weak in the kind of redundancy that is needed for information to be retained. Faced with a curriculum overloaded with data and weak in redundancy, students may find it difficult to know which items of information they are supposed to remember. Then, too, a student may be exposed to the same information in several courses while failing to recognize it as "the same," since it is contextualized differently in each course. When students fail to identify a cultural literacy item on a test, the problem may be not that they don't know the information but that they don't know they know it; they may have learned it in a context whose relevance to the test question they don't recognize. What is learned seems so specific to a particular course that it is difficult for students to see its application beyond.

12   The critic Kenneth Burke once compared the intellectual life of a culture to a parlor in which different guests are forever dropping in and out. As the standard curriculum represents the intellectual life, however, there is no parlor; the hosts congregate in separate rooms with their acolytes and keep their differences and agreements to themselves. Making one's way through the standard curriculum is rather like trying to comprehend a phone conversation by listening at only one end.[7] You can manage it up to a point, but this is hardly the ideal way to do it.

To venture a final comparison, it is as if you were to try to learn the game of baseball by being shown a series of rooms in which you see each component of the game separately: pitchers going through their windups in one room; hitters swinging their bats in the next; then infielders, outfielders, umpires, fans, field announcers, ticket scalpers, broadcasters, hot dog vendors, and so on. You see them all in their different roles, but since you see them separately you get no clear idea of what the game actually looks like or why the players do what they do. No doubt you would come away with a very imperfect understanding of baseball under these conditions. Yet it does not seem farfetched to compare these circumstances with the ones students face when they are exposed to a series of disparate courses, subjects, and perspectives and expected not only to infer the rules of the academic-intellectual game but to play it competently themselves.

---

[7] I adapt an observation made in a somewhat different context by Mary Louise Pratt, "Humanities for the Future: Reflections on the Western Culture Debate at Stanford," in *Politics of Liberal Education,* p. 19.

It is tempting to blame these problems on bad teaching, seemingly rectifiable by encouraging instructors to be more sensitive to their students' predicament. Certainly more sensitivity on the part of teachers would help. But even the most sympathetic and sensitive teacher cannot be sure which of his or her views may be flatly contradicted by the next teacher encountered by his or her students. Then, too, though good teaching may have its inherently individualistic aspects, we all need others at times to counteract our biases and to make up for our gaps in knowledge. For this reason the problems I have been discussing cannot be effectively addressed at the level of individual teaching. They are curricular problems, and a curriculum is not simply the sum total of separate acts of teaching but a systematic organization of teaching. In fact, the habit of reducing all questions about education to questions about individual *teaching* discourages us from thinking systematically about the curriculum. Our very use of the term "the classroom" to stand for the entire educational process is a symptom of this constricted way of thinking, which I call the "course fetish," though it might also be called the "cult of the great teacher."

How well one can teach depends not just on individual virtuosity but on the possibilities and limits imposed by the structure in which one works. It may not hold for everyone, but I believe I am a better teacher when I am able to take my colleagues as reference points in my classroom. As long as teaching is viewed as an inherently solo performance, too much is made to depend on the teacher's personal resources, something which puts teachers under inordinate pressure and makes for burnout. Only a weak system would depend on perpetual feats of personal virtuosity to keep it functioning at its best.

16   This point has been made by a powerful critic of the course system, Joseph Tussman, a reformer who helped develop an experimental program at the University of California at Berkeley. . . . In a book on the program published in 1969, Tussman pointed out that the course system had become so pervasive "that we have come to regard the conditions of course teaching as the conditions of teaching in general." He argued that the problem with the course system is that since "the courses are generally unrelated and competitive, . . . each professor knows that he has a valid claim to only a small fraction of the student's time and attention. The effect is that no teacher is in a position to be responsible for, or effectively concerned with, the student's total educational situation. The student presents himself to the teacher in fragments, and not even the advising system can put him back together again." These limiting conditions, noted Tussman, are ones "of which every sensitive teacher is bitterly aware. But there is nothing he can do about it. He can develop a coherent course, but a collection of coherent courses may be simply an incoherent collection."[8]

As Tussman maintained, the only effective unit for educational plan-

---

[8] Joseph Tussman, *Experiment at Berkeley* (New York: Oxford University Press, 1969), p. 6.

ning is the *program,* not the course. We tend, however, to associate programs and systems with bureaucracy, mechanization, and institutionalization, terms lacking in the sentimental emotional resonance that we attach to the idea of "the classroom" presided over by the great teacher. The magical aura of "the classroom" lies in the illusion that it is not part of a system at all, that it is an island somehow exempt from the incursions of bureaucracy. We know that the truth is otherwise, that courses have to be scheduled, assigned to rooms, listed in the catalog, and assimilated to the grid of credit hours, requirements, and grades. The course, however, is experienced not as an extension of bureaucratic organization but as a force that transcends and redeems bureaucratic organization and makes it tolerable.

This explains why we frequently hear academics speak irreverently about the existence of *departments* but hardly ever about their courses, though the course is an expression of the same process of bureaucratic specialization and privatization that produced the department. The department is thought to epitomize the divisive, competitive, meanly professionalized aspects of academic life. Its existence is a reminder of the arbitrary fences with which each discipline selfishly guards its disciplinary turf, of factional rivalry and a narrowly self-serving and proprietary view of intellectual life. The faculty meeting, an expression of the departmental ethos, typifies this realm of petty strife from which the course is felt to be a saving escape. As Tussman put it, "the faculty meeting—college, departmental, or committee—is the abrasive ordeal from which one flees to the delicious, healing privacy of one's own course."[9]

Whereas the department epitomizes the bureaucratic aspects of academic life, the course does not feel like a bureaucratic entity at all. Thus "the classroom" is believed to be what the university is really all about after we factor out the necessary evils of administration, departments, publish or perish, research, faculty meetings, and even the curriculum itself, which are seen as realms of conflict. This symbolic opposition in all its sentimentality is neatly exemplified in the recent popular film *Dead Poets Society,* in which a brilliantly creative and eccentric teacher of literature is pitted against a puritanical, repressive, and life-denying prep school administration.

20   But the most familiar representation of the sentimental image of the course as a scene of conflict-free community is the one presented on untold numbers of college catalog covers: A small, intimate class is sprawled informally on the gently sloping campus greensward, shady trees overhead and ivy-covered buildings in the background. Ringed in a casual semicircle, the students gaze with rapt attention at a teacher who is reading aloud from a small book—a volume of poetry, we inevitably assume, probably Keats or Dickinson or Whitman. The classroom, in these images, is a garden occupying a redemptive space inside the bureaucratic and professional

---

[9] Ibid., p. 11.

machine. It is a realm of unity and presence in a world otherwise given over to endless difference, conflict, competition, and factionalism. The classroom resembles the primitive Protestant Church, freed from the ecclesiastical externals that only tend to intervene between the believer and the authentic experience of the sacred texts. The curriculum, by contrast, is identified with the bureaucratic machine and is represented in the catalog not in pastoral images but in mechanically numbered lists of departments, courses, and requirements, although the cold linearity of this organization in its own way obscures the conflicts between departments and courses.

To the extent that the curriculum is associated with alien bureaucracy, the course fetish carries with it a certain disbelief in the very need for a curriculum. Underlying the course fetish finally is a conviction (as I recently heard a prominent philosopher and educational theorist say) that there is nothing wrong with today's education that cannot be cured by getting good teachers together and simply turning them loose. And there is a certain truth to this view. No doubt the best things that happen in universities *are* the things that happen in "the classroom." But the romance of "the classroom" blinds us to the steep educational price we pay when classrooms are isolated from one another.

"The classroom" embodies a contradiction: In the process of creating one kind of community it thwarts the community that it could be constituting with other courses.[10] For students, this results in the effects of cognitive dissonance that I described at the beginning of this chapter. For faculty as well as students it results in a stifling lack of intellectual community. It is not surprising that professors flock in increasing numbers to professional conferences and symposia, where they find the kind of collegial discussion that rarely occurs at home. No wonder they feel a lack of community at home when they spend so much of their time there isolated from one another in their courses.

To say this, to be sure, is to go against the widespread belief that professors now spend all too *little* of their time in their courses. This is sometimes indeed the case—though I think far less commonly than is thought. The more fundamental question we should be asking in most cases is not *how much* time teachers are spending in the classroom but *under what conditions*. Spending adequate time in the classroom is obviously crucial, but that time would be spent less wastefully if each classroom were not off limits to other classrooms, if classrooms formed a conversation instead of a set of ships passing in the night.

---

[10] I fail to do justice here and elsewhere in this book to a popular and valuable innovation that goes under the name of "collaborative learning" and is identified with work by Ken Bruffee, John Trimbur, Andrea Lunsford, Lisa Ede, and others. I agree with much of this work but believe that its logic points to something beyond "the classroom" as the locus of dialogue. On collaborative learning, see the essays by Bruffee and Trimbur mentioned in n. 7 to Chapter 4 [of Graff's *Beyond the Culture Wars*] Andrea Lunsford and Lisa Ede, *Singular Texts/Plural Authors: Perspectives on Collaborative Writing* (Carbondale, Ill.: Southern Illinois Press, 1990).

Personal Response

Do you agree with Graff that students are cynical about the courses they take? Are you more interested in grades and your career than you are about your convictions (paragraph 3)? Explain your answer.

Questions for Class or Small Group Discussion

1. Summarize in your own words what Graff's point is about the "disjunction of the curriculum" (paragraph 3). Explain any experiences you have had with the kind of disjunction Graff illustrates in his opening paragraphs or the confusion he describes in paragraph 9.

2. Discuss what you understand Graff to mean by the term "psyching out" (paragraph 10). Do you agree with Graff that students have to "psych out" their courses? If you have ever "psyched out" a course, explain how you did it.

3. Have you ever taken a cross-disciplinary course, one in which instructors from different disciplines collaborated? If so, describe that course. If not, try to imagine such a course. What disciplines do you think would work well together? How might such a course be constructed? What are the advantages and disadvantages of cross-disciplinary or team-taught courses?

4. How do you think classrooms might form a conversation (last paragraph)? Is such a "conversation" possible? Is it practical? How would you envision such a conversation taking place?

5. Find a classmate who has a different major from yours. Together, design a course that integrates your two disciplines.

Writing Topics

1. Argue in support of or against Gerald Graff's comment that students "have become cynical relativists who care less about convictions than about grades and careers" (paragraph 3).

2. Taking into account Graff's point about the "disjunction of the curriculum," narrate your personal experience with the kind of disjunction he illustrates in his opening paragraphs or the confusion he describes in paragraph 9.

3. Write an essay illustrating ways in which students "psych out" their courses, using personal experience if possible.

4. If you have ever taken a cross-disciplinary course, describe the course and evaluate your experiences in it. What do you think are the advantages and disadvantages of cross-disciplinary or team-taught courses?

CHAPTER 3

DOCUMENTING SOURCES AND WRITING A SYNTHESIS

Whenever you paraphrase or quote the ideas or words of someone else, you are required to state what the source is and on what page number the paraphrased or quoted material appears in that source. You will recall that the examples of paraphrases and quotations in Chapter 2 are followed by parenthetical citations to the source material. This naming of source material is called documenting your source. Many of the writing assignments you will do for this and other courses will involve borrowing the ideas and words of other authors. For the course in which you are using this textbook, you will have to document sources when you write papers that incorporate references to the readings in the book, and if you write a research paper, you will most certainly have much opportunity to document sources. The discussion in this chapter focuses on documenting the sources in this textbook but applies to documentation in general, no matter what your writing purpose and source material. The examples in this chapter demonstrate the documentation style endorsed by the Modern Language Association (MLA) and used in most disciplines in the humanities. For the documentation style of the American Psychological Association (APA), see Chapter 4.

To document the source of material you are borrowing, provide a parenthetical citation in your paper immediately after the quoted or paraphrased

---

Guidelines for Documenting Sources
- Provide a citation every time you paraphrase or quote directly from a source.
- Give the citation parenthetically following the quotation or paraphrase.
- In the parentheses, give the author's last name and the page number or numbers from which you took the words or ideas. Do not put any punctuation between the author's last name and the page number.
- If you name the author as you introduce the words or ideas, the parentheses will contain only the page number(s).
- At the end of your paper, make an alphabetical list of the authors you quoted or paraphrased and give complete bibliographic information, including not only author and title but also where it was published. This is the Works Cited page.

---

material. This citation includes the author's name and the page number on which the material appears. At the end of your paper, provide an alphabetical list of the works you quoted from or paraphrased from, following the formatting guidelines for documenting sources discussed in Chapter 4. While a complete discussion and guidelines for documenting sources appear in Chapter 4, the following guidelines will be useful for shorter papers using materials reprinted in this textbook.

DOCUMENTING SOURCES FROM
THIS TEXTBOOK USING MLA STYLE

You must give a citation when you use the exact words of another (in which case you use quotation marks before and after the borrowed words) or when you borrow the ideas of another person and put the ideas in your own words. Using the ideas or words of another person without acknowledging the source is plagiarism. Simply defined, plagiarism is the borrowing of another person's words without giving proper credit to that person. (A full discussion of plagiarism, including examples, appears in Chapter 4.)

When you document a source, you are giving credit to the material or ideas of someone else by naming the author, the title of the work, and where it was published. Any time you borrow the words or ideas of someone else, you need a citation. This section addresses the matter of how to document material that appears in this textbook, but the same principles apply to sources you get elsewhere. For more information on documenting sources, see the sections on taking notes and avoiding plagiarism in Chapter 4, which is on writing the research paper. Because *Perspectives on Contemporary Issues* is a collection of other people's works, not the editor's, you will probably not have occasion to use the words or ideas of Ackley herself. Because you are not reading the material in its original source, however, you must indicate that you have read it in her book.

Citing One Source. Suppose you want to quote or paraphrase a statement from Robert Hughes's essay "Behold the Stone Age." After you give either the exact words of Hughes or your paraphrase of his words, put a parenthesis, then his last name and the page number where you read the words *with no punctuation between them,* and then close the parenthesis: (Hughes 96). Do not write the word "page" or "pages" nor insert a comma between the author's name and the number of the page. If Hughes's piece is the only one you use in your paper, write "Work Cited" at the end of your paper and enter complete bibliographic information for the Hughes article:

> Hughes, Robert. "Behold the Stone Age." <u>Perspectives on Contemporary
> Issues: Readings Across the Disciplines</u>. Ed. Katherine Anne Ackley.
> Fort Worth: Harcourt Brace College Publishers, 1997. 96–100.

Citing Two or More Sources. If you use two or more essays from Ackley (or from any collection of essays), you do not need to repeat the full information for the collection with each essay. Instead, list the collection by the editor's name, giving full bibliographic information for it. Then list separately each article you use by author and title, but after the essay title, give only the collection editor's name and the inclusive page numbers of the essay.

For example, suppose in a paper on the "Art and Artists" chapter you use information or words from not only the Hughes article but also from Norman Cousins' "The Poet and the Computer" and Diana Jean Schemo's "Between the Art and the Artist Lies the Shadow." Here is how your Works Cited page would look:

> Ackley, Katherine Anne, ed. <u>Perspectives on Contemporary Issues:</u> <u>Readings Across the Disciplines</u>. Fort Worth: Harcourt Brace College Publishers, 1997.
> Cousins, Norman. "The Poet and the Computer." Ackley 101–103.
> Hughes, Robert. "Behold the Stone Age." Ackley 96–100.
> Schemo, Diana Jean. "Between the Art and the Artist Lies the Shadow." Ackley 104–106.

WRITING A SYNTHESIS

A synthesis draws conclusions from, makes observations on, or shows connections between two or more sources. In synthesis, you attempt to make sense of the ideas of two or more sources by extracting information that is relevant to your purpose. The ability to synthesize is an important skill, for we are continuously bombarded with a dizzying variety of information and opinions that need sorting out and assessment. To understand your own thinking on a subject, it is always useful to know what others have to say about it. You can see how important it is to read and think critically when synthesizing the ideas of others. The sources for a synthesis may be essays, books, editorials, lectures, movies, group discussions, or any of the myriad forms of communication that inform our academic and personal lives. At the minimum, you will be required in a synthesis to reflect on the ideas of two writers or other sources, assess them, make connections between them, and arrive at your own conclusions on the basis of your analysis. Often you will work with more than two sources; certainly you will do so in a research paper.

Your purpose for writing a synthesis will be determined by the nature of your assignment, though syntheses are most commonly used to either explain or argue. Perhaps you want to explain how something works or show the causes or effects of a particular event. You may argue a particular point, using the arguments of others as supporting evidence or as subjects for disagreement in your own argument. You may want to compare or contrast the positions of other writers for the purpose of stating your own opinion on the subject. When you write a research paper, you most certainly must synthesize the ideas and words of others. Whether your research paper is a report or an argument, you will have to sort through and make sense of what your sources say. Sometimes you will want to read many sources to find out what a number of people have to say about a particular subject in order to discover your own position on it.

Synthesis, then, involves not only understanding what others have to say on a given subject but also making connections between them, analyzing their arguments or examples, and/or drawing conclusions from them. These are processes you routinely employ in both your everyday life and in your courses whenever you take into consideration the words, ideas, or opinions of two or more people or writers on a topic. Beginning with Chapter 5, each chapter in Parts II–V ends with a list of suggestions for synthesis on the basis of the readings in that chapter. These topics ask you to argue, to compare and contrast, to explore reasons, to explain something, to describe, or to report on something, using at least two of the essays in the chapter.

In all cases, no matter what your purpose for writing the synthesis, you will need to state your own central idea or thesis early on in your paper. In preparation for writing your essay, you will find it very helpful to locate the central idea or thesis of each of the works under analysis and to summarize their main points. The summary is itself a kind of synthesis, in that you locate the key ideas in an essay, put them in your own words, and then put the ideas back together again in a shortened form. This process helps you understand what the authors believe and why they believe it. Furthermore, it is useful for your own readers to have a summary of the central idea or chief points of the articles you are assessing. As you write your essay, you will not only be explaining your own view, opinion, or position, but you will also be using the ideas or words of the authors whose works you are synthesizing. These will have to be documented, using the appropriate formatting for documenting sources illustrated in this chapter and in Chapter 4.

Guidelines for Writing a Synthesis

- **Determine your purpose for writing by asking yourself what you want to do in your essay.** Without a purpose, your synthesis will be a loosely organized, incoherent jumble of words. While your purpose is often governed by the way in which the assignment is worded, make sure you understand exactly what you intend to do.
- **Consider how best to accomplish your purpose.** Will you argue, explain, compare and contrast, illustrate, show causes and effects, describe, or narrate? How will you use your sources to accomplish your purpose?
- **Read each source carefully and understand its central purpose and major points.** If you are unclear about the meaning of an essay, reread it carefully, noting passages that give you trouble. Discuss these passages with a classmate or with your instructor if you are still unclear.

- Write a one-sentence statement of the central idea or thesis and a brief summary of each source you will be using in your paper. This process will help clarify your understanding of your sources and assist you in formulating your own central idea. These statements or summaries can then be incorporated into your synthesis where appropriate.
- Write a one-sentence statement of your own thesis or central purpose for writing the synthesis. This statement should be a complete sentence and will usually appear in the first paragraph of your essay. The thesis statement helps you focus your thoughts as you plan your essay by limiting the nature and scope of what you intend to accomplish. It also is a crucial aid to your readers because it is essentially a succinct summary of what you intend to do.
- Develop or illustrate your thesis by incorporating the ideas of your sources into the body of your paper, either by paraphrasing or quoting directly. Part of your purpose in writing a synthesis is to demonstrate familiarity with your sources and to draw upon them in your own essay. This requires that you make reference to key ideas of the sources.
- Document your sources. Keep in mind the guidelines for documenting all borrowed material.

ILLUSTRATION: SYNTHESIS

Heather Anne Schilling

Professor Lee

English 102

November 28, 1996

The Place of Spirituality in the College Curriculum

The opening paragraph provides background information and indicates that the issue is controversial.

Education today is more complicated than ever before. The rapid rate at which knowledge increases and the almost constantly changing nature of our society and the jobs required to sustain it put great pressure on both institutions of higher education and students alike. Colleges consider how best to adapt and change their curricula to meet the needs of students preparing to enter the workforce, while students are conflicted not only about what they should study but also about the relevance of their studies to their futures. One controversy centers on what subjects are appropriate in the college curriculum, including how much, if any, emphasis should be given to students' spiritual lives as they prepare

The thesis statement in the last sentence of the first paragraph is a straightforward declarative sentence that makes clear the position of the author.

for their professional lives. Given the increasingly complicated and troubled nature of contemporary society, colleges and universities should give as much consideration to students' spiritual development as they do to their intellectual development.

Levine's survey is summarized briefly and its relevance to the subject of the paper is made clear.

Research indicates that many college students are worried about America's future. One such study is that of Arthur Levine, a professor in the Harvard Graduate School of Education, who profiles today's college undergraduates and their views of the future in a report of his 1993 survey of undergraduates at 28 campuses. In his survey, Levine asked what social and political events had most influenced their lives. Levine's survey reveals that many of today's generation of college undergraduates have negative feelings about the significant events that have affected their lives.

Schilling 2

They also feel somewhat overwhelmed by the knowledge
that they are inheriting a "deeply troubled nation" whose
problems they will be expected to find solutions for (27).

Only page number is given in the citation because Levine's name is mentioned in the text.

This sense of fear about their futures and students'
resentment at the state of the country whose problems they
will inherit suggest a real need for the kind of emotional
support that a strong spirituality or deep religious belief can
provide. The support that comes from a solid understanding
of the role of religion in people's lives would very likely be a
comfort to students as they complete their education. It
would also help them prepare for a future in which they
may have to make decisions that will affect others as well
as themselves.

Heather expresses her own conclusion about the implications of Levine's survey for her own thesis.

Proponents of including courses that teach students
about religious values in college curricula point out that
"some patterns of religious commitment have been found to
be associated with high levels of mental health and ego
strength" (Sollod 16). Given that today's young people are
tomorrow's problem solvers, it makes sense to nurture good
mental health and the kind of self-confidence that comes
from spirituality or religious beliefs. As Levine notes in the
conclusion to his report, "The big issue facing students [he]
interviewed was how to choose" between "making money
and performing good deeds" (28). College-level courses on
religion and spirituality may help students make the choices
that best benefit the larger society.

Robert Sollod's name is not mentioned in the text, so in the citation, his last name is given along with the page number where the quotation appears in the source.

The quotation from Levine uses brackets to indicate that a word has been changed to keep the grammar of the sentence consistent.

Courses in religion and spirituality might also help
address some of the criticisms leveled at colleges, such as
the complaint that too many college classrooms are isolated
from one another, making most of them, according to
Gerald Graff, like "a set of ships passing in the night"

Schilling 3

(40). Graff cites the critic Kenneth Burke as having once

"compared the intellectual life of a culture to a parlor in

which different guests are forever dropping in and out,"

adding: "As the standard curriculum represents the

intellectual life, however, there is no parlor; the hosts

congregate in separate rooms with their acolytes and keep

their differences and agreements to themselves" (37).

Educators have responded to such criticism by offering

cross-curricular or interdisciplinary courses and by team-

teaching classes. As a result, students gain a sense of

community beyond the individual classroom and see

connections among the courses they take. This is the kind

of community that courses in spirituality and religion

encourage.

    Robert N. Sollod would likely agree that schools should

do more to meet students' personal needs, as he makes

clear in "The Hollow Curriculum" when he argues that

college "curricula . . . do little" to correct the lack of

"religious and spiritual teachings" (14). Sollod believes

that an understanding of religion and spirituality would

help professionals in many fields. Most colleges and

universities ignore these important aspects of students'

lives, resulting in "a kind of segregation of the life of the

spirit from the life of the mind in American culture"

(Sollod 16). A happy joining of the life of the spirit and

the life of the mind would surely be of benefit in an age

often criticized for its lack of a strong moral center and

intellectual activity.

    Despite the many courses colleges currently offer,

they would do well to add a component to the curriculum

that meets the spiritual needs of students. Students

The first time an author's name is used, his or her full name is given. For second and subsequent references, use last name only.

Notice that Heather balances her own observations or general remarks with both paraphrases and quotations from her source materials.

Naming the source as well as author provides additional helpful information for readers.

The three spaced dots are ellipsis points and serve to indicate that words have been omitted from the original. Rather than quote the entire sentence, Heather touches on the essence of Sollod's article and stresses the point relevant to her own central idea.

Schilling 4

The conclusion makes reference to the ideas of each of the three authors mentioned in the text of the paper and restates Heather's own position on the subject.

themselves express anger about the state of the world they are being educated to take major roles in, and they are confused about whether to serve society at large or to look after only themselves. Some educators are calling for colleges and universities to help students make connections between the courses they take and to realize the place of these courses in their larger contexts. Others call for colleges to pay attention to the spiritual lives of their students. Offering courses on spirituality and religion would thus benefit students, satisfy educators, and ultimately serve the greater need of a troubled and complex nation.

Works Cited. The Works Cited page gives full bibliographic information for each source. For the paper "The Place of Spirituality in the College Curriculum," the list of works cited appears as follows. Notice that works are listed alphabetically and that each citation conforms in punctuation and spacing to MLA style of documentation, discussed in Chapter 4.

Schilling 5

Works Cited

Ackley, Katherine Anne, ed. Perspectives on Contemporary
    Issues: Readings Across the Disciplines. Fort Worth:
    Harcourt Brace College Publishers, 1997.
Graff, Gerald. "Ships in the Night." Ackley 33-40.
Levine, Arthur. "The Making of a Generation." Ackley 20-
    28.
Sollod, Robert N. "The Hollow Curriculum." Ackley 14-17.

CHAPTER 4

WRITING A RESEARCH PAPER

No matter what course you write a research paper for, your goal is the same: to skillfully support a carefully formulated thesis with documented evidence. Writing such a paper can seem both overwhelming and exciting, especially if you have never written one before. This chapter presents a brief overview of the key steps in selecting a topic, researching it, and writing a paper incorporating the sources you have used. Keep in mind the discussion in Chapter 2 on summarizing, paraphrasing, and quoting. A research paper is likely to be much longer than a writing assignment generated from readings in this book, but otherwise there is little difference between using materials from this textbook and using materials from other sources in terms of accuracy and fairness to your sources.

DEFINING YOUR PURPOSE

Your instructor will tell you whether your purpose in the research paper is to argue, explain, analyze, or come to some conclusion about something. In an argumentative paper, you will make a judgment about your topic on the basis of what you find in your research. You will begin your research with an idea of what your position is, then research your subject extensively, arrive at an informed opinion, and finally defend that position by presenting evidence you believe to be valid (that is, logical and convincing). If you want to go a step further and convince your audience to adopt your position or to act on suggestions you propose, then your purpose is persuasive.

Caution: In addition to proving the validity of your own position, you must also present some of the opposing arguments. Obviously you cannot present every aspect and every position of an issue, but you must demonstrate that you are aware of the major viewpoints on your subject and that the position you have taken is a reasonable one. Ignoring opposing opinion is a major fault in argumentation because it suggests that you have not explored enough aspects of the topic to warrant the position you are taking.

The subjects for argumentative papers are virtually unlimited, but they often include controversial issues, such as those addressed in this textbook, topics on which opinion varies widely. On the other hand, in an informative paper, your subject will not necessarily be controversial. If you are to write an explanatory paper, you will gather information about your topic and present it in such a way that your reader understands it fully. You will explain, describe, illustrate, or narrate something in full detail, such as what the black hole is, how photosynthesis works, the circumstances surrounding a historical event, significant events in the life of a famous person, and the like.

No matter what your purpose, though, you will have one central idea, most often articulated early in the paper in the form of a single thesis statement. You will have to take a position on your topic and defend or illustrate it convincingly with evidence from your source materials. Because the argumentative paper is a common research assignment, much of the discussion in this chapter will be about selecting an appropriate topic on which to base an argument.

DISCOVERING A TOPIC

Once you know your purpose, the next, and perhaps most important, step in writing a research paper is to find a subject you will be comfortable working with for many weeks and narrow it to a specific topic. While some instructors assign topics, most leave the choice to students. Being free to choose your own research paper topic can be intimidating because so much depends on selecting the right one. You want a topic that not only holds your interest but that also offers you an opportunity to investigate it in depth.

The process of discovering what you are going to write about involves first determining the broad subject you are particularly interested in pursuing. Once you have settled on the subject, you will need to narrow it to one specific aspect of that subject. For many research paper assignments, that topic will have to be arguable, one that requires you to investigate both sides and arrive at and defend your own position. This position will be worded in the form of a hypothesis or thesis, stated most often as a declarative statement but sometimes as a question. Discovering your final topic takes time, so do some serious thinking about this important step as soon as the paper is assigned. You will be reshaping, narrowing, and refining your topic for much of the research process, so you do not want to switch subjects halfway through.

Brainstorming. As you consider the various suggestions for generating a research paper topic, you will find it useful to apply a technique for discovery that you have probably used before in your writing classes. Most students are familiar with **brainstorming or freewriting,** which involves simply writing without stopping, putting on paper everything that occurs to you as you think about your subject. To brainstorm or freewrite, spend five or ten minutes listing on a blank sheet of paper all of the subjects you are interested in without stopping to think too hard about what you are doing. Then select one or more of the subjects on your list and brainstorm for another five to ten minutes in order to find out what you already know about your subject.

Generating a Topic from Personal Interest. One way to find a topic for your research paper is to begin with subjects you already know well, are interested in, or think you would like to know more about. Begin by writing down such things as hobbies, sports, issues in your major, contemporary social issues, or topics in classes you are taking. Consider topics that attracted your interest in high school or in previous college classes, any reading you have already done on subjects that appeal to you, or the kinds of things that capture your attention when you watch television news, read news magazines or newspapers, or select nonfiction books for leisure-time reading.

Narrowing Your Subject to a Specific Topic. Most research paper assignments are short enough that you simply must narrow your focus in order to avoid being too shallow in your treatment of your topic or too hopelessly general. Keep in mind the distinction between *subject* and *topic:* subject is the general area under investigation, while topic is the narrow aspect of that subject that you are investigating. For example, Jack the Ripper is a subject, but entire books have been written on the notorious 1888 murders in the Whitechapel area of London. A suitable topic on the subject would be to explore the controversy surrounding the alleged links of the Duke of Clarence with the murders, taking a position in favor of the theory you find most plausible.

One way to get a sense of how a general topic can be narrowed is to look at the table of contents of a book on a subject that interests you. Notice the various chapter headings, which are themselves subtopics of the broad subject. Chapters themselves are often further subdivided. You want to find a topic that is narrow enough that you can fully explore it without leaving unanswered questions, yet broad enough that you can say enough about it in a reasonably long paper.

To narrow your subject to a topic, take a general subject and go through the brainstorming process again, this time listing everything that comes to mind about that particular subject. What subtopics does your subject have? What questions can you ask about your general subject? How might you narrow your focus on that subject? Ultimately, you want to generate an idea that gives focus to your preliminary library search.

Generating Topics from Personal Opinions. Virtually any topic can be turned into an argument, but opinions are always subject to debate. So one way to generate a research paper topic is to begin with your own strongly held opinions. **Caution:** Avoid a topic that is based entirely on opinion. Evaluative statements are especially good for argumentative papers because they are almost always likely to have differing opinions. Once you say that something is the best, the most significant, the most important, or the greatest, for instance, you have put yourself in the position of defending that statement. You will have to establish your criteria for making your judgment and defend your choice against what others might think. Here are some ideas for this particular approach:

- The most influential person in the twentieth century (or in America, in the world, in a particular field such as education, government, politics, arts, entertainment, or the like)
- The most significant battle in the Civil War (or World War I, World War II, the Korean War, the Vietnam War, the Gulf War)
- The greatest basketball (or football, tennis, soccer, baseball) player (either now playing or of all time)
- The greatest or worst president
- The best movie, book, or album of all time
- The business or industry with the greatest impact on American life in the last decade (or last twenty years, last fifty years, or of the century)

Because your conclusion on any of these or similar topics is your opinion, you will need to establish criteria for your conclusion, make clear what process you used to make it, and explain why the process is logical.

Generating Topics from Commonly Held Opinions. Another possibility for a research paper topic is to take a commonly held opinion (though not necessarily one that you believe), especially one based on stereotyped assumptions about a group or class of people, and explore the validity of that belief. Your goal here will be to determine whether the commonly held opinion is valid, partially valid, or invalid. Even if you cannot arrive at a definitive evaluation of the validity of the statement, you can still present the evidence you find and explain why your research is inconclusive. Here are examples of commonly held beliefs:

- Watching violence on television produces violent behavior.
- People who were abused as children often grow up to be abusers themselves.
- Men are naturally better at mechanical skills than women are.
- Women are naturally better at nurturing children than men are.
- Young people do not have much hope for a bright future.
- Women are more emotional than men.
- People stay on welfare because they are too lazy to work.
- Homosexuals could become "straight" if they wanted to.
- Homeless people could get off the streets if they really tried.

When determining the validity of a commonly held opinion or belief, your research will focus on gathering evidence that is unbiased. Although you may want to interview people about their opinions on a particular belief, the basis of your conclusion must rest on evidence that is clearly reliable.

Generating Topics from Controversy. Yet another way to discover a topic you find intriguing enough to commit many hours of time to is to think of controversial issues that always generate heated debate. These topics may be frequently discussed in newspapers, news magazines, and on television news programs and talk shows. They may be issues that candidates for public office, from local county board members to state and federal officials, are pressed to take stands on. Here are some examples of controversial statements:

- Affirmative action laws are unfair to white males and should be repealed.
- Media coverage of celebrity trials should be banned.
- Birth parents should always have a legal right to take back children they have given up for adoption.
- Children whose parents are on welfare should be placed in state-run orphanages.
- Women should be barred from participating in combat duty.

- Graphic violence in the movies (or in video games or MTV videos) poses a serious threat to our nation's moral values.
- The federal government should stop funding projects in the arts and the humanities.
- The federal government should provide unlimited funds to support research to find a cure for AIDS.
- Children who commit murder should be tried as adults no matter what their age.

DEVELOPING A WORKING BIBLIOGRAPHY

Now that you have your topic narrowed, you are ready to start the actual research process. The most logical place to start is the library, but do not overlook other excellent sources of information such as interviews, taped television shows, and government publications. For example, if you are researching the human genome project, you may want to interview a biology professor for information about the scientific aspects of the project and a philosophy professor for an opinion on its ethical implications. In addition to interviews, you may use material from a lecture, a television documentary, a film, or your own survey.

A working bibliography is a list of the sources you **might** use in your actual research paper, those that look particularly promising when you do your preliminary searching. At this point, you have not had time to read or even carefully skim all of your sources, nor have you had time to imagine how your sources fit together to support your hypothesis. Some instructors require that you prepare a separate bibliography card for each source that looks promising. Others suggest that you simply list titles and locations of potential sources and wait until you have looked at them more closely before making out bibliography cards. Your instructor will tell you which to do.

Guidelines for a Working Bibliography
- As you discover titles that sound promising for your research, write down the titles of each source.
- If it is a book, write down the title, the author, and the call number.
- If it is an article, write the title of the piece, the name of its author, the title of the magazine or journal it appears in, the dates of the issue, and the inclusive pages numbers of the article. You will need all of this information to find the article.
- For other sources such as videotapes, audio tapes, government documents, or pamphlets, write down as much information as you are given to make locating it easier.
- Write the location of the source, such as special collections, government documents, stacks, periodicals, and so on.

Begin your search for sources on your general subject (or topic, if you have sufficiently narrowed your focus) by using the on-line catalog or card catalog of your library for titles of books and guides to periodical literature (located in the reference room) or the on-line catalog for titles of magazine or journal articles. If your library has an on-line catalog and you do not know how to use it, ask someone who works in the library for instructions. Most computer terminals will have directions for using the on-line catalog, but if you need help, just ask. Card catalogs, guides to periodical literature, and on-line catalogs all organize their lists of sources by author, by title, and by subject matter. Because you are in the searching stage of your research, you will look under subject headings for titles that sound relevant to your research subject. The point of a working bibliography is to make as inclusive and complete a list of potential sources as possible.

MAKING BIBLIOGRAPHY CARDS

Once you have assembled a good number of sources to investigate, start locating and evaluating them. If you discover that you cannot use a source, cross it off your list or discard the card on which you wrote information about it. **When you find a source that definitely looks promising for your research topic, make a bibliography card for it before you begin taking notes.** Use three-by-five-inch cards, one for each source. Include complete bibliographic information, preferably in the form in which it will appear on your Works Cited page. For directions for creating bibliography cards in the same format as sources that will appear on your Works Cited page, see the section entitled "Documenting Sources: The Works Cited Page using MLA Style." Here are sample bibliography cards for six common sources.

FIGURE 4–1
BOOK WITH ONE AUTHOR

Heilbrun, Carolyn G. <u>Hamlet's Mother and Other Women</u>.
New York: Ballantine Books, 1990.

JOURNAL ARTICLE WITH ONE AUTHOR

Weaver, Constance. "Weighing the Claims About Phonics
First." <u>The Education Digest</u> 56 (April 1991): 19–22.

FIGURE 4–1 (*continued*)
NEWSPAPER ARTICLE WITH AUTHOR NAMED

> Warrick, Pamela. "Questions of Life and Death." The Los
>
> Angeles Times 4 Aug. 1991: E1+.

MAGAZINE ARTICLE WITH NO AUTHOR NAMED

> "Another Challenge to Coffee's Safety." Science News 20
>
> October 1990: 253.

JOURNAL ARTICLE WITH TWO AUTHORS

> Fabes, Richard A., and Jeremiah Strouse. "Formal vs.
>
> Informal Sources on Sex Education: Competing Forces in
>
> the Sexual Socialization of Adolescents." Adolescence 20
>
> (1985): 250–261.

GOVERNMENT DOCUMENT

> United States. Cong. House. Committee on Armed Services.
>
> Women in the Military: Hearing Before the Military
>
> Personnel and Compensation Subcommittee. 101st
>
> Cong., 2nd sess. 20 March 1990: 14–56.

TAKING NOTES

When you find an article, book, pamphlet, or other source you believe may be useful in your research, you will take notes from that source. Note cards are useful for several kinds of information: direct quotations, paraphrases, summaries of several pages or an entire article, and personal thoughts on your subject. Note

Guidelines for Taking Notes
- **Use four-by-six-inch cards.** Smaller cards do not give you much room and larger cards give you too much.
- **Write in ink.** Pencil tends to smudge.
- **Write the author's last name and the page number from which the information is taken.** That is all the information you need as long as you have a bibliography card for the source that lists complete bibliographic information.
- **Put only one idea or several small related ones on a card.** This will make it easier to organize your cards when you begin writing.
- **Write the subject of your notes at the top of each card.** This notation will be useful when you are organizing your note cards in preparation for writing your paper.
- **Use quotation marks before and after the material taken directly from the source.** Don't rely on remembering later whether the words are identical to the original or paraphrased.
- **Try not to write on the backs of your cards.** You may miss something when you begin to write your paper.
- **Use your cards to summarize.** It is appropriate at times to refer to an entire passage, an article, or a book without giving specific details. Make a note on the card to remind you that the information is a summary.
- **Use note cards to record original ideas that occur to you while you are reading.** Make sure you indicate that it is your own idea.

taking is crucial to the success of your paper. You must take notes accurately and carefully, reproducing the words of the author exactly as they appear if you quote or completely restating the author's words if you paraphrase. In either case, you will give a citation in your paper, so *it is essential that you record the source and page number of any information you put on a note card.*

PARAPHRASING

A paraphrase restates the ideas of a passage and is most useful for clarifying or emphasizing the main point of a short passage. To paraphrase, put the ideas of the author in your own words, being careful not to use phrases or key words of the original. Paraphrases are sometimes as long as the original passage, though often they are slightly shorter. The purpose of paraphrasing is to convey the essence of a sentence or passage in an accurate, fair manner and without the distraction of quotation marks. If in your paraphrase you use the exact words of the original, then you are quoting and must put quotation marks around those words. Your paper will be more interesting and readable if you paraphrase more often than you quote.

Guidelines for Paraphrasing
- Use your own words to restate the essence of a passage.
- Do not repeat the exact words of any part of the original.
- Try to paraphrase as often as possible, saving direct quotations for truly remarkable language, startling or unusual information, or otherwise original or crucial wording.
- Provide the source of *all* paraphrased material, either in your text as you introduce the material or parenthetically after it.

QUOTING

When it is not appropriate to paraphrase the words of another person, you will want to quote them. Quoting requires that you repeat the exact words of another, using quotation marks before and after the material being quoted. It is crucial that you copy the words *exactly* as they appear in the text. To omit words or approximate the original while using quotation marks is sloppy or careless handling of your source material.

How do you know when to quote rather than paraphrase? You should quote only those words, phrases, or sentences that are particularly striking or that must be reproduced exactly because you cannot put them into your own words without weakening their effect or changing their intent. Quote directly passages that are so succinctly or precisely worded that paraphrasing them would be more complicated or require more words than a direct quotation would. Quote those passages or parts of them that are original, dramatically worded, or in some way essential to your paper. Otherwise, rely on paraphrasing to refer to the ideas of others. Whether you quote directly or paraphrase, you will need to document your source, that is, identify the source and the location of your information within that source.

When taking notes, it is sometimes tempting to write down everything as it appears in the original, thinking that you will paraphrase at some later time.

Guidelines for Quoting
- Quote directly only those words, phrases, or sentences that are particularly striking and whose beauty, originality, or drama would be lost in a paraphrase.
- Put the exact words you are quoting between quotation marks.
- Do not change one word of the original unless you indicate with brackets, ellipses, or other conventions that you have done so. Otherwise, your words must be identical to those of the original.
- Be selective in the material you choose to quote directly. It is better to paraphrase the words of another rather than copy the words exactly.

Students who do that will find themselves faced with spending valuable time later rephrasing material when they should be concentrating on writing their paper, or else they take the easier route and use the direct quotations. The result may be a paper that is too full of direct quotations and lacking in effective paraphrases. Remember that you should quote directly only information that is particularly well expressed or material that you do not feel you can adequately put into your own words. Your final paper should have far more paraphrases than direct quotations.

AVOIDING PLAGIARISM

Giving proper credit to your sources is a crucial component of the research process. It is also one of the trickiest aspects of the process because it requires absolute accuracy in note taking. Many students have been disheartened by a low grade on a paper that took weeks of time to prepare because they were careless or inaccurate in the handling and documenting of source materials.

Simply defined, **plagiarism** is the borrowing of another person's words without giving proper credit to that person. The worst form of plagiarism is deliberately using the words or important ideas of someone else without giving any credit to that source. Handing in a paper someone else has written or copying someone else's paper and pretending it is yours are the most blatant and inexcusable forms of plagiarism, crimes that on some campuses carry the penalty of automatic failure in the course or even immediate expulsion from school. Most student plagiarism is not deliberate, but rather results from carelessness either in the research process, when notes are taken, or in the writing process, when notes are incorporated into the student's own text. Even this unintentional plagiarism can result in a failing grade, however, especially if it is done repeatedly in a paper.

Keep the following in mind when you take notes on your source materials and when you write your research paper:

- **It is plagiarism to use the exact words or ideas of another writer without putting quotation marks around the words or citing your source.** The reader of your paper assumes that words without quotation marks or a source citation are your own words. To use the words of another without proper documentation suggests that you are trying to pass the words off as your own without giving credit to the writer.
- **It is plagiarism to use the exact words of another writer without putting quotation marks around those words, even if you cite the source of the material.** Readers assume that words followed by a parenthetical citation are paraphrased from the original, that is, that they are your own words and that the general idea was expressed by the author of the source material.
- **It is plagiarism to paraphrase by changing only a few words of the original or by using the identical sentence structure of the**

Guidelines for Avoiding Plagiarism
- For direct quotations, write the words exactly as they appear in the original. Put quotation marks before and after the words. Do not change anything.
- For paraphrased material, put the original words in your own words, using your own writing style. Do not use the exact sentence pattern of the original, and do not simply rearrange words. You have to retain the central idea of the paraphrased material, but do so in your own words.
- When using borrowed material in your paper, whether direct quotations or paraphrases, acknowledge the source by naming the author or work in your introduction to the material. Doing so not only makes it clear to your reader that you are using borrowed material but often provides clear transition from your own words and ideas to the borrowed material that illustrates or expands on your ideas.
- Provide an in-text citation for all borrowed material. Give author's last name if it is not mentioned in the text of the paper, followed by page number(s). If the source material is anonymous, use a shortened version of the title in place of a name.
- Put all sources cited in your paper in an alphabetical list at the end of the paper. This is your list of works cited, containing only those works actually used in the paper.

---

   original, whether you give a source or not. Again, readers assume that words without quotation marks followed by a parenthetical citation are your own words, not those of someone else. In a paraphrase, the *idea* is that of another; the *words* are your own.
- It is inaccurate handling of source material to use quotation marks around words that are not exactly as they appear in the original. Readers assume that all words within quotation marks are identical to the original.

Obviously, accuracy and fairness in note taking are essential. Great care must be taken when you read your source materials and again when you transfer your notes to your final paper.

ILLUSTRATION: PLAGIARISM, INACCURATE DOCUMENTATION, AND CORRECT HANDLING OF SOURCE MATERIAL
The passage that follows is from page 8 of Jean Kilbourne's "Beauty and the Beast of Advertising." Here is complete bibliographic information as it would appear on a bibliography card and on the Works Cited page of a research paper.

Kilbourne, Jean. "Beauty and the Beast of Advertising."

Media&Values Winter 1989: 8–10.

Note that the title of the magazine is correct as written, with the ampersand (&) instead of "and" and with no spaces between the words.

> "You're a Halston woman from the very beginning," the advertisement proclaims. The model stares provocatively at the viewer, her long blonde hair waving around her face, her bare chest partially covered by two curved bottles that give the illusion of breasts and cleavage.
>
> The average American is accustomed to blue-eyed blondes seductively touting a variety of products. In this case, however, the blonde is about five years old.
>
> Advertising is an over $130 billion a year industry and affects all of us throughout our lives. We are each exposed to over 1,500 ads a day, constituting perhaps the most powerful educational force in society. The average adult will spend one and one-half years of his/her life watching television commercials. But the ads sell a great deal more than products. They sell values, images and concepts of success and worth, love and sexuality, popularity and normalcy. They tell us who we are and who we should be. Sometimes they sell addictions.

Now look at each of these sentences from a hypothetical research paper using information from the Kilbourne article and the commentary that follows on whether it is plagiarism, inaccurate handling of the original, or correct handling of source material:

1. Advertising is an over $130 billion a year industry and affects us throughout our lives.

   [This is **plagiarism**: Quotation marks are needed around words identical to the original and a source must be cited.]

2. We are each exposed to over 1,500 ads a day (Kilbourne 8).

   [This is **plagiarism**: Quotation marks are needed around words taken directly from the original.]

3. The average American is used to blue-eyed blondes seductively selling a variety of things (Kilbourne 8).

   [This is **plagiarism**: Original words are changed only slightly and the original sentence structure is retained.]

4. Kilbourne's analysis of advertising begins with the following quotation from a popular advertisement: "You're a Halston woman from the very beginning" (8).

[This is **inaccurate documentation:** Single quotation marks are needed within the double marks to indicate that quotation marks are in the original.]

5. In her analysis of the ways in which advertising uses women's bodies to sell products, Jean Kilbourne argues that ads sell much more than just products. Ads "sell values, images and concepts of success and worth" (8).

> [This is **correct:** Author is acknowledged in text of paper and the general idea of the article is adequately summarized. Quotation marks are used around material taken directly from original.]

Students are sometimes frustrated by these guidelines governing note taking and plagiarism, arguing that virtually everything in the final paper will be in quotation marks or followed by citations. But keep in mind that your final paper is a synthesis of information you have discovered in your research with your own thoughts on your topic, thoughts that naturally undergo modification, expansion, and/or revision as you read more and think more about your topic. Probably half of the paper will be your own words. These words will usually include all of the introductory and concluding paragraphs, all topic sentences and transitional sentences within and between paragraphs, and all introductions to direct quotations. Furthermore, you need give no citation for things that are general or common knowledge, such as facts about well-known historical or current events. If you keep running across the same information in all of your sources, you can assume it is general knowledge.

DOCUMENTING SOURCES: IN-TEXT CITATIONS USING MLA STYLE

When it comes time to write your paper, keep in mind the guidelines for what constitutes plagiarism and how to avoid it. In addition, look at the examples of quoting and paraphrasing in Chapter 2, the sample synthesis in Chapter 3, the sentences used to illustrate various tools of note taking and documentation in this chapter, and the student research paper that follows. Remember that you must be fair to your source and accurate in your representation of it.

MLA style of documentation requires that you give a brief reference to the source of any borrowed material in a parenthetical note that follows the material. This parenthetical note contains only the last name of the author and the page number(s) on which the material appears, or only the page number(s) if you mention the author's name in the text.

The parenthetic citation is placed within the sentence, that is, after the quotation or paraphrase but before the period. If the quotation itself contains punctuation, ignore a comma, period, or semicolon but include a question mark or exclamation mark. In all cases, the period for your sentence follows the parenthetical citation.

Here are formats for citing common sources in the text of your paper. The Works Cited format for many of the references illustrated here can be found in the section on creating a Works Cited page.

- **Book or article with two authors.** Name both authors followed by page number:

    (Barrett and Rowe 19)

- **Book or article with three or more authors.** If three, name all three or just the first and "et al." If more than three, name just the first and "et al." and then the page number:

    (Fletcher, Miller, and Caplan 78) or (Fletcher et al. 78)

Note: Reproduce the names in the order in which they appear on the title page. If they are not in alphabetical order, do not change their order.

- **Article or other publication with no author named.** Give a short title followed by page number:

    ("Teaching" 10)

Note: If you cite two articles beginning with the same word and with anonymous authors, use the full title of each to distinguish one from the other.

- **Two works by the same author.** Give name, short title, and page number:

    (Heilbrun "Hamlet's Mother" 123)

- **Works by people with the same last name.** Handle them in the same way as you would two works by the same author. In the parenthetical citation, give the last name followed by a short title of the work and then the page number(s).

INTEGRATING SOURCE MATERIALS INTO YOUR PAPER

In addition to fairness and accuracy, you want to smoothly integrate reference materials into the text of your paper. Pay special attention to the way in which you introduce your source materials. There are many ways of skillfully integrating the words and ideas of other people with your own words. Your research paper should not read as if you simply cut the words of someone else and pasted them in your paper, nor should you put everything from one source together, everything from another together, and so on. Your goal is to integrate the words and ideas of other people with your own words in a coherent, smooth, unified discussion.

- **Caution: Never put a quotation in your paper which is not in some way introduced or commented on.** A quotation that is not introduced or followed by some concluding comment is referred to as a "bald quotation" and detracts from the smooth flow of your paper.

You can achieve smooth integration of source materials into your text if you keep the following in mind:

- **Mention the author's name in the text of your paper to signal the beginning of a paraphrase or quotation.** The first time you mention the name, give both first and last names. After the first mention, give only last name:

  > Robert Sollod points out in "The Hollow Curriculum" that colleges would not think of excluding courses on multiculturalism in today's curriculum, given the importance of "appreciation and understanding of human diversity." Sollod asks: "Should such an appreciation exclude the religious and spiritually based concepts of reality that are the backbone upon which entire cultures have been based?" (A60).

- **Mention the source if no author is named.** This practice gives credit to the source while providing an introduction to the borrowed material:

  > A *U.S. News & World Report* article notes that, while there are no genes to determine what occupation one will go into, there are groups of genes that produce certain tendencies—risk-taking, for instance—that might predispose one to select a particular kind of work ("How Genes Shape Personality" 64).

- **Give a citation for all borrowed material.** Use the authority's name, use quotation marks, give the source and page number in a parenthetical citation, give some sort of general information, and/or use a pronoun to refer to the authority mentioned in the previous sentence. Do not rely on one parenthetical citation at the end of several sentences or an entire paragraph:

  > **Regna Lee Wood** has also researched the use of phonics in teaching children to read. **She** believes that the horrible failure of our schools began years ago. **Wood** notes that "it all began in 1929 and 1930 when hundreds of primary teachers, guided by college reading professors, stopped teaching beginners to read by matching sounds with letters that spell sounds" **(51). She** adds that since 1950, when most reading teachers switched to teaching children to sight words rather than sound them by syllable, "50 million children with poor sight memories have reached the 4th grade still unable to read" (52).

- **Vary introductory phrases and clauses.** Avoid relying overmuch on such standard introductory clauses as "Smith says" or "Jones writes." Some useful ways of introducing quotations and paraphrases include the following: "As Jerry Baker notes," "Professor Xavier argues," "According to Dr. Carroll," and "As Marcia Smith points out." Note that the first mention of your authority in your text should include the author's first name as well as last name. The second and subsequent references should be to last name only (**never** first name alone). So the first time you use the words or ideas of Susan Jaspers, for example, you would write: "Susan Jaspers correctly points out . . . ," while the next time you mention her work, write something like "Jaspers contends elsewhere that. . . ."

- **Combine quotations and paraphrases.** Doing so provides a smoother style than quoting directly all of the time:

  > Robert Levine's 1993 survey of college students reveals that today's generation of young people differs from those he surveyed in 1979. Levine discovered that today's college students "are living through a period of profound demographic, economic, global, and technological change." Since these students of the '90s see themselves living in a "deeply troubled nation," they have only guarded optimism about the future (27).

USING ELLIPSIS POINTS, BRACKETS, SINGLE QUOTATION MARKS, AND "QTD. IN"

Here are some additional guidelines for the mechanics of handling source materials and incorporating them into your paper:

- **If you want to omit words, phrases, or sentences from the original in your quotation, use ellipsis points to indicate the omission.** Ellipsis points consist of three spaced periods, with a space before, between, and after the periods. Most frequently they are used within a sentence, seldom at the beginning, and sometimes at the end of a sentence, in which case you must have a grammatically complete sentence. If the ellipses comes at the end of a sentence, you will use four periods. One period indicates the end of your sentence and should be placed immediately after the last word, as you would a period for any sentence. Then put a space before and between the next three periods but not after the last one. The quotation mark follows the last period, with no space between it and the period:

  > You know the old saying, "Eat, drink, and be merry. . . ."

If a parenthetical reference follows the ellipsis points at the end of your quoted sentence, use three periods with a space before each and place the sentence period after the final parenthesis:

> According to recent studies, "Statistics show that Chinese women's status has improved . . ." (*Chinese Women* 46).

Ellipsis points are not necessary if you are using a fragment of a sentence, that is, a few words or a subordinate clause, because it will be clear that some of the original sentence has been left out. For example, here is a passage from Steph Niedermair's paper "Nature vs. Nurture" that needs no ellipsis points:

> But they [sociobiologists] add that social and nurturing experiences can "intensify, diminish or modify" personality traits (Wood and Wood 272).

Elsewhere in her paper, Steph quotes a source but leaves out some words of the original. Her remaining quotation is a grammatically complete sentence, so she uses ellipsis points to indicate the omission:

> David T. Lykken, a professor of psychology and psychiatry at the University of Minnesota, also a member of the win team, puts Scan's idea another way: "'It's an endless circle. . . . Your genes determine who you are, which . . . determines the kind of environment you'll have, which determines who you are'" (Gallagher "Manner Born" 61).

Here is the original passage from Winifred Gallagher's article "To the Manner Born" (<u>Rolling Stone</u> 19 Nov. 1987: 56+):

> "It's an endless circle," he says. "Your genes determine who you are, which in many respects determines the kind of environment you'll have, which determines who you are."

- **If you want to change a word or phrase to conform to your own sentence, use brackets to indicate the change.** The brackets go before and after only the changed portion of the original.

  Original: In a miasma of Walt Disney images, Bambi burning, and Snow White asleep, the most memorable is "Cinderella."
  (Bernikow, Louise. "Cinderella: Saturday Afternoon at the Movies." *Among Women.* New York: Crown, 1980. 17–37.)
  Quotation: Louise Bernikow recalls spending Saturday afternoons at the theatre when she was growing up "in a miasma of Walt Disney images, . . . the most memorable [of which] is 'Cinderella'" (17).

  Note: This example illustrates the use not only of brackets but also of ellipsis points and a single quotation mark within a double.

- **If something is in quotation marks in the original, use single marks within the double in your own quotation.** Occasionally you will have to quote something that is already a quotation within a quotation, where the original contains a single quotation mark within a double. In that case, use a double quotation within a single within a double:

  > Johnson records an interview with a chief witness in this case. Smith is said to have proclaimed, "'"It wasn't me! I didn't do it!"'" (23). (The original on page 23 of the Johnson book reads:

> In my interviews with the chief witness, he swears he heard Smith say: "'It wasn't me! I didn't do it!'" Johnson quotes the witness, who is quoting Smith.)

- **If you quote or paraphrase material that is already quoted, use the abbreviation *qtd.*** Use "qtd. in" whenever you quote or paraphrase an author's account of someone else's words or ideas. Your Works Cited will not include the original source of the material you quoted or paraphrased but rather the indirect source, the one you found it in:

> Nationally, according to Dr. Randolph D. Smoak, Jr., "'"Passive smoking" is the third leading cause of premature death in the United States, exceeded only by direct smoking and alcohol'" (qtd. in "Pros/Cons" 142).

DOCUMENTING SOURCES: THE WORKS CITED PAGE USING MLA STYLE

The Works Cited page lists in alphabetical order all of the works you cited in your paper and comes at the end of your paper. You must have an entry for every work quoted from, paraphrased, summarized, or otherwise alluded to in your paper. **Do not include on your works cited list any works you read but did not use in the paper.** If you want to include a list of useful works that informed your understanding of your topic but that you did not quote or paraphrase from in your final paper, create a separate page entitled Works Consulted. Use the same format as for your list of works cited. Place the Works Consulted page last in your paper.

Guidelines for Creating Works Cited Entries for Books

- The first line of each entry begins flush with the left margin. Second and subsequent lines within each entry are indented five spaces.
- Each item in an entry is separated by a period: Author. Title. Publisher and date. Note that each period is followed by two spaces.
- The author's name is written with last name first, followed by a comma and then first name.
- Underline titles of books. Do not use italics or quotation marks.
- Titles of essays within books are placed within quotation marks.
- Double space within and between all entries.
- Shorten publishers' names and drop such words as *Inc., Co.,* and *Press.* Abbreviate *University* and *Press* for university presses, as U of Wisconsin P for University of Wisconsin Press or Oxford UP for Oxford University Press.
- Abbreviate names of states, provinces, and countries, for example, WI for Wisconsin, SK for Saskatchewan, Can. for Canada.

Books with a single author.

> Leonardi, Susan J. <u>Dangerous by Degrees: Women at Oxford and the Somerville College Novelists.</u> New Brunswick, NJ: Rutgers UP, 1989.

Author of an essay in a collection.

> Spacks, Patricia Meyer. "Sisters." <u>Fetter'd or Free?: British Women Novelists, 1670–1815.</u> Eds. Mary Anne Schofield and Cecilia Macheski. Athens, OH: Ohio UP, 1986. 136–151.

Note: Use this format when you cite an essay published in a collection of essays. Patricia Meyer Spacks's article appears on pages 136–151 of the collection of essays. The abbreviation "Eds." means that Mary Anne Schofield and Cecilia Macheski are co-editors. For one editor, use "Ed." Always give the inclusive page numbers of the entire article in a collection, as well as the place of publication and date of the collection.

Editor(s) of a collection.

> Schofield, Mary Anne, and Cecilia Macheski, eds. <u>Fetter'd or Free?: British Women Novelists, 1670–1815.</u> Athens, OH: Ohio UP, 1986.

Note: Use this format when you cite the ideas of the editors or when you refer to the entire collection.

Book with two or more authors.

> Gilbert, Sandra M., and Susan Gubar. <u>The Madwoman in the Attic: The Woman Writer and the Nineteenth-Century Literary Imagination.</u> New Haven: Yale UP, 1979.

Two works by the same author.

> Heilbrun, Carolyn. <u>Hamlet's Mother and Other Women.</u> New York: Ballantine, 1990.
>
> ---. <u>Writing a Woman's Life.</u> New York: Ballantine, 1988.

Note: List the books alphabetically. For the second and subsequent books by the same author, type three hyphens followed by a period in place of the name.

Creating a Works Cited List for Periodicals. Periodicals are magazines or journals that are published frequently and at fixed intervals. Distinguish between journals and magazines by considering audience, subject matter, and frequency of publication. Journals are fairly specialized, are usually written for people in a specific profession, are more technical and research-oriented than magazines, and generally appear much less frequently than magazines, perhaps bimonthly or four times a year. Magazines, on the other hand, are intended for a general audience, are not heavily research-oriented, and usually appear monthly or even weekly.

Guidelines for Creating Works Cited Entries for Periodicals
- Give both the title of the article and the name of the periodical in which it appears.
- Use quotation marks for the article title and underline the periodical name.
- Entries for articles in periodicals have three main divisions. Use periods to separate the main parts of the entry followed by two spaces: Author. Article title. Publication information (title of periodical, date it was published, and page numbers of the article).
- Author's name is written with last name first, followed by a comma and then the first name.
- If the article is anonymous, begin the entry with the title of the article. For placing the entries in alphabetical order on the list, ignore *The, A,* and *And* at the beginnings of titles.
- Follow date with a colon and the inclusive page numbers of the article. Do not use the abbreviations *p.* or *pp.* for pages.

Journal article. Follow this model:

> Author's Name. "Title of Article." Name of Periodical volume number (date): inclusive page numbers of article.
>
> Groff, Patrick. "The Maturing of Phonics Instruction." The Education Digest 52 (Jan. 1991): 402.
>
> Hamby, Alonzo L. "An American Democrat: A Reevaluation of the Personality of Harry S. Truman." Political Science Quarterly 106 (Spring 1991): 33–55.

Magazine article. Follow this model:

> Author's name. "Title of Article." Name of Magazine date: page number(s).

For articles in monthly or bimonthly magazines, give the month or months and the year. For weekly or biweekly publications, give the complete date, beginning with the day and abbreviating the month. For articles not appearing on consecutive pages, give only the first page number and a plus sign.

> Barrett, Wayne M., and Bernard Rowe. "What's Wrong With America and Can Anything Be Done About It?" USA Today Magazine Nov. 1994: 18–21.
>
> Bazell, Robert. "Sins and Twins." The New Republic 21 Dec. 1987: 17–18.
>
> Fletcher, John C., Franklin G. Miller, and Arthur L. Caplan. "Facing Up to Bioethical Decisions." Issues in Science and Technology Fall 1994: 75–80.

Article with no author.

"Teaching for Millions." Success Oct. 1992: 10.

Newspaper article. Following author's name and article title, give the name of the newspaper, underlined. If the city it is published in is not included in the name of the newspaper, add the name of the city in brackets after the name. Then give the date, beginning with the day, and abbreviating the month. Follow the date with a colon and page number(s) the article appears on. If the paper has more than one section and each section is paginated separately, give both section and page number. If it is a special edition of the newspaper, indicate that as well. Finally, if an article begins on one page and continues on another, use a plus sign.

> Dew, Diane. "Moral Responsibility the Best Contraceptive." The Milwaukee Journal 28 Sept. 1986: J6+.
> Schemo, Diana Jean. "Between the Art and the Artist Lies the Shadow." The New York Times 1 January 1995: sec. 4: 1.

Works Cited Form for Sources Other than Books and Periodical Articles

Congressional Record.

> United States. Senate. Transportation Systems for Alaskan Natural Gas. 95th Cong., 1st sess. S-2411. Washington: GPO, 1977.

Government document.

> U.S. Department of Health and Human Services. Caffeine and Pregnancy. Rockville, Md.: HHS Publications, 1981.

Lecture.

> Schilling, Brian. "The Role of First Responders in Medical Emergencies." Lecture at Whitko High School, 22 December 1995.

Letter.

> White, Jeremy. Letter to author. 1 October 1995.

Personal interview.

> Yahi, Mourad. Personal interview. 10 November 1995.

Reprint of an article provided by an information service.

> Koop, Everett C. "Life and Death and the Handicapped Newborn." Law & Medicine (Summer 1989): 101–113. Medical Science of Social Issues Resources Series. Boca Raton: SIRS, 1989. Art. 50.

Telephone interview.

> Yahi, Laurel. Telephone interview. 12 January 1995.

Pamphlet. Treat a pamphlet as you would a book:

> Tweddle, Dominic. <u>The Coppergate Helmet</u>. York, UK: Cultural Resource Management: 1984.

Television and radio programs.

> <u>60 Minutes</u>. CBS. WSAW, Wausaw. 17 Dec. 1995.

Note: For complete MLA guidelines on a wide range of sources, consult this book:

> Gibaldi, Joseph. *MLA* <u>Handbook for Writers of Research Papers</u>. 4th ed. New York: The Modern Language Association of America, 1995.

SAMPLE PAGES FROM STUDENT RESEARCH PAPERS USING MLA STYLE

Title Page. While MLA style does not require a separate title page, some instructors ask for it. If your instructor requires a title page, follow these guidelines:

- Center your title about a third to halfway down the page.
- Do not underline your title, put quotation marks around it, capitalize every letter in it, or use a period after it.
- Capitalize the first letter of all important words in the title.
- Beneath the title, double-space, type the word *by,* double-space again, and center your own name.
- Drop farther down the page and center your instructor's name, the course name, and the date. (See the example on the following page.)

Pagination and Spacing. The entire paper should be double-spaced, with pages numbered in the upper right-hand corner, one-half inch from the top and flush with the right margin. MLA style requires that pagination begin with page one and recommends that you include your last name before the page number.

First Page of a Research Paper with a Separate Title Page.

- If your instructor requires a separate title page, follow these guidelines for the first page of your paper: Type your last name and the number 1 in the upper right-hand corner, one-half inch from the top of the page, flush with the right margin.
- Drop down two inches from the top of the page and center your title, exactly as it appears on your title page.
- Do not underline your title, put quotation marks around it, capitalize every letter in it, or use a period after it.
- Capitalize the first letter of all important words in the title.
- Double-space and begin the body of your paper.

Nature vs. Nurture

by

Steph Niedermair

Professor Mitchell

English 102

2 May 1996

```
                                                    Heiman 1
                    The Effects of Secondhand Smoke
                Ever since the Surgeon General's first report in 1964 on

         the effects of cigarette smoking, smokers and nonsmokers

         have clashed in heated debates.
```

First Page of a Research Paper Without a Separate Title Page. If your instructor does not require a separate title page, follow these guidelines:

- Place your name, your instructor's name, the course title, and the date in the upper left-hand corner, one inch from the top of the paper and flush with the left margin.
- Double-space between each line.
- Double-space below the date and center your title.
- Do not underline your title, put quotation marks around it, capitalize every letter in it, or use a period after it.
- Capitalize the first letter of all important words in the title.
- Double-space again and begin the body of your paper.

```
                                                    Phonics 1
         Cory L. Vandertie

         Professor Kathy Mitchell

         English 102

         19 April 1996
                          The Phonics Controversy
                In recent years, school officials, teachers, and parents

         have been wrestling with the issue of how best to teach

         reading, with the controversy often centering on the conflict
```

Outline Page. If your instructor requires a formal outline, place it immediately after the title page. Your instructor will tell you how detailed your outline should be, but the basic directions include the following:

- Begin your outline with the thesis statement of your paper.
- Double-space between all lines of the outline.
- Use uppercase Roman numerals (I, II, III) for each major division of your outline and capital letters (A, B, C) for each subdivision under

each major division. If you find it necessary to further subdivide, use Arabic numerals (1, 2, 3) under capital letters and lowercase letters (a, b, c) under Arabic numerals.

- Do not number the outline page unless you have two or more pages. If your outline is two or more pages long, number all pages after the first in lowercase Roman numerals (ii, iii, iv), placed in the upper right-hand corner, one-half inch from the top of the paper and flush with the right margin.
- End with a statement summarizing your conclusion.

Here are outline pages from two student papers, the first with a fairly brief outline, the other with a more detailed outline.

Outline

Thesis: Nature and nurture play equal roles in personality development.

I. Genetics of personality

    A. Minnesota's twin study

    B. Specific tendency studies

    C. Twin meetings

II. Nurturing of personality

    A. Mead

    B. Pavlov and B.F. Skinner

III. Equality in personality development

    A. Corn

    B. Dog

    C. Jean and Joan

Conclusion: Research demonstrates that genetics alone do not fully determine personality.

Outline

Thesis: Parents, educators, and reading experts disagree on the issue of whether phonics instruction is beneficial to beginning readers.

I. Introduction
   A. Rudolph Flesch's observations
   B. National Assessment of Education Progress reports

II. Background
   A. Introduction to phonics
   B. Failure of schools to teach reading
   C. Regna Lee Wood

III. Phonics instruction
   A. How phonics works
   B. Problems associated with the teaching of phonics
   C. Factors associated with teaching phonics
      1. Direct
      2. Systemic
      3. Intensive

IV. Negative effects of phonics instruction
   A. Lack of information and knowledge
   B. Hooked on Phonics

V. Positive effects of phonics instruction
   A. Present-day improvements over early techniques
   B. Myths about phonics dispelled
   C. Andrew Schuster's story

VI. Jeanne Sternlicht Chall's research
   A. History of research
   B. *The Great Debate*

Conclusion: The debate over the benefits of phonics remains unresolved.

Introductory Paragraphs and Body of the Paper. As with any other kind of writing assignment, begin with an introduction that provides background information that makes clear what the topic of your paper is or what direction your argument will take, or that in some way sets the stage for what follows. State your thesis or central idea early in the paper. If your topic is controversial, explain the nature of the controversy. Once you have introduced your topic sufficiently, begin a development of your argument. Here are the opening pages of Steph Niedermair's paper, "Nature vs. Nurture."

Steph's introduction explains something of the nature of the controversy between those who believe environment plays a greater role in personality development and those who believe heredity plays a greater role. Steph's thesis indicates that she sides with those who believe both play equal roles. Readers can expect to see a development in the rest of the paper of each of these positions, as well as persuasive evidence from a variety of authorities in support of Steph's conclusion.

Here, Steph has combined a direct quotation and a paraphrase. The parenthetical citation tells us the source and the page number on which the quoted and paraphrased material is found.

Neidermair 1

Nature vs. Nurture

"Nature vs. nurture" is one of the most heatedly debated topics in the area of human biology today. Most scientists and nurturists agree that temperament and environment interact in some way to form personality. Their opinions differ, however, when it comes to how much and in what ways each factor influences personality and behavior. Geneticists are convinced that most of one's personality is formed at the moment of conception. On the other hand, nurturists claim that people who believe that genes are in control of personality do not take into consideration the fact that society and environment have a major effect on personality development. A review of both sides of the issue leads me to the conclusion that the human personality is so complex that it can be explained by neither heredity nor environment but rather by a combination of both.

Sociobiologists, for example, are convinced that nature and nurture are of equal importance. They agree with the geneticists' view that babies are born with a predisposed personality. But they add that social and nurturing experiences can "intensify, diminish, or modify" personality traits (Wood and Wood 272). Gerald McClearn, a psychologist and twin researcher at Pennsylvania State University, explained personality development realistically when he said, "'A gene can produce a nudge in one

The information about Gerald McClearn establishes his credentials.

McClearn's words are in both single and double quotation marks because he was quoted in the anonymous article "How Genes Shape Personality."

Neidermair 2

direction or another, but it does not directly control

The words *qtd. in* in the citation for McClearn's words mean "quoted in." Steph did not read his words in the original but as they were quoted in the article "How Genes Shape Personality."

behavior. It doesn't take away a person's free will'" (qtd. in "How Genes Shape Personality" 62). This component of an individual's free will is crucial to understanding the relative roles of nature and nurture in personality development.

The debate began over a century ago when Sir Francis Galton conducted the first twin studies, and it continues today with the work on human biology that is being done in many university research laboratories. The "nature vs. nurture" controversy is being heavily studied at the

Paragraph 3 is entirely in Steph's own words. She has done enough reading in her sources to know that twins are crucial to research in the area of personality formation and human behavior and that the University of Minnesota twin studies are common knowledge. Thus, paragraph 3 does not require any documentation.

University of Minnesota's Twin Research Center, for instance, where scientists are trying to quantify genetic and environmental factors that influence human behavior. Most research involves studying both identical and fraternal twins, some of whom were reared together and some of whom were reared apart. Identical twins who were reared apart are ideal for these studies because they share the same genetic codes but not the same environments. At the University of Minnesota, the twins go through six days of physical, psychological, and intellectual testing.

Winifred Gallagher reports that these twins answer 15,000 questions about their interests, values, principles, and eating habits. She explains that the Multidimensional

Steph does not need to give a citation at the end of the first sentence in paragraph 4 because she has named her authority and made it clear in her second sentence that she is still paraphrasing from that same authority. The parenthetical citation tells us the source.

Neidermair 3

Personality Questionnaire (MPQ), developed by Auke
Tellegen of the University of Minnesota, evaluates eleven
traits that can be broken down into three categories:
"positive emotionality," "negative emotionality," and
"constraint" ("Manner Born" 61). For their tests, Tellegen
and a team of scientists gathered 407 pairs of twins. Of
these, 261 pairs were identical, 44 of whom had been
reared apart. The other 146 pairs were fraternal, of
whom 27 sets had been reared apart (Konner 64). From
the MPQ, scientists obtained approximate percentages
relating to how much of each of the eleven traits was
caused by genetics. The results looked like this:
extroversion–61%; conformity–60%; worry–55%;
creativity–55%; paranoia–55%; optimism–54%;
cautiousness–51%; aggressiveness–48%;
ambitiousness–46%; orderliness–43%; and intimacy–33%
("How Genes Shape Personality" 62). These percentages
vary from person to person, but most times when twins
are subjected to testing, the results are remarkably alike
for each person. Minnesota scientists have concluded that
this data shows that genes are more influential than
nurture on most personality traits (Bazell 17).

    Theodore Reich, a psychiatric geneticist at Washington
University in St. Louis, is not surprised by new evidence
showing that genes influence personality. He says that,
after all, people have been breeding animals to obtain
certain traits or behaviors for many years (Holden 601).
The genetics of personality gets even more complicated
when one takes into consideration the fact that each trait
tested by MPQ is not controlled by one gene alone.

Note that the title of the Gallagher article, "Manner Born," is included because there are two articles by WInifred Gallagher on Steph's Works Cited page.

Complete bibliographic information for the Bazell article is given on Steph's Works Cited page.

In the following excerpt from Missy Heiman's paper, "The Effects of Secondhand Smoke," notice the parenthetical references to testimony recorded in the *Congressional Record* and to a government document:

Heiman 3

According to an investigation into whether to prohibit smoking in federal buildings conducted by the United States House Subcommittee of the Committee on Public Works and Transportation, almost 50 million nonsmokers over the age of 35 are regularly passive smokers, that is, they are exposed to environmental tobacco smoke (ETS) (412). According to biochemical markers, ETS is the equivalent of smoking two cigarettes a day (Hayward 7), so a person who chooses not to smoke is subjected to the same harmful effects of smoking as a smoker is. Since much of people's time is spent indoors, it is difficult for nonsmokers to escape ETS if they live or work with smokers. The Environmental Protection Agency (EPA) has shown that pollutant levels are higher indoors than out, causing real concern for the health of nonsmokers: "[We have] concluded that the widespread exposure to environmental tobacco smoke in the U.S. presents a serious and substantial public health risk" (U.S. House Subcommittee on Public Works and Grounds 173-74).

The risk includes adults and children alike. An estimated 50,000 adult Americans die from secondhand smoke each year: 35,000 from heart disease, 3,000 from lung cancer, and 12,000 from other types of cancers

To cite a government document, use the committee or agency name followed by a page reference. For agencies or committees with long names, it is better to use the name in the text of your paper, rather than interrupt the flow of your text with a long parenthetical reference.

Missy uses brackets to insert the words "We have" in the quotation from the EPA.

To refer to something by its initials, write it out the first time you mention it and put in parentheses immediately after it the initials you will use thenceforth to refer to it: environmental tobacco smoke (ETS) and Environmental Protection Agency (EPA).

Heiman 4

("Pros/Cons" 142). Those 50,000 nonsmoking people are
paying a price that people used to think was reserved only
for smokers. In Wisconsin alone, more than 10 percent of
lung cancer deaths are attributed to passive smoke
(Hayward 7). Nationally, according to Dr. Randolph D.
Smoak Jr., ""Passive smoking" is the third leading cause
of premature death in the United States, exceeded only by
direct smoking and alcohol'" (qtd. in "Pros/Cons" 142).
Those lives could have been saved had smoking been
permitted only outdoors.

Children are also victims of passive smoke. The EPA
concluded in 1993 that secondhand smoke can cause
respiratory problems in children ("Second Hand" 130).
Besides respiratory ailments, children are subject to many
other risks from secondhand smoke, such as increased
chances of chronic middle-ear infections, worsened
conditions in asthmatics, or even increased chances of
developing asthma ("Second Hand" 133). The question is,
do smokers have the right to endanger the lives and well-
being of children and adults by smoking in public places?
Representative Henry Waxman, a Democrat from
California who is the main sponsor of the Smoke-Free
Environment Act, declares, "'Smokers do not have the
right to jeopardize the health of nonsmokers, particularly
children'" ("Pros/Cons" 142). Representative Waxman's
Act was approved by the House committee in May 1994. It
prohibits smoking in buildings visited by ten or more
people per week, except in designated areas that must
have separate ventilation systems.

The words of Dr.
Randolph D.
Smoak Jr. are
quoted in the
source Missy read.
His words also
include a phrase in
quotation marks.
As a result, Missy's
quotation of
Smoak's words
begins with a triple
set of quotation
marks: single
within double to
indicate the
passage is quoted
in her source and
double within the
single to indicate
the phrase is
quoted within the
quotation.

"Second Hand"
and "Pros/Cons"
are short titles for
articles with no au-
thors' names.

Works Cited Page. The works cited pages for Steph Niedermair's and Missy Heiman's papers illustrate how to cite some of the most common sources used in undergraduate research papers, including books, weekly news magazine articles, newspaper articles, journal articles, essays in a collection, and government documents.

Niedemair 10

Works Cited

Bazell, Robert. "Sins and Twins." The New Republic 21 Dec.
1987: 17–18.

Gallagher, Winifred. "How We Become What We Are." The
Atlantic Monthly Sept. 1994: 38–40+.

——— "To the Manner Born." Rolling Stone 19 Nov. 1987: 56+.

Holden, Constance. "The Genetics of Personality." Science
237 (1987): 598–601.

"How Genes Shape Personality." U.S. News & World Report
13 Apr. 1987: 58–62.

Konnert, Melvin. "Under the Influence." Omni Jan. 1990:
62–64+.

Macionis, John J. "Socialization." Sociology. Englewood
Cliffs, N.J.: Prentice Hall, 1993. 131.

Wood, Samuel E. and Ellen R. Green Wood. "Child
Development." The World of Psychology. Needham
Heights, N.J.: Allyn and Bacon, 1993. 272.

Heiman 10

Works Cited

"Airline Smoking Ban Widens." Wall Street Journal 2 Nov.
    1994, eastern ed.,: B4.

"A Big Mac, Fries—And Clean Air." The New York Times 7
    Mar. 1994, late ed.: A16.

Hayward, Julie. Exposure to Tobacco Smoke: Effects on
    Children and Nonsmoking Adults. Madison: Wisconsin
    Dept. of Health and Social Services, August 1989.

Hilts, Philip J. "McDonald's Bans Smoking At All the Sites It
    Owns." The New York Times 24 Feb. 1994, late ed.:
    A16.

Nieves, Evelyn. "Going Smoke-Free: More Malls Joining in
    the Bans on Tobacco." The New York Times 2 Aug.
    1993, late ed.: A1+.

"Pros & Cons: Should H.R. 3434, the Smoke-Free
    Environment Act, Be Approved?" Congressional Digest
    May 1994: 142–160.

"Second-Hand Smoke." Congressional Digest May 1994:
    130–141.

Schmitt, Eric. "Military Tightens Its Rules Against
    Smoking." The New York Times 9 Mar. 1994, late ed.:
    A13.

"Travel Adviser." Travel Holiday Apr. 1994: 18.

U.S. House. Committee on Public Works and Transportation.
    Subcommittee on Public Buildings and Grounds. To
    Prohibit Smoking in Federal Buildings. 103rd Cong., 1st
    sess. H.R. 881. Washington, D.C.: GPO, 1993.

USING APA DOCUMENTATION STYLE

The documentation style of the American Psychological Association (APA), also referred to as the *author/date system,* is used widely in the behavioral and social sciences. It differs from that of the Modern Language Association (MLA), used primarily in the humanities, in some significant ways. While APA style uses parenthetical notes in the sentences to which they refer, as does MLA style, the contents of the notes differ. In the APA system, the year of publication is given in the parenthetical note, and page numbers are given only for quotations, not for paraphrases. Finally, sources are listed at the end of the paper on a page called References rather than Works Cited, and formatting for that page is quite different from formatting in MLA style. See guidelines below for both in-text citations and composing a References list using APA style.

For complete details on APA style, consult this source:

> American Psychological Association. *Publication Manual of the American Psychological Association.* 4th ed. Washington, D.C.: American Psychological Assn., 1994.

Parenthetical Citations Using APA Style.

- For quotations, include author's last name, a comma, the year the work was published, another comma, and the page number, preceded by the abbreviation *p.* or *pp.:*

  Many experts agree that "it is much easier and more comfortable to teach as one learned" (Chall, 1989, p. 21).

- If the source has two authors, name them both and use the ampersand (&) to separate their names:

  President Truman and his advisors were aware that the use of the bomb was no longer required to prevent an invasion of Japan by the Soviets (Alperovitz & Messer, 1991/92).

- Omit from the parenthetical citation any information given in the text:

  Samuel E. Wood and Ellen R. Green Wood (1993a) note that socio-biologists believe that social and nurturing experiences can "intensify, diminish or modify" personality traits (p. 272).

- If author's name is given in the text, follow it with the year of publication in parentheses:

  Nancy Paulu (1988) believes that children who are taught phonics get off to a better start than those who are not taught phonics.

- For works with three to five authors, name all of the authors the first time you refer to the work, but after that give only the last name of the first author followed by "et al." For a work with six or more authors, give only the first author's last name, followed by "et al." for all citations, including the first.

- If the author's name is repeated in the same paragraph, it is not necessary to repeat the year. However, if the author is cited in another paragraph, give the year of the work again.

- For summaries and paraphrases, give author and year but not page number of the information:

Minnesota scientists have concluded that this data shows that genes are more influential than nurture on most personality traits (Bazell, 1987).

- If the source has no author, use a short form of the title:

The twins were both born with musical abilities, but their unique experiences determined whether they acted on this ability ("How Genes Shape Personality," 1987).

Note: The first letter of each word in the short title is capitalized, but in the references list, only the first letter of the first word is capitalized.

- If you use two or more sources by the same author and they were published in the same year, use lowercase letters to refer to the order in which they appear on the references page:

Wood & Wood (1993a) observe that . . .
Other authorities (Wood & Wood, 1993b) agree, pointing out that . . .

- If one of your sources quotes or refers to another and you want to use that source in your paper, use the words *cited in,* followed by the source you read and the year the source was published. If you quote directly, give the page number of the source you read on which the quotation appeared:

Gerald McClearn, a psychologist and twin researcher at Pennsylvania State University, explained personality development realistically when he said: " 'A gene can produce a nudge in one direction or another, but it does not directly control behavior. It doesn't take away a person's free will' " (cited in "How Genes Shape Personality," 1987, p. 62).

SAMPLE PAGES FROM STUDENT RESEARCH PAPER USING APA STYLE

Here is a shortened version of Cory L. Vandertie's research paper entitled "The Phonics Controversy," illustrating in-text citations using APA style. Cory's outline appears in the earlier section in this chapter, illustrating outlines.

In papers written in APA style, provide a shortened version of the title, known as a *running head*, in the upper-right-hand corner of the page along with the page number.

If your instructor requires a separate title page, the title page is numbered 1.

Phonics 1

Cory L. Vandertie

Professor Kathy Mitchell

English 102

19 April 1996

The Phonics Controversy

The introductory paragraphs provide a background for the research topic.

In recent years, school officials, teachers, and parents have been wrestling with the issue of how best to teach reading, with the controversy often centering on the conflict over the effectiveness of phonics in such instruction. Rudolph Flesch, in his best-selling 1955 book *Why Johnny Can't Read*, was one of the first educators to advocate the use of phonics in reading classes. His book not only brought national attention to the reading problems of America's children but also endorsed the use of phonics to overcome those problems

Cory read about the Flesch book in Groff's book.

(cited in Groff, 1989). Neither the problem of children's inability to read effectively nor the effectiveness of phonics instruction has been satisfactorily addressed in the forty

Write author's full name the first time it is mentioned.

years since Flesch's book, however. According to Regna Lee Wood (1992), literacy rates continue to decline. In "That's Right—They're Wrong: Decline in Reading Ability Due to Abandonment of Phonics," Wood includes these startling

While only the first letter of the first word in the title of a work is capitalized in the references list, in your paper you must capitalize as you would other titles.

results of studies by the National Assessment of Educational Progress (NAEP): "Twenty years of NAEP reading tests show that most 7th-graders today can't read 6th grade lessons; most 8th-graders can't read 7th-grade lessons; and most 11th-graders can't read 9th-grade lessons written with 6th-

Give page number on
which a direct quotation
appears in the source.

Phonics 2

grade vocabularies" (p. 52). Statistics such as these have

This is a new
paragraph so the
date of Wood's
publication needs
to be mentioned
again.

created tension among educators as they debate how to

improve reading skills.

The declining literacy rate is an alarming indicator that

something must be done differently in our schools. Wood

(1992) points out that in 1930, only three million Americans

This is a
paraphrase, so
no page number
need be given.

could not read, but in 1990, 30 to 35 million U.S. citizens

could not read and were considered to be truly illiterate. She

also reports that two out of every three 17-year-olds could

not read well enough to do high school work in any subject.

The pronoun
she makes it
clear that Cory
is referring to
Wood,
mentioned in
the previous
sentence.

Educators and parents who are concerned about this

dramatic increase in the illiteracy rate and the inability of

the majority of students to read at their own grade levels

cannot refuse to explore all possible explanations for the

failure of our schools to teach reading adequately. One

avenue for exploration that may prove fruitful is the phonics

controversy. Parents, teachers, and reading experts familiar

with phonics all differ sharply in their views, compounding

the dilemma of whether phonics instruction should be

included in American schools. What role *does* phonics

education play in the teaching of reading?

More than 450 years ago, phonics instruction was

introduced to help young readers learn more about the

Cory asks a question as his
thesis, reflecting the
controversy over teaching
phonics. He will answer the
question in the course of
the paper.

Phonics 3

relationship between letters and sound (Groff, 1989). Some
researchers think that phonics has been used to teach
reading since the time of ancient Greeks. Chall (1989)
describes the method "as a tool for helping beginners identify
words accurately so that they can read texts with
comprehension earlier and more efficiently" (p. 4). Groff
agrees that phonics instruction can be very useful for the
development of children's word recognition skills. The
problem is how to convince parents and teachers of the
benefits of phonics. Wood (1992) believes that the horrible
failure of our schools to teach children to read skillfully
began years ago. She writes that "[the failure of schools to
teach reading] began in 1929 and 1930 when hundreds of
primary teachers, guided by college reading professors,
stopped teaching beginners to read by matching sounds with
letters that spell sounds" (p. 52).

 Phonics is not the entire answer to the question of how
best to teach children to read, however. Most reading experts
agree that "the most the application of phonics can do is help
children produce the approximate pronunciation of words"
(Groff, 1989, p. 6). Roberts (1989), writing for Parents
magazine, reports that phonics may not help all children
learn to pronounce words. He explains that anyone who has

The year of
Groff's publica-
tion has already
been mentioned
in this
paragraph, so it
is not repeated
here.

The brackets
indicate that
Cory has added
his own words
to the direct
quotation.

For smoother
transition and to
avoid too many
parenthetical
interruptions,
mention author
and source in
your text
whenever
possible.

Phonics 4

a visual or auditory handicap will find it harder to read using phonics. For instance, Roberts points out that a child who has suffered from an ear infection that caused temporary hearing loss at an early age may find it difficult to learn to read by using phonics because of missing out on experiencing sound discrimination.

* * * * *

In conclusion, many experts believe that we have the ability and the knowledge to educate our schoolchildren more effectively by using phonics. But while both traditional and experimental evidence supports the use of phonics, the debate continues. Educators who are not familiar with phonics instruction must be enlightened, perhaps with in-service workshops from experts on phonics instruction. Parents, too, may need to be convinced. Reading experts must be willing to work together to resolve some of the issues in the phonics debate, perhaps by putting together a combination of approaches to the teaching of reading that includes phonics. The bottom line is that we all must work to find a solution to the appalling rate of adult illiteracy in this country and the unsettling inability of students to read at their own grade levels. We must find solutions to these problems, or we risk jeopardizing not only our children's futures but our own.

Reference List

- Bibliographic entries for all works cited in a paper are listed in alphabetical order on a page entitled References.
- The first line of each entry in the reference list is indented five spaces and second and subsequent lines are flush with the left margin.
- Give last name and only the initials of the first and middle names of authors.
- The year of publication, in parentheses, follows author's name.
- For books, capitalize only proper nouns and the first word of the title and subtitle and underline the title.
- If a book is edited, place the abbreviation *Ed.* or *Eds.* in parentheses after the name of the editor(s).
- If there are two or more authors, each name is reversed and an ampersand (&), not the word *and,* is placed before the last name.
- For articles, book chapters, or titles of essays in collections, capitalize as for book titles and do not use quotation marks or underlining.
- Capitalize first letters of all key words in the name of the periodical and underline the name.
- Use the abbreviations *p.* and *pp.* for inclusive page numbers of articles in magazines and journals except when volume and issue number is given. If volume number is given, place it after name of the periodical and underline it. If an issue number is also given, place it in parentheses after volume number:

  > Hamby, A. L. (1991, Spring). An American Democrat: A reevaluation of the personality of Harry S. Truman. <u>Political Science Quarterly</u>, *106,* 33–55.

- If two or more works by the same author appear on the reference list, put them in chronological order. Repeat the author's name each time, followed by the date in parentheses.
- If an author has two works in the same year, put them in alphabetical order and give each entry a lowercase letter: (1996a), (1996b).

Phonics 12

References

Carbo, M. (1987, February). Reading styles research: What works isn't always phonics. Phi Delta Kappan, 68, 431–435.

Chall, J.S. (1989). The role of phonics in teaching reading. Washington, DC: U.S. Department of Education, Office of Educational Research and Improvement.

Groff, P. (1977). Phonics: Why and how. Morristown, NJ: General Learning.

Groff, P. (1989). Modern phonics instruction. Washington: U.S. Department of Education, Office of Educational Research and Improvement.

Kantrowitz, B. (1991, May 20). The profits of reading. Newsweek, p. 67.

Roberts, F. (1989, January). Does phonics cure reading problems? Parents, p. 49.

Weaver, C. (1991, April). Weighing the claims about phonics first. The Education Digest, pp. 19–22.

Wood, R.L. (1992, September 14). That's right—they're wrong: Decline in reading ability due to abandonment of phonics. National Review, pp. 49–52.

Young, P. (1993, January 11). The reading debate. McClean's, pp. 42–43.

PART TWO

ARTS AND THE MEDIA

CHAPTER 5

Art and Artists

CHAPTER 6

Music

CHAPTER 7

Film and Popular Culture

CHAPTER 8

Advertising

CHAPTER 9

Television

CHAPTER 5

ART AND ARTISTS

Human beings have always used a variety of creative ways in which to express themselves imaginatively through such forms as storytelling, drawing, sculpture, and music. Researchers have discovered paintings in prehistoric caves that provide evidence of the earliest humans' compulsion to tell stories or depict significant aspects of their lives through pictures, as Robert Hughes's discussion of prehistoric cave paintings in "Behold the Stone Age" reports. Because the very nature of artistic expression changes over time from culture to culture and from generation to generation within each culture, art provides a rich record of the lives of humans and their relationship with their world from the very earliest period of human existence. As you read Hughes's essay, consider whether you agree with him on the implications of the cave paintings. Can you think of other such discoveries that reveal something of the nature of both prehistoric humans and humans today? Consider, too, how our society might be changed without art—or even how your own life might change if art were not a part of it. Think, too, of the variety of artistic forms you are familiar with. Can any one in particular be said to reflect the essence of our culture? Why or why not?

Despite the persistence of art throughout time, the role of the artist in society and the relative value of art are often hotly debated topics. Tastes change and differ from generation to generation and individual to individual, as do values and beliefs about what is important to sustain and nurture a society and the standards by which people judge the merits of works of art. Determining what makes something "good" or "bad" is often a subjective response to it rather than a conscious application of objective standards. For instance, do you have any trouble determining whether a new movie, painting, or song is good or bad? How do you judge such works?

While this chapter focuses on the visual arts, literature is also a significant art form. Indeed, some would claim that imaginative writing, whether it be a short story, a novel, a poem, or some other form of creative expression, is just as crucial to the nurturing of the human soul as are visual arts and music. Certainly this is Norman Cousins' position in "The Poet and the Computer." Elsewhere in this textbook, in the section on the natural sciences, several writers whose chief interests are science and scientific writing explore the nature of human intelligence as measured by our ability to create metaphor and to think imaginatively. Whatever its form, imagination and creativity are clearly important components of human identity. As you read Cousins' essay, think about the degree to which you would describe yourself as creative. Do you agree with him that humans' imaginative capabilities are as essential to their identity as is their scientific ingenuity?

As you will see, the essays in this chapter raise some intriguing questions, such as, given the quantity of art, music, and literature produced historically and currently, how do we measure quality? Would our society be better off without artists, or would it lose its soul without them? The readings touch on some of the broader issues related to the role of the artist and the nature of art, too, including Diana Jean Schemo's thoughts on the connection between artists' moral nature and their work in "Between the Art and the Artist Lies the Shadow." Do you think that an artist's private morality should in any way influence the way you perceive her or his work?

The subject of art and artists is so vast that these few readings serve only to indicate the breadth and depth of possible topics and issues related to it. As you consider the points made by the writers in this section on art and the one that follows on music, think also about the kinds of imaginative writing you like to read and perhaps write yourself. Think about the role all of these forms of expression play in humans' lives: How might their absence affect us? Do you think you would be impoverished without art, music, and literature? Why or why not?

BEHOLD THE STONE AGE

Robert Hughes

Robert Hughes is a writer for Time *magazine and author of many books, including* The Art of Australia *(1966),* Heaven and Hell in Western Art *(1969),* The Shock of the New *(1981), and* The Fatal Shore *(1987). A widely known and respected art critic and cultural commentator, Hughes wrote this cover story for the February 13, 1995, issue of* Time. *In the essay, Hughes not only reports on the paintings discovered in a Paleolithic cave in France but also raises questions about the purpose and nature of art not only for Cro-Magnon humans but for us today.*

Not since the Dead Sea Scrolls has anything found in a cave caused so much excitement. The paintings and engravings, more than 300 of them, amount to a sort of Ice Age Noah's ark—images of bison, mammoths and woolly rhinoceroses, of a panther, an owl, even a hyena. Done on the rock walls with plain earth pigments—red, black, ocher—they are of singular vitality and power, and despite their inscrutability to modern eyes, they will greatly enrich our picture of Cro-Magnon life and culture.

When the French government last month announced that a local official, Jean-Marie Chauvet, had discovered the stunning Paleolithic cave near Avignon, experts swiftly hailed the 20,000-year-old paintings as a trove rivaling—and perhaps surpassing—those of Lascaux and Altamira. "This is a virgin site—it's completely intact. It's great art," exulted Jean Clottes, an adviser to the French Culture Ministry and a leading authority on prehistoric art. It has also reopened some of the oldest and least settled of questions: When, how and above all why did Homo sapiens start making art?

In the span of human prehistory, the Cro-Magnon people who drew the profusion of animals on the bulging limestone walls of the Chauvet cave were fairly late arrivals. Human technology—the making of tools from stone—had already been in existence for nearly 2 million years. There are traces of symbolism and ritual in burial sites of Neanderthals, an earlier species, dating back to 100,000 B.P. (before the present). Not only did the placement of the bodies seem meaningful, but so did the surrounding pebbles and bones with fragmentary patterns scratched on them. These, says Clottes, "do indicate that the Neanderthals had some creative capacity."

4   Though the dates are vastly generalized, most prehistorians seem to agree that art—communication by visual images—came into existence somewhere around 40,000 B.P. That was about the time when Cro-Magnons, Homo sapiens, reached Ice Age Europe, having migrated from the Middle East. Some experts think the Cro-Magnons brought a weapon that made Neanderthals an evolutionary has-been: a more advanced brain, equipped with a large frontal lobe "wired" for associative thinking. For art, at its root, is association—the power to make one thing stand for and symbolize another, to create the agreements by which some marks on a surface denote, say, an animal, not just to the markmaker but to others.

Among the oldest types of art is personal decoration—ornaments such as beads, bracelets, pendants and necklaces. The body was certainly one of the first surfaces for symbolic expression. What did such symbols communicate? Presumably the wearer's difference from others, as a member of a distinct group, tribe or totemic family: that he was a bison-man, say, and not a reindeer-man.

The Cro-Magnons were not the inarticulate Alley Oops of popular myth. They were nomadic hunter-gatherers with a fairly developed technology. They wore animal-skin clothing and moccasins tailored with bone needles, and made beautiful (and highly efficient) laurel-leaf-shaped flint blades. Living in small groups, they constructed tents from skins, and huts from branches and (in what is now Eastern Europe) mammoth bones.

Most striking was their yearning to make art in permanent places— the walls of caves. This expansion from the body to the inert surface was in itself a startling act of lateral thinking, an outward projection of huge cultural consequence, and Homo sapiens did not produce it quickly. As much time elapsed between the first recognizable art and the cave paintings of Lascaux and Altamira, about 15 to 20 millenniums, as separates Lascaux (or Chauvet) from the first TV broadcasts. But now it was possible to see an objective image in shared space, one that was not the property of particular bodies and had a life of its own; and from this point the whole history of human visual communication unfolds.

8   We are apt to suppose that Cro-Magnon cave art was rare and exceptional. But wrongly; as New York University anthropologist Randall White points out, more than 200 late–Stone Age caves bearing wall paintings, engravings, bas-relief decorations and sculptures have been found in southwestern Europe alone. Since the discovery of Lascaux in 1940, French archaeologists have been finding an average of a cave a year—and, says professor Denis Vialou of Paris' Institute of Human Paleontology, "there are certainly many, many more to be discovered, and while many might not prove as spectacular as Lascaux or Chauvet, I'd bet that some will be just as exciting."

No doubt many will never be found. The recently discovered painted cave at Cosquer in the south of France, for instance, can be reached only by scuba divers. Its entrance now lies below the surface of the Mediterranean; in the Upper Paleolithic period, from 70,000 B.P. to 10,000 B.P., so much of Europe's water was locked up in glaciers that the sea level was some 300 ft. lower than it is today.

Why the profuseness of Cro-Magnon art? Why did these people, of whom so little is known, need images so intensely? Why the preponderance of animals over human images? Archaeologists are not much closer to answering such questions than they were a half-century ago, when Lascaux was discovered.

Part of the difficulty lies in the very definition of art. As anthropologist Margaret Conkey of the University of California, Berkeley puts it, "Many cultures don't really produce art, or even have any concept of it. They have spirits, kinship, group identity. If people from highland New Guinea looked at some of the Cro-Magnon cave art, they wouldn't see anything recognizable"—and not just because there are no woolly rhinos in New Guinea either. Today we can see almost anything as an aesthetic configuration and pull it into the eclectic orbit of late-Western "art experience"; museums have trained us to do that. The paintings of Chauvet strike us as aesthetically impressive in their power and economy of line, their combination of the sculptural and the graphic—for the artists used the natural bulges and bosses of the rock wall to flesh out the forms of the animals' rumps and bellies. But it may be that aesthetic pleasure, in our sense, was the last thing the Ice Age painters were after.

12   These were functional images; they were meant to produce results. But what results? To represent something, to capture its image on a wall in colored earths and animal fat, is in some sense to capture and master it; to have power over it. Lascaux is full of nonthreatening animals, including wild cattle, bison and horses, but Chauvet pullulates with dangerous ones—cave bears, a panther and no fewer than 50 woolly rhinos. Such creatures, to paraphrase Claude Lévi-Strauss, were good to think with, not good to

eat. We can assume they had a symbolic value, maybe even a religious value, to those who drew them, that they supplied a framework of images in which needs, values and fears—in short, a network of social consciousness—could be expressed. But we have no idea what this framework was, and merely to call it "animistic" does not say much.

Some animals have more than four legs, or grotesquely exaggerated horns; is that just style, or does it argue a state of ritual trance or hallucination in the artists? No answer, though some naturally occurring manganese oxides, the base of some of the blacks used in cave paintings, are known to be toxic and to act on the central nervous system. And the main technique of Cro-Magnon art, according to prehistorian Michel Lorblanchet, director of France's National Center of Scientific Research, involved not brushes but a kind of oral spray-painting—blowing pigment dissolved in saliva on the wall. Lorblanchet, who has re-created cave paintings with uncanny accuracy, suggests that the technique may have had a spiritual dimension: "Spitting is a way of projecting yourself onto the wall, becoming one with the horse you are painting. Thus the action melds with the myth. Perhaps the shamans did this as a way of passing into the world beyond."

Different hands (and mouths) were involved in the production, but whose hands? Did the whole Cro-Magnon group at Chauvet paint, or did it have an élite of artists, to be viewed by nonartists as something like priests or professionals? Or does the joining of many hands in a collaborative work express a kind of treaty between rival groups? Or were the paintings added to over generations, producing the crowded, palimpsest-like effect suggested by some of the photos? And so on.

A mere picture of a bison or a woolly rhino tells us nothing much. Suppose, France's Clottes suggests, that 20,000 years from now, after a global cataclysm in which all books perished and the word vanished from the face of the earth, some excavators dig up the shell of a building. It has pointy ogival arches and a long axial hall at the end of which is a painting of a man nailed to a cross. In the absence of written evidence, what could this effigy mean? No more than the bison or rhino on the rock at Chauvet. Representation and symbolism have parted company.

16   Chauvet cave could be viewed as a religious site—a paleolithic cathedral. Some have even suggested that a bear's skull found perched on a rock was an "altar." Says Henry de Lumley, director of France's National Museum of Natural History: "The fact that the iconography is relatively consistent, that it seems to obey certain rules about placement and even the way animals are drawn . . . is evidence of something sacred." Yet nobody lived in the cave, and no one in his right mind could imagine doing so; the first analyses of the contents have yielded no signs of human habitation, beyond the traces of animal-fat lamps and torches used by temporary visitors, and some mounds of pigmented earth left behind by the artists.

Modern artists make art to be seen by a public, the larger (usually) the better. The history of public art as we know it, across the past 1,000 years and more, is one of increasing access—beginning with the church open to the worshippers and ending with the pack-'em-in ethos of the modern museum, with its support-system of orientation courses, lectures, films, outreach programs and souvenir shops. Cro-Magnon cave art was probably meant to be seen by very few people, under conditions of extreme difficulty and dread. The caves may have been places of initiation and trial, in which consciousness was tested to an extent that we can only dimly imagine, so utterly different is our grasp of the world from that of the Cro-Magnons.

Try to imagine an art gallery that could be entered only by crawling on your belly through a hole in the earth; that ramified into dark tunnels, a fearful maze in the earth's bowels in which the gallerygoer could, at any moment, disturb one of the bears whose claw marks can still be seen on the walls; where the only light came from flickering torches, and the bones of animals littered the uneven floor. These are the archaic conditions that, one may surmise, produced the array of cave fears implanted in the human brain—fears that became absorbed into a later, more developed culture in such narratives as that of the mythical Cretan labyrinth in whose core the terrible Minotaur waited. Further metabolized, and more basically misunderstood, these sacred terrors of the deep earth undergird the Christian myth of hell. Which may, in fact, be the strongest Cro-Magnon element left in modern life.

Personal Response

Describe your own interests in the visual arts by explaining whether you like "art" in general and who, if any, are your favorite artists and works of art.

Questions for Class or Small Group Discussion

1. This essay raises a number of questions about the purpose and nature of Cro-Magnon art. What implications do you think those questions have for art today? Explain your answer.

2. What impact, if any, do you think the discovery of the paintings in a Paleolithic cave in France will have on us today? What do you think we can learn from them?

3. In what ways has art remained essentially the same since the period Hughes describes in this essay? How has it changed significantly? Be as specific as possible in your answer.

4. Hughes describes the paintings in the cave in France and theorizes why they were painted. Can you offer any other plausible reasons for the cave paintings? Explain your answer in detail.

THE POET AND THE COMPUTER

Norman Cousins

Norman Cousins (1915–1990) was editor of the Saturday Review *for thirty-five years. He wrote twenty-five books and numerous essays on a wide range of subjects, including* Talks with Nehru *(1951),* Who Speaks for Man? *(1953), and* Present Tense *(1967). More recently,* The Celebration of Life *(1974) and* The Anatomy of Illness *(1979) describe his experiences with and recovery from an illness that doctors told him was fatal. A holistic health pioneer, Cousins served on the medical faculty at UCLA from 1978 until his death. In 1990, he received the Albert Schweitzer Prize for Humanitarianism for his efforts on behalf of international peace. In this essay, which first appeared in* Beyond Literacy: The Second Gutenberg Revolution *(1989), Cousins argues the crucial importance of not only the poet but of all imaginative creativity in the electronic age.*

"A poet," said Aristotle, "has the advantage of expressing the universal; the specialist expresses only the particular." The poet, moreover, can remind us that man's greatest energy comes not from his dynamos but from his dreams. The notion of where a man ought to be instead of where he is; the liberation from cramped prospects; the intimations of immortality through art, all these proceed naturally out of dreams. But the quality of man's dreams can only be a reflection of his subconscious. What he puts into his subconscious, therefore, is quite literally the most important nourishment in the world.

Nothing really happens to a man except as it is registered in the subconscious. This is where event and feeling become memory and where the proof of life is stored. The poet, and I use the term to include all those who have respect for and speak to the human spirit, can help to supply the subconscious with material to enhance its sensitivity, thus safeguarding it. The poet, too, can help to keep man from making himself over to the image of his electronic marvels. The danger is not so much that man will be controlled by the computer as that he may imitate it.

There once was a time, in the history of this society, when the ability of people to convey meaning was enriched by their knowledge of and access to the work of creative minds from across the centuries. No more. Conversation and letters today, like education, have become enfeebled by emphasis on the functional and the purely contemporary. The result is a mechanization not just of the way we live but of the way we think and of the human spirit itself.

4   The delegates to the United States Constitutional Convention were able to undergird their arguments with allusions to historical situations and to the ideas of philosophers, essayists, and dramatists. Names such as Thucydides, Aristotle, Herodotus, Plutarch, or Seneca were commonly

cited to support their positions. They alluded to fictional characters from Aristophanes, Marlowe, or Shakespeare to lend color to the exploration of ideas. The analytical essays by Hamilton, Madison, and Jay that appeared in *The Federalist Papers* were an excursion into the remote corners of history.

Men such as Jefferson, Adams, Franklin, and Rush, could summon pertinent quotations from Suetonius or Machiavelli or Montaigne to illustrate a principle. If they referred to Bacon's opinion of Aristotle, they didn't have to cite particulars; they assumed such details were common knowledge. Their allusions were not the product of intellectual ostentation or ornamentation but the natural condiments of discourse, bringing out the full flavor of the cultivated intelligence.

The same was true of correspondence. People regarded letters as an art form and a highly satisfying way of engaging in civilized exchange. The correspondence of Jefferson and Adams and Priestley was not so much a display of personal matters as a review of the human condition. It was not unusual for the writers to range across the entire arena of human thought as a way of sharing perceptions. Allusion was common currency. Today, we rarely turn to letters as a way of embarking on voyages of intellectual discovery.

The essential problem of man in a computerized age remains the same as it has always been. That problem is not solely how to be more productive, more comfortable, more content, but how to be more sensitive, more sensible, more proportionate, more alive. The computer makes possible a phenomenal leap in human proficiency; it demolishes the fences around the practical and even the theoretical intelligence. But the question persists, and indeed grows, whether the computer makes it easier or harder for human beings to know who they really are, to identify their real problems, to respond more fully to beauty, to place adequate value on life, and to make their world safer than it now is.

8   Electronic brains can reduce the profusion of dead ends involved in vital research. But they can't eliminate the foolishness and decay that come from the unexamined life. Nor do they connect a man to the things he has to be connected to, the reality of pain in others; the possibilities of creative growth in himself; the memory of the race; and the rights of the next generation.

The reason these matters are important in a computerized age is that there may be a tendency to mistake data for wisdom, just as there has always been a tendency to confuse logic with values and intelligence with insight. Unobstructed access to facts can produce unlimited good only if it is matched by the desire and ability to find out what they mean and where they would lead.

Facts are terrible things if left sprawling and unattended. They are too easily regarded as evaluated certainties rather than as the rawest of raw materials crying to be processed into the texture of logic. It requires a very unusual mind, Whitehead said, to undertake the analysis of a fact. The computer can provide a correct number, but it may be an irrelevant number until judgment is pronounced.

To the extent, then, that man fails to make the distinction between the intermediate operations of electronic intelligence and the ultimate responsibilities of human decision and conscience, the computer could obscure man's awareness of the need to come to terms with himself. It may foster the illusion that he is asking fundamental questions when actually he is asking only functional ones. It may be regarded as a substitute for intelligence instead of an extension of it. It may promote undue confidence in concrete answers. "If we begin with certainties," Bacon said, "we shall end in doubts; but if we begin with doubts, and we are patient with them, we shall end in certainties."

12 The computer knows how to vanquish error, but before we lose ourselves in celebration of victory, we might reflect on the great advances in the human situation that have come about because men were challenged by error and would not stop thinking and probing until they found better approaches for dealing with it. "Give me a good fruitful error, full of seeds, bursting with its own corrections," Ferris Greenslet wrote. "You can keep your sterile truth for yourself."

Without taking anything away from the technicians, it might be fruitful to effect some sort of junction between the computer technologist and the poet. A genuine purpose may be served by turning loose the wonders of the creative imagination on the kinds of problems being put to electronic tubes and transistors. The company of poets may enable the men who tend the machines to see a larger panorama of possibilities than technology alone may inspire.

Poets remind men of their uniqueness. It is not necessary to possess the ultimate definition of this uniqueness. Even to speculate on it is a gain.

Personal Response

What are some examples of your creativity? Do you consider yourself a "poet" as Cousins defines the term?

Questions for Class or Small Group Discussion

1. Do you agree or disagree with the central argument of this essay? Explain your answer. Do you think Cousins is an alarmist, or does he have good cause for concern?

2. Discuss Cousins' lament that too few people today recognize "allusions to historical situations and to the ideas of philosophers, essayists, and dramatists" (paragraph 4). Do you agree with Cousins that this lack of knowledge is cause for concern? What does he think was gained when history, philosophy, and literature were common knowledge?

3. How many of the people named in paragraphs 4 and 5 do you recognize? In class, go through the list and try to identify them. For those whose names no one is familiar with, volunteer to find out who they are and report back to your classmates.

4. Cousins defines "the poet" to include "all those who have respect for and speak to the human spirit" (paragraph 2). Who do you think are today's poets? What do they contribute to our culture?

BETWEEN THE ART AND THE ARTIST LIES THE SHADOW

Diana Jean Schemo

Diana Jean Schemo writes for the New York Times. *In this piece, which first appeared in the January 1, 1995, issue of the* Times, *Schemo raises an intriguing point about the relation of artists and their creations. Should we, she asks, separate artists' political or moral beliefs from their art?*

Reports of the death of the playwright John Osborne last week, which chronicled a life of unrelenting venom, probably did not stir a great amount of soul-searching among those who loved his work. The author of the 1956 play "Look Back in Anger" seemed to have looked forward, sideways, up and down in anger through his life, and gave rise to a school of British playwrights of such familiar bitterness they had their own acronym, the A.Y.M.—Angry Young Men.

But why do suggestions that other artists whose work we admire—writers, composers, painters, actors and singers—had politics or personal habits we find despicable stir uneasiness within? Why can the knowledge of the anti-Semitism of Edgar Degas or T. S. Eliot, or allegations of the near-criminal opportunism of Bertolt Brecht or of Picasso's misogyny cause such profound turmoil in many people?

For some, the disparity between the beauty of art and the human foibles of an artist undoubtedly causes no alarm. The poet Kenneth Koch, among many others, argues that art exists on its own plane, and should be considered independent of the person who created it. Art may well be like nature, wrapped in its own splendor and mystery, no more beholden to moral tribulations than the crocuses that herald spring. Perhaps, unlike Dorothy in "The Wizard of Oz," one should never trouble over the befuddled shaman behind the curtains who fashions our illusions, but thank genius for its gifts and ignore the rest.

4   After all, discarding art on a political basis lands us in dubious company of both left and right, from Josef Stalin to Joseph McCarthy. And while mores shift through age and place, true art defies time; centuries after the

scandal wore off Michelangelo's homosexuality, the Sistine Chapel still takes the breath away.

Logically, we can recount the intellectual arguments with ease: that the composer's gifts have more to do with an intuitive ability to imagine complex patterns of sound than to form sound political judgments; that an ear for language and rhythm, which can make a fine writer, has nothing to do with an eye for morality, let alone humanity.

But while good art requires skills such as these, art at its best connects words, sounds, movement or color to emotions crystalized within us. It allows us to glimpse something sublime within human reach, to fulfill the unuttered promise of experience, to find the poetry in our loneliness. We come to believe the person capable of elevating the mundane acts of our lives, fitting them into the grander record of human experience, must also possess a greater measure of wisdom.

We discover a writer and feel as if we've made a new friend, welcoming his witticisms, stacking them on our night tables. We follow the progression of his thinking, wonder about his observations on the way to work and feel a twinge of pride for having recognized talent. We want to know more. We want to know everything about the person behind the curtains, as if putting together the pieces of their lives will unravel the mystery of their creations.

8   And the art we love becomes intensely intimate.

Like the gloriously extravagant writer of radio scripts in Mario Vargas Llosa's "Aunt Julia and the Script Writer," when we are about to be swallowed by the muck of life, we turn to art. We fall in love and hear Puccini in our heads. We grow old and find "The Love Song of J. Alfred Prufrock" ineffably moving:

> *There will be time, there will be time*
> *To prepare a face to meet the faces that you meet;*
> *There will be time to murder and create,*
> *And time for all the works and days of hands*
> *That lift and drop a question on your plate.*

William Styron's severe depression, recounted in his slender volume, "Darkness Visible" (Random House, 1990), culminated in his contemplating suicide through a wrenching, sleepless night. He found the strength to prevail upon hearing Brahms' "Alto Rhapsody," which seemed to draw him back into the human family. (Styron left it at that, never addressing the question of politics. But what if his savior had been Richard Strauss, who had headed the Reich Music Chamber under Hitler, in charge of making sure that no "subversive" music or Jewish musicians were heard in the concert halls and opera houses of Nazi Germany?)

12   And so to learn that Eliot was an anti-Semite becomes a kind of betrayal, as if we were taken in by fine phrases alone. The exhilaration of personal discovery one might have felt gives way to shame at having not

picked up on some fundamental flaw that, on some level, we reason, must have been transmitted in the work.

"If you're dealing with a writer, more so than an artist or a musician, you can find symptoms of the despicable private trait, which is often a blemish on the work," said George Stade, a professor of English and comparative literature at Columbia University and author of "Confessions of a Lady-Killer" (Norton, 1979). He noted that Eliot's "Gerontion," for example, contains an anti-Semitic caricature of the rootless Jew as landlord of Europe; his "Sweeney Among the Nightingales" speaks of "Rachel, née Rabinovitch," who "tears at the grapes with murderous paws."

Professor Stade said the relation between talent and integrity bothered him more when he was 15 than it does now, though he confessed that recent allegations that Brecht signed his name to other people's work has lowered his esteem for the playwright. "It's like a person you fall in love with for his or her physical beauty, who you're then disappointed to find isn't a good person," Professor Stade said.

More disturbing than the prospect that one fell for a pretty face are the doubts about one's own character that may arise. Does finding that literature that resonates to our very core was written by a philanderer suggest there is a liar or a cheat crouching silently within us?

16   Philip Larkin, the English poet laureate, maintained that most people, faced with contradictory judgments about an artist and his work, will adjust their views until the two elements fall in line rather than accept the ambiguity. Thus a fine poet who was a misanthrope and racist—as the posthumous publication of Larkin's own correspondence suggests he was—will come to be seen as either a bitter poet or a good person, Larkin contends.

It is usually not that simple. We almost don't want to know, we long for the state of unknowing appreciation. We want to say, "Come back. All is forgiven," but we can't.

And so at times we flatter ourselves with the notion that we are rising above petty strictures to value art in all its breadth and mystery, and we listen to Strauss with pleasure. Or it's possible to admit this is a shameful indulgence, and listen guiltily, as if we are holed up in the pantry with chocolate ice cream. The only other choice is to avoid the work as sham altogether.

Still, the private questions persist—testimony to the power of art, and its limits.

Personal Response

Is your regard for a work of art (of any kind) in any way influenced by what you know about the artist? Give an example to illustrate your answer.

Questions for Class or Small Group Discussion

1. Schemo's concluding statement suggests that questions about artists' political beliefs or private morality are "testimony to the power of art, and its limits." Discuss what you think the limits of art are, in this context.

2. Discuss the ways in which artists' private behavior or personal beliefs affect your own responses to their art. Give examples from as many different kinds of art as you can.

3. If you discovered that an artist whom you have always admired holds views you strongly disagree with or does something you think is horrible, do you think you would continue to appreciate his or her art? Why or why not? What sorts of things would make you change your attitude toward that art?

4. Conduct a classroom debate on Kenneth Koch's argument "that art exists on its own plane, and should be considered independent of the person who created it" (paragraph 3).

Perspectives on Arts and Artists

Suggestions for Synthesis

1. Drawing on two or all three of the selections in this chapter, explain your viewpoint on the importance of art. Be sure to defend your position by supplying evidence not only from the essays but from your own observations as well.

2. Taking Norman Cousins' definition of "poet" in "The Poet and the Computer" and Diana Jean Schemo's "Between the Art and the Artist Lies the Shadow" as starting points, argue who you think today's most creative people are. Your argument might be for a particular group of people (artists, scientists, musicians, television talk show hosts) or for a particular person. In either case, give supporting evidence to substantiate your viewpoint.

3. Invite two artists from the community or campus to speak to your class on what art means to them and how they see the place of art in America today. Then write an essay in which you not only synthesize their remarks but provide a reasoned critique of them as well.

4. Using Diana Jean Schemo's observations in "Between the Art and the Artists Lies the Shadow" as background, survey a group of your friends and acquaintances for their opinion of the place of an artist's private beliefs and behavior in judging the artist's work. Then report the results of your survey in an essay that synthesizes Schemo's comments and those of the people you interview.

Additional Writing Topics

1. In "Behold the Stone Age," Robert Hughes points out that the oldest form of art is personal decoration. The body is still being used as a surface for symbolic expression by some young people, who use such techniques as branding, piercing, and tattooing. Defend or attack these practices by considering their relative artistic or creative merits.

2. Define "excellence" in a specific art form (for instance, a painting, a novel, a poem, a song, or a film) by stating the criteria you use for judging that abstract quality and giving examples you believe best illustrate it.

3. Explore the question of what makes some art live for all time and other art disappear. That is, what makes a work of art "timeless"? Select a particular painting as an example and explain in as much detail as possible why you believe as you do.

4. Define *art* (an admittedly abstract term but one that people never tire of wrestling with) and explain what you think is gained by a culture's interest in and support of art and what you think would be lost without it. Or, argue that nothing is gained by a culture's art and that little or nothing would be lost without it. Make sure you explain why you feel as you do on this subject.

5. Write a response to Norman Cousins' statement that "the danger is not so much that man will be controlled by the computer as that he may imitate it" (paragraph 2 of "The Poet and the Computer"). Agree or disagree with Cousins, stating why and giving examples to support your position.

6. In paragraph 13 of "The Poet and the Computer," Norman Cousins writes that "it might be fruitful to effect some sort of junction between the computer technologist and the poet." Support or argue against that statement by explaining whether you think such a junction is possible or even desirable and, if so, how it might be effected.

Research Topics

1. Taking into consideration Diana Jean Schemo's "Between the Art and the Artist Lies the Shadow" and the revelations about the private lives of either people she mentions or an artist you know of, do your own research and then argue your position on the connection between the artist's public life and his or her private behavior. Or, do the same thing for any public figure such as a sports star or a performer who has done something or been accused of doing something immoral. Consider whether evidence of immorality affects or alters in any way the quality of a person's work.

2. In recent years, some people have been highly critical of what they see as obscenity or immorality in contemporary art. The works of Robert Mapplethorpe, for instance, were the object of such widespread, heated public debate that the National Endowment for the Arts was threatened with funding cuts because

of similar projects it had awarded grants to. Research the issue of censorship and the arts and write an opinion paper on the subject. Consider: Do we have a moral obligation to limit what people can say, do, or use in their art, or do First Amendment rights extend to any subject or medium an artist wants to use?

3. Robert Hughes in "Behold the Stone Age" offers his theory about the nature and purpose of prehistoric art on the basis of cave drawings recently discovered in France. Such discoveries of prehistoric cave drawings that are fairly sophisticated in technique and meaning have led some art historians to suggest that art did not necessarily develop progressively, as has been commonly believed. Research this topic by reading about some of the prehistoric cave drawings that have been discovered and the theories of art historians about their importance. Then weigh the evidence and arrive at your own opinion about the nature and purpose of prehistoric art or what its place is in the historical development of art.

CHAPTER 6

MUSIC

Music has been an integral part of humans' lives from the earliest periods of our existence. Song and instrumental music have spoken to, soothed, excited, or otherwise influenced humans of virtually all cultures and time periods in a seemingly endless variety of styles, subject matter, and methods of delivery. Each new musician, composer, or singer hopes to create a style uniquely his or her own, though often acknowledging the influence of a previous form or artist. Sometimes a wholly new form of musical expression is created, from which generations of musicians and music lovers in turn take their inspiration.

The essays in this chapter suggest the multitude of issues surrounding the subject of music. One topic of interest to professional musicians and educators is the way in which audiences listen to music. That is the subject of the first selection, an excerpt from a book about music written by Aaron Copland, an American composer of considerable fame whose works appeal to a wide audience. Writing from a position of authority, Copland argues in "How We Listen to Music" for what he calls an "active kind of listening." Perhaps it has not occurred to you that music requires a certain kind of attention in order to be fully appreciated, but Copland believes it does. Before you read his essay, think for a moment about how you listen to music. Do you commit yourself fully to the music? Do you listen differently to different kinds of music? As you read Copland's essay, consider whether you are an "active" listener, according to his definition. Consider, too, whether the concerts you go to might require a different kind of attention from the attention Copland says all music requires.

The subject of contemporary music gives rise to sometimes heated debate, especially when rock and roll or alternative music is being discussed. Isabelle Leymarie in "Rock 'n' Revolt" addresses the issue of the connection between rock and roll music and actual violence. Some people are firmly convinced that certain lyrics of both mainstream and alternative music actually cause violence by promoting and glorifying it. Others argue just as vehemently that such music simply reflects popular culture, not influences it. As you read about the kinds of music Leymarie cites as having been banned or stigmatized, think about the music you listen to. Have you ever been criticized for the kinds of music you like (or perhaps perform)? Are you critical of certain kinds of music yourself? Where do you stand on the issue of the connection between rock lyrics and violent behavior?

Like Leymarie, Jack Santino discusses the way in which some music has been perceived as "a menace to society" in his look at the history of rock and roll. In

"Rock and Roll as Music; Rock and Roll as Culture," Santino traces the development and influence of rock. As you read the essay, think about the enormous influence rock music has had on so many people's lives, from its earliest beginnings in the 1950s through today. What is it about rock music that so many people find appealing? Why has it endured for close to five decades? Consider, too, why some musicians and fans choose alternative forms of music to express themselves. As Alex Ross points out in "Generation Exit," alternative music has characteristics that make it markedly—some would say alarmingly—different from rock. In his reflections on the suicide of musician Kurt Cobain in 1994, Ross also makes some pointed comments about the nature of alternative music. Consider whether you agree with him, and if not, why you differ.

As you read the essays in this chapter, think of what music means to you, how what these authors have to say relates to the kind of music you like, and what issues about music they raise that you think worth exploring with your classmates or in an essay. Music in its virtually infinite variety is a rich source of material for discussion and writing.

HOW WE LISTEN TO MUSIC

Aaron Copland

Aaron Copland (1900–1990) was an American composer whose works are frequently performed still today. Influenced by American jazz and folk music, he is best known for the ballets Billy the Kid *(1938),* Rodeo *(1942), and* Appalachian Spring *(1944). Copland also wrote about music, including the book* What to Listen for in Music *(1939, 1957), from which this excerpt is taken. Here he defines "active" listening.*

We all listen to music according to our separate capacities. But, for the sake of analysis, the whole listening process may become clearer if we break it up into its component parts, so to speak. In a certain sense we all listen to music on three separate planes. For lack of a better terminology, one might name these: (1) the sensuous plane, (2) the expressive plane, (3) the sheerly musical plane. The only advantage to be gained from mechanically splitting up the listening process into these hypothetical planes is the clearer view to be had of the way in which we listen.

The simplest way of listening to music is to listen for the sheer pleasure of the musical sound itself. That is the sensuous plane. It is the plane on which we hear music without thinking, without considering it in any way. One turns on the radio while doing something else and absent-mindedly bathes in the sound. A kind of brainless but attractive state of mind is engendered by the mere sound appeal of the music.

You may be sitting in a room reading this book. Imagine one note struck on the piano. Immediately that one note is enough to change the atmosphere of the room—providing that the sound element in music is a powerful and mysterious agent, which it would be foolish to deride or belittle.

4   The surprising thing is that many people who consider themselves qualified music lovers abuse that plane in listening. They go to concerts in order to lose themselves. They use music as a consolation or an escape. They enter an ideal world where one doesn't have to think of the realities of everyday life. Of course they aren't thinking about the music either. Music allows them to leave it, and they go off to a place to dream, dreaming because of and apropos of the music yet never quite listening to it.

Yes, the sound appeal of music is a potent and primitive force, but you must not allow it to usurp a disproportionate share of your interest. The sensuous plane is an important one in music, a very important one, but it does not constitute the whole story.

There is no need to digress further on the sensuous plane. Its appeal to every normal human being is self-evident. There is, however, such a thing as becoming more sensitive to the different kinds of sound stuff as used by various composers. For all composers do not use that sound stuff in the same way. Don't get the idea that the value of music is commensurate with its sensuous appeal or that the loveliest sounding music is made by the greatest composer. If that were so, Ravel would be a greater creator than Beethoven. The point is that the sound element varies with each composer, that his usage of sound forms an integral part of his style and must be taken into account when listening. The reader can see, therefore, that a more conscious approach is valuable even on this primary plane of music listening.

The second plane on which music exists is what I have called the expressive one. Here, immediately, we tread on controversial ground. Composers have a way of shying away from any discussion of music's expressive side. Did not Stravinsky himself proclaim that his music was an "object," a "thing," with a life of its own, and with no other meaning than its own purely musical existence? This intransigent attitude of Stravinsky's may be due to the fact that so many people have tried to read different meanings into so many pieces. Heaven knows it is difficult enough to say precisely what it is that a piece of music means, to say it definitely, to say it finally so that everyone is satisfied with your explanation. But that should not lead one to the other extreme of denying to music the right to be "expressive."

8   My own belief is that all music has an expressive power, some more and some less, but that all music has a certain meaning behind the notes and that the meaning behind the notes constitutes, after all, what the piece is saying, what the piece is about. The whole problem can be stated quite simply by asking, "Is there a meaning to music?" My answer to that would be, "Yes." And "Can you state in so many words what the meaning is?" My answer to that would be, "No." Therein lies the difficulty.

Simple-minded souls will never be satisfied with the answer to the second of these questions. They always want music to have a meaning, and the more concrete it is the better they like it. The more the music reminds them of a train, a storm, a funeral, or any other familiar conception the more expressive it appears to be to them. This popular idea of music's meaning—stimulated and abetted by the usual run of musical commentator—should be discouraged wherever and whenever it is met. One timid lady once confessed to me that she suspected something seriously lacking in her appreciation of music because of her inability to connect it with anything definite. That is getting the whole thing backward, of course.

Still, the question remains, How close should the intelligent music lover wish to come to pinning a definite meaning to any particular work? No closer than a general concept, I should say. Music expresses, at different moments, serenity or exuberance, regrets or triumph, fury or delight. It expresses each of these moods, and many others, in a numberless variety of subtle shadings and differences. It may even express a state of meaning for which there exists no adequate word in any language. In that case, musicians often like to say that it has only a purely musical meaning. They sometimes go further and say that *all* music has only a purely musical meaning. What they really mean is that no appropriate word can be found to express the music's meaning and that, even if it could, they do not feel the need of finding it.

But whatever the professional musician may hold, most musical novices still search for specific words with which to pin down their musical reactions. That is why they always find Tschaikovsky easier to "understand" than Beethoven. In the first place, it is easier to pin a meaning-word on a Tschaikovsky piece than on a Beethoven one. Much easier. Moreover, with the Russian composer, every time you come back to a piece of his it almost always says the same thing to you, whereas with Beethoven it is often quite difficult to put your finger right on what he is saying. And any musician will tell you that that is why Beethoven is the greater composer. Because music which always says the same thing to you will necessarily soon become dull music, but music whose meaning is slightly different with each hearing has a greater chance of remaining alive.

12   Listen, if you can, to the forty-eight fugue themes of Bach's *Well Tempered Clavichord*. Listen to each theme, one after another. You will soon realize that each theme mirrors a different world of feeling. You will also soon realize that the more beautiful a theme seems to you the harder it is to find any word that will describe it to your complete satisfaction. Yes, you will certainly know whether it is a gay theme or a sad one. You will be able, in other words, in your own mind, to draw a frame of emotional feeling around your theme. Now study the sad one a little closer. Try to pin down the exact quality of its sadness. Is it pessimistically sad or resignedly sad; is it fatefully sad or smilingly sad?

Let us suppose that you are fortunate and can describe to your own satisfaction in so many words the exact meaning of your chosen theme. There is still no guarantee that anyone else will be satisfied. Nor need they be. The important thing is that each one feel for himself the specific expressive quality of a theme or, similarly, an entire piece of music. And if it is a great work of art, don't expect it to mean exactly the same thing to you each time you return to it.

Themes or pieces need not express only one emotion, of course. Take such a theme as the first main one of the *Ninth Symphony*, for example. It is clearly made up of different elements. It does not say only one thing. Yet anyone hearing it immediately gets a feeling of strength, a feeling of power. It isn't a power that comes simply because the theme is played loudly. It is a power inherent in the theme itself. The extraordinary strength and vigor of the theme results in the listener's receiving an impression that a forceful statement has been made. But one should never try to boil it down to "the fateful hammer of life," etc. That is where the trouble begins. The musician, in his exasperation, says it means nothing but the notes themselves, whereas the nonprofessional is only too anxious to hang on to any explanation that gives him the illusion of getting closer to the music's meaning.

Now, perhaps, the reader will know better what I mean when I say that music does have an expressive meaning but that we cannot say in so many words what that meaning is.

16   The third plane on which music exists is the sheerly musical plane. Besides the pleasurable sound of music and the expressive feeling that it gives off, music does exist in terms of the notes themselves and of their manipulation. Most listeners are not sufficiently conscious of this third plane. . . .

Professional musicians, on the other hand, are, if anything, too conscious of the mere notes themselves. They often fall into the error of becoming so engrossed with their arpeggios and staccatos that they forget the deeper aspects of the music they are performing. But from the layman's standpoint, it is not so much a matter of getting over bad habits on the sheerly musical plane as of increasing one's awareness of what is going on, in so far as the notes are concerned.

When the man in the street listens to the "notes themselves" with any degree of concentration, he is most likely to make some mention of the melody. Either he hears a pretty melody or he does not, and he generally lets it go at that. Rhythm is likely to gain his attention next, particularly if it seems exciting. But harmony and tone color are generally taken for granted, if they are thought of consciously at all. As for music's having a definite form of some kind, that idea seems never to have occurred to him.

It is very important for all of us to become more alive to music on its sheerly musical plane. After all, an actual musical material is being used. The intelligent listener must be prepared to increase his awareness of the musical material and what happens to it. He must hear the melodies, the rhythms, the harmonies, the tone colors in a more conscious fashion. But above all he must, in order to follow the line of the composer's thought, know something of the principles of musical form. Listening to all of these elements is listening on the sheerly musical plane.

20   Let me repeat that I have split up mechanically the three separate planes on which we listen merely for the sake of greater clarity. Actually, we never listen on one or the other of these planes. What we do is to correlate them—listening in all three ways at the same time. It takes no mental effort, for we do it instinctively.

Perhaps an analogy with what happens to us when we visit the theater will make this instinctive correlation clearer. In the theater, you are aware of the actors and actresses, costumes and sets, sounds and movements. All these give one the sense that the theater is a pleasant place to be in. They constitute the sensuous plane in our theatrical reactions.

The expressive plane in the theater would be derived from the feeling that you get from what is happening on the stage. You are moved to pity, excitement, or gayety. It is this general feeling, generated aside from the particular words being spoken, a certain emotional something which exists on the stage, that is analogous to the expressive quality in music.

The plot and plot development is equivalent to our sheerly musical plane. The playwright creates and develops a character in just the same way that a composer creates and develops a theme. According to the degree of your awareness of the way in which the artist in either field handles his material you will become a more intelligent listener.

24   It is easy enough to see that the theatergoer never is conscious of any of these elements separately. He is aware of them all at the same time. The same is true of music listening. We simultaneously and without thinking listen on all three planes.

In a sense, the ideal listener is both inside and outside the music at the same moment, judging it and enjoying it, wishing it would go one way and watching it go another—almost like the composer at the moment he composes it; because in order to write his music, the composer must also be inside and outside his music, carried away by it and yet coldly critical of it. A subjective and objective attitude is implied in both creating and listening to music.

What the reader should strive for, then, is a more *active* kind of listening. Whether you listen to Mozart or Duke Ellington, you can deepen your understanding of music only by being a more conscious and aware listener—not someone who is just listening, but someone who is listening *for* something.

Personal Response

Does Copland's analysis accurately reflect the way you listen to music? If not, how do you listen to music?

Questions for Class or Small Group Discussion

1. Do you think Copland's three planes of listening to music are relevant only to "classical" music, or do they apply to any kind of music? Explain your answer.

2. Copland states that we should strive for "a more *active* kind of listening" (paragraph 26). Discuss the degree to which you believe yourself an active listener.

3. Do you agree with Stravinsky that music is an "'object'" or "'thing'" with "no other meaning than its own purely musical existence" (paragraph 7)? Or do you agree with Copland, who thinks that "all music has an expressive power" (paragraph 8)? Explain your answer.

4. Volunteer to bring to class a piece of music for everyone to listen to. Afterwards, discuss the ways in which you and your classmates listened to it. What do you think Copland would say about the way you listen?

ROCK 'N' REVOLT

Isabelle Leymarie

Isabelle Leymarie is a Franco-American pianist, dancer, and musicologist. Her study, Salsa and Migration, *appeared in an anthology of writing on Puerto Rico entitled* The Commuter Nation *(1992), and she has written a book entitled* La Salsa et le Latin Jazz *(1993). In this essay, which appeared in the February 1993 issue of* UNESCO Courier, *Leymarie explores the question of the relationship between music and violence.*

Rock, a musical and social phenomenon of unprecedented scope and intensity, raises in acute form the question of the relationship between music and violence. Its history has been fraught with violence. Jim Morrison, leader of The Doors, apostle of sex, alcohol and LSD, died young, of a heart attack in his bathtub in Paris. Stars Jimi Hendrix and Janis Joplin both died of drug overdoses. Acid rock has become synonymous with punks and English football riots. The fans of Metallica and Guns n' Roses have burned cars, and during a recent concert in Montreal they wrecked a stadium and injured twelve people. The Sex Pistols proclaimed in their song "Anarchy in the UK:" "I wanna destroy passers-by, for I wanna be anarchy." John Phillips, a member of The Mamas and The Papas, was reported by musicologist David Tame as claiming that any rock group can whip a crowd into a hysterical frenzy by carefully controlling a sequence of rhythms. In 1967 he went ahead and did just that in Phoenix. When Hell's Angels roughed up spectators during a Rolling Stones concert in California, rocker Mick Jagger remarked that "Something like this happens every time I play that song."

Although physically less conspicuous, violence is also expressed in the lyrics of urban music such as rap (a recent hit by star rapper Ice-T is entitled "Cop Killer") and free jazz ("We are not angry young men, we are enraged!" proclaimed saxophonist Archie Shepp in the late 1960s). Here, violence is palpable in lyrics, song titles, public statements by musicians, and in the music itself: the mega-volumes, "fuzz" effects and distortions of rock, the hammer beats of rap, the shrieking saxophones and cascading notes of jazz, and the amplified bass of reggae. Violence is also associated with other types of music. In Stanley Kubrick's film *A Clockwork Orange,* the hero, Alex, driven crazy by the sounds of Beethoven, jumps out of a window. In Cuba during the 1920s and 1930s, concerts by rival bands playing the popular music known as *son* degenerated into brawls which had to be broken up by the police.

Violence, in more controlled forms, is present in many musical traditions, old and new: in the wailing of women in the funeral lamentations of Macedonia; in certain Senegalese songs whose lyrics pour out a stream of bitter invective against new wives brought into a household; in the drumbeats of African *griot* storytellers which once stimulated the ardor of warriors and today perform a similar role for the participants in traditional wrestling matches. It is found in martial music, in hunting calls, and in filmed thrillers where it plays a crucial role in setting the mood.

4   Violence is also present in classical music such as Handel's "Saul," Beethoven's *Eroica Symphony,* in operas generally, such as those of Verdi, who once said that he sought to express "passions above all else" and almost all of whose heroines die tragic deaths, in Mahler's *Fourth Symphony,* in Berlioz's *Symphonie Fantastique,* with its dramatic *Dies irae,* and in Stravinsky's *The Rite of Spring,* in which a virgin, sacrificed to the gods, dances herself to death (a riot broke out during the first performance). One could continue the list indefinitely.

An Extraordinary Power

Is it possible, asks musicologist Gilbert Rouget in his book on music and trance, that music may be endowed with a magical power capable of whipping people into the state of madness which the ancient Greeks called "mania"? Or does it have no objective reality? Rouget cites Timotheus of Miletus, who lived in the fourth century BC and once said that music "was capable of tempting Alexander away from a banquet to take up arms, and then of luring him back again to his guests with a lilting harmony." Rouget also quotes Boethius, who claimed that the Dorian mode inspired virtue, whereas the Phrygian mode aroused passion and violence, and refers to Aristotle's theory of the ethos of modes, which was similar to that of Boethius. He concludes that music can induce a trance in some cases and calm in others, and that it "derives its power from its integration into a given set of representations."

It is true that in order to grasp the symbolism in a particular type of music it is essential to be familiar with the set of representations into which it is integrated and the context in which it is performed. In the West, for example, the major modes evoke elation and rejoicing and the minor modes inspire melancholy, while in the East other modes such as Arab *maqam* and Indian *ragas* evoke totally different emotional moods. Similarly, drums and trumpets are regarded as martial instruments and flutes are associated with pastoral. All this is bound up with mental associations that are to a large extent culturally determined.

Leibniz spoke of the "anxiety-causing effect" of dissonance, and yet today dissonances, which have become commonplace in contemporary music, have lost much of their disquieting character (even Chopin's mazurkas, when first performed, were criticized for their "dissonance"). Verdi's use of double basses to introduce the final scene of *Othello,* Berlioz's use of percussion instruments in the *Symphonie Fantastique,* and Alfred Hitchcock's use of violins to heighten dramatic tension, are all illustrations of the way in which musical choices are both personal and culturally determined.

8   And yet music, when considered as a group of organized sounds and hence as a purely acoustic phenomenon, is also known to produce certain physiological and psychological effects which have been scientifically documented. Certain rhythms and sound frequencies, for example, can accelerate or slow down the human metabolic rate and even induce hypnosis. John Diamond, a specialist in behavioral physiology, has shown how the relative strength of certain muscles, a function which is easily measurable, varies according to the type of music to which people are listening. Animals and plants are also known to react physically to music. According to studies carried out in India, Russia and the United States, plants seem to hate "heavy metal" rock music and twist themselves as far away as possible from the offending loudspeaker, while they adore classical violin and will grow even more lushly to the sounds of disco.

Noise engenders violence; it can even drive people to suicide. Some artificial noises, especially those which emanate from continuous-frequency engines, have been found to have a pathological effect on the body's cellular structure, and can sometimes cause cancer, while natural sounds, like those of waves, the warbling of birds and certain types of classical or African music, can create a sense of well-being and even a healing effect by harmonizing with our biorhythms.

In recent years, the practice of music therapy has enjoyed considerable popularity. Members of the Research Group in Pediatric Anaesthesiology at the Hospital for Sick Children in Paris and doctors in many American hospitals have used carefully selected types of music to reduce their patients' dependency on tranquillizers. In *The Burmese Harp* (1956), a fine film by the Japanese director Kon Ichikawa, a soldier-musician saps his comrades' will to fight whenever he plays and sings.

Study of the relationship between music and violence also raises the question of the political aspect of music. In many parts of the world, musicians such as the bards of Nepal, the *griots* or the musicians of Ethiopia are perceived as pariahs or as socially inferior, and are believed to lead dissolute lives and be addicted to drugs and alcohol. Music has often been used as an instrument of domination. In some African societies, *mirliton* reed pipes and other instruments provide a musical accompaniment during the ritual parading of masks, which women and children must not see and which perpetuate male dominance.

12   The French writer Jacques Attali has observed that in Western societies the upper classes have always encouraged artistic creation, but only in order to maintain the established order and legitimize their own authority. In the 1950s, the Dominican dictator Rafael Trujillo y Molina encouraged the practice of the *merengue,* a dance closely related to the samba, but gave orders that the musicians should sing his praises and exiled those who opposed him. In many countries, music has become a form of propaganda or been appropriated by the Church, and judgements about music have been an endorsement of manipulation and intolerance.

Authoritarian colonial regimes arbitrarily associated drums with violence and debauchery, and long banned black music. The "New Age" writer Corinne Hélène claims that jazz and juvenile delinquency go hand in hand. But this baseless claim is fraught with prejudice, for how can the beautiful and expressive phrasing of a Sarah Vaughan or an Ella Fitzgerald be associated with juvenile delinquency? Why should jazz as a whole be connected with this social problem when most young jazz musicians are now graduates of music conservatories and universities and the overwhelming majority of jazz fans are intellectuals? How indeed, when music, for many deprived black and Hispanic adolescents of America's urban ghettos, far from leading to delinquency, is often a lifeline?

In the United States, moral-majority pressure groups have stigmatized some rock records as "obscene," in the hope of getting them withdrawn from the market, but they also tried to ban the Robert Mapplethorpe photo exhibition and other artistic events which did not correspond with their ideals. On the other hand, some kinds of music such as "Muzak," which supposedly increase consumer sales and induce people in restaurants to eat more but are actually a form of audio-brainwashing and noise pollution, are broadcast all day long in shopping centres and other public areas.

Jacques Attali has also remarked that "show business, the star system and the hit parade are signs of deep-rooted institutional and cultural colonization." In this context music, through a sometimes violent protest against official art and the mechanization of society, becomes a means of fighting authority. "Music exists," adds Jacques Attali, "to help us hear the sound of change. It forces us to invent new categories, to come up with a new momentum capable of rejuvenating a view of society that has become ossified, trapped, moribund." This is partly true of rock and its rebellious anti-establishment stance, and of jazz, rap and reggae—all musical forms which proclaim their black identity and have rejected old models along with the hypocrisy and inhumanity of materialism. In certain ritualized settings, notably during festivals, subversive songs are often used to express grievances against the establishment.

A Yearning for Harmony

16   Does music engender violence or does it express violence? And if it does express violence, does it, by sublimating violent impulses and dissipating tensions, play a cathartic role and "soothe the savage breast"? Music, for Attali, is the "audible tape of society's vibrations and signs." It is undeniably deeply rooted in the collective psychology: rock, rap, free jazz and reggae all express the violence of the cultures which have bred them. But people and their environment are inseparable: the pent-up violence in the individual affects society and vice versa. While music reflects the collective *gestalt* of a society, its particular form of expression also reflects the emotions of the musician.

    In China, Egypt, India and ancient Greece, music was believed to possess a certain ethical value and the power to uplift or debase the soul. In ancient China, the imperial government existed in harmony with the twelve celestial tones, and during the Confucian Chin dynasty, certain "virtuous" songs and musical instruments were reputed to temper the harshness of the regime. Classical music is also imbued with spirituality: Mozart's Don Giovanni brings down divine vengeance upon himself by assassinating a nobleman and burns in hell for it. Liszt aspired to compose inspirational works, and although Wagner's "Tetralogy" (the four-opera *Ring* cycle) expresses both the fall of humanity cut adrift from the gods and the distress of the artist faced with the world's misfortunes, Wagner had a deeply moral view of art.

    The French sociologist Jean Duvignaud has written that art expresses "nostalgia for a lost form of communication in the shape of a forbidden dream that is continually revived by the irrepressible desire of the human emotional impulse." He goes on to say that a successful work of art "rebuilds behind the self a unity which pieces together the shards of a divided humanity." Now that idealism has been demolished and the philosophy of music has become a thing of the past, while the media (which tend to put the visual image before the musical message) bombard us with vulgar and iconoclastic music, it is more than ever incumbent on musicians and artists in general to adopt an ethical position. The most influential creators of the twentieth century, notably the film-makers whose art is one of our era's most powerful forms of expression—artists such as Kurosawa, Ozu and Satyajit Ray—have been passionate humanists.

    Musical eurhythmics presupposes both inner and outer harmony, peace with oneself and with the universe. Violence, in its latent form, is an intrinsic part of human nature and of the universe generally. But when violence is unleashed and expressed, often in a paroxysm, in music or other art forms, it is a symptom either of social unrest or of inner imbalance or torment, emotional deprivation and arrested development.

20   And just as the wind can rise from a gentle breeze to a raging hurricane, so music can enchant or destroy us. It is for musicians to create works which enrich life, which contribute to the harmony of humanity, without compromising the quality of their art (some forms of therapeutic music, such as "New Age" music, do not really have any aesthetic value).

However, when music achieves perfection, it allows us to catch a glimpse of the divine; it becomes, according to a Buddhist belief, the most refined art, the path to enlightenment. According to the Taoist sage, Zhuangzi, "Music allows man to remain pure, simple, sincere and in this way to rediscover his primitive emotions." (A few centuries later, Wagner would also use music to explore primitive forms of expression.) The great violinist Yehudi Menuhin once observed that "music creates order out of chaos." Nietzsche's humorous conclusion was that "Without music, life would be a mistake."

Personal Response

Describe your favorite kind of music and what appeals to you about it. Are you ever criticized for listening to it? What do you think it is about some music that produces negative or even hostile reactions in some people?

Questions for Class or Small Group Discussion

1. How would you answer Leymarie's question, "Does music engender violence or does it express violence" (paragraph 16)? Discuss whether you think music creates violent behavior or simply reflects the culture that produces it.

2. Leymarie gives examples of ways in which certain mental associations with music "are to a large extent culturally determined" (paragraphs 6 and 7). Can you give other examples of the point she makes in this section of her essay?

3. Give examples of musicians or musical groups who have made political statements through their music (paragraphs 11–15), especially those who use music as "a means of fighting authority" (paragraph 15). Discuss the effect you think their political statements have had.

4. Leymarie is objective for the most part, but she offers her own opinion from time to time, as for instance, when she says that "New Age" music does "not really have any aesthetic value." Find passages in which she makes her own subjective comments, and discuss whether you agree with her opinion or not.

ROCK AND ROLL AS MUSIC; ROCK AND ROLL AS CULTURE

Jack Santino

Jack Santino is a professor in the Department of Popular Culture at Bowling Green State University in Ohio. He won four Emmy Awards for his 1982 film Miles of Smiles, Years of Struggle: The Untold Story of Black Pullman Porters *and is author of the 1989 book* Miles of Smiles, Years of Struggles: Stories of Black Pullman Porters. *This essay was published first in the July 1990 issue of* The World and I.

Here we are, in the 1990s, and rock and roll music, in some form or other, is still the dominant popular musical form in the USA, and maybe the world. Who would have thought, almost forty years ago, when Big Joe Turner, Fats Domino, and Bo Diddley began having hit records that crossed over to the white charts, that rock and roll music would become the business and cultural force that it is today? Who would have thought, when Bill Haley's "Rock Around the Clock," or Hank Ballard and the Midnighters' "Work With Me Annie" were attacked for their supposed ill effects on youth, that a similar debate would be raging almost forty years later about songs and music that evolved and developed out of their efforts?

Rock and roll was seen as a menace to society by many in the fifties. Much of the reaction to the early crossover and cover hits was overtly racist. When a song intended for one market, such as blacks, becomes popular with another market, such as whites, it is called a crossover hit. When a song that has been recorded by one artist, for example, Little Richard, is recorded by another—for instance, Pat Boone—the re-recording is called a cover record. There were crossovers and covers of country and western material, but most of the early rock and roll crossovers did in fact go from the "race" or rhythm and blues charts to the pop charts. This meant an influx of black music on popular radio. Likewise, the cover records tended to be by whites of black artists' work. During the wave of rock and roll bashing and record smashing that began almost simultaneously with the music's sudden popularity, the very fact that much of the music was derived from black tradition was frequently raised as an issue. That the music had a beat, and that this syncopation was African American in origin, was pointed to as self-evident proof that the music was both inferior and corrupting.

On the other hand, rock and roll was also considered by many to be simply a fad, the latest in a long line of trivialities embraced by whimsical youth. This attitude continued well into the 1960s. The Beatles, for instance, were dismissed for years before it dawned on people that they were (1) not a fad, (2) important, and (3) good. It took a long time before adults figured out what the kids knew all along—rock and roll is here to stay.

The Origins of Rock and Roll

4   I remember seeing Elvis Presley on the *Ed Sullivan Show* in 1956. Although I was young, I knew who he was because my two older sisters had told me all about him. They were very interested in seeing him, and so was I. Watching him on television, I was fascinated by the performance and my sisters loved him, but my parents decided he was "on dope." "Look at his eyes!" my mother said, as if offering proof. Recently I was discussing Elvis with a colleague who also remembered seeing him on television for the first time. His story was identical to mine, right down to his mother's exclamation: "He must be on dope. Look at his eyes!" Actually, despite Presley's later addiction to drugs, at that time he was not "on" anything. But he managed to divide parents from children with his looks, his singing, and his stage movements. At that moment in 1956, a generation gap was created.

A similar thing happened in 1964, when the Beatles performed on the *Ed Sullivan Show*. Kids loved them and parents hated them—both their music and their appearance. In 1982, however, when Michael Jackson achieved a similar kind of superfame, also after national exposure on television, many parents took their children to see him on the Jacksons' Victory Tour. They viewed Jackson as the functional equivalent of the Elvis or the Beatles they remembered and cherished in their own youth and wanted to give their children the opportunity to see this generation's rock hero live. In fact, this is one of the reasons Michael Jackson declined in popularity rather quickly—too many parents liked him. Along with overexposure and his well-publicized idiosyncrasies, Jackson was immediately cast into a "good boy" role, as Elvis and the Beatles had been before him, thus clearing the way for such "bad boy" artists as Jerry Lee Lewis, the Rolling Stones, and Prince.

Rock and Roll's Evolving Audience

We live in a rock and roll culture. Since the 1950s, generations have grown up with the music—and to some extent it has grown up with them—while new artists and new styles continue to emerge. A generation gap still exists, however, although somewhat narrowed. Young people today may enjoy musicians who were popular before they were born, such as Chuck Berry, but how many parents today who grew up with fifties and sixties rock music enjoy Prince, or Bon Jovi, or the Dead Milkmen? "Rock and roll" means different things to people, depending on, among other things, how old they are, and although a great many adults consider themselves rock fans, they have difficulty in understanding, much less appreciating, the music that their kids enjoy.

I teach popular music, from a sociocultural as well as an aesthetic perspective, in the nation's only academic Department of Popular Culture, at

Bowling Green State University in Bowling Green, Ohio. I believe that the best teaching involves learning on the part of both the students and the instructor, and this is certainly true in my case. Through my teaching I am continually exposed to the various tastes and perceptions of the current generation of college students. From them, I find out not merely who is currently popular, who they like and dislike and why, but also how they view the artists of the past in the light of their own experience. For instance, during the sixties, the Monkees were viewed as a "plastic" band, consisting of nonmusician actors hired by a corporate entrepreneur (Don Kirshner) to play the roles of imitation Beatles, singing songs written for them by professional songwriters. Although they sold a lot of records, the counterculture hated them. Today, the issues of authenticity and sincerity I alluded to above simply are not relevant to the audience that hears, buys, and enjoys listening to the Monkees' records. Most of my students see no difference whatsoever between the Beatles and the Monkees, while many consumers in the sixties viewed the two bands as polar opposites. Moreover, this example points to another fact: The audience for popular music is diversified. The so-called counterculture may have despised the Monkees, but somebody liked them. They had the best selling album of 1966, along with several No. 1 singles.

8   If we accept the fact that there is such diversity in the tastes of the consumers of rock and roll music, we must then realize that the term is frequently used in a general way to encompass a great number of musical styles, both black and white. This is how I am using it. With this in mind, I would say that despite the fact that their view of the rock/pop music is different from mine, my students and I share a rock and roll culture.

Rock music (I am using the terms rock and roll and rock interchangeably, although not everyone does[1]) is one of the distinctive features of postwar life, along with television, the Cold War, space travel, and the atomic bomb. For instance, I can expect that everyone in my classroom will be familiar with most of the more popular songs of Elvis Presley, Chuck Berry, or Buddy Holly. They hear them on the radio and on television, they are used in commercials, they are covered by later artists—in short, it is difficult to be alive in America and not know these songs. The same thing is true for popular sixties music, especially the Beatles, the Beach Boys, and Detroit's Motown artists such as the Supremes, the Four Tops, and the Temptations.

However, if I play songs that were popular a year or two preceding the first nationally popular rock hits, or if I drop back to the forties and play something from the Big Band era, these college-age young people are totally unfamiliar with the material, no matter how popular it was in its day. Neither do they know much about other genres, such as blues or country. This is not to say, however, that within the apparently limited

---

[1] Ed Ward, Geoffrey Stokes, and Ken Tucker, eds., *Rock of Ages: The Rolling Stone History of Rock and Roll* (Englewood Cliffs, N.J.: Prentice-Hall, Inc., 1986), 249.

category of "rock" that there is not a wide variety of musical styles available to them. Often, these styles give rise to specific subcultures which have their own dress code and concomitant values, such as the punks.

Interweaving and Evolving Styles

This has always been the case. In his important and influential work *The Sound of the City,* Charlie Gillett says that when the music we call rock and roll achieved national popularity in the mid-fifties, it actually included five distinct regional styles: Memphis rockabilly (Elvis, Carl Perkins, Jerry Lee Lewis), Chicago rhythm and blues (Bo Diddley, Chuck Berry), New Orleans piano boogie (Fats Domino, Little Richard), the group harmony singing known as doo-wop, centered in New York but found in other urban areas as well (the Platters, the Moonglows, the Penguins), and Northern band rock and roll (Bill Haley and the Comets, from Chester, Pennsylvania). While one may question the specific number of styles Gillett identifies or argue for the inclusion of other styles as well, the principle is a sound one. Different styles of music, derived from blues, country, and gospel—often tied to a geographical region and sometimes to ethnicity as well—all became identified as rock and roll largely because they shared an emphasis on a beat that was appealing to a generation of young people.[2]

12   Since then, we have seen styles come and go, some to return again, others to wield an influence on later music. If rock is, generally speaking, a synthesis of rhythm and blues (i.e., black) music and country and western (i.e., white) music, and I believe it is, the music that resulted was the beginning, not the end, of a dynamic process. For instance, an interest in American blues inspired young, white British musicians to form bands such as the Rolling Stones and Cream. Their music led in turn to the development of heavy metal music in the 1970s through such blues-based British bands as Led Zeppelin. And heavy metal itself has changed greatly and spun new subgenres in the past twenty years: speed metal, glam metal, bubblegum metal, and so forth. England's Beatles, who were heavily influenced by Americans such as Buddy Holly and the Everly Brothers, went on to influence virtually every rock act in the world, including the early art-rockers, who also contributed to the rise of heavy metal. New styles are created out of the syntheses of the old, but these new styles became the raw materials for further developments.

There are and have been so many styles of rock or rock-derived music in the past thirty years that I could not exhaustively list them all in the space of this article, let alone describe, define, or discuss each of them. A partial list would include surf music, girl-group, Merseybeat, California country rock, psychedelic, punk, new wave, doo-wop, Motown, soul, funk, rap, disco, industrial, and synth-pop. Each has its audience, though neither the audiences nor the musical styles are mutually exclusive. For

---

[2] Charlie Gillett, *The Sound of the City* (New York: Pantheon Books, 1970), 23–35.

many adolescents, music becomes a basis of personal and group identity. The music is something they can relate to and feel is their own; they signal their taste by their dress, their hair styles, perhaps even the words they use. They associate with others who share their tastes and, implicitly, their values. Many such subcultures have formed around musical styles over the years. Rockabilly musicians in Memphis were "cats." In the sixties rock had unprecedented influence, giving rise to the hippie life-style. Rock in Britain became associated with Teddy Boys, mods, rockers, and, later, punks. Often, these rock subcultures are shocking and threatening to the rest of us, because the symbols that are used to identify one as a member are loaded with antisocial or rebellious meaning: motorcycle jackets, shoulder-length hair on men, spiked bracelets, and razor blades.

However, we should be aware that the members of these sub-groups—the people wearing such things—have redefined these symbols in their own terms and are usually not the threats they appear to be. Wearing forbidden items, breaking the rules for acceptable public appearance, helps define the group in many ways. Of course, it helps individuals identify each other as having reasonably similar tastes, but it also defines an in-group/out-group dichotomy, an "us against them" outlook. The choice of sacrilegious and taboo paraphernalia, such as crucifixes or swastikas, brings forth the wrath of outsiders and helps the kids perpetuate in their own mind their sense that they are both prejudged and misunderstood by adults.

Rock and Roll as Big Business

Rock and roll is a way of life; certainly it is music, but it is also big business. Selling records, compact discs, tapes, and concert appearances is at the center of a multi-billion-dollar international industry. The success of a popular musician depends as much on monetary backing, good publicity, and sharp business agents as it does on talent. Creating an image is an all-important part of the process. The leather-jacketed Beatles, for instance, were cleaned up and put into suits by their manager, Brian Epstein, to help them achieve commercial success. Ironically, their being marketed as cheeky but cute and cuddly British boys led to the self-conscious image-mongering of the Rolling Stones as unkempt ruffians.

16   Today, the music video has become a major marketing tool which has intensified the importance of visual image, often at the expense of the musicianship. Legend has it that Fabian was discovered sitting on the front step of his Philadelphia row house. His dark good looks appealed to the "talent scouts," but when the sixteen-year-old Fabian Forte explained that he could not sing, he was assured that this was not a problem. More recently, certain bands such as Duran Duran are said to be the contemporary versions of essentially the same process. They are routinely described as having been created by and for videos.

Such assessment may not be fair. Most popular musicians are groomed for a mass audience; not all make it. Artists who create music aimed at the widest possible market are not necessarily poor musicians. I have noticed that my students feel that artists have "sold out" when they achieve great popularity, for example, artists such as Bruce Springsteen and such former college favorites as Genesis and U2. The question really has to do with the extent to which an artist is willing to change in order to achieve this popularity, and whether the artist considers this change morally or aesthetically compromising. Forgotten in such judgments is the fact that rock music is indeed an industry whose first concern is making money, and that most if not all popular recording artists hope to appeal to a broad audience and, yes, make a lot of money. Sociologist Simon Frith sees this as a central contradiction in rock and roll music: It is and always has been an outlaw form, rebellious, renegade, at odds with authority. On the other hand, it is very much a part of the Establishment it apparently rejects: It is a commercial endeavor that generates fortunes for large corporations. Thus, Frith feels that the image of rock as an outlaw form is illusory, designed to add to its mystique and help sell more units.[3] Nevertheless, rock's most enduring artists are unquestionably talented musicians.

The Cultural Impact of Rock and Roll

Beyond all of this, however, is the question of rock as a social force. As a genre that breaks social rules, rock remains true to itself and appealing to its mostly younger audience specifically by stirring up controversy and angering adults. The kids' aesthetics are the reverse of the adults': the more tasteless and shocking the better. As a product of big business, however, rock is scrutinized for songs and lyrics that might tarnish the corporations' image or offend consumers, or rather, consumers' parents. Despite such well-publicized philanthropic and humanitarian efforts such as the Live-Aid concert or the song "We Are the World," both of which raised money for famine-plagued Ethiopia, rock music is seen as a threat to the young, and to society in general. Satanic imagery, references to violence, rape, drugs, and sex, along with provocatively explicit music videos, frighten the very parents who grew up with rock in the fifties and sixties. The current situation is different, they say, more extreme, more vile, and I have no doubt that it is. However, my students have taught me that the situation is more complex than it seems.

Often songs are judged out of the context of the entire album in which the kids will usually hear them. The Rolling Stones' "Under Cover of the Night" has been cited for its violence; my students answer that if you listen to the entire 1983 album *Undercover,* although the song showcases violence, the entire album is actually antiviolent. Likewise, some songs that are about suicide are not necessarily promoting it but rather attempting to demonstrate the futility of it. Nevertheless, many people feel that these

---

[3] Simon Frith, *Sound Effects: Youth, Leisure, and the Politics of Rock 'n' Roll* (New York: Pantheon Books, 1981).

songs (and others with less redeeming social qualities) contribute to the proliferation of society's evils. Companies have responded by initiating a labeling system that cautions consumers about potentially offensive material contained in the recordings. Opponents maintain this is censorship and a curtailment of free speech. From practical experience I can say that the labels in actuality do little to prevent the sale of these recordings to minors, but proponents of the system feel it is a necessary step, and that the free speech issue is outweighed by social urgency.

20   What is the effect of music—or any other popular medium, such as television or movies—on its audience? No one really knows. It has not been systematically measured and it may be immeasurable. One thing we do know: It depends on the person listening. There are a great many other factors involved as well, such as which specific music are we talking about, under what conditions is it being listened to, and in what situation? A youngster may be more vulnerable to suggestion at certain times, such as after the death of a parent, for instance, than at others. Lawsuits have been brought against singers such as Ozzy Osbourne by parents who feel that his work influenced—in fact, caused—their child to commit suicide. Under such circumstances, parents are distraught and feel understandably passionate about the issue. I am not a fan of Ozzy Osbourne's, and I believe that artists do have a responsibility to consider the effects of their work on their young audience, but it is hard to believe that a child could be driven to such an extreme act by a single piece of music unless there were many other problems already involved. I am not a psychologist, but it occurs to me that a teenager who spends a great deal of time listening to death-oriented music may in fact be asking for help. A fascination with this kind of material may be symptomatic of a deeper problem, one that parents should address before things get to the point of irrevocable tragedy.

It is too easy to blame rock stars for the existence of troubled teenagers. Millions of young people listen to the same records without killing themselves or committing crimes against others. I think we have to consider the personality of the listener as the primary rather than the secondary factor. People seek out music that reinforces their own attitudes and moods; they bring themselves to the music. Charles Manson heard the Beatles' "Helter Skelter" as a call for mass murder, but the rest of us did not.

Furthermore, we need to look closely at the great variety of material that is routinely lumped together in discussions of rock lyrics. There are many different genres, styles, and songs involved, and they may not all be of the same order. Is a song about masturbation to be treated the same as a song that urges its audience to kill? How much of the negative reaction to some of this material has to do with personal morality or individual political points of view? People have defended the use of Satanic imagery to me as simply an artistic use of mythological symbolism, and they frequently point to Milton's *Paradise Lost* as the epitome of an artistic use of the story of Satan. Indeed, Milton portrays Satan sympathetically. Are we to deny

Milton the use of the Bible for poetic purposes? Should we take Milton off the library shelves? Many of the people who want to curtail such symbolism believe in the literal, biblical truth of Satan, and see any reference to him as evil. However, not everyone in the United States shares this belief. Are we then dealing with constitutional issues of religious freedom?

It seems obvious that people have a right to write and sing what they want. But parents also have a right and a duty to monitor their children's entertainments. To the extent that rock remains a music of the young, we find a clash of two principles: the artists' right to free expression versus the parents' right to raise their children as they see fit. However, it is important to remind ourselves that rock stars are no longer exclusively in their teens and twenties. A forty-year-old Bruce Springsteen might well write about sex, as poets have always done. It would be unrealistic to expect him not to. In the past, rock performers were themselves young, and this is still true to a large extent, but as the decades have passed, both the audience and the musicians have aged. Last year (1989) saw tours by the Who, the Jefferson Airplane, the Kinks, the Rolling Stones, Bob Dylan, Ringo Starr, and Paul McCartney, all veterans of the sixties. Certainly there are younger musicians playing today, but the point is that these adult musicians cannot be expected to write or sing about teenage concerns.

24   Furthermore, such things as suicide, drugs, sex, and violence *are* teenage concerns. While artists have a responsibility not to glamorize them, that does not mean these themes should not be explored. Rock songs often work as fantasy explorations of situations that a young person has confronted or at least can imagine confronting. A teenager imagines him- or herself into the song, explores it, but does not necessarily live it. Adolescence is a time of identity formation, when peer-group pressure is very powerful, and when one explores any number of alternative identities: Today, I am a vegetarian, deeply concerned about world ecology; tomorrow I wear leather and chains. Rock music is a part of this testing out of identities, of ideas. It is a fictive form, and it may in fact *help* young people gain a sense of their identity.

Moreover, rock does not exist in a vacuum. It is not the only popular entertainment that has grown more violent and more sexually explicit in recent years. Compare the slasher films of today with the horror films of the sixties or fifties. Even a superheroic movie such as *Robocop,* whose audience would obviously contain a great many children, came very close to receiving an X-rating for violence. Language restrictions have loosened in film and television, and popular television shows are certainly much more explicit than ever before. Comic books are undergoing a similar controversy, due again to their traditional appeal to youngsters. Today's comics are often labeled "Intended For Mature Audiences," and feature the same range of subjects and themes as described above for rock. Creators say that comics are a medium like any other, and that they are free to produce what they want, for readers of all age groups, while others feel that comics are and will always be for kids, and therefore should not contain certain materials under any circumstances. My point is that, in the midst of all this opening up across all the popular media, why should anyone expect that rock music would not reflect the same changes? Is it any more exploitative when rock deals with these themes than television shows such as, say, *Dynasty,* or *Geraldo?* Songs may in fact be written about gang rape, and I find these reprehensible, but I find the slasher films reprehensible also. Rock music is a part of society. It should not be singled out as the single effective agent of change within society.

Redeeming Qualities

Rock also has its positive side, seldom addressed in this debate. Beyond such altruistic efforts as the above-mentioned Live-Aid concert, or Quake-Aid, held to raise money for earthquake victims in Northern California, or benefits to save the whales, or George Harrison's Concert for Bangladesh (way back in 1971), rock can be inspirational on a personal level. Most rock songs do *not* contain off-color lyrics or deal with extremely antisocial behavior. What of all the songs that celebrate fidelity, or that reject drug-taking as a way of life? The truth is, it is far more convincing for kids to hear Rolling Stone Keith Richards talk of the dangers of heroin than to hear Nancy Reagan pronounce "Just say no."

Ultimately, rock and roll is as much a creation of its audience as it is of the artists or the businessmen. Songs that deal with taboo subjects, such as Prince's "Darling Nikki" (masturbation), do not necessarily corrupt their listeners. Prince's fans are quite aware of his tendency to write explicitly about sex. He also writes frequently about God, leading some to see him as a kind of contemporary mystic, using sexual imagery to describe spiritual yearning. As I said, these issues are much more complex than the simpleminded arguments being raised on both sides suggest, and until we deal with them in all their complexity, we will continue to get nowhere. We need to hear out the young people who listen to Prince, or Madonna, or heavy metal, or rap. How do *they* perceive the music? What does it mean to them? They can tell us more about it than we can tell them. Which kids are attracted to which styles, and which musicians? While some rock and roll is nihilistic, much of it is romantic and often melodramatic. This is what has always appealed to me about it, and I think today's youth feel the same. How often do they hear something positive, something altruistic, in rock and roll? Two decades ago, Crosby, Stills, and Nash exhorted parents to "teach your children well," and also, for children, to "teach your parents well." The advice is still good. Let us learn from each other.

Personal Response

In his conclusion, Santino remarks that "rock can be inspirational on a personal level" (paragraph 26). To what degree do you find rock music personally inspirational?

Questions for Class or Small Group Discussion

1. Discuss ways in which rock music might be perceived as "a menace to society" (paragraph 2).

2. Who are today's popular musicians? What makes them so appealing to young people? Do you think they will still be popular in a year? In ten years? Why or why not?

3. Discuss the singers or groups from the 1950s, 1960s, or 1970s whose songs you are familiar with. How many do most of your class-mates know? Why do you think young people today are so familiar with music their parents and grandparents enjoyed?

4. Why do you think rock music is such an enormous force in so many young people's lives? What is it about music that makes it "a basis of personal and group identity" (paragraph 13)?

5. Some of Santino's students believe that "artists have 'sold out' when they achieve great popularity" (paragraph 17). Do you agree? Which artists do you think have "sold out"? Which have not?

6. How do you feel about the labeling system that cautions consumers about potentially offensive material in recordings (paragraph 19)? Do you agree with Santino that it has little effect on the sale of such record-ings to minors, or do you think it serves a useful purpose? Do you think parents have a legitimate right to hold musicians responsible for their children's behavior?

GENERATION EXIT

Alex Ross

Alex Ross writes for The New Yorker. *This essay, published in the April 25, 1994, issue of that magazine, was written for the "Postscript" column, a regular feature highlighting the life and achievements of a notable person who has recently died. Here, Ross writes of the larger implications of the suicide of "grunge" musician Kurt Cobain.*

When Kurt Cobain, the lead singer of the band Nirvana, killed himself with a shotgun blast to the head, the major media outlets gave the story wide play and warmed to its significance. Dan Rather led off hesitantly, his face full of dim amazement as he read aloud phrases like "the Seattle sound" and "Smells Like Teen Spirit." But ABC ventured bravely into interpreta-tion, explaining the grunge phenomenon to "people over thirty" and ob-taining one man-in-the-street reaction. "When you reach that kind of fame and you're still miserable, there's something wrong," a long-haired stoner-looking dude observed. And NBC's correspondent ambitiously invoked "the violence, the drugs, and the diminished opportunities of an entire generation," with Tom Brokaw appending a regretful smirk. This was only the evening of the first day; the newsstands were soon heavy with fresh musings on the latest lost generation, the twilit twenty-somethings, the new unhappiness.

From the outset of his career, the desperately individualistic Cobain was caught in a great media babble about grunge style and twenty-something discontent. His intensely personal songs became exhibits in the nation's ongoing symposium on generational identity—a fruitless project blending the principles of sociology and astrology. Those of us at the receiving end of Generation X theories find them infuriating enough; Cobain, hounded with titles like "crown prince of Generation X," buckled under them. He was loudly and publicly tormented by his notoriety, his influence, his importance. Everything written about him and his wife, Courtney Love, seemed to wound him in some way. "I do not want what I have got," he sang on his last album, yearning for oblivion of one kind or another.

And yet he chose a way of death guaranteed to bring down a hailstorm of analytical blather far in excess of anything he had experienced while he was alive. This is the paradoxical allure of suicide: to leave the chattering world behind and yet to stage-manage the exit so that one is talked about in the right way. This was also the paradox of Cobain's bizarre pop-star career—his choice both to abandon everyday life and to try to cast some larger spell over it. He thought he could appropriate blank categories like "Generation X" and "alternative culture" and fill them with the earnest ideals of the punk-rock subculture he came from. He thought he could take the road less travelled and then persuade everyone to follow him. It's amazing he got as far as he did.

4   "Alternative": A breathtakingly meaningless word, the emptiest cultural category imaginable. It proposes that the establishment is reprehensible but that our substitute establishment can somehow blissfully coexist with it, on the same commercial playing field. It differs from sixties notions of counter-culture in that no one took "alternative culture" seriously even at the beginning; it sold out as a matter of principle. MTV, the video clubhouse that brought Nirvanamania to fever pitch, seized on the "alternative" label as a way to laterally diversify its offerings, much as soft-drink companies seek to invent new flavors. The aesthetic microscope has not been invented that could find a really significant difference between an alternative band like Pearl Jam and the regular-guy rock that it supposedly replaces.

Alternative music in the nineties claims descent from the punk-rock movement that traversed America in the seventies and eighties. The claim is weakened by the fact that punk in its pure form disavowed mass-market success, a disavowal that united an otherwise motley array of youth subcultures: high-school misfits of all kinds, skateboard kids, hardcore skinheads, doped-out postcollegiate slackers. Punk's peculiar obsession was musical autonomy—independent labels, clubs installed in suburban garages and warehouses, flyers and fanzines photocopied after hours. Some of the music was vulgar and dumb, some of it brilliantly inventive; rock finally had a viable avant-garde. In the eighties, this do-it-yourself network solidified into independent, or indie, rock, anchored in the myriad college-rock stations and alternative newspapers. Dumbness persisted, but there were always scattered bands picking out weird, rich chords and giving no thought to a major-label future.

Nirvana, which enjoyed local celebrity on the indie-rock scenes of Aberdeen, Olympia, and Seattle, Washington, before blundering into the mainstream, was perfectly poised between the margin and the center of rock. The band didn't have to dilute itself to make the transition, because its brand of grunge rock already drew more on the thunderous tread of hard rock and heavy metal than on the clean, fast, matter-of-fact attack of punk or hardcore. Where punk and indie bands generally made vocals secondary to the disordered clamor of guitars, Nirvana depended on Cobain's resonantly snarling voice, an instrument full of commercial potential from the start. But the singer was resolutely punk in spirit. He undermined his own publicity campaigns, and used his commercial clout to support lesser-known bands; he was planning to start his own label, Exploitation Records, and distribute the records himself while he was on tour.

The songs on Nirvana's breakthrough second album, "Nevermind," walked a difficult line between punk form and pop content. For the most part, they triumphed, and, more than that, they struck a nerve, not only with trend-seeking kids but with people in their twenties or older who recognized the mixture of components that went into the music. Dave Grohl, the dead-on drummer who kept Nirvana on an even keel, has a pragmatic view of the album's appeal: "The songs were catchy and they were simple, just like an ABC song when you were a kid." Cobain was a close, direct presence, everyone's friendless friend. The songs, despite their sometimes messy roar, were cunningly fashioned. They had a seductive way of switching in midstream from plaintive meditation to all-out frenzy. If people still listen to Nirvana ten years from now, it will be on the strength of the music, not of Cobain's nascent martyr legend.

8   It was in the fall of 1991 that Nirvana mysteriously took hold of the nation's youth consciousness and began selling records in the millions. It's best not to analyze this sudden popularity all that closely; as Michael Azerrad points out in his book on the group, "Come As You Are," the kind of instantaneous word-of-mouth sensation that lifted the band to the top of the charts also buoyed the careers of such differently talented personalities as Peter Frampton and Vanilla Ice. Adolescents are an omnipotent commercial force precisely because their tastes are so mercurial. In the deep dusk of the Bush Administration, some segments of the nation's youth undoubtedly identified with Cobain's punkish world view, his sympathies and discontents, and, yes, the diminished opportunities of an entire generation. Others just got off on the crushing power of the sound.

Cobain was at once irritated and intrigued by the randomness of his new audience. He lashed out at the "jock numbskulls, frat boys, and metal kids" (in Azerrad's words) who jammed clubs and arenas for his post-"Nevermind" tours. But he also liked the idea of bending their minds toward his own punk ideals and left-leaning politics: "I wanted to fool people at first. I wanted people to think that we were no different than Guns n' Roses. Because that way they would listen to the music first, accept us, and then maybe start listening to a few things that we had to say." After the initial period of fame, he let loose with social messages, not as heavy-handed or as earnest as R.E.M.'s, but carefully aimed. He was happy to discover that high schools were divided between Nirvana kids and Guns n' Roses kids.

The zeal for subversion was well meant but naïve. By condemning racists, sexists, and homophobes in his audiences, he may have promoted the cause of politically correct language in certain high-school cliques, but he did not and could not attack the deep-seated prejudices smoldering beneath that language. When he declared himself "gay in spirit," as he did in an interview with the gay magazine *The Advocate*, he made a political toy out of fragile identity. And his disavowals of masculine culture rang false alongside a stage show that dealt in sonic aggression and equipment-smashing mayhem. Who was he kidding?

The attempt to carry out social engineering through rock lyrics is an impossible one. Rock and roll has never been and will never be a vehicle for social amelioration, despite many fond hopes. Music is robbed of its intentions and associations as it goes out into the great wide open; like a rumor passed through a crowd, it emerges utterly changed. Pop songs become the property of their fans and are marked with the circumstances of their consumption, not of their creation. An unsought listenership can brand the music indelibly, as the Beatles discovered with "Helter Skelter." Or as Cobain discovered when a recording of "Smells Like Teen Spirit" was played at a Guns n' Roses show in Madison Square Garden while women in the audience were ogled on giant video screens.

12   In his suicide note Cobain gestured toward all these crises, his lack of passion, and his disconnectedness from the broad rock audience. The story underneath is probably simpler and sadder: he was trying to get off drugs and found himself helpless without their support. He leaned on drugs long before he became famous—the malevolent media circus of his last few years cannot be easily blamed. Even when he started out, he looked tired and haggard. The rest of the story lies between him and his dealer. It's easy to make too much of these inevitable chemical tragedies; witness the overexamined case of River Phoenix, whom some of us necrologized last November. Next time, it will not shock me when a vulnerable, talented misfit about my age infiltrates celebrity culture, then dies playing the abusive games of rebellion. But it will make me just as sad.

Killing himself as and when he did, Cobain at least managed to deliver a final jolt to the rock world he loved and loathed. Rock stars are glamorized for dying young, but they aren't supposed to kill themselves on purpose. Greil Marcus's invaluable compendium "Rock Death in the 1970s" records—among a hundred and sixteen untimely demises—dozens of drug mishaps and only a handful of suicides. A transcendent drug-induced descent is the preferred exit. Certainly the shotgun blast casts a different light on Cobain's career; the lyrics all sound like suicide notes now. ("What else could I write/I don't have the right/What else should I be/All apologies.") He made his death unrhapsodizable.

The rage we feel at suicides may be motivated by love, but it is the love that comes of possession, not compassion. It is the urge of the crowd to take control of the defective individual. The most mordant words on the subject are still John Donne's, in defense of righteous suicide: "No detestation nor dehortation against this sin of desperation (when it is a sin) can be too earnest. But yet since it may be without infidelity, it cannot be greater than that." This sin cannot be greater than our own urge to rationalize and allegorize the recently dead, especially those who were somehow faithful to themselves.

Personal Response

What was your reaction to the news of Kurt Cobain's suicide? If you have no opinion on that subject, explain how you view rebellious or alternative musicians in general.

Questions for Small Group or Class Discussion

1. If you are familiar with them, discuss the music of Kurt Cobain and the group Nirvana. In what way do you think Cobain was "desperately individualistic" (paragraph 2)? How would you evaluate the music of Nirvana? What is the "grunge style" (paragraph 2)?

2. Ross notes that Cobain has been called the " 'crown prince of Generation X' " (paragraph 2). Discuss your understanding of the term *Generation X*. In what way was that term appropriate for Cobain? Do you consider yourself a member of Generation X?

3. Ross calls "alternative" a "breathtakingly meaningless word, the emptiest cultural category imaginable" (paragraph 4). Do you agree with him? How does alternative music differ from punk rock, from which it has descended (paragraph 5)?

4. Ross writes: "If people still listen to Nirvana ten years from now, it will be on the strength of the music" (paragraph 7). Discuss whether

you think people will still be listening to Nirvana ten years from now and explain your answer.

5. Discuss this statement: "Rock and roll has never and will never be a vehicle for social amelioration, despite many fond hopes" (paragraph 11). Can you give any examples to prove Ross wrong?

6. Discuss whether you feel as Ross does when he writes: "Next time, it will not shock me when a vulnerable, talented misfit about my age infiltrates celebrity culture, then dies playing the abusive game of rebellion" (paragraph 12).

Perspectives on Music

Suggestions for Synthesis

1. All of the writers in this chapter address the subject of the power of music to affect those who listen to it. Using the comments of at least two of the authors in this chapter, consider both positive and negative effects of music on concert audiences and why music is able to affect mass behavior.

2. Write a paper in which you draw on the comments of Isabelle Leymarie, Jack Santino, and Alex Ross as you argue for or against the power of music to influence violent behavior in individuals.

3. Explain what you think Aaron Copland ("How to Listen to Music") would say about the rock music Isabelle Leymarie uses as examples in the opening paragraphs of "Rock 'n' Revolt." Do you think he would say that such musicians and their audiences "listen actively," that they reflect all three levels of listening he outlines in his essay? Explain why by referring specifically to passages from Copland's essay.

4. Hold a class forum or debate on the issue of the conflict between "the artists' right to free expression versus the parents' right to raise their children as they see fit" ("Rock and Roll as Music," paragraph 23). Take into account as well the comments of both Isabelle Leymarie and Alex Ross. Or, write an essay in which you draw on the comments of all three as you explore and come to some conclusion about your own viewpoint on the conflict.

Additional Writing Topics

1. Write a reflective paper on the power of music for you personally. What kinds of music do you like? Why? How does music affect you?

2. Select a song you like especially well and write a detailed analysis of what it means to you.

3. In paragraph 1 of "Rock 'n' Revolt," Isabelle Leymarie refers to a claim by John Phillips "that any rock group can whip a crowd into a hysterical frenzy by carefully controlling a sequence of rhythms." If you have ever seen such a phenomenon, where a crowd became hysterically frenzied, describe what happened and explore why you think music has that kind of control over people's emotions.

4. Write a response to Jack Santino's comment in "Rock and Roll as Music; Rock and Roll as Culture" that young people who wear "rebellious" clothing and listen to rock music do so to prove that "they are both prejudged and misunderstood by adults."

5. In "Generation Exit," Alex Ross frequently refers to today's young people as "Generation X." Write an essay explaining in detail what that term means and whether you agree with its appropriateness as a label for an entire generation.

6. Argue your viewpoint on the relative place or importance in the evolution of music of counterculture music of the 1960s or alternative culture music of the 1990s. Define and give examples of either one or both, or compare and contrast the two.

7. Read and write a critical review of Michael Azerrad's book *Come As You Are* (mentioned in Alex Ross's "Generation Exit"). Do not simply report what the book says but, rather, give a considered analysis of the book. Consider among other things how well you think it is written, how well it engaged your interest, and what major points you agree or disagree with.

Research Topics

1. In the opening paragraph of "Rock 'n' Revolt," Isabelle Leymarie gives examples of rock musicians and groups whose music and/or lives have been "fraught with violence," while Jack Santino in "Rock and Roll as Music; Rock and Roll as Culture" refers to the perception of rock and roll as "a menace to society" (paragraph 2). Research one, two, or several of the performers or groups named by either Leymarie or Santino and argue in support of or against the view that they are violent or menaces to society.

2. Isabelle Leymarie refers to "certain physiological and psychological effects [of music] which have been scientifically documented" (Rock 'n' Revolt," paragraph 8). Research the phenomenon of the physiological and psychological effects of music. Look not only for information about scientific research on the subject but also for the comments or criticisms of people skeptical of such research. Weigh the evidence, and arrive at your own opinion on the subject.

3. Research a rock group (or single performer) from the 1950s, 1960s, or 1970s. Find out the group's history, the audience its music appealed to, what the distinctive features of its music were, how many hit records it had, and if it is still

performing. Formulate your own assessment of the group's significance in the history of rock and roll, and make that your thesis or central idea.

4. Research the life of a rock musician who died young and tragically. Make sure you read differing interpretations of that musician's motivations, goals, successes, and failures, and then argue your own conclusions about his or her life and death.

5. Research "grunge" or other alternative music for the purpose of identifying its chief characteristics, the way in which it differs from and is influenced by other kinds of music, and its artistic merit or social significance. Include opposing viewpoints, and argue your own position on its merits or significance.

CHAPTER 7

FILM AND POPULAR CULTURE

By its very nature, popular culture reflects the interests and tastes of large seg-ments of the population. Makers of Hollywood films, contemporary music, and other products of the entertainment industry hope to tap into or even to create trends that will have widespread appeal and thus result in huge profits. Because of its high visibility, ready availability, and ease of access to all age groups, the entertainment industry has always been closely scrutinized and subject to attack by its critics. Popular Hollywood films are particularly prime targets for both criticism and praise. Hollywood watchdogs and film critics pay attention to not only the craft of film production but also to the content of films. The current ratings system evolved in response to alarm at the graphic sex and violence that young people were being exposed to, sometimes unwit-tingly, before such guidelines were in place. In recent years, many people have been sharply critical of the entire entertainment industry, especially Hollywood films, for what they see as the irresponsible depiction of shocking images, ex-cessive violence, and unnecessarily graphic sex. Its defenders have been just as heated in their responses.

The readings in this chapter suggest the nature of the controversy over Hol-lywood films and other products of popular culture and raise a number of is-sues for you to consider in both class discussion and writing. First, Michael Parenti in "Class and Virtue" analyzes the messages he thinks many Hollywood movies send about the relationship between class and virtue, arguing that movies present the working class as morally inferior to those in the middle and upper classes. As you read Parenti's critique, weigh the evidence he supplies and consider whether you agree with him. After all, the movie Pretty Woman, *which Parenti is particularly critical of, was wildly popular. Do you find his analy-sis sensible, or do you think he overstates his case?*

Extending Parenti's critical analysis of how movies essentially endorse class and gender bigotry, Michael Medved in "Hollywood Poison Factory" argues that many of today's movies pose a threat to mainstream American values. His fairly conservative viewpoint may differ sharply from your own, or you may find yourself agreeing with him. As you read Medved's observations, think about movies you have seen recently. Do they contain scenes of graphic sex and violence? Do they contain foul and abusive language? If so, do such things bother you?

The other two pieces take a general look at popular culture and report the opinions of both its supporters and detractors. Richard Lacayo's cover story for

Time *addresses the issue of graphic sex and violence in all popular media, but it pays more attention to Hollywood films and filmmakers, which then presidential hopeful Bob Dole singled out for special attention in his criticism of sex and violence in popular culture. The chapter ends with a* Time *magazine forum on the subject of the entertainment industry. Represented in the forum are divergent voices on the issue of what to do about vulgarity and violence in movies and other forms of popular culture. Consider your own position on this controversial issue as you read the differing perspectives of these representative voices.*

CLASS AND VIRTUE

Michael Parenti

Michael Parenti writes frequently on cultural and political issues. His books include Power and the Powerless *(1978),* The Politics of the Mass Media *(1986),* Democracy for the Few, *fifth edition (1987), and* The Sword and the Dollar: Imperialism, Revolution, and the Arms Race *(1988). In this reading, excerpted from his book* Make Believe Media: The Politics of Entertainment *(1992), Parenti argues that certain films endorse class and gender bigotry.*

The entertainment media present working people not only as unlettered and uncouth but also as less desirable and less moral than other people. Conversely, virtue is more likely to be ascribed to those characters whose speech and appearance are soundly middle- and upper-middle class.

Even a simple adventure story like *Treasure Island* (1934, 1950, 1972) manifests this implicit class perspective. There are two groups of acquisitive persons searching for a lost treasure. One, headed by a squire, has money enough to hire a ship and crew. The other, led by the rascal Long John Silver, has no money—so they sign up as part of the crew. The narrative implicitly assumes from the beginning that the squire has a moral claim to the treasure, while Long John Silver's gang does not. After all, it is the squire who puts up the venture capital for the ship. Having no investment in the undertaking other than their labor, Long John and his men, by definition, will be "stealing" the treasure, while the squire will be "discovering" it.

To be sure, there are other differences. Long John's men are cutthroats. The squire is not. Yet, one wonders if the difference between a bad pirate and a good squire is itself not preeminently a matter of having the right amount of disposable income. The squire is no less acquisitive than the conspirators. He just does with money what they must achieve with cutlasses. The squire and his associates dress in fine clothes, speak an educated diction, and drink brandy. Long John and his men dress slovenly, speak in guttural accents, and drink rum. From these indications alone, the viewer knows who are the good guys and who are the bad. Virtue is visually measured by one's approximation to proper class appearances.

4   Sometimes class contrasts are juxtaposed within one person, as in *The Three Faces of Eve* (1957), a movie about a woman who suffers from multiple personalities. When we first meet Eve (Joanne Woodward), she is a disturbed, strongly repressed, puritanically religious person, who speaks with a rural, poor-Southern accent. Her second personality is that of a wild, flirtatious woman who also speaks with a rural, poor-Southern accent. After much treatment by her psychiatrist, she is cured of these schizoid personalities and emerges with a healthy third one, the real Eve, a poised, self-possessed, pleasant woman. What is intriguing is that she now speaks with a cultivated, affluent, Smith College accent, free of any low-income regionalism or ruralism, much like Joanne Woodward herself. This transformation in class style and speech is used to indicate mental health without any awareness of the class bias thusly expressed.

Mental health is also the question in *A Woman Under the Influence* (1974), the story of a disturbed woman who is married to a hard-hat husband. He cannot handle—and inadvertently contributes to—her emotional deterioration. She is victimized by a spouse who is nothing more than an insensitive, working-class bull in a china shop. One comes away convinced that every unstable woman needs a kinder, gentler, and above all, more *middle-class* hubby if she wishes to avoid a mental crack-up.

Class prototypes abound in the 1980s television series *The A-Team*. In each episode, a Vietnam-era commando unit helps an underdog, be it a Latino immigrant or a disabled veteran, by vanquishing some menacing force such as organized crime, a business competitor, or corrupt government officials. As always with the make-believe media, the A-Team does good work on an individualized rather than collectively organized basis, helping particular victims by thwarting particular villains. The A-Team's leaders are two white males of privileged background. The lowest ranking members of the team, who do none of the thinking nor the leading, are working-class palookas. They show they are good with their hands, both by punching out the bad guys and by doing the maintenance work on the team's flying vehicles and cars. One of them, "B.A." (bad ass), played by the African-American Mr. T., is visceral, tough, and purposely bad-mannered toward those he doesn't like. He projects an image of crudeness and ignorance and is associated with the physical side of things. In sum, the team has a brain (the intelligent white leaders) and a body with its simpler physical functions (the working-class characters), a hierarchy that corresponds to the social structure itself.[1]

Sometimes class bigotry is interwoven with gender bigotry, as in *Pretty Woman* (1990). A dreamboat millionaire corporate raider finds himself all

---

[1] Gina Marchetti, "Class, Ideology and Commercial Television: An Analysis of 'The A-Team'," *Journal of Film and Video,* 39, Spring 1987, pp. 19–28.

alone for an extended stay in Hollywood (his girlfriend is unwilling to join him), so he quickly recruits a beautiful prostitute as his playmate of the month. She is paid three thousand dollars a week to wait around his super-posh hotel penthouse ready to perform the usual services and accompany him to business dinners at top restaurants. As prostitution goes, it is a dream gig. But there is one cloud on the horizon. She is low-class. She doesn't know which fork to use at those CEO power feasts, and she's bothersomely fidgety, wears tacky clothes, chews gum, and, y'know, doesn't talk so good. But with some tips from the hotel manager, she proves to be a veritable Eliza Doolittle in her class metamorphosis. She dresses in proper attire, sticks the gum away forever, and starts picking the right utensils at dinner. She also figures out how to speak a little more like Joanne Woodward without the benefit of a multiple personality syndrome, and she develops the capacity to sit in a poised, wordless, empty-headed fashion, every inch the expensive female ornament.

8   She is still a prostitute but a classy one. It is enough of a distinction for the handsome young corporate raider. Having liked her because she was charmingly cheap, he now loves her all the more because she has real polish and is a more suitable companion. So suitable that he decides to do the right thing by her: set her up in an apartment so he can make regular visits at regular prices. But now she wants the better things in life, like marriage, a nice house, and, above all, a different occupation, one that would allow her to use less of herself. She is furious at him for treating her like, well, a prostitute. She decides to give up her profession and get a high-school diploma so that she might make a better life for herself—perhaps as a filing clerk or receptionist or some other of the entry-level jobs awaiting young women with high school diplomas.[2]

After the usual girl-breaks-off-with-boy scenes, the millionaire prince returns. It seems he can't concentrate on making money without her. He even abandons his cutthroat schemes and enters into a less lucrative but supposedly more productive, caring business venture with a struggling old-time entrepreneur. The bad capitalist is transformed into a good capitalist. He then carries off his ex-prostitute for a lifetime of bliss. The moral is a familiar one, updated for post-Reagan yuppiedom: A woman can escape from economic and gender exploitation by winning the love and career advantages offered by a rich male. Sexual allure goes only so far unless it develops a material base and becomes a class act.[3]

Personal Response

Do you agree with Parenti's analysis of the movie *Pretty Woman,* that it not only illustrates class bigotry but also gender bigotry? Explain your answer.

---

[2] See the excellent review by Lydia Sargent, *Z Magazine,* April 1990, pp. 43–45.

[3] Ibid.

Questions for Class or Small Group Discussion

1. Discuss Parenti's thesis (stated in his opening sentences) by considering examples of Hollywood films you and your classmates are familiar with. Do they illustrate or refute Parenti's contention about Hollywood's portrayal of class and virtue in films?

2. Parenti uses a 1980s hit series to illustrate his thesis about the portrayal of class and virtue on television (paragraph 6). Discuss a current television hit series in terms of the kind of analysis Parenti applies to *The A-Team*. If you are familiar with the series *The A-Team*, discuss whether you agree or disagree with Parenti's analysis of that program.

3. Discuss Parenti's comments about the film *Pretty Woman*. Do you and your classmates agree or disagree with his analysis (paragraphs 7–9)?

4. The focus of Parenti's essay is class and gender bigotry. What other kinds of bigotry might be portrayed in the media? Give examples to illustrate what you mean.

HOLLYWOOD POISON FACTORY

Michael Medved

Michael Medved is a movie critic who serves as cohost of Sneak Previews, *a weekly PBS program. This article, which appeared first in the November 1992 issue of* Imprimis, *is based on his book* Hollywood vs. America *(1992). Here, Medved objects to the foul language, graphic sex, and startling violence that characterize many contemporary films.*

America's long-running romance with Hollywood is over. For millions of people, the entertainment industry no longer represents a source of enchantment, of magical fantasy, of uplift, or even of harmless diversion. Popular culture is viewed now as an implacable enemy, a threat to their basic values and a menace to the raising of their children. The Hollywood dream factory has become the poison factory.

This disenchantment is reflected in poll after poll. An Associated Press Media General poll released in 1990 showed that 80 percent of Americans objected to the amount of foul language in motion pictures; 82 percent objected to the amount of violence, 72 percent objected to the amount of explicit sexuality, and by a ratio of 3 to 1 they felt that movies today are worse than ever.

Hollywood no longer reflects—or even respects—the values that most Americans cherish.

4   Take a look, for example, at the most recent Oscars. Five very fine actors were nominated for best actor of the year. Three of them portrayed murderous psychos: Robert DeNiro in *Cape Fear,* Warren Beatty in *Bugsy,*

and Anthony Hopkins in *The Silence of the Lambs* (this last a delightful family film about two serial killers—one eats and the other skins his victims). A fourth actor, Robin Williams, was nominated for playing a delusional homeless psycho in *The Fisher King*. The most wholesome character was Nick Nolte's, a good old-fashioned manic-depressive-suicidal neurotic in *The Prince of Tides*.

These are all good actors, delivering splendid performances, compelling and technically accomplished. But isn't it sad when all this artistry is lavished on films that are so empty, so barren, so unfulfilling? Isn't it sad when at the Academy Awards—the annual event that celebrates the highest achievement of which the film industry is capable—the best we can come up with is movies that are so floridly, strangely whacked out?

I repeat: The fundamental problem with Hollywood has nothing at all to do with the brilliance of the performers, or the camera work, or the editing. In many ways, these things are better than ever before. Modern films are technically brilliant, but they are morally and spiritually empty.

The Messages

What are the messages in today's films? For a number of years I have been writing about Hollywood's antireligious bias, but I must point out that this hostility has never been quite as intense as in the last few years. The 1991 season boasted one religion-bashing movie after another in which Hollywood was able to demonstrate that it was an equal-opportunity offender.

8   For Protestants there was *At Play in the Fields of the Lord,* a lavish $35 million rainforest spectacle about natives and their wholesome primitive ways and the sick, disgusting missionaries who try to ruin their lives. And then for Catholics there was *The Pope Must Die,* which was re-released as *The Pope Must Diet.* It didn't work either way. It features scenes of the Holy Father flirting with harlot nuns and hiding in a closet pigging out on communion wafers. For Jews there was *Naked Tango,* written and directed by the brother of the screenwriter for *The Last Temptation of Christ.* This particular epic featured religious Jews operating a brutal bordello right next door to a synagogue and forcing women into white slavery.

And then most amazingly there was *Cape Fear,* which was nominated for a number of the most prestigious Academy Awards. It wasn't an original concept. *Cape Fear* was a remake of a 1962 movie in which Robert Mitchum plays a released convict intent on revenge who tracks down his old defense attorney. Gregory Peck portrays the defense attorney, a strong, stalwart, and upright man who defends his family against this crazed killer. In the remake, by *Last Temptation* director Martin Scorsese, there is a new twist: The released convict is not just an ordinary maniac, but a "Killer Christian from Hell." To prevent anyone from missing the point, his muscular back has a gigantic cross tattooed on it, and he has Biblical verses tattooed on both arms.

When he is about to rape the attorney's wife, played by Jessica Lange, he says, "Are you ready to be born again? After just one hour with me, you'll be talking in tongues." He carries a Bible with him in scenes in which he is persecuting his family, and he tells people that he is a member of a Pentecostal church.

The most surprising aspect of this utterly insulting characterization is that it drew so little protest. Imagine that DeNiro's character had been portrayed as a gay rights activist. Homosexual groups would have howled in protest, condemning this caricature as an example of bigotry. But we are so accustomed to Hollywood's insulting stereotypes of religious believers that no one even seems to notice the hatred behind them.

12   The entertainment industry further demonstrates its hostility to organized religion by eliminating faith and ritual as a factor in the lives of nearly all the characters it creates. Forty to fifty percent of all Americans go to church or synagogue every week. When was the last time you saw anybody in a motion picture going to church, unless that person was some kind of crook, or a mental case, or a flagrant hypocrite?

Hollywood even removes religious elements from situations in which they clearly belong. The summer of 1991 offered a spate of medical melodramas like *Regarding Henry, Dying Young,* and *The Doctor.* Did you notice that all these characters go into the operating room without once invoking the name of God, or whispering one little prayer, or asking for clergy? I wrote a nonfiction book about hospital life once, and I guarantee that just as there are no atheists in foxholes, there are no atheists in operating rooms—only in Hollywood.

Religion isn't Hollywood's only target; the traditional family has also received surprisingly harsh treatment from today's movie moguls. Look again at *Cape Fear.* The remake didn't only change the killer; it also changed the hero, and this brings me to the second message that Hollywood regularly broadcasts. As I mentioned, the original character Gregory Peck plays is a decent and honorable man. In the remake, Nick Nolte's character is, not to put too fine a point on it, a sleazeball. He is repeatedly unfaithful to his wife; when his wife dares to question that practice, he hits her. He tries to beat up his daughter on one occasion because she is smoking marijuana. He is not a likable person. That a happily married, family-defending hero— the kind of person that people can identify with—is transformed into a sadistic, cheating, bitter man, says volumes about the direction of American movies.

Did you ever notice how few movies there are about happily married people? There are very few movies about married people at all, but those that are made tend to portray marriage as a disaster, as a dangerous situation, as a battleground—with a long series of murderous marriage movies.

16   There was *Sleeping with the Enemy,* in which Patrick Bergin beats up Julia Roberts so mercilessly that she has to run away. When he comes after her, she eventually kills him. There was also *Mortal Thoughts,* in which

Bruce Willis beats up *his* wife and he is killed by his wife's best friend. In *Thelma and Louise,* there is another horrible, brutal, and insensitive husband to run away from. In *A Kiss Before Dying,* Matt Dillon persuades twin sisters to marry him. He kills the first one and then tries to kill the second, but she gets to him first.

In *She-Devil,* Roseanne Barr torments her cheating husband Ed Begley, Jr., and in *Total Recall,* Sharon Stone pretends to be married to Arnold Schwarzenegger and tries to kill him. When he gets the upper hand, she objects, "But you can't hurt me! I'm your wife." Arnold shoots her through the forehead and says, "Consider that a divorce." And then there was a more recent film, *Deceived,* starring Goldie Hawn. The advertisement for the movie says, "She thought her life was perfect," and, of course, her model husband turns out to be a murderous monster. *Deceived* is an appropriate title, because we all have been deceived by Hollywood's portrayal of marriage. It even applies to television. The *New York Times* reports that in the past TV season there were seven different pregnancies. What did six of the seven pregnancies have in common? They were out of wedlock. The message is that marriage is outmoded, it is dangerous, oppressive, unhealthy.

But is it true? Recently, I made an interesting discovery. The conventional wisdom is that the divorce rate in America stands at 50 percent. This figure is used repeatedly in the media. But the 1990 U.S. Census Bureau has a category listing the number of people who have ever been married and who have ever been divorced. Less than 20 percent have been divorced! The evidence is overwhelming that the idea of a 50 percent divorce rate is more than a slight overstatement; it is a destructive and misleading myth.

Yet for years Hollywood has been selling divorce. Remember *The Last Married Couple in America,* starring the late Natalie Wood? That may be a Hollywood prophecy, but it is not the reality of the American heartland. In this matter, as in so many others, by overstating the negative, the film industry leads viewers to feel terrified and/or insecure, and their behavior is adversely affected. I know many people who say, "I'm reluctant to get married because I know there's a 50 percent chance I'm going to get divorced." Wouldn't it make a difference if they knew there was an 80 percent chance of staying together?

Rekindling Our Love Affair with Hollywood

20   There are many indications that the entertainment industry may be eager to reconnect with the grass roots—and to entertain an expanded notion of its own obligations to the public. The industry has, in some areas, behaved responsibly. In the past five years it changed its message about drugs. No longer is it making movies in which marijuana, cocaine, and

other drugs are glamorized. Hollywood made a decision. Was it self-censorship? You bet. Was it responsible? Yes.

We can challenge the industry to adopt a more wholesome outlook, to send more constructive messages. We can clamor for movies that don't portray marriage as a living hell, that recognize the spiritual side of man's nature, that glorify the blessings in life we enjoy as Americans and the people who make sacrifices to ensure that others will be able to enjoy them.

The box-office crisis put Hollywood in a receptive mood. Already two film corporations have committed to a schedule of family movies for a very simple reason: They are wildly successful. Only 2 percent of movies released in 1991 were G-rated—just fourteen titles—but at least eight of these fourteen proved to be unequivocally profitable. (By comparison, of more than six hundred other titles, *at most* 20 percent earned back their investment.) Look at *Beauty and the Beast,* my choice for Best Movie of 1991. It was a stunning financial success. We need many more pictures like this, and not just animated features geared for younger audiences. Shouldn't it be possible to create movies with adult themes but without foul language, graphic sex, or cinematic brutality? During Hollywood's golden age, industry leaders understood that there was nothing inherently *mature* about these unsettling elements.

People tell me sometimes, "Boy, the way you talk, it sounds as though you really hate movies." The fact is that I don't. I'm a film critic because I *love* movies. And I want to tell you something: All of the people who are trying to make a difference in this business love movies and they love the industry, despite all its faults. They love what it has done in the past, and they love its potential for the future. They believe that Hollywood can be the dream factory again.

24   When I go to a screening, sit in a theater seat, and the lights go down, there's a little something inside me that hopes against all rational expectation that what I'm going to see on the screen is going to delight me, enchant me, and entice me, like the best movies do. I began by declaring that America's long-running romance with Hollywood is over. It is a romance, however, that can be rekindled, if this appalling, amazing industry can once again create movies that are worthy of love and that merit the ardent affection of its audience.

Personal Response

Respond to Medved's question, "Shouldn't it be possible to create movies with adult themes but without foul language, graphic sex, or cinematic brutality" (paragraph 22)? Is it possible? Would you prefer movies to be less brutal, foul, and sexually graphic, or do those things not bother you?

Questions for Class or Small Group Discussion

1. Discuss the extent to which you agree with Medved that Hollywood films today are "morally and spiritually empty." Is he being unfair or generalizing too much on the basis of just a few films? Can you give examples of movies that either support or refute his allegation?

2. Medved refers several times to *Cape Fear.* If you have seen the film, discuss whether you agree with Medved's analysis of it. If you have not seen the film, rent the videotape and watch it, perhaps with some of your classmates. Then prepare your own response to the film, keeping in mind Medved's comments. Or, do the same for any of the other films Medved refers to or the most recent film you have seen.

3. What is your response to Medved's allegation that Hollywood films are antireligion and antifamily? Can you supply examples of recent films that prove him wrong? Can you give examples of films that support his assertion? Has any film accurately portrayed your own family? Were you surprised at Medved's comments about the divorce rate (paragraph 18)?

4. What other values would you say Hollywood projects in the films it produces? Do you see a continuation or increase of the trend toward more family entertainment, as Medved indicates in the section subtitled "Rekindling Our Love Affair with Hollywood"?

5. What do you think Medved has in mind when he longs for a return to Hollywood as "a dream factory"? Do you agree with Medved on this point, that films should be a source of "enchantment, of magical fantasy, of uplift" (paragraph 1)? Can you think of any films that might fit that ideal?

VIOLENT REACTION

Richard Lacayo

Richard Lacayo wrote this special report on Senator Bob Dole's attack on sex and violence in popular culture for the June 12, 1995, issue of Time. Emblazoned on the cover in red, white, and blue letters was the question: "Are Music and Movies Killing America's Soul?"

Care to see the chief theater of operations in the culture wars? Just take a stroll through the Sherman Oaks Galleria, a twinkling mall in California's San Fernando Valley. This is where the great outpouring of pop culture comes to market, a market that caters to all the moods of the American disposition, from moonglow to bloodlust. At Sam Goody's, the chain record store, the CD bins are stuffed with amiable releases by Hootie and the Blowfish and Boyz II Men. But they also hold the gangsta rap of Bloods and Crips and Tupac Shakur. Nearby, at the Time Out video arcade, Jordan Trimas, 16, is playing *Primal Rage,* a game in which dinosaurs tear one another to pieces. "Sure, the violence influences kids," he shrugs. "But nobody can do anything about it."

At the Sherman Oaks multiplex, it's the same mixed bag. On the wide screen there's a face-off between the two top-grossing films of the week. *Casper* (the Friendly Ghost) offers his doe-eyed version of mortality against the merry bloodbath that is *Die Hard with a Vengeance.* But over at Taco Bell, 15-year-old Christopher Zahedi will tell you he prefers the rougher stuff. "I liked the part in *Pulp Fiction* where the guy points a gun and says a prayer from the Bible and then kills everybody," he offers. "You hear the gun go *brrrr.* It's cool."

In their worst nightmares a lot of parents can also hear that gun go *brrrr.* They aren't so sure it's cool, just as they aren't so sure it's cool when they come across the more stomach-turning specimens of pop music in their kids' CD collections. That's why, when Bob Dole went to Los Angeles last week to blast the entertainment industry, he touched a chord that transcended the party politics his remarks were shrewdly crafted to serve. Though popular culture has a long and proud history of offending the squares, during the current decade it has particularly kept its sharpest edges to the front. Whatever is scabrous and saw-toothed and in-your-face is probably brought to you by the major labels and the big studios. For parents, the pervasive electronic culture can start to look like some suspect stranger who hangs around their kids too much, acting loutish, rude and drunk.

4   It was that anxiety Dole was speaking to when he accused the powers behind American movies, music and television of flooding the country with "nightmares of depravity." Warning that the more extreme products of pop culture threaten to undermine American kids, he called on the large media companies to swear off the hard stuff. "We must hold Hollywood and the entire entertainment industry accountable for putting profit ahead of common decency," Dole said, then raised the heat considerably by singling out one company, Time Warner, the media giant that includes the largest American music operation, the Warner film studio and a stable of magazines, including *Time.* One day after Dole's speech, William Bennett, the former Education Secretary and drug czar, sent letters to Time Warner board members asking the company to stop distributing rap with objectionable lyrics.

Later in the week, Dole's wife Libby announced that she would be selling more than $15,000 in Walt Disney stock after learning that Disney, through its subsidiary Miramax, is the distributor of *Priest.* The controversial film, which her husband had already denounced several weeks ago, depicts a gay clergyman and a sexually active straight one. And coming soon from Miramax is *Kids,* a raw depiction of a sex-obsessed, drug-bleary day in the life of some New York City teens. It's the sort of thing Mickey Mouse would have to peek at through trembling white-gloved fingers.

To be sure, Dole's remarks were an unmistakable pitch to the culturally conservative wing of the Republican Party, which will have a lot to say about who becomes the next G.O.P. presidential candidate. Dan Quayle, their favorite son, never entered the race. Pat Buchanan, their guilty pleasure, is probably too extreme to be elected. Even before it turned out that he once invested in an R-rated film, Phil Gramm of Texas had left them cold. Until recently, so had Dole, who never showed much interest in the politics of virtue before the Christian right emerged as a power bloc in the party. In an effort to gain their attention, he has been sniping for months at Hollywood. Last week's salvo was like a proposal of marriage.

But Dole's attacks resonate beyond the party faithful, in all senses of the word. In a *Time* poll conducted at the end of last week by Yankelovich Partners, Inc., 77% of those questioned said that they were very concerned or fairly concerned about violence in the media; 70% said the same about media representations of sex. With numbers like those, it's a safe bet that Campaign '96 will also be Murphy Brown II, a further chapter of the conservative assault on Hollywood that Quayle launched in 1992.

8   "What we need is a national debate over the relationship of liberty to virtue," says Gary Bauer, the former Reagan White House aide who is president of the Family Research Council. "If you expose children to uplifting and noble material, you're more likely to have noble citizens. If children are wallowing in sexual images and violence, that is bound to have an impact on those who are most vulnerable."

In Hollywood, whose denizens have already been ridiculed for getting too close to the Clinton White House, the outraged response to Dole has been quick and complete. The speech was "a '90s form of McCarthyism," said Oliver Stone, whose *Natural Born Killers* was on Dole's hit list of objectionable films. "I don't think the public is that stupid," said Clint Eastwood. TV producer Norman Lear said he was "turned off by the excesses in some films" but insisted that Hollywood these days is making more pictures like *The Lion King* and *A Little Princess*.

In his attack on purveyors of offensive pop culture, Dole took pains, at least for now, not to hit some prominent Republicans. When he cited a list of recent family films that were also sizable box-office hits, Dole included not only *The Lion King* and *Forrest Gump* but also *True Lies,* a movie that reduced a small army of bad guys to blood-splattered pieces. Then again, it starred Arnold Schwarzenegger, a G.O.P. muscleman. Another sometime Republican, Bruce Willis, is the star of *Die Hard with a Vengeance,* one of the many brutal-fun action pictures that escaped Dole's wrath. So did the gleefully smutty-minded Fox television network and its contributions to the history of crotch-grabbing, such as *Married . . . With Children.* Fox is owned by Rupert Murdoch, a major contributor to conservative causes.

One day after the speech, which was written largely by Mari Maseng, wife of conservative columnist George Will, a Dole aide admitted that the

Senator also had not seen most of the movies he talked about, nor had he heard most of the music. On Friday aboard his Gulfstream jet, Dole finally popped *Natural Born Killers* into the VCR. "Probably ought to take a look so I can say I've seen this thing," he joked to a *Time* reporter over the phone. "Then we can always throw it out the window."

12   Count on it to keep coming back. The violent and raunchy streak in civilization runs deep and long into the past. More teenage boys might be attracted to the classics if they knew about Homer's graphic descriptions of spear points ripping through flesh in *The Iliad* or the quarts of stage blood needed for any production of *Titus Andronicus*. As for sex, the lewd posturings in some paintings of Hieronymous Bosch would be rated NC-17 if they showed up at the multiplex.

But the rise of capitalism over the past two centuries has meant that all the resources of technology and free enterprise could at last be placed at the disposal of the enduring human fascination with grunt and groan. By the early decades of the present century, there had emerged in the U.S. an entertainment industry that would eventually prove to be all-pervasive and ever more given to decking out our base impulses with sweaty and imaginative detail. It awaited only the youth culture that began stirring and shaking in the 1950s to take full advantage of the possibilities in rock, films and TV. The result was a pop culture more pointed and grown up, but also more shameless and adolescent; sometimes both at the same time. The great skirmishes against the blue-nosed guardians of culture—the Hays Office that policed movies in the '30s or the network censors who tormented the Smothers Brothers in the late '60s—became the stuff of baby-boomer folklore.

The complications set in during the '90s, when the boomers who were once pop culture's most dedicated consumers became the decision makers at media companies—but also the parents of the next generation. Pulled one way by their lifelong instinct for whatever is sensational, unsanitized or unofficial, they find themselves dragged in the other direction by their emerging second thoughts as citizens and parents.

Dole says he's not interested in government censorship, which in any event hasn't worked very well in the past. In the best tradition of Patrick Henry, Americans generally don't have much patience with government interference in First Amendment rights of expression, even when they may not much like what's being expressed. In the most highly publicized attempt in recent years to set the law on pop music, three members of 2 Live Crew were arrested in Florida in 1990 after a live performance. It took a local jury just two hours to acquit them on obscenity charges.

16   But the First Amendment applies only to attempts by government to restrain expression. It says nothing about decisions made by private media companies, and it does nothing to prevent them from choosing which songs or programs they will or will not promote. Five years ago, Simon & Schuster canceled plans to publish *American Psycho,* the sado-chic novel by Bret Easton Ellis, after advance complaints about passages detailing the

sexual torture and mutilation of women. (It was subsequently published by Knopf, a division of Random House.) "It's our responsibility," says Martin Davis, then chairman of Simon & Schuster's corporate parent Paramount. "You have to stand for something." This is just the sort of thing that Dole says he has in mind: self-restraint on the part of producers and distributors. "I'm just saying sometimes you have to have corporate responsibility and remember the impact on children."

Some media execs claim there isn't much that companies can do to restrain artists once they have them on their rosters. "*Artists* make records, not record companies," says David Geffen, the film and record producer who is now one-third of Dream-Works with Steven Spielberg and former Disney executive Jeffrey Katzenberg. "No record company tells them what to record."

But Geffen, whose label stopped distributing the *Geto Boys* in 1991 because he couldn't stomach their lyrics, also knows it's not so simple. Record companies routinely tell artists to remix their albums or record new tracks. Something like that happened two years ago at A&M records. Its president, Al Cafaro, heard a track intended for an album by the rap artist Intelligent Hoodlum. *Bullet in the Brain* was about killing a police officer. In the wake of the uproar over Ice-T's song *Cop Killer,* record executives everywhere were thinking twice. "It was nothing that we could be party to," says Cafaro of the song. "I told him I couldn't release it." What did Intelligent Hoodlum do? "He took the song off the record."

Two weeks ago, in a conversation with *Time* editors and correspondents, House Speaker Newt Gingrich went one step further when he suggested that major radio advertisers band together to boycott stations that play "explicitly vicious" rap. "They could drive violent rap music off radio within weeks," he said. Talk like that makes record execs very nervous. They know their product can also be vulnerable to boycotts by record stores that are under pressure from consumer groups. "You can make waves, but you can't mess with retail," says Eric Brooks, president of Noo Trybe Records. "You need to have your album stocked in the store."

20   Though advertisers haven't banded together yet, some citizen groups are trying it. Dennis Walcott, president of the New York Urban League, organized a protest last week at radio station WQHT in New York to persuade the station to stop playing *Shimmy Shimmy Ya,* a rap song that the protesters say encourages sex without condoms. "I'm not asking for censorship," says Walcott. "I'm asking for corporations who make money from these things to think about content and message."

The prominence of African-American organizations as critics of gangsta rap is a new element in this year's version of the culture wars. In his new campaign against Time Warner, Bill Bennett is allied with C. DeLores Tucker, head of the National Political Congress of Black Women. After a woman working at radio station WBLS in New York complained last year about the lyrics of one rap song, management established a committee to screen the playlist. For station head Pierre Sutton, who is black, it's simply a matter of "not in my house you don't." Says Sutton: "Artists have the right to say what they want to, and we have the right to decide with regard to the playing of same." When 1993 statistics showed that violent crime in Kansas City, Missouri, had risen 200% in one year, FM station KPRS decided no longer to broadcast violent, sexually explicit or misogynist rap. Under the new policy, KPRS rose from third to first place in the local ratings.

Though the cultural-pollution issue looks like an easy win for the Republicans, it's not a clean sweep. As the debate develops in weeks to come, the soft spots in their arguments are likely to become more apparent. For a party committed to free-market principles—and which also wants to defund public television and end government oversight of the airwaves—a problem is that pop culture represents the free market at its freest, meaning most able to make a profitable pitch to the grosser appetites. Some of the most violent American films, like the Stallone-Willis-Schwarzenegger action pictures, are also among the most successful American film exports because their bang-bang simplicities translate easily across cultural boundaries. Says Democratic Senator Bill Bradley of New Jersey: "The free market that the economic conservatives champion undermines the moral character that the social conservatives desire."

They can point out, for example, that Tipper Gore was among the first crusaders against obscene rock lyrics. First Lady Hillary Clinton has made frequent, if muted, denunciations of media vulgarity, and now seems to be turning up the volume, most recently in her appearance on *Oprah*. And sandwiched into Bill Clinton's long State of the Union message in January was a plea to Hollywood "to assess the impact of your work and to understand the damage that comes from the incessant, repetitive, mindless violence and irresponsible conduct that permeates our media all the time."

24   In an interview with *Time* last week, Vice President Gore stepped up the rhetoric. "Some of the decisions made by executives in the entertainment industry, the advertising industry, the creative community, have been obscene and atrocious." It was fine with him, Gore added, to try to shame corporate executives into reining in their product, though he rejected the notion that "shaming alone is a magic solution."

It's also not as easy as it sounds. Some decisions by media companies may seem like no-brainers. How many rap songs about slicing women's throats does the world really need? But most other judgments of taste are more difficult calls. Both of the films that Dole deplored, *Natural Born Killers* and *True Romance,* happen to have been written by Quentin Tarantino. He's also the explosively gifted director of *Pulp Fiction,* the great cock-eyed movie where that guy quotes from the Bible and the gun goes *brrrr* and some younger viewers think it's cool—lots of older viewers too. In the effort to achieve a kid-friendlier culture, do we want to end up with a sanitized one, free of the worst excesses of "death metal" but also purged of Tarantino? Or of sassy but not salacious rappers like Salt-N-Pepa? Or even, let it be said, deprived of the mixed bag of gifts and gas that is Oliver Stone?

The culture wars won't just be conducted in board rooms and at candidates' debates. For some time to come, they will surely be going on within our families and homes, and sometimes within ourselves as well.

In the aftermath of the Oklahoma City bombing, the conservatives are also stuck with their own problem of violence in the media—and it's not just Schwarzenegger's body counts. "Jackbooted thugs," the description of federal law-enforcement agents in a fund-raising letter from the National Rifle Association, is a kind of cop-killer lyric in itself. So is "aim at the head"—radio talk-show host G. Gordon Liddy's suggestion for greeting federal law-enforcement agents at your door.

28   Republicans who talk about the real-life consequences of pop-culture vulgarity still scream at the suggestion of any link between talk-show belligerence and Oklahoma City. Americans aren't so sure. In the *Time* poll, 52% of those questioned said they believed that strong antigovernment rhetoric inspires people to violence. And a lot of Americans are already suspicious of any attempt to use the culture issue as a way to evade discussion of everything else that contributes to the fraying of American life, from threadbare schools to the flood of guns. In the *Time* poll, 55% of those questioned agreed that if candidates want to improve the nation's moral climate, there are more important issues to concentrate on than sex and violence in the entertainment industry.

With those weak points in mind, Bill Clinton took a swipe at Dole last week at a town meeting in Billings, Montana. Without mentioning the Senator by name, Clinton observed pointedly that "there are some public officials in our country who are only too happy to criticize the culture of violence being promoted by the media but are stone-cold silent when these other folks are talking and making violence seem O.K."

For Democrats, criticizing Hollywood amounts to biting the hand that feeds them. Media-company executives and major stars contributed heavily to Clinton's 1992 campaign and to Democratic coffers generally in last year's congressional elections. Even so, the Democrats appreciate the potential power of the cultural-pollution issue and hope to position themselves prominently before Republicans get a lock on it.

Personal Response

What is your response to Bob Dole's assertion that music, television, and film are "flooding the country with 'nightmares of depravity'"?

Questions for Class or Small Group Discussion

1. Discuss the extent to which you believe that the sexually explicit and violent content of music, television programs, and films is as big a

problem or has as extensive an influence as people like Bob Dole and others cited in this article maintain.

2. In paragraph 8, a former White House aide is quoted as saying that the country needs a "'national debate over the relationship of liberty to virtue.'" Conduct your own class debate or discussion on this topic.

3. Lacayo reports that Senator Dole "has not seen most of the movies he talked about, nor had he heard most of the music" (paragraph 11). Do you think that makes a difference? Does one have to read a book like *American Psycho* or see a movie like *Natural Born Killers* before forming an opinion on it?

4. Many defenders of the music and films that are under attack for their sexual and violent content make the same point that Lacayo does in paragraph 12, that "the violent and raunchy streak in civilization runs deep and long into the past." Discuss that particular argument in light of what Lacayo goes on to say in the next few paragraphs about the "resources of technology and free enterprise" (paragraph 13).

5. To what extent do you think that "the culture wars" is solely a political issue, that sexually explicit and violent lyrics, television programs, and Hollywood films are just highly visible and easy targets for presidential hopefuls and not serious threats to American culture?

TOUGH TALK ON ENTERTAINMENT

This forum appeared in conjunction with the June 12, 1995, Time *magazine cover story on the entertainment industry. It represents the voices of many people, as each expresses a different opinion on the topic.*

De gustibus non est disputandum was the way the ancient Romans put it: there is no point arguing about matters of taste. But that was easy for the Romans to say; they—and their children—weren't awash in a tide of explicit films, TV programs and recorded music. We are. And the consequences of this condition—even the question whether there *are* any consequences—have spurred arguments that grow more intense as mass entertainment becomes more pervasive. In the aftermath of Bob Dole's latest attack on Hollywood, *Time* asked some prominent people who produce or comment on the arts for their reactions:

LYNNE CHENEY
Fellow, American Enterprise Institute
In one scene of Oliver Stone's film *Natural Born Killers* the hero drowns his girlfriend's father in a fish tank and kills her mother by tying her down on her bed, pouring gasoline on her and burning her alive. Meanwhile, a

raucous, laugh-filled sound track tells the audience to regard this slaughter as the funniest thing in the world. Is it any wonder that millions of Americans are concerned about kids growing up in a culture that sends such messages—or that someone who wants to be our President would talk about it?

A lot of the commentary about Bob Dole's remarks on Hollywood has focused on whether he has gained political advantage from them, and I think there is no question but that he has. Not so much because he has positioned himself better with the cultural right, but because, as Americans across the political spectrum realize, he is right—just as President Clinton was right a few years ago when he castigated rap singer Sister Souljah for saying that blacks have killed one another long enough and that it was time for them to start killing whites. When you glamourize murder, as *Natural Born Killers* does; or glorify violence against women, as does 2 Live Crew; when lyrics are anti-Semitic, as Public Enemy's are, or advocate hatred of gays and immigrants, as those of Guns n' Roses do, it's not just conservatives who know something has gone wrong; any thinking liberal does too.

4   Those producing this garbage tell us we're naive. *Natural Born Killers* isn't an attempt to profit from murder and mayhem, says Oliver Stone. It's a send-up of the way the tabloid press exploits violence—a claim that would be a lot more convincing if Stone would contribute to charity the multimillion dollar profits the movie earned last year. Time Warner CEO Gerald Levin, whose company produced *Natural Born Killers* and has put out much of the most offensive music, says that rappers like Ice-T are misunderstood: when Ice-T chants "Die, die, die, pig, die," he is not really advocating cop killing, but trying to put us in touch with the "anguished" mind of someone who feels this way.

This is nonsense—rationalization of the most obvious sort. What we need to do, each of us as individuals, is let those who are polluting the culture know that we are going to embarrass them and shame them until they stop, until they use their vast talents and resources to put us in touch with our best selves—instead of with the worst parts of our nature.

JOHN EDGAR WIDEMAN
Author and professor

Which is more threatening to America—the violence, obscenity, sexism and racism of movies and records, or the stark reality these movies and music reflect? If a messenger, even one who happens to be black and a rapper, arrives bearing news of a terrible disaster, what do we accomplish by killing the messenger?

I wasn't around when black people were barred from playing drums. But I know the objections to African drumming weren't aesthetic; Southern legislators feared the drums' power to signal a general slave revolt. I was around when finding black music on the radio was a problem.

Growing up in Pittsburgh, Pennsylvania, the only way to hear the latest rhythm-and-blues sounds after dark was searching the scratchy hyperspace for *Randy's Record Shack* beaming up from Nashville, Tennessee.

8   Banning, ignoring, exploiting, damning black art has a long history. Protecting black freedom of expression and participation at all levels of society began just yesterday. So it's not accidental that politicians reaffirm the doublespeak and hypocrisy of America's pretensions to democracy. Let's deregulate everything; let the marketplace rule. Except when rap music captures a lion's share of the multi-billion dollar music market. Then, in the name of decency and family values, we're duty bound to regulate it. On the other hand, in areas of the economy where black people are appallingly underrepresented—the good jobs, for instance, that enable folks to maintain families—we should abhor intervention because it's not fair.

The best art interrogates and explodes consensus. Recall how traditional African-American gospel music, transformed in the 1960s to freedom songs, the oratory of Martin Luther King and the essays of James Baldwin inspired and guided us. But we can't have the best art unless we are willing to risk living with the rest, the second rate and 15th rate, the stuff that eventually Xs itself because its worthlessness teaches us not to buy or listen.

We must not lose patience and stop paying attention. We must not mistake jingoism or propaganda or sensationalism for art. We must not fear change, fear the shock and disruption true art inflicts. We must not smother what we don't want to hear with the drone of morally bankrupt, politically self-serving Muzak.

DONNA BRITT
Syndicated columnist

As a columnist who often writes about how American parents of every color, income and political stripe feel they're engaged in a losing war with cultural swill, I was glad to hear Bob Dole lambaste the entertainment industry. Every parent I know feels bombardment; who cares who thrusts it under the microscope?

12   Sure, it's hypocritical. Dole, who long ignored the issue, is playing politics by reducing a complex and unwieldy problem to too-easy sound bites. But who isn't? People who excoriate Dole for hypocrisy in blasting movies in which fictional characters use the same assault weapons he supports in real life ignore that his most passionate attackers make fortunes off the depravity they're protecting. Free speech invokers who say only parents are responsible for policing what their children hear and see overlook that even good parents—who've never been busier or had a more pervasive pop culture to contend with—are sometimes too overwhelmed to fight. Bad parents—and there are millions—aren't even trying. But we all must share the planet with the kids they're raising badly.

PAUL SCHRADER
Screenwriter and director

I don't know which is more appalling—the conservatives' hypocrisy or the entertainment industry's sanctimony.

There are solid arguments here, both Dole's and the libertarian response. You'll never know it from what you hear or read. That's because the debate, as framed by Dole and the entertainment industry, is not about values or freedom. It's about popularity. Hollywood calls popularity money; politicians call it votes.

The entertainment conglomerates are fond of invoking the First Amendment. That's because there's precious little excuse for what they've been up to the past 20 years. We've worked so long and hard at making audiences dumber, they have actually become dumber.

16   Is Dole up to anything different? Several years ago, I was involved in a public debate over a film I adapted from Nikos Kazantzakis' *The Last Temptation of Christ*. It was assailed as blasphemous by religious conservatives, most of whom had not seen the film. I realized at the time it didn't matter whether they had seen it. This was not a debate about the spiritual values of *Last Temptation;* this was a fight about who controls the culture. *Last Temptation,* like other cultural totems—flag burning, Robert Mapplethorpe, gun control, NEA, abortion—had become a symbol of cultural hegemony.

Yes, the entertainment industry is an empty, soulless empire. I can't bring myself to defend many of the films now made; I can't even defend those Dole approves of. Hollywood must examine itself. Its greed is sickening. It must judge the social impact, not just the popularity impact, of what it does. So must politicians who seek to exploit cultural values.

KATHA POLLITT
Poet, writer and social critic

People like pop culture—that's what makes it popular. Movies drenched in sex and gore, gangsta rap, even outright pornography are not some sort of alien interstellar dust malevolently drifting down on us, but products actively sought out and beloved by millions. When fighting to abolish the NEA and other government support for the arts, conservatives are quick to condemn "cultural élitism" and exalt the majority tastes served by the marketplace. So how can they turn around and blame entertainment corporations for following the money and giving mass audiences what they want? Talk about élitism!

I too dislike many pop-culture products, although probably not the ones that bother Senator Dole. But the fact is, no system of regulation or voluntary restraint is going to have much effect on mass entertainment. And I'd like to hear how Dole squares his antiviolence stand with his ardent support for the N.R.A. and the overturning of the assault-weapons ban. Guns don't kill people; rap music kills people? Oliver Stone movies kill people? Please.

20   Ultimately, culture reflects society—for a violent nation, violent amusements. But if Senator Dole and his fellow conservatives are serious about elevating American tastes, they'd do better to encourage greater variety in culture than to seek to homogenize it even further. Let them increase the NEA budget until it at least equals that for military bands. Let them restore to the public schools the art and music and performance programs that have been cut in the name of "getting back to basics." Let them support public radio and television—or not complain when the kids watch *Beavis and Butthead* and their parents watch *Married . . . With Children,* a show whose raw humor at the expense of family values enriches not some Hollywood liberal, by the way, but Newt Gingrich's publisher, Rupert Murdoch.

That Dole and other cultural conservatives claim to speak out of concern for women is particularly galling. What have they ever done for women? These are the same people who were silent when Republican Congressmen compared poor single mothers to mules and alligators, who want to ban abortion. If these men want to do something about entertainment that insults women, why not start with Rush Limbaugh and his references to pro-choice women as "feminazis"? Oh, but I forgot. Criticizing gangsta rap for demeaning women is defending "American values." Criticizing right-wing talk radio for doing the same is "politically correct."

DANYEL SMITH
Music editor, VIBE magazine

Senator Bob Dole's recent attacks on hip-hop music and violent films are as ugly and transparent as some of the so-called gangsta rappers he wants to huff and puff and blow away. Like those of the worst rappers, Dole's views sound tinny and half-desperate. Like the lamest films, Dole goes for the spectacular (guns, violence, melodrama) rather than the substantive (love, sex, race, class). The main thing Dole, weak rappers and weak movies share is an ultimate goal: money. Staten Island hip-hoppers Wu-Tang Clan said it best with their 1994 hit single, *C.R.E.A.M. (Cash Rules Everything Around Me).*

The mass of folks going to the movies and buying records are in their teens, 20s and early 30s. The optimism of *Forrest Gump* rang false for a lot of us. *The Lion King* offered moments of uplift that faded when the lights came up. But hip-hop songs such as KRS-One's *Build & Destroy,* Gang Starr's *Just to Get a Rep* and Tupac Shakur's *Holler If Ya Hear Me* sound fierce and true, reflecting in mood and content the real world around me and many hundreds of thousand of fans.

24   Yes, sexism runs rampant through hip-hop. But it, like the violence in the music, runs rampant through the world, and needs to be protested and dealt with—not just silenced on the whim of an ambitious politician. The assumption that simply because the Notorious B.I.G. raps around gunfire in a song, people are going to run out and shoot stuff up is insulting and

tired. We are trying to make sense of the world—just like every generation has had to do. Forgive us if our salve is your sandpaper, but we are not you—and we're not sure we want to be.

BILL BRADLEY
Democratic Senator from New Jersey

I applaud Senator Dole. Almost by any measure, the airwaves have become the pathways for too much trash. Violence without context and sex without attachment come into our homes too frequently in ways that we cannot control unless we are monitoring the television constantly.

Studies show that by the time a kid reaches 18, he's seen 26,000 murders on TV. That has implications. It creates a sense of unreality about the finality, pain, suffering and inhumanity of brutal violence. The question really is, What is government's role? The answer has got to be more citizenship in the boardroom, not censorship. The public has got to hold boards of directors, executives and corporations accountable for making money out of trash.

For example, if you see something that offends you, find out who the sponsor is, find out who's on its board of directors, find out where they live, who their neighbors are, their local clubs, churches and synagogues. Send a letter to the members of the board at their homes and ask whether they realize they are making huge profits from the brutal degradation of other human beings. Then send a copy of that letter to all of their neighbors and friends. You can also begin to put economic pressure on a corporation. Because the market that the economic conservative champions undermines the moral character that the social conservative desires, you have to try to introduce into the functioning of the market a moral sensibility that is usually absent.

DAVID MAMET
Playwright

28   Politics seems to me much like the practice of stage magic. The magician is rewarded for appearing to perform that which we know to be impossible. We onlookers agree to endorse his claims and applaud his accomplishments if he can complete his performance before getting caught out. Similarly, we know, in our hearts, that politicians running for office are, in the main, mountebanks. They promise us an impossible future, or in the case of Senator Dole, a return to an imaginary pristine past.

It is in our nature to credit the ridiculous for the sake of the momentary enjoyment it affords. We do so at the magic show, at the car showroom and during the electoral process. It has long been the favored trick of the Republican Party to seek support through the creation of a villain. This imaginary being, whose presence stands between us and a Perfect World, this pornographer, this purveyor of filth, this destroyer of the family is he or she who used to be known by the name of communist, fellow traveler, labor agitator. Other historical names include nigger lover, papist, Yellow Peril, faggot and Jew.

It is the pleasure of the demagogue to turn otherwise sane people one against the other by this ancient trick, in order to further his or her own personal ends.

Yes, popular culture, in the main, is garbage. Perhaps it always has been, I don't know. I know we have a legitimate human desire for leadership, and Senator Dole's demagoguery corrupts this desire into a search for a victim and a longing for revenge. Whether as entertainment or politics, I find such actions objectionable.

STANLEY CROUCH
Critic

32   Regardless of the political opportunism that may propel the rising attack on the entertainment industry, the attention is more than a good thing because our mass popular culture is the most influential in the world. But when questions are raised about that industry's irresponsible promotion of certain material, the industry's executives tell us it has no influence. Everyone has to know that is a steaming pile of shuck. At its best, popular art has been part of our ongoing redefinition of American life, moving us to question our prejudices and our political policies, our social fears and the ways in which we live our personal lives.

But what we are faced with now is the panting exploitation of all our worst inclinations. We see the cult of slut chic in which Madonna has been such an influence across all lines of race and style that video after video looks like a combination of film-school virtuosity and bimbo routines with a backbeat. We see films in which dramatic intensity is replaced by the shock of gore that takes place in a ruthless universe of amoral one-liners derived from James Bond.

Narcissism and anarchic resentment are promoted in such a calculated fashion that numskull pop stars pretend to be rebels while adhering to the most obvious trends. The executives who promote these performers say that the issue is one of "freedom of expression," while others claim that we are getting "reports from the streets." But the rapper Ice Cube told an interviewer that his work was for young people and that if his audience wanted something else he would give it to them. That is not the statement of a rebel.

These people are not about breaking taboos, they are about making money, and they know where to draw the line. A few years ago, there was an understandable controversy about the anti-Semitic statements of Professor Griff when he was a member of the rap group Public Enemy. He was soon gone from the group. That is a perfect example of how responsibly the industry can work. We will hear no "reports from the streets" that give voice to the mad ravings of Khalid Muhammad or Louis Farrakhan, regardless of the young black people who cheer them at rallies. We have no idea how often the words "nigger," "bitch" and "ho" have been recorded in gangsta rap, but we can be comfortably sure that no rap group will ever be signed and promoted if it uses the word "kike" as frequently. Nor should it be.

36   Why is this? Because the Third Reich proved beyond all reasonable doubt what the constant pumping of hate-filled images and inflammatory statements can do to a culture. I do not believe censorship is the answer. But I have no doubt good taste and responsibility will not limit the entertainment industry's ability to provide mature work that attacks our corruption, challenges our paranoia and pulls the covers off the shortcomings that Balkanize us. What we need is simply the same sense of responsibility and dire consequences that we bring to the issue of anti-Semitism.

—Compiled by Andrea Sachs and Susanne Washburn

Personal Response

Whose opinions of those expressed in this forum do you agree with? Explain why you agree with those particular opinions.

Questions for Class or Small Group Discussion

1. Discuss the opinions of the people participating in this forum. With whom do you and your classmates find yourself siding? Why? Is there much disagreement among the members of your class on whose opinions they agree with?

2. What does the knowledge that the issue under discussion here is to some degree a political issue add to your understanding of the public debate over violence in the media? Do you feel that either major political party has recommended a wholly satisfactory solution to the problem?

3. Discuss the merits of a recent controversial film, such as Oliver Stone's *Natural Born Killers* or Quentin Tarantino's *Pulp Fiction*. Choose a film most of you have seen, or rent the video version and watch it together. What appeals to you about it? What shocks or angers you? What makes it a good or bad film?

Perspectives on Film and Popular Culture
Suggestions for Synthesis

1. Do a comparison/contrast analysis of two films of the same type (that is, comedy, romance, drama, action, or mystery, for example). Choose one produced in a previous decade and one produced within the last few years. Then, discuss the conclusions you draw about differences and similarities, especially in terms of the comments of various critics represented in this chapter.

2. Drawing on at least two of the readings in this chapter, write an essay on the subject of the sexual and violent content of Hollywood films, exploring whether you think anything ought to be done about such films and if so, what can or should be done.

3. Drawing on at least two of the readings in this chapter, write an essay on the subject of the morality of Hollywood films, including your own position on the subject.

Additional Writing Topics

1. Applying Michael Parenti's analytic approach in "Class and Virtue," do a detailed analysis of the representation of class and/or gender issues in any Hollywood film or television show.

2. Michael Medved ("Hollywood Poison Factory") refers several times to *Cape Fear.* If you have seen the film, discuss whether you agree with Medved's analysis of it. If you have not seen the film, rent the videotape and watch it, perhaps with some of your classmates. Then prepare your own response to the film, keeping in mind Medved's comments. Or, do the same for any of the other films Medved refers to or to the most recent film you have seen.

3. In paragraph 2 of "Hollywood Poison Factory," Michael Medved reports that many Americans believe that "movies today are worse than ever." Argue in support of or against that statement, making sure to support your argument with specific examples of movies.

4. Discuss the extent to which you agree with Michael Medved ("Hollywood Poison Factory") that Hollywood films today are "morally and spiritually empty." Use examples to support your generalizations.

5. Select a recent, popular film and do a close analysis of the values you think the film endorses.

6. Write a position paper on the topic of sexually explicit and graphically violent Hollywood films by selecting one specific film for analysis and two or three others to use as examples to support your position.

7. Explore the effects, either positive or negative, of movies on you as you were growing up.

8. In paragraph 8 of Richard Lacayo's "Violent Reaction," a former White House aide is quoted as saying that the country needs a "'national debate over the relationship of liberty to virtue.'" Write an opinion paper on what you see as the relationship of liberty to virtue.

Research Topics

1. Select a particular genre (type) of film, such as comedy, western, romance, fantasy or action, and research what various film historians, film critics, and

other film commentators have observed about the films in that genre. Your purpose will be to assess the historical development of the genre and its current state: Has the genre already had a "golden age," or are filmmakers still perfecting the genre? As you do your preliminary reading, look for a controversial issue to focus your research on. Then draw your own conclusions after you have done a thorough research of your subject.

2. Much has been written about certain images in films, such as the portrayal of women, of minorities, and of class issues, as the readings in this chapter suggest. Select a particular image or theme to research for its representation in films. Choose a particular period (films this year or last or films from a previous decade, for instance) and narrow your focus as much as possible, a task that will become more manageable once you begin searching for sources and discover the nature of articles, books, and other materials on this general subject.

3. Research the debate over the degree to which parents have a responsibility to monitor the movies their children watch and/or the degree to which filmmakers have a responsibility to produce movies appropriate for children. Then formulate your own position on the issue and support it with references from your source materials.

CHAPTER 8

ADVERTISING

Advertising is big business. Companies spend millions of dollars promoting their products, often on a single ad campaign. Advertising spots on spectacular televised events such as the Super Bowl or the Olympics can cost advertisers dearly, as does space in magazines and newspapers with wide circulation. Clearly advertising has an effect on the success of sales, or advertising space and time would not cost what they do and companies would not commit so many dollars to print and television ads. Because of its potential to influence consumers, the advertising industry has always been the object of criticism from a number of quarters: Analysts protest the potentially harmful images of some ads, consumer advocate groups object to the advertisement of certain products, and government regulatory committees have created guidelines ensuring fairness in advertising. The essays in this chapter address some of the issues surrounding the advertising industry. While the first three readings analyze advertisements for the messages they send or for the way in which they manipulate consumers to buy, the last defends the practices of advertisers.

Jean Kilbourne, in "Beauty and the Beast of Advertising," explains and illustrates her belief that the advertising industry sells an image of woman as beautiful and sexy that is impossible for almost all women to achieve. Kilbourne contends that this narrow image of woman, based on superficial beauty and almost impossible thinness, produces emotional and psychological problems in females who believe they fall short of the "ideal." As you read Kilbourne's essay, consider whether the females you know are driven by media images to achieve a particular image. Consider, too, whether what Kilbourne says about females is true of advertisements aimed at males as well.

With a different focus but using a similar approach to that of Jean Kilbourne, William Lutz in "With These Words I Can Sell You Anything" analyzes the way advertisers use words to manipulate consumers. In particular, he is concerned about "weasel" words that are imprecise and essentially meaningless. As you read his analysis and consider his examples, think about how often you see and read those words in advertisements and on products themselves. Think about the extent to which you are influenced by such words as you make decisions about what brands or products to buy.

While Jean Kilbourne is worried about the effects of advertising images on female self-image and psychological well-being, and William Lutz is primarily concerned with honesty and fairness in advertising, David Beers and Catherine Capellaro focus on advertisements for potentially harmful products. In their essay "Greenwash," Beers and Capellaro analyze advertising campaigns of corporations whose products pose a threat to the environment and to the health of humans. They believe that certain advertisements are actually deceitful and unethical. See if you agree with them and, if so, what you think ought to be the response of concerned citizens to their allegations.

The chapter ends with a defense of advertising. Attacking consumer advocates and government regulators who are critical of the manipulative power of advertising, John O'Toole in "What Advertising Isn't" insists that the strategies advertisers use to sell their products are fair and legitimate. As you read O'Toole's opposing opinion, consider whether you think that what he says is a reasonable counterargument to the arguments of the other writers in this chapter.

BEAUTY AND THE BEAST OF ADVERTISING

Jean Kilbourne

Jean Kilbourne has lectured for many years on advertising images of women and on alcohol and liquor advertisements. Among her films on advertising images are Killing Us Softly *and* Still Killing Us Softly. *This essay, a short version of what Kilbourne does in her lectures, first appeared in 1989 in* Media&Values, *a leading resource in the United States for media literacy education. The magazine is published by the Center for Media Literacy.*

"You're a Halston woman from the very beginning," the advertisement proclaims. The model stares provocatively at the viewer, her long blonde hair waving around her face, her bare chest partially covered by two curved bottles that give the illusion of breasts and a cleavage.

The average American is accustomed to blue-eyed blondes seductively touting a variety of products. In this case, however, the blonde is about five years old.

Advertising is an over $130 billion a year industry and affects all of us throughout our lives. We are each exposed to over 1,500 ads a day, constituting perhaps the most powerful educational force in society. The average adult will spend one and one-half years of his/her life watching television commercials. But the ads sell a great deal more than products. They sell values, images and concepts of success and worth, love and sexuality, popularity and normalcy. They tell us who we are and who we should be. Sometimes they sell addictions.

4   Advertising is the foundation and economic lifeblood of the mass media. The primary purpose of the mass media is to deliver an audience to advertisers.

Adolescents are particularly vulnerable, however, because they are new and inexperienced consumers and are the prime targets of many advertisements. They are in the process of learning their values and roles and developing their self-concepts. Most teenagers are sensitive to peer pressure and find it difficult to resist or even question the dominant cultural messages perpetuated and reinforced by the media. Mass communication has made possible a kind of nationally distributed peer pressure that erodes private and individual values and standards.

But what does society, and especially teenagers, learn from the advertising messages that proliferate in the mass media? On the most obvious level they learn the stereotypes. Advertising creates a mythical, WASP-oriented world in which no one is ever ugly, overweight, poor, struggling or disabled either physically or mentally (unless you count the housewives who talk to little men in toilet bowls). And it is a world in which people talk only about products.

Housewives or Sex Objects

The aspect of advertising most in need of analysis and change is the portrayal of women. Scientific studies and the most casual viewing yield the same conclusion: Women are shown almost exclusively as housewives or sex objects.

8   The housewife, pathologically obsessed by cleanliness and lemon-fresh scents, debates cleaning products and worries about her husband's "ring around the collar."

The sex object is a mannequin, a shell. Conventional beauty is her only attribute. She has no lines or wrinkles (which would indicate she had the bad taste and poor judgment to grow older), no scars, or blemishes—indeed, she has no pores. She is thin, generally tall and long-legged, and, above all, she is young. All "beautiful" women in advertisements (including minority women), regardless of product or audience, conform to this norm. Women are constantly exhorted to emulate this ideal, to feel ashamed and guilty if they fail, and to feel that their desirability and lovability are contingent upon physical perfection.

Creating Artificiality

The image is artificial and can only be achieved artificially (even the "natural look" requires much preparation and expense). Beauty is something that comes from without: more than one million dollars is spent every hour on cosmetics. Desperate to conform to an ideal and impossible standard, many women go to great lengths to manipulate and change their faces and bodies. A woman is conditioned to view her face as a mask and her body as an object, as *things* separate from and more important than her real self, constantly in need of alteration, improvement, and disguise. She is made to feel dissatisfied with and ashamed of herself, whether she tries to achieve "the look" or not. Objectified constantly by others, she learns to objectify herself. (It is interesting to note that one in five college-age women have an eating disorder.)

"When *Glamour* magazine surveyed its readers in 1984, 75 percent felt too heavy and only 15 percent felt just right. Nearly half of those who were actually underweight reported feeling too fat and wanting to diet. Among a sample of college women, 40 percent felt overweight when only 12 percent actually were too heavy," according to Rita Freedman in her book *Beauty Bound.*

12   There is evidence that this preoccupation with weight begins at ever-earlier ages for women. According to a recent article in *New Age Journal,* "even grade-school girls are succumbing to stick-like standards of beauty enforced by a relentless parade of wasp-waisted fashion models, movie stars and pop idols." A study by a University of California professor showed that nearly 80 percent of fourth-grade girls in the Bay Area are watching their weight.

A recent *Wall Street Journal* survey of students in four Chicago-area schools found that more than half the fourth-grade girls were dieting and three-quarters felt they were overweight. One student said, "We don't expect boys to be that handsome. We take them as they are." Another added, "But boys expect girls to be perfect and beautiful. And skinny."

Dr. Steven Levenkron, author of *The Best Little Girl in the World,* the story of an anorexic, says his blood pressure soars every time he opens a magazine and finds an ad for women's fashions. "If I had my way," he said, "every one of them would have to carry a line saying, 'Caution: This model may be hazardous to your health.'"

Women are also dismembered in commercials, their bodies separated into parts in need of change or improvement. If a woman has "acceptable" breasts, then she must also be sure that her legs are worth watching, her hips slim, her feet sexy, and that her buttocks look nude under her clothes ("like I'm not wearin' nothin'").

16   This image is difficult and costly to achieve and impossible to maintain—no one is flawless and everyone ages. Growing older is the great taboo. Women are encouraged to remain little girls ("because innocence is sexier than you think"), to be passive and dependent, never to mature. The contradictory message—"sensual, but not too far from innocence"—places women in a double bind: somehow we are supposed to be both sexy and virginal, experienced and naive, seductive and chaste. The disparagement of maturity is, of course, insulting and frustrating to adult women, and the implication that little girls are seductive is dangerous to real children.

Influencing Sexual Attitudes

Young people also learn a great deal about sexual attitudes from the media and from advertising in particular. Advertising's approach to sex is pornographic: it reduces people to objects and de-emphasizes human contact and individuality. This reduction of sexuality to a dirty joke and of people to objects is the real obscenity of the culture. Although the sexual sell, overt and subliminal, is at a fevered pitch in most commercials, there is at the same time a notable absence of sex as an important and profound human activity.

There have been some changes in the images of women. Indeed, a "new woman" has emerged in commercials in recent years. She is generally presented as superwoman, who manages to do all the work at home and on the job (with the help of a product, of course, not of her husband or children or friends), or as the liberated woman, who owes her independence and self-esteem to the products she uses. These new images do not represent any real progress but rather create a myth of progress, an illusion that reduces complex sociopolitical problems to mundane personal ones.

Advertising images do not cause these problems, but they contribute to them by creating a climate in which the marketing of women's bodies—the sexual sell and dismemberment, distorted body image ideal and children as sex objects—is seen as acceptable.

20   This is the real tragedy, that many women internalize these stereotypes and learn their "limitations," thus establishing a self-fulfilling prophecy. If one accepts these mythical and degrading images, to some extent one actualizes them. By remaining unaware of the profound seriousness of the ubiquitous influence, the redundant message and the subliminal impact of advertisements, we ignore one of the most powerful "educational" forces in the culture—one that greatly affects our self-images, our ability to relate to each other, and effectively destroys awareness and action that might help to change that climate.

Personal Response

What do you think of Kilbourne's assertion that advertisements contribute to emotional and physical problems for teenage girls? Do you agree with her?

Questions for Class or Small Group Discussion

1. In paragraph 3 Kilbourne states that ads "sell values, images and concepts." What values and images is she critical of? What other "values, images and concepts" do you think the advertising industry sells?

2. Kilbourne asserts that women in ads are primarily either housewives or sex objects. Bring to class examples of ads that you think illustrate or refute that assertion.

3. Kilbourne's focus is on the negative effects of ads on females. Discuss the ways in which men are portrayed in advertisements. Are the portrayals stereotyped? What images of men do ads project? Are these images harmful?

4. Do the female teenagers you know seem to be influenced by advertisements? If so, how?

5. Bring several advertisements from magazines to class and do a careful analysis of the ways in which they portray men and women and reinforce cultural values.

WITH THESE WORDS
I CAN SELL YOU ANYTHING
William Lutz

William Lutz has become nationally known for his acute analyses of language in advertisements and other public statements. A professor of English at Rutgers University, Lutz chairs the Committee on Public Doublespeak of the National Council of Teachers of English and edits the Quarterly Review of Doublespeak. *His books are* Beyond Nineteen Eighty-Four *(1984) and* Doublespeak *(1990), from which this essay is taken.*

One problem advertisers have when they try to convince you that the product they are pushing is really different from other, similar products is that their claims are subject to some laws. Not a lot of laws, but there are some designed to prevent fraudulent or untruthful claims in advertising. Even during the happy years of nonregulation under President Ronald Reagan, the FTC did crack down on the more blatant abuses in advertising claims. Generally speaking, advertisers have to be careful in what they say in their ads, in the claims they make for the products they advertise. Parity claims are safe because they are legal and supported by a number of court decisions. But beyond parity claims there are weasel words.

Advertisers use weasel words to appear to be making a claim for a product when in fact they are making no claim at all. Weasel words get their name from the way weasels eat the eggs they find in the nests of other animals. A weasel will make a small hole in the egg, suck out the insides, then place the egg back in the nest. Only when the egg is examined closely is it found to be hollow. That's the way it is with weasel words in advertising: Examine weasel words closely and you'll find that they're as hollow as any egg sucked by a weasel. Weasel words appear to say one thing when in fact they say the opposite, or nothing at all.

"Help"—The Number One Weasel Word
The biggest weasel word used in advertising doublespeak is "help." Now "help" only means to aid or assist, nothing more. It does not mean to conquer, stop, eliminate, end, solve, heal, cure, or anything else. But once the ad says "help," it can say just about anything after that because "help"

qualifies everything coming after it. The trick is that the claim that comes after the weasel word is usually so strong and so dramatic that you forget the word "help" and concentrate only on the dramatic claim. You read into the ad a message that the ad does not contain. More importantly, the advertiser is not responsible for the claim that you read into the ad, even though the advertiser wrote the ad so you would read that claim into it.

4   The next time you see an ad for a cold medicine that promises that it "helps relieve cold symptoms fast," don't rush out to buy it. Ask yourself what this claim is really saying. Remember, "helps" means only that the medicine will aid or assist. What will it aid or assist in doing? Why, "relieve" your cold "symptoms." "Relieve" only means to ease, alleviate, or mitigate, not to stop, end, or cure. Nor does the claim say how much relieving this medicine will do. Nowhere does this ad claim it will cure anything. In fact, the ad doesn't even claim it will *do* anything at all. The ad only claims that it will aid in relieving (not curing) your cold symptoms, which are probably a runny nose, watery eyes, and a headache. In other words, this medicine probably contains a standard decongestant and some aspirin. By the way, what does "fast" mean? Ten minutes, one hour, one day? What is fast to one person can be very slow to another. Fast is another weasel word.

Ad claims using "help" are among the most popular ads. One says, "Helps keep you young looking," but then a lot of things will help keep you young looking, including exercise, rest, good nutrition, and a facelift. More importantly, this ad doesn't say the product will keep you young, only "young *looking*." Someone may look young to one person and old to another.

A toothpaste ad says, "Helps prevent cavities," but it doesn't say it will actually prevent cavities. Brushing your teeth regularly, avoiding sugars in food, and flossing daily will also help prevent cavities. A liquid cleaner ad says, "Helps keep your home germ free," but it doesn't say it actually kills germs, nor does it even specify which germs it might kill.

"Help" is such a useful weasel word that it is often combined with other action-verb weasel words such as "fight" and "control." Consider the claim, "Helps control dandruff symptoms with regular use." What does it really say? It will assist in controlling (not eliminating, stopping, ending, or curing) the *symptoms* of dandruff, not the cause of dandruff nor the dandruff itself. What are the symptoms of dandruff? The ad deliberately leaves that undefined, but assume that the symptoms referred to in the ad are the flaking and itching commonly associated with dandruff. But just shampooing with *any* shampoo will temporarily eliminate these symptoms, so this shampoo isn't any different from any other. Finally, in order to benefit from this product, you must use it regularly. What is "regular use"—daily, weekly, hourly? Using another shampoo "regularly" will have the same effect. Nowhere does this advertising claim say this particular shampoo stops, eliminates, or cures dandruff. In fact, this claim says nothing at all, thanks to all the weasel words.

8   Look at ads in magazines and newspapers, listen to ads on radio and television, and you'll find the word "help" in ads for all kinds of products. How often do you read or hear such phrases as "helps stop . . . ," "helps overcome . . . ," "helps eliminate . . . ," "helps you feel . . . ," or "helps you look . . ."? If you start looking for this weasel word in advertising, you'll be amazed at how often it occurs. Analyze the claims in the ads using "help," and you will discover that these ads are really saying nothing.

There are plenty of other weasel words used in advertising. In fact, there are so many that to list them all would fill the rest of this book. But, in order to identify the doublespeak of advertising and understand the real meaning of an ad, you have to be aware of the most popular weasel words in advertising today.

Virtually Spotless

One of the most powerful weasel words is "virtually," a word so innocent that most people don't pay any attention to it when it is used in an advertising claim. But watch out. "Virtually" is used in advertising claims that appear to make specific, definite promises when there is no promise. After all, what does "virtually" mean? It means "in essence or effect, although not in fact." Look at that definition again. "Virtually" means *not in fact.* It does *not* mean "almost" or "just about the same as," or anything else. And before you dismiss all this concern over such a small word, remember that small words can have big consequences.

In 1971 a federal court rendered its decision on a case brought by a woman who became pregnant while taking birth control pills. She sued the manufacturer, Eli Lilly and Company, for breach of warranty. The woman lost her case. Basing its ruling on a statement in the pamphlet accompanying the pills, which stated that, "When taken as directed, the tablets offer virtually 100% protection," the court ruled that there was no warranty, expressed or implied, that the pills were absolutely effective. In its ruling, the court pointed out that, according to *Webster's Third New International Dictionary,* "virtually" means "almost entirely" and clearly does not mean "absolute" (*Whittington v. Eli Lilly and Company,* 333 F. Supp. 98). In other words, the Eli Lilly company was really saying that its birth control pill, even when taken as directed, *did not in fact* provide 100 percent protection against pregnancy. But Eli Lilly didn't want to put it that way because then many women might not have bought Lilly's birth control pills.

12   The next time you see the ad that says that this dishwasher detergent "leaves dishes virtually spotless," just remember how advertisers twist the meaning of the weasel word "virtually." You can have lots of spots on your dishes after using this detergent and the ad claim will still be true, because what this claim really means is that this detergent does not *in fact* leave your dishes spotless. Whenever you see or hear an ad claim that uses the word "virtually," just translate that claim into its real meaning. So the television set that is "virtually trouble free" becomes the television set that is

not in fact trouble free, the "virtually foolproof operation" of any appliance becomes an operation that is in fact not foolproof, and the product that "virtually never needs service" becomes the product that is not in fact service free.

New and Improved

If "new" is the most frequently used word on a product package, "improved" is the second most frequent. In fact, the two words are almost always used together. It seems just about everything sold these days is "new and improved." The next time you're in the supermarket, try counting the number of times you see these words on products. But you'd better do it while you're walking down just one aisle, otherwise you'll need a calculator to keep track of your counting.

Just what do these words mean? The use of the word "new" is restricted by regulations, so an advertiser can't just use the word on a product or in an ad without meeting certain requirements. For example, a product is considered new for about six months during a national advertising campaign. If the product is being advertised only in a limited test market area, the word can be used longer, and in some instances has been used for as long as two years.

What makes a product "new"? Some products have been around for a long time, yet every once in a while you discover that they are being advertised as "new." Well, an advertiser can call a product new if there has been "a material functional change" in the product. What is "a material functional change"? you ask. Good question. In fact it's such a good question it's being asked all the time. It's up to the manufacturer to prove that the product has undergone such a change. And if the manufacturer isn't challenged on the claim, then there's no one to stop it. Moreover, the change does not have to be an improvement in the product. One manufacturer added an artificial lemon scent to a cleaning product and called it "new and improved," even though the product did not clean any better than without the lemon scent. The manufacturer defended the use of the word "new" on the grounds that the artificial scent changed the chemical formula of the product and therefore constituted "a material functional change."

16   Which brings up the word "improved." When used in advertising, "improved" does not mean "made better." It only means "changed" or "different from before." So, if the detergent maker puts a plastic pour spout on the box of detergent, the product has been "improved," and away we go with a whole new advertising campaign. Or, if the cereal maker adds more fruit or a different kind of fruit to the cereal, there's an improved product. Now you know why manufacturers are constantly making little changes in their products. Whole new advertising campaigns, designed to convince you that the product has been changed for the better, are based on small changes in superficial aspects of a product. The

next time you see an ad for an "improved" product, ask yourself what was wrong with the old one. Ask yourself just how "improved" the product is. Finally, you might check to see whether the "improved" version costs more than the unimproved one. After all, someone has to pay for the millions of dollars spent advertising the improved product.

Of course, advertisers really like to run ads that claim a product is "new and improved." While what constitutes a "new" product may be subject to some regulation, "improved" is a subjective judgment. A manufacturer changes the shape of its stick deodorant, but the shape doesn't improve the function of the deodorant. That is, changing the shape doesn't affect the deodorizing ability of the deodorant, so the manufacturer calls it "improved." Another manufacturer adds ammonia to its liquid cleaner and calls it "new and improved." Since adding ammonia does affect the cleaning ability of the product, there has been a "material functional change" in the product, and the manufacturer can now call its cleaner "new," and "improved" as well. Now the weasel words "new and improved" are plastered all over the package and are the basis for a multimillion-dollar ad campaign. But after six months the word "new" will have to go, until someone can dream up another change in the product. Perhaps it will be adding color to the liquid, or changing the shape of the package, or maybe adding a new dripless pour spout, or perhaps a————. The "improvements" are endless, and so are the new advertising claims and campaigns.

"New" is just too useful and powerful a word in advertising for advertisers to pass it up easily. So they use weasel words that say "new" without really saying it. One of their favorites is "introducing," as in, "Introducing improved Tide," or "Introducing the stain remover." The first is simply saying, here's our improved soap; the second, here's our new advertising campaign for our detergent. Another favorite is "now," as in, "Now there's Sinex," which simply means that Sinex is available. Then there are phrases like "Today's Chevrolet," "Presenting Dristan," and "A fresh way to start the day." The list is really endless because advertisers are always finding new ways to say "new" without really saying it. If there is a second edition of this book, I'll just call it the "new and improved" edition. Wouldn't you really rather have a "new and improved" edition of this book rather than a "second" edition?

Acts Fast

"Acts" and "works" are two popular weasel words in advertising because they bring action to the product and to the advertising claim. When you see the ad for the cough syrup that "Acts on the cough control center," ask yourself what this cough syrup is claiming to do. Well, it's just claiming to "act," to do something, to perform an action. What is it that the cough syrup does? The ad doesn't say. It only claims to perform an action or do something on your "cough control center." By the way, what and where is your "cough control center"? I don't remember learning about that part of the body in human biology class.

20   Ads that use such phrases as "acts fast," "acts against," "acts to prevent," and the like are saying essentially nothing, because "act" is a word empty of any specific meaning. The ads are always careful not to specify exactly what "act" the product performs. Just because a brand of aspirin claims to "act fast" for headache relief doesn't mean this aspirin is any better than any other aspirin. What is the "act" that this aspirin performs? You're never told. Maybe it just dissolves quickly. Since aspirin is a parity product, all aspirin is the same and therefore functions the same.

Works Like Anything Else

If you don't find the word "acts" in an ad, you will probably find the weasel word "works." In fact, the two words are almost interchangeable in advertising. Watch out for ads that say a product "works against," "works like," "works for," or "works longer." As with "acts," "works" is the same meaningless verb used to make you think that this product really does something, and maybe even something special or unique. But "works," like "acts," is basically a word empty of any specific meaning.

Like Magic

Whenever advertisers want you to stop thinking about the product and start thinking about something bigger, better, or more attractive than the product, they use that very popular weasel word, "like." The word "like" is the advertiser's equivalent of a magician's use of misdirection. "Like" gets you to ignore the product and concentrate on the claim the advertiser is making about it. "For skin like peaches and cream" claims the ad for a skin cream. What is this ad really claiming? It doesn't say this cream will give you peaches-and-cream skin. There is no verb in this claim, so it doesn't even mention using the product. How is skin ever like "peaches and cream"? Remember, ads must be read literally and exactly, according to the dictionary definition of words. (Remember "virtually" in the Eli Lilly case.) The ad is making absolutely no promise or claim whatsoever for this skin cream. If you think this cream will give you soft, smooth, youthful-looking skin, you are the one who has read that meaning into the ad.

The wine that claims "It's like taking a trip to France" wants you to think about a romantic evening in Paris as you walk along the boulevard after a wonderful meal in an intimate little bistro. Of course, you don't really believe that a wine can take you to France, but the goal of the ad is to get you to think pleasant, romantic thoughts about France and not about how the wine tastes or how expensive it may be. That little word "like" has taken you away from crushed grapes into a world of your own imaginative making. Who knows, maybe the next time you buy wine, you'll think those pleasant thoughts when you see this brand of wine, and you'll buy it. Or, maybe you weren't even thinking about buying wine at all, but now you just might pick up a bottle the next time you're shopping. Ah, the power of "like" in advertising.

24 How about the most famous "like" claim of all, "Winston tastes good like a cigarette should"? Ignoring the grammatical error here, you might want to know what this claim is saying. Whether a cigarette tastes good or bad is a subjective judgment because what tastes good to one person may well taste horrible to another. Not everyone likes fried snails, even if they are called escargot. (De gustibus non est disputandum, which was probably the Roman rule for advertising as well as for defending the games in the Colosseum.) There are many people who say all cigarettes taste terrible, other people who say only some cigarettes taste all right, and still others who say all cigarettes taste good. Who's right? Everyone, because taste is a matter of personal judgment.

Moreover, note the use of the conditional, "should." The complete claim is, "Winston tastes good like a cigarette should taste." But should cigarettes taste good? Again, this is a matter of personal judgment and probably depends most on one's experiences with smoking. So, the Winston ad is simply saying that Winston cigarettes are just like any other cigarette: Some people like them and some people don't. On that statement R. J. Reynolds conducted a very successful multimillion-dollar advertising campaign that helped keep Winston the number-two-selling cigarette in the United States, close behind number one, Marlboro.

Can It Be Up to the Claim?

Analyzing ads for doublespeak requires that you pay attention to every word in the ad and determine what each word really means. Advertisers try to wrap their claims in language that sounds concrete, specific, and objective, when in fact the language of advertising is anything but. Your job is to read carefully and listen critically so that when the announcer says that "Crest can be of significant value . . ." you know immediately that this claim says absolutely nothing. Where is the doublespeak in this ad? Start with the second word.

Once again, you have to look at what words really mean, not what you think they mean or what the advertiser wants you to think they mean. The ad for Crest only says that using Crest "can be" of "significant value." What really throws you off in this ad is the brilliant use of "significant." It draws your attention to the word "value" and makes you forget that the ad only claims that Crest "can be." The ad doesn't say that Crest is of value, only that it is "able" or "possible" to be of value, because that's all that "can" means.

28 It's so easy to miss the importance of those little words, "can be." Almost as easy as missing the importance of the words "up to" in an ad. These words are very popular in sale ads. You know, the ones that say,

"Up to 50% Off!" Now, what does that claim mean? Not much, because the store or manufacturer has to reduce the price of only a few items by 50 percent. Everything else can be reduced a lot less, or not even reduced. Moreover, don't you want to know 50 percent off of what? Is it 50 percent off the "manufacturer's suggested list price," which is the highest possible price? Was the price artificially inflated and then reduced? In other ads, "up to" expresses an ideal situation. The medicine that works "up to ten times faster," the battery that lasts "up to twice as long," and the soap that gets you "up to twice as clean" all are based on ideal situations for using those products, situations in which you can be sure you will never find yourself.

Unfinished Words

Unfinished words are a kind of "up to" claim in advertising. The claim that a battery lasts "up to twice as long" usually doesn't finish the comparison—twice as long as what? A birthday candle? A tank of gas? A cheap battery made in a country not noted for its technological achievements? The implication is that the battery lasts twice as long as batteries made by other battery makers, or twice as long as earlier model batteries made by the advertiser, but the ad doesn't really make these claims. You read these claims into the ad, aided by the visual images the advertiser so carefully provides.

Unfinished words depend on you to finish them, to provide the words the advertisers so thoughtfully left out of the ad. Pall Mall cigarettes were once advertised as "A longer finer and milder smoke." The question is, longer, finer, and milder than what? The aspirin that claims it contains "Twice as much of the pain reliever doctors recommend most" doesn't tell you what pain reliever it contains twice as much of. (By the way, it's aspirin. That's right; it just contains twice the amount of aspirin. And how much is twice the amount? Twice of what amount?) Panadol boasts that "nobody reduces fever faster," but, since Panadol is a parity product, this claim simply means that Panadol isn't any better than any other product in its parity class. "You can be sure if it's Westinghouse," you're told, but just exactly what it is you can be sure of is never mentioned. "Magnavox gives you more" doesn't tell you what you get more of. More value? More television? More than they gave you before? It sounds nice, but it means nothing, until you fill in the claim with your own words, the words the advertiser didn't use. Since each of us fills in the claim differently, the ad and the product can become all things to all people, and not promise a single thing.

Unfinished words abound in advertising because they appear to promise so much. More importantly, they can be joined with powerful visual images on television to appear to be making significant promises about a product's effectiveness without really making any promises. In a television ad, the aspirin product that claims fast relief can show a person with a headache taking the product and then, in what appears to be a matter of minutes, claiming complete relief. This visual image is far more powerful than any claim made in unfinished words. Indeed, the visual image completes the unfinished words for you, filling in with pictures what the words leave out. And you thought that ads didn't affect you. What brand of aspirin do you use?

32   Some years ago, Ford's advertisements proclaimed "Ford LTD—700% quieter." Now, what do you think Ford was claiming with these unfinished words? What was the Ford LTD quieter than? A Cadillac? A Mercedes Benz? A BMW? Well, when the FTC asked Ford to substantiate this unfinished claim, Ford replied that it meant that the inside of the LTD was 700% quieter than the outside. How did you finish those unfinished words when you first read them? Did you even come close to Ford's meaning?

Combining Weasel Words

A lot of ads don't fall neatly into one category or another because they use a variety of different devices and words. Different weasel words are often combined to make an ad claim. The claim, "Coffee-Mate gives coffee more body, more flavor," uses unfinished words ("more" than what?) and also uses words that have no specific meaning ("body" and "flavor"). Along with "taste" (remember the Winston ad and its claim to taste good), "body" and "flavor" mean nothing because their meaning is entirely subjective. To you, "body" in coffee might mean thick, black, almost bitter coffee, while I might take it to mean a light brown, delicate coffee. Now, if you think you understood that last sentence, read it again, because it said nothing of objective value; it was filled with weasel words of no specific meaning: "thick," "black," "bitter," "light brown," and "delicate." Each of those words has no specific, objective meaning, because each of us can interpret them differently.

Try this slogan: "Looks, smells, tastes like ground-roast coffee." So, are you now going to buy Taster's Choice instant coffee because of this ad? "Looks," "smells," and "tastes" are all words with no specific meaning and depend on your interpretation of them for any meaning. Then there's that great weasel word "like," which simply suggests a comparison but does not make the actual connection between the product and the quality. Besides, do you know what "ground-roast" coffee is? I don't, but it sure sounds good. So, out of seven words in this ad, four are definite weasel words, two are quite meaningless, and only one has any clear meaning.

Remember the Anacin ad—"Twice as much of the pain reliever doctors recommend most"? There's a whole lot of weaseling going on in this ad. First, what's the pain reliever they're talking about in this ad? Aspirin, of course. In fact, any time you see or hear an ad using those words "pain reliever," you can automatically substitute the word "aspirin" for them. (Makers of acetaminophen and ibuprofen pain relievers are careful in their advertising to identify their products as nonaspirin products.) So, now we know that Anacin has aspirin in it. Moreover, we know that Anacin has twice as much aspirin in it, but we don't know twice as much as what. Does it have twice as much aspirin as an ordinary aspirin tablet? If so, what is an ordinary aspirin tablet, and how much aspirin does it contain? Twice as much as Excedrin or Bufferin? Twice as much as a chocolate chip cookie? Remember those Unfinished Words and how they lead you on without saying anything.

36   Finally, what about those doctors who are doing all that recommending? Who are they? How many of them are there? What kind of doctors are they? What are their qualifications? Who asked them about recommending pain relievers? What other pain relievers did they recommend? And there are a whole lot more questions about this "poll" of doctors to which I'd like to know the answers, but you get the point. Sometimes, when I call my doctor, she tells me to take two aspirin and call her office in the morning. Is that where Anacin got this ad?

Read the Label, or the Brochure

Weasel words aren't just found on television, on the radio, or in newspaper and magazine ads. Just about any language associated with a product will contain the doublespeak of advertising. Remember the Eli Lilly case and the doublespeak on the information sheet that came with the birth control pills. Here's another example.

In 1983, the Estée Lauder cosmetics company announced a new product called "Night Repair." A small brochure distributed with the product stated that "Night Repair was scientifically formulated in Estée Lauder's U.S. laboratories as part of the Swiss Age-Controlling Skincare Program. Although only nature controls the aging process, this program helps control the signs of aging and encourages skin to look and feel younger." You might want to read these two sentences again, because they sound great but say nothing.

First, note that the product was "scientifically formulated" in the company's laboratories. What does that mean? What constitutes a scientific formulation? You wouldn't expect the company to say that the product was casually, mechanically, or carelessly formulated, or just thrown together one day when the people in the white coats didn't have anything better to do. But the word "scientifically" lends an air of precision and promise that just isn't there.

40   It is the second sentence, however, that's really weasely, both syntactically and semantically. The only factual part of this sentence is the introductory dependent clause—"only nature controls the aging process." Thus, the only fact in the ad is relegated to a dependent clause, a clause dependent on the main clause, which contains no factual or definite information at all and indeed purports to contradict the independent clause. The

new "skincare program" (notice it's not a skin cream but a "program") does not claim to stop or even retard the aging process. What, then, does Night Repair, at a price of over $35 (in 1983 dollars) for a .87-ounce bottle do? According to this brochure, nothing. It only "helps," and the brochure does not say how much it helps. Moreover, it only "helps control," and then it only helps control the "*signs* of aging," not the aging itself. Also, it "encourages" skin not to *be* younger but only to "look and feel" younger. The brochure does not say younger than what. Of the sixteen words in the main clause of this second sentence, nine are weasel words. So, before you spend all that money for Night Repair, or any other cosmetic product, read the words carefully, and then decide if you're getting what you think you're paying for.

Other Tricks of the Trade

Advertisers' use of doublespeak is endless. Remember the explanation of advertising's function given by Rosser Reeves earlier in this chapter: to make something out of nothing. The best way advertisers can make something out of nothing is through words. Although there are a lot of visual images used on television and in magazines and newspapers, every advertiser wants to create that memorable line that will stick in the public consciousness. I am sure pure joy reigned in one advertising agency when a study found that children who were asked to spell the word "relief" promptly and proudly responded "r-o-l-a-i-d-s."

The variations, combinations, and permutations of doublespeak used in advertising go on and on, running from the use of rhetorical questions ("Wouldn't you really rather have a Buick?" "If you can't trust Prestone, who can you trust?") to flattering you with compliments ("The lady has taste." "We think a cigar smoker is someone special." "You've come a long way baby."). You know, of course, how you're *supposed* to answer those questions, and you know that those compliments are just leading up to the sales pitches for the products. Before you dismiss such tricks of the trade as obvious, however, just remember that all of these statements and questions were part of very successful advertising campaigns.

A more subtle approach is the ad that proclaims a supposedly unique quality for a product, a quality that really isn't unique. "If it doesn't say Goodyear, it can't be polyglas." Sounds good, doesn't it? Polyglas is available only from Goodyear because Goodyear copyrighted that trade name. Any other tire manufacturer could make exactly the same tire but could not call it "polyglas," because that would be copyright infringement. "Polyglas" is simply Goodyear's name for its fiberglass-reinforced tire.

44 Since we like to think of ourselves as living in a technologically advanced country, science and technology have a great appeal in selling products. Advertisers are quick to use scientific doublespeak to push their products. There are all kinds of elixirs, additives, scientific potions,

and mysterious mixtures added to all kinds of products. Gasoline contains "HTA," "F-310," "Platformate," and other chemical-sounding additives, but nowhere does an advertisement give any real information about the additive.

Shampoo, deodorant, mouthwash, cold medicine, sleeping pills, and any number of other products all seem to contain some special chemical ingredient that allows them to work wonders. "Certs contains a sparkling drop of Retsyn." So what? What's "Retsyn"? What's it do? What's so special about it? When they don't have a secret ingredient in their product, advertisers still find a way to claim scientific validity. There's "Sinarest. Created by a research scientist who actually gets sinus headaches." Sounds nice, but what kind of research does this scientist do? How do you know if she is any kind of expert on sinus medicine? Besides, this ad doesn't tell you a thing about the medicine itself and what it does.

Advertising Doublespeak Quick Quiz

Now it's time to test your awareness of advertising doublespeak. (You didn't think I would just let you read this and forget it, did you?) The following is a list of statements from some recent ads. Your job is to figure out what each of these ads really says.

Domino's Pizza:	"Because nobody delivers better."
Sinutab:	"It can stop the pain."
Tums:	"The stronger acid neutralizer."
Maximum Strength Dristan:	"Strong medicine for tough sinus colds."
Listermint:	"Making your mouth a cleaner place."
Cascade:	"For virtually spotless dishes nothing beats Cascade."
Nuprin:	"Little. Yellow. Different. Better."
Anacin:	"Better relief."
Sudafed:	"Fast sinus relief that won't put you fast asleep."
Advil:	"Advanced medicine for pain."
Ponds Cold Cream:	"Ponds cleans like no soap can."
Miller Lite Beer:	"Tastes great. Less filling."
Philips Milk of Magnesia:	"Nobody treats you better than MOM (Philips Milk of Magnesia)."
Bayer:	"The wonder drug that works wonders."
Cracker Barrel:	"Judged to be the best."
Knorr:	"Where taste is everything."
Anusol:	"Anusol is the word to remember for relief."

Dimetapp:	"It relieves kids as well as colds."
Liquid Drāno:	"The liquid strong enough to be called Drāno."
Johnson & Johnson Baby Powder:	"Like magic for your skin."
Puritan:	"Make it your oil for life."
Pam:	"Pam, because how you cook is as important as what you cook."
Ivory Shampoo and Conditioner:	"Leave your hair feeling Ivory clean."
Tylenol Gel-Caps:	"It's not a capsule. It's better."
Alka-Seltzer Plus:	"Fast, effective relief for winter colds."

The World of Advertising

In the world of advertising, people wear "dentures," not false teeth; they suffer from "occasional irregularity," not constipation; they need deodorants for their "nervous wetness," not for sweat; they use "bathroom tissue," not toilet paper; and they don't dye their hair, they "tint" or "rinse" it. Advertisements offer "real counterfeit diamonds" without the slightest hint of embarrassment, or boast of goods made out of "genuine imitation leather" or "virgin vinyl."

48   In the world of advertising, the girdle becomes a "body shaper," "form persuader," "control garment," "controller," "outerwear enhancer," "body garment," or "anti-gravity panties," and is sold with such trade names as "The Instead," "The Free Spirit," and "The Body Briefer."

A study some years ago found the following words to be among the most popular used in U.S. television advertisements: "new," "improved," "better," "extra," "fresh," "clean," "beautiful," "free," "good," "great," and "light." At the same time, the following words were found to be among the most frequent on British television: "new," "good-better-best," "free," "fresh," "delicious," "full," "sure," "clean," "wonderful," and "special." While these words may occur most frequently in ads, and while ads may be filled with weasel words, you have to watch out for all the words used in advertising, not just the words mentioned here.

Every word in an ad is there for a reason; no word is wasted. Your job is to figure out exactly what each word is doing in an ad—what each word really means, not what the advertiser wants you to think it means. Remember, the ad is trying to get you to buy a product, so it will put the product in the best possible light, using any device, trick, or means legally allowed. Your only defense against advertising (besides taking up permanent residence on the moon) is to develop and use a strong critical reading, listening, and looking ability. Always ask yourself what the ad is *really* saying. When you see ads on television, don't be misled by the pictures, the visual images. What does the ad *say* about the product? What does the ad *not* say? What information is missing from the ad? Only by becoming an active, critical consumer of the doublespeak of advertising will you ever be able to cut through the doublespeak and discover what the ad is really saying.

Professor Del Kehl of Arizona State University has updated the Twenty-third Psalm to reflect the power of advertising to meet our needs and solve our problems. It seems fitting that this chapter close with this new Psalm.

THE ADMAN'S 23RD

The Adman is my shepherd;
I shall ever want.
He maketh me to walk a mile for a Camel;
He leadeth me beside Crystal Waters
    In the High Country of Coors;
He restoreth my soul with Perrier.
He guideth me in Marlboro Country
For Mammon's sake.
Yea, though I walk through the Valley of the Jolly Green Giant,
In the shadow of B.O., halitosis, indigestion, headache pain, and
    hemorrhoidal tissue,
I will fear no evil,
For I am in Good Hands with Allstate;
Thy Arid, Scope, Tums, Tylenol, and Preparation H—
They comfort me.
Stouffer's preparest a table before the TV
In the presence of all my appetites;
Thou anointest my head with Brylcream;
My Decaffeinated Cup runneth over.
Surely surfeit and security shall follow me
All the days of Metropolitan Life,
And I shall dwell in a Continental Home
With a mortgage forever and ever.

                                           Amen.

Personal Response

Make a list of the brand name products you have used today. Which, if any, did you buy because of claims made in their advertisements?

Questions for Class or Small Group Discussion

1. Bring copies of magazine or newspaper advertisements to class and do a careful analysis of their language and the way in which they manipulate consumers. What "weasel" words do you find in them? What unfinished words or words with no special meaning do you find?

2. Play the role of an advertiser who must sell a new product. (You make up the product.) Write an advertisement that uses "weasel"

words, unfinished words, or words with no special meaning. Then write an advertisement for the same product without using any of those words. Share your advertisements with classmates and discuss which was easier to write and why.

3. Listen to ads on radio and television, look at ads in magazines and newspapers, or walk down a supermarket aisle as Lutz suggests and notice the use of the words *help, virtually, new* and *improved.* How often do you see those words used? Do you agree with Lutz that the ads "are really saying nothing" (paragraph 8)?

4. Do the advertising doublespeak quick quiz (paragraph 46).

5. Discuss the extent to which you think it matters that advertisements use meaningless, empty words. That is, do you think the use of "weasel" words in advertisements is fair? Is anyone harmed by such words? Why should consumers care "what the ad is *really* saying" (paragraph 50)?

GREENWASH

David Beers and Catherine Capellaro

David Beers and Catherine Capellaro are reporters for Mother Jones, *a monthly magazine noted for its exposés of discreditable practices. In this essay, which first appeared in* Mother Jones *in 1991, Beers and Capellaro criticize what they see as deceit in ads for products that are harmful to the environment and to human health.*

You're bright, you're ambitious, your finger is on the pulse of Peoria, and ever since you fibbed your way out of your first spanking, you've realized there's a useful vacuum in the part of your brain where shame usually resides. May we suggest a career in greenwashing, the hottest new trend in dissembling for profit?

You gotta be willing to imply that your own dear mother would have liked the way your company clear-cuts redwoods. Louisiana-Pacific's president did it in magazine ads. You gotta be able to write an ad headline like EVERY DAY IS EARTH DAY WITH NUCLEAR ENERGY. It really ran. Let's say a year and a half ago, you immersed a prime San Francisco Bay Wetlands area in spilled oil. Could you, without laughing now, or even noticeably perspiring, ceremoniously give the nearest town a bronze statue of John Muir inscribed with your company name? Shell did. Do you have the humongous chutzpah to broadcast the image of wildlife literally clapping for Du Pont, one of the nation's top polluters? How about this extra touch: Beethoven's "Ode to Joy" swells in the background. It's been on TV.

The advertising and public-relations industries have long been paid to jujitsu potential anticorporate movements into image builders for their clients. But their attempted co-opting of environmentalism has been so frenzied, so nakedly nineties as to make Orwell's imagination seem stunted. And yet, because most of the media rely on the greenwashers for ad revenue, it's been hard to find anyone who is willing to shout that the emperor has dropped trow. Until now . . .

The Scratch 'n' Sniff Pollution Solution

4   ARCO shared its clean-air manifesto in a full-page ad in the eco-supplement to *Fortune* right around Earth Day. Under the headline IT'LL HELP CUT OUT AIR POLLUTION, the petroleum giant listed ten things it wants us to do more of, like "Rideshare" and "Combine errands into one trip" and "Avoid unnecessary accelerations and braking." ARCO printed these on one of those tree-shaped air-fresheners that you hang from your rearview mirror, with a thoughtful dotted line to follow when cutting it out, and the invitation, "Scratch tree to release scent." That'll come in especially handy in the Los Angeles smog belt, where ARCO's Carson refinery has been the second-highest emitter of particulate matter (596 tons), the second-highest of sulfur dioxide (893 tons), and third-highest for total hydrocarbons (1,348 tons). Take the little tree along to Alaska, too, where, in 1985 and 1986 alone, ARCO was cited for 229 excesses of state air-quality standards, most of them involving spewing a particularly foul, black carbon smoke, which the right technology could prevent.

What few realized, until informative ads started appearing, is that without a benevolent hand from big oil, nature itself would get all confused and despondent and just give up. Chevron's "People Do" series works this theme especially brazenly, as Justin Lowe, with Hillary Hansen, documented in the *Earth Island Journal* and the *San Francisco Bay Guardian.* Turns out that most of the animal-friendly initiatives that Chevron brags about in its five-to-ten-million-dollar TV and print campaign are required by law, and not voluntary as the ads imply. Example: "On a moonlit California desert, a kit fox senses a prowling coyote," the narrator intones, as we see fox dodge wily coyote by diving into "a cozy den that's designed to keep her snug and safe." Then: "Do people think of things like this just to help an endangered species make it through the night? People do." The artificial-den program is part of Chevron's forced compliance with the Endangered Species Act. When Chevron produced the television ad in 1986, it had only three artificial dens. Two of them were acquired from Gulf Oil when Chevron bought that company, and the third was not so snug: it had been specially built with a cutaway side view for the camera. Producing such a commercial can cost up to $200,000, which would buy a few hundred kit-fox dens. The fox that Chevron filmed, incidentally, was a borrowed and trained captive.

It's hard to pick the boldest lies advertised by slippery oil. In the op-ed-page corner that it rents in the *New York Times,* for example, Mobil asserts, "Just because we get our hands dirty doesn't mean we dirty the environment, too." This is the Mobil that spilled 455,696 gallons of oil from 1984 to 1988, and whose workers contend that lead and benzene at the Beaumont, Texas, plant have been handled so sloppily that they are linked to cancer and birth defects in the area. Mobil's Torrance, California, plant settled a civil complaint in 1989 for hazardous-waste violations.

Still, Texaco deserves a special star. DO IT RIGHT, blares the fat headline over a picture of smiley Texaco senior petroleum engineer Victor Simon and his assurance: "We have a corporate responsibility to do business with a conscience. This includes ensuring that the issues we are all passionate about—the environment and quality of life—are not overlooked. . . . In every step of our operations, from obtaining emission permits to ensuring on-site safety, simply meeting legislated standards isn't enough. We can and *do* exceed such standards. . . ." Why is this man smiling? In 1989, Texaco was fined $750,000 in the first-ever felony conviction under the Outer Continental Shelf Lands Act, for failing to perform tests of crucial oil-rig blowout-protection equipment, and then fabricating records of those tests. In 1989, Texaco was cited for violations of the Migratory Bird Treaty Act, which protects certain species of birds, including the ones found dead in the oil companies' waste pits. That year, more birds died in oil companies waste pits than from the *Valdez* spill. Also, in 1988, a Texaco subsidiary was ordered to pay the largest settlement ever under California's Hazardous Waste Control Act, $8.95 million for neglecting to properly clean up the area around five thousand corroded, leaking drums of hazardous waste. According to the EPA, Texaco's Port Neches, Texas, refinery poses what may be the highest industrial-site cancer risk in the country.

Garbage In, Garbage Out

8   Waste Management, Inc., an ad explains, does the favor of "helping the world dispose of its problems." That's green-washspeak for the fact that WMI and its chemical (ChemWaste Management) and nuclear (Chem-Nuclear) subsidiaries make up the biggest waste-dumping company in the world. Granted, the Waste Management empire didn't create the trillion pounds of toxic waste generated in the United States every year; it just hauls it, burns it, injects it into the earth, and sticks it into landfills. In so doing, it paid out between $20 million and $40 million in environment-related penalties, fines, and settlements in the 1980s. It also was hit with $8.5 million in fines and other settlements for efforts to destroy competitors by price-fixing, etc.

"What sort of a wildlife preserve is this?" asks the narrator for a WMI TV spot, while a soft-focus lens pans over rolling green hills and a butterfly flutters in the foreground. "Part of a scientifically managed sanitary landfill . . . developed by Waste Management." The viewer isn't told that, in 1988, toxics from one WMI landfill leaked into the soil below a canyon occupied by an endangered type of butterfly. Dozens of other landfills tend to endanger hard-strapped communities. In rural, mostly black Emelle, Alabama, CWM has dumped over 3.5 million tons of toxics, and paid one million dollars in environmental penalties. The Emelle hazardous-waste dump—one of the world's largest and still growing—occasionally catches fire, and authorities are resigned to the fact that it will leak into local water sources. Although the data has been challenged, residents say that an independent lab has found toxic chemicals in residents' bodies. Linda Wallace Campbell, an Emelle organizer, says it's no accident that hazardous waste gets dumped in areas like hers, where the average yearly income is nine thousand dollars. "Yeah, they're helping the world dispose of people of color, poor people," says Campbell. "We've got a piece of Love Canal right here."

Another WMI TV classic shows the earth with a list of nasty chemicals scrolling up the screen. Voice-over: "In just three years, we've made over two hundred million pounds of hazardous waste vanish from the face of the earth, destroying it with high-temperature incineration . . . without harm to the environment. We call that making progress." WMI paid a $4,475,000 fine in 1989 because, among other violations, those in charge of its big "state of the art" Chicago incinerator failed to monitor emissions and stop burning deadly PCB wastes when protective scrubbers and stack monitors weren't working. More progress: In 1988, the Illinois EPA temporarily closed the incinerator because (oops) operators disconnected pollution detectors in the stack.

Sell My Mother? How Much?

"We need everything that's out there. . . . We log to infinity. Because we need it all. It's ours. It's out there, and we need it all. Now." That's what Louisiana-Pacific chairman Harry Merlo, whose company is the biggest producer of redwood, told *Santa Rosa Press Democrat* reporter Mike Geniella a while back. What does a public-relations pro say to a guy like that, especially since, true to his convictions, Merlo has harvested trees faster than they grow, while giving big money to defeat forest-protection initiatives? Get me rewrite!

12   Here's Merlo in full-page ads that have appeared in *Fortune* and other magazines: "Respect for the environment is nothing new to me. From the time I was a small boy in a poor family of Italian immigrants, I've understood how precious our God-given resources are, and how important it is never to waste them. The lessons I learned from my mother, Clotilde Merlo—lessons of thrift, common sense, hard work, and strength of purpose—I have not forgotten for a single day."

Little Harry also learned from Mrs. Merlo, according to the ad, that "God is in the water." God had better get out and shower off: L-P's Samoa, California, pulp mill, along with the nearby Simpson paper plant, discharges over forty million gallons of effluent into the Pacific Ocean every day. Surfers tired of getting rashes from the resulting "black goo," as they describe it, are, through the Surfrider Foundation, suing. L-P could pay up to seventy-five million dollars if it loses. The judge who denied L-P's motion for dismissal of the suit wrote: "They have essentially exempted themselves from all environmental protection requirements and are therefore free to discharge potential chronically toxic effluent into the waters of the Pacific Ocean with impunity. The position is disingenuous and flies in the face of the Clean Water Act."

God seems to have forsaken a good portion of Silicon Valley's water, too, since IBM arrived on the scene. The Silicon Valley Toxics Coalition has been documenting IBM's foot-dragging on cleanup of soil and groundwater contamination that they say potentially exposed more than 100,000 residents to chemicals linked to cancer and birth defects. And yet, IBM's denial of this connection may explain its glorious double-pager, which has run in *Scientific American* and other magazines, showing, of all things, a pristine body of water. The headline: IN A CHANGING WORLD, SOME THINGS DESERVE TO REMAIN JUST THE WAY THEY ARE.

Might the ozone layer be one of those deserving things? Well, IBM has promised to phase out its massive chlorofluorocarbon use by 1993, which environmentalists are calling a victory won only after heavy pressure. IBM's San Jose, California, Endicott, New York, and Rochester, Minnesota, facilities were the top three CFC-113 emitters in 1987—over a decade after CFCs were known to shred the ozone layer. Now that IBM is swearing off CFCs, its substitute for washing computer chips will be detergent and distilled water, dried with ultrasound vibration. That technology was around before CFC-113 was introduced.

16   Even if IBM is finally getting around to leaving the ozone alone, Du Pont isn't about to stop messing with it. All those critters on TV applauding to Beethoven are ostensibly jazzed because Du Pont-Conoco is finally double hulling its new oil tankers. Somebody tell the animals that Du Pont is one of the world's largest makers of ozone-shredding chemicals, and plans to continue producing them until at least the year 2000. Du Pont also happened to be the United States' leading toxic polluter in 1988, according to the Citizens Fund report *Poisons in Our Neighborhoods*. Something else to clap about: despite the EPA phaseout of leaded gasoline, Du Pont is still producing lead additives, selling them more and more out of the country. David Schwartzman of Howard University's Geology and Geography department calls these exports "a crime against children," since immature brains and nervous systems are extremely vulnerable to lead poisoning. Now how does "Ode to Joy" go again?

For That Get-Up-and-Glow Feeling

Polluters are the real animals. This folksy reminder, scrawled on a sign hoisted by a cute little cartoon bear, adorns a full-page ad for the nuclear industry. Where, then, does that put nuke executives on the food chain? After all, the total accumulation of high-level radioactive waste has nearly doubled since 1980, and will last 250,000 years while we try to solve where to put it. Meanwhile, the volume of low-level radioactive waste has more than doubled, and today bloats three commercial landfills. Nuclear advocates are getting an official ear for their solution: label one-third of it "below regulatory concern" and treat it like the coffee grounds in your own trash can. Thus reclassified, low-level radiation could find its way into incinerators, dumps, sewers, and rivers. That could kill up to 250,000 people, a figure based on EPA estimates.

Every day is mishap day with nuclear energy. In fact, the industry has reported 34,300 nuclear "mishaps," nearly ten a day, since 1980. The Nuclear Regulatory Commission concluded that the chances of a severe core meltdown occurring at one of the 112 licensed U.S. plants in the next fifteen years is as high as 45 percent. West German and Swedish scientists have said there is a 70 percent chance of a Chernobyl-scale accident happening in the world every six years. No wonder polls show that U.S. public opposition to nuclear power is at an all-time high.

Which explains those expensive ads trumpeting nuclear power as foe of air pollution and greenhouse gases, and alternative to dependence on messy foreign oil. Just running such ads by nuclear power's propaganda organization, The U.S. Council for Energy Awareness, hasn't afforded enough exposure, as far as the *Wall Street Journal* is concerned. The paper sent reprints to members of Congress, along with a letter, from *WSJ* vice-president for marketing Bernard T. Flanagan, calling them "informative and thought-provoking." Lucrative, too.

20   The differences between what the greenwashers say and really do is so consistently, as Mrs. Merlo would say, clear cut, that one wonders where they peg the public's gullibility limit. While General Electric trills, "We bring good things to life," it profits from deadly nuclear-weapons work, having helped create the radioactive nightmares at Hanford Nuclear Reservation and the Knolls Atomic Power Lab—hence the on-going boycott of GE. With lovingly rendered animal portraits, GE proudly advertises its sponsorship of National Audubon Society specials on PBS, but neglects to mention that according to Citizens Fund, it ranks number one in Superfund sites and released more cancer-causing chemicals into the environment in 1988 than any other U.S. company. One of the most breathtaking exercises in mock humility is the two-pager taken out by that friend of the environment, the Chemical Manufacturer's Association. The ad literally promises the world: over a picture of the earth runs the headline HANDLE WITH RESPONSIBLE CARE, followed by the group's "guiding principles," like "To develop and produce chemicals that can be manufactured, transported, used, and disposed of safely." Union Carbide, of the Bhopal disaster, is one of the 170 signees.

"It's not that all these ads are untrue. They depict 5 percent of environmental virtue to mask the 95 percent of environmental vice," says Greenpeace's media director, Peter Dykstra. "There's a real moral vacuum in how people deal with advertising." Dykstra passes along a prime example of the greenwasher's ethical code, a letter that Greenpeace received from the big New York public relations firm Hill and Knowlton, Inc.

"We need your help. We know from your work that you recognize how critically important it is to reverse the declining quality of our air, land, and water, and to safeguard these resources before they are spoiled forever," wrote H&K vice-president Jeffrey L. Christmas, entreating Greenpeace USA's executive director, Peter Bahouth, to help promote a globally televised enviro-concert called Earth '90.

Not long before, the same Hill and Knowlton had written to suspected Mississippi River polluters, warning that Greenpeace might make them a protest target and offering seasoned expertise: "Hill and Knowlton veterans have worked on almost every major crisis in recent years, including Three Mile Island, Texas Eastern's PCB problem, the dioxin crisis, and Ashland's Ohio River oil spill." In case there is any doubt which side H&K represented in all those cases, the letter, leaked by a temp worker, goes on to suggest that firms hire the PR agency to "develop strategy for counteracting Greenpeace when it reaches [your] facilities. . . ."

24   H&K's Howard Marder, who wrote the letter, told *Mother Jones* that he sees "no contradiction" in the fact that his company tried to make money by both courting and countering Greenpeace. He says that he always advises clients to tell the "whole truth immediately." Did he research the pollution records of any of the companies along the Mississippi before offering to speak for them? No, says Marder, whose letter to one promises: "We can help select the most effective spokesman to convince the community and media of [your] *credibility*. The *way* the message is delivered by the company's spokesman is as important as the message itself." The italics are Hill and Knowlton's own. It's an old trick of the trade. Makes a word like credibility seem more credible.

Personal Response

What do you think of the contrast between what the large corporations cited by Beers and Capellaro say in their advertisements and what they actually do in practice? Are you angered or not bothered by what the authors see as deceit? Explain your answer.

Questions for Class or Small Group Discussion

1. Although Beers and Capellaro never define "greenwash," its meaning is made clear from the example they give. What do you understand the term to mean?

2. Discuss the ethics of the advertising campaigns run by the corporations cited in this article.

3. How balanced do you find this essay? What do you think the heads of corporations named here would say to Beers and Capellaro in their defense? What would you say to the heads of these corporations if you had an opportunity to comment to them on the information in this essay?

4. Bring several advertisements from magazines to class and do a careful analysis of the ways in which they "greenwash" the environmental impact of the products.

5. What other industries advertise potentially harmful or even destructive products in ways that downplay their negative aspects? Can you coin terms for what they do, as Beers and Capellaro have done for advertisements of products hazardous to the environment?

WHAT ADVERTISING ISN'T

John O'Toole

John O'Toole is president of the American Association of Advertising Agencies. Before that, he served as chairman of the board of Foote, Cone, and Belding Communications, Inc., one of the world's largest advertising agencies. In this essay, reprinted from his book The Trouble With Advertising, *second edition (1985), O'Toole defends the practices advertisers use to sell products.*

Advertising . . . is salesmanship functioning in the paid space and time of mass media. To criticize it for being that, for being true to its nature, is to question whether it should be permitted—a position taken by only the most rabid, none of whom has come up with a reasonable substitute for its role in the economy. And to criticize it for not being something else—something it might resemble but by definition can never be—is equally fruitless. Yet much of the professional criticism I spoke of has its feet planted solidly on those two pieces of shaky ground.

As a format for conveying information, advertising shares certain characteristics with journalism, education, entertainment and other modes of communication. But it cannot be judged by the same standards because it is essentially something else. This point is missed by many in government, both the regulators and the elected representatives who oversee the regulators.

The Federal Trade Commission was pushing not too long ago for one of those quasi-laws they call a Trade Regulation Ruling (when they were empowered to write the law of the land, I don't know; but that's another argument). This particular TRR would have required an ad or commercial for any product claiming to be nutritious to list all its nutritive elements.

For two reasons advertising cannot comply with such a requirement and still end up as advertising.

4   One, advertising is salesmanship, and good salesmanship does not countenance boring the prospect into glassy-eyes semiconsciousness. Yet I am sure—and consumers on whom sample ads and commercials were tested agreed—that a lengthy litany of niacin, riboflavin, ascorbic acid and so on is as interesting as watching paint dry.

Less subjective is the fact that such a listing can't be given for many good, wholesome products within the confines of a thirty-second commercial. Since that's the standard length today, the end result of the proposed TRR would have been to ban those products from television advertising. The FTC staff did not consider that advertising necessarily functions in the paid space and time of mass media. Adding twenty or more seconds of Latin makes that impossible.

This example illustrates the problems that can arise when regulators try to dictate what must go into advertising. An FTC attorney named Donald F. Turner was quoted by Professor Raymond Bauer in a piece for the *Harvard Business Review* as saying, "There are three steps to informed choice. (1) The consumer must know the product exists. (2) The consumer must know how the product performs. (3) He must know how it performs compared to other products. If advertising only performs step one and appeals on other than a performance basis, informed choice cannot be made."

This is probably true in an ad for a new floor wax from S. C. Johnson or an antiperspirant from Bristol-Myers. But what about a new fragrance from Max Factor? How do you describe how Halston performs compared to other products? Is it important for anyone to know? Is it salesmanship to make the attempt? Or suppose you're advertising Coca-Cola. There can't be many people left in the world who don't know Coke exists or how it performs. Granted, there may be a few monks or aborigines who don't know how it performs in relation to other products, but you can't reach them through advertising. So why waste the time or space?

8   The reason Coca-Cola advertises is to maintain or increase a level of awareness about itself among people who know full well it exists and what it tastes like, people whom other beverage makers are contacting with similar messages about their products. Simple information about its existence and its popularity—information that triggers residual knowledge in the recipient about its taste and other characteristics—is legitimate and sufficient. It does what a salesman would do.

On the other hand, advertising for a big-ticket item—an automobile, for instance—would seemingly have to include a lot of information in order to achieve its end. But the advertising is not attempting to sell the car. It is an advance salesman trying to persuade the prospect to visit a showroom. Only there can the principal salesman do the complete job. Turner's definition is neither pertinent nor possible in the case of automobiles. In such cases mass communications media cannot convey the kind of information one needs in order to "know how the product performs" or to "know how it performs compared to other products." You have to see it, kick the tires, ask the salesman questions about it, let the kids try out the windshield wipers. And surely you have to drive it.

In the paid space and time of mass media, the purpose of automobile advertising is to select the prospect for a particular car and, on the basis of its appeal to his income, life-style or basic attitudes, to persuade him he's the person the designers and engineers had in mind when they created this model. If the information is properly chosen and skillfully presented, it will point out the relevance of the car to his needs and self-image sufficiently to get him into the showroom. Then it's up to the salesman to sell him the car—but with a different package of information, including the tactile and experiential, than could be provided in the ad.

From time to time some government regulator will suggest that advertising information should be limited to price and function. But consider how paleolithic that kind of thinking is. Restricting advertising to a discussion of price and function would eliminate, among other things, an equally essential piece of information: what kind of people make and market this product or provide this service.

12   The reputation, quality standards, taste and responsibility of the people who put out a product is information that's not only important to the consumer but is increasingly demanded by the consumer. It's information that can often outweigh price and function as these differences narrow among products within the same category. It's information that is critical to the advertising my agency prepares for clients like Johnson's Wax, Sunkist Growers, Hallmark, Sears and many others. Advertising would not be salesmanship without it. Put it this way: if surgeons advertised and you had a hot appendix, would you want the ads to be limited to price and function information?

The government regulators, and the consumer advocates dedicated to influencing them, do not understand what advertising is and how it is perceived by the consumer. And their overwhelming fear that the one is always trying to deceive the other leads them to demand from advertising the kind of product information that characterizes *Consumer Reports*. They expect advertising to be journalism, and they evaluate it by journalistic standards. Since it is not, advertising, like the ugly duckling, is found wanting.

It is not in the nature of advertising to be journalistic, to present both sides, to include information that shows the product negatively in comparison with other entries in the category (unless, of course, the exclusion of such information would make the ad misleading or product usage hazardous). For example, advertising for Sunkist lemons, which might point out the flavor advantages of fresh lemons over bottled juice, should not be expected to remind people that fresh lemons can't be kept as long as a bottle of concentrate. Information is selected for journalism—or should be—to provide the recipient with as complete and objective an account as possible. Information is selected for advertising to persuade the recipient to go to a showroom or make a mental pledge to find the product on a store shelf.

Advertising, like the personal salesman, unabashedly presents products in their most favorable light. I doubt that there's a consumer around who doesn't understand that. For instance, would you, in a classified ad offering your house for sale, mention the toilet on the second floor that doesn't flush? I doubt that even a conscience as rigorous as Ralph Nader's would insist, in an ad to sell his own used car, on information about that worn fan belt or leaky gasket. No reader would expect it. Nor does anyone expect it from our clients.

16   Information, as far as advertising is concerned, is anything that helps a genuine prospect to perceive the applicability of a product to his or her individual life, to understand how the product will solve a problem, make life easier or better, or in some way provide a benefit. When the knowledge can't safely be assumed, it also explains how to get the product. In other words, it's salesmanship.

It is not witchcraft, another craft government regulators and otherwise responsible writers are forever confusing with mine. For the same reasons people like to believe that someone is poisoning our water supply or, as in the Joseph McCarthy era, that pinkos proliferate in our government and are trying to bring it down, someone is always rejuvenating the idea of subliminal advertising.

Subliminal advertising is defined as advertising that employs stimuli operating below the threshold of consciousness. It is supposed to influence the recipient's behavior without his being aware of any communication taking place. The most frequently cited example, never fully verified, involved a movie theater where the words "Drink Coke" were flashed on the screen so briefly that while the mind recorded the message, it was not conscious of receiving it. The result was said to be greatly increased sales of Coca-Cola at the vending counter.

I don't like to destroy cherished illusions, but I must state unequivocally that there is no such thing as subliminal advertising. I have never seen an example of it, nor have I ever heard it seriously discussed as a technique by advertising people. Salesmanship is persuasion involving rational and emotional tools that must be employed on a conscious level in order to effect a conscious decision in favor of one product over its competitive counterparts, and in order to have that decision remembered and acted upon at a later time. Furthermore, it's demeaning to assume that the human mind is so easily controlled that anyone can be made to act against his will or better judgement by peremptory commands he doesn't realize are present.

20   Even more absurd is the theory proposed by Wilson Bryan Key in a sleazy book entitled *Subliminal Seduction*. From whatever dark motivations, Key finds sexual symbolism in every ad and commercial. He points it out to his readers with no little relish, explaining how, after reducing the prospect to a pliant mass of sexual arousal, advertising can get him to buy anything. There are some who might envy Mr. Key his ability to get turned on by a photograph of a Sunkist orange.

Most professional critics are much less bizarre in their condemnations. Uninformed about the real nature of advertising, perhaps, but not mad. For instance, they often ascribe recondite powers to advertising—powers that it does not have and that they cannot adequately define—because it is not solely verbal. Being for the most part lawyers and academics, they are uncomfortable with information conveyed by means other than words. They want things spelled out, even in television commercials, despite the fact that television is primarily a visual medium. They do not trust graphic and musical information because they aren't sure that the meaning they receive is the same one the consumer is receiving. And since they consider the consumer much more gullible and much less astute than they, they sound the alarm and then charge to the rescue. Sorcery is afoot.

Well, from time immemorial, graphics and music have been with us. I suspect each has been part of the salesman's tool kit for as long as there have been salesmen. The songs of medieval street vendors and Toulouse-Lautrec's Jane Avril attest.

A mouth-watering cake presented photographically as the end benefit of Betty Crocker Cake Mix is just as legitimate as and more effective than a verbal description. The mysteriously exuberant musical communication "I Love New York" honesty conveys the variety of experiences offered by New York State; it is not witchcraft. It is not to be feared unless you fear yourself. But perhaps that is the cradle that spawns consumer advocates and government regulators. There is something murky in that psyche, some kink in the mentality of those who feel others are incapable of making mundane decisions for themselves, something Kafka-like in the need to take over the personal lives of Americans in order to protect them from themselves.

24   I read with growing disquiet a document put out by the staff of the Federal Trade Commission in 1979 entitled *Consumer Information Remedies*. In discussing how to evaluate consumer information, they wrote,

> The Task Force members struggled long and hard to come up with a universally satisfactory definition of the *value* of consumer information. Should the Commission consider a mandatory disclosure to be a valuable piece of information, for instance, if it were later shown that although consumers understood the information, they

did not use it when making purchase decisions? Is there a value in improving the *quality* of market decisions through the provision of relevant information, or is it necessary for the information to change behavior to have value?

The ensuing "remedies" make it clear that the staff really judges the value of a mandatory disclaimer by the degree to which it changes consumer behavior in the direction they are seeking.

But wait a minute. I'm a consumer, too. Who are they to be wondering what to do with me next if I understand but choose to ignore some dumb disclaimer they've forced an advertiser to put in his ad? It's my God-given right to ignore any information any salesman presents me with—and an ad, remember, is a salesman. And what's this about changing behavior? Well, mine is going to change if the employees of a government I'm paying for start talking like that out loud. It's going to get violent.

Later in the same document, the staff addresses "Sub-Optional Purchases." While I have no quarrel with their intent, I find my hackles rising as they define the problem in terms of people "misallocating resources," consumers wasting their dollars on "products that do not best satisfy their needs." Listen, fellows, those are *my* resources you're talking about. Those are *my* dollars, what there is of them after you guys in Washington have had your way with my paycheck. I'm going to allocate them as I damn well please. And if I want to waste a few on products that do not best satisfy my needs—an unnutritious but thoroughly delicious hotdog at the ball park, for example—try to stop me.

28   Perhaps I, in turn, am seeking evidence of conspiracy. Perhaps I'm looking under beds. But I think I understand the true nature of government bureaucrats. They, on the other hand, do not understand that of advertising. They and other professional critics—the journalists, consumerists, academicians—don't understand that it's not journalism or education and cannot be judged on the basis of objectivity and exhaustive, in-depth treatment. Thorough knowledge of a subject cannot be derived from an advertisement but only from a synthesis of all relevant sources: the advertising of competitors, the opinions of others, the more impartial reports in newspapers, magazines and, increasingly, television.

The critics also don't understand that advertising isn't witchcraft, that it cannot wash the brain or coerce someone to buy what he doesn't want. It shouldn't be castigated for what it cannot and does not purport to do. And it isn't entertainment, either. A commercial should offer some reward to the viewer in return for his time, but that reward need not always take the form of entertainment. Sometimes the tone should be serious, even about seemingly frivolous subjects. Hemorrhoids are not funny to those who have them.

Advertising sometimes resembles other fields, just as an elephant resembles a snake to the blind man who feels its trunk, and a tree to another who feels its leg. But advertising is really salesmanship functioning in the paid space and time of mass media. . . . We can find enough reasons to criticize advertising without flailing it for not being what it isn't.

Personal Response

What do you think of O'Toole's defense of advertisements? Are you persuaded by him, especially after reading some of the attacks against advertising in the rest of this chapter? Explain your answer.

Questions for Class or Small Group Discussion

1. Analyze O'Toole's argument and discuss the points on which you agree or disagree with him. What do you find persuasive about it? What weaknesses do you find?

2. O'Toole is highly critical of consumer advocates and government regulators. Do you agree with his opinion of those groups? Do you think we need such groups? What might happen if such groups did not exist?

3. Respond to O'Toole's statement that advertising "isn't entertainment." Do you agree? Can you give examples of advertisements that do attempt to entertain?

4. Most people have heard of the idea of subliminal advertising and believe that advertisers employ it. Were you surprised when O'Toole stated "unequivocally that there is no such thing as subliminal advertising" (paragraph 19)? Explain your answer.

Perspectives on Advertising
Suggestions for Synthesis

1. Write an imaginary dialogue among the following: Jean Kilbourne ("Beauty and the Beast of Advertising"), William Lutz ("With These Words I Can Sell You Anything"), David Beers and Catherine Capellaro ("Greenwash"), and John O'Toole ("What Advertising Isn't"). Imagine what you think O'Toole would say to the criticisms each of the others makes about advertising.

2. In "Beauty and the Beast of Advertising," Jean Kilbourne concedes that advertising images do not cause problems but rather contribute to them. Advertisers, like producers of music, movies, and television shows, contend that they do not create problems but simply reflect the values of society. Drawing on at least two of the readings in this chapter, conduct a class forum or write an essay in which you explore the subject of how much responsibility advertisers bear for the images they produce in their advertisements.

3. Debate or write an essay on the ethics of advertising, as examined in any or all of the essays in this chapter.

4. Conduct a panel discussion on advertising in which members of your class play the roles of the authors whose essays appear in this section. The rest of the students in the audience should ask questions from their perspectives as consumers.

Additional Writing Topics

1. With "Greenwash" by David Beers and Catherine Capellaro in mind, write a letter to the head of a major corporation whose product poses a serious threat to the environment. In the letter, express your views on the advertisements Beers and Capallaro use as examples.

2. Do an analysis of a recent advertising campaign of a major corporation, perhaps one named by Beers and Capallaro or another industry whose product poses a threat to the environment or to human health and well-being.

3. Write an essay in response to the central argument of any of the essays in this unit.

4. Explore ways in which consumers can address some of the concerns about advertising raised by David Beers and Catherine Capellaro in "Greenwash."

5. Use examples of well-known advertisements to explore the question of whether advertisers underestimate the intelligence of consumers.

Research Topics

1. Research the subject of advertising ethics by locating articles and books representing the opinions of both those who are critical of advertisements and those who defend them. Argue your own position on the subject, supporting it with relevant source materials.

2. Research advertising images of a specific group. For instance, you could focus on images of women, as Jean Kilbourne has done, and locate additional research and opposing viewpoints. Consider also the topics of advertising images of men, advertisements that encourage destructive behavior, or advertisements aimed at children.

CHAPTER 9

TELEVISION

A welcome innovation to many people when it first appeared, television has nevertheless been the target of suspicion, attack, or ridicule from the time it was invented. At first, people thought "the tube" would never replace the radio, especially when its early live-only broadcasts made comical errors inevitable. Once the problems were worked through and television broadcasting became increasingly sophisticated in both technology and programming, television became commonplace. Television programs now number in the thousands, with not only cable access but computer-controlled satellite dishes bringing a dizzying array of viewing choices into people's homes. Many families own not only two or three (or more) televisions but also at least one VCR. With the seemingly endless demand for television shows from viewers, network producers and local station managers are always looking for programs that will attract viewers and draw sponsors.

One of the criticisms of television is that people, especially children, spend too much time watching it and doing nothing else. In fact, because so many people do spend so much of their time sitting and watching, we now have the term couch potato in our vocabulary. Pete Hamill is highly critical of the power of television on viewers. In his essay "Crack and the Box," Hamill makes the unusual comparison of television addiction to drug addiction. He believes that mindlessly watching vapid programs on television is analogous to the mind-numbing effects of drugs on addicts. See if you agree with his view on the tremendous hold television has on many people's lives.

Television's critics have also lambasted it as a "vast wasteland." This chapter has an essay by the person who first used that phrase, Newton N. Minow. With Craig L. Lamay, Minow has written a book that is sharply critical of television programming for children. In "Making Television Safe for Kids," the Introduction to that book, Minow makes an urgent plea for network television to provide better programming for children.

The next two essays articulate opposing views on the subject of television and violence. Susan R. Lamson, in "TV Violence: Does It Cause Real-Life Mayhem?", and William F. Buckley Jr., in "Don't Blame Violence on the Tube," express opposing opinions on whether television violence causes violent and criminal behavior. Lamson writes from the perspective of her official position in the National Rifle Association, and Buckley writes as a long-time host of a television show. A further indication of the positions from which they are writing is *where their pieces were first published: Lamson's appeared in* American Hunter *and Buckley's in* TV Guide. *As you might guess from this information and the titles of their essays, Lamson argues that television violence has enormous influence on children and bears large responsibility for the high U.S. homicide rate, while Buckley argues that television does not cause violent behavior. Where do you stand on this issue?*

The last essay in this chapter, Nik Gowing's "Instant TV and Foreign Policy," takes up a different matter on the subject of television. A popularly held belief is that live television coverage of ethnic and territorial conflicts necessarily influences policy makers. As a result of his interviews with many policy makers and government officials, however, Gowing concludes that such coverage has little effect in prompting diplomatic action.

CRACK AND THE BOX

Pete Hamill

Pete Hamill is a journalist who has written for both newspapers and magazines. "Crack and the Box" first appeared in Esquire *magazine in 1990 and was reprinted later that year in* Networker *magazine. In the essay, Hamill compares the mind-numbing, addictive effect of television to drug addiction.*

One sad, rainy morning last winter I talked to a woman who was addicted to crack cocaine. She was 22, stiletto-thin, with eyes as old as tombs. She was living in two rooms in a welfare hotel with her children, who were two, three, and five years of age. Her story was the usual tangle of human woe: early pregnancy, dropping out of school, vanished men, smack and then crack, tricks with johns in parked cars to pay for the dope. I asked her why she did drugs. She shrugged in an empty way and couldn't really answer beyond "makes me feel good." While we talked and she told her tale of squalor, the children ignored us. They were watching television.

Walking back to my office in the rain, I brooded about the woman, her zombie-like children, and my own callous indifference. I'd heard so many versions of the same story that I almost never wrote them anymore; the sons of similar women, glimpsed a dozen years ago, are now in Dannemora or Soledad or Joliet; in a hundred cities, their daughters are moving into the same loveless rooms. As I walked, a series of homeless men approached me for change, most of them junkies. Others sat in doorways, staring at nothing. They were additional casualties of our time of plague, demoralized reminders that although this country holds only two percent of the world's population, it consumes 65 percent of the world's supply of hard drugs.

Why, for God's sake? Why do so many millions of Americans of all ages, races, and classes choose to spend all or part of their lives stupefied?

I've talked to hundreds of addicts over the years; some were my friends. But none could give sensible answers. They stutter about the pain of the world, about despair or boredom, the urgent need for magic or pleasure in a society empty of both. But then they just shrug. Americans have the money to buy drugs; the supply is plentiful. But almost nobody in power asks, *Why?* Least of all, George Bush and his drug warriors.

4   In the last Nielsen survey of American viewers, the average family was watching television seven hours a day. This has never happened before in history. No people has ever been entertained for seven hours a *day*. The Elizabethans didn't go to the theater seven hours a day. The pre-TV generation did not go to the movies seven hours a day. Common sense tells us that this all-pervasive diet of instant imagery, sustained now for 40 years, must have changed us in profound ways.

Television, like drugs, dominates the lives of its addicts. And though some lonely Americans leave their sets on without watching them, using them as electronic companions, television usually absorbs its viewers the way drugs absorb their users. Viewers can't work or play while watching television; they can't read; they can't be out on the streets, falling in love with the wrong people, learning how to quarrel and compromise with other human beings. In short, they are asocial. So are drug addicts.

One Michigan State University study in the early '80s offered a group of four- and five-year-olds the choice of giving up television or giving up their fathers. Fully one third said they would give up Daddy. Given a similar choice (between cocaine or heroin and father, mother, brother, sister, wife, husband, children, job), almost every stone junkie would do the same.

There are other disturbing similarities. Television itself is a consciousness-altering instrument. With the touch of a button, it takes you out of the "real" world in which you reside and can place you at a basketball game, the back alleys of Miami, the streets of Bucharest, or the cartoony living rooms of Sitcom Land. Each move from channel to channel alters mood, usually with music or a laugh track. On any given evening, you can laugh, be frightened, feel tension, thump with excitement. You can even tune in "MacNeil/Lehrer" and feel sober.

8   But none of these abrupt shifts in mood is *earned*. They are attained as easily as popping a pill. Getting news from television, for example, is simply not the same experience as reading it in a newspaper. Reading is *active*. The reader must decode little symbols called words, then create images or ideas and make them connect; at its most basic level, reading is an act of the imagination. But the television viewer doesn't go through that process. The words are spoken to him or her by Dan Rather or Tom Brokaw or Peter Jennings. There isn't much decoding to do when watching television, no time to think or ponder before the next set of images and spoken words appears to displace the present one. The reader, being active, works at his or her own pace; the viewer, being passive, proceeds at

a pace determined by the show. Except at the highest levels, television never demands that its audience take part in an act of imagination. Reading always does.

In short, television works on the same imaginative and intellectual level as psychoactive drugs. If prolonged television viewing makes the young passive (dozens of studies indicate that it does), then moving to drugs has a certain coherence. Drugs provide an unearned high (in contrast to the earned rush that comes from a feat accomplished, a human breakthrough earned by sweat or thought or love).

And because the television addict and the drug addict are alienated from the hard and scary world, they also feel they make no difference in its complicated events. For the junkie, the world is reduced to him or her and the needle, pipe, or vial; the self is absolutely isolated, with no desire for choice. The television addict lives the same way. Many Americans who fail to vote in presidential elections must believe they have no more control over such a choice than they do over the casting of "L.A. Law."

The drug plague also coincides with the unspoken assumption of most television shows: Life should be *easy*. The most complicated events are summarized on TV news in a minute or less. Cops confront murder, chase the criminals, and bring them to justice (usually violently) within an hour. In commercials, you drink the right beer and you get the girl. *Easy!* So why should real life be a grind? Why should any American have to spend years mastering a skill or craft, or work eight hours a day at an unpleasant job, or endure the compromises and crises of a marriage?

12   The doper always whines about how he or she *feels*; drugs are used to enhance feelings or obliterate them, and in this the doper is very American. No other people on earth spend so much time talking about their feelings; hundreds of thousands go to shrinks, they buy self-help books by the millions, they pour out intimate confessions to virtual strangers in bars or discos. Our political campaigns are about emotional issues now, stated in the simplicities of adolescence. Even alleged statesmen can start a sentence, "I feel that the Sandinistas should . . ." when they once might have said, "I *think* . . ." I'm convinced that this exaltation of cheap emotions over logic and reason is one by-product of hundreds of thousands of hours of television.

Most Americans under the age of 50 have now spent their lives absorbing television; that is, they've had the structures of drama pounded into them. Drama is always about conflict. So news shows, politics, and advertising are now all shaped by those structures. Nobody will pay attention to anything as complicated as the part played by Third World debt in the expanding production of cocaine; it's much easier to focus on Manuel Noriega, a character right out of "Miami Vice," and believe that even in real life there's a Mister Big.

What is to be done? Television is certainly not going away, but its addictive qualities can be controlled. It's a lot easier to "just say no" to television than to heroin or crack. As a beginning, parents must take immediate control of the sets, teaching children to watch specific television *programs,* not "television," to get out of the house and play with other kids. Elementary and high schools must begin teaching television as a subject, the way literature is taught, showing children how shows are made, how to distinguish between the true and the false, how to recognize cheap emotional manipulation. All Americans should spend more time reading. And thinking.

For years, the defenders of television have argued that the networks are only giving the people what they want. That might be true. But so is the Medellin Cartel.

Personal Response

Have you ever been addicted to television? If so, explain why you found it so appealing. If not, explain why you think you were never "hooked" on television viewing.

Questions for Class or Small Group Discussion

1. Discuss whether you think Hamill is exaggerating when he says that television addiction is like drug addiction. Outline Hamill's major points of comparison between the two and then consider whether you think the comparison holds on all points.

2. What do you think of Hamill's argument in paragraph 3 that the government is asking the wrong questions in its war on drugs? Do you agree with him?

3. Do you agree with Hamill that television viewing is an entirely passive activity (paragraphs 8–9)? Can you give examples of television programs that prove him wrong?

4. Discuss your own television viewing habits. Do your own experiences bear out Hamill's views on the deadening effects of television?

5. Discuss Hamill's contention that because television is drama and so many people watch television, "nobody will pay any attention to anything . . . complicated" (paragraph 13). Do you agree with him? Why or why not?

MAKING TELEVISION SAFE FOR KIDS

Newton N. Minow

Newton N. Minow, former chairman of the Federal Communications Commission, is an attorney and chairman of the board of the Carnegie Corporation. He has written a book with Craig L. Lamay, Abandoned in the Wasteland: Children, Television, and the First Amendment

(1995). The Introduction to that book is reprinted here. Minow's use of the term "vast wasteland" in 1961 to describe what he saw as vapid television programming prompted a national debate on television and its responsibilities to the American public. More than three decades later, Minow is still concerned with the role television can and ought to play in the public interest.

In 1961, shortly after President John F. Kennedy appointed me chairman of the Federal Communications Commission, I told the nation's broadcasters, the people who in those days ran the television business, that they had made television into a "vast wasteland."

Almost overnight, those two words became television's first enduring sound bite. For decades, they have been used, over and over and over again, to describe what Americans find when they come home after work in the evenings and turn on their television sets, what our children find there after school or on Saturday morning. "Vast wasteland" appears in newspaper headlines, in book titles, in magazine articles, in Bartlett's *Familiar Quotations,* even as the answer to a Trivial Pursuit question. My wife and our three daughters threaten to inscribe my tombstone, "On to a Vaster Wasteland."

But the last straw came when our daughter Mary showed me a reading comprehension test for prospective law students that included five multiple-choice questions about a paragraph in my vast-wasteland speech. Imagine my shock when I got three of the answers wrong! At that point, I realized that my too-quoted speech had been a failure. The two words I wanted people to remember from that speech were not "vast wasteland." The two words I cared about were "public interest."

4   The law governing radio and television broadcasting, the Federal Communications Act of 1934, gives broadcasters free and exclusive use of broadcast channels on condition that they serve the "public interest, convenience and necessity." When I arrived at the FCC, I sought out the man who had drafted the law twenty-seven years earlier, Washington's former senator Clarence C. Dill, long retired by then. I asked him what he had meant by the "public interest." Senator Dill told me that he and his colleagues had been of two minds: on the one hand, it was the middle of the Great Depression and they wanted to encourage people to risk their money in the new medium; on the other hand, they knew they had to have some legal standard with which to award licenses to some people while rejecting others, because there were not enough channels to go around. "A young man on the committee staff had worked at the Interstate Commerce Commission for several years," Dill recalled, "and he said, 'Well, how about "public interest, convenience and necessity"? That's what we used there.' That sounded pretty good, so we decided we would use it, too."

The plan backfired. No one in Congress defined what the public-interest clause was supposed to mean in broadcasting. It had been developed to regulate the railroads and later the telegraph and telephone services, industries that the law deemed public utilities subject to detailed rate and public-service regulation. But the Federal Communications Act specifically exempted broadcasters from obligations as public utilities, which meant that they had the best of both worlds—all the benefits of a utility monopoly but none of the rate and public-service obligations. In the absence of a clear, specific definition of the public interest, broadcasters had the *quid*—exclusive, free use of the public airwaves—without the *quo*. So it has remained for sixty years.

Today, the Communications Act stands as a monument to the mistake of writing into law vaguely worded quid pro quos. Because the act did not define what the public interest meant, Congress, the courts, and the FCC have spent sixty frustrating years struggling to figure it out.

For more than half of those years, I've been privileged to participate in this debate and to observe it from a ringside seat. It has been my good luck to serve our government, public television, commercial broadcasting, advertising, and telephone, publishing, and cable companies, to help organize televised presidential debates, to teach students who now are leaders in communications and law, and to direct think tanks and foundations concerned with communications policy. I've seen every side of the elephant from every angle: as a chairman of a leading public television station (WTTW in Chicago); as a chairman of the Public Broadcasting Service (PBS); as a director of a commercial network (CBS); as a director of independent commercial broadcasting stations (of the Tribune Company); as a director of a leading advertising and communications company (Foote, Cone & Belding); and as a professor at the Annenberg Washington Program of Northwestern University. After these decades, to me the answer is clear. The public interest meant and still means that we should constantly ask: What can television do for our country, for the common good, for the American people?

8   Most important, I believe, the public interest requires us to ask what we can do for our children. By the time most Americans are eighteen years old, they will have spent 15,000 hours in front of a television set, about 4,000 hours more than they have spent in school, and far more than they have spent talking with their teachers, their friends, or even their parents. If we can't figure out what the public interest means with respect to those who are too young to vote—the youngest of whom are illiterate, who are financially, emotionally, and even physically dependent on adults—then we will never figure out what it means anywhere else. Children above all know this. They hear us talk incessantly about broken schools, broken homes, and broken values, and they watch as we do nothing about their broken spirits.

Why haven't we acted to give our children a healthier television environment? For half a century, anyone who has questioned the American commercial television system has been shouted down as a censor. Instead of talking seriously about how to improve television for our children, Americans argue to a stalemate about broadcasters' rights and government censorship. We neglect discussion of moral responsibility by converting the public interest into an economic abstraction, and we use the First Amendment to stop debate rather than to enhance it, thus reducing our first freedom to the logical equivalent of a suicide pact.

We have become accustomed to using the First Amendment to avoid asking ourselves hard questions which might require uncomfortable answers. For example, when I served on the CBS board of directors, I was concerned about the practice our television networks had of announcing the predicted results of elections before the polls were closed. After I asked for a review of this policy at a CBS board meeting, CBS News executives presented the methodology that the network used—with its exit-poll interview, computerized databases, and comparisons with prior election data from carefully selected precincts. On this basis, they defended their announcing likely election results while polls were still open.

12   I asked, "But why do this?" The answer was, "We have a right to do this under the First Amendment."

I asked again, "But why do we do it?" The answer again was, "We have a right to do this under the First Amendment."

I said, "Perhaps my question is not clear. My question is, *Why* do we do it?" For a third time, the answer was, "We have a right to do this under the First Amendment."

To say I was bothered is to put it mildly. So I asked, "Acknowledging that the First Amendment gives us the right to do it, my question is *Why* do it? For competitive reasons, so ABC and NBC won't beat us?" The answer was no.

So, I asked again, "If we don't do it to beat ABC and NBC, then why?" This time the answer was, "We must share immediately with the public all the information we have. We can't sit on information and keep the public in the dark when we know the election results. We must inform the public at once!"

16   "Then why," I asked, "do we say, 'We have an important announcement for you, but first, a commercial'? If it's so important, why wait for the commercial?"

I never got an answer to that one. I expect that the answer would have been, It is our right to do this under the First Amendment.

This example dramatized for me how correct Justice Potter Stewart was when he said that we confuse the right to do something with whether it is the right thing to do.

We should be asking ourselves whether what we do is the right thing. In 1961, when I called television a "vast wasteland," I was thinking of an endless emptiness, a fallow field waiting to be cultivated and enriched. I never dreamed that we would fill it with toxic waste. If I had it to do over again, I would concentrate every effort on improving children's television.

For, as Gabriela Mistral, the Chilean poet who won the Nobel Prize, wrote: "We are guilty of many errors and many faults, but the worst crime is abandoning the children."

20   If I had to do it over again, that's where I would draw the battle line.

My interest in television's effect on children began in 1956, when Robert Kennedy and I traveled together, often as roommates, as members of Adlai Stevenson's presidential campaign staff. Bob and I had a lot in common, especially because my wife, Jo, and I have three children the same ages as three of Bob and Ethel's children. When the Stevenson campaign reached Springfield, Illinois, Bob asked if we could skip the speeches and go visit Abraham Lincoln's home. On the way, Bob said something I've never forgotten: he said that when he grew up, the three great influences on children were home, school, and church, but in observing his own children, he believed that there was now a fourth major influence, television.

In the thirty-eight years since that walk in Springfield, more than 3,000 sociological studies have confirmed Bob Kennedy's observation. Television's influence on our children is staggering. Even those who do not accept the link described in 1972 by the Surgeon General between screen violence and aggressive behavior in children concede that television teaches our children that guns and violence solve problems, that it affects the way they perceive people of other races, that it regards them as consumers rather than as citizens, and that it shapes their fears and expectations about the future. Every afternoon when they come home from school, millions of American children turn on their television sets to see what the adult world holds for them. What do they find there?

During one randomly selected week, January 31 through February 4, 1994, my daughter Nell recorded what they saw: programs about a thirteen-year-old girl who has slept with twenty men and a seventeen-year-old who has slept with more than a hundred (both girls carried beepers); about transsexual prostitutes; about parents who hate their daughters' boyfriends; about men whose girlfriends want too much sex; about white supremacists who hate Mexicans; about a woman who tried to kill herself nine times; about a sadomasochistic couple who explained that instead of putting a ring on her finger at their wedding, they had his penis pierced; about a man who fathered four children by three women and who "couldn't stop cheating"; and programs called "Dad by Day, Cross-Dresser by Night" and "Using Sex to Get What You Want."

24   Peggy Noonan described the difference between what children see on television now and what they saw a generation ago:

> When I was a kid there were kids who went home to empty houses, and they did what kids do, put on the TV. There were game shows, cartoons, some boring nature show, an old movie, *The Ann Sothern Show,* Spanish lessons on educational TV, a soap opera.

Thin fare, boring stuff; kids daydreamed to it. But it was better to have this being pumped into everyone's living room than, say, the Geto Boys on channel 25, rapping about killing women, having sex with their dead bodies and cutting off their breasts.

Really, you have to be a moral retard not to know that this is harmful, that it damages the young, the unsteady, the unfinished. You have to not care about anyone to sing these words and to put this song on TV for money.

In an ideal world, no American children would be left alone for long periods of time with only television for companionship. In an ideal world, every parent would be responsible, every parent would have the time and financial resources to control his or her child's television viewing, and every parent would be as vigilant as *Miami Vice* producer Dick Wolf, who says that he won't allow his own children to see the shows he has produced. In an ideal world, the people who work in television would have to take an oath like the Hippocratic oath, the first tenet of which would be, "Do no harm." In an ideal world, the people who use the airwaves to send toxic programming into our living rooms would be forced to sit down with their *own* children and explain to them why it is they are proud of what they do. I think then producers and programmers would come out from behind the First Amendment and try to do better for all our children.

They started off with the best intentions. In the early 1950s, when television was still new, broadcasters, in the hope of inducing people with children to purchase television sets, aired exemplary, high-quality children's programs. My friend Burr Tillstrom created Chicago's own *Kukla, Fran and Ollie.* A decade later, when more than 90 percent of American homes had sets, most commercial broadcasters stopped thinking about what was best for children and shifted their emphasis to selling products for advertisers. Indeed, the most important children's program in the United States might not have come about at all except for a string of lucky coincidences.

Late in 1968, Dean Burch (whom I knew from our service together on a bipartisan commission) called me in Chicago from Tucson and asked for some advice. President-elect Richard M. Nixon had offered him the appointment of chairman of the FCC. Dean had turned it down and was having second thoughts. I advised him to call immediately and accept.

28   A few months later, he invited me to dinner in Washington. "Okay, big shot," he said. "You talked me into this. You told me I could do good in the world. Any ideas?" I told Dean about a new program not yet on the air, funded in part by the Carnegie Corporation and which I had heard described by an exceptionally talented, dedicated broadcaster named Joan Cooney at a meeting of the board of National Educational Television— NET, the precursor to the Public Broadcasting Service.

"Is she married?" Dean asked. "Do you think her maiden name might be Ganz?" When I said that she had indeed been introduced at the meeting as Joan Ganz Cooney, Dean smiled.

"That must be Joanie Ganz," he said. "I asked her to marry me when we both were students at the University of Arizona."

When Dean got in touch with Joan, she told him that she was having problems getting additional funding approved by the Department of Health, Education and Welfare. Dean, who had managed Barry Goldwater's 1964 presidential campaign, went with Joan to meet with the Arizona senator. The minute Senator Goldwater was introduced to her, he said, "Ganz, from Phoenix. Are you related to Harry Ganz?" When Joan said yes, the senator replied, "Harry was my dear friend and the first to encourage me to run for office. How can I help you?" Not long after that, HEW approved the necessary funding. Twenty-five years later, it remains the best example of how television can be used to help and nurture all children. Since it went on the air in 1969, *Sesame Street* has been seen by billions of children in more than one hundred countries.

32   Why aren't there more *Sesame Streets?* Apart from public television, our television system is a business attuned exclusively to the marketplace. Children are treated as a market to be sold to advertisers at so many dollars per thousand eyeballs. In such a system, children are not seen as the future of democracy, nor does the television industry consider that it has a special responsibility for their education, values, and nurturing. When Congress wrote the Communications Act in 1934, it took great pains to ensure equal time for only one group of Americans: politicians. Children were not on the agenda, because Congress did not think about connecting broadcasting with the needs of children. In the years after World War II, when television exploded into American homes and transformed American culture, Congress again did not think about children.

The Children's Television Act, a small step in the right direction, did not become law until 1990. The act marked the first time Congress recognized children as a special audience, and it requires commercial broadcasters to provide "educational and informational" programs for children. Until recently, however, broadcasters all but ignored the law. After researchers discovered that stations throughout the country were claiming that cartoons and old episodes of *Leave It to Beaver* and *The Jetsons* met the law's requirements, the FCC began a proceeding to make them clean up their act. There are more good children's television shows today than there have been in more than a decade, but even now 60 percent of the programs broadcasters claim meet the minimal requirements of the Children's Television Act air between 5:30 a.m. and 7 a.m.

We have only one *Sesame Street* and a few programs like *Ghostwriter, Mister Rogers' Neighborhood,* and *The Magic School Bus.* But the reason we have so few is that we have only whatever the sponsors think the market will bear, and there is a clear market failure. For millions of children, that means talk shows and violent cartoons which are often nothing but thinly disguised commercials. Ask any commercial television executive what the key to success is in children's television, and he will tell you that it's not the show but the merchandising that surrounds it—the millions of dollars' worth of toys, video games, canned spaghetti, lunch boxes, and other products the show was created to sell.

Anyone who doubts this merchandising imperative should read an issue of *Broadcasting and Cable,* the television industry's trade magazine. In a special August 1992 issue devoted to "Children's TV," the Fox and Buena Vista production studios were fighting to "carve out at least three-quarters of the kids' viewing pie," the magazine reported, while smaller suppliers were "battling for the remaining fringe availabilities." Said one executive of his company's strategy for children's programming: "We have to be sharpshooters to pick off time periods we can get into." This image—of sharpshooters gunning for our children—perfectly sums up the American approach to children's television.

36   All this illustrates Fred Friendly's wise observation about the American television system: broadcasters make so much money doing their worst that they cannot afford to do their best. While producers try to re-create runaway merchandising hits like *Teenage Mutant Ninja Turtles, Mighty Morphin Power Rangers,* or *Beavis and Butt-Head,* good programs like *Cro* or *Beakman's World* struggle to gain an audience in the worst possible time slots.

This system is what television executives, writers, and producers call, with no sense of irony, the "marketplace of ideas." As the term is used today, this is a crude caricature of the metaphor first used by John Stuart Mill and later by Supreme Court Justice Oliver Wendell Holmes, Jr. But in one respect the caricature is accurate: the ideas that matter the most in the television marketplace are those that make the most money.

When it could be serving the best interests of children, our system chooses to serve the best interests of advertisers. Unless we correct this, unless we make explicit provisions for what the "public interest" truly means with regard to children, we shall repeat—in the digital era of "telecomputers" and information-on-demand—the worst mistakes that plagued the age of analog broadcasting. In 2054, some future FCC chairman will look back at us from the vantage point of a much vaster wasteland and wonder why, when we had a second chance, we failed to seize it.

Law and public policy usually lag behind new technologies. The Constitution is subject to amendment only through specific, prescribed procedures, but I suggest to you that sometimes the Constitution and the law are amended without any of us realizing it. Sometimes this happens through the evolution of political practices—as in the case of the electoral college—and sometimes when the Constitution is amended by technology, silently and instantly.

40   For example, consider political jurisdictions. When the technology of television developed, the television and advertising industries quickly saw that television signals did not correspond with political boundaries. A television signal spreads through the air in a circle with a radius of about sixty miles. Viewers of a signal broadcast from my hometown of Chicago live in the city of Chicago, the suburbs in Cook County, five other counties in the metropolitan area of Chicago, and in other parts of Illinois, Wisconsin, Indiana, and Michigan. The same situation exists throughout the United States and across our national boundaries into Canada and Mexico.

When this became apparent, the broadcasting and television industries quickly drew their own map of the United States, ignoring city, county, state, and national boundary lines, and dividing the country into DMA's—designated marketing areas. They didn't call for a constitutional convention or persuade Congress to change any laws. They simply threw away the official governmental maps and boundaries and began defining their business in terms of DMA's instead of cities, counties, states, and the nation. Today there are 211 DMA's, the ten largest of which cover a third of the nation's population. And thus communities became markets, citizens became customers, and children became fair game.

During World War II, the Army battalion in which I served built the first telephone lines along the Burma Road, miraculously connecting the ancient civilizations of India and China with modern communications technology. This was an early version of the information superhighway of the future. After World War II, I entered college and then law school, all the while intensifying my interest in communications. I met Marshall McLuhan when he participated in a panel discussion at Northwestern University in 1960. When President Kennedy asked me to serve as chairman of the Federal Communications Commission, I knew this was the one government job I had to take.

My first day on the job at the FCC, I received a visit from one of the senior commissioners, T.A.M. Craven, a crusty ex-Navy engineer who had been appointed by President Dwight D. Eisenhower. Commissioner Craven asked, "Young man, do you know what a communications satellite is?" I said no. He groaned, "I was afraid of that."

44   When I said I'd like to learn, he told me of his unsuccessful efforts to get the FCC to approve a test launch of Telstar, an experimental communications satellite developed by the American Telephone and Telegraph Co. with the encouragement of the National Aeronautics and Space Administration. Commissioner Craven convinced me that this was the one part of the space race with the Soviet Union where we were far ahead, but that our own government was standing in the way. The FCC quickly approved the Telstar experiment, and to this day I treasure a picture of Tam Craven with me in Bangor, Maine, where Telstar was successfully launched on July 10, 1962.

The development of communications satellites like Telstar in the 1960s led to the development of CNN, C-SPAN, HBO, and countless other cable networks in the 1970s and 1980s, to cheaper long-distance telephone rates, and to the explosion of global communications in the 1990s. Through communications satellites, we learned that modern technology has no respect for political boundaries, or Berlin Walls, or Tienanmen Squares, or dictators in Iraq.

Today, we are finding that the things we did a generation ago have led to another communications revolution, fueled by the technologies not only of satellites but of digitization and fiber-optic cable. This revolution is going on not just here in the United States but around the world. In most countries it is especially challenging to the not-for-profit, public telecommunications systems established in the early days of broadcasting, such as the BBC in Britain, the CBC in Canada, or NHK in Japan. All these national systems are having to meet new competition, much of it originating with programmers outside their borders, and all are having to ask what their function should be as public servants in a multichannel marketplace.

Their officials recognize that the meaning of the public interest will change—indeed, must change—in a new communications environment in which viewers rather than programmers choose what to watch and when, and in which viewers may one day even produce and distribute programs themselves. There are few firm points of agreement on how this new communications environment should be structured or whom it should serve. My daughter Martha often reminds me that, particularly in the United States, the public is much more cynical and divided now than during the years of the Kennedy administration, when it was much easier to agree on the meaning of the public interest.

48 But everyone everywhere, even in 1995, can agree on one precept: the public interest requires us to put our children first. Left to the marketplace, children will receive either very bad service or none at all. Policymakers in every country know this is true because they have the example of American broadcast television to show them it is true. For that reason, all of them are working to make special provisions for children in their national communications policies.

Now, after sixty-one years of missed opportunities, Congress should seize the opportunity to do the same. In the midst of the current technological revolution, as we build a new communications capacity undreamed of in human history, Congress has a second chance to define what Americans mean by the public interest, a second chance to give meaning to the public interest as the information superhighway enters our lives.

Second chances are rare in life, and are often—as Samuel Johnson said of second marriages—a "triumph of hope over experience." But there should be little argument that if we are wisely to take advantage of our gift of a second chance, Congress should concentrate on children. The time to act is now, not later. Later will be too late. By not specifying what it meant by the public interest in the Communications Act of 1934, Congress gave license to a broadcast system that sees children not as human beings but as financial opportunities. It is a bad system, and many good men and women in television must be liberated from it. If we want to change it, we should not be deterred by false choices. The choice is not between free speech and the marketplace on the one hand, and governmental censorship and bureaucracy on the other. The choice is to serve the needs of children and use the opportunities presented by the superhighway in the digital age to enrich their lives. If we turn away from that choice, the consequences of our inaction will be even greater educational neglect, more craven and deceptive consumerism, and inappropriate levels of sex and violence—a wasteland vaster than anyone can imagine, or would care to. Let us do for our children today what we should have done long ago.

I am reminded of a story President Kennedy told a week before he was killed. The story was about French Marshal Louis-Hubert-Gonzalve Lyautey, who walked one morning through his garden with his gardener. He stopped at a certain point and asked the gardener to plant a tree there the next morning. The gardener said, "But the tree will not bloom for one hundred years." The Marshal looked at the gardener and replied, "In that case, you had better plant it this afternoon."

Personal Response

What do you think of television programs for children? Are you aware of any that seem to take a moral responsibility for enriching children's lives?

Questions for Class or Small Group Discussion

1. Minow states that people have had a hard time figuring out what "public interest" means (paragraph 4). How would you define the term? What do you think television can do for the common good of the American people?

2. Minow believes that television producers have an ethical responsibility to children to ensure that children's needs are met and their lives enriched. Do you agree with Minow? How feasible do you find his goals for public policy? How do you anticipate that heads of networks and television producers would regard his suggestions?

3. In paragraph 33, Minow comments that despite a law that requires broadcasters to provide "'educational and informational'" programs, far too few such programs exist. Consider whether such a law can really be enforced. That is, if the major networks have not worked to meet the spirit of the law, what makes Minow think they ever will?

4. Discuss examples of current television programs for children that you think Minow would approve of. What programs do you think he would disapprove?

TV VIOLENCE: DOES IT CAUSE
REAL-LIFE MAYHEM?

Susan R. Lamson

Susan R. Lamson is director of federal affairs for the National Rifle Association. At a congressional hearing on television violence in 1993, Lamson explained the position of the National Rifle Association on the topic. In this July 1993 American Hunter *article, Lamson attacks television for promoting violent behavior.*

Turn on your TV virtually any time of any day and you can bring a carnival of murder, mayhem and bloodshed right into your living room. Maybe, like many Americans, you've grown accustomed to it and even expect it. But step back and look at this kaleidoscope of killing through the eyes of a child—and consider what role it's played for America's new generation of ultra-violent killers—and you see what a menace TV violence really is.

Televised mayhem is seen as a leading cause of America's epidemic of violent crime. It was the subject of May 12 hearings before the House Energy & Commerce Committee's Telecommunications & Finance subcommittee and the Senate Judiciary Committee's Constitution subcommittee. I represented NRA at the hearings and was joined by the nation's leading experts on human behavior and psychology to call for an end—or at least a reduction—of the broadcast brutality that's taking such a vicious toll on society.

As Dr. Brandon S. Centerwall, professor of epidemiology at the University of Washington, explained: "The U.S. national homicide rate has doubled since the 1950s. As a member of the Centers for Disease Control violence research team, my task was to determine why. A wide array of possible causes was examined—the 'baby boom' effect, trends in urbanization, economic trends, trends in alcohol abuse, the role of capital punishment, the effects of civil unrest, the availability of firearms, exposure to television.

4   "Over the course of seven years of investigation," Dr. Centerwall continued, "each of these purported causes was tested in a variety of ways to see whether it could be eliminated as a credible contributor to the doubling of rates of violence in the U.S. And, one by one, each of them was invalidated, except for television."

If that's frightening to you, consider this: In his landmark 1989 study, Centerwall concluded, "it is estimated that exposure to television is etiologically [causally] related to approximately one half of the homicides committed in the U.S., or approximately 10,000 homicides annually, and to a major proportion—perhaps one half—of rapes, assaults and other forms of inter-personal violence in the U.S."

While not all agree with Centerwall's assessment of the problem's severity, few challenge his claim that Hollywood bloodshed *does* spill out from the screen and into our lives. As the American Psychological Association testified, the cause-and-effect link between TV violence and human aggression has been well-established for nearly 20 years. But until recently the TV networks have been reluctant to change. That's why in 1990 Congress passed the Television Violence Act, that allowed the networks to cooperate and develop programming standards with which they and the public could live.

The problem is, violence sells. Media executives know it and profit from it. More viewers means higher ratings, which add up to more advertising dollars. So, as the National Institute of Mental Health has found, 80% of all television programs contain violent acts. But the violence is like a drug: viewers develop a tolerance for it, so media "pushers" give them steadily more.

8   Typically, prime-time programming has averaged eight to 12 violent acts per hour. A recent study by the Annenberg School of Communications found violence in children's programming at an historic high—32 violent acts per hour. And a recent *TV Guide* study counted 1,845 acts of violence in 18 hours of viewing time, an average of 100 violent acts per hour, or one every 36 seconds.

While adults may see all this TV mayhem as just the latest "action entertainment," children don't get it. Psychologists agree that up to ages three and four, children can't distinguish fact from fantasy on TV. For them, TV is a reflection of the world, and it's not a friendly place. Still, juvenile viewership is high. Children average nearly four hours of TV per day, and in the inner cities that increases to as many as 11 hours. Which means that in many cases, TV is the reality.

And this TV violence "addiction" is taking an increasingly grisly toll. FBI and census data show the homicide arrest rate for 17-year-olds more than doubled between 1985 and 1991, and the rate for 15- and 16-year-olds increased even faster. Psychologists point to several effects of televised mayhem: Children are taught that society is normally violent. They become disproportionately frightened of being victimized and become less likely to help victims of crime. They also grow more aggressive and violent themselves.

Through the Television Violence Act, the major networks have agreed on a set of standards to reduce the level of gratuitous violence in their programs. But so far, there's been little change; network executives promise better for the fall 1993 season.

12   Ironically, this year's congressional hearings on TV violence were in May—"sweeps month,"—when the networks compete for the viewership ratings that determine their advertising profits for the year to come. Some critics are calling May 1993 one of the most violent sweeps months in TV history.

Whereas in years past, entertainment executives flatly refuted the dangers of TV violence, the network heads who testified during the May hearings were more receptive of change—or so they said. Still, their words somehow ring hollow, especially given the brutality of their "sweeps month" programming.

Howard Stringer, president of CBS, Warren Littlefield of NBC and Thomas S. Murphy of ABC all spoke at the congressional hearings. Stringer talked of his network's "principles," "seriousness," "responsibility" and "careful and extensive discussion"—yet there seems to be no end to the bloodshed. Then, in a *Washington Post* story days later, Stringer blamed firearms: "There are 200 million guns, 66 million handguns in America. That has a lot to do with violence." (Readers will remember that the Washington, D.C., affiliate of Stringer's network recently rejected NRA's new commercial on the failings of the criminal justice system. The remarkable excuse given by CBS's affiliate was that the commercial "tends to inflame or incite.")

Barring legislation, congressional hearings can't accomplish much without unified grassroots pressure from citizens. Ultimately, your letters, phone calls and faxes are the best ammunition in the fight to cut televised brutality and thus curb crime and safeguard your Second Amendment rights. When you see examples of pointless, gratuitous violence in your TV programming, write to the network executives and let them know how you feel. The appropriate names and addresses are as follows:

Chairman of the Board
Capital Cities/ABC, Inc.
77 W. 66th St.
New York, NY 10023–6201

President
CBS Broadcast Group
524 W. 57th St.
New York, NY 10019–2902

President
NBC Entertainment
30 Rockefeller Plaza
New York, NY 10012–0002

16   Better yet, make a note of what products or services are advertised during violent programs, and voice your outrage to the leaders of those companies. You can get the proper names and addresses through your library's reference section. Excellent resources include *Standard and Poor's Register of Corporations, Directors and Executives,* Dun and Bradstreet's *Million Dollar Directory,* and *Moody's Manuals.*

In the end, only you—as a consumer, TV viewer and voter—can demand an end to the televised violence that's bloodying our society. If all NRA members and gun owners do their part in this fight, we *can* cut into the TV destruction that so gravely threatens both our children and our Bill of Rights.

Personal Response

Do you agree with Lamson that television is entirely too violent? If so, does such violence bother you? Explain your answer.

Questions for Small Group and Class Discussion

1. Lamson asks readers to consider the role that television has played "for America's new generation of ultra-violent killers" (paragraph 1). Discuss whether you think Lamson offers conclusive proof to support her belief in the causal relationship between television violence and real-life violence.

2. Lamson says in paragraph 2 that "televised mayhem is seen as a leading cause of America's epidemic of violent crime." Discuss other causes that may also account for the epidemic of crime.

3. Watch prime-time television for one evening or children's programs for one Saturday morning and record the number of violent acts you see. Decide beforehand exactly what will be considered a violent act (for instance, will you include verbal assaults?). If several of your classmates do the same, on different evenings or different channels, you should get a good indication of whether the figures Lamson cites in paragraph 8 are still accurate today. Do a follow-up discussion of your observations.

4. Evaluate the argument Lamson makes here. Do you think her interest in the National Rifle Association in any way influences her argument? Does it influence your evaluation of the argument?

DON'T BLAME VIOLENCE ON THE TUBE
William F. Buckley Jr.

William F. Buckley Jr., is founder of The National Review *and host of the long-running television show* Firing Line. *He has written several books of nonfiction, including* Overdrive *(1983) and* Up from Liberalism *(1959, 1984). His novels include* Atlantic High *(1983),* See You Later, Alligator *(1985),* High Jinx *(1986), and* A Very Private Plot *(1993). In this essay, which first appeared in* TV Guide *in 1994, Buckley defends television against those who accuse television of causing real-life violence.*

There's something about violence that—abstractly—appeals. Children reflect this most directly. Children don't lie: They haven't reached the age of guile, so when they gravitate to toy guns and gory comics, and movies with arrows through chests, and boiling oil and exploding turrets, the eyes marvel with fascination, and the nickels pour out for more. One needs to reflect on the phenomenon, and apply it not to children, but to their parents.

The chestnut about how if you kill one person you're a murderer, if you kill a million you are a great general, applies, if indirectly, to the uproar about TV. What hurts is the *particularization* of violence. When what you see on the screen is machine guns or artillery blazing forth and dozens, even hundreds, of people—Indians, or Nazis, or Japanese—dropping in their tracks, that's stuff you look at without ever disturbing the rhythm of your hand passing from the popcorn to your mouth. It's when the screen focuses on an individual that one's emotional attention is arrested.

And then it's what happens to the victim that makes the difference. If he is merely going to be shot, that doesn't, in most cases, bother people or even grip their imagination. Especially if he is the fifth or 15th person shot in that television hour. It is when the act of violence causes the viewer to fasten his attention not so much on the capacity of so many people to kill, but on the capacity of some people to engage in individuated cruelty—that's when you feel the impulse to close your eyes, and when the memory is haunting. These are distinctions Attorney General Reno didn't make when she yakked about how the TV world has to clean up its act, or she will report it to Congress.

4   Consider the elementary distinction: We are viewing *Roots,* the story of slavery in the United States. A mean white master sets out to punish the unruly or insolent or courageous slave, and somebody steps up with a big long whip. The first stroke brings out an instant diagonal welt on the slave's back and as you see it, you hear his grunt of pain. What then does the camera do?

What it ought to do is what it generally does—turn to look in on the faces of the bystanders; or of the slavemaster's wife, mistress, children; whatever. And what you hear is the repeated slash of the whip and the yelps of pain.

That is violence going on, no question about it, but it is a violence that at least has the grace to blush. It is the lady's fan lifted up to conceal the view of the bull's horn that has got the matador in the groin and is tossing him skyward, the shuttered eyes of the man viewing the same scene. It is what distinguishes the sadist from the viewer who wants realism and excitement and drama but doesn't want that element of violence that indulges instincts it is the purpose of civilization to quieten.

The 6-year-old who takes pleasure in seeing his brother disciplined will, if all goes well with his moral development, want to avoid seeing any such scene by the time he is 16. What he has learned in the interval is that pain is something we seek to avoid. Pain—violence—is what is done by people who aren't socialized, and are insensible to the pain of others. When pain is unavoidable, the doctors are there with narcotics. When it is unnecessary—as with the crime that surrounds us—it is nevertheless the stuff of real life, and we learn about real life primarily, these days, from television.

8   The statistic is that by the time the average child finishes elementary school, he will have seen some 8,000 people "killed" on TV. And the fuss seems to be about the impact that viewing has on the young American growing up. It is tempting to postulate a correlation: 1) We live in a society in which crime is rampant and generally increasing. And 2) we live in a society in which crime-on-TV is increasing. There are, granted, little oscillations in both generalities: Crime has slightly decreased this year, in several categories. And violence is less frequent on network television, but it is nevertheless all over the place, on TV as in city streets. 3) Therefore: Television is responsible for the proliferation of crime.

We do not in fact know whether this is so. As has been pointed out by critics of television critics, the same stuff we see here on TV is seen in Great Britain and Japan, yet we have more than three times as much crime as Great Britain, and nine times as much as Japan: So why didn't all that violence corrupt the Brits and the Japanese?

It isn't easy to answer that objection, not if your design is like that of Sen. Hollings of South Carolina. He seems to want to hold television responsible for national violence. And of course it springs quickly to mind that if a politician denounces somebody or something for the crime wave, people will get the impression that he is *doing something* about crime, which is generally not the case. It can't be established that crime on the screen has zero connection with crime on the street. No one can tell us how much crime we would have in America, or in England or Japan, if there were *no* crime on television. Perhaps less. Certainly a little less, because we know that specific acts of violence depicted on television have been imitated.

We can't know what it is in the nature of some individuals that causes them to take insane risks. We can't know why early in December a jilted ensign shot his girlfriend and one of his Annapolis classmates and then himself, instead of behaving like however many other jilted ensigns who *don't* slaughter the girl who draws away from them. And we cannot establish that he was attracted to violence because of all the killings he saw on television. The Hutus and Tutsis twice in 30 years have killed each other in tribal warfare on a scale that dwarfs American murder (23,750 per year) into insignificance. During most of that time there was no television in Burundi.

12   Our problem is this insensibility to others' feelings, to their rights, to their person. The Christian religion, like most others, teaches us that it is sinful to cause pain, except as civil punishment. We develop in such a way as to cultivate this moral sense that tells us violence is wrong. And if our education succeeds, we feel a progressive distaste for any lascivious treatment of pain. If that moral development isn't cultivated, we are callous. To the extent that we are that, we indulge ourselves in gross forms of realism, and involve ourselves in bloody spectacles that seemed routine to the Romans, who enjoyed witnessing the torture of Christians by lions. It wasn't television that moved the crowds to shout out their joy at seeing men and

women torn limb from limb, or that caused Elizabethan society to devise excruciating ways in which to end the lives of heretics. These were the fruit of different, and undeveloped, moral perspectives.

Roots, I have heard it said, caused many Americans to realize just what it was that Americans were capable of doing to other human beings during the days of slavery. I don't doubt that the horror we feel for the Holocaust is significantly the responsibility of such scenes as Herman Wouk gave us in the miniseries based on his great *Winds of War* novels. The thing to keep your eyes on, surely, is just that one detail: the barring of the entirely redundant detail.

"GoodFellas" told us a story of life in the Mafia. It is as violent as violence gets. But there was a single scene in it that startled the viewer. Or put it this way: One hopes not to encounter anyone who saw it and *wasn't* startled when one of the protagonists opened the trunk of the car where the wounded antagonist lay and plunged a kitchen knife borrowed from his mother into his whimpering prisoner. The viewer saw it—almost all. There was no closeup of the blade entering the stomach and chest—that much was left to the imagination. And such are the critical distinctions in a society that affirms some threshold in matters of taste.

That taste can never be generated by acts of Congress or claps of thunder issuing from the Attorney General. We suffer from many ailments in America, and a whole lot can be said about the insufficiencies of TV, but not that it is responsible for original sin, whose harvest in every human being varies from season to season, leaving us only to know that here and there, there will always be sin. Don't blame it on the tube. Television violence can do as much to enhance our inclination to oppose violence as to reinforce any inclination to engage in it.

Personal Response

Do you agree with the critics who say television is too violent, or do you agree with Buckley?

Questions for Class or Small Group Discussion

1. How convincing do you find Buckley's argument? Where do you see weaknesses, if any, in his reasoning?

2. What do you think of Buckley's observation that people were violent long before television was invented? Does that fact necessarily mean that television does not cause violence?

3. Comment on Buckley's concluding statement: "Television violence can do as much to enhance our inclination to oppose violence as to reinforce any inclination to engage in it."

4. As Buckley concedes, it is true that some people commit violent acts after watching a television show (paragraph 10). However, most people do not commit violent acts. What do you think keeps people from committing crimes, and how do you account for the extreme cruelty and violence of a few? What role, if any, do you think violent media play in such violence?

INSTANT TV AND FOREIGN POLICY
Nik Gowing

Nik Gowing based this essay, which first appeared in the October 1994 issue of The World Today, *on a paper entitled* Real-time Television Coverage of Armed Conflicts and Diplomatic Crises: Does It Pressure or Distort Foreign Policy Decisions? *He wrote that paper during his fellowship at the Joan Shorenstein Barone Center in the John F. Kennedy School of Government at Harvard University in spring 1994.*

"Something must be done." The pressure for foreign policy action seems to become inevitable following ghastly television images of carnage in Bosnia, Rwanda or Somalia. Unlike in Vietnam, Lebanon or the Falklands, the gruesome television pictures appear more rapidly and contemporaneously than ever. They are "real-time"—beamed back virtually instantaneously from mobile satellite dishes shipped to the heart of a conflict zone.

It is conventional wisdom that horrific real-time television images shock leading Western governments into reacting and modifying their policies. But do they really? In many cases there are good reasons to believe not. Foreign policy is not the servant of television imagery that many assume. In 1991, live pictures from the mountain quagmire in southern Turkey of Kurds fleeing Saddam Hussein's troops after the Gulf war forced first Europe and then the United States to create "safe havens."[1] Appalling images of the plight of Bosnian Moslems in Srebrenica in April 1993 generated intense pressure on the UN Security Council to create "safe areas." But after conducting more than 100 interviews with diplomatic and military insiders for a recent research project at Harvard University, I conclude that the conventional wisdom that shocking real-time television coverage of the new generation of ethnic and civil conflicts drives the making of foreign policy is something of a self-perpetuating myth. A clutch of important examples do not in themselves confirm an automatic cause-and-effect paradigm.

[1] Nik Gowing, "The media dimension: TV and the Kurds," *The World Today,* July 1991, pp. 111–112.

Usually (but not always) the so-called "CNN factor" is not what many assume. The undeniable and unrivalled ability of television news to provide rapid, raw, real-time images as a video ticker-tape service must not be misread as a power to sway policy-makers. Television highlights a policy dilemma but does not resolve it. The challenge for television news crews is to cover crises as rapidly, comprehensively and as accurately as possible. Usually the challenge for governments is to appear to react while quietly adhering to the continuum of a "cold and rational" policy line drafted at the start of a crisis.

4   Vivid television coverage did not force a Western policy to end the war in Slovenia; or to save Vukovar and Dubrovnik in Croatia; or to inter- vene to halt either the Bosnian Serb bombardment of Gorazde or the mass-slaughter of hundreds of thousands in Rwanda and Burundi. Rather, television has merely highlighted the West's impotence and its failure to find a political consensus to prevent or pre-empt wars at a time of diplo- matic overstretch. Vivid and horrific real-time coverage has been a catalyst for humanitarian and financial aid. But, by-and-large, it has not forced crisis prevention beyond a steely diplomatic determination to keep to minimal- ist, low-risk, low-cost policies which have had no realistic chance to halt conflicts that belligerents remained determined to keep fighting.

The dispatch of humanitarian aid in a flurry of self-congratulation and justification to alleviate a catastrophe is also frequently misread as a change in policy. During the Rwanda catastrophe in July 1994, flying fire- trucks from California, water-purification machinery from Frankfurt and military teams to organise the logistics of an emergency relief effort was a highly visible and reactive response to the ghastly images of death and squalor from the refugee camps of Goma in Zaire. But it was not a change of foreign policy. Instead, as shown in Bosnia, it was a palliative to alleviate the effects of a crisis which diplomacy had failed to identify and prevent.

"When governments have a clear policy, they have anticipated a situa- tion and they know what they want to do and where they want to go, then television has little impact. In fact they ride it." This is the conclusion reached by Kofi Annan, Under-Secretary-General for UN Peacekeeping, after observing government responses to conflicts seen on television.

Ministers and diplomats have developed what one senior British official described as "an iron will" to resist the undoubted power of a vivid, unrelenting flow of emotive television images that show mangled bodies and distraught, emaciated victims of the new generation of ethnic and civil wars.

8   There are currently more than two dozen regional wars. Television news cameras put a handful of them on the diplomatic radar screen and thereby go some way to prioritising crisis management. Television thus powerfully influences recognition of problems, which in turn helps to shape the foreign policy agenda. But it does not necessarily dictate policy responses. As the war historian, Sir Michael Howard, has concluded with

reference to the war in former Yugoslavia: "Television brings it closer to us, but provides us with no new means to resolve it."[2]

Real-time television highlights more vividly and contemporaneously than ever the new fault-lines in what is described variously as the developing "Clash of Civilisations",[3] the "Clash within Civilisations",[4] the "Coming Anarchy",[5] or some other variant of the ethnic instability fast developing across the globe. But governments tend to be delighted that television has the interest and resources to cover only one or two at once.

"Television is a big influence on a daily basis, but the key is keeping a balanced, even keel over the long term," a British official confirmed to this author. On Bosnia, another conceded: "Television almost derailed policy on several occasions, but the spine held. It had to. The secret was to respond to limit the damage, and be seen to react without undermining the specific [policy] focus." Or, as Britain's UN Ambassador, Sir David Hannay, observed: "We are a pretty stubborn lot. When it comes to an earth-shattering event we will not be swept off our feet."

Washington is little different. "Television does not have much day-to-day impact," according to Charles Kupchan, Director of the European Affairs desk at the National Security Council until earlier this year. "As a source of information for the National Security Council [television] is not that important. Gross pictures of suffering [in Bosnia] were not going to force intervention because the policy-makers have decided these fights are not worth picking."

12   The relationship between policy-making and real-time television coverage of the new post-Gulf war generation of armed conflicts goes to the heart of governance. But what is commonly known as the "CNN factor" (even though it embraces the impact of many other international broadcasters) is also unpredictable, fickle and therefore difficult to unravel with great certainty. The impact is erratic. Often the effect is not what many expect. "There are many times when there are horrific images and there is no policy impact," said Rick Inderfurth, Alternate American Representative to the United Nations. "It is very difficult to work out and anticipate how the CNN factor will come into play. It is like waking up with a big bruise, and you don't know where it came from and what hit you."

The ultimate paradox is that foreign-policy makers at all levels continue to claim—often with a wry smile—that television coverage has a profound impact on their work, even though they have a steely determination to resist it. Most of them openly curse television coverage, even

---

[2] Quoted from "Cold War, Chill Peace," delivered as the Ditchley Foundation Annual Lecture on 9 July 1993.

[3] Samuel Huntingdon, "The Clash of Civilisations," *Foreign Affairs,* Summer 1993, pp. 22–49.

[4] Professor Stanley Hoffman, presentation at Harvard University, 15 March 1994.

[5] Robert Kaplan, "The Coming Anarchy," *Atlantic Monthly,* February 1994.

though few have the time or inclination to watch the pictures in question. And, most important, ministers and officials do not trust television. Not because it lies, but because they say it is over-emotional. It plays too much to the heart and not enough to the head. It also forces their agenda in directions they sometimes cannot control, and it skews crisis management in ways they have often failed to predict. "Television is often wrong. We have to make sure we are right," said one senior American official. "Television does not focus for long enough, and it is often too sensational," said another. A senior Downing Street insider added: "Something must be done, [but] television means we can do the wrong thing."

On the other hand, many at the highest levels admit simultaneously to being as shocked, humbled and emotionally troubled as the average viewer—often prompted by the reactions of their family or staff who do see the pictures. "There is a fair determination to resist and limit the power of television," said Sir Robin Renwick, Britain's Ambassador to the United States, before recalling pressure on Bosnia from his own teenage daughter at home. "But we are susceptible, and we hate horrors too."

In June 1994, a month before Rwanda evolved into the biggest humanitarian disaster ever confronted by aid organisations, the British Foreign Secretary, Douglas Hurd, described the unending process of slaughter as a "true heart of darkness" whose details "I can barely bring myself to watch on television or read about."[6] Yet during the first three months of mass-slaughter the television coverage did not prompt a determined response aimed at forcing an end to the fighting and murder. Indeed, apart from France, which responded for its own complex internal political reasons, there was active international indifference to the carnage. The UN's appeal for a 5,500-strong peace operation was virtually ignored.

16   Similarly, on Bosnia, ministers "saw images of people who could have been themselves". "Yugoslavia kept officials awake at night," said one British source. "People were genuinely upset by the substance of what television showed. [At times] John Major was upset," said a former senior Downing Street official.

Such emotional impact is one thing, yet modifying policies in response is quite a different matter. "Politicians were prepared to withstand images. The Prime Minister and Foreign Secretary will always take a long view. We were driven by television pressure, but it was never overwhelming," confirmed one senior official at the heart of Bosnia policy.

When television pictures have cried out for determined, proactive foreign policy responses to end a conflict, sources have described to me a process by which ministers usually ensured there was an appearance of *tactical* response, when in reality there was little or no *strategic* change to overall policy.

---

[6] Speech at the Foreign and Commonwealth Office to London's Diplomatic Corps, 15 June 1994.

Television coverage seldom changes political will. Governments do as much as they can to resist the impact of television images. Yet ministers and officials know they have to be seen to respond. They have learned to adapt by making instant responses which appear to satisfy any public sense of horror while making the most limited commitments possible. As one official put it: "Governments have to be prepared to cope and have bloody sticky moments. They must be willing to sustain the policy line during [television coverage], then after television has gone away."

20   Only on rare occasions is such a steely determination in government overwhelmed by public pressure. As Bosnia and Somalia showed, real-time television not only provides governments with valuable corroboration of diplomatic and military telegrams, it also sharpens policy dilemmas at the most inconvenient moments. These are the moments of what I label "policy panic," when governments find their minimalist policies are pushed beyond the limit. They can no longer rely on what one senior Downing Street official described as the "pseudo-policies for pseudo-action" often used to give the impression of a response to television when the reality is different.

"When there is a problem, and the policy has not been thought, there is a knee-jerk reaction. They have to do something or face a public-relations disaster," said Kofi Annan after his experiences marshalling UN peacekeeping efforts in former Yugoslavia. On such occasions ministers and officials have confirmed how they find themselves fighting the tide of what one referred to as "a fantastically powerful medium which is often crude and where the words that go with it are often trite." Here powerful television coverage can—and does—break the governmental determination to resist.

For example, the plight of Bosnian Moslems in Srebrenica in April 1993 failed to move the UN Security Council's Big Five to take action to save them. Douglas Hogg, the British Foreign Office Minister, encapsulated the international unwillingness to take action when he went on BBC Radio and said: "If you are asking me if we have a policy that will certainly save Srebrenica in a few hours, the answer, I regret to say, is 'no'."[7]

But then the appalling television images shot by the enterprising freelance reporter/cameraman Tony Birtley emerged. They showed the squalor and near-starvation of Srebrenica and thereby undermined the international community's resistance. Fired by their anger at what television showed them, the majority nonaligned nations on the Security Council pushed through a resolution to create "safe areas," even though the big powers continued to warn against creating such a precedent.

24   But now, in retrospect, those involved are not convinced they acted so wisely. "I did not know that what we were creating was a trap,"

---

[7] Speaking on the *Today* programme on BBC Radio 4. Quoted in "Siege of Srebrenica," *The Guardian*, 17 April 1994.

concedes Diego Arria, the Venezuelan Ambassador who led the pressure on the Security Council at the time.

Another prime example of the pressure created by television coverage came after the transmission of the bodies of United States Army Rangers killed in Mogadishu in October 1993. The images revolted those in the Clinton Administration who saw them, but not to the point of forcing a change of policy as is widely assumed. Instead, what eventually forced a decision to withdraw were the thousands of phone calls made to lawmakers on Capitol Hill. In turn the lawmakers—not the original pictures—put pressure on the White House, and Clinton relented.

Clinton's National Security Adviser, Anthony Lake, confirmed the fickle impact of those dreadful images which came a few days after a dozen American soldiers had also been killed, but out of sight of television cameras. First Mr. Lake conceded privately that he himself never saw the television pictures of the dead Rangers, and therefore could not be influenced by them. Second, and quite remarkably, Mr. Lake confessed that even to the world's most sophisticated military power "the [television] pictures helped make us recognise that the military situation in Mogadishu had deteriorated in a way that we had not frankly recognised."[8]

A key reason for television's limited impact on conflict policy is the fact that public opinion in general is viewed as ill-informed and unreliable as a basis for drawing up a policy like air strikes. Except for the universal public fury over the dead Rangers in Somalia, the American public, for example, has been unmoved politically by much of the current war horrors on television. Even outrages like the Sarajevo market massacre in February 1993 barely shifted public opinion. Overall, the ministerial postbags on Bosnia, Somalia or Rwanda have been minimal. The demands for action have been "shallow."

28   Mass public opinion—however it is measured—therefore scarcely matters in foreign-policy calculations. "We [the White House] do not poll on foreign policy as a matter of policy-principle [sic]," according to George Stephanopoulos, Special Policy Adviser to Bill Clinton. Over Yugoslavia, for example, it is not sure what the public wanted anyway. Mark Gearan, Mr. Clinton's Communications Director, characterised the citing of public opinion to justify foreign-policy decisions as "an additive to bolster an argument. [But] public opinion is not that important."

There is, however, one important way in which television does have an impact on policy-making. It is indirectly through what one senior official described to me as the "political sonic ripples." As Marlin Fitzwater, George Bush's White House Press Secretary, put it: "The pressure of television on decision-making by the President is always indirect."

These ripples come from the small elite of newspaper editors, leader-writers, op-ed columnists and motivated politicians who closely monitor

---

[8] Mr. Lake's remarks were quoted in the Theodore H. White Lecture by Daniel Schorr at the Joan Shorenstein Barone Center, Harvard University, 18 November 1993.

real-time television output as part of their routine professional duties. Their influential views play back to policy-makers through the cuttings of newspaper columns and their quoting of broadcast interviews with politicians. Mr. Stephanopoulos, for example, confirms that President Clinton "pays real attention to the op-eds to see what people are saying."

The same view on the power of newspaper reporting based on television coverage is repeated widely in the ministerial offices of the main Western capitals. Whether justified or not, it is conventional wisdom in government that print is more reliable than television images.

32   Without satellite dishes and the potential for real-time coverage, it is unlikely that the plight of war zones like Sarajevo, Srebrenica and Somalia would have been given such prominence in crisis management. Real-time television reporting—despite its inevitably random, piecemeal and, therefore, flawed coverage—has painted skewed pictures which diplomats valued as intelligence but rarely trusted as a basis for policy. Officials understand well the shortcomings of instant reporting and instant punditry on instant deadlines by satellite, hence their scepticism and mistrust. Edward Bickham, special adviser to the British Foreign Secretary from 1991 to 1993, put it like this: "The power of television in foreign policy is a mixed blessing. It plays too much to the heart, and too little to the head."[9]

Many diplomats believe the brinkmanship in Sarajevo during late July and early August of 1993 was exaggerated because of powerful, overzealous reporting by a massively swollen press corps, many of whom journeyed to the Bosnian capital with what one correspondent called "more than a whiff of Baghdad Mark II." UN officials have recalled what they described as "blood lust" and a warring crusade among some journalists. One leading correspondent was heard to ask a colleague over breakfast: "What is it going to take us to get the United States and their allies to intervene here?"

Such pressure led directly to NATO's preparations for air strikes. But in retrospect diplomats say the picture portrayed by television at that time and throughout the siege was distorted. Either knowingly or by default, crucial facts that would have given context and balance to events were omitted from much of the reporting. "Air strikes have been wound up by television," said one. "Sarajevo was not strangled. That's an emotive phrase," another complained long after the crisis. "The Serbs on Igman was one of the worst examples of bad reporting," according to the European Union peace negotiator, Lord Owen.

Many journalist colleagues reject such criticism. They are affronted by complaints of distortion, whether inadvertent or premeditated. However, in a rare, belated public acknowledgment of the problem, a *Daily Telegraph* editorial questioned "the credulity of some sections of the media." It concluded: "The media do no service to the international community by

---

[9] Edward Bickham, "Playing to the Heart of the Nation," *Spectrum,* Autumn 1993, p. 3.

oversimplifying the issues. If journalists are to be the catalyst for foreign policy initiatives they must retain a measure of detachment." [10]

36   In the United States, in particular, some correspondents say their newspapers or television stations rarely accepted reporting that undermined the beleaguered image of the Bosnian Moslems. As many sources shamefacedly confirmed, America can only cope with "one black hat" in a crisis.

Stories that were critical of the Bosnians or implicated them were often spiked or diluted. "Editors did not want to believe it," one American reporter told me. "Anyone who defies the conventional wisdom will find themselves in deep trouble," said another. Such unbalanced perceptions helped serve the political aims of Western governments to blame and isolate the Serbs but did nothing for accurate, balanced coverage of such a complex war.

Continuing ambiguities over the Sarajevo market massacre on 5 February, which killed 68 people, illustrate this critical point. First, the horrific television images played a less critical role in the subsequent diplomatic progress than is commonly believed. Under intense French pressure, other diplomatic and military factors had already quietly been at work for several weeks. "It did not take just the television coverage of the Sarajevo massacre to push things forward. Things were moving," said White House Communications Director Mark Gearan. And Sir Robin Renwick, British Ambassador in Washington, stated: "The fact of the incident weighed with us most. It would not have triggered action if people were not already thinking about action."

But the more critical question is, who fired the mortar? Was it indeed a Serb emplacement or was it a mobile Bosnian mortar? Officially, the question remains unanswered. After several independent crater analyses and investigations by military experts, UN officials no longer say categorically that a Serb mortar killed the 68 people. The UN's verdict is described as "neutral" or "inconclusive."

40   Use of such words sends a clear signal. The UN is no longer convinced beyond all doubt that the mortar was fired from a Serb position. But such public ambiguity long after the event poses a vital and awkward question in relation to the power of real-time television coverage. The immediate assumption on 5 February was that the mortar attack had been planned, authorised and fired by the Serbs. The "neutral" verdict now questions that.

What if world leaders like Bill Clinton, John Major and Eduard Balladur had felt themselves forced by public anger over the television images to launch immediate air strikes against the Serbs, when later investigations questioned the Serb culpability for the market massacre? This is the ultimate fear of ministers, diplomats and soldiers: that emotive pictures,

---

[10] "Rose's Welcome Candour," editorial in *The Daily Telegraph,* 28 April 1994.

provided virtually instantaneously by real-time television coverage, force them into an impulsive, costly policy response which kills people, when the reality on the ground is different from what was first assumed.

Bosnia, Somalia and Rwanda will not end the horrors reported by television. In Africa, the International Committee of the Red Cross has identified up to 2,000 possible future ethnic conflicts. In the Russian "near abroad," ethnographers have pointed to 260 possible "battle-lines of the future." More conflicts loom elsewhere.

Bosnia and Somalia were probably diplomatic watersheds. They defined starkly the limits to any moral imperative for foreign intervention in future conflicts. Mr. Clinton's subsequent Presidential Decision Directive 25 on American involvement in foreign "peace operations"[11] has further narrowed the possibilities.

44 The Rwanda slaughter and mass exodus of refugees in the summer of 1994 produced the most horrific television pictures of all. Yet with the exception of France, the public pressure on policy-makers was negligible. In Rwanda and elsewhere, television cameras will continue to cover the carnage. The pictures will create deep emotions. But they are unlikely to make the kind of differences to the fundamental calculations in foreign policy that many expect or hope for. Rather, they will merely highlight conflicts that Western governments have no ability to prevent or decisive political will to solve—that is, until the participants reach what Clausewitz called the culminating point and are prepared to stop fighting.

As the number of ethnic and territorial disputes, armed conflicts and civil wars increases, the chances that horrific television images will stir governments into decisive action are diminishing fast and are already probably negligible. Television coverage of conflicts is not the catalyst for diplomatic action that many assume.

Personal Response

How do you usually react when viewing television coverage of ethnic wars, such as in Somalia, Bosnia, and Rwanda?

Questions for Class or Small Group Discussion

1. Comment on this statement: "Most [foreign-policy makers] openly curse television coverage. . . . And, most important, ministers and officials do not trust television" (paragraph 13).

2. Gowing reports that policy makers and government officials believe that live television coverage of horrific events is "over-emotional. It plays too much to the heart and not enough to the head" (paragraph 13). Discuss whether you think it is possible to not be overemotional

---

[11] Announced on 5 May 1994.

when reporting brutalities, mass murders of children and the elderly, and other atrocities of ethnic and regional wars.

3. If, as Gowing learned in his interviews with diplomatic and military insiders, live television coverage of foreign regional wars does not change foreign policy, what effect does such coverage have? Who do you think is influenced and in what ways?

4. Gowing learned that policy makers and government officials are more influenced by print journalism than they are by television journalism. Why do you think that is so? Discuss what you see as the advantages and disadvantages of live television coverage of war atrocities versus print articles on such events.

Perspectives on Television

Suggestions for Synthesis

1. Compare and contrast Susan R. Lamson's argument in "TV Violence: Does It Cause Real-Life Mayhem?" with William F. Buckley Jr.'s in "Don't Blame Violence on the Tube." State whose argument you agree with and why.

2. Create a dialogue in which you imagine what William F. Buckley ("Don't Blame Violence on the Tube") would say in response to Newton N. Minow ("Make Television Safe for Kids"), especially Minow's conviction that television has a moral responsibility to children.

3. Conduct a class forum or write an essay on the issue of violence as learned versus innate behavior, drawing on several of the essays in this chapter.

Additional Writing Topics

1. Write a paper in which you either defend or challenge Pete Hamill ("Crack and the Box"), Newton N. Minow ("Making Television Safe for Kids"), Susan R. Lamson ("TV Violence: Does It Cause Real-Life Mayhem?"), or William F. Buckley Jr. ("Don't Blame Violence on the Tube").

2. Write a letter to the president of one of the major television networks in which you express your views on the nature and quality of its programming for children.

3. Write a letter to either or both the sponsors and the producer(s) of a television program you find particularly violent, mindless, or vulgar, explaining your complaint and what you would like to see changed.

4. Write a letter to the sponsors or producer(s) of a television program you find especially intellectually stimulating, educational, or informative, praising the program and pointing out its best features.

5. In 1961, Newton N. Minow coined the term "vast wasteland" to refer to television (see "Making Television Safe for Kids"). Argue either that television remains a vast wasteland or that the phrase is no longer appropriate.

6. Either defend or refute the statement by Newton N. Minow that "children are treated as a market to be sold to advertisers" (paragraph 32, "Making Television Safe for Kids").

7. Explore the effects of television viewing on you personally, either now or in the past.

8. Respond to the comment by Pete Hamill that while America makes up only "two percent of the world's population, it consumes 65 percent of the world's supply of hard drugs" ("Crack and the Box").

Research Topics

1. Susan R. Lamson states in "TV Violence: Does It Cause Real-Life Mayhem?" that "the cause-and-effect link between TV violence and human aggression has been well-established for nearly 20 years" (paragraph 6). Research the subject of the causal connection between television violence and human aggression and either support or refute her statement.

2. Research to find out more about the Television Violence Act and what people have to say about its potential effectiveness. Then explain what conclusions you draw from your research.

3. Research the issue of violence as learned versus innate behavior. Try to determine, if possible, the extent to which violence on television (and other media) produces violent behavior and the extent to which people have a natural propensity for it. Start by reading what behavioral scientists and others who do work on human behavior have to say about the subject, and formulate your own position on it.

4. Interview a representative group of people for their responses to television coverage of ethnic conflicts abroad, and write a paper on your findings and your own conclusions. Draw up a list of questions before you begin, perhaps using some of the comments Nik Gowing makes about public reaction to such coverage in "Instant TV and Foreign Policy." Combine material from your interviews with library research to gain a broader understanding of the topic.

PART THREE
SOCIAL AND BEHAVIORAL SCIENCES

CHAPTER 10

Poverty and the Family

CHAPTER 11

Criminal Behavior

CHAPTER 12

Gender

CHAPTER 13

Race and Ethnicity

CHAPTER 14

International Relations

CHAPTER 10

POVERTY AND THE FAMILY

Once largely ignored, the issues of poverty, homelessness, and welfare have in-creasingly been subjects of often heated discussion in recent years. At the com-munity level, social workers and staffs at shelters for the homeless and impoverished struggle to meet the needs of desperate people, while at the state and federal levels, legislators argue over whether to cut welfare funding. The numbers of people in poverty, especially women and children, continue to rise. Many families whose incomes provide just enough for basic necessities like shelter and food are only a paycheck or two away from living on the streets. Compounding the difficulty of these issues are certain attitudes toward or stereotyped beliefs about people on welfare or who are homeless. Charges of laziness and fraud are often leveled at welfare recipients, despite studies that demonstrate the vast majority of people on welfare want to work and be independent.

The essays in this chapter examine some of the issues associated with poverty, welfare, and homelessness. In her essay "Homeless Families," for in-stance, Ellen Bassuk explores the plight of homeless mothers and children and calls for changes in government policies to address their needs. As you read Bassuk's essay, think about the perspective from which she writes—that of a teacher of psychiatry—and how professionals in other fields might assess the problems of homeless families differently. Do you find Bassuk's treatment of the subject to be an objective, fair picture of the effects of poverty on families? Do you agree with the suggestion she makes for changing government policies?

Whereas Bassuk writes as a professional who is concerned about the prob-lem of homeless and welfare families, the rest of the readings provide insights of a different nature. They are all written from personal experience. In "I Just Wanna Be Average," Mike Rose tells what it was like to be in the vocational education track in high school, where he was erroneously placed for two years. Rose makes a compelling point about the debilitating effects of race, class, and poverty on individual self-esteem. Next, writing from her perspective as a single parent receiving welfare aid and struggling to complete her college education, Teresa McCrary explains why she feels people are unfairly picking on her and others like her in "Getting Off the Welfare Carousel." As you read these essays, think about your own attitudes toward people on welfare or in poverty. Do Rose's and McCrary's personal experiences in any way influence or reinforce attitudes you already have? Do you know people who have experienced situa-tions similar to Rose's and McCrary's?

The last piece in this chapter, "In Defense of Orphanages," takes up the is-sue of poverty and welfare as it relates to children and the elderly, as Charles D. Aring assesses the positive and negative aspects of the orphanage he lived in as a child. Writing from the perspective of some seventy years later, Aring moves from his defense of orphanages to a vision of an institution that meets the needs of both the elderly and the young, with guidance from the middle-aged. As you read of his experiences as an orphan and his hopes for the elderly, consider to what degree you share Aring's sympathy for the plight of those groups and his hopes for their well-being.

HOMELESS FAMILIES

Ellen L. Bassuk

Ellen L. Bassuk is an associate professor of psychiatry at Harvard Medical School. Her published works include The Mental Health Needs of a Homeless Person *(1986) and* Emergency Psychiatry *(1984). She is president and cofounder of The Better Homes Founda-tion, which awards grants to programs that provide services and sup-port to homeless families. This essay, which appeared originally in* Scientific American *in 1991, addresses some of the problems home-less families must cope with and identifies government policies that have failed to alleviate the problems.*

Twenty-six-year-old Martha lives in a shelter with her daughter, Sarah, and son, Matthew. Martha, whose father regularly beat her, graduated from high school with honors and completed three years of college. Soon after she was married, her husband was imprisoned for theft. After his release, the marriage became violent and floundered, and over the course of three years Martha left her husband fifteen times. Martha is withdrawn and re-luctant to apply for a job or an apartment. She describes a deep and en-during sense of shame, particularly about her black and carious teeth—the result of many years without dental care.

Five-month-old Sarah is frail, listless, and underweight. She cannot hold down her food, is unable to grasp a rattle, and rarely vocalizes or smiles. Her brother, Matthew, who has moved seven times in his fifteen months of life, is painfully shy. After arriving at the shelter, he stopped say-ing the few words he knew, refused to eat, and had trouble sleeping.

Martha, Sarah, and Matthew—who were interviewed during the course of a study I conducted with my colleagues at Harvard Medical School—are part of the fastest-growing subset of the homeless: families most often headed by women. These single-parent families now account for approximately 34 percent of the homeless population—an increase from 27 percent in 1985, according to a thirty-city survey conducted in 1990 by the U.S. Conference of Mayors. Another study, conducted in 1987 by the Urban Institute, found that 23 percent of all homeless individuals are family members. Every night between 61,500 and 100,000 homeless children sleep in emergency shelters, welfare hotels, abandoned buildings, or cars. Some sleep exposed to the perils of the streets.

4   The consequences of this situation are dire. During critical, formative years, homeless children lack the basic resources needed for normal development. They undergo experiences resulting in medical, emotional, behavioral, and educational problems that may plague them forever. Their mothers, often victims of abuse, sometimes lack the resources to reenter society.

Research by myself and others has shown that "houselessness" is only one aspect of homelessness. Home implies basic shelter, but it also entails connection to a community of supports, including friends and family, organizations that share common values and beliefs, such as churches, as well as caretaking institutions. Homelessness marks a rupture in community and family ties in addition to a loss of residence.

By examining the plight of homeless mothers and children, we can begin to understand the far-reaching societal impact of their situation. And by delineating the many factors leading to homelessness, we can suggest long-term policy decisions that realistically address the diverse needs of those families.

Roots of family homelessness are myriad and apply to discussions of homeless adult individuals, runaway youths, as well as parents with children. During the past decade, cutbacks in benefits coupled with severe shortages of low-income housing jeopardized the stability of all people with reduced or fixed incomes—pushing many onto the streets. Although the size of the homeless population is unknown, experts agree it is growing. An advocacy group, the Partnership for the Homeless, reported that the number of homeless people increased 18 percent between 1988 and 1989. Estimates of the numbers of homeless vary wildly according to the source, design, and agenda of the study: from 250,000 to as many as three million nationwide.

8   Ironically, increases in social welfare spending, both in real dollars and in percent of gross national product, did not benefit the poor during the 1980s. Social security expenditures, for example, helped only the elderly. Even financial assistance programs, such as Aid to Families with Dependent Children (AFDC), accomplished little. Although most homeless families receive such aid, the amounts are well below the 1990 federal poverty income level of $13,359 for a family of four. Indeed, the maximum amount of AFDC available to a family of three—even when taken together with food stamp benefits—bought 26 percent less in 1990 than it did in the early 1970s.

At the same time financial assistance plummeted for many persons, housing costs outdistanced income. The median rents of unsubsidized, low-income apartments climbed from $225 to $360. And the number of poor renters increased from 4.5 million in 1974 to 7 million in 1987.

Gentrification and conversion of apartments to condominiums further depleted the supply of affordable housing. This shortage was never addressed by the federal government. In the past ten years the government virtually ceased funding construction or rehabilitation programs for low- and moderate-income housing. Between 1980 and 1987, new commitments for the construction of public and Section 8, or subsidized, housing fell from about 173,249 to 12,244 apartments, reports Michael A. Stegman of the University of North Carolina at Chapel Hill.

Dwindling aid and housing shortages are not problems specific to mothers and their children, but this group is particularly at risk. More women are running households than ever before in U.S. history. In 1970, for example, one in ten families were headed by women, according to Senator Daniel Patrick Moynihan of New York, who has written a book on the subject; by 1989, more than one in five families were headed by women.

12   Approximately one-third of the families headed by women are living below the poverty line, and studies by the Urban Institute have found that they are generally poorer than families of aged or disabled persons. Although the numbers of poor people and the overall poverty rate decreased slightly between 1983 and 1989, the poverty rate surged during 1990: 2.1 million more Americans became poor. Meanwhile the poverty rate among children and female-run households remained consistently high. The number of poor, female-run families grew 25.5 percent between 1970 and 1979 and another 15 percent between 1980 and 1989. The Census Bureau recently reported that children younger than 18 years make up 38 percent of the 33.6 million poor in the United States.

Because homelessness is a manifestation of extreme poverty and because families headed by women are disproportionately poor, these families are especially vulnerable to economic vicissitudes. The situation is exacerbated by today's housing market. Even if a mother is working full-time and has child care provided free by a family member, rent constitutes a large proportion of her budget. Any unexpected drop in income or rise in expenses may easily dislodge her and her family.

Furthermore, because many cities have low vacancy rates and because waiting lists for public housing are years long, families able to survive with little after-rent income are often unable to find housing. Housing vouchers are sometimes available, but supply cannot meet demand; mothers with more than three children are sometimes considered undesirable tenants.

Economic dislocation alone cannot explain how one poor, female-run family manages to maintain a home while another must turn to an emergency shelter for refuge. Within the subset of such households are families particularly susceptible to homelessness. Research suggests that a lack of relationships and resources such as savings or child care can hamper a family's capacity to remain housed.

16   In a vicious cycle, the housing famine itself destroys some of these supports by dislocating entire families. Initially, some homeless families may live with friends or family, doubling up in already overcrowded living quarters. As time passes, such relationships tend to weaken. Indeed, most families move several times in a year before becoming homeless. Martha, for example, lived with her relatives and friends before she turned to abandoned buildings and shelters.

From the outset, however, many homeless mothers have never had people to turn to for help. In 1985 we conducted a study of the needs of eighty families and 151 children living in Massachusetts family shelters. We found that most mothers were disconnected not only from caretaking institutions—such as day care—but from friends and family.

The reasons for the isolation may stem from the mother's own childhood. Studies of homeless mothers have documented a relatively high frequency of early and current disruptive experiences, including divorce, desertion, illness, parental death, or victimization. In a recent Boston University study, Lisa A. Goodman reported that 89 percent of homeless mothers had been the victims of physical or sexual abuse at some point in their lives, 67 percent while children.

As a result of a traumatic childhood, some homeless mothers may never have had adequate supports or the capacity to find and keep them. Difficult early experiences can impede the development of social skills, hindering a person's ability to find employment and seek social services as well as to form sustaining long-term relationships.

20   The lack of social skills can thwart these women's efforts to maintain jobs. Research indicates that although most homeless mothers have completed two or three years of high school, they generally have limited work experience, which is compounded by sexual discrimination in the job market. Employment alone, however, does not guarantee financial security. Even if these women are employed in service-sector jobs, which pay the minimum wage of $4.25 per hour, many cannot make ends meet. Without job training and adequate child care, it is difficult to imagine how they could afford current rents or become self-sufficient.

Some homeless families are also hindered by substance abuse and mental illness. Although few systematic epidemiological studies have been completed, an estimated 10 to 30 percent of homeless mothers abuse alcohol or drugs such as crack cocaine. The use of drugs further complicates the situation of these families and sometimes impairs their ability to raise children. In contrast to single homeless adults, homeless mothers in family shelters have lower rates of chronic mental illness, particularly schizophrenia, and most have not become homeless as a result of deinstitutionalization.

The high incidence of pregnancy among these women may contribute to homelessness. According to a 1989 New York City study by

James R. Knickman and Beth C. Weitzman of New York University, pregnant women receiving AFDC had an 18 percent chance of becoming homeless as compared with a 2 percent chance for women who were not pregnant. Data from seventeen cities suggest that the pregnancy rate among homeless women is 12 percent—other studies put the rate at 35 percent. The rate for the general population was 10.8 percent in 1985, the most recent year for which figures can be obtained.

Homeless women are frequently poorly nourished and receive little or no prenatal care. A 1987 report by the New York City Department of Health revealed that 40 percent of the homeless women studied had no prenatal care at all. Consequently, they are at high risk for adverse pregnancy outcomes and low-birthweight babies.

24   The problems of the mothers are in turn mirrored in their children—the cycle is perpetuated. The prevalence of alcohol and drug abuse among homeless women threatens the health of their babies. A 1989 report by the Select Committee on Children, Youth and Families found that the number of drug-exposed babies tripled or quadrupled in most surveyed hospitals between 1985 and 1988. Some of these infants manifest congenital abnormalities, mental retardation, and long-term neurobehavioral problems.

Although foster care families take in some of these infants, the system is overburdened. One Miami hospital, for instance, has twenty to thirty boarder babies on any given day: a new Florida state law mandates that all drug-exposed newborns are wards of the state.

The select committee also reported a high correlation between substance abuse and child abuse and neglect—in all families, housed and homeless alike. In the District of Columbia, for example, substance abuse was implicated in more than 80 percent of the reported cases of child abuse.

Homeless children experience more acute and chronic medical problems than do poor children who have homes. Health care workers find high incidences of diarrhea and malnourishment, as well as asthma and elevated blood levels of lead in shelter children. The Children's Defense Fund reported that homeless children are three times more likely to have missed immunizations than are housed children.

28   The psychological well-being of homeless children is no better, as the case of twelve-year-old Robert, living in a Boston shelter, illustrates. When interviewed, Robert said he was ugly and often thought about killing himself and would do so if he had the chance. He was not sure how he would carry out this intent but said he felt desperate enough to hold it as an idea.

Robert said he hated school. He stated that he had no friends and was bored and that he worried his classmates would discover he had no real home. Robert said he was teased by his peers and criticized by adults. He disliked the shelter and the other children there and spoke wistfully of the family's last home in a trailer. Robert was failing in school and had repeated a grade.

In our 1985 study we discovered that almost half of the homeless preschoolers manifested serious emotional and developmental delays. When compared with poor, housed children, homeless children were slower in language development, motor skills, fine-motor coordination, and personal and social ability. Studies from Los Angeles, New York City, St. Louis, and Philadelphia have subsequently reported similar findings.

A 1989 Department of Education report estimated that 30 percent of the nation's 220,000 school-age homeless children do not attend school regularly. The National Coalition for the Homeless, an advocacy group, estimates that the actual numbers of homeless school-age children are two to three times as great and that as many as 50 percent are not attending school.

32   As homeless children move from place to place, and switch from school to school, they are likely to become victims of bureaucracy. The sluggish transfer of academic records or files can delay their enrollment and set them back further. In addition, the lack of subsidized transportation and child care threatens their mothers' ability to get them to school and back to the shelter.

Many homeless children who do attend school, such as Robert, are failing or doing below-average work. The few studies conducted on this problem found that between 30 and 50 percent of homeless children had repeated a grade. In New York City most homeless children scored below grade level in mathematics and reading.

Because some homeless children fall behind their peers, they may be designated as having special needs. When this is the case, an educational plan must be formulated to address the child's unique problems, and, whenever possible, access must be provided to special educational services. In the nation's underfunded public school system, however, these resources are not often available. It is unlikely that the parent alone will be able to help the child catch up. Thus, many children remain behind and are at high risk of becoming dropouts. Although the precise figure is not known, the dropout rate for homeless children is suspected to be much higher than the nation's already elevated rate of 28.6 percent.

Although there are no easy solutions to the plight of homeless families, the crisis-oriented policies of the past decade have clearly failed. One facet of this policy is the emergency shelter system. Homelessness has been incorrectly viewed as a transient response to a situational crisis, that is, a temporary lack of low-income housing or employment. The shelter system was predicated on this erroneous assumption, yet these emergency facilities are becoming institutionalized. The Department of Housing and Urban Development (HUD) counted 1,900 shelters in 1984; by 1988, there were 5,400 shelters. During these four years, the percentage of sheltered families rose from 21 to 40.

36   Even some facilities better designed to meet the complex needs of homeless families are an incomplete solution. So-called transitional services provide longer lengths of stay as well as a combination of housing

assistance, education, job training, psychosocial help, and health care. In many ways, the structured, supervised environment of these facilities is best suited to helping families in crisis as well as those who are particularly troubled. These expensive, interim facilities, however, necessitate a move to permanent housing.

At present the high volume of clients for both emergency shelters and transitional housing often leads to an unfortunate paradox. Forced to choose, the staff of these residences often exclude families with problems such as substance abuse, family violence, and physical or mental disabilities. The overflow of clients is sometimes placed in welfare hotels, where there are few services. Even mothers leaving transitional facilities are infrequently monitored or followed by caseworkers. Facing their troubles alone again, these mothers can easily fall prey to the same situation that first led them to homelessness. In both cases, those mothers and children most in need of help are often least likely to find it.

The federal government's efforts to provide housing that goes beyond emergency shelter or transitional facilities to offer more complete services have been minimal. In 1987 the passage of the Stewart B. McKinney Act (the Homeless Assistance Act) offered new hope with the designation of $490.2 million for aid to the homeless. An additional $1.2 billion was appropriated over the next three years. The money was spent on supportive housing, residential programs, health and mental health care, education for children, and job training for all homeless people. Although the McKinney Act was a promising first step, the funds were spread too thin and were not directed to supplying permanent housing or long-term services.

Indeed, for the most part, the federal government has proved unwilling to combat homelessness. Consequently, states, cities, and private non-profit organizations have been left with an enormous, often impossible, task. New York City, for instance, just announced the failure of its plan for homeless families. The more than $25-million, year-old "Alternative Pathways" program, designed to prevent the eviction of 10,000 families and to pay the unpaid rent of 32,000 families, was understaffed and underfunded. As a result of its failure, an anticipated 6,000 families will be living in shelters by June 1992—more than ever before in the city's history.

40   To address realistically homelessness and its parent, extreme poverty, the nation needs to rethink its policy completely. First, citizens must elect representatives who allocate adequate funds for domestic needs: housing, a higher minimum wage, education, health care, child care, and social services. Such spending will assist both homeless families and those living in poverty. Ultimately, it will prevent many instances of homelessness.

Second, comprehensive programs for homeless persons must be made available and must be integrated with permanent housing. This situation fosters community ties and offers families autonomy while providing the services they need. One model of such an approach is a joint effort started in 1989 by the Robert Wood Johnson Foundation and HUD.

Under the Homeless Families Program, nine cities, including Atlanta, Baltimore, and Denver, will receive a projected $600,000 grant each over five years to implement services for homeless families. The program also makes available 1,200 Section 8 certificates, public housing assistance funds, worth about $35 million over five years.

In each city, parents and children are housed in residences that are clustered so that the families can provide support for one another. Families are followed by case managers who ensure that mothers receive appropriate treatment for mental health or substance abuse problems—one program provides testing for HIV infection. Employment training and child care are also made available. To date, the initiative has helped more than one hundred homeless families move from emergency shelters to permanent housing.

The Better Homes Foundation, which I cofounded, supports similar efforts. Since its inception in 1988, the foundation has awarded $1.7 million to fifty-five programs that provide a range of services, including prenatal and pediatric health care, housing and entitlements assistance, substance abuse programs, parenting services, and long-term case management.

44   The foundation also collaborates with other organizations. In a joint venture with IBM, for example, the foundation established the Kidstart program. Case managers assess the social, emotional, and cognitive development of homeless preschoolers. They then help children gain access to programs such as Headstart, a federally funded educational service; they provide counseling and help homeless mothers with their parenting responsibilities. The Kidstart model is particularly effective because many homeless children have special needs and are therefore entitled by law to receive appropriate services. By negotiating bureaucracy and helping parents, case managers can protect children from some of the disastrous effects of homelessness.

Unfortunately, such programs are available only to a small number of homeless families. Before comprehensive programs can be widely implemented, a perceptual change must occur among policymakers and the general public. The fact that most homeless families are extremely poor and that a significant subgroup have other vulnerabilities as well has contributed to an ideological tension and prejudice ever present below the surface of American politics. Before effective solutions can be achieved, we must eradicate biases against homeless people.

In the early 1980s a largely economic explanation of homelessness was pitted against one that focused on individual frailties. One side believed homeless people were economically dislocated by a system that concentrated the wealth among a small class of highly privileged citizens. The other side asserted that the homeless were chronically disabled by various social pathologies. At its most extreme, this view was expressed by President Ronald Reagan: "Some of those people are there, you might say, by their own choice."

The debate was fueled by data showing that homeless families, not unlike poor families, suffer disproportionately from substance abuse and mental disorders. Researchers, such as myself, studying these problems were accused of stigmatizing an already disenfranchised population—of blaming the victim. In an effort to protect the homeless, some advocates and providers refused to acknowledge mental illness or substance abuse. They simply concluded that permanent housing would eliminate homelessness.

48   Rather than employing new data that chronicled the complexities of homelessness, some advocates and critics tended simplistically to ascribe homelessness to single factors. When they identified a problem such as mental illness, for example, they interpreted the studies as indicative of one-to-one causality—with no regard to the context of extreme poverty. Along these lines, various editorials even concluded that homelessness was not a housing problem and that the homeless merely needed to be institutionalized.

At the heart of this debate are society's views of economic misfortune, individual frailties, and personal disabilities. Traditionally, emotional and social problems have been judged as the moral shortcomings of an individual. Someone suffering from a psychiatric illness or an addiction is rarely viewed as a person who has a disorder or who is taxed by overwhelming circumstances. Instead the affliction becomes a metaphor for a host of evils; it serves as testimony of the individual's unworthiness, a cause for condemnation.

Unless a multidimensional understanding of the heterogeneity of homelessness is reached along with acknowledgment of the heterogeneity of homeless family needs, we will continue to formulate ineffective policies. We must recognize that families on the street need more than just shelter. They need employment, a community, sustaining relationships, health care, child care, and education.

The serious systemic ills plaguing this country virtually ensure homelessness for a growing number of families. Until the federal government provides ample housing, welfare, and employment, vulnerable families will continue to struggle. Although we know the direction we must take to ameliorate extreme poverty and homelessness, our unwillingness to do so reflects our values and our priorities. The debate about the origins of homelessness has diverted attention away from the most basic issue: are we willing to care for the most disenfranchised among us, whether it be on the basis of economic need or individual need, or both? Are we willing to lose another generation of young women and children?

Personal Response

What image of the homeless did you have before reading this essay? Has your understanding of them changed in any way now that you have read Bassuk's essay? If so, in what way? If not, explain why.

Questions for Class or Small Group Discussion

1. In paragraphs 19 and 20, Bassuk suggests that a traumatic childhood impedes the development of social skills in women, which in turn has serious economic implications for them. What kinds of trauma do you think Bassuk is referring to? What specific skills is she referring to? Explore reasons why not having these skills proves to be a hindrance to the women under discussion.

2. Bassuk says that there are no easy solutions to the problem of homelessness and cites policies that have failed (paragraph 35). Why do you think the policies have failed? What do you think cities, states, and/or the federal government must do to solve the problem of homelessness?

3. Assume that you are a member of the board of directors of a temporary housing facility. What criteria would you establish for acceptance into the facility? What services might the facility provide to help the people who come to it? How do you think your perspective would shift if you were a worker at the facility, a caseworker for a family assigned to it, or one of the people seeking help?

4. In paragraph 45, Bassuk says that "we must eradicate biases against homeless people." What biases is she referring to? How do you think we can eradicate them?

5. Bassuk views the problem of homelessness from her own discipline, psychiatry. How do you think the perspective would change if viewed from one or more of these disciplines: criminology, economics, gerontology, history, human behavior, sociology, and/or women's studies? That is, what do you think people trained in these fields would consider essential when assessing the problem and attempting to find solutions? Do you think certain considerations become more important than others, depending on the discipline of the analyst? Explain your answer.

I JUST WANNA BE AVERAGE
Mike Rose

Mike Rose earned his doctorate in educational psychology at the University of California at Los Angeles, where he is associate director of UCLA Writing Programs. He has taught in a variety of educational programs for economically impoverished people and has written extensively on language, literacy, and the teaching of writing. This reading is excerpted from Rose's 1989 book, Lives on the Boundary: The Struggles and Achievements of America's Underprepared.

My parents used to say that their son would have the best education they could afford. Maybe I would be a doctor. There was a public school in our neighborhood and several Catholic schools to the west. They had heard that quality schooling meant private, Catholic schooling, so they somehow got the money together to send me to Our Lady of Mercy, fifteen or so miles southwest of Ninety-first and Vermont.

It took two buses to get to Our Lady of Mercy. The first started deep in South Los Angeles and caught me at midpoint. The second drifted through neighborhoods with trees, parks, big lawns, and lots of flowers. The rides were long but were livened up by a group of South L.A. veterans whose parents also thought that Hope had set up shop in the west end of the county. There was Christy Biggars, who, at sixteen, was dealing and was, according to rumor, a pimp as well. There were Bill Cobb and Johnny Gonzales, grease-pencil artists extraordinaire, who left Nembutal-enhanced swirls of "Cobb" and "Johnny" on the corrugated walls of the bus. And then there was Tyrrell Wilson. Tyrrell was the coolest kid I knew. He ran the dozens like a metric halfback, laid down a rap that out-rhymed and outpointed Cobb, whose rap was good but not great—the curse of a moderately soulful kid trapped in white skin. But it was Cobb who would sneak a radio onto the bus, and thus underwrote his patter with Little Richard, Fats Domino, Chuck Berry, the Coasters, and Ernie K. Doe's mother-in-law, an awful woman who was "sent from down below." And so it was that Christy and Cobb and Johnny G. and Tyrrell and I and assorted others picked up along the way passed our days in the back of the bus, a funny mix brought together by geography and parental desire.

Entrance to school brings with it forms and releases and assessments. Mercy relied on a series of tests, mostly the Stanford-Binet, for placement, and somehow the results of my tests got confused with those of another student named Rose. The other Rose apparently didn't do very well, for I was placed in the vocational track, a euphemism for the bottom level. Neither I nor my parents realized what this meant. We had no sense that Business Math, Typing, and English-Level D were dead ends. The current spate of reports on the schools criticizes parents for not involving themselves in the education of their children. But how would someone like Tommy Rose, with his two years of Italian schooling, know what to ask? And what sort of pressure could an exhausted waitress apply? The error went undetected, and I remained in the vocational track for two years. What a place.

4   Students will float to the mark you set. I and the others in the vocational classes were bobbing in pretty shallow water. Vocational education has aimed at increasing the economic opportunities of students who do not do well in our schools. Some serious programs succeed in doing that, and through exceptional teachers—like Mr. Gross in *Horace's Compromise*—students learn to develop hypotheses and troubleshoot, reason through a problem, and communicate effectively—the true job skills. The vocational track, however, is most often a place for those who are just not making it, a dumping ground for the disaffected. There were a few

teachers who worked hard at education; young Brother Slattery, for example, combined a stern voice with weekly quizzes to try to pass along to us a skeletal outline of world history. But mostly the teachers had no idea of how to engage the imaginations of us kids who were scuttling along at the bottom of the pond.

And the teachers would have needed some inventiveness, for none of us was groomed for the classroom. It wasn't just that I didn't know things—didn't know how to simplify algebraic fractions, couldn't identify different kinds of clauses, bungled Spanish translations—but that I had developed various faulty and inadequate ways of doing algebra and making sense of Spanish. Worse yet, the years of defensive tuning out in elementary school had given me a way to escape quickly while seeming at least half alert. During my time in Voc. Ed., I developed further into a mediocre student and a somnambulant problem solver, and that affected the subjects I did have the wherewithal to handle: I detested Shakespeare; I got bored with history. My attention flitted here and there. I fooled around in class and read my books indifferently—the intellectual equivalent of playing with your food. I did what I had to do to get by, and I did it with half a mind.

But I did learn things about people and eventually came into my own socially. I liked the guys in Voc. Ed. Growing up where I did, I understood and admired physical prowess, and there was an abundance of muscle here. There was Dave Snyder, a sprinter and halfback of true quality. Dave's ability and his quick wit gave him a natural appeal, and he was welcome in any clique, though he always kept a little independent. He enjoyed acting the fool and could care less about studies, but he possessed a certain maturity and never caused the faculty much trouble. It was a testament to his independence that he included me among his friends—I eventually went out for track, but I was no jock. Owing to the Latin alphabet and a dearth of *R*s and *S*s, Snyder sat behind Rose, and we started exchanging one-liners and became friends.

There was Ted Richard, a much-touted Little League pitcher. He was chunky and had a baby face and came to Our Lady of Mercy as a seasoned street fighter. Ted was quick to laugh and he had a loud, jolly laugh, but when he got angry he'd smile a little smile, the kind that simply raises the corner of the mouth a quarter of an inch. For those who knew, it was an eerie signal. Those who didn't found themselves in big trouble, for Ted was very quick. He loved to carry on what we would come to call philosophical discussions: What is courage? Does God exist? He also loved words, enjoyed picking up big ones like *salubrious* and *equivocal* and using them in our conversations—laughing at himself as the word hit a chuckhole rolling off his tongue. Ted didn't do all that well in school—baseball and parties and testing the courage he'd speculated about took up his time. His textbooks were *Argosy* and *Field and Stream,* whatever newspapers he'd find on the bus stop—from the *Daily Worker* to pornography—conversations with uncles or hobos or businessmen he'd meet in a coffee shop, *The Old Man and the Sea.* With hindsight, I can see that Ted was developing into one of those rough-hewn intellectuals whose sources are a mix of the learned and the apocryphal, whose discussions are both assured and sad.

8   And then there was Ken Harvey. Ken was good-looking in a puffy way and had a full and oily ducktail and was a car enthusiast . . . a hodad. One day in religion class, he said the sentence that turned out to be one of the most memorable of the hundreds of thousands I heard in those Voc. Ed. years. We were talking about the parable of the talents, about achievement, working hard, doing the best you can do, blah-blah-blah, when the teacher called on the restive Ken Harvey for an opinion. Ken thought about it, but just for a second, and said (with studied, minimal affect), "I just wanna be average." That woke me up. Average?! Who wants to be average? Then the athletes chimed in with the clichés that make you want to laryngectomize them, and the exchange became a platitudinous melee. At the time, I thought Ken's assertion was stupid, and I wrote him off. But his sentence has stayed with me all these years, and I think I am finally coming to understand it.

Ken Harvey was gasping for air. School can be a tremendously disorienting place. No matter how bad the school, you're going to encounter notions that don't fit with the assumptions and beliefs that you grew up with—maybe you'll hear these dissonant notions from teachers, maybe from the other students, and maybe you'll read them. You'll also be thrown in with all kinds of kids from all kinds of backgrounds, and that can be unsettling—this is especially true in places of rich ethnic and linguistic mix, like the L.A. basin. You'll see a handful of students far excel you in courses that sound exotic and that are only in the curriculum of the elite: French, physics, trigonometry. And all this is happening while you're trying to shape an identity, your body is changing, and your emotions are running wild. If you're a working-class kid in the vocational track, the options you'll have to deal with this will be constrained in certain ways: You're defined by your school as "slow"; you're placed in a curriculum that isn't designed to liberate you but to occupy you, or, if you're lucky, train you, though the training is for work the society does not esteem; other students are picking up the cues from your school and your curriculum and interacting with you in particular ways. If you're a kid like Ted Richards, you turn your back on all this and let your mind roam where it may. But youngsters like Ted are rare. What Ken and so many others do is protect themselves from such suffocating madness by taking on with a vengeance the identity implied in the vocational track. Reject the confusion and frustration by openly defining yourself as the Common Joe. Champion the average. Rely on your own good sense. Fuck this bullshit. Bullshit, of course, is everything you—and the others—fear is beyond you: books, essays, tests, academic scrambling, complexity, scientific reasoning, philosophical inquiry.

The tragedy is that you have to twist the knife in your own gray matter to make this defense work. You'll have to shut down, have to reject intellectual stimuli or diffuse them with sarcasm, have to cultivate stupidity, have to convert boredom from a malady into a way of confronting the world. Keep your vocabulary simple, act stoned when you're not or act more stoned than you are, flaunt ignorance, materialize your dreams. It is a powerful and effective defense—it neutralizes the insult and the frustration of being a vocational kid and, when perfected, it drives teachers up the wall, a delightful secondary effect. But like all strong magic, it exacts a price.

Personal Response

Were you "occupied" or "liberated" (paragraph 9) by the courses you took in high school? Explain your answer.

Questions for Class or Small Group Discussion

1. In paragraph 4, Rose writes that "students will float to the mark you set." What do you understand him to mean by that statement?

2. Rose says that at the time Ken Harvey told his teacher "I just wanna be average," he thought it a stupid remark, but now he has come to understand it. What does Rose think the statement means now? Do you know anyone like Ken Harvey? If so, describe that person.

3. Rose makes a strong connection between class or poverty level and quality of education, especially in paragraph 9. Look closely at that paragraph and summarize the points he makes there. To what degree do your own experiences support or refute Rose's contentions?

4. Evaluate the relative advantages and disadvantages of the tracking system. If you were tracked in high school, explain how your courses were similar to and different from those that students in other tracks had to take. If possible, use specific examples of students to illustrate the effects of being tracked, as Rose does in this piece.

GETTING OFF THE WELFARE CAROUSEL

Teresa McCrary

Teresa McCrary was a 35-year-old student at the University of Minnesota receiving welfare when she wrote this essay for the "My Turn" column of Newsweek *magazine in 1993. In the essay, McCrary*

explains why she feels it is unfair to criticize welfare recipients, outlin-
ing compelling reasons why she stayed on welfare.

I am a welfare mom. And I have one thing to say: stop picking on us! There
are 5 million families on welfare in the United States, most of them single
women with kids. Is this really such a major financial burden? I believe
we're targeted because we're an easy mark. Because we have no money,
there are no lobbyists working on our behalf either in Washington, D.C.,
or in local legislatures. I want to tell you who we are and why we stay
home with our children.

The stereotypical welfare mom has 10 kids, including a pregnant
teenage daughter, all taking advantage of the dole. I have never personally
known such a woman. Most of the mothers I know are women who forgo
the usual round of job searches and day care so they can mind their homes
and children in a loving and responsible way. We may not have paying jobs,
but any mother, married or single, working or retired, will tell you that
motherhood is a career in itself.

Yet we are constantly told we should go out and get real jobs. Yes,
most of us are unemployed; do we really have a choice? Last time I looked,
the unemployment rate was more than 6 percent. If the unemployed can't
find work, where are we moms supposed to look? The only jobs open to
us are maid work, fast-food service and other low-paying drudgery with no
benefits. How are we expected to support our children? Minimum wage
will not pay for housing costs, health care, child care, transportation and
work clothes that an untrained, uneducated woman needs to support even
one child.

4   Many of us take money under the table for odd jobs, and cash from
generous friends and relatives to help support our families. We don't report this money to the Aid to Families with Dependent Children, because
we can't afford to. Any cash we get, even birthday money from grandparents, is deducted from the already minuscule benefits. We're allowed
between $1,000 and $3,000 in assets including savings and property, automobiles and home furnishings. We are told that if we have more than that
amount, we should be able to sell some things and live for a year from the
proceeds. Can you imagine living on $3,000 for a year?

As for child support, unless the money sent to the state by the father
is greater than AFDC benefits, the family receives only $50 monthly. This
bonus decreases food-stamp benefits. We are told that the state intends
to prosecute "deadbeat dads" for back support. Seldom do news stories
mention that, in the case of welfare families, the state keeps collected back
support. Although this reduces the tax burden, none of the money goes to
the children. Outsiders are led to believe that the children will benefit, and
they do not. No wonder some welfare moms—and their children's fathers—believe it's not worth the effort to try to get the dads to pay up. If

we could have depended on these men in the first place, we would not be on welfare.

So what about family values? Those of us who do not have a man in our lives do the emotional job of both mother and father. My daughter says she should give me a Father's Day card, because I am just as much a father to her as a mother. On top of these two careers, we are told we should work.

We could hold down a minimum-wage job, unarguably the hardest work for the least amount of money. If we could find an employer willing to hire us full time (most low-wage jobs are part time). Unable to afford child care, we'd have latchkey children whose only good meal of the day would be school lunch. The whole paycheck would go to housing and job expenses. When we got home exhausted, we'd clean house, help with homework, listen to how the kids' day went—feeling relieved if none of them had been teased for their garage-sale clothes. We'd pray that nobody got sick, because we couldn't afford a day off work or doctor fees (welfare pays very little, but it has the important benefit of health care). We'd worry about getting laid off at any moment—in tough times, minimum-wage jobs are the first to go.

8   These fears cause stress that may result in child abuse. Many times we feel, no matter how hard we try, that in some way our children are being neglected if we are holding down a job. So we stay home. We've learned that we can depend only on ourselves. We don't enjoy living at the poverty level, but we can't see a minimum-wage job as the answer.

I believe that we single mothers must become self-sufficient through education and training. And that means both money and patience on the taxpayers' part. I'm in my fourth year at college. I, and the other welfare moms I know at school, maintain a 3.0 grade average or better. Are we exceptions to the rule? Maybe not; perhaps people in my circumstances are more motivated to make better lives for themselves. Fighting the low self-esteem brought on by divorce and poverty, we have taken the difficult step, usually without a support system, of going back to school. By carefully scheduling classes and studying late at night, I have been able to care for my kids while learning TV and radio production.

College may be out of reach for many. By raising tuition and entrance requirements, most colleges and universities are barring us from their campuses. Even President Clinton's proposed two-year training program may not help much. Vocational or technical schools mean training for low-paying jobs. Still, we'll be told to find work or lose our benefits.

If the government keeps decreasing or eliminating the programs we and the children depend upon for survival, here's what will happen: in a few years, instead of 5 million single women and their children on welfare, there will be 5 million single women and their children on the streets. I don't know how many starving millions the United Nations is trying to help in Somalia. But if people keep picking on us, the United Nations will have to help the United States feed *us.*

Personal Response

What is your image of welfare recipients? Has it changed in any way or been reinforced as a result of reading this essay?

Questions for Class or Small Group Discussion

1. Explain the meaning of McCrary's title, "Getting off the Welfare Carousel." Why is "carousel" an appropriate metaphor, from McCrary's viewpoint? Would you characterize the welfare system as a "carousel"?

2. In paragraph 1, McCrary writes: "I believe we're targeted because we're an easy mark." In what ways does McCrary think welfare mothers are easy marks? Explain whether you agree or disagree with her.

3. If you personally know people who are on welfare, compare their situations with that of Teresa McCrary. Do you think their reasons are the same as hers for staying on welfare? How do they differ?

4. Look closely at the reasons McCrary lists for staying on welfare. Do you consider them sound reasons for not taking a job outside the home? Explain your answer.

5. McCrary implies that the federal government pays too much attention to foreign affairs and not enough to domestic problems (paragraph 11). Discuss the degree to which you agree or disagree with her on that point.

IN DEFENSE OF ORPHANAGES

Charles D. Aring

Charles D. Aring is a professor emeritus of neurology at the University of Cincinnati. He has written a book, The Understanding Physician. *In this essay, first published in* The American Scholar *in 1991, Aring recalls his own experience in an orphanage and calls for a national plan to meet the needs of both orphans and the elderly.*

I took up residence in an orphanage a few days before my seventh birthday and remained there until the age of fifteen and a half, a total of eight and a half years. I was a full orphan by reason of my father's desertion before my birth and my mother's death in her forty-ninth year. I have no memory of having seen my father. During the year after my mother's death, I was assigned to two foster homes seriatim, which involved my attending four primary schools during my sixth and seventh years. I was tolerated at these

homes until I could be moved along. I can recall little in the way of masculine influence during my first six years until I got to the orphanage, which
may account for my slow acclimatization there. It was a rough, tough existence after the totally feminine environment of my earliest years.

It has not been considered particularly advantageous to spend one's
formative years in an orphanage. The immediate experience made me actively dislike almost everything about it. Nowadays, the phasing out of orphanages has thinned the ranks of the alumni.

Orphanages have fallen into desuetude after struggling along under a
Dickensian cloud. The foster home has largely replaced the orphanage.
The social service attitude routinely supports the primacy of the nuclear
family, no matter how disorganized it may be. Social problems these days
are dealt with less on principle than on the basis of cost. But I doubt
whether orphanages were more expensive per capita than other modes of
child care.

4   Before all witnesses and memories disappear, I want to record the
debits and credits of the orphanage I knew and draw some conclusions
about the care and nurture of children without parents. My experience
was garnered in the second decade of this century. A long career in teaching enables me to know how disconcerting to some people this ancient
history may be; I have in mind those who always trust what is new and feel
contempt for what is old. But history has its uses nonetheless—if only the
satisfaction of curiosity.

To begin with fundamentals, the orphanage food was simple, coarse,
and, as I recall, insufficient. Meals were closer to feeding than to dining.
Our meager fare can be inferred from the invariable Christmas gift: an apple or an orange; the child who got an orange was considered lucky. But I
recall no obesity in this population in children or staff. This was surely an
advantage owing to what might otherwise be construed as a debit. Food
limitation in childhood may indeed have something to do with setting the
"appestat" (by analogy with thermostat) control.

Clothing was likewise plain. The boys' uniform included blue overalls,
suggesting in its way our minority status. A blue short-trousered, serge
suit was the emblem of confirmation in Sunday school at the age of fourteen; I do not remember what happened to it after the ceremony—very
likely it wore out. But I do remember attending high school in the cast-
off trousers of a mailman's uniform, and that did not help me to be
self-confident.

The administration during most of my residence consisted of a childless couple. The husband had advanced (if that is the word) to the super-
intendency of the orphanage from a job as a teamster: he drove a local
beer wagon. His main qualification for his new post was that he was himself an alumnus of the institution. His education could not have been beyond the elementary school level, if that, and his wife was unable to read
or write. The women caretakers were also uneducated but kindly. A

board of directors met periodically and were not, as a group, intellectually impressive.

8   Discipline was strict, as I suppose it had to be with a hundred charges, six to fourteen years of age, about equally divided between girls and boys. Much of the work of the institution fell to the children under the supervision of the caretakers, the superintendent, and the matron. It was mainly drudgery, although some of the older children became adept at such things as shoe repairing, sewing, and mechanic's work.

Two superintendents followed one another during my residence at the orphanage, the first, not long after my arrival, having been dismissed for molesting some of the older girls. This brings up the subject of sexual education: it was nonexistent, except as normal children somehow pick up such things. The sexes were kept segregated, and all forms of sexual expression rigidly suppressed. This did not prevent an occasional roll in the bushes, which we heard about through the grapevine when the couple was apprehended. I was too naive to get involved in conduct contrary to the rules. My report cards from elementary school suggest that I was considered a good boy with frequent E's (excellent) for conduct and effort.

It can be imagined that education was not a priority in the establishment. There were bound to be some exceptional children among the lot, but intellectual achievement was neither stressed nor rewarded. The children knew who the achievers were without help or sign from the administration.

Religious training, which was wholly rote learning, occupied almost the whole of Sunday. The children were marched to the neighboring German Evangelical Lutheran Church in a long line, just as they were marched to school. It was there that I was fortunate enough to be assigned to the best teacher of my early years. Somehow she led me to appreciate the Bible as literature. But the appalling sermons in English or German, like the other religious exercises routinely performed at the orphanage, guaranteed my agnostic outlook as an adult. The vaccination, so to speak, took. Perhaps this perfunctory religious training had the benefit of preventing prejudice, religious or social.

12   From these various defects it should not be inferred that I was unappreciative of the home I was given, and I turn now to the credits. The shelter was secure, and the environment neat and clean, owing mainly to our own efforts under steady supervision. No task was considered too menial for us to take on and be held responsible for. "Goofing off" was unknown and malingering unthought of. Discipline was strict, and we strove to keep out of trouble's way. Punishment in the form of work could be prolonged until a replacement arrived by virtue of another's misdeed. There were no really bad guys among us, which reminds me that I know nothing about the admissions policy. Whatever it was, it seems to have excluded the problem child. It also seems to me that disturbed children were much less

common than today. I do not recall any such children in the eight grades of a very mixed elementary school.

The business of childhood is play; at the orphanage it was of course limited by all the work that had to be done about the place. At the same time it was an advantage to have so many playmates at hand for every kind of game. And we played every kind, without much equipment—we simply made do. Exciting ball games were had with an old rubber ball and a broomstick (it sharpened the batting eye). I became adept at constructing hard baseballs by winding the unravelings of a worn-out stocking over a rubber core, such as a ball used for playing jacks. Leather covers were salvaged from old baseballs, and these I knew how to stitch. Later, I had no trouble making the baseball team since I could always hit, thanks to this stickball training. My poliomyelitic lower limb was a handicap, to be sure, but not enough to keep me off the team.

We also made up games, such as the competitive stalking and catching of cicadas. We termed them locusts and garnered considerable lore about the habits and life cycle of this beautiful insect, to say nothing of its facility for tree climbing, which, like so much else, was forbidden.

Another plus was the brass band. Though quite young, I was given the cymbals to play, then moved to the alto horn as soon as I could manage it, and finally to the slide trombone. The younger children were instructed mainly by the older, although there was a bandmaster—a member of the orchestra in one of the local picture houses. Musical engagements away from the orphanage compound afforded us a respite from the routines and chores. We marched in parades, including the one for the Liberty Loan of the First World War, and we played at flag raisings as well as at other festivals. Eventually I became deeply interested in classical music, most likely as a result of this early haphazard musical experience.

16   The orphanage had a bit of a library, and I believe I read all that was in it. I had begun reading at the age of three or four, perhaps at my invalid mother's knee, and the taste for books may have been fostered by the physical limitations that followed the poliomyelitis that I contracted at the age of one year. The orphanage library was composed of books of the Frank Merriwell, Tom Swift, Rover Boys, and Horatio Alger genre. My experience leads me to recommend any sort of reading for young children; they will choose as they develop. Once begun, reading becomes a habit. When I got to high school, some use of the public library was possible, on the way to or from school, though nobody at the orphanage showed interest in whether we read or not.

Perhaps the most useful feature of the place was the camaraderie amongst the children and the variety of older boys. This was not part of the program; rather, it was a natural development in that setting. Not long after my joining the institution, one of the older boys "took my part," as it was termed. Up to that time, I had lived under feminine influence, and I was lame to boot, which tended to attract the unfavorable attention of other children. It made a difference to those tempted to torment if they had to deal with one of the larger boys of the "family."

If not a family, we were a clan and would close ranks in competitions with children outside the walls. They were the "English kids," in contrast to our designation as "German Protestant orphans." We usually prevailed in snowball fights (more fun than fight), baseball, boxing, and other athletic events. It made up for our social inferiority. I had a few friends among the "English kids," but many more among my fellow orphans.

The superlative merit of the institution was the great good health that prevailed among us during my entire tenure. This was the major benefit conferred by my life in an orphanage; it set a pattern and perhaps influenced my eventual choice of occupation as well. I had come from an unhealthy environment: my mother had been an invalid practically since my birth. Her mother, who was also ill, died during my second or third year. She and my mother's younger sister, both subject to repeated depressions, often required hospital care.

20 At the orphanage, everyone was *expected* to be healthy—and usually we were. There was a sick room and a "nurse" on the premises, but aside from contagious diseases and some cuts and bruises, there was little illness. I myself had chicken pox, sustained a lacerated scalp in a fall owing to my own foolishness, sprained my ankle while sledding, and that was all. During my more than eight years of residence, there were no deaths. I remained healthy thereafter, except for a few iatrogenic ills. Evidently we confirmed the thesis enunciated by the English poet and satirist Charles Churchill:

> The surest road to health, say what they will,
> Is never to suppose we shall be ill;
> Most of those evils we poor mortals know,
> From doctors and imagination flow.

Had I derived nothing more from my orphan life than the reversal of my family legacy of poor health, the experience would have been worth it. That I was made wary of wine, women, and smoking, I suppose, was mainly because of penury, although strict admonitions may also have had something to do with it.

I can count other benefits, one of them being the necessity of learning a second language—German. Surely one of the great defects of public education in this country is indifference to languages, including our own. Ludwig Wittgenstein, as I recently discovered, supplies the rationale for my conviction. "The limits of my language," he writes, "mean the limit of my world."

I am not sure by what factors maturity was skewed, as it certainly was, by orphanage life. Adolescence was curbed, certainly, and its manifestations mishandled or not handled at all. But early acceptance of responsibility was continually reinforced, and that was a good thing. Generally, the more responsibility given to normal children, the more responsible they become. On the other hand, our life did little for socialization outside the group; I was quite inhibited on leaving the protective walls, and forever after tended to substitute institutions for personal contact.

24   The development of talent, too, was neglected. The half-orphan had a better chance if the surviving parent took care to make up for the total lack of intellectual stimulation. I was not aware of any advantage because of being a whole-orphan until after I had left, when I came to realize that it was possible to undertake the care and nurture of the self.

After "graduating" from the orphanage, educational and occupational opportunities were inversely proportional to the number of one's relatives. And their problems might well augment the burden. Within the orphanage, a surviving parent could convey a measure of comfort merely by being. But when the parent resumed responsibility for a child in his early teens, the change was fraught with risk, not the least of which was to deal emotionally with the original abandonment.

So I found an advantage in being a whole-orphan. I noticed that few of the children who were predominantly half-orphans continued their education on leaving the institution, usually because of the presence of a surviving parent. He or she may have remarried and was apt to enlist the support of the child rather than the other way around. In any case, this parent was no more adequate emotionally or financially than when he or she first relinquished the child.

What is more, once out of the orphanage, which was located in the suburbs, the youngster often found himself living in one of the slums of the city, and suddenly exposed to the dangers that he had been shielded from by walls and regulations. All too often this devastating pressure in mid-adolescence—Shakespeare's "the ambush of young days"—was more than the child could overcome. I was lucky to find myself domiciled and in the shadow of another large institution (the Cincinnati General Hospital), which brought into my ken a whole host of behavior models.

28   What about orphan children today? For the orphan, like the poor, is always with us. Having seen so many of my fellows fall by the wayside, my main concern is, How can opportunity be provided for the child to fulfill his potential? Considering the problem historically, I know of no better scheme than that of Girard College in Philadelphia. It is no doubt the outstanding orphanage in the United States. There the primary goal has been the education and training of the children to the full extent of their talents. Plainly, orphans everywhere should, after primary and secondary schooling, receive vocational training if not interested or equipped for a college education.

The Girard program was drafted well over a century and a half ago by Stephen Girard (1750–1831), a self-made international trader who was reputed to be the wealthiest man in the American colonies. He put his mind to the care of orphans when drawing up his last will and testament at the age of seventy-six, and revised it in his eightieth year. The college opened on January 1, 1848.

To achieve his purposes, Girard gave a generous endowment and left little to chance in its use. The details of his plan were clearly spelled out. It needs little in the way of modernization, save for conforming to changes in the law of the land, as has been pointed out by John Keats in "The Legend of Stephen Girard," an article first published in 1978 in *American Heritage*. Girard's philosophy of nurture for orphaned children is as valid today as it was 164 years ago.

Girard College accepts normal children, whole-orphans or half-orphans, between the ages of six and eleven. The college now consists of seventeen buildings on forty-three acres. Currently there are more than five hundred children there, a third of whom are girls. The school maintains high educational credentials. Mental and physical health are evaluated carefully before admission. Girard's non-denominational chapel is held twice weekly. The students may attend religious congregations of their choice off campus. There are courses in comparative religion in the curriculum.

32   Every opportunity is afforded by a large enthusiastic faculty for students to develop to the extent of their capacity. From the day of admission, it is expected that the student will go on to a university, and practically all of them do go on scholarships underwritten by Girard. Similar arrangements are made for graduate school.

The program directs orphans toward what should be a gratifying life. Girard has graduated a host of successful persons. One development is an enthusiastic and vigorous alumni association. Girard is a happy ship for those who have had the exceptional good fortune of boarding and partaking in Mr. Girard's great concept. But what of those who for any reason cannot partake in a legacy according to Mr Girard's grand design?

Looking forward, I, too, have dreamed of an institution for the future. I can imagine a facility for housing not only orphan children but also a limited number of healthy elders who might be interested in their own development after retiring. It should be a facility modeled on the extended family of bygone years, particularly as it existed in rural areas. The administration would represent the middle generation, the children being the younger generation. In my scheme, the opportunity for communication between the generations should be always available. Some elders would want none of it. This is quite understandable. By definition my retreat would select naturally the sort of clientele that would foster its program. From the standpoint of mental health, the availability of younger generations to older and vice versa is useful and beyond dispute. Children and the elderly are natural allies.

To keep the extended family going, incentive programs could be set up in which the children and the retired folk would participate under the supervision of the middle generation serving as the administrators. The elders, expert by reason of experience in one or another discipline or technique, would be ready-made personnel for instruction and recreation. Not only literacy but art and music could be taught and practiced under their tutelage. Members of such an extended family would form friendships and groupings, by free choice and affinity, which would be lasting, a family unit in the best sense.

36   The pattern of an extended family "home" would resemble the real world more than the usual modern concentration of a single generation. Its clientele would be exposed to the quirks, vagaries, pleasures, ills, and interests of persons of all varieties of age, personality development, competence, and health. It goes without saying that such an establishment would require wise administration. That of the usual immuring institutions as we know them would not fill the bill. The best administrative talent has not gravitated to orphanages and retirement homes. The prevalent oppressive social philosophy of economism, which views human life in terms of production, acquisition, and distribution of wealth, has not dealt kindly with persons at the extremes of the age scale. But there they are and will always be. They deserve better than our heedless age has managed to organize for their well-being.

Personal Response

What do you think of Aring's experiences at the orphanage? Can you imagine yourself leading such a life? Does it appeal to you? Explore reasons why or why not.

Questions for Class or Small Group Discussion

1. Summarize the advantages and disadvantages of orphanages that Aring cites. Then discuss them in terms of your own reactions to what he describes or your own perspective on orphanages.

2. Compare and contrast the advantages of orphanages over foster homes. If you are not familiar with the way orphanages operate, draw on Aring's descriptions of the one he attended and the Girard program, which Aring describes in paragraphs 28–33.

3. What do you understand Aring to mean when he writes that "educational and occupational opportunities were inversely proportional to the number of one's relatives" (paragraph 25)?

4. What do you think of the institution Aring envisions at the end of his essay (paragraphs 34–36)? What are the merits of his plan? Does such an institution appeal to you? Do you think it would appeal to your older relatives? Explain your answer.

5. Discuss the general question of orphaned children's welfare. Whose responsibility do you think it is to see that all children receive good starts in life? Who sets the standards for health and education for orphaned children? Who oversees the welfare of those children?

Perspectives on Poverty and the Family

Suggestions for Synthesis

1. In his essay "In Defense of Orphanages," Charles D. Aring uses the example of a specific institution to answer his question, "How can opportunity be provided for the [orphan] child to fulfill his potential?" (paragraph 28). Write an essay in which you answer Aring's question, taking into consideration the points Ellen L. Bassuk ("Homeless Families") and Mike Rose ("I Just Wanna Be Average") make about the effects of poverty on self-esteem or other matters affecting the well-being of children.

2. Consider the problems associated with meeting the needs of either welfare recipients or homeless people. Begin by summarizing the reasons and possible solutions offered in two or more of the articles in this chapter. Then propose your own remedies or ways to reduce the large numbers of people in poverty or without homes.

3. Compare the conditions that create a need for Teresa McCrary ("Getting Off the Welfare Carousel") and others like her to go on welfare with the conditions Ellen L. Bassuk outlines in her essay "Homeless Families." How are they similar? How are they different? What conclusions can you draw from those two essays about women, children, and welfare?

Additional Writing Topics

1. Teresa McCrary wrote "Getting Off the Welfare Carousel" for "My Turn," a regular column in *Newsweek* magazine that provides a forum for readers to express their opinions on controversial topics. Write your own opinion paper on one of the issues addressed in this chapter.

2. Prepare a hypothetical case study of a welfare recipient or homeless person. Provide details on the person's current economic, physical, and emotional makeup and create a background for the person that explains how he or she came to be on welfare or homeless. Offer remedies for the person's situation and attempt to predict the person's future.

3. Using Mike Rose's discussion of "liberated" and "occupied" students in "I Just Wanna Be Average," compare and contrast teachers you have had who liberated you and those who simply occupied you, pointing out the qualities that distinguish them and exploring possible effects of their teaching styles on you personally.

4. Using your own experiences or those of people you know well, argue in support of or against Mike Rose's contention that poverty level and quality of education are closely linked ("I Just Wanna Be Average").

5. With Mike Rose's "I Just Wanna Be Average" in mind, argue for or against the use of tracking systems in schools, considering both advantages and disadvantages of such a system.

6. Write an essay in which you propose a way in which cities, states, and/or the federal government can help solve or alleviate the problem of homelessness in America.

7. Working in small groups, create a scenario involving one or more of the following people: welfare recipient or homeless person, welfare caseworker or worker at a homeless shelter, police officer, and either or both a wealthy person and a working-class person with a regular income and a home. Provide a situation, create dialogue, and role-play in an effort to understand the varying perspectives of different people on the issue of welfare or homelessness. Then present your scenario to the rest of your classmates. For an individual writing project, do an analysis of the scenario or fully develop the viewpoint of the person whose role you played.

Research Topics

1. Research your state's policy on welfare, including residency requirements, eligibility for payments, monitoring of welfare persons, and related issues. Then write a paper outlining your opinion of your state's welfare policy, including any recommendations you would make for changing it.

2. With Ellen L. Bassuk's "Homeless Families" in mind, research one aspect of the subject of women and poverty. For instance, Bassuk suggests that a traumatic childhood impedes the development of social skills in women, which in turn has serious economic implications for them. Find out what kinds of trauma and what specific skills she is referring to and why not having these skills proves to be a hindrance to women. In your paper on this subject, propose ways to help women gain the skills they need to get out of poverty.

3. From time to time, politicians propose establishing orphanages that would house not only orphaned children but the children of single parents on welfare or parents who have been deemed unfit. Research this subject, and then write a paper in which you argue for or against the establishment of such orphanages. Make sure you consider as many perspectives as possible on this complex issue, including the welfare of the child, the rights of the parent or parents, and society's responsibility to protect children.

CHAPTER 11

CRIMINAL BEHAVIOR

America has the highest violent crime rate in the world. The number of murders and rapes in some areas of the country is at an all-time high, while muggings, armed robbery, and drug trafficking continue to characterize the perils of city living. As a result, people who can afford to move are leaving the city, while those who cannot afford to move live in dread and fear, shutting themselves up in their homes at night or arming themselves in case of attack. But crime is not limited to large cities. Small communities have been shocked and dismayed by violent crimes such as kidnapping, murder, and rape in their own home towns. Children are abducted from their own bedrooms or neighborhoods and discovered later, murdered, or never found again. Even very young children are murdering other children.

The essays in this chapter suggest some of the ways in which this terrible problem of criminal behavior is being addressed. Some blame the ready availability of firearms for the increase in murder and other violent crimes. Thus, writing from the perspective of a long-time researcher into the relationship between firearms and violence, Franklin E. Zimring in "Firearms, Violence, and Public Policy" raises a number of questions about gun control, points out where insufficient evidence exists, and examines several strategies for firearms control. As you read his essay, consider your own views on gun control and whether what Zimring says makes sense to you.

Nathan McCall writes from an entirely different and very personal perspective. As a young black male who grew up in a suburb of Portsmouth, Virginia, the son of caring, working-class parents, McCall had become by the age of 14 a gang member who participated in gang fights, gang rape, and petty theft before finally being imprisoned. His youth and early adulthood were typical of the lives of far too many young males. Fortunately for McCall, as he explains in "Native Son," his story has a different, happier outcome than most. As you read about the experience that proved to have a profound, life-changing effect on him, think about the ways in which young people choose violence and self-destructive behavior and reasons why they make those choices.

In "What's Wrong With America and Can Anything Be Done About It?" Wayne M. Barrett and Bernard Rowe trace a host of social problems, including crime and violence, to a decline in decency and discipline. They suggest a number of remedies that many readers may find controversial. As you read what they have to say, consider whether you agree or disagree with them. If you disagree, what do you think are causes and possible solutions for the nation's serious social problems?

One theory to explain why some people are violent is that such behavior is genetic, as Dennis Overbye reports in "Born to Raise Hell?" Overbye makes some pointed comments on news that scientists may have located a gene responsible for criminal behavior and raises some intriguing questions about such research. What answers would you offer to the questions he raises? Do you share his concern over research into genetic causes for violent and criminal behavior?

FIREARMS, VIOLENCE, AND PUBLIC POLICY

Franklin E. Zimring

Franklin E. Zimring teaches law at the University of California at Berkeley and directs the Earl Warren Legal Institute. He has published a number of works, including The Search for Rational Drug Control *(1992),* The Scale of Imprisonment *(1991), and* The Citizen's Guide to Gun Control *(1987). This essay was originally published in 1991 in* Scientific American.

Even though the United States has many more gun-control laws than any other nation, Americans are more likely to be victims of gun-related violence. We have no hope of greatly improving this situation as long as we continue to construct gun-control policy on a weak foundation of facts.

Since the 1960s some social and behavioral scientists have been investigating how violence is related to firearms. But their conclusions have largely been ignored. Neither supporters nor opponents of gun-control laws have felt any great need to cite facts. Strong emotions have kept the conflicting parties at each other's throats.

Recent congressional debates on gun control have also relied on undocumented assertions. The 1991 Brady bill aims to reduce the violence associated with guns by making handgun purchases subject to waiting periods and police notification. The congressional debate over these issues is no more informed than it was during the deliberations that led to the Gun Control Act of 1968. A distaste for facts is also evident in the emphasis Americans have placed on research: much more money is spent on newspaper advertisements about gun control than on research about firearms and violence.

4   During the past three decades, investigators have learned about the relation between guns and the death rate from violent crime, accidents, and suicides. They recorded the kinds of firearms used in these situations, and they measured how gun-control laws have influenced crime and the ownership of guns.

The accumulating evidence provides reasons for discomfort on both sides of the political struggle. Ample data confirm that as guns become more available, people are more likely to die during violent crimes—a connection that opponents of gun control have tried to deny. Research also shows that many laws do not significantly diminish the number of guns used in violence, although many advocates of gun control have assumed they would.

Lawmakers have agreed to many measures that try to keep guns out of the hands of criminals. But these regulations have not brought violence down to a level that most Americans can tolerate. At the same time, we have not confronted the controversial issue of reducing the thirty-five million handguns that play the greatest role in violence caused by firearms.

The Federal Bureau of Investigation reports that in 1990 criminals in the United States committed more than 1.8 million acts of homicide, robbery, forcible rape, and serious assault. More than 28 percent of these violent crimes involved firearms. And, most notably, guns were the cause of death in 64 percent of the twenty-three thousand homicides. Although the statistics portray the magnitude of gun-related violence, they provide no information about why or how the flow of firearms should be regulated.

8   The issue of gun control hinges on whether the death rate from violence would subside if people were forced to abandon firearms and choose other weapons such as knives. As Philip J. Cook and Daniel Nagin of Duke University once asked, "Does the weapon matter?"

The answer is not obvious. In 1958 Marvin E. Wolfgang of the University of Pennsylvania claimed that the choice of weapon did not make much difference in criminal homicide. He argued that if guns were unavailable, assailants would wield other deadly weapons to achieve their goal. His analysis assumed that most people who commit criminal homicide have a single-minded and unconditional intention to kill.

A decade after Wolfgang's work, I found evidence that the weapon used is important in determining whether a violent assault will lead to death. I reviewed Chicago police records of more than sixteen thousand violent assaults, both fatal and nonfatal, to determine the outcomes of attacks with guns and knives, the two weapons most commonly used in criminal homicide. The study showed that most attackers seemed to stop short of ensuring the victim's death. In eight out of ten assaults with guns, the attacker shot the victim only once. Attackers also inflicted one wound in seven out of ten cases in which the victim died.

In general, fatality seemed to be an almost accidental outcome of a large number of assaults committed with guns or knives. The Chicago study indicated that most nonfatal attacks, like most homicides, resulted in wounds to vital parts of the body. According to the study, homicide and serious assaults involved the same kinds of motives (mostly spontaneous arguments), and they occurred in the same places at the same times.

12   One important difference among assaults was the weapon used: an assault with a gun was five times more likely to result in a fatality than an assault with a knife. And assaults with guns to all vital body areas—head, neck, shoulders, chest, and abdomen—were many times more likely to kill than attacks to the same locations with knives. In 1990 more than

23 percent of the one million serious assaults involved guns, whereas knives played a role in 20 percent of assaults.

Do attackers who carry guns simply have more lethal intentions than assailants who use knives? The Chicago data indicated otherwise: compared with assaults with guns, attacks with knives were more likely to result in multiple wounds, and they were equally likely to damage a part of the body where death can result. The five-to-one difference in death rate thus seems to stem from the greater dangerousness of the firearm as a weapon, what is known as an instrumentality effect.

If such instrumentality effects are large, a shift from guns to knives would cause a drop in the homicide rate even if the total rate of violent assault did not change. Other studies have corroborated the presence of large instrumentality effects in urban violence.

When Hans Zeisel of the University of Chicago and other sociologists compared assaults in cities that had different mixes of guns and knives, they found a difference in death rate between the two kinds of assaults. Zeisel, who examined New York and Houston, wrote, "If the level of gun attacks in Houston were reduced from 42 percent to New York's level of 24 percent, 322 gun attacks would have been knife attacks. At present, these 322 gun attacks resulted in sixty-three fatalities. . . . If they were knife attacks, roughly twelve fatalities would result—a reduction from twenty deaths per hundred attacks to four per hundred."

16   Although all guns are deadly, some types of firearms are more harmful than others because they are more likely to be used in crime and violence. In the United States, handguns—small, concealable weapons that can be fired with one hand—account for one-third of the 120 to 150 million firearms estimated to be owned by civilians. Handguns are used in more than 75 percent of firearm-related homicides and more than 80 percent of firearm-related robberies. On the average, rifles and shotguns are seven times less likely than handguns to be used in criminal violence. In states and cities that have made special efforts to restrict handguns, the major problem is still illegal handguns rather than long guns. (No one has recorded how many crimes are committed with what are called military assault weapons. These semiautomatic rifles and handguns require a separate trigger pull for each bullet discharged but can fire many rounds of ammunition quickly.)

To determine whether the type of gun influences the outcome of violent assaults, my colleagues and I conducted a follow-up study in Chicago in 1972. Not surprisingly, we found that a large-caliber gun was twice as likely to kill as a small-caliber gun in cases in which the guns inflicted the same number of wounds to the same part of the body. This statistic indicated that mortality from criminal violence is strongly correlated with the dangerousness of the weapon, not just the attacker's intent.

Some sociologists have criticized the conclusion that the motivations behind most homicides are ambiguous. They argue that the similarity between fatal and nonfatal assaults might be superficial. Furthermore, they maintain that attackers who wield guns may have substantially different intentions from criminals who use knives. But so far no evidence derived from data on assault has been presented that argues against instrumentality effects in homicide.

The role of weapons is largely unknown in another kind of assault, forcible rape. More than one hundred thousand cases are reported to the police every year, and roughly eight thousand of them involve firearms. Although a change in firearm use could prevent many rapes at gunpoint, most rapists use personal force or other means. No studies have yet determined the different rates of death from forcible rape involving different types of weapons.

20   A central issue in the gun-control debate is robbery. Each year the FBI tallies more than five hundred thousand robberies and three thousand deaths of robbery victims. (This type of crime produces by far the most killings of strangers.)

In 1990 criminals carried firearms in 37 percent of 640,000 robberies reported to the police. Criminals do not rely heavily on firearms for robberies of vulnerable individuals on the street. But they often carry guns to rob stores. My colleagues and I found that in Chicago firearms are involved in two-thirds of robberies of commercial establishments but fewer than two-fifths of street robberies.

Because robberies need involve only the threat of injury, it cannot be assumed that the choice of weapon in a robbery will influence the outcome in the same way as the choice in assaults does. Only in recent years have investigators published special reports on the influence of guns on the death rate from robbery.

The National Crime Survey reports that crime victims are less likely to resist robbers who carry guns than those who wield other weapons. Apparently, a firearm makes the threat of force by a robber conspicuously credible. The risk of any victim injury is therefore lower when a robber has a gun instead of, say, a knife.

24   But in cases where robberies result in injuries, guns are far more deadly than other weapons. James Zuehl and I at the University of Chicago found that the death rate is three times higher for robberies at gunpoint than for robberies with knives, the next most dangerous robbery weapon. Cook has found that in areas where gun ownership is unusually prevalent, death rates from robbery are high.

These findings independently confirm the instrumentality effects found in assaults because robbers presumably do not select their weapons with the intent of injuring their victim. Robberies with firearms, like assaults with guns, contribute greatly to the crime-related death rate, independent of the motivations of the criminal.

One question not yet answered is how much the availability of guns influences the rate of robberies. Presumably, when guns are widely available, robberies become easier to commit and increase in frequency. Yet in one study of U.S. cities, Cook did not find a correlation between gun availability and total robbery rate. No one has yet investigated the more specific comparison of commercial robbery rates.

Very few scholars have studied how firearms are related to two important forms of noncriminal violence: suicide and accidents. In the United States, death by self-inflicted gunshot wounds accounts for over half the more than thirty thousand suicides committed every year. Firearms are no more effective a means of suicide than are such methods as hanging or jumping. But when firearms are not at hand, people most frequently attempt suicide by drug overdoses. If guns were not available to people with suicidal intentions, how many attempts might be redirected to less lethal means and how many lives would be saved? This question deserves far more attention than it has received.

28   Accidents involving firearms claim about two thousand lives every year in the United States, a much lower death rate than that for homicides or suicides. About 60 percent of accidental fatalities occur in or around the home. The population groups that have the highest fatality rates from accidents are male children and adolescents, who are generally inexperienced in using guns and are often tempted to play with them. Clearly, if young people did not have access to guns, the death rate would drop.

Two other findings about the misuse of firearms have some significance when considering strategies of firearm control. First, the percentage of gun-related crimes in an area is related to the proportion of owners of firearms in that area. In 1969 the Task Force on Firearms demonstrated that if a city ranks high in gun use for one kind of crime, such as aggravated assault, the use of guns tends to be high for other types of crime, such as robbery. Cook has also found that high rates of gun use in suicide are positively correlated with rates of gun use in violent crime. As more firearms are available to the civilian population, more guns are also available for misuse.

Second, in the 1970s the Federal Bureau of Alcohol, Tobacco, and Firearms conducted studies of handguns confiscated on city streets. The bureau showed that handguns are most likely to be misused in the first few years after the weapons are introduced to the civilian market. In four U.S. cities studied by the bureau, handguns three years old or younger constituted half of those confiscated on the streets but less than a quarter of the total number owned by civilians. Consequently, handguns play their greatest role in street crime when they are a few years old, even though they often function for many years.

All gun-control measures seek to reduce the influence of the use of firearms in crimes and violence. The ideal gun-control measure would prevent all crime and violence involving guns without interfering with their legitimate use in contemporary life. More realistically, regulations should reduce the problems caused by illegitimate uses as much as possible while minimizing the restraints on legitimate uses of guns. To achieve this goal, lawmakers have proposed many different types of regulations. The laws are usually based on one of three strategies: prohibiting high-risk uses of firearms, keeping guns out of the hands of high-risk users, or banning high-risk firearms.

32   Regulations that prohibit high-risk uses of firearms include "place and manner" prohibitions and extra penalties for unlawful use. Most gun laws in the United States seek to regulate the place and manner in which firearms may be used. They prohibit such high-risk uses as carrying firearms in a motor vehicle or discharging a firearm in populated areas or concealing weapons on one's person. Place-and-manner laws attempt to deter high-risk behavior with guns, and they rely on the police to intervene before violence occurs. These laws prevent violence only to the extent that the police can discover and arrest persons who violate such laws. How much violence is deterred because guns are not carried is not known. But the rate of gun-related violence would almost certainly increase if carrying loaded weapons became widespread.

High-risk behavior with guns can also be discouraged by instituting particularly stiff penalties for criminals who use firearms. Such laws attempt to deter the would-be robber or attacker from using a gun during a crime. More than half of the states have passed such laws. This approach is popular with gun owners because the penalties concern only gun-related crime and place no restrictions on firearm ownership.

Extra-penalty laws are limited, however, in their potential to curb firearm violence. To reduce the number of crimes involving guns, such laws would have to discourage persons who would not be deterred by the already severe penalties for robbery and assault. Can the threat of additional punishment succeed? A robber might be deterred from using a gun if the penalty for robbery with a gun were several times greater than that of robbery without a gun. But punishment for robbery is already severe, at least as set forth in the statutes. In addition, a robber who carries a gun should not be punished so harshly that the additional penalty he risks if he injures or kills his victim is relatively small. It seems unlikely, therefore, that such laws have much more potential to deter gun use in robberies.

The issue of additional deterrence is also complicated for the crime of assault with a gun because the person who attacks someone with a gun is already risking the maximum punishment if the victim dies. A series of studies—the most notable by Colin Loftin and his associates at the University of Maryland—find that at best extra-punishment laws reduce gun-related crime by a small amount.

36   Extra punishment and place-and-manner regulation do have a role in comprehensive firearm control. But they cannot be used as the primary controls in a system that aspires to influence the death rate from violence substantially.

Laws attempting to discourage high-risk uses of firearms can be more effective when they are combined with selective ownership prohibitions. This second gun-control strategy seeks to deny high-risk users access to firearms. Usually the law considers high-risk users to include convicted felons, minors, adjudicated mental incompetents, drug addicts, and fugitives from justice. The theory is that high-risk users should not be allowed to own firearms, because the societal damage they cause through violence outweighs the social value of their interests in using guns legitimately.

The federal government and nearly every state prohibit some type of high-risk ownership. But many of these laws do not make a person prove his eligibility to own a gun before obtaining one. The ownership ban is supposed to be effective because the ineligible person will be subject to criminal penalties if caught possessing a firearm. Although such a law will not keep guns out of the hands of high-risk users who lie about their status, it is hoped high-risk users will be deterred by the threat of criminal punishment.

The ownership bans represent some improvement over simply passing stiffer penalties for gun-related crimes because the law attempts to separate the potential criminal from his gun before he commits a crime with it. And if such laws could reduce the number of gun owners by excluding the people subject to the prohibition, they would indeed reduce violence.

40   But it is no easy matter to keep guns away from a group of "bad guys" while allowing a larger group of "good guys" to own millions of them. Furthermore, bans are not very effective when the purchaser does not have to prove his eligibility as a gun purchaser. For instance, a convicted felon, who is prohibited from acquiring a gun under federal law, can easily obtain one if he is willing to lie about his record.

To prevent high-risk groups from freely obtaining firearms, many state and local governments now attempt to identify ineligible gun buyers before they acquire weapons. The screening system included in the Brady bill permits the police to determine whether a prospective gun purchaser has a criminal record. If the check turns up nothing, or even if it is not done, the purchaser can obtain the gun.

Screening systems are more effective than simple bans because screening prevents some high-risk users from obtaining guns even if they are willing to break the law. But because the screening systems mean additional costs and delays to all who wish to buy firearms, gun-owner groups usually oppose screening.

Screening systems and ownership prohibitions have a limited effect on homicides because most are committed by people who were not previously convicted of a felony and who therefore can purchase a gun legally. Still, screening systems are helpful to the extent that they keep firearms away from convicted felons and minors.

44   Many systems of owner screening suffer from another limitation. They affect only the purchase of weapons from commercial retailers. The measures do not apply to transactions between private citizens, who are continually selling and passing on some thirty-five million handguns. Prospective criminals can easily steal or purchase these guns.

To prevent the transfer of guns from private citizens to ineligible users, a few states require owners of firearms to register their weapons. In such schemes, owners must give information identifying each firearm they own. Gun accountability works like car registration, whereas owner screening is analogous to driver's licenses. But owner-licensing schemes will have a limited impact on violence because they leave a large arsenal of firearms to which potential criminals have easy access.

The dangers of widespread access to firearms can be alleviated, in part, by regulating guns that are particularly dangerous. Laws that limit the supply of high-risk weapons can complement the strategy of decreasing high-risk uses and users. Supply-reduction laws strive to make the most dangerous guns so scarce that potential criminals cannot obtain them easily. The laws are justified on the grounds that the harm caused by owning and using these particularly dangerous firearms is greater than the benefit, even in the non-criminal population.

Supply-reduction laws usually deny citizens the opportunity to own a high-risk firearm unless they prove a special need for the weapon or belong to an exempt group, such as the military or the police. The idea behind supply reduction is that gun-related violence will decrease significantly only if the firearms most often used in violence are not available to most people.

48   The first weapons singled out for high-risk classification were machine guns and sawed-off shotguns as specified in the National Firearms Act of 1934. More than three decades later federal law put special restrictions on destructive devices of military origin and forbade the importation of handguns that were classified as unsuitable for sporting purposes. Several current proposals are designed to prohibit civilian ownership of military assault weapons.

Some state and local governments also single out the handgun as a high-risk firearm and require special licenses to purchase handguns. The system in New York City is the most prominent example of this approach. City residents must demonstrate a special need for a handgun, whereas in permissive licensing systems only high-risk users are disqualified. Gun-control supporters frequently advocate restricting the supply of handguns on a nationwide basis.

But a decrease in handguns will reduce firearm violence only if other guns are not substituted. It has been difficult so far to determine what effect restrictive licensing has had. Cities and states that have such licensing schemes have found that long guns are not replacing handguns as crime weapons. But one reason for this lack of substitution is that the laws have failed, so far, to reduce the supply of handguns significantly.

It is all too easy to move guns across state and city borders from areas where guns are easily available to places where firearm supplies are regulated. Law enforcement agencies in Massachusetts and New York City have shown that, in jurisdictions that have tight controls, more than 80 percent of guns confiscated by police were originally acquired out of state. Current federal law is trying to inhibit the flow of firearms between states, but the problem remains substantial.

52   In most northeastern cities with restrictive handgun laws, the use of guns in violent crime is lower than that in other U.S. cities. In Washington, D.C., the Federal Bureau of Alcohol, Tobacco, and Firearms strictly enforced federal laws for nine months in 1976, and it reported success in reducing the flow of firearms. But the effort was not sustained. Washington currently experiences high rates of gun-related violence despite a restrictive handgun law.

Analysts do not have sufficient information to make predictions about the impact of gun control in the United States. Some have compared the United States with such countries as England, France, Germany, and Holland. They have discovered that nations with much lower rates of firearm ownership have lower rates of crimes involving guns. But these Western nations also have much lower rates of violent crimes that do not involve firearms.

Indeed, it is the very high rate of violence in the United States that makes the costs of gun use so large. The United States has both a "crime problem" and a "gun problem," and each exacerbates the other. No Western nation has ever instituted strict controls under conditions similar to those in the United States.

Although most citizens support such measures as owner screening, public opinion is sharply divided on laws that would restrict the ownership of handguns to persons with special needs. If the United States does not reduce handguns and current trends continue, it faces the prospect that the number of handguns in circulation will grow from thirty-five million to more than fifty million within fifty years. A national program limiting the availability of handguns would cost many billions of dollars and meet much resistance from citizens. These costs would likely be greatest in the early years of the program. The benefits of supply reduction would emerge slowly because efforts to diminish the availability of handguns would probably have a cumulative impact over time.

56   At the heart of the debate over handgun restrictions is a disagreement about the character of American life in the twenty-first century. Roughly half of Americans believe that strict handgun control is not worth the hardship of changing policy in the United States. They assume that the weapons can remain a part of American life for the indefinite future. But

just as many Americans see the removal of the current stockpile of handguns as a necessary down payment on the American future. They regard free availability of handguns as a severe threat to urban life. American policy on handgun control will ultimately depend on which of these attitudes prevails.

Personal Response

In his concluding paragraph, Zimring briefly summarizes two differing viewpoints in the handgun debate, based on different visions of America in the twenty-first century. Which vision of America's future do you have? Explain your answer.

Questions for Class or Small Group Discussion

1. In paragraph 2, Zimring asserts that both sides of the gun control issue have ignored facts. Summarize the facts Zimring believes people ignore. Why do you think people ignore these facts? What do you think would happen if people paid attention to them? Would it make any difference in the way people feel about gun control?

2. Zimring raises a number of questions and points out many areas that no one has investigated. Summarize the areas Zimring believes need more study, and discuss the potential effect you think such studies might have on the gun control controversy.

3. As Zimring notes, the issue of gun control is highly charged, with both those in favor of and those against strict regulations tending to argue with strong emotion. What is it about this issue that makes it so highly controversial?

4. Zimring says that the United States has both a "crime problem" and a "gun problem" (paragraph 54). What is the difference between those two problems, and how do they bear on the gun control issue?

5. Although Zimring remains neutral and sustains an objective tone, where do you think he stands on this issue? How can you tell? Where do you stand on the issue of gun control?

NATIVE SON

Nathan McCall

Nathan McCall was imprisoned for armed robbery at the age of 20, but after prison, he earned a college degree and became a journalist. He now writes for the Washington Post. *His autobiography,* Makes Me Wanna Holler: A Young Black Man in America *(1994), describes his youth, his time in prison, and his pivotal discovery of books. In this excerpt from* Makes Me Wanna Holler, *McCall describes the influence that reading Richard Wright's* Native Son *had on him while serving his prison term.*

There were moments in that jail when the confinement and heat nearly drove me mad. At those times, I desperately needed to take my thoughts beyond the concrete and steel. When I felt restless tension rising, I'd try anything to calm it. I'd slap-box with other inmates until I got exhausted, or play chess until my mind shut down. When all else failed, I'd pace the cellblock perimeter like a caged lion. Sometimes, other inmates fighting the temptation to give in to madness joined me, and we'd pace together, round and round, and talk for hours about anything that got our minds off our misery.

I eventually found a better way to relieve the boredom. I noticed that some inmates broke the monotony by volunteering for certain jobs in the jail. Some mopped the halls, and others worked in the dispensary or the kitchen. When the inmate librarian was released from jail, I asked for and was given his job. I began distributing books on the sixth floor as part of a service provided by the Norfolk Public Library. A couple of times a week, I pushed a cart to each cellblock and let inmates choose books and place orders for literature not on the cart. I enjoyed the library work. It gave me a chance to get out into the halls and walk around, and to stick my face to the screens on the floor windows and inhale fresh air.

Beyond the short stories I'd read in high school, I hadn't done much reading. Naturally, while working for the library, I leafed through more books than I normally would have. One day, shortly after starting the job, I picked up a book featuring a black man's picture on the cover. It was titled *Native Son,* and the author was Richard Wright. I leafed through a few pages in the front of the book, and couldn't put it down. The story was about a confused, angry young black man named Bigger Thomas, whose racial fears lead him to accidentally suffocate a white woman. In doing so, he delivers himself into the hands of the very people he despises and fears. I identified strongly with Bigger and the book's narrative. He was twenty, the same age as me. He felt the things I felt, and, like me, he wound up in prison. The book's portrait of Bigger captured all those conflicting feelings—restless anger, hopelessness, a tough facade among blacks and a deep-seated fear of whites—that I'd sensed in myself but was unable to express. Often, during my teenage years, I'd felt like Bigger—headed down a road toward a destruction I couldn't ward off, beaten by forces so large and amorphous that I had no idea how to fight back. I was surprised that somebody had written a book that so closely reflected my experiences and feelings.

I read that book every day, and continued reading by the dim light of the hall lamps at night, while everyone slept. On that early morning when I finished reading *Native Son,* which ends with Bigger waiting to go to the electric chair, I broke down and sobbed like a baby. There is one passage that so closely described how I felt that it stunned me. It is a passage where a lawyer is talking to Bigger, who has give up hope and is waiting to die:

> You're trying to believe in yourself. And every time you try to find a way to live, your own mind stands in the way. You know why that is? It's because others have said you were bad and they made you live in bad conditions. When a man hears that over and over and looks about him and sees that life is bad, he begins to doubt his own mind. His feelings drag him forward and his mind, full of what others say about him, tells him to go back. The job in getting people to fight and have faith is in making them believe in what life has made them feel, making them feel that their feelings are as good as others'.

After reading that, I sat up in my bunk, buried my face in my hands, and wept uncontrollably. I cried so much that I felt relieved. It was like I had been carrying those feelings and holding in my pain for years, keeping it pushed into the back of my mind somewhere.

I was unaccustomed to dealing with such deep feelings. Occasionally, I'd opened up to Liz, but not a lot. I was messed up inside, empty and afraid, just like Bigger. *Native Son* confirmed for me that my fears *weren't* imagined and that there were rational reasons why I'd been hurting inside.

I developed through my encounter with Richard Wright a fascination with the power of words. It blew my mind to think that somebody could take words that described exactly how I felt and put them together in a story like that. Most of the books I'd been given in school were about white folks' experiences and feelings. I spent all that time learning about damned white folks, like my reality didn't exist and wasn't valid to the rest of the world. In school, the only time we'd really focused on the lives of black people was during Black History Week, which they set aside for us to learn the same old tired stories about Booker T. Washington and a few other noteworthy, dead black folks I couldn't relate to. But in *Native Son* I found a book written about a plain, everyday brother like myself. That turned me on in a big way and inspired me to look for more books like that.

Before long, I was reading every chance I got, trying to more fully understand why my life and the lives of friends had been so contained and predictable, and why prison—literally—had become a rite of passage for so many of us. I found books that took me places I'd never dreamed I could travel to and exposed me to a range of realities that seemed as vast as the universe itself.

Once, after reading a book of poems by Gwendolyn Brooks, I wrote to her, not really expecting to receive a reply. She wrote me back and sent *i don't see the mention necessity to race*

me an inspirational paperback of hers titled *Aloneness.* I was thrilled that a well-known black writer like her had taken the time to respond to me.

I was most attracted to black classics, such as Malcolm X's autobiography. Malcolm's tale helped me understand the devastating effects of self-hatred and introduced me to a universal principle: that if you change your self-perception, you can change your behavior. I concluded that if Malcolm X, who had also gone to prison, could pull his life out of the toilet, then maybe I could, too.

Up to that point, I'd often wanted to think of myself as a baad nigger, and as a result, I'd tried to act like one. After reading about Malcolm X, I worked to get rid of that notion and replace it with a positive image of what I wanted to become. I walked around silently repeating to myself, "You are an intelligent-thinking human being; you are an intelligent-thinking human being . . . ," hoping that it would sink in and help me begin to change the way I viewed myself.

Malcolm X made his conversion through Islam. I'd seen Muslims selling newspapers and bean pies on the streets, but I didn't know anything about their religion. I was drawn to Christianity, mostly because it was familiar. I hadn't spent much time in church. It seemed that all they did in churches I'd been to was learn how to justify suffering at the hands of white folks. But now there were Christian ministers active at the jail, and I became interested. They came around about once a week and talked to inmates through the bars, prayed with them and read Scripture. I started talking with them about God and about life in general.

It wasn't hard to accept the possibility that there was a higher force watching over me. When I looked back at my life, I concluded that there had been far too many close calls—times when I could have offed somebody or gotten killed myself—for me to believe I had survived solely on luck. I wondered, *Why didn't that bullet strike Plaz in the heart when I shot him? Why didn't I pull the trigger on that McDonald's manager when he tried to get away? And why wasn't I on the corner the night my stick partners were shot?* Unable to come up with rational answers to those questions, I reasoned that God must have been pulling for me.

My interest in spiritual things also came from a need to reach out at my most powerless point and tap into a higher power, something beyond me and, at the same time, within me. I longed for a sense of wholeness that I had never known but sensed I was entitled to. I set out to learn more about my spiritual self, and I began exploring the Bible with other inmates who held Bible studies some nights in the cellblock.

At some point, I also got a library copy of the book—*As a Man Thinketh*—that Reverend Ellis had given me in college. I immediately understood what he had been trying to get across: that thinking should be an *active* process that, when cultivated, can change a person's behavior, circumstances, and, ultimately, his fate.

[marginal note:] here he shows the importance of positive thinking

[marginal note:] I decays with

[marginal note:] 5) here, McCall took what he learned in Malcolm X's book and applied it to his life.

[marginal note:] 6) The change didn't stop with attitude he developed an interest in Christianity and his spiritual life flourished as well #2

[marginal note:] CONTEMPLATES SEVERAL SITUATIONS WHERE God pulled for him such as

[marginal note:] then to next page

[handwritten margin note: here it seems as though he is ← reemphisizing his main point]

When I first started reading, studying, and reflecting on the information I got from books, I had no idea where it all might lead. Really, it didn't matter. I was hungry for change and so excited by the sense of awakening I glimpsed on the horizon that the only thing that mattered was that I had made a start. I often recited the Scripture that Reverend Ellis had given me to read before I was sentenced: "Everything works together for the good of those that love God, for those who are called according to His purpose." *If that's true, I thought, maybe I can get something positive out of this time in prison.* It sure didn't seem like it. But it made me feel better just thinking it might be possible.

[handwritten margin note: THE POSITIVE THING WAS IN his INTEREST IN THE READING and THE INEVITABLE CHANGE IN HIS LIFESTYLE]

Personal Response

Comment on your response to McCall's personal narrative.

Questions for Class or Small Group Discussion

1. Nathan McCall clearly attributes the turning point of his life to reading *Native Son*. Considering the problem of crime and violence in America, to what degree do you think reading books might be a solution?

2. Why do you think McCall was so moved by *Native Son?* What did it offer him that had been missing in his life? What did Christianity do for him?

[handwritten margin note: this SEEMS TO BE THE AUTHOR theory on why he started reading this but was reached in retrospect]

3. McCall believes that low self-esteem or self-hatred was largely responsible for his criminal behavior and that once he began to think positively about himself, he was able to turn his life around. Discuss the implications of that statement: Is it not true that many behavior problems stem from low self-esteem, regardless of race, class, or gender?

4. McCall believes that thinking positively helps people overcome any difficulty. Do you agree or disagree with that philosophy? Give examples to support your position.

WHAT'S WRONG WITH AMERICA AND CAN ANYTHING BE DONE ABOUT IT?

Wayne M. Barrett and Bernard Rowe

Wayne M. Barrett is associate editor of USA Today, *and Bernard Rowe, a British citizen, is a retired chartered accountant and textile industry consultant who lives in Valley Stream, New York. They wrote this essay, which details their opinions about causes and solutions for America's social ills, for* USA Today *magazine in 1994.*

It is a clichéd tale as old as the hills. The elder generation looks at society's youngsters and shakes its head in disappointed wonder and disgust. "When I was a kid . . . ," the admonishment inevitably begins. Today, however, the Establishment is in no position to criticize anyone or anything. If American youth is poisoned with skewed values and a lack of respect, one doesn't have to look very far to see where such behavior originates. Consider the following incidents:

- Unmarried pregnant teenage girls, no longer outcasts among their high school peers, instead are made cheerleaders and crowned homecoming queens by court order.
- The Chief Council for the President of the United States commits suicide and, before the body is even cold, Clinton Administration officials rifle through his office to remove all "incriminating" paperwork that related to the Chief Executive and First Lady.
- In 1993, New York Mets outfielder Vince Coleman threw an M-80 firecracker into a crowd of fans outside Dodger Stadium in Los Angeles. A handful of people, including a little girl, were injured in the explosion. In response to the heat the Mets took following this ugly and unforgivable occurrence, the club's Vice President of Baseball Operations, Gary Hunsicker, stated: "This incident didn't happen during working hours. It didn't happen in the clubhouse. It only involves the Mets because he is an employee of the Mets. This is Vince Coleman's incident. this is Vince Coleman's problem."
- "The Program," a Disney movie about a college football team, contained a scene in which a drunken player lies on a busy highway's dividing line, with traffic zooming past. A New Jersey man and Pennsylvania teenager, imitating the dangerous stunt, were killed, while a New York teenager was paralyzed. The film's producers and distributors were blamed. (The scene subsequently was removed from the film and videotape version.)
- A New York City mugger was awarded $4,300,000 by the state's Court of Appeals, which ruled that the arresting officer used too much force by shooting him. The U.S. Supreme Court refused to overturn the decision.
- A 1993 survey released by Who's Who Among American High School Students found that the nation's top secondary school pupils get their good grades the old-fashioned way—they cheat. Eighty percent said cheating was common at their schools, and 78% admitted to doing so themselves.
- The handshake, long the symbol of sportsmanship and good will, has been banned at the closing of school sporting events in California's Ventura County. It seems that some players were

spitting in their hands before shaking or slapping opponents in the face during the post-game ritual.

- Madison Square Garden Network announced John Andariese has covered the National Basketball Association since 1972. Recently, he compared the "old days" to contemporary times, where players "diss" each other with trash talk. Bench-clearing brawls often are the result. "It wasn't that long ago when respect came from winning the game; a series; a championship. Self-respect was about being part of the game; now it's a reason to be thrown out of the game.

  "Today, self-respect is so misplaced," he told the *New York Post.* "It's about putting your own feelings above all else. The individual's interests, including commercial interests, come before the team. . . . We've made heroes out of guys who do bad things; selfish things. The attention they receive is often equated with their ability to be entertaining, and that's when commercial opportunities present themselves."

- Fox Television, in a live update on the New York Rangers' 54-year quest for the Stanley Cup, cut to a reporter outside Madison Square Garden just before the opening faceoff of Game 5 of the finals. No sooner did the camera go on than a bunch of Big Apple rooters standing behind the reporter started chanting: "Let's Go Rangers! F— Vancouver!" Loudly, over and over again. Did Fox switch back to the studio? Of course not. Instead, the obscene chant came cascading right into the viewer's living room, over and over.

- Fallen football hero O.J. Simpson, wanted by the Los Angeles Police on a double-murder charge, took cops on a cross-county highway chase, captured live by news helicopter cameras. As O.J.'s car passed under an overpass, a group of revelers cheered him on, apparently delighted to be part of the action.

It all comes down to a breakdown in discipline and the advent of liberalism. The general idea is of total *laissez-faire*—the concept that everyone has a personal right to do whatever he or she wants. America has institutionalized selfishness.

People need not look out for anyone but themselves. My interest then becomes myself. I no longer have to worry about anyone else. When there is the understanding that people just live for themselves, when that attitude permeates a society, individuals attempt to protect themselves without regard for others. If they can't protect their rights in a civilized way, they're prepared to carry it through using a violent route, oftentimes with little or no regard for right and wrong, or how that action will impact upon themselves or those around them. After all, that person reasons, I'm free and have my own rights.

4   One can track this growth in liberalism with the breakdown of the great religions. The church taught a certain level of morals. "Thou shalt not steal" didn't come from the schools. Parents taught that. They took their kids to church, synagogue, or the mosque, and the youngsters were taught there that you mustn't kill; you mustn't do certain things. Along came liberalism, and no one bothered to teach those things anymore. This effectively has led to a bankrupt society. True, there are numerous social welfare programs, but, because Americans have let go of all other moral values, much of the good that these programs could have generated or produced has been lost.

There used to be corporal punishment in the schools. If teachers tried that today, they would be sued. If parents do it, they risk having the state take away their offspring. Accordingly, such discipline wasn't only given up in school, but in the home as well.

Everywhere, there is unbridled freedom bordering on license. Children are allowed to watch any television program, no matter what it is. By allowing kids unrestricted access to TV, the movies, and new computer information systems, they not only are being exposed to greater knowledge, they are being exposed to all of the world's ills without countervailing criticism. No one comes on at the end to say, "This is wrong; this should not have happened." No one tries to utilize the media to show youngsters a piece of news that might be startling and use it as a lesson, asking them: "What happens if . . . ?"

Not surprisingly, then, the nation's work ethic has suffered as well. Today, employees have rights against their employer, oftentimes out of balance with what rights should be. True, there was a time when employers exploited individuals, and the unions had to right major wrongs. People were made to work in a certain way that was beyond what was reasonable. The unions have come full circle and introduced a system whereby the employees almost control what they will do, what rights they have, and how much they will work.

8   Within the workplace, certain individuals may be motivated, but they often are held back by the others, who complain, "What are you doing? Why are you being so productive? If management sees this, it will want more from us." They then will use whatever means are at their disposal— violence not excepted—to stop the more productive workers. While the advent of unions brought back a certain sense of balance, it took away the decency of the individual, which no longer counts.

When individuals are institutionalized, it effectively removes a lot of their creativity and motivation. There is a tremendous loss, especially in the aspect of discipline. Doing what management wants is only one facet of discipline. The other is fulfilling your moral obligation when you take on a job or assignment.

That the work ethic has been weakened by Western society becomes particularly noticeable in considering newcomers to our shores. Immigrant labor has not been subject to generations of this kind of influence, so they come to this country willing to work, willing to give it their best. They feel they owe it. They have a job. They're determined to achieve for themselves, their families, and the relatives back home. They are willing to work hard, sacrificing and doing without for years.

These people never remove the yoke from their shoulders. They were born into societies where children, parents, and grandparents lived in one community. Children knew that, as they grew up, they had an obligation to take care of their parents. Today, as youngsters grow up and go to college, their main concern is for themselves and their own well-being.

12   Marriage is another dying institution. Today, many people decide to live together to see if they're compatible. Does that produce the best results? Obviously not. "If we live together," the attitude goes, "why should I commit myself? Why should I assume responsibility? Indeed, why should I give of myself more than I need to so that I can still have the physical contact my desires require without having to give a financial or moral commitment to just one person or to the children who may come from this relationship? I can come and go as I please. If someone better arrives on the scene, I can go with him or her."

Such an attitude inevitably leads to a lack of discipline and responsibility for another. If children see their parents act this way, why should they be any different? When they go to school, why should they care about their friends? Why do they have to worry that other kids may be hurt? To take it a step further, why would it worry them if they hurt other youngsters?

Meanwhile, lawsuit mania has gripped America. The phenomenon goes back to the same issue: I have a right! I'm entitled to sue for anything and everything that may impinge upon that right, no matter what society's needs.

Take the Rodney King case. This is a man who everyone agrees required force to be subdued after a high-speed auto chase, but excessive force was used by the Los Angeles police. There was a wrong committed here, but remember, King was in the wrong, too. Conceding that he had inflicted upon him a certain amount of pain, he did deserve something for his suffering. He should have been given a small amount of financial compensation, but not a seven-digit settlement.

16   This is a man who in his lifetime never dreamed of earning that kind of money or had been deprived of anything resembling that sort of income. He probably is way better off having been subjected to physical abuse at the hands of the police. That doesn't justify the wrong, but neither does it justify a multi-million-dollar lawsuit. It's not an issue of civil rights. The system has been made to look stupid. The courts and lawyers should be viewed with a certain amount of integrity. Once respect has disappeared, so has the sense of honesty.

Now, consider the impact of the legal system on physicians. Much of what the medical profession does today simply is to avoid lawsuits, because it's a "cover yourself just in case" kind of world. This is the price society pays for allowing malpractice lawyers to reach for the moon. The measure of compensation should be related to what is right and what is wrong. Instead, the dollar amounts are astronomical. In the end, society pays. When individuals who have observed the system at work find themselves with the potential for a claim, however spurious, they say, "Well, it's my turn to exploit it now." There are bumper stickers that sum it up quite succinctly: "Hit me; I need the cash." That's not what society should be all about.

The Drug Scourge

The drug problem in America also can be traced back to a lack of discipline, lack of education, and lack of knowledge between right and wrong. Again there is the attitude: I have rights. I want to take drugs. Meanwhile, the government says they must be outlawed. A tremendous amount of resources have been sunk into the war on drugs, with no victory in sight. As a result of interdictment efforts, however, drugs are becoming more and more expensive, and more and more people are turning to crime to finance their drug habits. One way of looking at it is the government has made criminals out of noncriminals.

When addicts kill for drug money, people act perplexed and ask, "How on Earth did this happen?" Actually, the surprise is that it doesn't happen more often. As the situation worsens, society does what it absolutely shouldn't—legislate against its own people.

20   In a society pervasive with so many freedoms, government simply can't say, with regard to drugs, "No, you can't do what you want." It hasn't worked and won't work. The easy solution is to legalize drugs. There's a strong case for that. Fundamentally, the price of drugs would drop to next to nothing. Sell it like alcohol and cigarettes, with a label: "Warning—this stuff may kill you." The criminals peddling it will be out of business overnight. The people addicted to it no longer will have to commit crimes to obtain it. If they want to rot their bodies and minds, or even kill themselves, let them.

Making drugs illegal recalls an old Hebrew saying: "Stolen waters are sweet." If you tell people they can't have drugs, especially in a *laissez-faire* society such as ours, the response will be, "I'll show you what I can have." Yet, if you were to say, "Take this poison," people would respond, "Are you crazy?"

Here is where education can be so valuable. Morality can be introduced into many subjects. So can the concepts of quality, decency, right, and wrong. Programs can be designed so that almost every teacher and every subject can introduce moral values.

In the old days, a child was told, "Sit here and pay attention." If a student dozed off or talked during lessons, there was instant retribution. To some extent, such a system was shown to have been very successful, though many children failed to achieve their full potential. Nevertheless, it certainly gave kids a better education than they're getting today.

24   Contemporary students, as they grow older and become more mature, discover that much of school has been a waste of time. They didn't learn very much, and thus have very little respect for teachers. Think what's going to happen when they have children to send to school. Can they convincingly tell their kids, "You must respect your teacher"? Absolutely not. Yet, the system doesn't change, except to give children more rights and greater freedom, and only in the negative form.

What is the price society pays?—criminals in the classroom. Never before did children come to school armed in order to protect themselves. Walk the streets of New York and you will see thousands of kids there on a normal school day. These youngsters have grown up with zero discipline. What happens when they get older?

In the past, the military system, while far from perfect, accomplished two things: It made people live a disciplined life and took them off the streets. American society has abandoned another of the fortresses of discipline. For whatever bad or good influence it had, the military at least showed people they couldn't do whatever they wanted. It also often gave them a vocation.

Discipline and decency are disappearing from the family as well. So much used to take place within the network of the family, including the education of the children. Parents sat down with them and went through their homework, helped them with assignments, and saw to it that they were progressing. Today, too many parents are jealous of their time. Watching a favorite TV show becomes more important than helping with their offspring's homework.

28   Children today seem to be kept only out of a grudging obligation. Parents will send their kids off to a private high school if they can afford it, or, in the summer, to camp. Look at it from the youngsters' viewpoint. They no longer see the constant cohesive unit of the family. On the contrary, they remember that their father sent them money and took care of their economic needs. The child comes to regard the economic thread as what is important. "My father was busy chasing the dollar. He gave me food. He sent me to camp. But other than that, I didn't really need him. I didn't need my mother, either." When there's a substitute for everything and children don't see the need for the family unit, it is an unreasonable expectation that they, in turn, will grow up and create a proper family unit.

Children very quickly perceive the way adults are. Parents who have no time for their kids and show no interest in them, who don't give up their time to help others, can't expect their children to grow up and do that. As a result, society winds up with a next generation whose main interests are themselves. They are liberated, free, have rights they are entitled to, and only have to make sure they will have means to provide for themselves. In their old age, they will not be able to depend on their children, anymore than their parents can depend on them.

A Revolution Is Needed

There has to be a total revolution in this country in attitudes and outlook. If we don't come up with a quick, solid remedy, some very serious unwanted changes will take place, almost as great as what happened in the Soviet Union. When the American Dream bursts, there's no predicting exactly where the pieces will fall.

Most of the standard remedies already have been tried. We have raised and lowered taxes, adjusted interest rates, added police officers in an effort to promote law and order, poured more money into the educational system, and interdicted the traffic of narcotics, even attempting to impede their flow at the source by shipping drug enforcement agents overseas. The net effect has been minor.

32   Some success stories can be demonstrated, but, overall, it's hard to dispute that the U.S. is a nation in decline. Fundamentally, there's a perception by most Americans that we are worse off than we were, and our hopes for the future are dim. Gone are the days when we looked to the future and saw the Great American Promise.

The basic ingredient for a happy society is that anyone who wishes to work should be able to find a job. In the U.S. today, unemployment is rampant, layoffs are all too common, and jobs flow overseas. One problem is lack of productivity by American workers.

Industry, struggling to survive in the face of cheap foreign competition, has changed its methods. Massive layoffs have resulted, and a healthier type of American company is emerging. "Leaner and meaner" is the cliché. Industry can look forward to reduced costs, and therefore be more competitive.

Government, meanwhile, remains extremely wasteful, maintaining multiple employees for each one required in industry. The numbers range all the way from 25 to 50, depending on which survey one chooses to read or believe. Even in the face of all the cuts in the private sector, there's been virtually no drastic actions by the Federal, state, or city government. They all remain overbloated. Elected officials are afraid to antagonize the army of civil servants and refuse to reduce their own staffs.

36   The public does not have confidence in the government or in the economy. People don't have the confidence that the future will be brighter. The key to reversing this malaise is that good jobs must be provided. How this can be accomplished is no secret. Too much of the employment in this country has been lost to foreigners. The U.S. exported many of its jobs through various government policies, often in the name of helping developing countries. At the same time, it allowed tremendous amounts of imports, often undercutting American companies.

America has a great history of charity, and many countries of the world are grateful, but the U.S. is in a time of crisis. The way to ensure that America will be here tomorrow to continue its tradition of decency and kindness is to make sure that many of those jobs exported overseas are returned home.

How can that be accomplished? The simplest way, one guaranteed to produce an almost immediate effect, is by imposing strict import controls. The U.S. should turn to its major trading partners—Taiwan, Korea, Japan, and China, which account for a very large part of the trade deficit—and say to them, "You may export into the U.S., dollar for dollar, what you purchase from America." It is ludicrous to think that the U.S. should allow a two- or three-to-one ratio of imports to exports. Under the dollar-for-dollar proposal, there would be an immediate shortage of many products and some short-term price increases. However, people can survive without a new camera this month or maintain their cars for another six months—or purchase an American car—until things stabilize.

The U.S. would have to maintain this policy for a minimum of three years, then ease off in increments of no greater than 10%. Then, the manufacturers and entrepreneurs will feel secure in the knowledge that, if they produce goods in this country, they will have a local market and potential for export. They will be willing to invest in the necessary plant and machinery—almost immediately—to manufacture goods. Meanwhile, foreign companies should be encouraged with incentives to introduce more and more production in the U.S. A new flow of jobs will be created within an extremely short period of time.

40   One important side effect may be a reduction in crime. American youths—especially minorities—face high rates of unemployment, poor prospects, and a lack of interest in life. Providing them with reasonably paying productive jobs can help make them feel they are valued members of society.

Next is the issue of taxation. Practically speaking, Americans don't like paying taxes and, above all, feel that much of what they pay is wasted. So long as there's mismanagement in government, there is resentment on the part of taxpayers. People recognize the need to finance national and local services, so they are prepared to pay, but there's the general sense out there—and not without justification—that the U.S. taxpayer isn't getting value for the buck.

Another major irritant is that the burden of taxation does not seem to be shared by all. There is massive avoidance of taxation in many industries, and the government doesn't even want to admit the scale of avoidance because it's embarrassingly large. People accept the idea of being taxed if everyone shares the burden. One way is to generate a taxation system that virtually encompasses the entire country. Take certain industries and tax them at source. This is not a value-added tax, which runs through all the multiple stages of production and becomes very expensive to collect. The U.S. has to look for something that is simple, efficient, and easy to collect.

For example, the utility companies could be taxed very highly. Abolish income tax altogether and corporation taxes because they require massive administration, massive coflection systems, massive policing and effectively turn the nation into a country of crooks. Under the new plan, every electric bill would be taxed heavily. Oil, if it's imported, would be taxed at the ports; domestic oil wells, at the source. There's no reason Americans can't pay up to $4 a gallon for gas as they do in many European countries. Everyone would be caught up in the net because nobody can avoid electricity or phone bills. Among the benefits would be a very simple method of collection. A far smaller IRS would emerge.

44   Right now, America is a nation in crisis, so all the old rules are off. An enormous number of government employees no longer would be necessary. Within industry, a tremendous amount of money is spent to assist in the collection of taxes. There would be substantial savings there. As government expenses go down, revenues could be rebudgeted.

As for the poor, government now pays out a substantial amount in welfare and other social programs. Instead of money, services should be provided. It would be a cleaner system, with much less fraud. A lot of the people on such programs have been shown to take the money and use it in ways that don't necessarily benefit their welfare.

Undoubtedly, a system that sucks in the needy, while failing to show them a way out, is inherently flawed. Temporary and short-term help must be axiomatic to the system. All who enter must be encouraged to leave as soon as possible. Life within the system can not be made more comfortable than outside it. There must be an end to the credo: "We are better off on welfare than at work." To achieve this, all citizens—on welfare and off—should be issued identity cards with photos. Such a card would be required in all dealings with officialdom as well as the maintenance of bank accounts, financial securities, homes, and other assets and liabilities. In order to secure welfare benefits, a potential recipient would have to submit to a means test to be verified by the identity card. If, and while, assets remain below established criteria, appropriate benefits would be granted, and only for that period.

These benefits would be distributed on community campuses, as it is vitally important to establish appropriate homes to house welfare recipients. All beneficiaries would be required to live on campus and to participate in maintaining it based on their abilities. The campus would be sparsely, yet adequately, furnished and would provide food prepared in a communal kitchen. The cash allowance would be extremely limited, sufficient for only the barest of necessities (which, for the most part, already would be supplied on campus). There would be counselors available to assist with interviews and appropriately sponsored job training. Travel to and from such locations would be arranged by the counselor social workers using vouchers instead of cash.

48   This system would be managed by appropriate community boards. Its members—all volunteers—would be drawn from the community, industry, local government, clergy, and the judiciary. The government would pay 50% of the cost, the balance to be covered by regional utilities and local donations.

It's Time to Bring Back the Draft

What should be done about the military? The first thing to do is forget about the idea of a volunteer army. The U.S. must reintroduce the draft. The purpose of conscription is two-fold. There is an immediate problem with a generation that has grown up without discipline. The best thing America can do about it is to draft youths aged 17 to 21 for a period of 18 months to two years. Run them through military training and teach them what they didn't learn in school. The military could be used to handle works projects. After a certain number of months in initial basic training, a schedule could be set up allocating perhaps two days a week for military training, four days for production, and one day off.

The military also could be used for policing. If an area is out of control, like Los Angeles during the Rodney King riots, call in the Army. In New York, for example, the police don't have the numbers to cope with street crime. Hire the military. Have a soldier on every corner 24 hours a day. See how anxious street thugs are to mug someone when they see an armed soldier standing on the corner.

Congress has passed numerous law enforcement bills, many calling for more prisons, which already are draining too much revenue. Obviously, there is a great need to put away people who are dangerous to society. The numbers being seen now, though, in terms of percentage of the general population in prison, is very high, and they are costing society a fortune.

52   America's criminal justice system has several significant flaws. It fails to convey the impression that justice is done, that it is swift, and that it acts as a deterrent to potential perpetrators. Speed is essential to an effective system of justice. "Delay defeats equity" is a long-held maxim of law. It also is vital to remember the victim. At present, virtually no effort is made to compensate the victim. Adoption of the following will improve the situation:

- Abolish the jury system. It is time-consuming, expensive, allows for clever manipulation of jurors by attorneys, and suggests that, having heard and understood the evidence, judges are incapable of rendering a fair verdict.

- Establish a court of petty/small crimes that can deal swiftly with many of the lesser cases in a manner similar to small claims court.
- Require mandatory sentencing for violent crimes without parole.
- Institute capital punishment for all deliberate murders. A death sentence should be subject to immediate priority appeals and then followed right away by execution. Keeping inmates on death row for years is immoral, cruel, and wasteful.
- Enact caning or birching for thieves. Besides being a just punishment, it will avoid clogging up the prison system.
- Make prison labor tougher. Prisoners should be made to work long and hard as part of their sentence. The soft and easy jobs presently offered do not make jail a place to avoid at any cost. The proceeds from this labor should pay for prisoner upkeep, and the balance should be turned over to crime victims as partial compensation.
- Community service sentences need to be stricter. Whenever criminals today are sentenced to community service, it usually means some cushy job with the Red Cross or similar agency. Let community service provide meaningful work for a city or state agency, such as sanitation, road repair, graffiti scrubbing, etc. Any wages earned would help compensate victims.
- Lower the age for adult crime. Anyone 14 years old and up should be treated as an adult. Children below that age should be limited to a flogging (under appropriate medical supervision).

America needs a better way to educate the nation's youth; a revamped military system; vastly altered social services; a slimmed down, more efficient bureaucracy; a stronger, more caring family unit; and a revitalized economy with no income taxes that nevertheless generates enough revenue to erase the deficit almost overnight. Will any of it happen, and, if it did, would society's ills be cured? If America is to be saved, we must try.

Personal Response

What is your response to Barrett and Rowe's assertion in their first paragraph that "American youth is poisoned with skewed values and a lack of respect"?

Questions for Class or Small Group Discussion

1. Discuss the authors' contention that America's abandonment of decency and discipline and its adoption of liberalism have led to an "institutionalized selfishness" (paragraph 2). Do you think their examples in

the opening section are ample evidence of "skewed values and a lack of respect"? Do you agree that Americans are, in general, selfish? How do Barrett and Rowe connect this allegation with the gun-control issue?

2. Summarize the complaints Barrett and Rowe lodge against American society. Which ones do you agree with? Which ones do you disagree with? Explain your answers.

3. What do you think of the solution Barrett and Rowe propose for the drug problem in America? Do you favor legalization of drugs? If so, would you legalize all or just some drugs? Explore the pros and cons of this issue.

4. Do you agree with Barrett and Rowe that "there has to be a total revolution in this country in attitudes and outlook" (paragraph 30)? Explain why or why not. Do you agree with the changes they call for, or would you suggest others?

5. How do you feel about Barrett and Rowe's proposal that America bring back the draft and the uses to which they propose putting the military?

6. What do you think of the solutions Barrett and Rowe propose for the high crime rate in this country? Which would you be in favor of adopting? Which seem extreme to you?

BORN TO RAISE HELL?

Dennis Overbye

Dennis Overbye is a writer who contributes to Time *magazine. This piece was written for a regular* Time *feature entitled "Essay," a weekly forum for writers to express their views on timely, often controversial, topics. Overbye responds here to scientists' search for a gene to account for violent or criminal behavior.*

Some of us, it seems, were just born to be bad. Scientists say they are on the verge of pinning down genetic and biochemical abnormalities that predispose their bearers to violence. An article in the journal *Science* last summer carried the headline EVIDENCE FOUND FOR A POSSIBLE "AGGRESSION" GENE. Waiting in the wings are child-testing programs, drug manufacturers, insurance companies, civil rights advocates, defense attorneys and anxious citizens for whom the violent criminal has replaced the beady-eyed communist as the boogeyman. Crime thus joins homosexuality, smoking, divorce, schizophrenia, alcoholism, shyness, political liberalism, intelligence, religiosity, cancer and blue eyes among the many aspects of human life for which it is claimed that biology is destiny. Physicists have been pilloried for years for this kind of reductionism, but in biology it makes everybody happy: the scientists and pharmaceutical companies expand their domain; politicians have "progress" to point to; the smokers, divorcés and serial killers get to blame their problems on biology, and we get the satisfaction of knowing they are sick—not like us at all.

Admittedly, not even the most rabid sociobiologists contend that babies pop out of the womb with a thirst for bank robbing. Rather, they say, a constellation of influences leads to a life of crime, among them poverty, maleness and a trait known as "impulsivity," presumably caused by bad brain chemistry, caused in turn by bad genes. What, you may ask, is impulsivity? The standard answer tends to involve people who can't control their emotions or who get into bar fights. A study conducted in Finland found that men so characterized tend to be deficient in the brain hormone serotonin—one of several chemical messengers that transmit signals between nerve cells. In another study researchers found that the men in a Dutch family with a history of male violence seemed to lack the ability to break down certain neurotransmitters, including serotonin, that build up in the brain during flight-or-fight situations. Couple this with persistent statistical surveys purporting to show that criminals tend to run in families and you have the logic behind the Violence Initiative dreamed up a couple of years ago by the Department of Health and Human Services, which included research to discover biological markers that could be used to distinguish violence-prone children as early as age five. Any doubts about the potential for abuse in such a program were erased when Frederick Goodwin, then director of the Alcohol, Drug Abuse and Mental Health Administration, lapsed into a comparison of inner-city youth to murderous oversexed monkeys during a speech about the initiative. "Maybe," he said, "it isn't just the careless use of the word when people call certain areas of certain cities jungles . . ." Amid the ensuing outcry, the National Institutes of Health canceled its financial support for a planned conference on the biology of violence. Now, however, bolstered by a cautious approval from the National Academy of Sciences, the conference is back on, and Goodwin is head of the National Institute of Mental Health.

Science marches on. Or does it? The whole affair is uncomfortably reminiscent—as the scientists admit—of the 1960s, when researchers theorized that carriers of an extra Y, or male, chromosome were predisposed to criminality, or of earlier attempts to read character from the bumps on people's skulls. As any doctor who ever testified for a tobacco company in one of those trials knows, the statistical association of two things, like smoking and cancer, or guns and murders, does not necessarily imply cause and effect. We know too little about the biochemical cocktail that is the brain, and all too much about how stigmatized children live down to our expectations.

4   Being a great fan of science, I'm all in favor of more research, testing, poking, drugging, jailing, genetic therapy, amniocentesis, just as soon as

someone can give me a scientific definition of impulsivity, one that provides, say, a cultural- and color-blind distinction between a spirited child and an impulsive one. If bar fights are the criteria, it's nice to think that a simple blood test might have spared us the antics of people like Billy Martin or George Steinbrenner.

My real complaint is that the violence initiative doesn't go nearly far enough. Some laboratory should be looking for the racism gene, or the homophobia gene. Goodwin was right; the inner city is a jungle. But so are the corporation, the newsroom and the White House staff. The language of trial lawyers or bond traders in full testosterone fury is as bloodcurdling as any mugger's. When it comes to social carnage, the convenience-store stickup can't compare with a leveraged buyout, trickling-down unemployment, depression, anger, alcoholism, divorce, domestic abuse and addiction. I'd like to see white men with suspenders and cellular phones tested for the greed gene. The genomes of presidential candidates should be a matter of public record.

I'm a middle-aged white man as afraid as anyone else of being not quite alone on a dark New York City street, and I've stared into the stone-cold eyes of a mugger while he told me, "It's just you and me." When you hear those words, it's too late to fight the war on crime. The rush to define criminals as sick obscures an uncomfortable truth about our society, which is that crime and violence often pay handsomely. Just ask the conquistadores, the Menendez brothers, Oliver North or the comfortable and respected descendants of bootleggers and slaveholders. Ask the purveyors of the most violent television program in recent memory: the Gulf War.

Personal Response

What is your opinion of the scientific search for a gene that may be responsible for criminal behavior?

Questions for Class or Small Group Discussion

1. Why do you think Overbye is so bothered by the possibility of isolating a gene responsible for criminal behavior? State in your own words what Overbye's objection to this kind of research is.

2. Do you think Overbye has a valid point when he asks for "a scientific definition of impulsivity . . . that provides, say, a cultural- and color-blind distinction between a spirited child and an impulsive one" (paragraph 4)? What is his point here?

3. Discuss this statement: "We know too little about the biochemical cocktail that is the brain, and all too much about how stigmatized children live down to our expectations" (paragraph 3).

4. Respond to this sentence in Overbye's concluding paragraph: "The rush to define criminals as sick obscures an uncomfortable truth about our society, which is that crime and violence often pay handsomely." What do you think of the examples he gives to illustrate his remark?

5. Volunteer to find out if the National Institutes of Health finally held the conference on the biology of violence (paragraph 2). If it did take place, try to find a summary of what went on during the conference and report back to your class.

Perspectives on Criminal Behavior

Suggestions for Synthesis

1. Discuss the relationship between what Nathan McCall writes in "Native Son" about the influence of books and spirituality on him and what Wayne M. Barrett and Bernard Rowe find wrong with America in "What's Wrong with America and Can Anything Be Done About It?"

2. Conduct a classroom forum on the problem of inner city violence. In preparation, decide what aspects of the problem you want to address in the forum and which perspectives you will examine the problem from. Consider including the perspectives of law enforcement officers, sociologists, behavioral scientists, educators, and social workers. For a writing assignment, examine one aspect of the problem of inner city violence and offer solutions for it, taking into consideration two or more of the essays in this chapter.

3. Select one specific aspect of the problem of crime and violence in America, as addressed in two or more of the essays in this chapter. Write a paper assessing the seriousness of the problem and offering possible solutions, to the degree that solutions are possible.

Additional Writing Topics

1. Argue for or against the legalization of certain drugs, such as marijuana.

2. Argue for or against reinstating the draft in America.

3. Argue for or against stricter gun control laws, taking into consideration Franklin E. Zimring's comments in "Firearms, Violence, and Public Policy."

4. If you have ever been inspired by a book or an article in a magazine, write about that experience. Describe your feelings and explain how or why you were moved or influenced by the writing.

5. Read Richard Wright's *Native Son* (see Nathan McCall's piece entitled "Native Son"), and write a report in which you summarize the book, evaluate its strengths and weaknesses, and state your personal reaction to it.

6. Respond to the allegation Wayne M. Barrett and Bernard Rowe make in "What's Wrong with America and Can Anything Be Done About It?" that American youth are disrespectful and lack values.

7. Argue in support of or against Dennis Overbye's position on the issue of scientific research to discover a genetic cause for violence.

Research Topics

1. Since Franklin E. Zimring's "Firearms, Violence, and Public Policy" was written, the Brady Bill has been passed into law. Research the Brady Bill by locating follow-up studies or periodical articles commenting on its effectiveness. Then arrive at your own conclusions about the bill, supporting your position with evidence from your research.

2. Research recent statistics on serious crimes such as armed robbery, rape, murder, and assault with a deadly weapon and argue ways to reduce the rate of violent crime in America.

3. Research the Violence Initiative of the Department of Health and Human Services, which Dennis Overbye criticizes in "Born to Raise Hell?" Summarize its goals, its current status, and what people have said about it as you explain your own opinion of its usefulness as a way to control violent behavior.

CHAPTER 12

GENDER

Many people use the word gender *interchangeably with the word* sex, *but the two have different meanings. Sex is a biological category, with a person's sex— whether male or female—determined genetically. On the other hand, gender refers to the socially constructed set of expectations for behavior based on one's sex. Masculinity and femininity are gender constructs whose definitions vary and change over time and with different cultures or groups within cultures. What is considered appropriate and even desirable behavior for men and women in one culture may be strongly inappropriate in another. Within American culture, definitions of masculinity and femininity have changed over time but continue to be shaped by a number of influences, such as parental expectations, peer pressure, and media images. While we are born either male or female, most of us learn to behave in ways consistent with our society's expectations for our sex.*

Fairy tales and children's stories are ways in which a culture transmits messages about gender differences and how boys and girls are expected to act. Many older, traditional tales portray rather narrow and often negative possibilities for females, in contrast to males, who have more choices and more freedom than females. In "Cinderella: Saturday Afternoon at the Movies," Louise Bernikow demonstrates one way of reading a fairy tale for its messages about femininity, especially the way in which the story encourages female rivalry to gain male favor. As you read her analysis of the classic fairy tale "Cinderella," try to recall your own fantasies when you heard or read it as a child. Think about other fairy tales as well, and consider whether you agree with Bernikow's reading of the messages they convey to boys and girls.

In a vein similar to Bernikow's, Robert Bly, in the excerpt from his book Iron John *reprinted here, also uses a fairy tale, but he is interested in American culture's definition of masculinity, not femininity. Bly uses a tale to introduce his theory that men need to reawaken the archetypal "wild man" that he believes lies buried inside all men through such activities as beating drums, chanting, and dancing. Male or female, you will probably find his viewpoint intriguing, whether you agree with it or not. As you read Bly's interpretation of one fairy tale, think about other fairy tales and what they suggest about masculinity. Consider also whether you agree with Bly's theory of the "wild man." Following Bly's piece is an essay by Alan Buczynski, who takes exception to Robert Bly's theories about American males. In "Iron Bonding," Buczynski disagrees by countering the prevailing belief, popularized by Bly, that men cannot communicate deep feelings to one another. As you read, consider whether you agree with Buczynski or with Bly, or if you think both make valid observations about the nature of masculinity and men's capacity to care deeply.*

Lois Gould creates her own modern fairy tale in "X: A Fabulous Child's Story," which plays on many of the traditional sex-role expectations about appropriate behavior for boys and girls. Her story about what happens when one set of parents refuses to reveal the sex of their child delightfully highlights the way in which most of us have very clear assumptions about what a child can or cannot do in terms of behavior, dress, talent, and potential solely on the basis of the child's sex. Before you read Gould's essay, jot down a list of characteristics you associate with males and do the same for females. Try to recall your early childhood, the toys you played with, the games you played, and the other children you played with. Then see how many of the sex-role stereotypes Gould identifies in her fantasy are true to your own experiences.

The chapter concludes with a piece that will likely provoke as heated a classroom discussion as any of the other readings in this chapter, for John Leland, in "Bisexuality Emerges as a New Sexual Identity," reports on the growing population of men and women who define themselves as neither straight nor gay but bisexual. The essay addresses the whole idea of sexual and gender identity and explains why some people have chosen to blur or ignore the differences between the sexes. Try to keep an open mind as you read the piece, and then consider to what extent you understand the viewpoint of the young people Leland reports on.

CINDERELLA: SATURDAY AFTERNOON AT THE MOVIES

Louise Bernikow

Louise Bernikow is a writer whose subjects center on women's culture. Her personal essays reflecting on women's psychology, women's friendships, and the ties between women are collected in Among Women *(1980), from which this piece is taken. Here, she recalls movies and fairy tales from her childhood and their implication for fostering potentially destructive behaviors in females.*

> *No, Cinderella, said the stepmother,*
> *you have no clothes and cannot dance.*
> *That's the way with stepmothers.*
>   *(Anne Sexton, "Cinderella")*

> *Turn and peep, turn and peep,*
> *No blood is in the shoe,*
> *The shoe is not too small for her,*
> *The true bride rides with you.*
>   *(Grimms'* Cinderella)

I begin with a memory of movies and mother, a dark theatre and a Saturday afternoon. In a miasma of Walt Disney images, Bambi burning and Snow White asleep, the most memorable is "Cinderella." I carry her story with me for the rest of my life. It is a story about women alone together and they are each other's enemies. This is more powerful as a lesson than the ball, the Prince or the glass slipper. The echoes of "Cinderella" in other fairy tales, in myth and literature, are about how awful women are to each other. The girl onscreen, as I squirm in my seat, needs to be saved. A man will come and save her. Some day my Prince will come. Women will not save her; they will thwart her. There is a magical fairy godmother who does help her, but this, for me, has no relation to life, for the fairy is not real and the bad women are. The magical good fairy is a saccharine fluff.

There are two worlds in the Cinderella cartoon, one of women, one of men. The women are close by and hostile, the men distant and glittering. Stepsisters and stepmother are three in one, a female battalion allied against Cinderella. The daughters are just like their mother. All women are alike. Lines of connection, energy fields, attach sisters to mother, leaving Cinderella in exile from the female community at home.

Father is far off. On film, neither he nor the Prince has much character. Father is her only tie, her actual blood tie, but the connection does her no good. Daddy is King in this world; I cannot keep Daddy and King apart in my memory. My own father was as far off, as full of authority, as surrounded by heraldry, the trumpets of fantasy, to me, to my mother. King Daddy.

4   The Prince is rich and handsome. Rich matters more than handsome. The girl among the cinders, dressed in rags, will escape—I am on her side, I want her to escape, get away from the cinders and the awful women—because the Prince will lift her out. The world of the Prince is the world of the ball, music, fine clothes and good feeling. Were everything to be right at home, were the women to be good to one another and have fun together, it would not be sufficient. The object is the ball, the Prince, the big house, the servants. Class mobility is at stake. Aspiration is being titillated.

To win the Prince, to be saved, requires being pretty. All the women care about this. Being pretty is the ticket and because Cinderella is pretty, the stepmother and stepsisters want to keep her out of the running. There is no other enterprise. Cinderella does not turn up her nose and hide in a corner reading a book. Being pretty, getting to the ball, winning the Prince is the common ground among the women. What we have in common is what keeps us apart.

Cinderella must be lonely. Why, I wonder, doesn't she have a friend? Why doesn't she go to school? Why doesn't her father tell the awful women to stop? A hurt and lonely girl, with only a prince to provide another kind of feeling. Why doesn't she run away? Why can't the situation be changed? It is as though the house they live in is the only world, there is not other landscape. Women are always in the house, being awful to each other.

Magic. Cinderella has a fairy godmother who likes her and wants her to be happy. She gives the girl beautiful clothes. She doesn't have to instruct Cinderella or give her advice about how to waltz or how to lift her skirt or even give her directions to the palace. Only the clothes and the accoutrements—and a prohibition about coming home at midnight. A powerful woman who wants Cinderella to be pretty and successful in the social world. I know, at whatever age it is that I watch this story unfold, that the mother beside me is not the woman on the screen. Her feelings on such matters are, at best, mixed up. She is not so powerful.

8   I am stirred and confused by the contrast between bad and good women and the way it all seems to revolve around the issue of being pretty. Some women are hostile and thwarting, others enabling and powerful. The stepmother hates Cinderella's prettiness; the fairy godmother adorns it. I look sideways at my mother, trying to decide which kind of woman she is, where she stands on the business of pretty. Often, she braids my hair and settles me into polka dot, parades me before my beaming father. It is good to be pretty. Yet, onscreen, it is bad to be pretty— Cinderella is punished for it. In the enterprise of pretty, other women are your allies and your enemies. They are not disinterested. The heat around the issue of pretty, the urgency and intensity of it, is located among the women, not the men, at whom it is supposedly aimed. Luckily, we move on to the ball and the lost slipper.

This is one of the oldest and most often-told stories, varying significantly from one version to another, one country to another, one period to another. What appears on movie theatre screens or television on Saturday afternoons comes from as far away as China, as long ago as four hundred years. Each teller, each culture along the way, retained some archetypal patterns and transformed others, emphasized some parts of the story, eradicated others. Disney took his version of Cinderella from one written down by a Frenchman named Perrault in the seventeenth century. Perrault's is a "civilized" version, cleaned up, dressed up and given several pointed "lessons" on top of the original material.

Many of the details about fashionability that we now associate with the story come from Perrault. His has the atmosphere of Coco Chanel's dressing rooms, is modern and glamorous. He concocted a froufrou, aimed at an aristocratic audience and airily decorated with things French. He named one of the sisters Charlotte and set the action in a world of full-length looking glasses and inlaid floors. He invented a couturière called Mademoiselle de Poche to create costumes for the ball, linens and ruffles, velvet suits and headdresses. Disney dropped the French touches.

Perrault's story is set in a world of women with their eyes on men. Even before the King's ball is announced, the stepmother and stepsisters are preoccupied with how they look. They are obsessed with their mirrors, straining to see what men would see. Once the ball is on the horizon, they starve themselves for days so that their shapes shall be, when laced into Mademoiselle de Poche's creations, as extremely slender as those in our own fashion magazines. The ball—and the prospects it implies—intensifies the hostility toward Cinderella. They have been envious. Now, they must keep the pretty girl out of competition. Most of the action of Perrault's story is taken up with the business of the ball.

12 　　Cinderella is a sniveling, self-pitying girl. Forbidden to go to the ball, she does not object but, instead, dutifully helps her stepsisters adorn themselves. She has no will, initiates no action. Then, magically, the fairy godmother appears. She comes from nowhere, summoned, we suppose, by Cinderella's wishes. Unlike the fairy godmother in other versions of the story, Perrault's and Disney's character has no connection to anything real, has no meaning, except to enable Cinderella to overcome the opposition of the women in her home, wear beautiful clothes and get to the ball. Cinderella stammers, unable to say what she wants—for she is passive, suffering and good, which comes across as relatively unconscious. The fairy divines Cinderella's desire and equips her with pumpkin/coach, mice/horses, rats/coachmen, lizards/footmen, clothes and dancing shoes. She adds the famous prohibition that Cinderella return by midnight or everything will be undone.

These details of the fairy godmother's magic—the pumpkin, image of All Hallows' Eve; midnight, the witching hour; mice, rats and lizards originated with Perrault. They are specific reminders of an actual and ancient female magic, witchcraft. Since Perrault wrote his story in the seventeenth century, it is not surprising to find echoes of this magic, which was enormously real to Perrault's audience.

Thousands had been burned at the stake for practicing witchcraft, most of them women. A witch was a woman with enormous power, a woman who might change the natural world. She was "uncivilized" and in opposition to the world of the King, the court, polite society. She had to be controlled. Perrault's story attempts to control the elements of witchcraft just as various kings' governments had, in the not too recent past, controlled what they believed to be an epidemic of witchcraft. Perrault controls female power by trivializing it. The witchcraft in this story is innocent, ridiculous, silly and playful. It is meant to entertain children.

The prohibition that Cinderella return by midnight is also related to witchcraft. She must avoid the witching hour, with its overtones of sexual abandon. The fairy godmother acts in this capacity in a way that is familiar to mothers and daughters—she controls the girl, warns her against darkness, uses her authority to enforce restraint, prevent excess, particularly excess associated with the ball, the world of men, sexuality.

16 　　Cinderella's dancing shoes are glass slippers. Perrault mistranslated the fur slipper in the version that came to him, substituting *verre* for *vire* and coming up glass. No pedant came along to correct the mistake, for the glass slipper is immensely appropriate to the story in its modern form and

the values it embodies. Call it dainty or fragile, the slipper is quintessentially the stereotype of femininity. I wonder how Cinderella danced in it.

The rags-to-riches moment holds people's imagination long after the details of the story have disappeared. It appeals to everyone's desire for magic, for change that comes without effort, for speedy escape from a bad place—bad feelings. We all want to go to the ball, want life to be full of good feeling and feeling good. But Cinderella's transformation points to a particular and limited kind of good feeling—from ugly to beautiful, raggedy to glamorous. The object of her transformation is not actually pleasure (she does not then walk around her house feeling better) but transportation to the ball with all the right equipment for captivating the Prince.

Transformed, Cinderella goes to the ball, which is the larger world, the kingdom ruled by kings and fathers. The stepmother has no power in that world and does not even appear. This part of the story focuses on men, who are good to Cinderella as forcefully as women have been bad to her. Perrault embellishes Cinderella's appearance in a way that would have been congenial to the French court. In fact, she seems to have gone to the French court. The story is suffused with perfume and "fashionability." The Prince is taken with Cinderella and gives her some candy—"citrons and oranges," according to the text. How French. She, forever good, shares the candy with her stepsisters, who do not, of course, know who she is.

Cinderella has a wonderful time. As readers, hearers, watchers, we have a wonderful time along with her. More than the music and the dancing, the aura of sensual pleasure, everyone's good time comes from the idea that Cinderella is a "knockout." This is exciting. Perrault's word for what happens is that the people are *étonnés,* which means stunned. Cinderella is a showstopper, so "dazzling" that "the King himself, old as he was, could not help watching her." He remarks on this to his Queen, whose reactions we are not told. Being "stunning" is being powerful. This is the way women have impact, the story tells us. This is female power in the world outside the home, in contrast to her former powerlessness, which was within the home, which was another country. This tells me why women spend so much time trying to turn themselves into knockouts—because, in Cinderella and in other stories, it *works.*

20   Presumably, Cinderella's giddiness over her own triumph at the ball makes her forget her godmother's command and almost miss her midnight deadline. Lest we lose the idea that all men adore Cinderella, Perrault adds a courtier at the end of the story, as the search for the missing Cinderella is carried out, and has him, too, say how attractive Cinderella is. She fulfills, then, the masculine idea of what is beautiful in a woman. She is the woman men want women to be.

Cinderella flees at midnight and loses her shoe. Perrault plays this part down, but Disney has a visual festival with the glinting glass slipper on the staircase and the trumpet-accompanied quest to find its owner. Perrault's Prince sends a messenger to find the shoe's owner, which puts the action at some distance, but Disney gives us a prince in all his splendor.

Cinderella is a heroine and in the world of fairy tales what the heroine wins is marriage to the Prince. Like any classic romance, wafted by perfume and fancy clothes, the young girl is lifted from a lowly powerless situation (from loneliness and depression, too) by a powerful man. He has no character, not even a handsome face, but simply represents the things that princes represent, the power of the kingdom.

Opposition to achieving this triumph comes from the women in the house; help comes from daydream and fantasy. The only proper activity for women to engage in is primping. What is expected of them is that they wait "in the right way" to be discovered. Cinderella obeys the rules. Her reward is to be claimed by the Prince. The lesson of Cinderella in these versions is that a girl who knows and keeps her place will be rewarded with male favor.

24   Like a saint, she shows neither anger nor resentment toward the women who treated her so badly. In fact, she takes her stepsisters along to the castle, where she marries each off to a nobleman. Now everyone will be happy. Now there will be no conflict, no envy, no degradation. If each woman has a prince or nobleman, she will be content and the soft humming of satisfaction will fill the air. Women otherwise cannot be alone together.

This is the sort of story that poisoned Madame Bovary's imagination. In Flaubert's novel, a woman married to a country doctor, with aspirations for a larger life, goes to a ball where a princely character pays her some attention. The ball and the Prince, seen by Emma Bovary as possibilities for changing everyday life, haunted her uneasy sleep. The ball was over. Wait as she might for its return, for a second invitation, all she got was a false prince—a lover who did not lift her from the ordinariness of her life—and then despair.

The romance depends on aspiration. The Prince must be able to give the heroine something she cannot get for herself or from other women. He must represent a valuable and scarce commodity, for the women must believe there is only one, not enough to go around, and must set themselves to keeping other women from getting it. In "Cinderella," like other fairy tales and other romances, the world of the Prince represents both actual and psychological riches.

Perrault's Cinderella is the daughter of a gentleman, turned into a peasant within the household. She has been declassed by female interlopers, reduced to the status of servant, for she belongs to her father's class only precariously. One of the ways women exercise their power, the story tells us, is by degrading other women. Cinderella will be saved from her female-inflicted degradation first by another female, the fairy godmother, who puts her on the road to her ultimate salvation. At the end of the story, she is restored to her class position, or, better, raised to an even higher position by the Prince.

28   Her fall from class is represented not only by her tattered clothes, but by the work she is forced to do. She is the household "drudge" and

housework is the image of her degradation. Her work has no value in the story; it is the invisible, repetitious labor that keeps things going and makes it possible for the sisters and stepmother to devote themselves to *their* work, which is indolence on the one hand and trying to be beautiful for men on the other. Historically, indolence has been revered as the mark of a lady. What is "feminine" and "ladylike" is far removed from the world of work. Or the world of self-satisfying work. A man prides himself on having a wife who does not work; it increases his value in the eyes of other men; it means he provides well; it enforces conventional bourgeois "masculinity." A lady has long fingernails, neither the typewriter nor the kitchen floor has cracked them. She has porcelain skin; neither the rough outdoors nor perspiration has cracked that. Out of the same set of values comes the famous glass slipper.

The stepmother's class position is as precarious as Cinderella's is. The story does not tell, but we can imagine that whether she was married before to a poorer man or one equally a gentleman, her status and security are now tied to the man she has married and the ones she can arrange for her daughters. History, experience, and literature are full of landless propertyless women trying to secure marriage to stand as a bulwark against poverty, displacement and exile, both actual and psychological. The actual situation bears emphasis. The economic reality behind the fairy tale and the competition among the women for the favor of the Prince is a world in which women have no financial lives of their own. They cannot own businesses or inherit property. The kingdom is not theirs. In order to survive, a woman must have a husband. It is in the interest of her daughters' future—and her own—that the stepmother works to prevent competition from Cinderella. She is not evil. Within the confines of her world and the value systems of that world, she is quite nice to her own daughters, only cruel to Cinderella.

Still, the stepmother is an archetypal figure in fairy tales, always a thwarter, often a destroyer of children. Psychologists, and Bruno Bettelheim in particular, have a psychological explanation for this. The "bad" stepmother, Bettelheim points out, usually coexists with the "good" mother, representing two aspects of a real mother as experienced by a child. The stepmother is shaped by the child's unacceptable anger against her own mother. But there are real facts of life at work in these stepmother stories, too, especially as they describe what can happen among women at home. To a man's second wife, the daughter of the first marriage is a constant reminder of the first wife. The second wife is continually confronted with that memory and with the understanding that wives are replaceable, as they frequently and actually *were* in a world where women died young in childbirth, and men remarried, moved on.

A woman marries a man who has a daughter and comes to his household, where the daughter's strongest connection is to her father; the stepmother's strongest connection is to the husband. The Eternal Triangle appears, husband/father at the center, mediating the relationship, step-mother and daughter as antagonists, competing for the husband/father's attention and whatever he may represent. Anxious, each in her own way and equally displaced, they face each other with enmity. The masculine imagination takes prideful pleasure in the story, placing, as it does, husband/father at center stage, making him King, arbiter of a world of women. . . .

32   I am writing an essay about Cinderella, spending mornings at the type-writer, afternoons in libraries, interpreting information on index cards of various colors and sheets of yellow paper. I discover something bizarre woven in the story as we now know it: that the story took root in ancient China. The remnants of that culture, especially of the ancient practice of footbinding, are in the story, in the value of the small foot, in the use of the shoe to represent the potential bride. I see, then, the historical truth behind the terrible moment at the end of "Cinderella."

The Prince brings the slipper to the house of Cinderella's father. First one stepsister, then the other attempts to slip her foot into it, but each foot is too large. The first stepsister's toe is too large. The stepmother hands her daughter a knife and says, "Cut off the toe. When you are Queen you won't have to walk anymore." The second stepsister's heel is too large and her mother repeats the gesture and the advice.

Mutilation. Blood in the shoe, blood on the knife, blood on the floor and unbearable pain, borne, covered, masked by the smile. It is too famil-iar, frightening in its familiarity. The mother tells the daughter to mutilate herself in the interests of winning the Prince. She will not have to walk. Again, indolence enshrined. As mothers, in fact, did in China until the twentieth century—among the upper classes as unquestioned custom and among peasants as great sacrifice and gamble.

It began when the girl was between five and seven years old. The ban-dages were so tight, the girl might scream. Her mother pulled them tighter and might have tried to soothe her. Tighter. At night, in agony, the girl loosens them. She is punished, her hands tied to a post to prevent unlac-ing. The bones crack. The pain is constant. Tighter. She cannot walk. Tighter. By her adolescence, the girl has learned to bind her feet herself and the pain has lessened. She has, as a reward, special shoes, embroi-dered and decorated, for her tiny feet.

36   I translate the actual foot-binding, the ritual interaction of mother and daughter, to metaphor. A black mother straightens her daughter's hair with a hot iron, singeing the scalp, pulling and tugging. The daughter screams. My mother buys me a girdle when I am fifteen years old because she doesn't like the jiggle. She slaps my face when I begin to menstruate, telling me later that it is an ancient Russian custom and she does not know its origin. I sleep with buttons taped to my cheeks to make dimples and with hard metallic curlers in my hair. Tighter. I hold myself tighter, as my mother has taught me to do.

Is the impulse to cripple a girl peculiar to China between the eleventh and twentieth centuries? The lotus foot was the size of a doll's and the woman could not walk without support. Her foot was four inches long and two inches wide. A doll. A girl-child. Crippled, indolent and bound. This is what it meant to be beautiful. And desired. This women did and do to each other.

Pain in the foot is pain in every part of the body. A mother is about to bind her daughter's feet. She knows the pain in her own memory. She says: "A daughter's pretty legs are achieved through the shedding of tears."

This women did to each other.
This women do.
Or refuse to do.
. . . .

Personal Response

Select a film for children that you recall from your childhood and discuss what you remember most about it. Do you think it has the same kinds of messages Bernikow says "Cinderella" has?

Questions for Class or Small Group Discussion

1. Discuss whether you agree with Bernikow's interpretation of "Cinderella," that the story is chiefly "about how awful women are to each other" (paragraph 1).

2. Discuss whether you think it is true that "rich matters more than handsome" (paragraph 4) for men in our society, while being pretty is most important for women (paragraph 5).

3. Do you agree that females' power resides in their being "stunning" (paragraph 19), while other kinds of power in women are feared? Discuss your own perceptions of powerful women: Do you view power in women differently from or the same as the way you see it in men?

4. Bernikow sees a parallel between the stepsisters in "Cinderella" cutting off parts of their feet to win the Prince and the practice of foot-binding in China, and she interprets foot-binding as a metaphor for other interactions between mothers and daughters (paragraphs 36–38). To what extent do you agree with her in this interpretation? Do women today have any painful rituals they go through to make themselves appealing to men? Do men go through painful rituals in order to appeal to women?

5. Can you name any current books or recent Hollywood films that have the same sorts of messages that Bernikow sees in "Cinderella"? What other fairy tales or children's stories reinforce Bernikow's point

about female rivalry and male power? What would happen if you reversed the sex roles in "Cinderella"?

IRON JOHN
Robert Bly

Robert Bly is a poet, writer, and lecturer whose best-selling book Iron John: A Book About Men *(1990) influenced many men to reconsider their definition of masculinity and to join the small but burgeoning men's movement of the early 1990s. Among Bly's poetry collections are* Silence in the Snowy Fields *(1962);* The Light Around the Body *(1968), for which he was awarded the National Book Award; and* Loving a Woman in Two Worlds *(1985). The piece reprinted here is excerpted from* Iron John.

We talk a great deal about "the American man," as if there were some constant quality that remained stable over decades, or even within a single decade.

The men who live today have veered far away from the Saturnian, old-man-minded farmer, proud of his introversion, who arrived in New England in 1630, willing to sit through three services in an unheated church. In the South, an expansive, motherbound cavalier developed, and neither of these two "American men" resembled the greedy railroad entrepreneur that later developed in the Northeast, nor the reckless I-will-do-without culture settlers of the West.

Even in our own era the agreed-on model has changed dramatically. During the fifties, for example, an American character appeared with some consistency that became a model of manhood adopted by many men: the Fifties male.

4   He got to work early, labored responsibly, supported his wife and children, and admired discipline. Reagan is a sort of mummified version of this dogged type. This sort of man didn't see women's souls well, but he appreciated their bodies; and his view of culture and America's part in it was boyish and optimistic. Many of his qualities were strong and positive, but underneath the charm and bluff there was, and there remains, much isolation, deprivation, and passivity. Unless he has an enemy, he isn't sure that he is alive.

The Fifties man was supposed to like football, be aggressive, stick up for the United States, never cry, and always provide. But receptive space or intimate space was missing in this image of a man. The personality lacked some sense of flow. The psyche lacked compassion in a way that encouraged the unbalanced pursuit of the Vietnam war, just as, later, the lack of what we might call "garden" space inside Reagan's head led to his callousness and brutality toward the powerless in El Salvador, toward old people here, the unemployed, schoolchildren, and poor people in general.

The Fifties male had a clear vision of what a man was, and what male responsibilities were, but the isolation and one-sidedness of his vision were dangerous.

During the sixties, another sort of man appeared. The waste and violence of the Vietnam war made men question whether they knew what an adult male really was. If manhood meant Vietnam, did they want any part of it? Meanwhile, the feminist movement encouraged men to actually look at women, forcing them to become conscious of concerns and sufferings that the Fifties male labored to avoid. As men began to examine women's history and women's sensibility, some men began to notice what was called their *feminine* side and pay attention to it. This process continues to this day, and I would say that most contemporary men are involved in it in some way.

8   There's something wonderful about this development—I mean the practice of men welcoming their own "feminine" consciousness and nurturing it—this is important—and yet I have the sense that there is something wrong. The male in the past twenty years has become more thoughtful, more gentle. But by this process he has not become more free. He's a nice boy who pleases not only his mother but also the young woman he is living with.

In the seventies I began to see all over the country a phenomenon that we might call the "soft male." Sometimes even today when I look out at an audience, perhaps half the young males are what I'd call soft. They're lovely, valuable people—I like them—they're not interested in harming the earth or starting wars. There's a gentle attitude toward life in their whole being and style of living.

But many of these men are not happy. You quickly notice the lack of energy in them. They are life-preserving but not exactly life-giving. Ironically, you often see these men with strong women who positively radiate energy.

Here we have a finely tuned young man, ecologically superior to his father, sympathetic to the whole harmony of the universe, yet he himself has little vitality to offer.

12   The strong or life-giving women who graduated from the sixties, so to speak, or who have inherited an older spirit, played an important part in producing this life-preserving, but not life-giving, man.

I remember a bumper sticker during the sixties that read "WOMEN SAY YES TO MEN WHO SAY NO." We recognize that it took a lot of courage to resist the draft, go to jail, or move to Canada, just as it took courage to accept the draft and go to Vietnam. But the women of twenty years ago were definitely saying that they preferred the softer receptive male.

So the development of men was affected a little in this preference. Nonreceptive maleness was equated with violence, and receptive maleness was rewarded.

Some energetic women, at that time and now in the nineties, chose and still choose soft men to be their lovers and, in a way, perhaps, to be their sons. The new distribution of "yang" energy among couples didn't happen by accident. Young men for various reasons wanted their harder women, and women began to desire softer men. It seemed like a nice arrangement for a while, but we've lived with it long enough now to see that it isn't working out.

16   I first learned about the anguish of "soft" men when they told their stories in early men's gatherings. In 1980, the Lama Community in New Mexico asked me to teach a conference for men only, their first, in which about forty men participated. Each day we concentrated on one Greek god and one old story, and then late in the afternoons we gathered to talk. When the younger men spoke it was not uncommon for them to be weeping within five minutes. The amount of grief and anguish in these younger men was astounding to me.

Part of their grief rose out of remoteness from their fathers, which they felt keenly, but partly, too, grief flowed from trouble in their marriages or relationships. They had learned to be receptive, but receptivity wasn't enough to carry their marriages through troubled times. In every relationship something *fierce* is needed once in a while: both the man and the woman need to have it. But at the point when it was needed, often the young man came up short. He was nurturing, but something else was required—for his relationship, and for his life.

The "soft" male was able to say, "I can feel your pain, and I consider your life as important as mine, and I will take care of you and comfort you." But he could not say what he wanted, and stick by it. *Resolve* of that kind was a different matter.

In *The Odyssey,* Hermes instructs Odysseus that when he approaches Circe, who stands for a certain kind of matriarchal energy, he is to lift or show his sword. In these early sessions it was difficult for many of the younger men to distinguish between showing the sword and hurting someone. One man, a kind of incarnation of certain spiritual attitudes of the sixties, a man who had actually lived in a tree for a year outside Santa Cruz, found himself unable to extend his arm when it held a sword. He had learned so well not to hurt anyone that he couldn't lift the steel, even to catch the light of the sun on it. But showing a sword doesn't necessarily mean fighting. It can also suggest a joyful decisiveness.

20   The journey many American men have taken into softness, or receptivity, or "development of the feminine side," has been an immensely valuable journey, but more travel lies ahead. No stage is the final stop.

Finding Iron John

One of the fairy tales that speak of a third possibility for men, a third mode, is a story called "Iron John" or "Iron Hans." Though it was first set down by the Grimm brothers around 1820, this story could be ten or twenty thousand years old.

As the story starts, we find out that something strange has been happening in a remote area of the forest near the king's castle. When hunters go into this area, they disappear and never come back. Twenty others go after the first group and do not come back. In time, people begin to get the feeling that there's something weird in that part of the forest, and they "don't go there anymore."

One day an unknown hunter shows up at the castle and says, "What can I do? Anything dangerous to do around her?"

24   The King says: "Well, I could mention the forest, but there's a problem. The people who go out there don't come back. The return rate is not good."

"That's just the sort of thing I like," the young man says. So he goes into the forest and, interestingly, he goes there *alone,* taking only his dog. The young man and his dog wander about in the forest and they go past a pond. Suddenly a hand reaches up from the water, grabs the dog, and pulls it down.

The young man doesn't respond by becoming hysterical. He merely says, "This must be the place."

Fond as he is of his dog and reluctant as he is to abandon him, the hunter goes back to the castle, rounds up three more men with buckets, and then comes back to the pond to bucket out the water. Anyone who's ever tried it will quickly note that such bucketing is very slow work.

28   In time, what they find, lying on the bottom of the pond, is a large man covered with hair from head to foot. The hair is reddish—it looks a little like rusty iron. They take the man back to the castle, and imprison him. The King puts him in an iron cage in the courtyard, calls him "Iron John," and gives the key into the keeping of the Queen.

Let's stop the story here for a second.

When a contemporary man looks down into his psyche, he may, if conditions are right, find under the water of his soul, lying in an area no one has visited for a long time, an ancient hairy man.

The mythological systems associate hair with the instinctive and the sexual and the primitive. What I'm suggesting, then, is that every modern male has, lying at the bottom of his psyche, a large, primitive being covered with hair down to his feet. Making contact with this Wild Man is the step the Eighties male or the Nineties male has yet to take. That bucketing-out process has yet to begin in our contemporary culture.

32   As the story suggests very delicately, there's more than a little fear around this hairy man, as there is around all change. When a man begins to develop the receptive side of himself and gets over his initial skittishness, he usually finds the experience to be wonderful. He gets to write poetry

and go out and sit by the ocean, he doesn't have to be on top all the time in sex anymore, he becomes empathetic—it's a new, humming, surprising world.

But going down through water to touch the Wild Man at the bottom of the pond is quite a different matter. The being who stands up is frightening, and seems even more so now, when the corporations do so much work to produce the sanitized, hairless, shallow man. When a man welcomes his responsiveness, or what we sometimes call his internal woman, he often feels warmer, more companionable, more alive. But when he approaches what I'll call the "deep male," he feels risk. Welcoming the Hairy Man *is* scary and risky, and it requires a different sort of courage. Contact with Iron John requires a willingness to descend into the male psyche and accept what's dark down there, including the *nourishing* dark.

For generations now, the industrial community has warned young businessmen to keep away from Iron John, and the Christian church is not too fond of him either.

Freud, Jung, and Wilhelm Reich are three investigators who had the courage to go down into the pond and to accept what they found there. The job of contemporary men is to follow them down.

36   Some men have already done this work, and the Hairy Man has been brought up from the pond in their psyches, and lives in the courtyard. "In the courtyard" suggests that the individual or the culture has brought him into a sunlit place where all can see him. That is itself some advance over keeping the Hairy Man in a cellar, where many elements in every culture want him to be. But, of course, in either place, he's still in a cage.

The Loss of the Golden Ball

Now back to the story.

One day the King's eight-year-old son is playing in the courtyard with the golden ball he loves, and it rolls into the Wild Man's cage. If the young boy wants the ball back, he's going to have to approach the Hairy Man and ask him for it. But this is going to be a problem.

The golden ball reminds us of that unity of personality we had as children—a kind of radiance, or wholeness, before we split into male and female, rich and poor, bad and good. The ball is golden, as the sun is, and round. Like the sun, it gives off a radiant energy from the inside.

40   We notice that the boy is eight. All of us, whether boys or girls, lose something around the age of eight. If we still have the golden ball in kindergarten, we lose it in grade school. Whatever is still left we lose in high school. In "The Frog Prince," the princess's ball fell into a well. Whether we are male or female, once the golden ball is gone, we spend the rest of our lives trying to get it back.

The first stage in retrieving the ball, I think, is to accept—firmly, definitely—that the ball has been lost. Freud said: "What a distressing contrast

there is between the radiant intelligence of the child and the feeble mentality of the average adult."

So where is the golden ball? Speaking metaphorically, we could say
that the sixties culture told men they would find their golden ball in sensitivity, receptivity, cooperation, and nonaggressiveness. But many men gave
up all aggressiveness and still did not find the golden ball.

The Iron John story says that a man can't expect to find the golden
ball in the feminine realm, because that's not where the ball is. A bride-
groom secretly asks his wife to give him back the golden ball. I think she'd
give it to him if she could, because most women in my experience do not
try to block men's growth. But she can't give it to him, because she doesn't
have it. What's more, she's lost her own golden ball and can't find that
either.

44   Oversimplifying, we could say that the Fifties male always wants a
woman to return his golden ball. The Sixties and Seventies man, with equal
lack of success, asks his interior feminine to return it.

The Iron John story proposes that the golden ball lies within the magnetic field of the Wild Man, which is a very hard concept for us to grasp.
We have to accept the possibility that the true radiant energy in the male
does not hide in, reside in, or wait for us in the feminine realm, nor in the
macho/John Wayne realm, but in the magnetic field of the deep masculine.
It is protected by the *instinctive* one who's underwater and who has been
there we don't know how long.

In "The Frog Prince" it's the frog, the un-nice one, the one that everyone says "Ick!" to, who brings the golden ball back. And in the Grimm
brothers version the frog himself turns into the prince only when a hand
throws him against the wall.

Most men want some nice person to bring the ball back, but the story
hints that we won't find the golden ball in the force field of an Asian guru
or even the force field of gentle Jesus. Our story is not anti-Christian but
pre-Christian by a thousand years or so, and its message is still true—getting the golden ball back is incompatible with certain kinds of conventional
tameness and niceness.

48   The kind of wildness, or un-niceness, implied by the Wild Man image
is not the same as macho energy, which men already know enough about.
Wild Man energy, by contrast, leads to forceful action undertaken, not
with cruelty, but with resolve.

The Wild Man is not opposed to civilization; but he's not completely
contained by it either. The ethical superstructure of popular Christianity
does not support the Wild Man, though there is some suggestion that
Christ himself did. At the beginning of his ministry, a hairy John, after all,
baptized him.

When it comes time for a young male to talk with the Wild Man he
will find the conversation quite distinct from a talk with a minister, a rabbi,
or a guru. Conversing with the Wild Man is not talking about bliss or mind

or spirit or "higher consciousness," but about something wet, dark, and low—what James Hillman would call "soul."

The first step amounts to approaching the cage and asking for the golden ball back. Some men are ready to take that step, while others haven't yet bucketed the water out of the pond—they haven't left the collective male identity and gone out into the unknown area alone, or gone with only their dog.

52   The story says that after the dog "goes down" one has to start to work with buckets. No giant is going to come along and suck out all the water for you: that magic stuff is not going to help. And a weekend at Esalen[1] won't do it. Acid or cocaine won't do it. The man has to do it bucket by bucket. This resembles the slow discipline of art: it's the work that Rembrandt did, that Picasso and Yeats and Rilke and Bach did. Bucket work implies much more discipline than most men realize.

The Wild Man, as the writer Keith Thompson mentioned to me, is not simply going to hand over the golden ball either. What kind of story would it be if the Wild Man said: "Well, okay, here's your ball"?

Jung remarked that all successful requests to the psyche involve deals. The psyche likes to make deals. If part of you, for example, is immensely lazy and doesn't want to do any work, a flat-out New Year's resolution won't do any good. The whole thing will go better if you say to the lazy part: "You let me work for an hour, then I'll let you be a slob for an hour—deal?" So in "Iron John," a deal is made: the Wild Man agrees to give the golden ball back if the boy opens the cage.

The boy, apparently frightened, runs off. He doesn't even answer. Isn't that what happens? We have been told so often by parents, ministers, grade-school teachers, and high-school principals that we should have nothing to do with the Wild Man that when he says "I'll return the ball if you let me out of the cage," we don't even reply.

56   Maybe ten years pass now. On "the second day" the man could be twenty-five. He goes back to the Wild Man and says, "Could I have my ball back?" The Wild Man says, "Yes, if you let me out of the cage."

Actually, just returning to the Wild Man a second time is a marvelous thing; some men never come back at all. The twenty-five-year-old man hears the sentence all right, but by now he has two Toyotas and a mortgage, maybe a wife and a child. How can he let the Wild Man out of the cage? A man usually walks away the second time also without saying a word.

Now ten more years pass. Let's say the man is now thirty-five . . . have you ever seen the look of dismay on the face of a thirty-five-year-old man? Feeling overworked, alienated, empty, he asks the Wild Man with full heart this time: "Could I have my golden ball back?"

---

[1] The Esalen Institute, located on the Big Sur coast of California, is a hot-springs resort that offers seminars and group and individual therapy.

"Yes," the Wild Man says, "if you let me out of my cage."

60   Now something marvelous happens in the story. The boy speaks to the Wild Man, and continues the conversation. He says, "Even if I wanted to let you out, I couldn't, because I don't know where the key is."

That's so good. By the time we are thirty-five we don't know where the key is. It isn't exactly that we have forgotten—we never knew where it was in the first place.

The story says that when the King locked up the Wild Man, "he gave the key into the keeping of the Queen," but we were only about seven then, and in any case our father never told us what he had done with it. So where is the key?

I've heard audiences try to answer that one:

"It's around the boy's neck."

No.

"It's hidden in Iron John's cage."

No.

"It's inside the golden ball."

No.

"It's inside the castle . . . on a hook inside the Treasure Room."

No.

"It's in the Tower. It's on a hook high up on the wall!"

No.

The Wild Man replies, "The key is under your mother's pillow."

64   The key is not inside the ball, nor in the golden chest, nor in the safe . . . the key is under our mother's pillow—just where Freud said it would be.

Getting the key back from under the mother's pillow is a troublesome task. Freud, taking advice from a Greek play, says that a man should not skip over the mutual attraction between himself and his mother if he wants a long life. The mother's pillow, after all, lies in the bed near where she makes love to your father. Moreover, there's another implication attached to the pillow.

Michael Meade, the myth teller, once remarked to me that the pillow is also the place where the mother stores all her expectations for you. She dreams: "My son the doctor." "My son the Jungian analyst." "My son the Wall Street genius." But very few mothers dream: "My son the Wild Man."

On the son's side, he isn't sure he wants to take the key. Simply transferring the key from the mother's to a guru's pillow won't help. Forgetting that the mother possesses it is a bad mistake. A mother's job is, after all, to civilize the boy, and so it is natural for her to keep the key. All families behave alike: on this planet, "The King gives the key into the keeping of the Queen."

68   Attacking the mother, confronting her, shouting at her, which some Freudians are prone to urge on us, probably does not accomplish much—she may just smile and talk to you with her elbow on the pillow. Oedi-

pus' conversations with Jocasta never did much good, nor did Hamlet's shouting.

A friend mentioned that it's wise to steal the key some day when your mother and father are gone. "My father and mother are away today" implies a day when the head is free of parental inhibitions. That's the day to steal the key. Gioia Timpanelli, the writer and storyteller, remarked that, mythologically, the theft of the key belongs to the world of Hermes.

And the key has to be *stolen*. I recall talking to an audience of men and women once about this problem of stealing the key. A young man, obviously well trained in New Age modes of operation, said, "Robert, I'm disturbed by this idea of stealing the key. Stealing isn't right. Couldn't a group of us just go to the mother and say, 'Mom, could I have the key back?'?"

His model was probably consensus, the way the staff at the health food store settles things. I felt the souls of all the women in the room rise up in the air to kill him. Men like that are as dangerous to women as they are to men.

72   No mother worth her salt would give the key away. If a son can't steal it, he doesn't deserve it.

"I want to let the Wild Man out!"

"Come over and give Mommy a kiss."

Mothers are intuitively aware of what would happen if they got the key: they would lose their boys. The possessiveness that mothers typically exercise on sons—not to mention the possessiveness that fathers typically exercise on daughters—can never be underestimated.

76   The means of getting the key back varies with each man, but suffice it to say that democratic or nonlinear approaches will not carry the day.

One rather stiff young man danced one night for about six hours, vigorously, and in the morning remarked, "I got some of the key back last night."

Another man regained the key when he acted like a whole-hearted Trickster for the first time in his life, remaining fully conscious of the tricksterism. Another man stole the key when he confronted his family and refused to carry any longer the shame for the whole family.

We could spent days talking of how to steal the key in a practical way. The story itself leaves everything open, and simply says, "One day he stole the key, brought it to the Wild Man's cage, and opened the lock. As he did so, he pinched one of his fingers." (That detail will become important in the next part of the story.) The Wild Man is then free at last, and it's clear that he will go back to his own forest, far from "the castle."

What Does the Boy Do?

80   At this point a number of things could happen. If the Wild Man returns to his forest while the boy remains in the castle, the fundamental historical split in the psyche between primitive man and the civilized man would reestablish itself in the boy. The boy, on his side, could mourn the loss of

the Wild Man forever. Or he could replace the key under the pillow before his parents got home, then say he knows nothing about the Wild Man's escape. After that subterfuge, he could become a corporate executive, a fundamentalist minister, a tenured professor, someone his parents could be proud of, who "has never seen the Wild Man."

We've all replaced the key many times and lied about it. Then the solitary hunter inside us has to enter into the woods once more with his body dog accompanying him, and then the dog gets pulled down again. We lose a lot of "dogs" that way.

We could also imagine a different scenario. The boy convinces, or imagines he could convince, the Wild Man to stay in the courtyard. If that happened, he and the Wild Man could carry on civilized conversations with each other in the tea garden, and this conversation would go on for years. But the story suggests that Iron John and the boy cannot be united—that is, cannot experience their initial union—in the castle courtyard. It's probably too close to the mother's pillow and the father's book of rules.

We recall that the boy in our story, when he spoke to the Wild Man, told him he didn't know where the key was. That's brave. Some men never address a sentence to the Wild Man.

84   When the boy opened the cage, the Wild Man started back to his forest. The boy in our story, or the thirty-five-year-old man in our mind—however you want to look at it—now does something marvelous. He speaks to the Wild Man once more and says, "Wait a minute! If my parents come home and find you gone, they will beat me." That sentence makes the heart sink, particularly if we know something about child-rearing practices that have prevailed for a long time in northern Europe.

As Alice Miller reminds us in her book *For Your Own Good,* child psychologists in nineteenth-century Germany warned parents especially about *exuberance.* Exuberance in a child is bad, and at the first sign of it, parents should be severe. Exuberance implies that the wild boy or girl is no longer locked up. Puritan parents in New England often punished children severely if they acted in a restless way during the long church services.

"If they come home and find you gone, they will beat me."

The Wild Man says, in effect, "That's good thinking. You'd better come with me."

88   So the Wild Man lifts the boy up on his shoulders and together they go off into the woods. That's decisive. We should all be so lucky.

As the boy leaves for the forest, he has to overcome, at least for the moment, his fear of wildness, irrationality, hairiness, intuition, emotion, the body, and nature. Iron John is not as primitive as the boy imagines, but the boy—or the mind—doesn't know that yet.

Still, the clean break with the mother and father, which the old initiators call for, now has taken place. Iron John says to the boy, "You'll never see your mother and father again. But I have treasures, more than you'll ever need." So that is that. . . .

Personal Response

What do you think of Bly's theory that a Wild Man lies hidden deep within the soul of every male?

Questions for Class or Small Group Discussion

1. Summarize the characteristics of the "Fifties male" and the "soft male" of the seventies, as described by Bly, and then discuss whether these "models of manhood" (paragraph 3) fit any men you know.

2. Discuss the characteristics you think would describe the "Nineties male."

3. Discuss your understanding of Bly's theory of the "Wild Man" and what happens when men do not get in touch with that deeply hidden part of their souls. Do you agree with Bly that the Eighties or Nineties male has not yet made contact with his Wild Man (paragraph 31)?

4. To what extent do you agree with Bly's interpretation of the "Iron John" story? Do you agree with his explanation of the symbolic meanings of the ancient hairy man at the bottom of the lake, the golden ball, and the key under the mother's pillow? If not, how would you interpret them?

IRON BONDING

Alan Buczynski

Alan Buczynski, who holds a degree in English, works as an ironworker in the Detroit area. In this essay, which originally appeared in The New York Times Magazine *in 1992, he argues against Robert Bly's theories about men in* Iron John. *Buczynski counters the prevailing belief that men cannot communicate deep feelings to one another by explaining the ways in which he and his coworkers express emotion.*

"I just don't get it." We were up on the iron, about 120 feet, waiting for the gang below to swing up another beam. Sweat from under Ron's hard hat dripped on the beam we were sitting on and evaporated immediately, like water thrown on a sauna stove. We were talking about the "men's movement" and "wildman weekends."

"I mean," he continued, "if they want to get dirty and sweat and cuss and pound on things, why don't they just get *real* jobs and get paid for it?" Below, the crane growled, the next piece lifting skyward.

I replied: "Nah, Ron, that isn't the point. They don't want to sweat every day, just sometimes."

4   He said: "Man, if you only sweat when you want to, I don't call that real sweatin'."

Although my degree is in English, I am an ironworker by trade; my girlfriend, Patti, is a graduate student in English literature. Like a tennis ball volleyed by two players with distinctly different styles, I am bounced between blue-collar haulers and precise academicians. My conversations range from fishing to Foucault, derricks to deconstruction. There is very little overlap, but when it does occur it is generally the academics who are curious about the working life.

Patti and I were at a dinner party. The question of communication between men had arisen. Becky, the host, is a persistent interrogator: "What do you and Ron talk about?"

I said, "Well, we talk about work, drinking, ah, women."

8   Becky asked, "Do you guys ever say, 'I love you' to each other?" This smelled mightily of Robert Bly and the men's movement.

I replied: "Certainly. All the time."

I am still dissatisfied with this answer. Not because it was a lie, but because it was perceived as one.

The notion prevails that men's emotional communication skills are less advanced than that of chimpanzees, that we can no more communicate with one another than can earthworms.

12   Ironworkers as a group may well validate this theory. We are not a very articulate bunch. Most of us have only a basic education. Construction sites are extremely noisy, and much of our communication takes place via hand signals. There is little premium placed on words that don't stem from our own jargon. Conversations can be blunt.

Bly's approach, of adapting a fable for instruction, may instinctively mimic the way men communicate. Ironworkers are otherwise very direct, yet when emotional issues arise we speak to one another in allegory and parable. One of my co-workers, Cliff, is a good storyteller, with an understated delivery: "The old man got home one night, drunk, real messed up and got to roughhousing with the cat. Old Smoke, well she laid into him, scratched him good. Out comes the shotgun. The old man loads up, chases Smoke into the front yard and blam! Off goes the gun. My Mom and my sisters and me we're all screamin'. Smoke comes walkin' in the side door. Seems the old man blew away the wrong cat, the neighbor's Siamese. Red lights were flashin' against the house, fur was splattered all over the lawn, the cops cuffed my old man and he's hollerin' and man, I'll tell you, I was cryin'."

Now, we didn't all get up from our beers and go over and hug him. This was a story, not therapy. Cliff is amiable, but tough, more inclined to solving any perceived injustices with his fists than verbal banter, but I don't need to see him cry to know that he can. He has before, and he can tell a story about it without shame, without any disclaimers about being "just a kid," and that's enough for me.

Ron and I have worked together for nine years and are as close as 29 is to 30. We have worked through heat and cold and seen each other injured in the stupidest of accidents. One February we were working inside a plant, erecting steel with a little crane; it was near the end of the day, and I was tired. I hooked onto a piece and, while still holding the load cable, signaled the operator "up." My thumb was promptly sucked into the sheave of the crane. I screamed, and the operator came down on the load, releasing my thumb. It hurt. A lot. Water started leaking from my eyes. The gang gathered around while Ron tugged gently at my work glove, everyone curious whether my thumb would come off with the glove or stay on my hand.

16   "O.K., man, relax, just relax," Ron said. "See if you can move it." Ron held my hand. The thumb had a neat crease right down the center, lengthwise. All the capillaries on one side had burst and were turning remarkable colors. My new thumbnail was on back order and would arrive in about five months. I wiggled the thumb, an eighth of an inch, a quarter, a half.

"You're O.K., man, it's still yours and it ain't broke. Let's go back to work."

Afterwards, in the bar, while I wrapped my hand around a cold beer to keep the swelling and pain down, Ron hoisted his bottle in a toast: "That," he said, "was the best scream I ever heard, real authentic, like you were in actual pain, like you were really *scared*."

If this wasn't exactly Wind in His Hair howling eternal friendship for Dances With Wolves, I still understood what Ron was saying. It's more like a 7-year-old boy putting a frog down the back of a little girl's dress because he has a crush on her. It's a backward way of showing affection, of saying "I love you," but it's the only way we know. We should have outgrown it, and hordes of men are now paying thousands of dollars to sweat and stink and pound and grieve together to try and do just that. Maybe it works, maybe it doesn't. But no matter how cryptic, how Byzantine, how weird and weary the way it travels, the message still manages to get through.

Personal Response

Explore the degree to which you are able to talk freely about your emotions.

Questions for Class or Small Group Discussion

1. Buczynski's friend Becky asks if he and his friends ever say "I love you" to one another. Do you think saying "I love you" is an important indicator of how emotionally deep a person is, or do you think, as Buczynski does, that there are other ways to convey emotion just as

meaningfully? Do you think women define love relationships and friendships differently from the way men do? If so, in what ways? Explain your answers.

2. What does Buczynski think of Robert Bly's view of masculinity? (See the previous essay, "Iron John," an excerpt from Bly's book.)

3. Summarize Buczynski's point about men's communication style. Do you agree with his viewpoint? On the basis of your own observations of men you know well, do you think men communicate indirectly and avoid talking about their emotions? Is there a difference in the way a man communicates depending on his age? Does it make a difference if the man is speaking to a woman rather than to another man?

4. Do you know much about the men's movement in the United States? What do you think prompted men to organize such a movement? What do you suppose its goals are? Do you think they are the same as those that prompted the contemporary women's movement?

5. In same-sex groups, discuss the misconceptions women and men have of each other. Have someone take notes and then compare lists. How much agreement between the all-female and all-male groups do you find? If there are significant differences, try to account for those differences.

X: A FABULOUS CHILD'S STORY

Lois Gould

Lois Gould is a writer and a journalist. In addition to short stories and newspaper articles, she has written several novels: Such Good Friends *(1970),* Necessary Objects *(1972), and* La Presidenta *(1981). This story first appeared as a "Story for Free Children" in* Ms. *magazine in 1972 and has since been reprinted countless times.*

Once upon a time, a baby named X was born. This baby was named X so that nobody could tell whether it was a boy or a girl. Its parents could tell, of course, but they couldn't tell anybody else. They couldn't even tell Baby X, at first.

You see, it was all part of a very important Secret Scientific Xperiment, known officially as Project Baby X. The smartest scientists had set up this Xperiment at a cost of Xactly 23 billion dollars and 72 cents, which might seem like a lot for just one baby, even a very important Xperimental baby. But when you remember the prices of things like strained carrots and stuffed bunnies, and popcorn for the movies and booster shots for camp, let alone 28 shiny quarters from the tooth fairy, you begin to see how it adds up.

Also, long before Baby X was born, all those scientists had to be paid to work out the details of the Xperiment, and to write the *Official Instruction Manual* for Baby X's parents and, most important of all, to find the right set of parents to bring up Baby X. These parents had to be selected very carefully. Thousands of volunteers had to take thousands of tests and answer thousands of tricky questions. Almost everybody failed because, it turned out, almost everybody really wanted either a baby boy or a baby girl, and not Baby X at all. Also, almost everybody was afraid that a Baby X would be a lot more trouble than a boy or a girl. (They were probably right, the scientists admitted, but Baby X needed parents who wouldn't *mind* the Xtra trouble.)

4   There were families with grandparents named Milton and Agatha, who didn't see why the baby couldn't be named Milton or Agatha instead of X, even if it *was* an X. There were families with aunts who insisted on knitting tiny dresses and uncles who insisted on sending tiny baseball mitts. Worst of all, there were families that already had other children who couldn't be trusted to keep the secret. Certainly not if they knew the secret was worth 23 billion dollars and 72 cents—and all you had to do was take one little peek at Baby X in the bathtub to know if it was a boy or a girl.

But, finally, the scientists found the Joneses, who really wanted to raise an X more than any other kind of baby—no matter how much trouble it would be. Ms. and Mr. Jones had to promise they would take equal turns caring for X, and feeding it, and singing it lullabies. And they had to promise never to hire any baby-sitters. The government scientists knew perfectly well that a baby-sitter would probably peek at X in the bathtub, too.

The day the Joneses brought their baby home, lots of friends and relatives came over to see it. None of them knew about the secret Xperiment, though. So the first thing they asked was what kind of a baby X was. When the Joneses smiled and said, "It's an X!" nobody knew what to say. They couldn't say, "Look at her cute little dimples!" And they couldn't say, "Look at his husky little biceps!" And they couldn't even say just plain "kitchy-coo." In fact, they all thought the Joneses were playing some kind of rude joke.

But, of course, the Joneses were not joking. "It's an X" was absolutely all they would say. And that made the friends and relatives very angry. The relatives all felt embarrassed about having an X in the family. "People will think there's something wrong with it!" some of them whispered. "There *is* something wrong with it!" others whispered back.

8   "Nonsense!" the Joneses told them all cheerfully. "What could possibly be wrong with this perfectly adorable X?"

Nobody could answer that, except Baby X, who had just finished its bottle. Baby X's answer was a loud, satisfied burp.

Clearly, nothing at all was wrong. Nevertheless, none of the relatives felt comfortable about buying a present for a Baby X. The cousins who sent the baby a tiny football helmet would not come and visit any more. And the neighbors who sent a pink-flowered romper suit pulled their shades down when the Joneses passed their house.

The *Official Instruction Manual* had warned the new parents that this would happen, so they didn't fret about it. Besides, they were too busy with Baby X and the hundreds of different Xercises for treating it properly.

12   Ms. and Mr. Jones had to be Xtra careful about how they played with little X. They knew if they kept bouncing it up in the air and saying how *strong* and *active* it was, they'd be treating it more like a boy than an X. But if all they did was cuddle it and kiss it and tell it how *sweet* and *dainty* it was, they'd be treating it more like a girl than an X.

On page 1,654 of the *Official Instruction Manual,* the scientists prescribed: "plenty of bouncing and plenty of cuddling, *both*. X ought to be strong and sweet and active. Forget about *dainty* altogether."

Meanwhile, the Joneses were worrying about other problems. Toys, for instance. And clothes. On his first shopping trip, Mr. Jones told the store clerk, "I need some clothes and toys for my new baby." The clerk smiled and said, "Well, now, is it a boy or a girl?" "It's an X," Mr. Jones said, smiling back. But the clerk got all red in the face and said huffily, "In *that* case, I'm afraid I can't help you, sir." So Mr. Jones wandered helplessly up and down the aisles trying to find what X needed. But everything in the store was piled up in sections marked "Boys" or "Girls." There were "Boys' Pajamas" and "Girls' Underwear" and "Boys' Fire Engines" and "Girls' Housekeeping Sets." Mr. Jones went home without buying anything for X. That night he and Ms. Jones consulted page 2,326 of the *Official Instruction Manual.* "Buy plenty of everything!" it said firmly.

So they bought plenty of sturdy blue pajamas in the Boys' Department and cheerful flowered underwear in the Girls' Department. And they bought all kinds of toys. A boy doll that made pee-pee and cried, "Pa-pa." And a girl doll that talked in three languages and said, "I am the Pres-i-dent of Gen-er-al Mo-tors." They also bought a storybook about a brave princess who rescued a handsome prince from his ivory tower, and another one about a sister and brother who grew up to be a baseball star and a ballet star, and you had to guess which was which.

16   The head scientists of Project Baby X checked all their purchases and told them to keep up the good work. They also reminded the Joneses to see page 4,629 of the *Manual,* where it said, "Never make Baby X feel *embarrassed* or *ashamed* about what it wants to play with. And if X gets dirty climbing rocks, never say 'Nice little Xes don't get dirty climbing rocks.'"

Likewise, it said, "If X falls down and cries, never say 'Brave little Xes don't cry.' Because, of course, nice little Xes *do* get dirty, and brave little Xes *do* cry. No matter how dirty X gets, or how hard it cries, don't worry. It's all part of the Xperiment."

Whenever the Joneses pushed Baby X's stroller in the park, smiling strangers would come over and coo: "Is that a boy or a girl?" The Joneses would smile back and say, "It's an X." The strangers would stop smiling then, and often snarl something nasty—as if the Joneses had snarled at *them.*

By the time X grew big enough to play with other children, the Joneses' troubles had grown bigger, too. Once a little girl grabbed X's shovel in the sandbox, and zonked X on the head with it. "Now, now, Tracy," the little girl's mother began to scold, "little girls mustn't hit little . . ." and she turned to ask X, "Are you a little boy or a little girl, dear?"

20   Mr. Jones who was sitting near the sandbox, held his breath and crossed his fingers.

X smiled politely at the lady, even though X's head had never been zonked so hard in its life, "I'm a little X," X replied.

"You're a *what?*" the lady exclaimed angrily. "You're a little b-r-a-t, you mean!"

"But little girls mustn't hit little Xes, either!" said X, retrieving the shovel with another polite smile. "What good does hitting do, anyway?"

24   X's father, who was still holding his breath, finally let it out, uncrossed his fingers, and grinned back at X.

And at their next secret Project Baby X meeting, the scientists grinned, too. Baby X was doing fine.

But then it was time for X to start school. The Joneses were really worried about this, because school was even more full of rules for boys and girls, and there were no rules for Xes. The teacher would tell boys to form one line, and girls to form another line. There would be boys' games and girls' games, and boys' secrets and girls' secrets. The school library would have a list of recommended books for girls, and a different list of recommended books for boys. There would even be a bathroom marked BOYS and another one marked GIRLS. Pretty soon boys and girls would hardly talk to each other. What would happen to poor little X?

The Joneses spent weeks consulting their *Instruction Manual* (there were 249½ pages of advice under "First Day of School"), and attending urgent special conferences with the smart scientists of Project Baby X.

28   The scientists had to make sure that X's mother had taught X how to throw and catch a ball properly, and that X's father had been sure to teach X what to serve at a doll's tea party. X had to know how to shoot marbles and how to jump rope and, most of all, what to say when the Other Children asked whether X was a Boy or a Girl.

Finally, X was ready. The Joneses helped X button on a nice new pair of red-and-white checked overalls, and sharpened six pencils for X's nice new pencilbox, and marked X's name clearly on all the books in its nice new bookbag. X brushed its teeth and combed its hair, which just about covered its ears, and remembered to put a napkin in its lunchbox.

The Joneses had asked X's teacher if the class could line up alphabetically, instead of forming separate lines for boys and girls. And they had asked if X could use the principal's bathroom, because it wasn't marked anything except BATHROOM. X's teacher promised to take care of all those problems. But nobody could help X with the biggest problem of all—Other Children.

Nobody in X's class had ever known an X before. What would they think? How would X make friends?

32   You couldn't tell what X was by studying its clothes—overalls don't even button right-to-left, like girls' clothes, or left-to-right, like boys' clothes. And you couldn't guess whether X had a girl's short haircut or a boy's long haircut. And it was very hard to tell by the games X liked to play. Either X played ball very well for a girl, or else X played house very well for a boy.

Some of the children tried to find out by asking X tricky questions, like "Who's your favorite sports star?" That was easy. X had two favorite sports stars: a girl jockey named Robyn Smith and a boy archery champion named Robin Hood. Then they asked, "What's your favorite TV program?" And that was even easier. X's favorite TV program was "Lassie," which stars a girl dog played by a boy dog.

When X said that its favorite toy was a doll, everyone decided that X must be a girl. But then X said that the doll was really a robot, and that X had computerized it, and that it was programmed to bake fudge brownies and then clean up the kitchen. After X told them that, the other children gave up guessing what X was. All they knew was they'd sure like to see X's doll.

After school, X wanted to play with the other children. "How about shooting some baskets in the gym?" X asked the girls. But all they did was make faces and giggle behind X's back.

36   "How about weaving some baskets in the arts and crafts room?" X asked the boys. But they all made faces and giggled behind X's back too.

That night, Ms. and Mr. Jones asked X how things had gone at school. X told them sadly that the lessons were okay, but otherwise school was a terrible place for an X. It seemed as if Other Children would never want an X for a friend.

Once more, the Joneses reached for their *Instruction Manual.* Under "Other Children," they found the following message: "What did you Xpect? *Other Children* have to obey all the silly boy-girl rules, because their parents taught them to. Lucky X—you don't have to stick to the rules at all! All you have to do is be yourself. P.S. We're not saying it'll be easy."

X liked being itself. But X cried a lot that night, partly because it felt afraid. So X's father held X tight, and cuddled it, and couldn't help crying a little, too. And X's mother cheered them both up by reading an Xciting story about an enchanted prince called Sleeping Handsome, who woke up when Princess Charming kissed him.

40   The next morning, they all felt much better, and little X went back to school with a brave smile and a clean pair of red-and-white checked overalls.

There was a seven-letter-word spelling bee in class that day. And a seven-lap boys' relay race in the gym. And a seven-layer-cake baking contest in the girls' kitchen corner. X won the spelling bee. X also won the relay race. And X almost won the baking contest, except it forgot to light the oven. Which only proves that nobody's perfect.

One of the Other Children noticed something else, too. He said, "Winning or losing doesn't seem to count to X. X seems to have fun being good at boys' skills *and* girls' skills."

"Come to think of it," said another one of the Other Children, "maybe X is having twice as much fun as we are!"

44   So after school that day, the girl who beat X at the baking contest gave X a big slice of her prizewinning cake. And the boy X beat in the relay race asked X to race him home.

From then on, some really funny things began to happen. Susie, who sat next to X in class, suddenly refused to wear pink dresses to school any more. She insisted on wearing red-and-white checked overalls—just like X's. Overalls, she told her parents, were much better for climbing monkey bars.

Then Jim, the class football nut, started wheeling his little sister's doll carriage around the football field. He'd put on his entire football uniform, except for the helmet. Then he'd put the helmet *in* the carriage, lovingly tucked under an old set of shoulder pads. Then he'd start jogging around the field, pushing the carriage and singing "Rock-a-bye Baby" to his football helmet. He told his family that X did the same thing, so it must be okay. After all X was now the team's star quarterback.

Susie's parents were horrified by her behavior, and Jim's parents were worried sick about his. But the worst came when the twins, Joe and Peggy, decided to share everything with each other. Peggy used Joe's hockey skates, and his microscope, and took half his newspaper route. Joe used Peggy's needlepoint kit, and her cookbooks, and took two of her three baby-sitting jobs. Peggy started running the lawn mower, and Joe started running the vacuum cleaner.

48   Their parents weren't one bit pleased with Peggy's wonderful biology experiments, or with Joe's terrific needlepoint pillows. They didn't care that Peggy mowed the lawn better, and that Joe vacuumed the carpet better. In fact, they were furious. It's all that little X's fault, they agreed. Just because X doesn't know what it is, or what it's supposed to be, it wants to get everybody *else* mixed up, too!

Peggy and Joe were forbidden to play with X any more. So was Susie, and then Jim, and then *all* the Other Children. But it was too late; the Other Children stayed mixed up and happy and free, and refused to go back to the way they'd been before X.

Finally, Joe and Peggy's parents decided to call an emergency meeting of the school's Parents' Association, to discuss "The X Problem." They sent a report to the principal stating that X was a "disruptive influence." They demanded immediate action. The Joneses, they said, should be *forced* to tell whether X was a boy or a girl. And then X should be *forced* to behave like whichever it was. If the Joneses refused to tell, the Parents'

Association said, then X must take an Xamination. The school psychiatrist must Xamine it physically and mentally, and issue a full report. If X's test showed it was a boy, it would have to obey all the boys' rules. If it proved to be a girl, X would have to obey all the girls' rules.

And if X turned out to be some kind of mixed-up misfit, then X should be Xpelled from the school. Immediately!

52   The principal was very upset. Disruptive influence? Mixed-up misfit? But X was an Xcellent student. All the teachers said it was a delight to have X in their classes. X was president of the student council. X had won first prize in the talent show, and second prize in the art show, and honorable mention in the science fair, and six athletic events on field day, including the potato race.

Nevertheless, insisted the Parents' Association, X is a Problem Child. X is the Biggest Problem Child we have ever seen!

So the principal reluctantly notified X's parents that numerous complaints about X's behavior had come to the school's attention. And that after the psychiatrist's Xamination, the school would decide what to do about X.

The Joneses reported this at once to the scientists, who referred them to page 85,759 of the *Instruction Manual.* "Sooner or later," it said, "X will have to be Xamined by a psychiatrist. This may be the only way any of us will know for sure whether X is mixed up—or whether everyone else is."

56   The night before X was to be Xamined, the Joneses tried not to let X see how worried they were. "What if . . . ?" Mr. Jones would say. And Ms. Jones would reply, "No use worrying." Then a few minutes later, Ms. Jones would say, "What if . . . ?" and Mr. Jones would reply, "No use worrying."

X just smiled at them both, and hugged them hard and didn't say much of anything. X was thinking. What if . . . ? And then X thought: No use worrying.

At Xactly 9 o'clock the next day, X reported to the school psychiatrist's office. The principal, along with a committee from the Parents' Association, X's teacher, X's classmates, and Ms. and Mr. Jones, waited in the hall outside. Nobody knew the details of the tests X was to be given, but everybody knew they'd be *very* hard, and that they'd reveal Xactly what everyone wanted to know about X, but were afraid to ask.

It was terribly quiet in the hall. Almost spooky. Once in a while, they would hear a strange noise inside the room. There were buzzes. And a beep or two. And several bells. An occasional light would flash under the door. The Joneses thought it was a white light, but the principal thought it was blue. Two or three children swore it was either yellow or green. And the Parent's Committee missed it completely.

60   Through it all, you could hear the psychiatrist's low voice, asking hundreds of questions, and X's higher voice, answering hundreds of answers.

The whole thing took so long that everyone knew it must be the most complete Xamination anyone had ever had to take. Poor X, the Joneses thought. Serves X right, the Parents' Committee thought. I wouldn't like to be in X's overalls right now, the children thought.

At last, the door opened. Everyone crowded around to hear the results. X didn't look any different; in fact, X was smiling. But the psychiatrist looked terrible. He looked as if he was crying! "What happened?" everyone began shouting. Had X done something disgraceful? "I wouldn't be a bit surprised!" muttered Peggy and Joe's parents. "Did X flunk the *whole* test? cried Susie's parents. "Or just the most important part?" yelled Jim's parents.

"Oh, dear," sighed Mr. Jones.

64   "Oh, dear," sighed Ms. Jones.

"*Sssh*," ssshed the principal. "The psychiatrist is trying to speak."

Wiping his eyes and clearing his throat, the psychiatrist began, in a hoarse whisper. "In my opinion," he whispered—you could tell he must be very upset—"in my opinion, young X here . . ."

"Yes? Yes?" shouted a parent impatiently.

68   "*Sssh!*" ssshed the principal.

"Young *Sssh* here, I mean young X," said the doctor, frowning, "is just about . . ."

"Just about *what?* Let's have it!" shouted another parent.

". . . just about the *least* mixed-up child I've ever Xamined!" said the psychiatrist.

72   "Yay for X!" yelled one of the children. And then the others began yelling, too. Clapping and cheering and jumping up and down.

"*SSSH!*" SSShed the principal, but nobody did.

The Parents' Committee was angry and bewildered. How *could* X have passed the whole Xamination? Didn't X have an *identity* problem? Wasn't X mixed up at *all?* Wasn't X *any* kind of a misfit? How could it *not* be, when it didn't even *know* what it was? And why was the psychiatrist crying?

Actually, he had stopped crying and was smiling politely through his tears. "Don't you see?" he said, "I'm crying because it's wonderful! X has absolutely no identity problem! X isn't one bit mixed up! As for being a misfit—ridiculous! X knows perfectly well what it is! Don't you, X?" "The doctor winked, X winked back.

76   "But what *is* X?" shrieked Peggy and Joe's parents. "We still want to know what it is!"

"Ah, yes," said the doctor, winking again. "Well, don't worry. You'll all know one of these days. And you won't need me to tell you."

"What? What does he mean?" some of the parents grumbled suspiciously.

Susie and Peggy and Joe all answered at once. "He means that by the time X's sex matters, it won't be a secret any more!"

80   With that, the doctor began to push through the crowd toward X's parents. "How do you do," he said, somewhat stiffly. And then he reached out to hug them both. "If I ever have an X of my own," he whispered, "I sure hope you'll lend me your instruction manual."

Needless to say, the Joneses were very happy. The Project Baby X scientists were rather pleased, too. So were Susie, Jim, Peggy, Joe, and all the Other Children. The Parents' Association wasn't, but they had promised to accept the psychiatrist's report, and not make any more trouble. They even invited Ms. and Mr. Jones to become honorary members, which they did.

Later that day, all X's friends put on their red-and-white checked overalls and went over to see X. They found X in the back yard, playing with a very tiny baby that none of them had ever seen before. The baby was wearing very tiny red-and-white checked overalls.

"How do you like our new baby?" X asked the Other Children proudly.

84   "It's got cute dimples," said Jim.

"It's got husky biceps, too," said Susie.

"What kind of baby is it?" asked Joe and Peggy.

X frowned at them. "Can't you tell?" Then X broke into a big, mischievous grin. "*It's a Y!*"

Personal Response

Explore your reaction to this fable. Did you enjoy it? Why or why not? Did the experiences of X seem familiar to you and, if so, in what ways?

Questions for Class or Small Group Discussion

1. Identify the traditional sex role expectations or assumptions about gender differences that the story explores or exposes.

2. Select a passage of several paragraphs and read it aloud, using masculine pronouns for all references to X. Then do to the same using feminine pronouns. Discuss the effects of substituting sex-specific pronouns for the indefinite X.

3. Discuss whether you think that society will some day be "genderless." How possible do you think it would be to raise a child not to be conscious of gender? What advantages and disadvantages do you see in having a "genderless" society?

4. Discuss your own experiences growing up. Did your parents treat you differently on the basis of your sex? Did teachers? Other children? How, if at all, do you think television and other media influence your feelings about being male or female?

BISEXUALITY EMERGES AS A NEW SEXUAL IDENTITY

John Leland

John Leland is a writer for Newsweek *magazine, which ran this cover story in its July 17, 1995, issue. The piece reports on the growing population of men and women who define themselves as neither straight nor gay but, rather, bisexual. It features couples and individuals whose sexual orientation defies traditional labels.*

Steven and Lori are what you might call the marrying type. They met on the first day of freshman orientation at the University of Chicago in 1988. By Thanksgiving, she was taking him home to meet her family; the following year they got engaged. This May they celebrated their first wedding anniversary.

In their one-bedroom apartment in Hyde Park, a collegiate affair down to the cinderblock bookshelves, Steven and Lori, now both 24, have developed an almost telepathic relationship. If anyone tells one of them anything, they joke, the other knows about it immediately. But during their freshman year, Steven says, he used to go off on his own every so often. "I think I told you I was going to a Democratic Socialist meeting," he recalls to Lori. He was really going to a campus gay and lesbian support group. Steven had come to college with a "practically nonexistent" romantic life, but a clear attraction to both men and women. After one of the group meetings, he decided to come clean to Lori.

STEVEN: [I said] Lori, I have something to tell you.

4   LORI: At which point, I thought he had cancer.

STEVEN: And I told her, and her response was "Oh, is that all?"

LORI: Yeah, it's not like cancer, after all. After that big buildup, it's like, gee, that's not a big deal.

When the couple got married at city hall last year, perhaps the most relieved person in the Midwest was Lori's mother. "Now she thinks I'm going to behave," says Lori. She says this with a playful smirk. In the years before their marriage—during their engagement—Lori had a serious relationship with another woman, and Steven had one with another man. Their marriage now is a home invention that they describe as "body-fluid monogamous." In conversation, they discuss condoms as matter-of-factly as the weather. Lori has an ongoing sexual relationship with another man and is looking for another woman; Steven has a friendship with a man that is sometimes sexual. Lori says, "At the time that I was coming out I was more interested in men, and now I'm more interested in women." Steven is "much more interested" in men right now. He still has sex with his wife, but he now identifies himself as gay, though he also calls himself a "once and future bisexual."

8   Bisexuality is the hidden wild card of our erotic culture. It is what disappears when we divide desire into gay and straight, just as millions of Americans of various ethnic origin disappear when we discuss race in terms of black and white. Now, in scattered pockets, bisexuality is starting to become more visible. Bisexual characters have popped up in TV series like "Roseanne" and "Melrose Place" and in films like "Three of Hearts" and "Threesome." Two decades after Mick Jagger and David Bowie flaunted their androgynous personas, pop stars like Michael Stipe, Courtney Love and Sophie B. Hawkins and model Rachel Williams have discovered anew that there's more to life than when a man loves a woman. As Stipe told NEWSWEEK, promoting R.E.M.'s latest album, "I've always been sexually ambiguous in terms of my proclivities; I think labels are for food." MTV and fashion advertising, pumping out fetishized images of men and women, have created a climate that Harvard professor Marjorie Garber, author of the provocative new book "Vice Versa: Bisexuality and the Eroticism of Everyday Life," calls "virtual bisexuality": the only way to watch these naked torsos, male and female alike, is erotically. Many college students, particularly women, talk about a new sexual "fluidity" on campus. And most significantly, the Internet has emerged as a safe harbor where users can play fluidly with gender, both their own and that of their virtual partners. As Garber puts it, "We are in a bisexual moment."

In the splintered multiculturalism of the 1990s, an independent bisexual movement is starting to claim its own identity. The Bisexual Resource Guide lists 1,400 groups spread throughout the United States and abroad, including Bi Women of Color, Bi Adult Children of Alcoholics, Bi Star Trekkies. There are bi cable shows, bi web sites, bi newsletters and magazines. "We are taught we have to be one thing," says Howard University divinity professor Elias Farajajé-Jones. "Now people are finding out that they don't have to choose one thing or another. That doesn't mean they are confused."

The Bridge

Freud called bisexuality a universal "disposition"; he believed that we all have male and female sides, each heterosexually attracted to people of the opposite gender, but that most of us repress one side. For him, it was exclusive *heterosexuality* that was "a problem that needs elucidating" (unfortunately, he never got around to it). Alfred Kinsey, in his famous 1948 report, mapped human sexuality on a scale of zero to 6, with zero representing exclusively heterosexual behavior and 6 exclusively homosexual behavior; bisexuality was the bridge that held the poles together. The anthropologist Margaret Mead urged in 1975 that we "come to terms with the well-documented, normal human capacity to love members of both sexes." And in 1995, "Adam," a bisexual teen in Oakland, Calif., says bisexuality is no guarantee of a date on a Saturday night: "A bisexual," he says, "doesn't have any more sex than the captain of the football team."

After a brief vogue during the sexual revolution—"Bisexual Chic: Anyone Goes," chortled NEWSWEEK in 1974—it moved back underground in the 1980s, pushed by fears of AIDS and by gay identity politics. Nobody knows how many bisexuals there are in the country, or just how bisexuality should be defined. Its existence alone makes many people uncomfortable; it suggests that all sexual identity might be subject to change or expansion, and that we may not ever really be able to fulfill our partners or be fulfilled ourselves. "I'll put it this way," says Faune, a bi New York grad student who asked to be identified by his online handle. "You're attracted to only one sex and you don't feel there's anything missing. To me that would be hell."

12   In a culture organized, however precariously, around monogamy, bisexuality lurks as a rupture in the social structure, conjuring fears of promiscuity, secret lives and instability. It can make the knotty issues of human relationships—jealousy, fidelity, finances, parental roles, custody—even more complex. And with these uncertainties comes an increased threat of AIDS. Failed monogamy is already a principal source of pain in this country; bisexuality suggests that nonmonogamy, or "polyamory," is an accepted part of life. Not for nothing does one bisexual journal call itself, with mock derision, Anything That Moves. In practice promiscuity is not an article of faith for all bisexuals; it's an option. Many bis are monogamous for all or parts of their lives. The sociologist Paula Rust, in the upcoming book "Bisexuality: The Psychology and Politics of an Invisible Minority," explains the paradox this way: "Imagine concluding that a person who finds both blue and brown eyes attractive would require two lovers, one with each eye color, instead of concluding that this person would be happy with *either* a blue-eyed or a brown-eyed lover."

Mostly, though, we'd rather not think about bisexuality. When Rolling Stone publisher Jann Wenner left his wife this spring for another man, bisexuality was the possibility missing from most accounts. Bisexuality has been written out of our literature: early publishers simply rewrote the genders of male love objects in Plato's "Symposium" and some of Shakespeare's sonnets; more often schools just teach around them. Bisexuality even disappears from many sex surveys, which count people with any same-sex behavior as homosexual. And yet it has had a tremendous impact on our culture. Many of the men who have taught us to be men—Cary Grant, James Dean—and the women who've taught us to be women—Billie Holiday, Marlene Dietrich—enjoyed sex with both men and women.

The bisexual blip of the '70s was an offshoot of the sexual revolution; it was straight, with a twist. By contrast, the current bisexual moment rises from the gay and feminist movements. For a generation that came of age during the gay-rights movement, same-sex relationships or experiments no longer carry the stigma they once did. More and more of us—at work, at school, in our families and in our entertainments—move comfortably between gay and straight worlds. "Those of us who are younger," says Rebecca Kaplan, 24, a psychology major at MIT, "owe a great deal to gays, lesbians and bisexuals who came before us. Because of them I was able to come out as a bisexual and not hate myself." Feminism has also made romantic attachments between two women—either provisional or lasting—more acceptable, even privileged. As president of the National Organization for Women, Patricia Ireland sets a quiet example: she has both a husband and a female companion. Nearly every college or university in the country, and some high schools, now have gay and lesbian student centers; sex with one's own gender, for anyone who's curious, is now a visible and protected part of campus culture. Queer studies and gender studies are now a part of the national curriculum. A popular T shirt, spotted recently in a Connecticut high school, puts it this way: DON'T ASSUME I'M STRAIGHT. As one 17-year-old bi says, "It's not us-versus-them anymore. There's just more and more of us."

Tim Höring, 21, a sophomore at City College in San Francisco, describes himself as "typical of bisexual youth. We just refuse to label ourselves as any of the five food groups . . . [We] revel in the fuzziness, in the blurred images." Working-class, Roman Catholic, son of a retired New York narcotics cop, Höring had his first sexual fantasies about Wonder Woman and the Bionic Woman. Then in his teens he admitted to himself, in a series of difficult steps, that he was also attracted to men. He came out to a few friends in high school; at his graduation, when his name was called, the last six rows in the auditorium mischievously yelled out, "the bisexual" (this news came as a surprise to his parents). For the most part he has been in monogamous relationships, usually with men—though now he is dating two gay men and a bisexual woman. "I never wanted a white picket fence," he says, "but I do want someone I can settle down with and raise my Benetton kids." His partner may be a man or a woman. "I don't feel forced to choose," he says. "I don't have to make any tough choices."

Softening Tensions

16 For many bisexuals, it hasn't been that easy. "When I came out in '88," says Melissa Merry, 31, an energetic Chicagoan who calls herself Mel, "I was told by people from [local lesbian] support groups not to come out as bisexual or I'd be asked to leave." Many gays and lesbians, she says, dismissed bisexuals as fence sitters, unwilling to give up a "phase" they themselves had outgrown. As a college student in Michigan, Merry remembers, she went to a singles-heavy bar one night. "And I saw this woman across the room and I thought, 'She is just so attractive.' I thought, 'Where did that come from?' I was involved with a guy, we were going to get married, and then all of a sudden that didn't make sense anymore." Now Merry works in two organizations for bis, but says tensions between bis and gays have softened. After years of resistance, gay and lesbian organizations have started to add bisexuality to their banners. As for the

lesbian groups that shunned her, Merry says, "I can't think of any . . . that I can't go to now."

Many bis, though, still feel rejected on two fronts: by straights for being too gay, and by gays for not being gay enough. During the late '80s, bisexual men—especially married men who stepped out with other men—were painted as stealth assassins bringing AIDS to their unsuspecting wives. As Cosmopolitan warned in 1989, "If a man's eyes follow other men, be very cautious." This fear has cooled somewhat, particularly among younger women—both because of the availability of condoms, and because AIDS never swept through the heterosexual population, except around IV drug use. Of women who contract AIDS sexually, the portion who get it from bisexual males remains at 10 to 20 percent; 80 to 90 percent get it from drug users, Centers for Disease Control and Prevention estimates. Still, for many women this is reason enough to worry. The bisexual response: it is unprotected sex, not bisexuality, that transmits AIDS.

Luis, 36, has felt pressures from both gays and straights. A marine biologist by training, Luis now runs a Miami prescription-drug service for patients with HIV. For the last 5½ years, he has been involved with a bi woman; recently, he invited a gay man into their relationship and home. Luis is HIV-positive; his partners are not. "My first lover and first relationship was with a [gay] man, Juan," says Luis. "I learned a lot from him, but there was this other part of me that needed to be expressed. Juan would tell me, 'You're just trying to conform and go back into the closet.' I didn't mind being called gay, but that's not all of who I am. I'm as queer as they come and as straight as they come. I'm 200 percent." Luis remembers once telling a man he'd slept with that he also had sex with a woman. "He got up in the middle of the meal and walked out," Luis says. The prejudice is no more palatable when it comes from straights. Shopping at a northwest Miami mall with his male lover recently, Luis found himself assaulted with anti-gay slurs. "How did the guy know about us?" asks Luis, who does not dress outrageously. "We don't have any stickers on the car."

These dual pressures push some to lead bifurcated lives. William Wedin, a psychologist and director of the Bisexual Information and Counseling Service, says that most of the bisexuals he sees would rather remain in the closet. "Sometimes they will lead separate lives where they are known as gay to one group of friends and seen as straight by another group of people. Sometimes they will go to two doctors: one who deals with medical problems, another who deals with sexually transmitted diseases. They will create separate worlds."

20   Amid these fears and prejudices, scholars and researchers are looking for ways to rethink bisexuality: how to make sense of the millions of Americans, maybe tens of millions, who over the course of their lifetimes have sex with both men and women. Many, even most, don't call themselves bisexual. According to sex researcher Martin Weinberg of Indiana

University, the majority of men who engage in sex with both men and women label themselves "heterosexual." Conversely, Paula Rust, in a 1992 survey of women who identified themselves as lesbians, found that two thirds of them said they were attracted to men, and 90 percent had been in sexual relationships with men. Further, most bisexuals are not attracted equally to men and women. Where do you draw the line? Should fantasy and desire count, even if they aren't acted upon? And what about married people who later come to recognize themselves as gay? "I don't have a definition [of bisexuality]," says John O. G. Billy, lead author of the 1991 study "The Sexual Behavior of Men in the United States," "because I'm not sure there is any one standard definition." The number of Americans who have sex with both men and women concurrently is very small. According to the University of Chicago's massive 1992 "Sex in America" study, about .7 percent of American men, and .3 percent of American women report having had both male and female sexual partners in the last 12 months. Most of the self-identified bisexuals interviewed for this article would not qualify under these terms.

Erotic Patterns

In practice, bisexuality has come to describe an incredibly broad range of erotic patterns: some monogamous, some polyamorous, some fleeting and some wholly fantastic. Indigo Som, 28, a paper artist currently in a monogamous relationship with another woman, considers the word bisexual far too vague to describe her life. "My sexual orientation," she says, "is toward creative people of color who can cook."

So who are bi, and how did they get that way? Are they really different from everybody else? "Some people say everyone has the biological potential for bisexuality, but that's untestable," says Weinberg, who led one of the few major studies of bisexuals (published last year as "Dual Attraction: Understanding Bisexuality"). "The answer is, we don't know." Weinberg conceives of bisexuality as often being an "add-on"—we commonly develop one orientation first, usually straight, and then "add on" an attraction to the other gender. "Learning bisexuality," he writes, is a matter of "failing to unlearn the desirable aspects of one's own gender."

J. Michael Bailey, a sociologist at Northwestern University, says bisexuality is in the genes. In a study of sexual orientation in nearly 5,000 Australian twins, he found that identical twins were more likely both to have bisexual feelings than fraternal twins, suggesting bisexuality might have a genetic basis. "I conceptualize bisexuality this way," he says: "if somebody has enough of the relevant genetic factors, they'll be homosexual. If they don't have enough, they'll be bisexual." His data are still preliminary and have not been subjected to peer scrutiny.

24   At bottom, though, bisexuality simply does not reduce neatly. There are no bisexual acts nor bisexual desires, only bisexual histories. Bisexuality is less a root than a construction—different in each individual—of

passions and actions we are accustomed to calling heterosexual or homosexual. In its ambiguities, it calls into question the certainties of both gay and straight identities. Pushed far enough, it absorbs both.

Matthew Ehrlich, 25, argues that his own desire has nothing to do with gender. Ehrlich, managing editor of VH1 Online in New York, said he was attracted to both men and women once he "started smooching at age 14." He came out as gay at Williams College, he says, because he saw a lot of abusive heterosexual relationships around him; for the last five years he has identified himself as bi though he prefers the term queer. "There are some times that I want a certain kind of hair at the back of someone's neck, a look in their eyes, the way they hold their mouth, but it's not necessarily limited to one gender," he says. "It's often much stronger that I want to run my hands through short hair at the back of the neck than that it's a man or woman's hair." Ehrlich says some of his partners don't understand this, which leads to problems of trust or jealousy. "[They'll say], 'How can you be sure you desire me when I'm only one gender?'" he says. But this is not the point. "I don't desire a gender, I desire a person."

Many Orientations

This remains the unresolved paradox of bisexuality: that in its most individuated moments, it is most indistinguishable from homosexuality or heterosexuality. Desire is desire. John Cheever, who described the breadth of his passions in his journals, deemed bisexuality a pitifully narrow way to look at human attraction. "To interrogate oneself tirelessly on one's sexual drives," he wrote, "seems to me self-destructive. One can be aroused, for example, by the sight of a holly leaf, an apple tree, or a male cardinal bird on a spring morning." As Garber argues, we all have manifold orientations: to green eyes, say, or to money or power. But deep down we remain defiantly attracted to individuals.

In San Francisco recently, Tim Höring was telling his friends about how he changed his approach to picking up boys. He used to say, "Are you queer?" Then he switched to, "Do you like boys?" Now his favorite line is "Do you like me?" As he sees it, "I've gone from the political to the historical attraction to the very personal. All that really matters is if they like me." This is the new bisexual moment in a nutshell: hard fought, hard thought, and distinctly individual. It is a thorny narrative, fraught with questions of identity and belonging. And in the end, it is really about the simple, mysterious pull between warm human bodies when the lights go out.

Personal Response

What is your opinion of the trend toward bisexuality reported on in this piece? Does the subject make you uncomfortable or not? Explain your answer.

Questions for Class or Small Group Discussion

1. Leland notes the number of pop stars who claim to be bisexual and quotes Michael Stipe as saying, "I think labels are for food" (paragraph 8). Comment on that statement and what you think Stipe means by it.

2. Respond to the views of Sigmund Freud, Alfred Kinsey, Margaret Mead, and "Adam" on human sexuality (paragraph 10).

3. Leland states in paragraph 11 that the very existence of bisexuality "makes many people uncomfortable." What other reasons besides that mentioned in paragraph 11 do you think account for people's discomfort with the idea of bisexuality?

4. Discuss whether you agree with Leland on the effect bisexuality has on monogamous relationships (paragraph 12).

5. Leland comments that "same-sex relationships no longer carry the stigma they once did" (paragraph 14). Do you agree with him? Explain your answer.

Perspectives on Gender

Suggestions for Synthesis

1. The essays in this chapter all, in one way or another, touch on the issue of gender and sexual identity. Drawing on two or more of the essays, write a reflective essay in which you explore your own concepts of masculinity and femininity (and perhaps androgyny) and the way in which those concepts have shaped the way you are today. Consider to what degree you think sex determines destiny.

2. With the observations of Louise Bernikow ("Cinderella: Saturday Afternoon at the Movies") and Robert Bly ("Iron John") in mind, conduct your own investigative analysis of fairy tales, children's stories, advertising images, music videos, television programs, or films for their depiction of female and male sex roles. Do you find stereotyped assumptions about masculinity and femininity? In what ways do you think the subject of your analysis reinforces or shapes cultural definitions of masculinity and femininity?

3. Invite representatives from your campus gay and lesbian organization to speak to your class about its group and the activities they sponsor, or interview representatives from that organization. Then, taking their comments and the ideas reported by John Leland in "Bisexuality Emerges as a New Sexual Identity" into consideration, write an essay exploring your views on the general topic of sexual orientation and sexual identity.

Additional Writing Topics

1. Examine media images for the ways in which gays and lesbians are portrayed. Focus on a particular medium, such as print advertisements, television situation comedies, or film.

2. Explore ways in which you would like to see definitions of masculinity and femininity changed. How do you think relationships between the sexes would be affected if those changes were made?

3. Write a personal narrative recounting an experience in which you felt you were being treated unfairly or differently from those of the other sex. What was the situation, how did you feel, and what did you do about it?

4. Write an essay in which you explain the degree to which you consider gender issues important. Do you think too much is made of gender? Does it matter whether definitions of masculinity and femininity are rigid?

7. Read Robert Bly's *Iron John* and write a critique of it. Include your assessment of its weaknesses and strengths and your personal response to the book.

8. Write an essay in which you explain why you agree or disagree with the opinion of Louise Bernikow in "Cinderella: Saturday Afternoon at the Movies," Robert Bly in "Iron John," or Alan Buczynski in "Iron Bonding."

Research Topics

1. Research the history of the contemporary women's movement, the men's movement, or the gay rights movement in America, and report on its origins, goals and influence. You will have to either extend or narrow your scope, depending on the time you have for the project and the nature of your purpose.

2. Research the subject of bisexuality, making sure to include differing viewpoints, and then explain your own viewpoint on the topic, supporting your position with relevant source materials.

3. Expand topic number 2 under "Suggestions for Synthesis" to include library research of articles and books by people who have done their own studies or have expressed opinions on the subject of sex-role stereotyping in books, movies, or other media.

CHAPTER 13

RACE AND ETHNICITY

Racial or ethnic heritage is as important to shaping identity as are sex and social class. One's race or ethnicity can also influence quality of life, educational opportunity, and advancement in employment. American society has a long history of struggling to confront and overcome racism and discrimination on the basis of ethnic heritage. Beginning well before the Civil War, American antislavery groups protested the enslavement of African Americans and worked to abolish slavery in all parts of the country. Other groups besides African Americans have experienced harsh treatment and discrimination solely because of their color or ethnic heritage. These groups include Chinese men brought to America to help construct a cross-country railroad in the nineteenth century, European immigrants who came to America in large numbers near the end of the nineteenth century in search of a better life than in their homelands, Japanese men who came in the twentieth century to work at hard labor for money to send home, and Latinos/Latinas and Hispanics migrating north to America. As a result of heightened awareness of the interplay of race, class, and gender, schools at all levels, from elementary through postgraduate, have incorporated materials into courses on race, class, and/or gender or created whole courses devoted to those important components of our individual identities and histories.

The first two essays in this chapter are personal essays on the issue of ethnic origin. Kesaya E. Noda's "Growing Up Asian in America" explores from various perspectives the conflicts she felt about her identity as a member of the only Asian-American family in a small American town. After graduating from high school, Noda lived in Japan for a year and a half while she learned Japanese and discovered much about her heritage. She subsequently returned for another year's stay in her effort to resolve some of the conflicts she describes in the essay reprinted here. As you read Noda's essay, think about ways in which your own race or ethnic background have affected the way you live, your interactions with others, and your goals and hopes for your future. Has that component of your identity played a large or a small role in making you the person you are today?

Next, in "Hispanic in America: Starting Points," Ada María Isasi-Diaz focuses on what she sees as the unique situation of Hispanics in America. Isasi-Diaz argues that Hispanics are different from other ethnic groups and contends that their difference is perceived as a threat. She outlines what she feels must be the starting points in America's acceptance and understanding of Hispanics. As you read her essay, think about the argument Isasi-Diaz makes and whether you agree with her. Be prepared to discuss with your classmates why you think as you do about Isasi-Diaz's assertions.

The chapter ends with a viewpoint different from those of other writers in this chapter. In "Cultural Baggage," Barbara Ehrenreich explains why she has no interest in celebrating her ethnic and religious heritage. As her title suggests, she views such matters as "baggage." As you read, keep in mind what the authors of other pieces in this chapter have to say about their own ethnic or racial heritage and consider how they might respond to her remarks. Consider also whether you agree or disagree with her viewpoint and why.

GROWING UP ASIAN IN AMERICA

Kesaya E. Noda

Kesaya E. Noda was born in California but grew up in New Hampshire, where she and her family were the only Asian Americans in their small town. Her book, The Yamato Colony *(1981), describes life in the small California community where her grandparents settled and her parents grew up. She is now studying for her doctorate in religious studies at Harvard Divinity School. This essay, first published in* Making Waves *(1989), an anthology of Asian-American writing, explains the conflicts Noda felt about her racial identity while she was growing up.*

Sometimes when I was growing up, my identity seemed to hurtle toward me and paste itself right to my face. I felt that way, encountering the stereotypes of my race perpetuated by non-Japanese people (primarily white) who may or may not have had contact with other Japanese in America. "You don't like cheese, do you?" someone would ask. "I know your people don't like cheese." Sometimes questions came making allusions to history. That was another aspect of the identity. Events that had happened quite apart from the me who stood silent in that moment connected my face with an incomprehensible past. "Your parents were in California? Were they in those camps during the war?" And sometimes there were phrases or nicknames: "Lotus Blossom." I was sometimes addressed or referred to as racially Japanese, sometimes as Japanese-American, and sometimes as an Asian woman. Confusions and distortions abounded.

How is one to know and define oneself? From the inside—within a context that is self-defined, from a grounding in community and a connection with culture and history that are comfortably accepted? Or from the outside—in terms of messages received from the media and people who are often ignorant? Even as an adult I can still see two sides of my face and past. I can see from the inside out, in freedom. And I can see from the outside in, driven by the old voices of childhood and lost in anger and fear.

I Am Racially Japanese

A voice from my childhood says: "You are other. You are less than. You are unalterably alien." This voice has its own history. We have indeed been seen as other and alien since the early years of our arrival in the United States. The very first immigrants were welcomed and sought as laborers to replace the dwindling numbers of Chinese, whose influx had been cut off by the Chinese Exclusion Act of 1882. The Japanese fell natural heir to the same anti-Asian prejudice that had arisen against the Chinese. As soon as they began striking for better wages, they were no longer welcomed.

4   I can see myself today as a person historically defined by law and custom as being forever alien. Being neither "free white," nor "African," our people in California were deemed "aliens, ineligible for citizenship," no matter how long they intended to stay here. Aliens ineligible for citizenship were prohibited from owning, buying, or leasing land. They did not and could not belong here. The voice in me remembers that I am always a *Japanese*-American in the eyes of many. A third-generation German-American is an American. A third-generation Japanese-American is a Japanese-American. Being Japanese means being a danger to the country during the war and knowing how to use chopsticks. I wear this history on my face.

I move to the other side. I see a different light and claim a different context. My race is a line that stretches across ocean and time to link me to the shrine where my grandmother was raised. Two high, white banners lift in the wind at the top of the stone steps leading to the shrine. It is time for the summer festival. Black characters are written against the sky as boldly as the clouds, as lightly as kites, as sharply as the big black crows I used to see above the fields in New Hampshire. At festival time there is liquor and food, ritual, discipline, and abandonment. There is music and drunkenness and invocation. There is hope. Another season has come. Another season has gone.

I am racially Japanese. I have a certain claim to this crazy place where the prayers intoned by a neighboring Shinto priest (standing in for my grandmother's nephew who is sick) are drowned out by the rehearsals for the pop singing contest in which most of the villagers will compete later that night. The village elders, the priest, and I stand respectfully upon the immaculate, shining wooden floor of the outer shrine, bowing our heads before the hidden powers. During the patchy intervals when I can hear him, I notice the priest has a stutter. His voice flutters up to my ears only occasionally because two men and a woman are singing gustily into a microphone in the compound, testing the sound system. A prerecorded tape of guitars, samisens, and drums accompanies them. Rock music and Shinto prayers. That night, to loud applause and cheers, a young man is given the award for the most *netsuretsu*—passionate, burning—rendition of a song. We roar our approval of the reward. Never mind that his voice had wandered and slid, now slightly above, now slightly below the given line of the melody. Netsuretsu. Netsuretsu.

In the morning, my grandmother's sister kneels at the foot of the stone stairs to offer her morning prayers. She is too crippled to climb the stairs, so each morning she kneels here upon the path. She shuts her eyes for a few seconds, her motions as matter of fact as when she washes rice. I linger longer than she does, so reluctant to leave, savoring the connection I feel with my grandmother in America, the past, and the power that lives and shines in the morning sun.

8   Our family has served this shrine for generations. The family's need to protect this claim to identity and place outweighs any individual claim to any individual hope. I am Japanese.

I Am a Japanese-American

"Weak." I hear the voice from my childhood years. "Passive," I hear. Our parents and grandparents were the ones who were put into those camps. They went without resistance; they offered cooperation as proof of loyalty to America. "Victim," I hear. And, "Silent."

Our parents are painted as hard workers who were socially uncomfortable and had difficulty expressing even the smallest opinion. Clean, quiet, motivated, and determined to match the American way; that is us, and that is the story of our time here.

"Why did you go into those camps?" I raged at my parents, frightened by my own inner silence and timidity. "Why didn't you do anything to resist? Why didn't you name it the injustice it was?" Couldn't our parents even think? Couldn't they? Why were we so passive?

12   I shift my vision and my stance. I am in California. My uncle is in the midst of the sweet potato harvest. He is pressed, trying to get the harvesting crews onto the field as quickly as possible, worried about the flow of equipment and people. His big pickup is pulled off to the side, motor running, door ajar. I see two tractors in the yard in front of an old shed; the flatbed harvesting platform on which the workers will stand has already been brought over from the other field. It's early morning. The workers stand loosely grouped and at ease, but my uncle looks as harried and tense as a police officer trying to unsnarl a New York City traffic jam. Driving toward the shed, I pull my car off the road to make way for an approaching tractor. The front wheels of the car sink luxuriously into the soft, white sand by the roadside and the car slides into a dreamy halt, tail still on the road. I try to move forward. I try to move back. The front bites

contentedly into the sand, the back lifts itself at a jaunty angle. My uncle sees me and storms down the road, running. He is shouting before he is even near me.

"What's the matter with you?" he screams. "What the hell are you doing?" In his frenzy, he grabs his hat off his head and slashes it through the air across his knee. He is beside himself. "Don't you know how to drive in sand? What's the matter with you? You've blocked the whole roadway. How am I supposed to get my tractors out of here? Can't you use your head? You've cut off the whole roadway, and we've got to get out of here."

I stand on the road before him helplessly thinking, "No, I don't know how to drive in sand. I've never driven in sand."

"I'm sorry, uncle," I say, burying a smile beneath a look of sincere apology. I notice my deep amusement and my affection for him with great curiosity. I am usually devastated by anger. Not this time.

16   During the several years that follow I learn about the people and the place, and much more about what has happened in this California village where my parents grew up. The issei, our grandparents, made this settlement in the desert. Their first crops were eaten by rabbits and ravaged by insects. The land was so barren that men walking from house to house sometimes got lost. Women came here too. They bore children in 114-degree heat, then carried the babies with them into the fields to nurse when they reached the end of each row of grapes or other truck-farm crops.

I had had no idea what it meant to buy this kind of land and make it grow green. Or how, when the war came, there was no space at all for the subtlety of being who we were—Japanese-Americans. Either/or was the way. I hadn't understood that people were literally afraid for their lives then, that their money had been frozen in banks; that there was a five-mile travel limit; that when the early evening curfew came and they were inside their houses, some of them watched helplessly as people they knew went into their barns to steal their belongings. The police were patrolling the road, interested only in violators of curfew. There was no help for them in the face of thievery. I had not been able to imagine before what it must have felt like to be an American—to know absolutely that one is an American—and yet to have almost everyone else deny it. Not only deny it, but challenge that identity with machine guns and troops of white American soldiers. In those circumstances it was difficult to say, "I'm a Japanese-American." "American" had to do.

But now I can say that I am a Japanese-American. It means I have a place here in this country, too. I have a place here on the East Coast, where our neighbor is so much a part of our family that my mother never passes her house at night without glancing at the lights to see if she is home and safe; where my parents have hauled hundreds of pounds of rocks from fields and arduously planted Christmas trees and blueberries, lilacs, asparagus, and crab apples; where my father still dreams of angling a stream to a new bed so that he can dig a pond in the field and fill it with water and fish. "The neighbors already came for their Christmas tree?" he asks in December. "Did they like it? Did they like it?"

I have a place on the West Coast where my relatives still farm, where I heard the stories of feuds and backbiting, and where I saw that people survived and flourished because fundamentally they trusted and relied upon one another. A death in the family is not just a death in a family; it is a death in the community. I saw people help each other with money, materials, labor, attention, and time. I saw men gather once a year, without fail, to clean the grounds of a ninety-year-old woman who had helped the community before, during, and after the war. I saw her remembering them with birthday cards sent to each of their children.

20   I come from a people with a long memory and a distinctive grace. We live our thanks. And we are Americans. Japanese-Americans.

I Am a Japanese-American Woman

Woman. The last piece of my identity. It has been easier by far for me to know myself in Japan and to see my place in America than it has been to accept my line of connection with my own mother. She was my dark self, a figure in whom I thought I saw all that I feared most in myself. Growing into womanhood and looking for some model of strength, I turned away from her. Of course, I could not find what I sought. I was looking for a black feminist or a white feminist. My mother is neither white nor black.

My mother is a woman who speaks with her life as much as with her tongue. I think of her with her own mother. Grandmother had Parkinson's disease and it had frozen her gait and set her fingers, tongue, and feet jerking and trembling in a terrible dance. My aunts and uncles wanted her to be able to live in her own home. They fed her, bathed her, dressed her, awoke at midnight to take her for one last trip to the bathroom. My aunts (her daughters-in-law) did most of the care, but my mother went from New Hampshire to California each summer to spend a month living with Grandmother, because she wanted to and because she wanted to give my aunts at least a small rest. During those hot summer days, mother lay on the couch watching the television or reading, cooking foods that Grandmother liked, and speaking little. Grandmother thrived under her care.

The time finally came when it was too dangerous for Grandmother to live alone. My relatives kept finding her on the floor beside her bed when they went to wake her in the mornings. My mother flew to California to help clean the house and make arrangements for Grandmother to enter a local nursing home. On her last day at home, while Grandmother was sitting in her big, overstuffed armchair, hair combed and wearing a green summer dress, my mother went to her and knelt at her feet. "Here, Mamma," she said. "I've polished your shoes." She lifted Grandmother's legs and helped her into the shiny black shoes. My Grandmother looked down and smiled slightly. She left her house walking, supported by her children, carrying her pocket book, and wearing her polished black shoes. "Look, Mamma," my mom had said, kneeling. "I've polished your shoes."

24   Just the other day, my mother came to Boston to visit. She had recently lost a lot of weight and was pleased with her new shape and her feeling of good health. "Look at me, Kes," she exclaimed, turning toward me, front and back, as naked as the day she was born. I saw her small breasts and the wide, brown scar, belly button to pubic hair, that marked her because my brother and I were both born by Caesarean section. Her hips were small. I was not a large baby, but there was so little room for me in her that when she was carrying me she could not even begin to bend over toward the floor. She hated it, she said.

"Don't I look good? Don't you think I look good?"

I looked at my mother, smiling and as happy as she, thinking of all the times I have seen her naked. I have seen both my parents naked throughout my life, as they have seen me. From childhood through adulthood we've had our naked moments, sharing baths, idle conversations picked up as we moved between showers and closets, hurried moments at the beginning of days, quiet moments at the end of days.

I know this to be Japanese, this ease with the physical, and it makes me think of an old Japanese folk song. A young nursemaid, a fifteen-year-old girl, is singing a lullaby to a baby who is strapped to her back. The nursemaid has been sent as a servant to a place far from her own home. "We're the beggars," she says, "and they are the nice people. Nice people wear fine sashes. Nice clothes."

If I should drop dead,
bury me by the roadside!
I'll give a flower
to everyone who passes.

What kind of flower?
The cam-cam-camellia [tsun-tsun-tsubaki]
watered by Heaven:
alms water.

28   The nursemaid is the intersection of heaven and earth, the intersection of the human, the natural world, the body, and the soul. In this song, with clear eyes, she looks steadily at life, which is sometimes so very terrible and sad. I think of her while looking at my mother, who is standing on the red and purple carpet before me, laughing, without any clothes.

I am my mother's daughter. And I am myself.

I am a Japanese-American woman.

Epilogue

I recently heard a man from West Africa share some memories of his childhood. He was raised Muslim, but when he was a young man, he found himself deeply drawn to Christianity. He struggled against his inner impulse for years, trying to avoid the church yet feeling pushed to return to it again and again. "I would have done *anything* to avoid the change," he said. At last, he became Christian. Afterwards he was afraid to go home, fearing that he would not be accepted. The fear was groundless, he discovered, when at last he returned—he had separated himself, but his family and friends (all Muslim) had not separated themselves from him.

32   The man, who is now a professor of religion, said that in the Africa he knew as a child and a young man, pluralism was embraced rather than feared. There was "a kind of tolerance that did not deny your particularity," he said. He alluded to zestful, spontaneous debates that would sometimes loudly erupt between Muslims and Christians in the village's public spaces. His memories of an atheist who harangued the villagers when he came to visit them once a week moved me deeply. Perhaps the man was an agricultural advisor or inspector. He harassed the women. He would say: "Don't go to the fields! Don't even bother to go to the fields. Let God take care of you. He'll send you the food. If you believe in God, why do you need to work? You don't need to work! Let God put the seeds in the ground. Stay home."

The professor said, "The women laughed, you know? They just laughed. Their attitude was, 'Here is a child of God. When will he come home?'"

The storyteller, the professor of religion, smiled a most fantastic tender smile as he told this story. "In my country, there is a deep affirmation of the oneness of God," he said. "The atheist and the women were having quite different experiences in the encounter, though the atheist did not know this. He saw himself as quite separate from the women. But the women did not see themselves as being separate from him. 'Here is a child of God,' they said. 'When will he come home?'"

1989

Personal Response

In what way, if any, have you experienced conflicting feelings about your own identity? How did you resolve the conflict? If you have not resolved it, explore reasons why it is difficult for you to do so.

Questions for Class or Small Group Discussion

1. Noda raises the issue of labels and their power to affect people. What stereotypes about the Japanese has Noda had to struggle with? What does being female add to her conflict? What is the "anti-Asian

prejudice" (paragraph 3) that both Chinese and Japanese in America historically fell victim to? Do you find yourself putting people into categories and labeling them? How would other people categorize you?

2. Summarize the contrasts between American and Japanese ways of viewing things, as Noda describes them. How do these contrasts help illuminate the complexity of her identity conflict?

3. Within each division of her essay, Noda not only explores conflicts over her identity but shifts perspectives ("I move to the other side" [paragraph 5], "I shift my vision and my stance" [paragraph 12], and "I think of her with her own mother" [paragraph 22]). How do these shifts in perspective help Noda understand the complexity of her personal conflict? How do they help resolve her conflict?

4. Discuss the meaning and implications of the epilogue. What point is Noda making with the anecdotes about the Muslim who converted to Christianity, the atheist who harassed the African village women, and the women's response? What solution to her problem do they suggest? Do you find it a fully satisfactory solution? Does Noda?

5. Discuss the stereotyped labels students in your class or others you know have experienced because of their ethnic or racial heritage. What happens to your discussion when your focus moves to white students? What do you think accounts for stereotypes and demeaning attitudes toward groups different from one's own? What prevents people from understanding the perspectives of other people? What aspects of American culture reinforce or even perpetuate stereotypes? How can you personally work against stereotyping and prejudice?

6. Try to imagine being of a different race or ethnic group from your own for a typical day. Then discuss your "day" with a classmate, preferably one whose race or ethnicity is different from yours.

HISPANIC IN AMERICA: STARTING POINTS

Ada María Isasi-Díaz

Ada María Isasi-Díaz is a writer living in New York. She has written, with Yolanda Tarango, a book entitled Women: Prophetic Voice in the Church *(1988). In 1982, she received the Chicago Catholic Women's Woman of the Year award. This piece, which Isasi-Díaz calls a "working paper," was published in* Christianity and Crisis *in 1991.*

The twenty-first century is rapidly approaching and with it comes a definitive increase in the Hispanic population of the United States. We will soon be the most numerous ethnic "minority"—a minority that seems greatly problematic because a significant number of us, some of us would say the majority, behave differently from other immigrant groups in the United States.

Our unwillingness to jump into the melting pot; our insistence on maintaining our own language; our ongoing links with our countries of origin—due mostly to their geographic proximity and to the continuous flow of more Hispanics into the United States; and the fact that the largest groups of Hispanics, Mexican Americans and Puerto Ricans, are geographically and politically an integral part of this country: These factors, among others, make us different. And the acceptance of that difference, which does not make us better or worse than other groups but simply different, has to be the starting point for understanding us. What follows is a kind of working paper, a guide toward reaching that starting point.

A preliminary note about terminology. What to call ourselves is an issue hotly debated in some segments of our communities. I use the term "Hispanic" because the majority of the communities I deal with include themselves in that term, though each and every one of us refers to ourselves according to our country of origin: Cubans, Puerto Ricans, Mexican Americans, etc. What I do wish to emphasize is that "Latina/o" does not have a more politicized or radical connotation than "Hispanic" among the majority of our communities. In my experience it is most often those outside our communities who insist on giving Latina/o such a connotation. The contrary, however, is true of the appellation, "Chicana/o," which does indicate a certain consciousness and political stance different from but not necessarily contrary to the one of those who call themselves Mexican Americans.

4   The way Hispanics participate in this society has to do not only with us, but also with U.S. history, economics, politics, and society. Hispanics are in this country to begin with mostly because of U.S. policies and interests. Great numbers of Mexican Americans never moved to the United States. Instead, the border crossed *them* in 1846 when Mexico had to give up today's Southwest in the Treaty of Guadalupe-Hidalgo. The spoils of the Spanish American War at the end of the nineteenth century included Puerto Rico, where the United States had both military and economic interests. Without having any say, that nation was annexed by the United States.

Cuba suffered a somewhat similar fate. The United States sent troops to Cuba in the midst of its War of Independence against Spain. When Spain surrendered, the United States occupied Cuba as a military protectorate. And though Cuba became a free republic in 1902, the United States continued to maintain economic control and repeatedly intervened in Cuba's political affairs. It was, therefore, only reasonable that when Cubans had to leave their country, they felt they could and should find refuge here.

The United States government accepted the Cuban refugees of the Castro regime, giving them economic aid and passing a special law making it easy for them to become residents and citizens.

As for more recent Hispanic immigrants, what can be said in a few lines about the constant manipulation by the United States of the economies and political processes of the different countries of Central America? The United States, therefore, has the moral responsibility to accept Salvadorans, Guatemalans, Hondurans, and other Central Americans who have to leave their countries because of political persecution or hunger. In short, the reasons Hispanics are in the United States are different from those of the earlier European immigrants, and the responsibility the United States has for our being here is vastly greater.

In spite of this difference, many people believe we Hispanics could have become as successful as the European immigrants. So why haven't we? For one thing, by the time Hispanics grew in numbers in the United States, the economy was no longer labor-intensive. Hispanics have lacked not "a strong back and a willingness to work," but the opportunity to capitalize on them. Then, unlike the European immigrants who went west and were able to buy land, Hispanics arrived here after homesteading had passed. But a more fundamental reason exists: racism. Hispanics are considered a nonwhite race, regardless of the fact that many of us are of the white race. Our ethnic difference has been officially construed as a racial difference: In government, businesses, and school forms "Hispanic" is one of the choices under the category *race.*

8   No possibility exists of understanding Hispanics and being in dialogue with us unless the short exposition just presented is studied and analyzed. The starting point for all dialogue is a profound respect for the other, and respect cannot flourish if the other is not known. A commitment to study the history of Hispanics in the United States—from the perspective of Hispanics and not only from the perspective presented in the standard textbooks of American history—must be the starting point in any attempt to understand Hispanics.

A second obstacle to dialogue is the prevalent insistence in this country that one American Way of Life exists, and it is the best way of life for everybody in the world. The melting pot concept has provided a framework in which assimilation is a must, and plurality of cultures an impossibility. Hispanic culture is not seen as an enrichment but as a threat. Few understand that Hispanic culture provides for us, as other cultures do for other peoples, guidelines for conduct and relationships, a system of values, and institutions and power structures that allow us to function at our best. Our culture has been formed and will continue to be shaped by the historical happenings and the constant actions of our communities—communities in the United States that are influenced by what happens here as well as in our countries of origin.

It is only within our own culture that Hispanics can acquire a sense of belonging, of security, of dignity, and of participation. The ongoing attempts to minimize or to make our culture disappear will only create problems for the United States. They engender a low sense of identity that can lead us to nonhealthy extremes in our search for some self-esteem. For us, language is the main means of identification here in the United States. To speak Spanish, in public as well as in private, is a political act, a means of asserting who we are, an important way of struggling against assimilation. The different state laws that forbid speaking Spanish in official situations, or militate against bilingual education, function as an oppressive internal colonialism that ends up hurting U.S. society.

The majority of Hispanics are U.S. citizens who have lived here all of our lives. To engage with us, Americans belonging to the dominant group, as well as to different marginalized racial and ethnic groups, must be open to new possibilities, to new elements becoming part of the American Way. Above all, they must reach beyond the liberal insistence on individualism, now bordering on recalcitrant self-centeredness. This is all the more urgent given the importance of community and family in Hispanic culture. Community for us is so central that we understand personhood as necessarily including relationship with some form of community. Family has to do not only with those to whom we are immediately related or related only by blood; it is a multilayered structure constituted by all those who care, all those to whom we feel close, who share our interests, commitments, understandings, and to whom we will always remain faithful. This sense of family is closer to the model that is becoming prevalent in the United States instead of the now almost mythical nuclear family. Indeed, Hispanics have much to contribute to the changing concept of family in this society.

12   The importance of community also finds expression in the way we relate to others at our work places. Our business contacts and dealings have at their center personal relationships much more than institutionalized procedures and structures. It is often better to know someone, even someone who knows someone, than to present the best plan, have the highest bid, or be the first one there. And the very prosperous Hispanic businesses that do exist here, though limited in number when one considers that more than 18 million Hispanics live in this country, clearly show that the way we do business can also be successful.

Hispanics know that we wear our emotions pinned on our sleeves, that we express what we believe and feel quite readily. Not to feel deeply seems to us to diminish our sense of humanity. We do not find it valuable to hide our subjectivity behind a so-called objectivity and uniform ways of dealing with everyone. We proudly and quickly express our opinions. For us time is to be used to further and enjoy our sense of community. It is more important to wait for everyone to be present than to start a meeting exactly on time. It is more important to listen to everybody and to take time to dwell on the personal than to end a meeting on time.

And those who want to deal with Hispanics need to know that conscience plays a very prominent role in our lives because we live life intensely. We do not take anything lightly, whether it is play, work, love, or, unfortunately, hate. We often think in ethical terms even in inconsequential matters. This intensity and insistence in giving serious consideration to almost all aspects of life are a constitutive element of our high sense of honor, our way of talking about our standard of morality and personhood, which we are willing to defend no matter the cost.

Finally, those who wish to understand Hispanics need to know that our religious practices—what is often referred to as *religiosidad popular*—express our close relationship with the divine. A personal relationship with God and the living-out of that relationship in day-to-day life is much more important to us than establishing and maintaining relationships with church structures and going to church on Sundays. Christianity, and specifically Roman Catholicism, are an intrinsic part of Hispanic culture—something not always understood and taken into consideration in this secular culture. Many of the cultural traditions and customs still prevalent today in Hispanic communities are closely entwined with religious rituals. Processions, lighting candles, relating to the saints, arguing and bartering with God through *promesas*—all of these are not only a matter of religion but a matter of culture.

16   The dominant groups in U.S. society must acknowledge that Hispanics have much to contribute to the United States and that in order to do so we must be allowed to be who we are. Meanwhile, the dominant groups in society, especially, need to be open to cultural, religious, social, and even organizational pluralism. The nations that have failed and disappeared from the map of our world are not those that have been open to change but rather those that insist on rigidity, uniformity, and believing they are better than others. That is what should be adamantly opposed in the United States—not a multiplicity of language, cultures, and customs.

Personal Response

Has your understanding of Hispanics changed or been reinforced as a result of reading this essay? Explain your answer. If you are Hispanic, describe your feelings as you read the essay.

Questions for Class or Small Group Discussion

1. Isasi-Diaz says that we must understand the history of Hispanics in the United States "from the perspective of Hispanics and not from the perspective presented in the standard textbooks of American history"

(paragraph 8). How do those two perspectives differ? What do you recall about Hispanics from reading history books?

2. Isasi-Diaz (like Kesaya E. Noda in "Growing Up Asian in America")
writes in favor of a pluralistic society, not a melting pot society in which
minorities are assimilated into the dominant culture. Conduct a class
debate or an intense discussion in your small group on the issue of melting pot versus pluralism, taking as a starting point the issues Isasi-Diaz
raises in her essay.

3. In paragraph 4, Isasi-Diaz asserts that "the way Hispanics participate in [American] society has to do not only with us, but also with
U.S. history, economics, politics, and society." To what extent do you
think that approach applies to other ethnic or racial groups trying to be
understood in America? How do you think each of those perspectives—
historical, economic, political, and societal—informs our understanding of Hispanics?

4. Discuss the subject of terminology for various racial or ethnic
groups. What impact do you think labels or other identity markers have
on members of those groups?

CULTURAL BAGGAGE

Barbara Ehrenreich

*Barbara Ehrenreich is a writer whose articles appear in a variety
of popular magazines and newspapers. She has contributed to* Time
magazine, Ms. *magazine, and* The New York Times, *among many
others. In this piece, which appeared in the "Hers" column, a regular
feature of* The New York Times Sunday Magazine, *in 1992, Ehrenreich explains why she has little interest in her own ethnic heritage.*

An acquaintance was telling me about the joys of rediscovering her ethnic
and religious heritage. "I know exactly what my ancestors were doing
2,000 years ago," she said, eyes gleaming with enthusiasm, "and *I can do the
same things now.*" Then she leaned forward and inquired politely, "And
what is your ethnic background, if I may ask?"

"None," I said, that being the first word in line to get out of my
mouth. Well, not "none," I backtracked. Scottish, English, Irish—that was
something, I supposed. Too much Irish to qualify as a WASP; too much of
the hated English to warrant a "Kiss Me, I'm Irish" button; plus there are a
number of dead ends in the family tree due to adoptions, missing records,
failing memories and the like. I was blushing by this time. Did "none" mean

I was rejecting my heritage out of Anglo-Celtic self-hate? Or was I revealing a hidden ethnic chauvinism in which the Britannically derived serve as a kind of neutral standard compared with the ethnic "others"?

Throughout the 60's and 70's, I watched one group after another—African-Americans, Latinos, Native Americans—stand up and proudly reclaim their roots while I just sank back ever deeper into my seat. All this excitement over ethnicity stemmed, I uneasily sensed, from a past in which *their* ancestors had been trampled upon by *my* ancestors, or at least by people who looked very much like them. In addition, it had begun to seem almost un-American not to have some sort of hyphen at hand, linking one to more venerable times and locales.

4   But the truth is, I was raised with none. We'd eaten ethnic foods in my childhood home, but these were all borrowed, like the pasties, or Cornish meat pies, my father had picked up from his fellow miners in Butte, Mont. If my mother had one rule, it was militant ecumenism in all matters of food and experience. "Try new things," she would say, meaning anything from sweetbreads to clams, with an emphasis on the "new."

As a child, I briefly nourished a craving for tradition and roots. I immersed myself in the works of Sir Walter Scott. I pretended to believe that the bagpipe was a musical instrument. I was fascinated to learn from a grandmother that we were descended from certain Highland clans and longed for a pleated skirt in one of their distinctive tartans.

But in "Ivanhoe," it was the dark-eyed "Jewess" Rebecca I identified with, not the flaxen-haired bimbo Rowena. As for clans: Why not call them "tribes," those bands of half-clad peasants and warriors whose idea of cuisine was stuffed sheet gut washed down with whisky? And then there was the sting of Disraeli's remark—which I came across in my early teens—to the effect that his ancestors had been leading orderly, literate lives when my ancestors were still rampaging through the Highlands daubing themselves with blue paint.

Motherhood put the screws on me, ethnicitywise. I had hoped that by marrying a man of Eastern European-Jewish ancestry I would acquire for my descendants the ethnic genes that my own forebears so sadly lacked. At one point, I even subjected the children to a seder of my own design, including a little talk about the flight from Egypt and its relevance to modern social issues. But the kids insisted on buttering their matzohs and snickering through my talk. "Give me a break, Mom," the older one said. "You don't even believe in God."

8   After the tiny pagans had been put to bed, I sat down to brood over Elijah's wine. What had I been thinking? The kids knew that their Jewish grandparents were secular folks who didn't hold seders themselves. And if ethnicity eluded me, how could I expect it to take root in my children, who are not only Scottish-English-Irish, but Hungarian-Polish-Russian to boot?

But, then, on the fumes of Manischewitz, a great insight took form in my mind. It was true, as the kids said, that I didn't "believe in God." But this could be taken as something very different from an accusation—a reminder of a genuine heritage. My parents had not believed in God either, nor had my grandparents or any other progenitors going back to the great-great level. They had become disillusioned with Christianity generations ago—just as, on the in-law side, my children's other ancestors had shaken off their Orthodox Judaism. This insight did not exactly furnish me with an "identity," but it was at least something to work with: we are the kind of people, I realized—whatever our distant ancestors' religions—who do *not* believe, who do not carry on traditions, who do not do things just because someone has done them before.

The epiphany went on: I recalled that my mother never introduced a procedure for cooking or cleaning by telling me, "Grandma did it this way." What did Grandma know, living in the days before vacuum cleaners and disposable toilet mops? In my parents' general view, new things were better than old, and the very fact that some ritual had been performed in the past was a good reason for abandoning it now. Because what was the past, as our forebears knew it? Nothing but poverty, superstition and grief. "Think for yourself," Dad used to say. "Always ask why."

In fact, this may have been the ideal cultural heritage for my particular ethnic strain—bounced as it was from the Highlands of Scotland across the sea, out to the Rockies, down into the mines and finally spewed out into high-tech, suburban America. What better philosophy, for a race of migrants, than "Think for yourself"? What better maxim, for a people whose whole world was rudely inverted every 30 years or so, than "Try new things"?

12   The more tradition-minded, the newly enthusiastic celebrants of Purim and Kwanzaa and Solstice, may see little point to survival if the survivors carry no cultural freight—religion, for example, or ethnic tradition. To which I would say that skepticism, curiosity and wide-eyed ecumenical tolerance are also worthy elements of the human tradition and are at least as old as such notions as "Serbian" or "Croatian," "Scottish" or "Jewish." I make no claims for my personal line of progenitors except that they remained loyal to the values that may have induced all of our ancestors, long, long ago, to climb down from the trees and make their way into the open plains.

A few weeks ago, I cleared my throat and asked the children, now mostly grown and fearsomely smart, whether they felt any stirrings of ethnic or religious identity, etc., which might have been, ahem, insufficiently nourished at home. "None," they said, adding firmly, "and the world would be a better place if nobody else did, either." My chest swelled with pride, as would my mother's, to know that the race of "none" marches on.

Personal Response

How do you feel about Ehrenreich's relative lack of interest in her heritage? How strongly do you feel about your own ethnic and religious heritage?

Questions for Class or Small Group Discussion

1. Assess Ehrenreich's remarks about other people's celebrations of their ethnic, race, and religious heritage in light of her own white Anglo-Celtic background. How, if at all, do you think that perspective affects her viewpoint?

2. What do you think Ehrenreich means in paragraph 2 when she refers to "a hidden ethnic chauvinism"?

3. Do you think Ehrenreich makes a valid point about heritage and identity, or do you disagree with her completely? Explain your answer.

4. Ehrenreich reveals that she identified with "the dark-eyed 'Jewess' Rebecca" in Scott's *Ivanhoe,* rather than with the character who is more like her in background (paragraph 6). Discuss your own heroes in books or movies and what attracts you to them.

5. What do you imagine the authors of the other essays in this chapter—Kesaya E. Noda and Ada María Isasi-Diaz—would say in response to Ehrenreich? Working in small groups, create an imaginary conversation among these three writers. Try to capture their voices as they are revealed through their essays.

Perspectives on Race and Ethnicity
Suggestions for Synthesis

1. All the authors in this chapter address the issue of labels. Synthesize their discussions into your own analysis of the role labels play in one's identity, self-esteem, and/or self-concept.

2. Kesaya E. Noda ("Growing Up Asian in America") and Ada María Isasi-Diaz ("Hispanic in America: Starting Points") both write in favor of a pluralistic society, not a melting pot society in which minorities are assimilated into the dominant culture. Explore your position on the issue of melting pot versus pluralism, taking into consideration the views of Noda and Isasi-Diaz.

3. Conduct a class workshop on prejudice in America. The entire class should agree on topics to cover and the format for the workshop. Individual students

may volunteer to write papers or speak from notes for presentation to the class, or you may want to invite guest speakers such as the affirmative action officer from your campus or the director of your campus minority studies program, if you have one.

4. Explore the possibilities of using as models for solving social problems Hispanics' concept of community and the important role religion or spirituality plays in their lives, as Isasi-Diaz explains them in "Hispanic in America: Starting Points." Select a particular problem from this chapter or from "Poverty and the Family," "Criminal Behavior," or "Public Health Issues" and explain how applying the Hispanic models might help solve the problem.

5. Interview at least one other person whose racial or ethnic heritage is different from yours about some of the points raised in the essays by Kesaya E. Noda and Ada María Isasi-Diaz. Then write an essay explaining what you learned and how (if) the interview has in any way changed your own views on the issue of racism.

Additional Writing Topics

1. Write a reflective essay on your own cultural heritage, explaining your family's background and how you feel about that heritage.

2. Prepare a working paper, as Ada María Isasi-Diaz has done in "Hispanic in America: Starting Points," in which you set forth what you believe are starting points for countering prejudice or ethnic and racial hatred in the United States.

3. Isasi-Diaz, in "Hispanic in America: Starting Points," says that we must understand the history of Hispanics in the United States "from the perspective of Hispanics and not only from the perspective presented in the standard textbooks of American history" (paragraph 8). Write an essay in which you explain how those two perspectives differ, including examples of what you recall about Hispanics from reading history books.

4. Write a letter to the editor of the *New York Times Sunday Magazine* in which you explain why you agree or disagree with Barbara Ehrenreich's viewpoint on celebrating racial or ethnic heritage in "Cultural Baggage."

Research Topics

1. Research and write a paper on one of the following topics related to some of the essays in this chapter: the influx of Chinese immigrants to America in the nineteenth century; the Chinese Exclusion Act of 1882 and its implications for Japanese immigrants; the Japanese religion Shinto; the internment of Japanese in America during World War II; or the economic, political, or historical relationship of the United States with Puerto Rico, Cuba, Central America, or Mexico.

2. Expand writing topic number 3 under "Additional Writing Topics" to include library research. Find sources that reread Hispanic history or point out discrepancies, as Isasi-Diaz suggests. Then explain the conclusions you draw on the basis of your research and personal knowledge.

CHAPTER 14

INTERNATIONAL RELATIONS

America has long held a strong position in international relations. Leaders of many countries see the United States as a powerful ally in times of war and as a source of aid, both financial and humanitarian, in peacetime, when weak countries struggle to become stronger and work toward financial and political independence. Some critics of American foreign policy see this strength as a mixed blessing, however. They point out that America's ability and willingness to help less advantaged nations means that far more countries than America can reasonably aid ask for assistance. As a result, critics argue, America's own resources are diminished and its domestic problems do not get the attention they deserve. Supporters of America's foreign policy argue that America is morally and ethically obligated to help weak countries, especially when they are targets of hostile aggression from other countries.

While the subject of international relations is very broad, the essays in this chapter narrowly focus on two topics: the controversy over the role America should play in defending and assisting other countries and the question of how to establish ties and improve relationships between American citizens and people in other countries. The first three essays consider the role of the United States in wartime and the degree to which it ought to take responsibility for aiding weak countries. The final essay addresses ways to strengthen friendly relations between the United States and Japan. In Part Five of this textbook, you will find additional essays on America's relations with foreign nations. The chapters entitled "The American Image Abroad" and "The United States in the Global Marketplace" consider those relationships from the perspective of business and economics.

Commenting on American involvement in the 1991 Gulf War, Charles Krauthammer argues that the United States does not have to be the world's police force. In "Must America Slay All the Dragons?" Krauthammer explains why he believes America should not feel responsible for the fates of many of the world's small countries. Before you read his essay, think about your own impressions when America became involved in the Gulf War. Then, as you read his argument, consider whether you agree with Krauthammer's position and why or why not.

Offering a contrasting viewpoint on the subject of America's responsibility for others, Paul Johnson, in "Colonialism's Back—and Not a Moment Too Soon," disagrees with the position Krauthammer takes. Johnson argues that the United States and other major world powers have a moral obligation to help weakened Third World countries regain their stability. Again, as you read

Johnson's essay, consider whether you agree with him and why or why not. Finally, on the subject of America's involvement in foreign wars, John Lukacs explains how in each postwar period Americans have typically reconsidered and finally disapproved of that involvement. In "Revising the Twentieth Century," Lukacs summarizes four periods of revisionism following four great struggles of this century and warns about a potential danger of revisionism.

The chapter ends with an essay by Hisako Yanaka, a Japanese American Studies professor in Tokyo who has made many extended visits to the United States. In "Building Bridges Between Young Japanese and African Americans," she proposes ways to strengthen U.S.–Japanese relations. She points out that a lack of knowledge about each other will prevent mutual understanding and suggests that educating the next generation without bias or prejudice is crucial to strengthening relationships between the two countries. As you read what she has to say about the United States and Japan, think of your own relationship with people from foreign countries you know or have met, and consider whether Yanaka's observations could apply to the United States' relationship to other countries as well.

MUST AMERICA SLAY ALL THE DRAGONS?

Charles Krauthammer

Charles Krauthammer is a contributing editor for The New Republic *and writes a syndicated column that appears in a number of national magazine. He also contributes to* Time *magazine, where the following essay appeared shortly before the end of the Gulf War in 1991. Krauthammer clearly believes that the United States has committed itself too broadly and too often to aiding foreign countries in times of both war and peace.*

Students massacred in China, priests murdered in Central America, demonstrators gunned down in Lithuania—these acts of violence are as wrong as Iraqi soldiers' killing civilians. We cannot oppose repression in one place and overlook it in another.
—*Senator George Mitchell, January 29, 1991*

So what does this mean, that we want to stop naked [Iraqi] aggression? Does this mean that . . . the United States will indeed become the policeman of the world?
—*Senator Tom Harkin, January 11, 1991*

Well, gentlemen, which is it? The Democrats first complain that it is hypocritical to oppose injustice *x* but tolerate injustice *y*. Then they complain that the U.S. has turned into the world's policeman. How can it be otherwise? If stopping one injustice morally commits us to stopping all injustice, what does that make the U.S. if not the world's policeman?

It does not take a Kissinger to figure that any nation has to be selective in its attention to the injustices of the world. Those who imply otherwise have an agenda—and it is not to turn the U.S. into the world's policeman. It is to turn the U.S. into the world's bystander. If opposing injustice anywhere obliges us to become involved everywhere, then only a fool would not prefer involvement nowhere.

This false everywhere–nowhere dichotomy is the moral pillar of American isolationism. Wherever the American banner has been raised in the past decade—Grenada, Panama, Nicaragua and now the Persian Gulf—isolationists have demanded to know, How can we in good conscience oppose bad guys there and not land Marines in Port-au-Prince or Cape Town?

4   The question is posed constantly. Only the place names change. Mitchell, in his response to the President's State of the Union address, brought up China, El Salvador and Lithuania. Mario Cuomo, questioning George Bush's motive for intervening in the gulf, asks ironically, Was it designed to curb aggression? Then why not intervene in Afghanistan or Tibet?

The answer is breathtakingly simple. Why are American exertions on behalf of the oppressed selective? National interest.

Americans, haunted by the stern visage of Woodrow Wilson, are loath to confess that they do not act for reasons of morality alone. We would rather not admit that one reason to resist Saddam Hussein is that we are not prepared to see the economies of the West wrecked by the ambition of a foreign tyrant. Indeed, some American critics think it a fatal moral criticism of the gulf war to say that if Kuwait had only sand and no oil, the U.S. would not have rushed to its defense.

The answer to that charge is, Of course not. And, So what? Foreign policy is not philanthropy. Any intervention must pass two tests: it must be 1) right and 2) in our interests. Each is a necessary condition. Neither is sufficient. Otherwise, foreign policy degenerates into mindless moralism on the one hand or cynical realpolitik on the other.

8   The U.S. does not intervene purely for reasons of morality. If it did, it would spend itself dry righting every wrong in the world. Nor does it act purely out of self-interest. If, for example, a genuine pro-Iraqi coup had led Kuwaitis to join voluntarily with Iraq, the U.S. would hardly have gone to war to reverse that action. (During the oil shocks of the 1970s, suggestions that the U.S. seize the oil fields of Arabia were never even taken seriously.)

Every intervention requires a just cause. That doesn't mean that every just cause warrants intervention. To warrant intervention, a cause must at the same time be important to the U.S. The idea that importance ought not matter and that consistency impels us to intervene against every injustice is simply American moralism gone wild.

Life presents us with a hierarchy of evils. Being finite, we are forced to assign them priority and even, if necessary, tolerate some lesser evil to fight the greater. Was it wrong to have blinked at the enormities of Stalin for the four years that he was needed in the war against Hitler?

Take a hard case, Lithuania. For the months of the gulf crisis, until Gorbachev went free-lancing with his peace plan, there seemed to be a tacit U.S.-Soviet understanding that the U.S.S.R. would stay within the anti-Iraq coalition and the U.S. would go easy on criticizing Moscow's repression of Lithuania. Is such a deal conscionable?

12   One could say that it is foolish, that we are misreading our interests, that in the long run a freed Soviet empire is more important to America than a small Arabian principality. Perhaps, but the critics' charge is not geopolitical. It is moral. Americans, they maintain, cannot in good conscience uphold freedom in one place and tolerate repression in another.

Yes, they can, and sometimes they must. America is not omnipotent. It cannot be everywhere. It has to have priorities. One cannot equate the utter devastation of Kuwait with the cruel but hardly fatal repression of Lithuania. There is no doubt that under Gorbachev or his generals, Lithuania will continue to exist as a society. There can be little doubt that under Saddam, Kuwait will not.

Foreign policy is an exercise in discrimination. Our resources, like our stores of compassion, are finite. We take up arms against those troubles that are both particularly evil and particularly threatening to us. And we husband our resources to meet those troubles. That will occasionally mean having to recruit others to help and having to make moral compromises to keep that help. Hence our long minute with the Soviets over the Baltics.

After the gulf crisis, we must be equally nimble in reordering our priorities. We must immediately turn to a vigorous advocacy of Baltic independence. But it would be irresponsible to jeopardize the war effort by doing so during the crisis. War is no time for moral luxuries. The first task in war is winning it.

16   We cannot slay all the dragons at once. There is no dishonor in slaying them one at a time.

Personal Response

What are your memories or impressions of the Gulf War?

Questions for Class or Small Group Discussion

1. The essay begins with a quotation from Senator George Mitchell, who maintains that "we cannot oppose repression in one place and overlook it in another." Do you agree or disagree with Senator Mitchell?

2. Discuss Krauthammer's response to Senator Mitchell and others like him who believe that if America goes to the aid of one oppressed country, it must go to the aid of all of them. Whose position do you agree with? Why?

3. Krauthammer brings up the point that America would not have become involved in the Gulf War "if Kuwait had only sand and no oil" (paragraph 6). Do you agree or disagree with him? Explain your answer.

4. Discuss Krauthammer's assertion that any American "intervention must pass two tests: it must be 1) right and 2) in our interests" (paragraph 7). Did U.S. involvement in Grenada, Panama, and Nicaragua meet those criteria (paragraph 3)? Can you think of other conflicts America has intervened in? Do they meet Krauthammer's criteria?

COLONIALISM'S BACK—AND NOT A MOMENT TOO SOON
Paul Johnson

Paul Johnson, author of Modern Times, *is currently at work on a history of the American people. This essay was first published in the April 19, 1993, issue of* The New York Times Magazine. *Taking a position opposed to that of Charles Krauthammer in the previous essay, Johnson explains why he believes that the United States has a moral obligation to Third World nations.*

We are witnessing today a revival of colonialism, albeit in a new form. It is a trend that should be encouraged, it seems to me, on practical as well as moral grounds. There simply is no alternative in nations where governments have crumbled and the most basic conditions for civilized life have disappeared, as is now the case in a great many third-world countries.

Third-world governments have long sought military assistance from the advanced powers to put down internal rebellions. But a historic line was crossed when American marines landed in Somalia—without any request, because no government existed. The intervention, made with the approval of the United Nations Security Council, was a humanitarian attempt to supply some kind of protection for life and property in a country that had shown it could not govern itself. The old-style United Nations approach, of sending officials to hold talks with the opposing factions, was visibly demonstrated to have failed when an angry Somali mob threw rubbish at the walls of the United Nations compound, thinking that the Secretary General, Boutros Boutros-Ghali, was within.

Nor is Somalia the only instance in which the international community is being obliged to take on a semi-colonial role. On March 31 the Security Council voted, without dissent (China abstained), for direct military intervention in the internal affairs of the former Yugoslavia. This decision indicated, among other things, that the new colonialism is not just about white men running the affairs of nonwhite countries but can involve intervention in Europe—or anywhere else.

4   But it is obvious that Africa, where normal government is breaking down in a score or more states, is the most likely theater for such action. The appeals for help come not so much from Africa's political elites, who are anxious to cling to the trappings of power, as from ordinary, desperate citizens, who carry the burden of misrule. Recently in Liberia, where rival bands of heavily armed thugs have been struggling for mastery, a humble inhabitant of the capital, Monrovia, named after the fifth President of the United States, approached a marine guarding the United States Embassy and said, "For God's sake come and govern us!"

The grass-roots origin of the appeal for the return of colonialism puts the whole phenomenon in a different perspective. The present generation, even in the former colonial powers, has been brought up to consider any form of colonialism as inherently evil, a gross form of oppression practiced by technologically superior powers on weaker races. That, of course, is not how its practitioners, throughout history, saw it.

The Greeks, who invented colonialism, founded city-colonies to spread their civilization. The Romans, who inherited the Greek empire, did the same. Most of the people thus colonized welcomed this form of rule and lamented the destruction of the Roman Empire in the fifth century A.D. as a catastrophe.

From the Renaissance through to the early years of the 20th century, first the European powers and then Russia and the United States competed for colonies, and all believed they were bestowing civilization on those less fortunate. By the early 20th century, however, colonialism was operating under growing restrictions imposed by liberal opinion.

8   Indeed, by the end of the First World War, when Woodrow Wilson insured the triumph of self-determination throughout Europe, colonialism was manifestly on the moral defensive. Hence, the Versailles treaty, instead of carving up the former colonies of Germany and Turkey among the victorious powers, created trusteeships. These were territories not yet considered fit for self-government but mandated by the League of Nations to various civilized powers to be prepared for independence. Britain got Iraq, Jordan, Palestine and Tanganyika (now Tanzania); France got Syria and Lebanon, and the United States and Japan were awarded various Pacific territories.

"Trusteeship" was a notion derived from English common law, in which a child was made a ward of the court until attaining the age of 21. It had first been applied to a territory in 1899, when Britain, with Egypt, created the Anglo-Egyptian Sudan, known as a condominium, the aim being to train cadres who would eventually lead it to independence. This British notion that there was no such thing as a colony in perpetuity, but that all territories would become independent when they were ready for it, was already implicit in British administration throughout its Asian and African empire, and had been put into force in its so-called White Dominions of South Africa, Canada, Australia and New Zealand.

From Versailles onward, then, there was a growing assumption that all colonies would eventually be freed. Hostility to colonialism increased throughout the Second World War, fueled by American high-mindedness and by the ideological beliefs of the Soviet regime, where Lenin's anticolonial tract "Imperialism" was part of the canon.

These new moral forces, and the physical impact of the Second World War, which weakened the old European colonial powers, especially Britain, brought about the age of decolonization. There was a paradox in this process. Colonies had never been better administered than during their last phase. Britain had set increasingly high standards. Ghana and Nigeria, for example, were meticulously prepared for their freedom. Morocco was admirably ruled by France in the person of Marshal Lyautey, who gave it a superb infrastructure of roads and ports. The Congo, originally looted by Belgium, got a model trustee-type administration in the 1950's.

12　　But at precisely the time when colonies were deriving the maximum benefit from European rule, the decision was taken to liberate them forthwith. Many experienced colonial administrators were appalled at the way in which the gradualist approach to self-rule was abruptly abandoned. But in the rush, their voices went unheeded. There are fashions in geopolitics as well as in clothes, and instant decolonization was one. By the mid-1960's it was virtually all over.

Then came the reckoning, borne not indeed by the colonial powers themselves, which on balance benefited financially from surrendering their "white man's burden" (as Kipling called it), but by their former subjects. In Africa, the instability that began immediately after the Belgian Congo was decolonized in 1960 has since continued throughout most of the continent. Not everyone has suffered. Three categories have flourished: the professional politicians, the army officers and the less scrupulous businessmen. But most ordinary Africans have done badly, as a result of the collapse of constitutional government and the rule of law, as well as civil and tribal conflicts, invasion, corruption and man-made famines.

In the Congo, now Zaire, average real incomes are now a fraction of what they were in the early 1960's, and this is probably true of a number of countries, though in present conditions statistics are worthless. Some of the smaller states have drifted out of the international economy almost altogether. Certain states, like Chad and Mauritania, have known nothing but internal warfare for a generation—a Hobbesian nightmare in which life is "nasty, brutish and short." The record of Angola and Mozambique is not much better.

Particularly sad has been the ruin of territories that once were advancing rapidly under colonialism. The Anglo-Egyptian Sudan, the most notable of them, has been the victim of a prolonged civil war, of the famine it inevitably produced and of systematic harassment of the Christian south by the Muslim north. Uganda, another tribute to colonialism, suffered the atrocious tyranny of Idi Amin, and is still impoverished and lawless.

Tanzania, a successful mandate, has gone slowly downhill under a quasi-socialist regime, despite having received more financial aid per capita than any other third-world country. There are numerous others: the Central African Republic, Nigeria, Algeria, Liberia, the Horn of Africa.

16   Western experts who had backed the rapid transfer of power argued that Africa, in particular, was going through a difficult transition, and that patience—plus assistance of all kinds—was imperative. That view is now discredited. During the 1980's it came to be recognized that government-to-government aid usually served only to keep in power unsuccessful, unpopular and often vicious regimes.

As for patience, the historical record shows it served nobody. By the early 1990's, two of the world's most chronically unstable and poorest black states were Haiti and Liberia, which had been governing themselves for 200 and 150 years respectively. In both, ordinary citizens, who had no security for property or even life, clamored for Western intervention.

During the 1980's, old-style aid was largely discontinued. Western governments underwrote specific, approved projects, and supervised the spending. At the same time, huge quantities of money and goods were distributed by international charities. But both methods, while an improvement on the old, in many cases ran into the insuperable problem of government breakdown, which meant that aid supplies were commandeered and looted or sold on the black market by tribal factions and brigands. By the early 1990's, some international agencies were beginning openly to argue that, in crisis situations, like the famines in East Africa, a Western military presence was essential to supplement a largely nonexistent government.

Recall, however, that it was United Nations theory and practice to deploy troops at the request of a legitimate government. But what was to be done in places like Haiti, where there was no legitimate government, or Somalia, where there was no government at all? Were the U.N. and the West to stand idly by?

20   During the 1970's the answer would almost certainly have been yes. But in the 1980's geopolitical fashion once more began to change, as Western powers showed a renewed willingness to use force in what they believed to be right. The new fashion was set by Margaret Thatcher's Britain in 1982, when it reversed the aggression in the Falklands. Thus emboldened, President Reagan intervened to reverse an extremist coup in Grenada, and both powers led a mighty coalition of states, including many in the third world, to reverse the Iraqi occupation of Kuwait in 1990.

The decision of the United States, with United Nations authority, to send marines into Somalia marked a new turning point. Here there could be no question of invitation from the local government, since no such body existed and the whole purpose of the landing was to insure aid supplies got to where they were needed, and to protect them, and aid workers, from the armed bands that divided the country between themselves. But such armed intervention, by its very nature, is bound to prove unsatisfactory, and the American effort has already run into difficulties.

French and Belgian forces used in "rescue missions" in central Africa have met exactly the same problem. They can restore order for a time, and in limited areas, but they cannot tackle the source of the disorder, which is political and requires a political solution. The moment they pull out, the disorders reappear.

It is worth remembering that the original Dutch, Portuguese and British traders who came to the African coasts in the early modern period, with the aim of doing business and with no intention of settling, faced exactly the same problem. They could not trade without stability, and to get stability they had to impose it. So they built little forts, which became bigger and eventually turned into the nucleus of colonies. European colonialism in its origins was to some extent a reluctant and involuntary process.

24   Happily, the civilized powers need not get stuck in the old colonial quagmire, because they have the example of the trusteeship system before them. The Security Council could commit a territory where authority has irretrievably broken down to one or more trustees. These would be empowered not merely to impose order by force but to assume political functions. They would in effect be possessed of sovereign powers.

Their mandate would usually be of limited duration—5, 10, 20 years, for example—and subject to supervision by the Security Council; and their ultimate object would be to take constitutional measures to insure a return to effective self-government with all deliberate speed. I stress "effective" because we must not repeat the mistakes of the 1960's. The trustees should not plan to withdraw until they are reasonably certain that the return to independence will be successful this time. So the mandate may last 50 years, or 100.

Reviving trusteeship means reversing the conventional wisdom of the last half-century, which laid down that all peoples are ready for independence and that any difficulties they encounter are the result of distortions created by colonialism itself. But this philosophy is false, as painful events have repeatedly demonstrated. Africa's problems—and the problems of some states outside Africa—are not created by colonialism or demographics or natural disasters or shortage of credit. Most of the horrors, including famine, are created by government: bad, incompetent and corrupt government, usually all three together, or by no government at all.

For more than 30 years the international community has been treating symptoms, not causes. The basic cause is obvious but is never publicly admitted: some states are not yet fit to govern themselves. Their continued existence, and the violence and human degradation they breed, is a threat to the stability of their neighbors as well as an affront to our consciences. There is a moral issue here: the civilized world has a mission to go out to these desperate places and govern.

28   By "civilized world" we ought eventually to include among potential trustees not only Germany and Japan, which will soon be eligible for permanent membership in the Security Council, but countries like Singapore, which have proved themselves models of public administration. Russia, China and India will eventually play their part—one way to educate them in the global responsibilities that their size and numbers oblige them to assume. There must be several models of trusteeship, ranging from the provision of basic government where none exists to the setting up of internal security networks and mandatory economic management.

If done firmly and confidently, such state-building will prove popular. It is important, therefore, that the first pilot projects should be carefully chosen, and its trustees experienced. Somalia is an obvious choice. So is Liberia and perhaps Haiti. Zaire, where the crumbling Mobutu tyranny will be followed by anarchy, is another candidate, as are Angola and Mozambique.

Making a start will not be easy because it means scrapping the easy assumptions of decades. Once again, the already overburdened United States will have to take the major responsibility, though it can count on staunch support from Britain and, in this case, from France. Labor and expense will be needed, as well as brains, leadership and infinite patience. The only satisfaction will be the unspoken gratitude of millions of misgoverned or ungoverned people who will find in this altruistic revival of colonialism the only way out of their present intractable miseries.

Personal Response

Do you agree with Johnson that the United States has a moral obligation to help stabilize Third World nations? Explain your answer.

Questions for Class or Small Group Discussion

1. Discuss the feasibility of instituting trusteeships in Third World countries, as Johnson suggests. Do you think such a plan would work? What do you think the United States would have to do in the countries Johnson mentions in order to stabilize them and bring them to the point where they can become self-governing? Do you think the United States is in a position to do what it would take?

2. Discuss or debate the following statement: "There is a moral issue here: the civilized world has a mission to go out to these desperate places and govern" (paragraph 27).

3. Discuss Johnson's closing statement: "The only satisfaction will be the unspoken gratitude of millions of misgoverned or ungoverned people who will find in this altruistic revival of colonialism the only way out of their present intractable miseries." Do you think that "unspoken gratitude" is reward enough for countries like the United States, Britain, or France to act altruistically?

4. Does Johnson convince you that countries like Somalia, Liberia, Haiti, Zaire, Angola, and Mozambique would welcome the kind of assistance Johnson calls for the United States and other world powers to give? Explain why or why not.

REVISING THE TWENTIETH CENTURY

John Lukacs

John Lukacs is a historian and author of numerous articles and books, including The Duel: May 10–31 July 1940: The Eighty-Day Struggle Between Churchill and Hitler *(1991). In this essay, which appeared in the September 1994 issue of* American Heritage, *he argues the point that people are constantly revising their views of historical events as he explains shifts in Americans' views of U.S. involvement in the major conflicts of the twentieth century.*

History *is* revisionism. It is the frequent—nay, the ceaseless—reviewing and revising and thinking of the past. The notion that the study and the writing of history consist of the filling of gaps or the adding of new small bricks to the building of the cathedral of historical knowledge was a nineteenth-century illusion ("We have now histories of the Federalists in every New England State, except for Connecticut. You must do Connecticut"), allied with the fantasy that once the scientific method has been followed precisely, with all extant documents exhausted, the result will be definite and final ("the definitive account of Waterloo, approved by British as well as by French and German and Dutch historians"). There are important differences between historical and legal evidence, one of them being that the historian deals in multiple jeopardy that the law eschews; the former is retrying and retrying again. There is nothing very profound in this observation, since that is what all thinking is about. Not the future, and not the present, but our past is the only thing we know. All human thinking involves the rethinking of the past.

There may be five hundred biographies of Lincoln, but there is no certainty that the 501st may not furnish our minds with something new and valid—and not necessarily because its author has found a new cache of Lincoln documents. What matters more than the accumulated *quantity* of the research (note the word: "re-search") is the crystallizing *quality* of the revision. What is its purpose? Is it exposé, scandal, sensation, or the more or less honest wish to demolish untruths? Is it the author's desire for academic or financial success, to further his advancement in front of his colleagues or in the greater world of affairs? Or (as is, alas, often the case) is it to further the cause of a political ideology? This is where the subject of this article comes in.

The term *revisionism* is of German origin. It was first applied to those German socialists who, around 1875, chose to mitigate the doctrine of the inevitability of the proletarian revolution. This Marxist usage does not concern us. But the other, and still present, use of historical "revisionism" has a German origin too. It arose after 1919, reacting to the punitive and condemnatory treaty imposed on Germany and on its World War I allies. The wish to revise their terms, to change the then drawn frontiers of Europe was a powerful impulse, eventually leading to Hitler and to World War II. However, the aim of this historical revisionism was not directed at injustices of geography; it was directed at injustices of the record—that is, at the unjust condemnation of Germany as responsible for the war, stated in the Treaty of Versailles. The Germans had every reason to combat that. As early as 1919 the new republican and democratic German government began to publish documents to prove that the guilt for the coming of the war in 1914 was not Germany's alone. A much more extensive and scholarly documentation was published in a series of volumes a few years later. The Germans felt so strongly about this that in 1923 a German amateur historian, Alfred von Wegerer, began issuing a scholarly journal, *Die Kriegsschuldfrage* (The War Guilt Question).

4   By that time the first wave of revisionism among American historians had begun to form. Of the four waves of revisionism in the twentieth century this was the longest and the strongest one. It began as an intellectual and academic (and sometimes also a political and an ethnic) reaction against the extreme condemnation of Germany in 1917 and 1918 that had been broadcast from many sources, including the Creel Committee, Wilson's own propaganda machine, with many exaggerations and falsehoods. It was a reaction by liberals and radicals against superpatriotism, not very different from (and often allied with) their opposition to American conformism, to the post-war Red Scare, to the Ku Klux Klan, to the American Legion of the twenties. As early as 1920, for example, *The Nation* started to attack the dangers of French, not of German, militarism. In September 1921 the magazine raised the question: "Who has contributed more to the myth of a guilty nation plotting the war against a peaceful Europe than the so-called historians who occupy distinguished chairs in our universities?" They were "willing tools" of "professional propaganda." The young and later distinguished Sidney Bradshaw Fay, then of Smith College (*not* a typical revisionist, I must add) had already published three successive articles in *The American Historical Review* ("New Light on the Origins of the World War"), a result of his reading of the recently published German, Austrian, and Russian documents. Within five years this first wave of revisionism swelled into a tide. From a scattered group of mavericks, revisionists now included respected members of the historical profession and reputable intellectuals: the prominent Charles A. Beard, the University of Chicago historian Ferdinand Schevill (who wrote in 1926 that "there are today among reputable historians only revisionists"), the sociologist turned historian Harry Elmer Barnes, whose *Genesis of the World War* was published by the reputable house of Knopf in 1926. Their cause was supported

by amateurs such as the German-American judge Frederick Bausman (*Let France Explain*), by literary figures such as Albert J. Nock and H. L. Mencken, and by the editors of *The Nation* and of *The New Republic,* while the lumbering *Atlantic Monthly* was tacking over gradually to that side too.

By the late twenties the revisionist tide was further swelled by the predictable confluence of another historical argument, about 1917 and not 1914. The time had come to revise not only the thesis of German war guilt but the story of American involvement in the war. Much of that argument had already been suggested by the above-mentioned historians, especially by Barnes; but the first substantial book denouncing Wilson and American intervention, *Why We Fought,* was published in 1929 by C. Hartley Grattan, a onetime student of Barnes. By the early thirties article after article, book after book, was attacking American intervention in World War I. The most serious work was Walter Millis's *The Road to War* in 1935. The most determined book by a professional historian was Charles Callan Tansill's *America Goes to War* in 1938. By that time their arguments had filtered down from the margins of academia and from intellectuals' periodicals through the reading public to the broad lowlands of popular sentiment. *The Road to War* was a best seller, with as many as sixty thousand copies in print by 1936. A few months later Dr. Gallup reported that 70 percent of Americans thought it had been wrong to enter World War I. Meanwhile Hitler, Mussolini, and the Japanese were rising in power.

In 1938 and 1939 another current in the revisionist tide came to the surface. Many revisionists were now worried over what they saw as an ominous change in Franklin Roosevelt's foreign policy. (In 1932 Roosevelt ran as an isolationist, and as late as 1935 he went so far as to suggest his acceptance of the revisionist thesis.) Foremost among them were Barnes, Tansill, and the big gun among American historians, Charles Beard. In September 1939 Beard published a powerful blast against American intervention in Europe, *Giddy Minds and Foreign Quarrels* (the Republican senator D. Worth Clark, of Idaho, used his franking privilege to distribute ten thousand copies of this little book). Yet by 1940 the revisionist camp was badly split. Many of the liberals were coming around to support Britain against Hitler. Others were not. In 1940 Beard came out with another book, *A Foreign Policy for America.* Eleven years later Sen. Robert A. Taft published a book with a virtually identical title, but already in 1940 it was evident that the formerly radical and Jeffersonian Democrat Beard and the rigid Republican Taft were seeing eye to eye. But before the next year was out, the news of Pearl Harbor roared over them both.

Revisionism was submerged but not sunk. After 1945 came the second wave of American revisionism, attacking Roosevelt for having maneuvered the country into war, indeed, for having contributed surreptitiously and willfully to the catastrophe at Pearl Harbor. Many of the historian figures were the same ones as before, the two principal professionals among them Beard (*American Foreign Policy in the Making, 1932–1940* and

President Roosevelt and the Coming of the War) and Tansill (*Back Door to War*). There were many others; but this second wave of revisionism received relatively little attention; many of the revisionist books were now printed by minor publishers. Yet the effect of this kind of revisionism was wider than what the publishing record might indicate. The majority of the so-called conservative movement that began to coalesce in the early 1950s was composed of former isolationists and revisionists. The principal element of the Republican surge after 1948 was a reaction against Roosevelt's foreign policy, including such different figures as Joseph R. McCarthy, John Foster Dulles, and the young William F. Buckley, Jr. It was part of the emergence of the New Right in American politics. Still, Hitler and Tojo had few public defenders, and this second wave of revisionism failed to swell into an oceanic current.

8   The third, and much larger, wave of revisionism came not from the New Right but from the New Left. These were the historians who during the fretful sixties attempted to rewrite the origins of the Cold War with Russia, arguing and claiming that American foreign policy and aggressiveness were at least as responsible for the coming of the Cold War as was the Soviet Union. The principal ones (again, there were many others) of those New Left historians were D. F. Fleming (*The Cold War and Its Origins*), William Appleman Williams (*The Tragedy of American Diplomacy*), Gar Alperovitz (*Atomic Diplomacy*), David Horowitz (*The Free World Colossus*), Gabriel Kolko (*The Politics of War*), Diane Shaver Clemens (*Yalta*), and Lloyd C. Gardner (*Architects of Illusion*), all their books issued between 1959 and 1970 by the most reputable university presses and trade houses.

Unlike the revisionists of the 1920s and 1940s, these authors had little opposition from most of their historian colleagues, for such was the, generally Leftist, intellectual tendency of the American sixties. These authors were praised, and portions of their works anthologized in college readers and textbooks. Whereas the revisionists of the 1920s and 1930s had their greatest effect among general readers, most of the consumers of this third wave of revisionist prose were college students. When Robert Maddox, in his calm and serious *The New Left and the Origins of the Cold War* (1973), pointed out some of the dishonesties of the documentation and the inadequacies of scholarship in these books, he was treated with tut-tutting and fence-sitting by most academic reviewers, so many vicars of Bray. However, as with so many fads and fashions of the sixties, the tide of Cold War revisionism, though temporarily overwhelming, did not endure for long.

Twenty or more years later we may detect the rise of a fourth wave of revisionism, coming again from the so-called Right rather than from the Left. Again this began in Germany, in the mid-1980s, developing there in *Historikerstreit* (historians' quarrel), whose main figures have been German professional historians who, while unwilling to whitewash Hitler and his regime (that has remained the work of self-appointed extreme pamphleteers for decades now, as well as of fanatical amateur historians such as the English David Irving), attempted to make their case against the uniqueness of the crimes committed by the Germans during the Third Reich. This tendency to revise some of the lately accepted and hitherto hardly questioned histories of the Second World War has recently appeared in Britain, with historians such as Maurice Cowling (in *The Impact of Hitler* and elsewhere: "the belief that Churchill had understood Hitler . . . was not true"), the younger Andrew Roberts (*The Holy Fox—A Biography of Lord Halifax*: "Churchill as Micawber," simply waiting for something to turn up; "Britain finally won, but at appalling cost, and ruin for her standing in the world"). John Charmley in his recently published *Churchill: The End of Glory* goes much farther: he questions not only Churchill's personal character but his policy to resist and fight Hitler's Germany at any cost; Charmley goes so far as to suggest that not to acquiesce in Hitler's domination of Europe was a mistake.

These books are more scholarly in their equipment than are the productions of pamphleteers who, among other things, deny the existence of the Holocaust. Excessive attention directed to such fanatics may be as useless as the criticism aimed at the new revisionists' theses without a detailed analysis of their sources and a careful refutation of their methods. Three years ago in my *The Duel: May 10–31 July 1940: The Eighty-Day Struggle Between Churchill and Hitler* I could write that "we are at (or, more precisely, already beyond) a watershed in the political and intellectual history of the world because of the evident collapse of the reputation, and consequently, of the influence of Marxism as well as of 'Leftist' liberalism; and this is bound to lead to all kinds of novel, though not necessarily salutary, tendencies of historical interpretation." This is a symptom of the rise of a New Right, not only in Germany and Britain but throughout Europe and Japan, when people, disillusioned with the malfunctioning liberal and socialist policies of their governments, project their disappointments backward, to the Second World War; when, for example, the condemnation of Churchill's statesmanship, at least indirectly, suggests some kind of a rehabilitation of Hitler's. During the Reagan years in this country we saw, here and there, a tendency to question not only the evident problems of the American welfare state but the establishment of its tenets by Roosevelt and the New Deal, and there is reason to believe that new indictments (and I fear not always well-warranted or judicious ones) of Roosevelt's foreign policy before and during the Second World War are also due to appear—in sum, that this newest wave of revisionism about the war will spill over to this side of the Atlantic too.

12   What revisionist historians claim, or at least emphatically suggest, is that their scholarship is better and their intellectual independence stronger than that of the majority of their opponents. To the contrary, few of the revisionists have been immune to the ideological tendencies of their times. In the preface to *The American Revisionists*, Warren I. Cohen, the careful historian of what I have called the first wave, wrote in 1967: "I am

equally convinced that if I had graduated from Columbia College in 1925 instead of 1955, the revisionist cause would have had one more adherent. It is not a question of the logic of the revisionist argument but . . . largely a matter of the prevailing climate of opinion. . . ." Or as W. J. Ghent (cited by Cohen) wrote in his 1927 attack on the revisionists in an article called "Menckenized History": "Vociferous and sweeping denunciation of existing beliefs, customs, standards, and institutions is the current mode, and 'revisionism' is merely one of its phases." After the First World War there was a growing revulsion to war and an embracing of new ideas, including pacifism. After the Second World War there was another reaction, against Roosevelt and the sometimes unspoken question of whether America should have entered the war against Germany, and on the side of Russia, at that. During the sixties there was the reaction against the Vietnam War and against the ideology of the Cold War. During the nineties nationalism is on the rise, and we shall see . . .

In 1917 Beard was an extreme interventionist: The United States "should help eliminate Prussianism from the earth. . . ." Germany represents "the black night of military barbarism . . . the most merciless military despotism the world has ever seen." By 1926 he was a Germanophile, influenced not only by the revelations of the German diplomatic documents but by German philosophies of history. Beard was not an opportunist, and even in the 1930s he insisted that he was not really an isolationist; rather, he was struggling with that seemingly concrete but, alas, often malleable concept of national interest. (In 1932 Beard received a twenty-five-thousand-dollar grant—a very large sum then—from the Social Science Research Council for the precise definition of "national interest." The result was one of his few unreadable books.) At that time he was a fervent supporter of Franklin Roosevelt, but soon he turned even more fervently against him. The case of Barnes is more telling. His first revisionist articles appeared in 1924, arguing for a division in the responsibilities for the outbreak of the war. By 1926 he was going farther: France and Russia were responsible. Thereafter he became more and more extreme and violent. He was invited to lecture in Hitler's Germany, as was Tansill. In 1940 Barnes volunteered to promote the circulation of German propaganda volumes. After the war he became an admirer of Hitler: "a man whose only fault was that he was too soft, generous and honorable." The Allies had inflicted worse brutality on the Germans "than the alleged exterminations in the gas-chambers." This, of course, was the extreme case of a once talented but embittered man, driven to such statements by what he called The Historical Blackout, one of his later pamphlets. Everything was grist to his mill, including the most dubious of "sources" and "evidences." The same was true of Tansill, who in 1938 wrote in his introduction to America Goes to War: "Crusading zeal is hardly the proper spirit for an impartial historian." Yet Tansill was the prototype of a zealous crusader, in both of his big revisionist works about the two world wars. Eventually he became a member of the John Birch Society.

Revisionists such as Barnes were often obsessed with the idea of a conspiracy against them. He called the anti-revisionists the "Smearbund." When the Chicago historian Bernadotte Schmitt first criticized his *Genesis of the World War,* Barnes wrote: "There is the very important fact [fact?] that Mr. Schmitt seems to live in daily dread of being mistaken for a member of the detestable Teutonic breed." Barnes even thought that there was a conspiracy among booksellers not to reorder his *Genesis.* Mencken's relationship to Barnes (they corresponded for decades) is also telling. In May 1940, when the German armies lurched forward into Holland, Belgium, and France, Mencken wrote Barnes that the American press "would be hollering for war within two months"; in June he wrote that "Roosevelt will be in the war in two weeks, and . . . his first act will be to forbid every form of free speech." Mencken, like Barnes and other revisionists, was bitterly against a war with Hitler's Reich, but after the war he thought that the United States should go to war against "the Russian barbarians." That inconsistency—if that was what it was—was typical of the inclinations of almost all the post–World War II revisionists. The opposite was true of the Cold War revisionists of the 1960s, who accused the United States of having provoked the Cold War with Russia, while almost all of them approved the American involvement in the war against Germany. They, too, did little else but project backward their then widespread and fashionable dislike of the Vietnam War to events that had happened twenty or more years earlier, manipulating that record for their own purposes. In the 1970s most of them turned to other topics, and at least one of them (Horowitz) became a neoconservative publicist.

There is, however, more involved here than a few historians adjusting their ideas to a prevalent climate of opinion. In some instances their writings affected American history, through a momentum that was slowly gaining ground. In the 1920s the writings of the revisionists had an influence on those members of Congress, mostly Western populists—George W. Norris, Gerald P. Nye, William E. Borah, for example—who had opposed the war and the Versailles Treaty. By 1934 the isolationist and revisionist tide ran so strong that a congressional committee, presided over by Nye, found it politic to investigate the doings of bankers and munition makers and other villainous promoters of the American entrance into the war seventeen years before. (One of the Nye Committee's counsels was an ambitious young lawyer, Alger Hiss.) In 1935 Congress passed the first Neutrality Act, a definite reaction against the memories of World War I. It was extended in 1937. By that time Sen. Homer Bone of Washington could report "a fact known even to school children in this country: Everyone has come to recognize that the Great War was utter social insanity, and was a crazy war, and we had no business in it at all."

16   This illustrates a significant phenomenon to which few, if any, historians have yet devoted attention. It is the time lag in the movement of ideas, the slowness of the momentum with which ideas move and then appear on the surface at the wrong time, giving the lie to Victor Hugo's famous saw about Ideas Whose Time Has Come. The high tide of revisionism occurred from 1935 to 1938, when the German danger was rising anew—not, say, in 1919 and 1920, when there had been cogent reasons to mitigate a mistreatment of Germany. The high tide of Second World War revisionism occurred in 1954 and 1955, when the reputations of Franklin Roosevelt and of Yalta were at a low ebb. The high tide of the revisionism about the origins of the Cold War came around 1965, when American-Russian relations were actually improving.

Of course, it takes time for historians to complete their researches and produce their books, but there is an agitated tone in many revisionist works that stands in odd contrast with the slow momentum of their eventual effects. One reason for this is the often weak and tergiversating reaction of the revisionists' historian opponents. At the beginning the seemingly radical performance of the former is often ignored, but then, gradually, the revisionists' ideas may be adopted by respectable historians when it seems politic for them to do so or when they feel safely convinced by their judiciousness. Thus, for example, Tansill's radical and Germanophile *America Goes to War* was praised in *The Atlantic* and the *Yale Review* and by such eminent historians as Allan Nevins and Henry Steele Commager: Tansill traced, "in magisterial style, the missteps which carried the United States along the road to war. It is an impressive performance, conducted with skill, learning, and wit, *illuminating the present as well as the past.*" The italics are Cohen's as well as mine, for this was written by Commager as late as 1938, the most ominous and successful year in Hitler's career along the road to another war. The title of Beard's trenchant 1939 *Giddy Minds and Foreign Quarrels* is not really appropriate. So many of his colleagues' minds were not at all giddy; they were alarmingly slow. Even more disheartening was the reaction of many historians to the New Left revisionists of the 1960s, when the scholarship of those books was wanting. As Maddox wrote, "Reviewers who have been known to pounce with scarcely disguised glee on some poor wretch who incorrectly transcribed a middle initial or date of birth have shown a most extraordinary reluctance to expose even the most obvious New Left fictions," including false statements to which tens of thousands of students were subsequently exposed in our colleges and universities. Finally, when it comes to the newest wave of revisionism, lamentably few historians have taken the trouble to track down and point out the selective methodology and frequently sloppy scholarship of Charmley's denigration of Churchill. Spending, instead, long paragraphs and pages debating his thesis, they pursue the obvious, as Wilde once said, with the enthusiasm of shortsighted detectives.

In science it is the rule that counts; in history, often the exceptions. And there have been exceptions to the shortcomings of scholars involved with revisionism. Millis, who, as we saw earlier, was the author of the most successful revisionist book in 1935, a few years later found himself appalled by the use people were making of his work, which, after all, had dealt with 1917, with the past and not with the then present. By 1938 Millis stood for resistance against Hitler and other dictators. "1939 is not 1914" was the title of his article in *Life* in November 1939, when Roosevelt had to struggle against a senseless Neutrality Act. Maddox, whose study of the New Left revisionists was ignored or criticized by other historians, refused to make common cause with the New Right; he remained unimpressed by the selective argumentation of Leftist and Rightist, of Marxist and anti-Communist, of neoliberal and neoconservative historians alike, because of his personal integrity, the essence of human integrity being its resistance to temptations, perhaps especially to intellectual ones.

Such temptations are the bane of historians, and not only of those who are in pursuit of attractive intellectual novelty. This does not mean a defense of "orthodox" history, because there is no such thing. Historians should be aware of the inevitably revisionist nature of their thinking and work. But the revision of history must not be an ephemeral monopoly of ideologues or opportunists who are ever ready to twist or even falsify evidences of the past in order to exemplify current ideas—and their own adjustments to them.

Personal Response

Give an example of a way in which you have changed your behavior or attitude as a result of reviewing or rethinking your past.

Questions for Class or Small Group Discussion

1. Besides history, what other disciplines do you think are constantly "reviewing and revising and rethinking" their subjects (paragraph 1)?

2. Discuss this statement: "All human thinking involves the rethinking of the past" (paragraph 1). Can you think of any area of knowledge that is not subject to constant reviewing, revising, and rethinking?

3. Summarize the four waves of revisionism Lukacs identifies. What are the characteristics of the revisionist historians of each period? How did the public respond in each period to the revisionists?

4. Lukacs is intrigued by revisionist historians' reactions to major conflicts of this century, but he is also alarmed by the way in which some of them "twist or even falsify evidences of the past in order to exemplify current ideas" (paragraph 19). Do you know of any historical event

that has been twisted or falsified to fit current ideas? Besides history, where else is there a danger of twisting evidence from the past to fit current ideas?

BUILDING BRIDGES BETWEEN YOUNG JAPANESE AND AFRICAN AMERICANS

Hisako Yanaka

Hisako Yanaka teaches American history in the American Studies program at Kyoritsu Women's University in Tokyo. She has visited the United States for extended periods many times, including a seven-month period in 1994 as a researcher in the Joint Center for Political and Economic Studies. This essay is based on her presentation at a panel discussion on strengthening U.S.–Japan relationships, held at Hunter College in 1995.

A positive relationship between Japanese and African Americans has not been well-established as yet, but there are great similarities among young people of both communities. I teach American history in a women's university in Japan. For seven months in 1994 I was a researcher in residence in the Joint Center for Political and Economic Studies, which is a nonpartisan and nonprofit think tank for African Americans, to research the relationship between Japanese-owned companies and African-American communities in Georgia. Through my experience as a university professor of American studies and researcher on African-American communities, I had many opportunities to learn about African Americans and Japanese. One thing I have learned is that young people in both groups have an enthusiastic attitude toward learning foreign cultures. It is important that these young people understand undistorted, unbiased realities of each other's society.

First of all, let me explain to what extent Japanese young people are exposed to the history and culture of African Americans. It is regrettable that in world history classes up through high school, Japanese students learn very little about the United States. They learn only about the American Revolution, the Civil War, the New Deal, and a few famous presidents. Therefore in the junior or senior high schools, Japanese pupils get very little knowledge of African Americans or have only a negative image of them as slaves.

In their daily lives the Japanese have few chances to meet African Americans directly. In the countryside almost no Japanese have encountered African Americans. The major sources on African Americans for young Japanese people are the mass media, that is, television news, movies, music videos, and magazines. For example, the movie on Malcolm X was a big hit in Japan, and many young Japanese bought clothing items relating to

Malcolm X. Young people in Japan are fascinated with African-American culture, and it is very popular to imitate their haircuts and clothing styles and to practice the latest dance steps and rap music. Therefore it is very important that mass media accurately convey the realities of African Americans. Quite often, the Japanese reader of Japanese newspapers comes away with negative impressions of African Americans and other minority people, such as that they are violent, are poor, and have low education levels. In Japanese media all social problems existing in the United States are apt to be connected with African Americans or illegal Hispanic immigrants. Only black athletes and entertainers tend to be considered successful African Americans in Japanese minds. Many Japanese young people have heard of Martin Luther King Jr., but they confuse the civil rights movement and the emancipation of the slaves. Nor do they know any contemporary African Americans who are accomplished professionals. In order to lead the recent growing interest in African Americans among young Japanese in the right direction, American history teachers should write books and articles on the history of African Americans and their contributions to American culture, not only for academic books but also for nonacademic magazines and books. In this regard, I am very glad to tell you that a recent issue of a popular magazine featured "black studies" and included well-balanced articles on the history and culture of African Americans.

4   Now let me turn to the Japanese university students and their interests in African Americans. When they enter the universities and take an American history course, they for the first time learn about African Americans. Many Japanese universities have opened new departments relating to international affairs, and they provide American studies programs in those new departments. Our university, Kyoritsu Women's University, started the Department of International Affairs five years ago. In our American Studies program we have about 100 students each year. When I teach American history, focusing on multiculturalism in the United States and including lots of materials on minorities and women in my lectures and reading lists, many students realize that they have had a wrong perception of African Americans or that they have considered them in an abstract context. At first, many students think the percentage of black population in the United States is between 30 percent and 40 percent because they read newspaper articles on crimes and drug problems related to African Americans. When they finish the American history course, they are impressed with the rich contribution of African Americans to the history and culture of the United States. Then some of my students choose their graduation thesis topics from black history. One student analyzed the thoughts and speeches of Sojourner Truth, and another student interpreted the works of Toni Morrison. The civil rights movement is a very popular topic for many students.

Young Japanese, including university students, seldom show racism or prejudice toward African Americans. Young Japanese people, unlike their elders, think of and treat blacks visiting Japan as equal to whites. The Japanese tend to describe a foreigner as "a person from outside the country," whether he or she is a white, black, Asian, or of Japanese descent from Hawaii or Brazil. Traditionally Japanese have divided people into two groups, those inside and those outside, and they have excluded those who are different from Japanese people. In this sense Japanese can be said to be discriminatory toward all foreigners. Quite often many Japanese are afraid to approach foreigners because they are uncertain about them. But nowadays Japanese young people frequently go abroad and feel more comfortable with foreigners than their elders do. Besides, more and more different kinds of foreigners, such as Southeast Asians and Middle Easterners, come to Japan as laborers and work with Japanese young people. Therefore the young generation of Japanese generally do not show any hostility or antagonism toward foreigners, even though they act reservedly and formally. From the viewpoint of young Japanese, African Americans just make up one group of foreigners.

As for young African Americans' attitudes toward Japanese, according to a 1991 survey conducted by the Joint Center for Political and Economic Studies, a considerable number of African Americans (74 percent) hold favorable attitudes toward the Japanese despite repeated racial insults by prominent Japanese public officials. Had this survey targeted younger people, the percentage of the respondents with favorable attitudes toward Japanese might be higher than 74 percent. In fact, during my research in the Joint Center, I interviewed a number of young black students and professors in Georgia. I found that many black students in the Atlanta area were interested in learning Japan's language and its culture. Many black students come to realize that knowledge of or interest in foreign language and culture will expand their perspectives and create job opportunities in their future. Spelman College started a Japanese studies program in September of 1994 with a gift of $120,000 from twelve Japanese companies. It is the first comprehensive Japanese studies program at the undergraduate level and includes two language courses and three lecture courses on Japanese literature, economics, and culture. Georgia Institute of Technology also has Japanese language courses, and more students want to take the Japanese classes than can be enrolled. Even public high schools in Atlanta provide Japanese language classes. During my research interviews I met several black students who wanted internships in Japanese companies while they studied international affairs.

While I researched for seven months in Washington, D.C., I met many promising young African Americans. For example, my director in the U.S.–Japan Project at the Joint Center for Political and Economic Studies, who has a law degree from George Washington University, spent one year in Japan as an adviser for the Board of Education in Mie prefecture. She is well-informed about Asian affairs. I had an excellent research assistant, who worked during the last summer as an intern at the Joint Center after graduating from the Kennedy School of Government of Harvard. Now she works in the Treasury Department as a specialist on the Japanese economy. She speaks perfect Japanese and writes the difficult Japanese language, which consists of Chinese characters plus two Japanese phonetic alphabets. There are many black students with the same kind of ability and high aspirations for the future. These well-qualified and able young African Americans are creating a good relationship between Japanese and black communities.

8   Finally, I would like to suggest one important thing for both the Japanese and African-American young generations. Again I will quote the data from the 1991 survey conducted by the Joint Center. As for knowledge of Japan, while 62 percent of white respondents in the survey claim substantial knowledge of Japan, only 39 percent of blacks do, with 61 percent saying they have little or no such knowledge. The same thing can be said for the scarcity of knowledge of Japanese people about African Americans. This lack of knowledge about each other will prevent mutual understanding in the future. Therefore the most important thing is to bring up the next generation with an interest in foreign cultures, without any bias or prejudice toward them. Education is the most effective means of achieving this purpose. A lot of plans are possible in the field of education. Japanese companies can provide African-American and Japanese students with scholarships to send them to colleges and high schools in each other's country as exchange students. Companies might also provide internships for African Americans to experience the Japanese workplace. Even short trips or language training in school would have a marked effect on young people. For example, since 1980 under the Japan Exchange and Teaching (JET) program, the Japanese government has offered U.S. college graduates a year of teaching English in one of twelve Japanese cities. African-American students should be encouraged to apply for JET programs. During my interviews, I was pleased to learn that one professor in a historically black college advises his students to become more mobile and have wider global perspectives. I would like to see historically black colleges establish sister-school relationships in Japan so that students and faculty members of schools in both countries can interact. At the same time, I hope that African-American professors will apply for grants or other funds to teach in Japanese universities. For example, my university welcomes one Fulbright lecturer every year. I have heard from the Fulbright Commission that few American professors are willing to spend a year in Japan teaching American studies and that the commission has some difficulty obtaining enough professors to meet the demands from Japanese universities for the Fulbright lecturers.

Frequent contact between young African Americans and Japanese as well as accurate and plentiful information about each other will improve the relationship between them. For this purpose, more energy and money should be provided by both Japanese and American governments and corporations. I have already seen some burgeoning efforts among young people of both groups to achieve a better understanding of and to build better relations with one another. Japan and the U.S. should encourage those efforts and hence build stronger relations between the young people of both nations.

Personal Response

What image of the Japanese do you have? Would you like to visit Japan someday? Explain your answer.

Questions for Class or Small Group Discussion

1. Yanaka mentions that mass media are the major sources of information about African Americans (paragraph 3). What image of Japanese do American young people get from mass media?

2. Yanaka states that Japanese media portray negative images of African Americans and Hispanics by attributing many social ills to those groups and that the only positive images are of black athletes and entertainers (paragraph 3). Discuss whether such a statement is true of American media's images of minority groups as well.

3. Yanaka maintains that "lack of knowledge about each other will prevent mutual understanding" and that educating the next generation without bias or prejudice is crucial to strengthening U.S.–Japan relationships (paragraph 8). How can American students gain more knowledge of Japan? Do you think it is possible to educate an entire generation without prejudice? Applying Yanaka's observations to young Americans in general, how might they build better relationships with young people of any foreign country?

4. Discuss your own junior high and senior high exposure to people of other countries. Did you learn much about them? Do you think American secondary school children in general get much education about other countries?

5. Invite an expert on foreign relations to speak to your class. Or, invite one, two, or several foreign students on your campus to engage in an informal or formal dialogue about strengthening relationships between American students and foreign students.

Perspectives on International Relations

Suggestions for Synthesis

1. Using the arguments of both Charles Krauthammer in "Must America Slay All the Dragons?" and Paul Johnson in "Colonialism's Back—and Not a Moment Too Soon," explain your own position on the issue of America's responsibility for other countries.

2. Drawing on the observations of two or more writers in the chapter, write a position paper explaining your stand on the question of America's responsibility to defend oppression wherever it occurs.

Additional Writing Topics

1. Write a letter to the editor of *Time* magazine in response to Charles Krauthammer's essay, "Must America Slay All the Dragons?"

2. Write a personal essay explaining a way in which you have changed your behavior or attitude as a result of reviewing or rethinking your past.

3. Respond to the statement of Senator George Mitchell that "we cannot oppose repression in one place and overlook it in another" (Charles Krauthammer's "Must America Slay All the Dragons?"). Explain whether you agree or disagree with Senator Mitchell and why.

4. Examine America's involvement in Grenada, Kuwait, Panama, or Nicaragua in terms of Charles Krauthammer's assertion that any American "intervention must pass two tests: it must be 1) right and 2) in our interests" (paragraph 7, "Must America Slay All the Dragons?").

5. Argue in support of or against the following statement: "There is a moral issue here: the civilized world has a mission to go out to these desperate places and govern" (paragraph 26, Paul Johnson's "Colonialism's Back—and Not a Moment Too Soon").

6. Using specific examples, write an essay on images of Japanese or other foreigners in American mass media.

7. Describe your own friendship with a person from a foreign country, including what you see as the benefits of such a relationship.

8. If you have traveled abroad, write an essay about that experience, focusing on what you learned about another country and what you see as the benefits of foreign travel.

Research Topics

1. Research the conditions surrounding America's involvement in the Gulf War, Panama, Nicaragua, or Grenada. Limit your focus to one aspect of the subject,

such as what led to America's involvement, what America's involvement meant to American citizens, or effects on the country of America's intervention. Then argue the extent to which you support that involvement.

2. Research the history of colonialism and the effects of decolonization in Chad, Mauritania, Angola, Uganda, or any of the other countries Paul Johnson mentions in "Colonialism's Back—and Not a Moment Too Soon."

3. Research the subject of U.S. relations with Japan, China, or another country that may figure importantly in the future of the United States. On the basis of your research, assess the relative importance to the United States of strengthening such relations and the potential effects of allowing relations with that country to deteriorate.

PART FOUR

SCIENCE AND TECHNOLOGY

CHAPTER 15

COMPUTER SCIENCE

The field of computer science is constantly changing, with new and faster programs being developed more frequently than most people can keep track of. While early researchers recognized the potential of computers, it is likely that few of them envisioned the staggering capabilities of computers today nor the extent to which computers would be so closely and inextricably linked with our everyday lives. Increasingly sophisticated computers make child's play of what just a few years ago were challenging or impossible tasks. Young children today learn skills—some of them before they enter school—that many of their grandparents will never even try to learn. Indeed, computer technology has advanced at such a rapid rate that its powers seem unlimited, a prospect that fills some with eager anticipation and leaves others feeling intimidated and frightened.

The authors of the first two pieces in this chapter take a cautious approach to new computer technology. In "If This Is the Information Highway, Where Are the Rest Stops?" Deborah Baldwin explains what consumer advocates see as both the problems and potential of the Information Superhighway; and in "It's Been Real," Sally Tisdale reports on her experiences at Cyberthon, a conference celebrating the new computer technology of virtual reality. Tisdale is not at all convinced of its benefits. As you read their essays, think about your own attitude toward computers, especially the Internet and the concept of virtual reality. Do you share Baldwin's and Tisdale's skepticism about these technologies, or do you welcome them?

In contrast to both Baldwin and Tisdale, Grant Fjermedal in "Artificial Intelligence" is rather excited about computer technology, in particular, the possibility of humans living indefinitely. In his essay, Fjermedal explains the hopes of some scientists that they may be able one day to implant computer copies of their brains into robots. Does Fjermedal's vision appeal to you? Do you think his idea falls more in the realm of science fiction than science, or do you think artificial intelligence has potential for being realized?

As you may be aware, some people are not just skeptical of computer technology; they are adamantly opposed to it. They contend that society is far too dependent on computers, that computers already invade our lives, and that computers have the dangerous potential to violate personal freedom. Vocal critics of computers sometimes refer to themselves as neo-Luddites, a reference to a group of nineteenth-century British textile workers who protested the Industrial Revolution. The workers rebelled on the grounds that the technology that *created machines to replace work that had previously been done by hand also produced dehumanizing working conditions that stripped people of their personal dignity and drove them to early deaths. In the final selection in this chapter, "The Luddites Are Back," Steven Levy finds fault with some critics' wholesale assault on computer technology and expresses his belief that they are using the term "Luddite" incorrectly to refer to themselves. As you read his summary of the faults critics find with computers, consider whether you agree with any of their complaints.*

As you read the essays in this chapter, your responses to them will undoubtedly be influenced by your own familiarity with and skill—or lack of it—in the use of computers. You may well know far more about them than some of the authors represented here, or you may have no interest in the subject at all. However, these four perspectives on the subject of computers are varied enough that they should provide plenty of material for fruitful class discussions or writing.

IF THIS IS THE INFORMATION HIGHWAY, WHERE ARE THE REST STOPS?

Deborah Baldwin

Deborah Baldwin is an editor of and regular contributor to Common Cause Magazine, *where this article appeared in the Spring 1994 issue. She details here what she sees as benefits and drawbacks of the Information Superhighway.*

It's hard to say when it happened exactly, but at some point around Halloween things started moving very quickly on the telecommunications front.

Suddenly, what was once a fanciful vision of the distant future—when Americans would be able to communicate with their appliances via cell phone and carry on conversations with their loved ones via computer—became as immediate as next season's sitcoms.

Things were already getting out of hand for those of us who had held onto record players during the ascendance of CDs, stubbornly refusing to invest in new consumer electronics "until things settle down." By the close of 1993, everything from pencils and postal carriers to Blockbuster and the Big Three networks began to look suspiciously out of date.

4   Meanwhile we were inundated with the details of the Viacom-QVC battle for Paramount—or was it the other way around?—as Bell Atlantic, a formerly reputable phone company, got hitched to cable behemoth TeleCommunications Inc. (TCI) in a $32 million ceremony. It was hard to know what to think, much less what to do, about all this merger mania beyond contemplating a future in which the number of info-phone-tainment-TV-companies-with-shopping-networks would be down to two.

As if all this weren't bad enough, computer hackers—known in some circles as mouse potatoes—got sex appeal. It was hard to keep dismissing people who whiled away their time at the keyboard (What—didn't they have jobs? Couldn't they get dates?) when their hero Bill Gates was the richest man in America. Gone were the days when the electronically challenged could feign politeness as discussions turned to modems, megabytes and ROMs vs. RAMs. Maybe most Americans would rather have lower monthly utility rates, safer schools and a new washing machine than a connection to global E-mail, but the Information Age had arrived, and the media brought the message forth in a tsunami of articles about the Internet, a loose network of computers that until recently was of concern only to science nerds, academics and computer junkies. Today, according to countless breathless accounts commissioned by editors clearly concerned about how all this may affect their profession, the number of Americans with access to the Internet is 15 million—and climbing.

The lonely crowd's worst fears about the electronic frontier—where citizens will be able to hook themselves up to a life-support system consisting of television, telephone and computer, and never have to leave the house in order to work, shop or even vote—were about to become reality. And inevitably, in a town where the term policy wonk was invented, fascination with things electronic took hold like the latest strain of Asian flu. As Information Superhighway hysteria spread down Pennsylvania Avenue, you could almost hear humming in the air: It's the dawning of a new era in communications law! Don't miss this opportunity to participate in the latest policy debate! Say "goodbye" to old-fashioned representative democracy—"hello" to Virtual Government!

Hey—be the first person in your political coalition to host an Internet news group!

8   "When I started in 1990, there were damn few people working on this," says Jamie Love, who in three short years has established himself as Ralph Nader's telecommunications policy guru and Internet gadfly. Nowadays, when Love drops by meetings of public interest types who want to join in the telecommunications fun, there are so many Johnny Come Latelys he can barely find a chair.

Part of the attraction is the prospect of participating in a bleeding-edge campaign that has none of the baggage of such aging issues as saving the spotted owl, reforming federal prisons and making automobiles more energy efficient. The revolution in telecommunications is all new and it's all up for grabs.

And before long, a growing chorus of advocates says, it will be too late for the public interest community to try to influence telecommunications policy—to make interactive TV channels available, for example, for democratic discourse and the like. Already, money from cable, broadcast, telephone, home shopping and Hollywood is pouring through Congress like Mississippi River floodwaters—at the rate of about $10 million in 1991–92, according to one analysis. And the raw economic power of media chieftains like John Malone, the zillionaire co-founder of TCI, coupled with their dazzling appeal in a city better known for pushing paper than global vision, is threatening to turn policymakers into whimpering schoolchildren.

Still, if Wall Street barons are on the edges of their seats awaiting some signal from the marketplace about what Americans really want (video-porn delivered by phone? a hair-care channel?), Washington's public interest community is at a similar turning point. Many groups have heard the call. But it's one thing to have a passionate interest in telecommunications policy. It's another to develop a grassroots Information Superhighway lobbying group—and raise enough money to keep it going.

There's No Escaping Now

12   In case you're still at the stage I was four months ago—curious about the Information Superhighway but genuinely worried about having to program anything more complicated than a VCR—here's what all the hype is about. It's been about 10 years since the PC and Mac turned typewriters into landfill; a new kind of computerized communications will similarly eclipse the telephone. It will tie our computers at home and work to the outside world, enabling us to plunder the world's entertainment and information resources at the push of a button.

After we get all our other work done, of course.

In the beginning was the Internet, a network of computer networks tied together by high-speed wire. Devised by the Pentagon as a way to protect the flow of military information during a nuclear holocaust, the Internet was embraced early on by academic researchers, who soon learned to use it to open up the electronic card catalogues at other colleges, communicate with colleagues in faraway places (exchanging dissertations became popular) and bellyache about tenure. Anyone with a modem and a subscription to a local Internet exchange can also communicate by E-mail—a cheap, convenient alternative to having to rummage for stamp and envelope or wait for discount phone rates to apply. You type your message, fire it off and wait for the inevitable snappy comeback, which will be typed at the sender's convenience and read at yours—making the notion of human beings walking from house to house to deliver mail as quaint as ice wagons. The Internet also offers the possibility of conversations with like-minded souls (there are news groups devoted to every imaginable topic, from Iran-contra to Jerry Seinfeld) and access to umpteen kinds of information that have been dumped onto the system.

"It's hard to get a good conceptual understanding" of all this, concedes Jim Keller, formerly with Sprint and now with the industry-funded Information Infrastructure Project at Harvard's Kennedy School. With the superhighway, it would be possible to distribute video and other media and—assuming the highway going out of your house were as big as the one coming in—an opportunity to broadcast everything from political diatribes to home video.

16   Other useful functions: When dinner debates erupted over who was the winning pitcher in the last game of the World Series in 1950, you'd be able to scroll over to the keyboard and call up a sports almanac. Endless amounts of information about political candidates and causes could be yours: no more wading through prime time in search of an engaging critique of the gubernatorial incumbent's voting record. Tired of having to recycle those unread sections of the paper piling up in the living room? Drop your subscription and read only what you want on a computer screen. Can't decide whether to vacation in Egypt? Ask the computer to put you in touch with people who've been there. And let's not mention buying stuff and renting videos without having to drive to the mall.

No one's foolish enough, however, to assume that the John Malones of the world will go out of their way to provide services that don't automatically make money—things like the local equivalent of C-SPAN, for example. Cable TV companies didn't think up community access stations on their own, and they're not likely to sweat about electronic democracy unless someone makes them. Same applies to the phone companies that are so anxious to build Information Superhighway on-ramps everywhere: The only reason they charge relatively low rates for basic service now is because regulators set the prices. Let 'em loose so they can start delivering video by phone, and they'll charge what the market will bear.

Enter the media reform movement, which began in the early 1970s as an effort to advance such things as the Fairness Doctrine (a requirement that broadcasters give time to both sides of a political debate) and equal time (access to the airwaves for opposing candidates). The 1980s were a bad time for media reform—"from my perspective, it was devastating," says Andrew Blau, coordinator of the Benton Foundation's Communications Policy Project—because the buzzwords changed from "public" to "access" to "deregulation," the latter responsible for the untrammeled growth of cable TV—not to mention cable TV rates.

Then, in the 1990s, something funny happened. Deregulation backlash led to a sweeping new cable TV law. And a fascination with reform arose outside Washington, in Cambridge and Silicon Valley, where traditionally libertarian computer users started worrying about government policies affecting privacy and access—about big government using the new technology to simultaneously learn more about its citizens and tell them less. A bit of the industry's technological know-how and money was grafted onto the media reform movement's thinning stalks, creating a strange new progressive-libertarian hybrid.

20   Attempting to take root under the Information Superhighway's grow lights today are a handful of groups, ranging from Ralph Nader's tiny Taxpayer Assets Project to the brash Electronic Frontier Foundation, which was bankrolled by the inventory of Lotus software. There's the 20-year-old Media Access Project—still lobbying to bring back the Fairness Doctrine—and the Consumer Federation of America, which wants to protect consumers from gouging by the regional Bell operating companies, or

RBOCs (pronounced Are Box), which are anxious to get into fancy new lines of work like video. Add the 14-year-old Benton Foundation, the two-year-old Center for Media Education and the nascent Center for Civic Networking . . . plus the ACLU, whose former Washington director is now director of the Electronic Frontier Foundation, the Center for Policy Alternatives and Computer Professionals for Social Responsibility. Also active are the librarians—yes, the librarians—who have provided the contemporary media reform movement with some of its few female leaders. (As a showcase for brainy, techie types, telecommunications boasts a large number of fast-thinking, faster-talking men, who compete to see who gets the most invites to testify on Capitol Hill and who has greater impact at the White House.)

Galvanizing this eclectic group is the sheer size and political clout of the opposition, a composite of media-communications-entertainment interests about as consumer-friendly as the Terminator. The RBOCs alone—collectively, individually—comprise a fantastic political force both in Washington and locally, where they badger regulators for rate hikes and sweet-talk about getting schools and hospitals onto the highway.

"It's just huge," says Gene Kimmelman, formerly with the Consumer Federation of America and now an aide to Sen. Howard Metzenbaum (D-Ohio). "In one year the seven [RBOCs] put together $22 million" to lobby in Washington—"and that doesn't include public relations." Kimmelman counts the number of phone company lobbyists in Washington in "the hundreds," and reminds his caller of where the money came from to pay their hourly fees: Thanks to consumers, the phone companies already have a $90-billion-a-year operating cash flow.

Some of that money helped the U.S. Telephone Association snap up top Clinton aide Roy Neel for a reported $500,000 salary and brought Peter Knight—a former top Senate aide to Vice President Albert Gore—to Bell Atlantic's account at one prestigious law firm and Clinton campaign adviser Thomas Casey to its account at another. Virtually every major Washington firm works in some way for the telecommunications industry, says Kimmelman, with phone company money providing a significant part of the business.

24   "When you talk about the phone companies you are talking about political power unlike any other," says Nick Johnson, a consumer advocate who served on the Federal Communications Commission (FCC) in the early '70s. Pointing to the Bell Atlantic-TCI merger, Johnson anticipates "absolutely overpowering" political pressure on Washington to let the Big Guys run the Superhighway anyway they want.

What way is anybody's guess at this point, because no one knows for sure how the highway will shape up. (Well, a few things are certain: People want to be able to put their videos on hold when they go to the bathroom, and they like to order things over the phone.) So what brings the Big Guys to Washington? A desire for carte blanche—for the right to compete in a new era of hands-off government as they keep splitting like amoebas, mating like rabbits and cashing in like casinos. The RBOCs, with control of local phone service, want access to money-making long-distance services now dominated by AT&T, Sprint and MCI—and vice versa; the cable companies want access to money-making phone services—and vice versa; the entertainment giants want to cut deals with the most lucrative producers—and vice versa; and everybody wants the right to merge with everybody else without having bothersome antitrust lawyers breathing down their necks. "The thing that frightens me most is the merger mania," Rutgers University political scientist Benjamin Barber said in a November speech.

Not Tonight, I Have a Headache

But if the looming threat of a vertically integrated, shared telecommunications monopoly leaves you longing for an evening with Jane Austen, this is no time to look the other way. Public interest advocates believe there's a way to harness all this new technology for the betterment of democracy, and no better time than now to press the communications industry for concessions like toll-free on-ramps for everyone, starting with schools and libraries—which might prefer some new books and lighting fixtures but would probably settle for a bank of Macs.

Advanced thinkers have been gathering not only on the Internet but at a series of in-person conferences designed to raise consciousness and engender hobnobbing. At a January confab in Arlington, Va., hosted by Vanderbilt University's Freedom Forum First Amendment Center and the National Emergency Civil Liberties Foundation, a rapt audience was treated to an hour-long rain dance by Sun Microsystems' technical wizard John Gage, who traced electronic communications back to the invention of speech (60,000 years ago), the written word (6,000 years ago), the printing press (600 years ago), TV (60 years ago) and user-friendly Internet software (last July) while explaining how quickly new technology was overtaking society's ability to cope with it.

Panelists from groups like the ACLU and EFF tackled issues of privacy and civil rights, while members of the audience argued over whether Ross Perot-style electronic town meetings would improve democracy or turn it into mob rule. "It sounds creepy," opined panelist David Burnham, author of *The Rise of the Computer State,* while others spoke forcefully about energizing the public.

If it's unclear whether the Information Superhighway will improve the political process, at a minimum keyboards and modems will speed things up. And activists like Jamie Love firmly believe that when they aren't busy watching TV, shopping at home and firing off E-mail, Americans will want to use the new technology to, say, debate the issues with their fellow "netizens," download government information on myriad topics, let their voices be heard at the local school board and seek out information about those who are willing to leave the house long enough to run for office.

"In 1991 I started posting notices [about telecommunications policy] on the Internet," Love says of his earliest experiments in desktop lobbying, "and all of a sudden we were reaching 10,000 people"—at virtually no cost. In sharp contrast to the customary ways of Washington, lobbying on the Internet proved amazingly, well, democratic and, Love says, gave "a tiny group like ours an opportunity to shape the debate." Today, thanks to his persevering presence on the Internet (and in-your-face style of politicking), he gets invited to gather around the table with Al Gore and telecommunications industry CEOs.

"In Washington what's 'politically possible' dominates the debate," Love says, while Internet users have higher expectations. Meanwhile there are no letterheads, pinstriped suits or other visual cues to give weight to one side—"it all looks the same, so the only thing that matters is the merit of your argument."

32   Love's major coup, the culmination of a three-year battle with the Securities and Exchange Commission, will give the public access to valuable financial databases at the SEC that had been controlled by Mead Data Central, which makes available on-line everything from *The Journal of Injectable Drugs* to *Common Cause Magazine*—at gulpingly high rates.

A different kind of electronic lobbying campaign unfolded in California last year when Jim Warren, a retired computer entrepreneur, saw a way to make state legislation (both enacted and proposed) available on-line. Operating out of his home on a redwood-covered ridge 30 miles south of San Francisco, Warren posted a call to action to Internet users, who responded with enough mail to California lawmakers to move the necessary legislation forward. "According to the author of the bill, the on-line activism was instrumental," Warren says in a phone interview conducted as he watches out his window for forest fires.

"There is a heavy push in the information on-line industry to privatize access to government records," Warren says, adding that until now an electronic copy of all California state statutes would have cost $200,000.

Warren traces his politicization to 1990, when questions of privacy and government raids on computer hackers compelled a number of formerly apolitical computer mavens to get organized. "I actually believe that constitutional stuff," he says with a laugh when asked why he got involved. Warren predicts that within a year no serious candidate will be able to campaign without the Internet—something President Clinton clearly has taken to heart with the installation of a hookup at the White House.

36   The Los Angeles-based Center for Governmental Studies has devised an experimental "Interactive Multimedia Political Communications Project" aimed at helping citizens dial up everything from 30-second political spots to lengthy speeches, press conferences and candidate biographies. The project is designed to let people get past paid political advertising and

ultimately participate in a kind of electronic balloting system. Envisioning an America that makes fans of representative government cringe, the center's Tracy Westen says, "In 100, or maybe 50, years, elected officials will be honorary. . . . We'll have Virtual Government."

Who knows how quickly the average information-overloaded citizen will leap at the opportunity to dial up next year's version of "The Man From Hope." At the same time, there's ample evidence that the mouse potatoes currently cruising the Internet are an especially opinionated, information-hungry bunch who don't mind speaking their minds (and speaking . . . and speaking). Wild debates over public policy issues go on for days and weeks on the Internet, which has generated its own informal etiquette and even, in the manner of Personals ads, its own acronyms. One of my favorites is IMHO—"in my humble opinion"—a useful euphemism for "you nut."

In communities where computers are old hat, citizens already are experimenting with electronic lobbying. Computer Professionals for Social Responsibility is setting up an interactive network in Seattle, home of Boeing. And Santa Monica, Calif., has such advanced computer communications that the homeless recently used terminals installed at libraries and other public places to lobby for shower facilities, bathrooms, a laundromat and lockers so they could get cleaned up for job interviews. Now people who can't afford housing on their own are using the terminals to find roommates, and donated computer equipment is being used to train the unemployed for jobs, says local activist Michelle Wittig.

In Government They Distrust

Santa Monica aside, right now the average electronic lobbyist is less likely to be one of the homeless than one of the computer gentry—folks who joined the electronic revolution years ago as the first ones on their block to buy a modem, who already enjoy access to the Internet through either an academic institution or a monthly subscription to a local network, who've conveniently forgotten the tens of millions of dollars the government has invested in creating the Internet and who don't understand what all the fuss is about in Washington.

40   Asked how he harnesses the Internet constituency to fight for change in Congress, Danny Weitzner, who lobbies for the Electronic Frontier Foundation, responds, "That's an interesting issue. . . . In terms of our supporters, a lot are skeptical when we talk about the need to legislate. They say, 'Ah—the government is just going to screw it up again.'"

At issue are two major bills, one introduced by House Judiciary Committee Chair Jack Brooks (D-Texas) and House Energy and Commerce Committee Chair John Dingell (D-Mich.), which would set the terms for RBOCs wanting entree into long-distance service, the other an ambitious rewrite of the 1934 Communications Act introduced by Rep. Edward Markey (D-Mass.), chair of the telecommunications subcommittee. In exchange for allowing phone companies to get into video delivery, and cable companies to get into phone service, the bill would encourage a system of universal (everyone can get it) access to the Information Superhighway and direct the FCC to figure out a way to bring about an "open platform"—a way for anyone to distribute information as well as receive it.

Another provision in the Markey bill would bar companies from owning both the local cable TV franchise and local phone service, a measure meant to protect the public from a media takeover by the 21st century equivalent of the Rockefellers. The provision lapses after five years, an arrangement Jamie Love rejects as a sellout and the Media Access Project's Andrew Jay Schwartzman compares to "coitus interruptus—just when things get going, it ends."

Because the bill contains affordable service and open platform provisions, however, it has won the endorsement of the Electronic Frontier Foundation (EFF), which takes some pride in the fact that it is a pragmatic, coalition-building group with good political connections and few delusions about who really controls the telecommunications debate. (Hint: It's not Ralph Nader.)

44   Co-founded by Mitchell Kapor, who bagged multimillions as a founder of the Lotus Development Corp. before dropping out and getting political, EFF has described itself as "a public interest organization dedicated to realizing the democratic potential of new computer and communications media." In political circles, EFF likes to play mainstream to Jamie Love's gadfly extremism.

Asked about the debate within the public interest Telecommunications Policy Roundtable over the Markey bill, EFF Executive Director Jerry Berman says, "We believe Markey is the vehicle [for negotiating]. The idea that we should go off and build a perfect bill is just wrongheaded. We've got to make common cause [with the Big Guys]."

Love, who dismisses all of Congress as a tool of special interests, naturally disagrees, and he just can't resist taking potshots at EFF, arguing that it is accommodating because it too takes money from such industry giants as AT&T, Bell Atlantic, MCI, Apple and IBM. Perched on a broken chair in a warehouse labyrinth that appears to be crammed with all the paper ever generated by Nader's Center for the Study of Responsive Law, Love takes the purist's position. He can afford to, as his two-person staff, which gets slim funding from the center and a few foundations, is perennially broke.

EFF, in contrast, recently opened smart offices in downtown Washington, where a staff of 11 uses state-of-the-art equipment to debate the big issues and keep track of its appointments on Capitol Hill. "We do not shade our positions," says Berman, referring to the flap over EFF's funding. "We take them and try to build coalitions behind them." Groups that rely on foundation money, he suggests, aren't as credible as those that depend on support from the real world of business and commerce.

48   Like some members of Congress, Berman suggests that contributions from lots of sources tend to cancel themselves out, and lots of contributions represent, in classic checkbook democracy fashion, lots of constituents. Clearly annoyed by ongoing debate on the Internet about EFF's politics, he continues, "I've been in the public interest community for many years, when I could have been with [the fat cat lawyer-lobbying firm] Covington and Burling, and I resent the implication that as an individual or organization we've been paid off." When it is suggested that the problem may be one of having to mingle in the corporate world, he responds, "I don't know where else to mingle!"

One alternative is to build a membership of small contributors, something EFF has toyed with doing. But that's an expensive endeavor, especially if it's done through direct mail, and EFF's efforts to advertise $40 memberships over the Internet have had only limited success. (The foundation has about 1,300 members.) One problem is that "netiquette" discourages requests for money—perhaps because of the Internet's historic ties to high-minded academia, or perhaps because the greatest fear among Internet users is that someday someone will figure out a way to make them pay.

"There's a debate going on among users of the Internet and groups like EFF about whether the Internet should be used to solicit funds; is it such sacrosanct ground that it shouldn't be sullied by commercialism?" says Roger Craver, a public-interest fundraising consultant who does most of his work through conventional snail mail. But the real problem, he believes, isn't netiquette but the nature of the system, which is so large and encompassing that it's impossible for fundraisers to target relatively narrow audiences. "There's the sheer size. . . . You hang out your message and hope someone sees it," he explains. "If you're trying to build membership you need targeting of some sort."

In other words, there is no direct mail fundraising without a list.

52   That phenomenon is one reason why so much of the public interest activity on the telecommunications front is funded by foundations and corporations: No one's figured out how to do it differently. And it's another reason so much of the lobbying is done by tax-exempt nonprofits like EFF: If EFF were set up only as a lobbying group, it wouldn't be able to take tax-deductible grants.

Andrew Schwartzman of the Media Access Project, which accepts small amounts of industry money, says the debate over funding is misplaced. "We all want the same thing; the question is how we get there." In the meantime, "There is a false sense of urgency: 'The train is leaving the station!' But another year isn't going to make a difference. The technology doesn't even exist yet. Wall Street is pressing this because the big companies want to take advantage before policymakers realize they are giving away the store."

No matter who ends up with the goods, says Schwartzman, "10 years from now you're still going to be looking to Dan Rather and his successors." What matters isn't the Superhighway of the year 2008 but the transition, he argues, and that means fighting for the same old reforms that put people to sleep during the '80s—things like the Fairness Doctrine and rules barring the phone company from controlling the content of the information it carries. By focusing too much on the distant future, he argues, we may end up giving everything to three or four companies. "That will transform the democratic process," he predicts, and not for the better.

Personal Response

If you have access to the Internet, describe the level of your involvement with it. If you do not have access to the Internet, how much and in what ways do you think you would use it if it were available to you?

Questions for Class or Small Group Discussion

1. Discuss the benefits you see in the Information Superhighway. In particular, what are the advantages of the Information Superhighway for college students? Do you see any drawbacks for college students?

2. Summarize the dangers of the Information Superhighway, as consumer groups see them. Do you think they have cause for worry?

3. According to Baldwin, "Public interest advocates believe there's a way to harness all this new technology for the betterment of democracy" (paragraph 26). How, specifically, might the Information Superhighway be used to better democracy?

4. Discuss whether you share the optimism of consumer advocates for a positive use of the new technology and explain your answer.

IT'S BEEN REAL

Sallie Tisdale

Sallie Tisdale is a writer whose books include The Sorcerer's Apprentice *(1986),* Harvest Moon *(1987),* Lot's Wife: Salt and the Human Condition *(1988), and* Stepping Westward: The Long Search for Home in the Pacific Northwest *(1991). She is a frequent contributor to such magazines as* Harper's *and* Esquire, *where this essay first appeared in 1991. In it, she narrates her experiences at a convention celebrating the benefits of virtual reality.*

Each of the six hundred people who attended the Cyberthon conference had to pass through layers of black plastic strips fluttering in the pearly static of a strobe. Each left the cool sunshine of San Francisco for dim lighting and dark shadows, exchanged the grim industrial neighborhood for the noisy growl of a crowd inside a warehouse. Cyberthon was a celebration of the technology called virtual reality, a hip term for a new wave of computer-generated experience. "Virtual reality" is an artless phrase, too clever by half for the technology itself. But it reflects the fantasy of its makers: the dream of making worlds, of visiting environments and living inside stories without leaving the living room. One company's motto for its virtual-world project was "Reality isn't enough anymore." For the people at Cyberthon, it didn't have to be.

Shouldering their way through the narrow halls and corners of a maze of ten-foot-high wooden walls, many of the conventioneers converged on the linen-covered tables of catered food: macaroni salad, cheese and crackers, and pots of coffee. Wavy Gravy, in a tie-dye-clown's dashiki, curly rainbow wig, and red nose, poked cheerfully by, balancing a plate of salad, and just behind him Bill Walton followed, shyly stooping under the door frame.

Cyberthon lasted twenty-four hours, around the clock, and only three working virtual-reality (VR) systems were available for all the participants to fight over. (Obtaining even three—one of which broke down during the conference—took a bit of luck. The simple lack of working programs reflects the current uncertain state of the technology.) A lottery was held every hour, names drawn from a hat to determine which of the attendees would get to try on glove and goggles and visit a programmed world for a few minutes in exchange for the $250 registration fee.

4   The labyrinth of squares and rectangles twisted and turned upon itself, the path blocked by people bending over computers, waiting for a turn at a particular joystick, an untried game. The center of the maze and its dark angles spilled into Mom's Kitchen, a bright square room decorated with all the comforts of the 1950s home: an electric stove, platters of potato chips and peanuts, bowls of M&M's, jars of peanut butter and grape jelly and an open loaf of white bread, and in the funky, curvaceous fridge, a glass jar of milk with a note attached—"Please don't drink from the bottle. Love, Mom." High above the table a film camera steadily panned.

In a blind hallway off the stage was the other rest stop—a section of a jet three seats across, complete with windows and tiny overhead lights; far in front was a little movie screen showing cartoons. A half-dozen people sat silently watching, staring ahead. Wandering around, I could hear snatches of a new slang, an aphoristic shorthand. "Nice cheap hack," one man said knowingly to another, and later I caught "vanilla reality" and "granularity." At one booth, an enthusiastic salesman assured me his program was "refreshable."

In an L-shaped room, two banks of computers flashed in bright hues; I sat in front of the single unoccupied screen, and immediately a young man leaned over my shoulder. "Can I show you how it works?" he asked. The software was RB2 Swivel, developed by VPL Research, which also offered one of the three working systems. Programmers build the worlds of virtual reality with geometric shapes—polygons—that can be infinitely molded. Under the patient gaze of the young man, I pulled up a menu on the computer, chose something called "Ken and Barbara," and watched my screen fill with two polygonal marionettes, vaguely male and female, held in a frozen leap on a dark background.

The three men beside me were also playing with Ken and Barbara, making them spin and dance on a flat floor, shifting an arm up, a leg out. I turned Barbara on her side, one degree at a time, by pointing her silhouette where I wanted her to go, and then made Ken follow in a growing embrace. When the white-haired man next to me saw what I was doing, his hands raced, and in a few moments his puppets were obscenely entangled, while mine still fell slowly to the floor. Leaving the room, I passed another man and heard him chortle; he had equipped Barbara with two ridged silver cones for breasts, just like Madonna's.

8   In the farthest corner of the Cyberthon labyrinth was the exhibit of Sense8, one of the show's three working virtual-reality systems. (The third was run by AutoDesk.) Sense8 is a software company founded by Eric Gullichsen and Patrice Gelband, who left AutoDesk to form their own software business and are already marketing a program that allows architects to walk through their own designs before a single brick is laid. The rectangular room was packed with lottery winners taking turns in Sense8's world.

The Sense8 staff had two setups available: one used a set of goggles, the other a large color monitor with a big funnel attached to block peripheral vision. Both ran the same "world." Virtual reality as an experience—as opposed to a technology—is rather more like going to the movies than going to a new world. Improvements in the technology will make VR more and more engaging, but the coarseness of the pictures themselves disappoints most users. Still, as with movies and all screens—television and computer both—the VR visitor tends to shut out the surrounding physical reality and disappear, for better or worse, inside the apparent one.

People using the goggles reclined in something called the flogiston chair, a $1,599 piece of furniture designed, says Sense8's literature, for the perfect "flow" posture. Rather than donning a glove, the user moves through Sense8's world with a kind of pressure-sensitive joystick.

I perched on the barstool in front of the fixed screen. Behind me I heard one of the staff say to a man lying in the chair, "Let me restart the world." I could see on the screen an office, a desk, a red chair, and a set of bookshelves lined up crookedly on a floor that ended in a void. The furniture was simple and bright, the details sharp. Programmers talk about high and low resolution, which means nothing more than how sharp the image appears to the user, how dull and grainy the picture becomes when seen up close. The graininess depends directly on the number of pixels used—

another bit of slang, short for picture elements—and the number of pixels is a matter of technical sophistication and money. The more pixels there are, the sharper the picture. Goggles actually provide the worst picture.

12   In one corner of the "office" I could see three rows of television sets piled one on top of the other. I floated toward them by pressing the joystick and then pushed a button with my right hand. A big, colored bullet floated out of my eyes and down with a missile's whoosh; it struck and shattered one of the televisions with the crystalline noise of breaking glass.

Hours later, in the middle of the night, I returned to Sense8 and sat on a folding chair next to a noisy fan providing a little breeze in the stale air. All through the building people were drifting off to sleep, on couches, under tables, stretched across the jet seats. Over the corner of the maze drifted electronic Irish music, fat oboes with a Celtic drum and bells. A baby-faced man sat straight up in the chair next to mine. Above his plump cheeks sat a small set of goggles shaped like aviator glasses. His feet were flat on the floor and parallel, his arms relaxed on the arms of the chair, and on his lap was a control labeled Synchro-Stim 2000. Behind the dark lenses of the glasses, tiny bulbs flashed in a rhythm set by the controls to stimulate alpha waves in the brain. He had a miniature smile on his face, and the muscles in his fingers and cheeks twitched and jerked as in sleep.

"I'm at liberty to say I'm an acidhead and not pretend otherwise," John Perry Barlow told me. "Drugs are not the issue here—it's the slippery epistemology that psychedelics induce. You don't have to take psychedelic drugs to have it. But most of the people I know in this scene have taken psychedelic drugs. I don't think this culture is being particularly honest about it." It was late on Saturday evening, and Barlow sat at a table on the back deck of the wharfside warehouse, where rows of little lights were reflected in the fragrant water. A man in a dark corner nearby played a wandering melody on his saxophone. "I don't know what's going to happen with this, but it's going to happen, and it will happen in a more positive light if we proceed as though it were fun and good."

A lot of people working in virtual reality think the establishment fears their technology, fears that virtual reality will intoxicate users, distort perceptions, and transform ideas the way certain drugs have done. Jaron Lanier, the young founder of VPL Research, is openly nervous about the easy comparisons between virtual reality and LSD—this in spite of the fact that Lanier is the most deliberately psychedelic of virtual reality's proponents. Lanier, at thirty, is a plump man with ropy blond dreadlocks and a high, mild, almost shy voice. In one interview after another he has dreamed out loud about the potential of virtual reality. Lanier and his fans talk of wanting to live outside limitations, to live in a world in which even the laws of physics are designed to one's liking. The connection to drug culture, both as source material and adjunct, is unmistakable.

16   Back inside the warehouse, most of the conference attendees had abandoned their games and monitors a few hours after midnight and

jammed into a big room to hear Timothy Leary speak. Wavy Gravy took the stage under bright lights, still dressed as a clown, sang a paean to Harpo Marx, and told a rambling pornographic tall tale, loosening up the crowd like a good opening act. Then Leary rose, a thin, vague, white-haired man with a ravaged face. He paced the stage, speaking very slowly in a Boston Brahmin voice of cultivated consonants and long-drawn vowels, a whispery, lost inflection. He let sentences trail off and seemed to gently caress his wandering thoughts, pulling them down to words. "It's a community," he murmured, "a new version of the old community of people who are chasing reality." He paused. A few people tittered. "There's such a range of eccentric and far-out talent." Another pause, and he seemed to excite for a moment. "But that should be expected, because the product that is being produced and sold is reality! It's not spreadsheets and work stations. Reality!" After a few more phrases, a few more pauses, he turned to the others on the stage and said, "Listen, I've done the best I could, really."

The drug culture frightens the Establishment for a number of reasons, only one of which is the power of drugs to make users question the status quo. New cultures have power themselves; cultures create new identities, new loyalties. This cultural identity—still felt decades later by people who used psychedelics in the sixties—affects the social fabric. In fact, virtual reality may be intoxicating, but it is more analogous to the dulling of alcohol than the dynamic, interactive experience of LSD. Virtual reality can never be an unprogrammed trip. There is no doubt that the proponents of virtual reality imagine this technology creating a culture just as powerful. Already it has its own vocabulary, its own words for determining who is of it and who is not.

After Leary wandered back to his seat on the stage, Terence McKenna rose. McKenna is a gnome of a man with a reedy, persuasive voice, an ethnobotanist who studies natural hallucinogens. "It's kind of a strange idea," he began, "but people have been doing VR for about a hundred and twenty-five thousand years. They just called it taking psychedelic drugs. Why is this the oldest form of entertainment?" The crowd was willing, tired, wide-eyed, laughing on cue. "The thing virtual reality holds out is the ability for one person to show another person the contents of their imagination. We've never been able to do that—oil paints, working in wood, marble, and steel, and then even in electronic pixels and film. It's not entirely satisfying. Our world is networked together using small mouth noises, which are speech, or symbols for small mouth noises. This is not a wide band for communication, this small mouth-noise thing." As he spoke, a looping series of fractal images was projected on the blank movie screen behind his head, a shifting snake of chaos changing from pink to lavender to white. "We need to recapture the conspiratorial ambience of the dope-dealing past that we keep trying to leave behind. Because it is a conspiracy, make no mistake about it. When one form of media supplants another, huge power blocks are disenfranchised, and huge new power blocks emerge."

Eventually a microphone was opened for comments from the audience, many of which were only slightly relevant, almost all of which were positive. After a time, a man named Michael Rossman, an acquaintance of Leary's and McKenna's, made one of the few critical speeches of the entire weekend. After establishing his own credentials as a user of psychedelics, Rossman talked with emotion about his work as an elementary-school science teacher. He said he avoids using computers, preferring to take his students out of the classroom and into the physical world. "These kids come to school with Nintendos! Jesus H. Christ, what is this argument that Nintendo teaches fine motor control? Hey, masturbation teaches fine motor control! How do we connect them with something that's real? Where is the moral center? This is a very dangerous drug we are messing with here. We've got no idea how dangerous it is."

20   Rossman was applauded, but when the panel was finished a number of people shook their heads over his concerns. One man, standing near the stage, grumbled to another, "The whole 'Let's protect the children!' trip. C'mon, guys!"

Under all the earnest pronouncements and speeches about the new technology, there is a sense of glee—the kids are in the driver's seat again, and no one can see over the steering wheel. Easy enough to imagine great things down the road, adventures and feats of derring-do, easy to imagine world-changing and dragon-slaying. Imagine a technology that allows us to do anything—to do what is illegal, immoral, lost in time, physically impossible, lethal. One young man told me, near dawn, that virtual reality could help people "experience what it is to be human in a more diverse, less centered, higher bandwidth sort of way." Lanier calls virtual reality "shared hallucinations, except that you can compose them like works of art." The list of dreams, of hoped-for programs, is long: to float in Saturn's rings, ride through medieval London or around the bonds of a molecule, follow a mote of dust in a tornado or a drop of blood in a vein; to crawl along the bottom of the Marianas Trench.

Researchers are working on direct EEG probes, on gloves that give tactile sensations to the fingers, body suits that give a kind of force feedback to the muscles of the legs and arms so that the wearer, standing still, feels as if he is running. Howard Rheingold talks of dildonics, a future of sex between gloved and anonymous participants in separate rooms. Jaron Lanier speaks of half-formed dreams: Would you like to be Alice, getting bigger or smaller with a single sip? Would you like to be a car, a piano, a rain cloud? He imagines worlds populated by several people at once, acting and reacting independently; he imagines virtual mirrors, in which I will see not only my computer-tracked hand, but my own tracked and ideal self.

A common theme, repeated again and again in virtual-reality circles, is the hope that it will be better than television, and at least as good as the telephone. It's not really a hope, no matter how it's phrased, that virtual reality will be a tool for good—it's an expectation. No one seems to expect anything less. No one speaks of things like information overload, data glut, of how overwhelmed the American animal already is with numbers, words and pictures, film and sounds, and promises on every billboard. No one mentions the brave new world.

24   Questions about virtual reality—and the answers given—are confused, worded as though they rise out of virtual reality itself, separate from our daily, messy lives. But they really arise here, in our skin and eyes. Will virtual reality, like opium, sicken its users of ordinary life? (Will it be the drug of choice for people already sickened?) Will it be better or worse to be alive, to be in our bodies, growing old, waking up in the morning to go to work, when a perfect, programmed reality is so nearby? Is it nothing more than brain candy? Such questions are quickly dismissed as paranoid. Lanier and others are fond of exclaiming that virtual reality serves to enhance our experience in the physical world by reminding us of it. I heard one person say late in the night, "You take the goggles off and boom! *There's* an epiphany—the texture of your skin."

I sat in the near dark behind the jet seats with Eric Gullichsen, cofounder of Sense8, and he told me, "The time will come when you will go to look at something and there won't be any way to distinguish whether it's something that's living, whether it's artificial, whether it's controlled by another person or an artificial intelligence. Those kinds of distinctions won't mean anything ten or twenty years in the future."

I asked him, "What's the point of it?"

"What do you mean, 'What's the point?'"

28   "Yeah, what's the point?"

"What kind of question is that?"

I felt a curious absence of narrative at Cyberthon, both in and out of the virtual worlds. It was an absence of plot—there is no story yet, no cosmology. When people talk about the technology getting "better," what is meant is simply an improved image—better reception. No doubt the current technology is overly awkward and inelegant, but I'm not convinced that new and better goggles will change that. This assumption—that all virtual reality needs is better gear—pervades all discussions about it.

I watched a slide show given by Scott Fisher, formerly of NASA, on Saturday afternoon. He was explaining a computer-generated skeleton designed to help physicians plan orthopedic surgery. The human body, he noted, was the most complex of systems to imitate; the fuel dynamics of a jet engine were simpler. "Actually, it would run a lot better if we cut off the foot," said Fisher. "Too many polygons."

32   Lanier professes a disdain for language, imagining, he says, a world of "postsymbolic communication," a world without words. A number of VR people agree with Lanier, dismissing not just words but the concept of

words. (Lanier's disdain for the written word, though, is not so great that he could resist a six-figure advance from Harcourt Brace Jovanovich to write a book on VR.) The inflated respect for the visual common to the computer community is at the same time a distaste for language. As Steven Levy, author of *Hackers* and a columnist for *Macworld,* writes, "A thousand words die with every picture." In this land of commands and abbreviations, books are antiques, reading is anachronistic. (And the writing is almost willfully poor.) Language is difficult, defined, at times infuriating; it is work, language. To read a story you have to perform a labor of imagination—you have to strain the story through your eyes. But in virtual reality there is no labor. The world you enter is virtual; so is the act of entering it.

Computers are complex beasts; their programmers—those who would give us these new worlds—suffer from a certain narrowness of focus. The exciting new questions they ask each other, about relation and language and space and reality, have been asked for ages, but philosophy has no place here. The programmers are all angles and math, all crystals, no curves. There is something terribly familiar about the flying pillars and smashed television sets, something smacking of comic books and Saturday-morning cartoons. What kind of virtual world would be drawn by an Inuit, a Mongolian village girl, a yogi, an aboriginal shaman? What mythical dreams and symbols would they choose, what synergy of light and sound? Here is a technology with massive power, stuck in the tiny paradigm of the white American male.

No wonder then that the conference seemed constrained by a strange naiveté, a fantasy presuming more of humans than human history should warrant. Lanier has said that the rape of the planet happens because we have nothing nonmaterial to rape, nothing virtual on which to act out our need to mold and shape. He imagines a world without forms, where rich and poor disappear.

The current complete virtual-reality system available from VPL costs about $225,000. (The DataGlove alone runs about $8,500.) Much of the cost is the hardware—the powerful generating computers—and the price will certainly drop as the techniques and tools improve. But more than price concerns me, though price clearly affects control. Virtual reality, like most computer technologies, is the province of white men—mostly young. There were a handful of women at Cyberthon, a few black men, several Japanese men. These are the same people who own the computers that run the programs, the same people who work for and in many cases run the companies that design the computers. The same people write the software, direct the academic programs of computer technology, write and publish the articles promoting the technology. I heard few complaints. The strongest public challenge to the conference came from a young man who decried the panels as "a bunch of technoweenies whining about who's going to fund their latest fad." Over loud protests from floor and stage, he added, "We're trying to forward the industrial revolution and there are still people fighting the agricultural revolution and losing." He found little support.

36   In the chalky white light of morning, I stood with Stewart Brand, founder of the *Whole Earth Review* and the Point Foundation, Cyberthon's sponsor, near the finger of San Francisco Bay, behind the warehouse. Each piling stood clear above the flat, mirrored water, and nearby a blue heron dived, and surfaced, and dived, splitting the surface like skin. Beside the latrines a pair of orange-vested security guards tossed a Frisbee. Brand was listening, talking, laughing, and then he smiled, his lined face full of pleasure, and said, "I don't know. Maybe virtual reality does make you appreciate the world more." He looked at the sky. "Or maybe it's just a beautiful day."

Personal Response

If you have ever experienced virtual reality, describe that experience. If you have not personally experienced it, explain how you feel about the idea of experiencing virtual reality, now that you have read this article.

Questions for Class or Small Group Discussion

1. Discuss Tisdale's questions about or criticisms of virtual reality and whether you agree that she has cause for concern.

2. Tisdale suggests that "the establishment" fears virtual reality in part because of its similarity to the drug culture (paragraph 17). In what ways is virtual reality like drug use? How is it different?

3. Discuss this comment by a man named Michael Rossman: "'Where is the moral center? This is a very dangerous drug we are messing with here. We've got no idea how dangerous it is'" (paragraph 19).

4. Tisdale notes that a common theme in discussions of virtual reality "is the hope that it will be better than television, and at least as good as the telephone" (paragraph 23) and that "questions about virtual reality—and the answers given—are confused" (paragraph 24). Discuss the possibilities you see for this new technology and the questions you have about it.

ARTIFICIAL INTELLIGENCE

Grant Fjermedal

Grant Fjermedal is author of Magic Bullets: A Revolution in Cancer Treatment *(1984) and* The Tomorrow Makers: A Brave New World of Living Brain Machines *(1986). This piece, excerpted from* The Tomorrow Makers, *was first published in* Omni *in 1986. In it,*

Fjermedal explores his views on the possibility of living forever by having one's brain copied and implanted in a computerized robot.

I'm sure that Hans Moravec is at least as sane as I am, but he certainly brought to mind the classic mad scientist as we sat in his fifth-floor office at Carnegie-Mellon University on a dark and stormy night. It was nearly midnight, and he mixed for each of us a bowl of chocolate milk and Cheerios, with slices of banana piled on top.

Then, with banana-slicing knife in hand, Moravec, the senior research scientist at Carnegie-Mellon's Mobile Robot Laboratory, outlined for me how he could create a robotic immortality for Everyman, a deathless universe in which life would go on forever. By creating computer copies of our minds and transferring, or downloading, this program into robotic bodies, Moravec explained, humans could survive for centuries.

"You are in an operating room. A robot brain surgeon is in attendance. . . . Your skull but not your brain is anesthetized. You are fully conscious. The surgeon opens your braincase and peers inside." This is how Moravec described the process in a paper he wrote called "Robots That Rove." The robotic surgeon's "attention is directed at a small clump of about one hundred neurons somewhere near the surface. Using high-resolution 3-D nuclear-magnetic-resonance holography, phased-array radio encephalography, and ultrasonic radar, the surgeon determines the three-dimensional structure and chemical makeup of that neural clump. It writes a program that models the behavior of the clump and starts it running on a small portion of the computer sitting next to you."

4   That computer sitting next to you in the operating room would in effect be your new brain. As each area of your brain was analyzed and simulated, the accuracy of the simulation would be tested as you pressed a button to shift between the area of the brain just copied and the simulation. When you couldn't tell the difference between the original and the copy, the surgeon would transfer the simulation of your brain into the new, computerized one and repeat the process on the next area of your biological brain.

"Though you have not lost consciousness or even your train of thought, your mind—some would say soul—has been removed from the brain and transferred to a machine," Moravec said, "In a final step your old body is disconnected. The computer is installed in a shiny new one, in the style, color, and material of your choice."

As we sat around Moravec's office I asked what would become of the original human body after the downloading. "You just don't bother waking it up again if the copying went successfully," he said. "It's so messy. Humans have got so many problems that you might just want to leave it retired. You don't take your junker car out if you've got a new one."

Moravec's idea is the ultimate in life insurance: Once one copy of the brain's contents has been made, it will be easy to make multiple backup copies, and these could be stashed in hiding places around the world, allowing you to embark on any sort of adventure without having to worry about aging or death. As decades pass into centuries you could travel the globe and then the solar system and beyond—always keeping an eye out for the latest in robotic bodies into which you could transfer your computer mind.

8   If living forever weren't enough, you could live forever several times over by activating some of your backup copies and sending different versions of yourself out to see the world. "You could have parallel experiences and merge the memories later," Moravec explained.

In the weeks and months that followed my stay at Carnegie-Mellon, I was intrigued by how many researchers seemed to believe downloading would come to pass. The only point of disagreement was *when*—certainly a big consideration to those of us still knocking around in mortal bodies. Although some of the researchers I spoke with at Carnegie-Mellon, MIT, and Stanford and in Japan thought that downloading was still generations away, there were others who believed achieving robotic immortality was imminent and seemed driven by private passions never to die.

The significance of the door Moravec is trying to open is not lost on others. Olin Shivers, a Carnegie-Mellon graduate student who works closely with Moravec as well as with Allen Newell, one of the founding fathers of artificial intelligence, told me, "Moravec wants to design a creature, and my professor Newell wants to design a creature. We are all, in a sense, trying to play God."

At MIT I was surprised to find Moravec's concept of downloading given consideration by Marvin Minsky, Donner Professor of Science and another father of artificial intelligence. Minsky is trying to learn how the billions of brain cells work together to allow a person to think and remember. If he succeeds, it will be a big step toward figuring out how to join perhaps billions of computer circuits together to allow a computer to receive the entire contents of the human mind.

12   "If a person is like a machine, once you get a wiring diagram of how he works, you can make copies," Minsky told me.

Although Minsky doesn't think he'll live long enough to download (he's fifty-seven now), he would consider it. "I think it would be a great thing to do," he said. "I've spent a long time learning things, and I'd hate to see it all go away."

Minsky also said he would have no qualms about waving goody-bye to his human body and taking up residence within a robot. "Why not avoid getting sick and things like that?" he asked. "It's hard to see anything against it. I think people will get fed up with bodies after a while. Then you'll have another population problem: You'll have all the people of the past, as well as the new ones."

Another believer is Danny Hillis, one of Minsky's Ph.D. students and the founding scientist of Thinking Machines, a Cambridge-based company that is trying to create the kind of computer that might someday receive the contents of the brain. During my research several computer scientists would point to Hillis's connection machine as an example of a new order of computer architecture, one that's comparable to the human brain. (Hillis's connection machine doesn't have one large central processing unit as other computers do but a network of 64,000 small units—roughly analogous in concept, if not in size, to the brain's network of 40 billion neuronal processing units.)

16   "I've added up the things I want to do in my life, and it's about fifteen hundred years' worth of stuff," Hillis, now twenty-eight, told me one day as we stood out on the sixth-floor sun deck of the Thinking Machines building. "I enjoy having a body as much as anyone else does, but if it's a choice between downloading into a computer—even one that's stuck in a room someplace—and still being able to think versus just dying, I would certainly take that opportunity to think."

Gerald J. Sussman, a thirty-six-year-old MIT professor and a computer hacker of historic proportions, expressed similar sentiments. "Everyone would like to be immortal. I don't think the time is quite right, but it's close. I'm afraid, unfortunately, that I'm in the last generation to die."

"Do you really think that we're that close?" I asked.

"Yes," he answered, which reminded me of something Moravec had written not too long ago: "We are on a threshold of a change in the universe comparable to the transition from nonlife to life."

Personal Response

Does the possibility of living forever by having your brain copied by a computer and implanted in a robot appeal to you or not? Explain your answer.

Questions for Class or Small Group Discussion

1. Many would argue that the subject of this essay is more in the realm of science fiction than of science, but often the stuff of science fiction eventually becomes reality. Discuss the implications of what Fjermedal describes here, were it to become a reality. Does it seem entirely possible to you, or do you consider it too fantastic to ever become reality? Explain your answer.

2. Respond to this remark of Marvin Minsky, one of the creators of artificial intelligence, speaking of the possibility of reproducing the human brain in a computer program: "'It's hard to see anything against it'" (paragraph 14). Do you agree with him? Why or why not?

3. Discuss whether you agree with Danny Hillis when he says that "'if it's a choice between downloading into a computer—even one

that's stuck in a room someplace—and still being able to think versus just dying, I would certainly take that opportunity to think'" (paragraph 16).

THE LUDDITES ARE BACK

Steven Levy

Steven Levy is a journalist who writes for Newsweek *magazine. This essay appeared in a section entitled "Random Access" in the June 12, 1995, issue of* Newsweek. *In it, Levy points out who some of computer technology's critics are and what they find wrong with it, and he explains why he thinks the term they like to use to describe themselves is being used erroneously.*

It took Kirkpatrick Sale two blows with a sledgehammer to destroy the IBM PC he brought to his appearance at New York City's Town Hall last January in a "Vision Fest" sponsored by the *Utne Reader*. Sale, a longtime leftist critic, doesn't like technology in general and computers in particular. On the very first page of his book "Rebels Against the Future"—a historical account of the 19th-century Luddite war against the Industrial Revolution, with misguided commentary on its relevance to our time—he apologizes that the book was published with modern technology. This meant that the means of production were "not entirely neutral and untainted." The world would be better, Sale thinks, if computers simply went away.

Sale's book places him in the vanguard of a group of antitechnologists who view the digital revolution with a sense of horror and dread. Though these works do not yet threaten to eclipse the flood of "How to Use the Internet" tomes, it does seem to be a mini-boom of late, replete with titles like "Resisting the Virtual Life" (edited by James Brook and Iain Boal), "Silicon Snake Oil" (by Clifford Stoll) and "The Future Does Not Compute" (by Stephen Talbott). The latter book contains my favorite negative image; Talbott likens the computer screen to a prison window. That little gem comes in a chapter entitled "Can Human Ideals Survive the Internet?" Are you getting the drift?

Sadly, this gang provides a shrill, unproductive counterpoint to the technophiliac hype coming from Silicon Valley and the trade press. There is nothing wrong with criticizing various aspects, or even the general direction, of the computer movement—on the contrary, it is essential to maintain not only our skepticism but a keen sense of what works and what doesn't, as we attempt to integrate the overwhelming flood of innovation into our lives. But these self-proclaimed neo-Luddites start out from a wrongheaded premise: that computers themselves are evil.

4   This demonization is based on an unwillingness to consider the pluses as well as the minuses of computer technology. Sale, for instance, seems locked to the idea that computers are inevitably linked to hierarchical models of control—he seems unaware that personal computers are a creation of the counterculture, and that many of the digital pioneers he would condemn were specifically concerned with empowering individuals. Neo-Luddites who do understand computers often fail to draw on that perspective when they launch their attacks. For instance, geek apostate Stoll takes a dim view of the Information Highway as it stands today, in the earliest stages of construction. He complains that it's hard to use, and you can't really buy anything. This is like someone at the turn of the century criticizing auto travel. The roads are bumpy! These cars need cranks to start!

By and large, the best critiques of technology seem to be coming from people who accept the inevitability of computerization and are devoted to spreading the technology in a more felicitous manner. If you want the most withering assessments of software interfaces, for instance, just talk to the people whose job it is to design them—only they know the distance we must travel before ease-of-use is anything but a misnomer. Those most intimate with computers believe that if our systems are open and continually evolving, they will wind up as a positive force. There are, of course, no guarantees that things will work out for the best. Are there ever? But I do think that there is some reason for optimism. While it is true that automation can displace workers, computer technology does provide new jobs—and can, through the Net, amplify the voice of the displaced.

In light of this it is interesting that the neo-Luddites align themselves with a group that had no such reason for optimism. As Sale vividly describes in his book, the original Luddites were a brave aggregation of textile workers in northern England who deserved a better fate than becoming a synonym for those who mindlessly oppose change. Between 1812 and 1814, groups proclaiming allegiance to a legendary King Ludd risked (and in some cases lost) their lives by wielding hammer and hatchet against modern looms that moved cloth production into inhumane factories. But their real enemy was a system that regarded them as chattel. The weavers' circumstances were far removed from the dispossessed in our society: when faced with the loss of their jobs, they had nowhere to go, and their children and their children's children were effectively stripped of a future.

Everybody agrees that the Luddites failed in their Quixotic rebellion. Yet in the long run, we came to accept their complaints—it is now legally and morally unacceptable to run sweatshops and engage in oppressive child-labor practices. More important, the fruits of technology are now more widely distributed: even the poor in this country live a considerably better life than the displaced 19th-century textile worker. This places the neo-Luddites in an uncomfortable position. A tenet of their philosophy is an abiding nostalgia for a pre-technical world: one not shared by those who uncomplainingly watch TV, drive cars and get food out of refrigerators. (Sale told a WIRED magazine interviewer that he believed civilization itself was a catastrophe.) It is a telling fact that the neo-Luddites consist not of blue-collar workers, but elite symbol-shufflers who will never themselves be displaced by computers.

8   That's why, when Kirkpatrick Sale performs the hollow circus act of smashing his own machine, he cheapens the desperate struggle of his subjects. Sale's book successfully argues that the Luddites should be rescued from the linguistic taint of being thought of as know-nothings. Not so with their successors.

Personal Response

Do you share the views of antitechnologists, as described in this essay? Explain your answer.

Questions for Class or Small Group Discussion

1. What do you think accounts for the strong criticism of and resistance to computer technology expressed by writers like Kirkpatrick Sale, Clifford Stoll, and Stephen Talbott (paragraphs 1–2)? What do they fear? Do you agree with their views? Explain your answer.

2. Discuss what you see as the "pluses [and] minuses of computer technology" (paragraph 4).

3. Insofar as you understand who the Luddites are, do you agree with Levy's taking exception to antitechnologists calling themselves neo-Luddites? Explain your answer.

4. What do you think Kirkpatrick Sale, Clifford Stoll, Stephen Talbott, and other critics of computer technology would have to say about the subjects of the other essays in this chapter: virtual reality, the Information Superhighway, and explorations into the possibility of programming computers to replicate the workings of the human brain?

Perspectives on Computer Science

Suggestions for Synthesis

1. Explain your position on the subject of computer technology, incorporating the views of at least two of the writers in this chapter. If possible, either invite a scientist or computer science instructor to speak to your class about computer

technology, or conduct an interview with one. Incorporate the views of the expert into your paper.

2. Explain your views on the moral or ethical implications of one of the new computer technologies discussed in this chapter, such as artificial intelligence or virtual reality. If possible, either invite an instructor from the philosophy department to speak to your class on the subject or interview one. Take the views of the philosophy instructor and at least one of the writers in this chapter into account in your essay.

3. Hold a class forum on the subject of the potential uses and dangers of computer technology, including virtual reality, artificial intelligence, and the Information Superhighway. For a writing exercise, explore the subject by incorporating the views of two or more writers in this chapter.

Additional Writing Topics

1. Read any of the books Steven Levy mentions in paragraphs one and two of his essay "The Luddites Are Back" and write a report in which you both summarize its major points and provide a thoughtful, detailed response to it.

2. Compare and contrast the benefits of the Information Superhighway with its potential dangers as you explain your own view of this computer technology.

3. Explore the direction you see computers taking in the next decade or two by considering the potential and possible dangers of computer technology in the twenty-first century.

4. Respond to this statement in Sallie Tisdale's "It's Been Real": "Computers are complex beasts; their programmers—those who would give us these new worlds—suffer from a certain narrowness of focus" (paragraph 33).

5. In speaking of the possibility of reproducing the human brain in a computer program, Marvin Minsky, one of the creators of artificial intelligence, said: "'It's hard to see anything against it'" (paragraph 14, Grant Fjermedal's "Artificial Intelligence"). Write an essay in which you explain why you agree or disagree with Minsky.

Research Topics

1. In paragraph six of Steven Levy's "The Luddites Are Back," he briefly explains the origin of the term *Luddite*. Research the activities of this early nineteenth-century group of British textile workers and summarize your findings. Then state whether you agree with Levy that the term is being used incorrectly by present-day critics of computer technology and explain your position.

2. Interview instructors in the humanities and in the sciences about their views on the potential uses and dangers of computer technology, summarize your

findings in a formal paper, and explain what conclusions you have come to on the basis of the interviews. Supplement your interviews with library research.

3. Expand topic number 3 under "Additional Writing Topics" by including library research on the topic.

4. Writing in 1991, Sallie Tisdale in "It's Been Real" comments that the technology of virtual reality is in an uncertain state (paragraph 3). Research the current state of virtual reality technology, and explain your own position on its possible benefits and drawbacks.

CHAPTER 16

NATURAL SCIENCES

The natural sciences include such disciplines as biology, physics, astronomy, and chemistry. Their focus of inquiry is on the workings and phenomena of the natural world, from the ocean floor to the farthest galaxies of the universe. The essays in this chapter cover that range and hint at the enormous possibility for increasing human knowledge of the world we inhabit. The authors here share a belief in the wonders and joy of science and in the close relationship of science and creative imagination.

For instance, in "Can We Know the Universe? Reflections on a Grain of Sand," Carl Sagan, an internationally known astronomer who has made the mysteries of space less mystifying to millions of people through his popular television series Cosmos, *counters those who think that everything worth knowing will soon be known. In illustrating how vast is the knowledge yet unknown, Sagan's exuberant belief in the value of scientific inquiry is clearly evident. Consider, as you read his essay, whether you share his enthusiasm for the potential of scientific inquiry or if you side with the scientists who think that everything worth knowing has already been discovered, or soon will be. Do you share Sagan's enthusiasm for science?*

Like Sagan, Jacob Bronowski in "The Reach of the Imagination" emphasizes the imaginative component of scientific thinking as he explains the workings of the imagination and why he believes it marks the chief difference between humans and other animals. Consider whether you agree with him on this point. Are there other areas of equal importance that distinguish humans' superiority to other animals? Similar in his view of science to Sagan and Bronowski, W. John Coletta, an English teacher who coordinates a technical and scientific writing program at his university, explores the link between science and imagination. In "Minding the Reef," based on his personal encounter with a barracuda, Coletta makes such observations as "biology is metaphor," "science . . . is literature," and "the natural world is just as figurative as a poem, literally." To what extent do you agree with all of these writers about the imaginative and creative components of science and its link with the humanities?

The final piece in this chapter, "The Chemist," is by another scientist who works to popularize science and make it more accessible to the public. In this brief chapter from his book celebrating the truly interdisciplinary nature of our lives, chemist Roald Hoffmann explores the metaphor of discovery used by scientists from historical, psychological, philosophical, and sociological perspectives. As you read the essay, think about the broader issue raised by Hoffmann, that is, the interconnectedness of the disciplines. Do you see such a connection in the courses you are now taking?

CAN WE KNOW THE UNIVERSE? REFLECTIONS ON A GRAIN OF SAND

Carl Sagan

Carl Sagan is professor of astronomy and space sciences at Cornell University. He received the Pulitzer Prize for literature for his book The Dragons of Eden *(1977). Sagan is also a recipient of a NASA Medal for Exceptional Scientific Achievement and for Distinguished Public Service, and a Peabody Award for his public television series* Cosmos. *This essay is excerpted from his 1979 book* Broca's Brain: Reflections on the Romance of Science.

> *Nothing is rich but the inexhaustible wealth*
> *of nature. She shows us only surfaces,*
> *but she is a million fathoms deep.*
>   Ralph Waldo Emerson

Science is a way of thinking much more than it is a body of knowledge. Its goal is to find out how the world works, to seek what regularities there may be, to penetrate to the connections of things—from subnuclear particles, which may be the constituents of all matter, to living organisms, the human social community, and thence to the cosmos as a whole. Our intuition is by no means an infallible guide. Our perceptions may be distorted by training and prejudice or merely because of the limitations of our sense organs, which, of course, perceive directly but a small fraction of the phenomena of the world. Even so straightforward a question as whether in the absence of friction a pound of lead falls faster than a gram of fluff was answered incorrectly by Aristotle and almost everyone else before the time of Galileo. Science is based on experiment, on a willingness to challenge old dogma, on an openness to see the universe as it really is. Accordingly, science sometimes requires courage—at the very least the courage to question the conventional wisdom.

Beyond this the main trick of science is to *really* think of something: the shape of clouds and their occasional sharp bottom edges at the same altitude everywhere in the sky; the formation of a dewdrop on a leaf; the origin of a name or a word—Shakespeare, say, or "philanthropic"; the reason for human social customs—the incest taboo, for example; how it is that a lens in sunlight can make paper burn; how a "walking stick" got to look so much like a twig; why the Moon seems to follow us as we walk; what prevents us from digging a hole down to the center of the Earth;

what the definition is of "down" on a spherical Earth; how it is possible for the body to convert yesterday's lunch into today's muscle and sinew; or how far is up—does the universe go on forever, or if it does not, is there any meaning to the question of what lies on the other side? Some of these questions are pretty easy. Others, especially the last, are mysteries to which no one even today knows the answer. They are natural questions to ask. Every culture has posed such questions in one way or another. Almost always the proposed answers are in the nature of "Just So Stories," attempted explanations divorced from experiment, or even from careful comparative observations.

But the scientific cast of mind examines the world critically as if many alternative worlds might exist, as if other things might be here which are not. Then we are forced to ask why what we see is present and not something else. Why are the Sun and the Moon and the planets spheres? Why not pyramids, or cubes, or dodecahedra? Why not irregular, jumbly shapes? Why so symmetrical, worlds? If you spend any time spinning hypotheses, checking to see whether they make sense, whether they conform to what else we know, thinking of tests you can pose to substantiate or deflate your hypotheses, you will find yourself doing science. And as you come to practice this habit of thought more and more you will get better and better at it. To penetrate into the heart of the thing—even a little thing, a blade of grass, as Walt Whitman said—is to experience a kind of exhilaration that, it may be, only human beings of all the beings on this planet can feel. We are an intelligent species and the use of our intelligence quite properly gives us pleasure. In this respect the brain is like a muscle. When we think well, we feel good. Understanding is a kind of ecstasy.

4   But to what extent can we *really* know the universe around us? Sometimes this question is posed by people who hope the answer will be in the negative, who are fearful of a universe in which everything might one day be known. And sometimes we hear pronouncements from scientists who confidently state that everything worth knowing will soon be known—or even is already known—and who paint pictures of a Dionysian or Polynesian age in which the zest for intellectual discovery has withered, to be replaced by a kind of subdued languor, the lotus eaters drinking fermented coconut milk or some other mild hallucinogen. In addition to maligning both the Polynesians, who were intrepid explorers (and whose brief respite in paradise is now sadly ending), as well as the inducements to intellectual discovery provided by some hallucinogens, this contention turns out to be trivially mistaken.

Let us approach a much more modest question: not whether we can know the universe or the Milky Way galaxy or a star or a world. Can we know, ultimately and in detail, a grain of salt? Consider one microgram of table salt, a speck just barely large enough for someone with keen eyesight to make out without a microscope. In that grain of salt there are about 10^{16} sodium and chlorine atoms. This is a 1 followed by 16 zeros, 10 million billion atoms. If we wish to know a grain of salt, we must know at least the three-dimensional positions of each of these atoms. (In fact, there is much more to be known—for example, the nature of the forces between the atoms—but we are making only a modest calculation.) Now, is this number more or less than the number of things which the brain can know?

How much *can* the brain know? There are perhaps 10^{11} neurons in the brain, the circuit elements and switches that are responsible in their electrical and chemical activity for the functioning of our minds. A typical brain neuron has perhaps a thousand little wires, called dendrites, which connect it with its fellows. If, as seems likely, every bit of information in the brain corresponds to one of these connections, the total number of things knowable by the brain is no more than 10^{14}, one hundred trillion. But this number is only one percent of the number of atoms in our speck of salt.

So in this sense the universe is intractable, astonishingly immune to any human attempt at full knowledge. We cannot on this level understand a grain of salt, much less the universe.

8   But let us look more deeply at our microgram of salt. Salt happens to be a crystal in which, except for defects in the structure of the crystal lattice, the position of every sodium and chlorine atom is predetermined. If we could shrink ourselves into this crystalline world, we could see rank upon rank of atoms in an ordered array, a regularly alternating structure—sodium, chlorine, sodium, chlorine, specifying the sheet of atoms we are standing on and all the sheets above us and below us. An absolutely pure crystal of salt could have the position of every atom specified by something like 10 bits of information.[1] This would not strain the information-carrying capacity of the brain.

If the universe had natural laws that governed its behavior to the same degree of regularity that determines a crystal of salt, then, of course, the universe would be knowable. Even if there were many such laws, each of considerable complexity, human beings might have the capacity to understand them all. Even if such knowledge exceeded the information-carrying capacity of the brain, we might store the additional information outside our bodies—in books, for example, or in computer memories—and still, in some sense, know the universe.

Human beings are, understandably, highly motivated to find regularities, natural laws. The search for rules, the only possible way to understand such a vast and complex universe, is called science. The universe

---

[1] Chlorine is a deadly poison gas employed on European battlefields in World War I. Sodium is a corrosive metal which burns upon contact with water. Together they make a placid and unpoisonous material, table salt. Why each of these substances has the properties it does is a subject called chemistry, which requires more than 10 bits of information to understand.

forces those who live in it to understand it. Those creatures who find everyday experience a muddled jumble of events with no predictability, no regularity, are in grave peril. The universe belongs to those who, at least to some degree, have figured it out.

It is an astonishing fact that there *are* laws of nature, rules that summarize conveniently—not just qualitatively but quantitatively—how the world works. We might imagine a universe in which there are no such laws, in which the 10^{80} elementary particles that make up a universe like our own behave with utter and uncompromising abandon. To understand such a universe we would need a brain at least as massive as the universe. It seems unlikely that such a universe could have life and intelligence, because beings and brains require some degree of internal stability and order. But even if in a much more random universe there were such beings with an intelligence much greater than our own, there could not be much knowledge, passion or joy.

12   Fortunately for us, we live in a universe that has at least important parts that are knowable. Our common-sense experience and our evolutionary history have prepared us to understand something of the workaday world. When we go into other realms, however, common sense and ordinary intuition turn out to be highly unreliable guides. It is stunning that as we go close to the speed of light our mass increases indefinitely, we shrink toward zero thickness in the direction of motion, and time for us comes as near to stopping as we would like. Many people think that this is silly, and every week or two I get a letter from someone who complains to me about it. But it is a virtually certain consequence not just of experiment but also of Albert Einstein's brilliant analysis of space and time called the Special Theory of Relativity. It does not matter that these effects seem unreasonable to us. We are not in the habit of traveling close to the speed of light. The testimony of our common sense is suspect at high velocities.

Or consider an isolated molecule composed of two atoms shaped something like a dumbbell—a molecule of salt, it might be. Such a molecule rotates about an axis through the line connecting the two atoms. But in the world of quantum mechanics, the realm of the very small, not all orientations of our dumbbell molecule are possible. It might be that the molecule could be oriented in a horizontal position, say, or in a vertical position, but not at many angles in between. Some rotational positions are forbidden. Forbidden by what? By the laws of nature. The universe is built in such a way as to limit, or quantize, rotation. We do not experience this directly in everyday life; we would find it startling as well as awkward in sitting-up exercises, to find arms outstretched from the sides or pointed up to the skies permitted but many intermediate positions forbidden. We do not live in the world of the small, on the scale of 10^{-13} centimeters, in the realm where there are twelve zeros between the decimal place and the one. Our common-sense intuitions do not count. What does count is experiment—in this case observations from the far infrared spectra of molecules. They show molecular rotation to be quantized.

The idea that the world places restrictions on what humans might do is frustrating. Why *shouldn't* we be able to have intermediate rotational positions? Why *can't* we travel faster than the speed of light? But so far as we can tell, this is the way the universe is constructed. Such prohibitions not only press us toward a little humility; they also make the world more knowable. Every restriction corresponds to a law of nature, a regularization of the universe. The more restrictions there are on what matter and energy can do, the more knowledge human beings can attain. Whether in some sense the universe is ultimately knowable depends not only on how many natural laws there are that encompass widely divergent phenomena, but also on whether we have the openness and the intellectual capacity to understand such laws. Our formulations of the regularities of nature are surely dependent on how the brain is built, but also, and to a significant degree, on how the universe is built.

For myself, I like a universe that includes much that is unknown and, at the same time, much that is knowable. A universe in which everything is known would be static and dull, as boring as the heaven of some weak-minded theologians. A universe that is unknowable is no fit place for a thinking being. The ideal universe for us is one very much like the universe we inhabit. And I would guess that this is not really much of a coincidence.

Personal Response

Examine in some detail your attitude toward science. What science courses have you had? Which did you like? Why?

Questions for Class or Small Group Discussion

1. Discuss what you think Sagan means by his opening statement: "Science is a way of thinking much more than it is a body of knowledge."

2. Consider this statement: "Science sometimes requires courage—at the very least the courage to question the conventional wisdom" (paragraph 1). What examples can you give of scientific discoveries or advances that required courage? Explain why you think they required courage.

3. The title of the book from which this essay is excerpted is *Broca's Brain: Reflections on the Romance of Science*. In what ways do you think science might be "romantic"? Explain why you think so.

4. Sagan counters those who say that everything we need to know is already known by suggesting the infinite nature of what we do not yet know. Discuss in your groups or the class as a whole the questions you have about the natural world you wish scientists would find answers to.

For instance, what puzzles you about the ocean, the earth, or the solar system that no one has yet been able to explain?

THE REACH OF THE IMAGINATION
Jacob Bronowski

Jacob Bronowski (1908–1974) was a Polish-born American scientist whose television series Ascent of Man *(1974) combined art, philosophy, and science to explain the connections between science and the humanities. His books include* The Common Sense of Science *(1951),* Science and Human Values *(1959), and* William Blake, A Man with a Mask *(1965). This essay was originally delivered as the Blashfield Address at a meeting of the American Academy of Arts and Letters and the National Institute of Arts and Letters in May 1966. It was reprinted in the Spring 1990 issue of* American Scholar.

For three thousand years, poets have been enchanted and moved and perplexed by the power of their own imagination. In a short and summary essay I can hope at most to lift one small corner of that mystery; and yet it is a critical corner. I shall ask, What goes on in the mind when we imagine? You will hear from me that one answer to this question is fairly specific: which is to say, that we can describe the working of the imagination. And when we describe it as I shall do, it becomes plain that imagination is a specifically *human* gift. To imagine is the characteristic act, not of the poet's mind, or the painter's, or the scientist's, but of the mind of man.

My stress here on the word *human* implies that there is a clear difference in this between the actions of men and those of other animals. Let me then start with a classical experiment with animals and children which Walter Hunter thought out in Chicago about 1910. That was the time when scientists were agog with the success of Ivan Pavlov in forming and changing the reflex actions of dogs, which Pavlov had first announced in 1903. Pavlov had been given a Nobel Prize the next year, in 1904; although in fairness I should say that the award did not cite his work on the conditioned reflex, but on the digestive gland.

Hunter duly trained some dogs and other animals on Pavlov's lines. They were taught that when a light came on over one of three tunnels out of their cage, that tunnel would be open; they could escape down it, and were rewarded with food if they did. But once he had fixed that conditioned reflex, Hunter added to it a deeper idea: he gave the mechanical experiment a new dimension, literally—the dimension of time. Now he no longer let the dog go to the lighted tunnel at once; instead, he put out the light, and then kept the dog waiting a little while before he let him go. In this way Hunter timed how long an animal can remember where he has last seen the signal light to his escape route.

4   The results were and are staggering. A dog or a rat forgets which one of three tunnels has been lit up within a matter of seconds—in Hunter's experiment, ten seconds at most. If you want such an animal to do much better than this, you must make the task much simpler: you must face him with only two tunnels to choose from. Even so, the best that Hunter could do was to have a dog remember for five minutes which one of two tunnels had been lit up.

I am not quoting these times as if they were exact and universal: they surely are not. Hunter's experiment, more than fifty years old now, had many faults of detail. For example, there were too few animals, they were oddly picked, and they did not all behave consistently. It may be unfair to test a dog for what he *saw,* when he commonly follows his nose rather than his eyes. It may be unfair to test any animal in the unnatural setting of a laboratory cage. And there are higher animals, such as chimpanzees and other primates, which certainly have longer memories than the animals that Hunter tried.

Yet when all these provisos have been made (and met, by more modern experiments) the facts are still startling and characteristic. An animal cannot recall a signal from the past for even a short fraction of the time that a man can—for even a short fraction of the time that a child can. Hunter made comparable tests with six-year-old children, and found, of course, that they were incomparably better than the best of his animals. There is a striking and basic difference between a man's ability to imagine something that he saw or experienced, and an animal's failure.

Animals make up for this by other and extraordinary gifts. The salmon and the carrier pigeon can find their way home as we cannot: they have, as it were, a practical memory that man cannot match. But their actions always depend on some form of habit: on instinct or on learning, which reproduce by rote a train of known responses. They do not depend, as human memory does, on calling to mind the recollection of absent things.

8   Where is it that the animal falls short? We get a clue to the answer, I think, when Hunter tells us how the animals in his experiment tried to fix their recollection. They most often pointed themselves at the light before it went out, as some gun dogs point rigidly at the game they scent—and get the name *pointer* from the posture. The animal makes ready to act by building the signal into its action. There is a primitive imagery in its stance, it seems to me; it is as if the animal were trying to fix the light on its mind by fixing it in its body. And indeed, how else can a dog mark and (as it were) name one of the three tunnels, when he has no such words as *left* and *right,* and no such numbers as *one, two, three?* The directed gesture of attention and readiness is perhaps the only symbolic device that the dog commands to hold on to the past, and thereby to guide himself into the future.

I used the verb *to imagine* a moment ago, and now I have some ground for giving it a meaning. *To imagine* means to make images and to move them about inside one's head in new arrangements. When you and I recall the past, we imagine it in this direct and homely sense. The tool that puts the human mind ahead of the animal is imagery. For us, memory does not demand the preoccupation that it demands in animals, and it lasts immensely longer, because we fix it in images or other substitute symbols. With the same symbolic vocabulary we spell out the future—not one but many futures, which we weigh one against another.

I am using the word *image* in a wide meaning, which does not restrict it to the mind's eye as a visual organ. An image in my usage is what Charles Peirce called a *sign,* without regard for its sensory quality. Peirce distinguished between different forms of signs, but there is no reason to make his distinction here, for the imagination works equally with them all, and that is why I call them all images.

Indeed, the most important images for human beings are simply words, which are abstract symbols. Animals do not have words, in our sense: there is no specific center for language in the brain of any animal, as there is in the human being. In this respect at least we know that the human imagination depends on a configuration in the brain that has only evolved in the last one or two million years. In the same period, evolution has greatly enlarged the front lobes in the human brain, which govern the sense of the past and the future; and it is a fair guess that they are probably the seat of our other images. (Part of the evidence for this guess is that damage to the front lobes in primates reduces them to the state of Hunter's animals.) If the guess turns out to be right, we shall know why man has come to look like a highbrow or an egghead: because otherwise there would not be room in his head for his imagination.

12   The images play out for us events which are not present to our senses, and thereby guard the past and create the future—a future that does not yet exist, and may never come to exist in that form. By contrast, the lack of symbolic ideas, or their rudimentary poverty, cuts off an animal from the past and the future alike, and imprisons him in the present. Of all the distinctions between man and animal, the characteristic gift which makes us human is the power to work with symbolic images: the gift of imagination.

This is really a remarkable finding. When Philip Sidney in 1580 defended poets (and all unconventional thinkers) from the Puritan charge that they were liars, he said that a maker must imagine things that are not. Halfway between Sidney and us, William Blake said, "What is now proved was once only imagined." About the same time, in 1796, Samuel Taylor Coleridge for the first time distinguished between the passive fancy and the active imagination, "the living Power and prime Agent of all human Perception." Now we see that they were right, and precisely right: the human gift is the gift of imagination—and that is not just a literary phrase.

Nor is it just a literary gift; it is, I repeat, characteristically human. Almost everything that we do that is worth doing is done in the first place in the mind's eye. The richness of human life is that we have many lives; we live the events that do not happen (and some that cannot) as vividly as those that do; and if thereby we die a thousand deaths, that is the price we pay for living a thousand lives. (A cat, of course, has only nine.) Literature is alive to us because we live its images, but so is any play of the mind—so is chess: the lines of play that we foresee and try in our heads and dismiss are as much a part of the game as the moves that we make. John Keats said that the unheard melodies are sweeter, and all chess players sadly recall that the combinations that they planned and which never came to be played were the best.

I make this point to remind you, insistently, that imagination is the manipulation of images in one's head; and that the rational manipulation belongs to that, as well as the literary and artistic manipulation. When a child begins to play games with things that stand for other things, with chairs or chessmen, he enters the gateway to reason and imagination together. For the human reason discovers new relations between things not by deduction, but by that unpredictable blend of speculation and insight that scientists call induction, which—like other forms of imagination—cannot be formalized. We see it at work when Walter Hunter inquires into a child's memory, as much as when Blake and Coleridge do. Only a restless and original mind would have asked Hunter's questions and could have conceived his experiments, in a science that was dominated by Pavlov's reflex arcs and was heading toward the behaviorism of John Watson.

16   Let me find a spectacular example for you from history. What is the most famous experiment that you had described to you as a child? I will hazard that it is the experiment that Galileo is said to have made in Sidney's age, in Pisa about 1590, by dropping two unequal balls from the Leaning Tower. There, we say, is a man in the modern mold, a man after our own hearts: he insisted on questioning the authority of Aristotle and St. Thomas Aquinas, and seeing with his own eyes whether (as they said) the heavy ball would reach the ground before the light one. Seeing is believing.

Yet seeing is also imagining. Galileo did challenge the authority of Aristotle, and he did look at his mechanics. But the eye that Galileo used was the mind's eye. He did not drop balls from the Leaning Tower of Pisa—and if he had, he would have got a very doubtful answer. Instead, Galileo made an imaginary experiment in his head, which I will describe as he did years later in the book he wrote after the Holy Office silenced him: *Discorsi . . . intorno a due nuove scienze,* which was smuggled out to be printed in the Netherlands in 1638.

Suppose, said Galileo, that you drop two unequal balls from the tower at the same time. And suppose that Aristotle is right—suppose that the heavy ball falls faster, so that it steadily gains on the light ball, and hits the ground first. Very well. Now imagine the same experiment done again, with only one difference: this time the two unequal balls are joined by a string between them. The heavy ball will again move ahead, but now the light ball holds it back and acts as a drag or brake. So the light ball will be speeded up and the heavy ball will be slowed down; they must reach the ground together because they are tied together, but they cannot reach the ground as quickly as the heavy ball alone. Yet the string between them has turned the two balls into a single mass which is heavier than either ball—and surely (according to Aristotle) this mass should therefore move faster than either ball? Galileo's imaginary experiment has uncovered a contradiction; he says trenchantly, "You see how, from your assumption that a heavier body falls more rapidly than a lighter one, I infer that a (still) heavier body falls more slowly." There is only one way out of the contradiction: the heavy ball and the light ball must fall at the same rate, so that they go on falling at the same rate when they are tied together.

This argument is not conclusive, for nature might be more subtle (when the two balls are joined) than Galileo has allowed. And yet it is something more important: it is suggestive, it is stimulating, it opens a new view—in a word, it is imaginative. It cannot be settled without an actual experiment, because nothing that we imagine can become knowledge until we have translated it into, and backed it by, real experience. The test of imagination is experience. But then, that is as true of literature and the arts as it is of science. In science, the imaginary experiment is tested by confronting it with physical experience; and in literature, the imaginative conception is tested by confronting it with human experience. The superficial speculation in science is dismissed because it is found to falsify nature; and the shallow work of art is discarded because it is found to be untrue to our own nature. So when Ella Wheeler Wilcox died in 1919, more people were reading her verses than Shakespeare's; yet in a few years her work was dead. It had been buried by its poverty of emotion and its trivialness of thought: which is to say that it had been proved to be as false to the nature of man as, say, Jean Baptiste Lamarck and Trofim Lysenko were false to the nature of inheritance. The strength of the imagination, its enriching power and excitement, lies in its interplay with reality—physical and emotional.

20   I doubt if there is much to choose here between science and the arts: the imagination is not much more free, and not much less free, in one than in the other. All great scientists have used their imagination freely, and let it ride them to outrageous conclusions without crying "Halt!" Albert Einstein fiddled with imaginary experiments from boyhood, and was wonderfully ignorant of the facts that they were supposed to bear on. When he wrote the first of his beautiful papers on the random movement of atoms, he did not know that the Brownian motion which it predicted could be seen in any laboratory. He was sixteen when he invented the paradox that he resolved ten years later, in 1905, in the theory of relativity, and it bulked much larger in his mind than the experiment of Albert Michelson and Edward Morley which had upset every other physicist since 1881. All his life Einstein loved to make up teasing puzzles like Galileo's, about falling lifts and the detection of gravity; and they carry the nub of the problems of general relativity on which he was working.

Indeed, it could not be otherwise. The power that man has over nature and himself, and that a dog lacks, lies in his command of imaginary experience. He alone has the symbols which fix the past and play with the future, possible and impossible. In the Renaissance, the symbolism of memory was thought to be mystical, and devices that were invented as mnemonics (by Giordano Bruno, for example, and by Robert Fludd) were interpreted as magic signs. The symbol is the tool which gives man his power, and it is the same tool whether the symbols are images or words, mathematical signs or mesons. And the symbols have a reach and a roundness that goes beyond their literal and practical meaning. They are the rich concepts under which the mind gathers many particulars into one name, and many instances into one general induction. When a man says *left* and *right,* he is outdistancing the dog not only in looking for a light; he is setting in train all the shifts of meaning, the overtones and the ambiguities, between *gauche* and *adroit* and *dexterous,* between *sinister* and the sense of right. When a man counts *one, two, three,* he is not only doing mathematics; he is on the path to the mysticism of numbers in Pythagoras and Vitruvius and Kepler, to the Trinity and the signs of the Zodiac.

I have described imagination as the ability to make images and to move them about inside one's head in new arrangements. This is the faculty that is specifically human, and it is the common root from which science and literature both spring and grow and flourish together. For they do flourish (and languish) together; the great ages of science are the great ages of all the arts, because in them powerful minds have taken fire from one another breathless and higgledy-piggledy, without asking too nicely whether they ought to tie their imagination to falling balls or a haunted island. Galileo and Shakespeare, who were born in the same year, grew into greatness in the same age; when Galileo was looking through his telescope at the moon, Shakespeare was writing *The Tempest* and all Europe was in ferment, from Johannes Kepler to Peter Paul Rubens, and from the first table of logarithms by John Napier to the Authorized Version of the Bible.

Let me end with a last and spirited example of the common inspiration of literature and science, because it is as much alive today as it was three hundred years ago. What I have in mind is man's ageless fantasy, to fly to the moon. I do not display this to you as a high scientific enterprise; on the contrary, I think we have more important discoveries to make here on earth than wait for us, beckoning, at the horned surface of the moon. Yet I cannot belittle the fascination which that ice-blue journey has had for the imagination of men, long before it drew us to our television screens to watch the tumbling astronauts. Plutarch and Lucian, Ariosto and Ben Jonson wrote about it, before the days of Jules Verne and H. G. Wells and science fiction. The seventeenth century was heady with new dreams and fables about voyages to the moon. Kepler wrote one full of deep scientific ideas, which (alas) simply got his mother accused of witchcraft. In England, Francis Godwin wrote a wild and splendid work, *The Man in the Moone,* and the astronomer John Wilkins wrote a wild and learned one,

The Discovery of a New World. They did not draw a line between science and fancy; for example, they all tried to guess just where in the journey the earth's gravity would stop. Only Kepler understood that gravity has no boundary, and put a law to it—which happened to be the wrong law.

24   All this was a few years before Isaac Newton was born, and it was all in his head that day in 1666 when he sat in his mother's garden, a young man of twenty-three, and thought about the reach of gravity. This was how he came to conceive his brilliant image, that the moon is like a ball which has been thrown so hard that it falls exactly as fast as the horizon, all the way round the earth. The image will do for any satellite, and Newton modestly calculated how long therefore an astronaut would take to fall round the earth once. He made it ninety minutes, and we have all seen now that he was right; but Newton had no way to check that. Instead he went on to calculate how long in that case the distant moon would take to round the earth, if indeed it behaves like a thrown ball that falls in the earth's gravity, and if gravity obeyed a law of inverse squares. He found that the answer would be twenty-eight days.

    In that telling figure, the imagination that day chimed with nature, and made a harmony. We shall hear an echo of that harmony on the day when we land on the moon, because it will be not a technical but an imaginative triumph, that reaches back to the beginning of modern science and literature both. All great acts of imagination are like this, in the arts and in science, and convince us because they fill out reality with a deeper sense of rightness. We start with the simplest vocabulary of images, with *left* and *right* and *one, two, three,* and before we know how it happened the words and the numbers have conspired to make a match with nature: we catch in them the pattern of mind and matter as one.

Personal Response

Discuss the aspects of this essay you find especially intriguing and why. If you do not find any aspect of this essay intriguing, explain why.

Questions for Class or Small Group Discussion

1. Elaborate on Bronowski's statement that imagination "is the faculty that is specifically human, and it is the common root from which science and literature both spring and grow and flourish together" (paragraph 22). What do you think he means, and why?

2. Discuss the ways in which scientists you know about were imaginative, making sure you explain why you think so.

3. Bronowski's essay was written before the first moon landing (see paragraphs 23–25). If Bronowski were writing today, what example do you think he would use in his closing paragraphs to demonstrate that scientific achievement is the result of both technology and imagination? What examples would you use? Why?

4. Working with members of a small group, interview a scientist about the importance of the imagination in his or her work. Before the interview, work in your group to draw up a list of appropriate questions. Select one member to set up the appointment, one to ask the questions, one to record the answers, and one to report to the rest of the class the results of your interview.

MINDING THE REEF

W. John Coletta

W. John Coletta, an associate professor of English at the University of Wisconsin-Stevens Point, has an interdisciplinary background. In addition to degrees in English, he also holds an M.S. degree in environmental education administration and a B.S. degree in recreation education. Most of Coletta's scholarly work reflects this interdisciplinary background and his commitment to doing language studies as an ecologist might study nature. In this essay, written for this textbook, Coletta muses on his experiences while directing a sailing camp for high school students in the British Virgin Islands.

Science (As the muscled barracuda charged), *is literature* (I gave no thought to the fact that millions of years of encoding protected the flower of my throat from his feigned desire. I was frightened.) *but better organized. And like literature, science must be lived.* (After the barracuda's thrust and retreat, however, I realized that the relationship of the barracuda's territoriality to my terror was not, after all, important, was not the product of that kind of force that has called the razor-like sharpness of the barracuda's tooth out of the evasiveness of the reef fishes upon which it preys. I was merely out of place and frankly embarrassed for having so little respected the barracuda as to have made his mock charge necessary; I was merely too large to call out from *Sphyraena barracuda* more than a bluff.) *And the natural world is just as figurative as a poem, literally.* She steps then dips below the brush of the tangled bank of the marsh, and tilting her head, Mary Oliver (*Homo sapiens poetica*) sees "a spindle of bleached reeds . . . wrinkl[e] into three egrets." Is this wrinkling of reeds into egrets a biological phenomenon or merely some figurative one, some poet's dream of a visual Eden where the reeds lie down with the egret?

The	*early sun pries open the morning woods*
Bringing	*a flower to me in tiny bundles.*
And	*to see the flower but one time only—*
Receiving	*the image in motion as you*
Are	*bringing the stillness of thought—*
One	*must do much collecting.*

Or perhaps this transformation of reeds into egrets is merely some projective vision akin to thinking one sees (while scuba diving) a barracuda in a boat's keel? But the world on its keel ever pitches and yaws; reed and egret are pushed and pulled by the transforming eyes of a million predators and prey in a glorious cycle of blood and water in which bodies are offered as a community's communion with its emergent self—an ecological wine of great age and refinement whose "legs" are legs (an egret's), whose "bouquet" is a bouquet (of reeds), and whose legs are a bouquet (the reed-legged-and-necked egret). Indeed, a "rose is a rose is a rose"; but an "egret is a reed is an egret" is richer. And surely those egrets who looked most like reeds were the more successful hunters, poised behind a perceptual curtain that caused some unsuspecting fish or toad to think the moment's drama not for him or her. Indeed, for a fish (as opposed to a poet) the failure to solve the complex visual puzzle (or metaphor) presented by the egrets and the reeds may prove fatal. *For in nature as in poetry, metaphor makes all the difference.* And whether we read Mary Oliver's poem, or see for ourselves the biological mimicry of egret and reed—that is, whether we experience a figure of speech or a figure of sight—what is striking is that this ecological drama that unfolds before us is translatable into human language. (And so the bee's flower—merely a foraging index for a bee—is a symbol of love for thee.)

Biology must expand its range to include the ecology of metaphor, for while the "reed-egret" metaphor may not have profound implications for human beings (*but there was a time, Wilson cries, when the buzz of a bee or the scent of water made a difference*), the inability of some human beings to solve the visual puzzle called "organism-habitat" may prove grave (literally). Visually, we humans can separate rather efficiently a spotted owl from its background; but such a separation, while visually convincing, is made at no little cognitive and ecological cost. In spite of the recent Supreme Court's upholding of federal rules limiting land use to protect endangered species, some people insist that habitat modification or degradation should not be held up unless such activities *actually kill or injure* an endangered species, in other words, unless we can actually see a tree fall on an actual spotted owl or a bulldozer run over an actual golden lion tamarin. But while it is easy to separate visually owl from habitat, there is literally no separation that is not death. (*And the shaman sees only the small wing-like wrinkling of the forest as it folds itself upon a vole.*) **To cut the oxygen hose of a scuba diver is to leave the scuba diver perfectly unmolested; I haven't touched a hair on her head, your honor.** *The life support system of the spotted owl is old growth, the oxygen hose the transpiring leaves of the falling trees.* The owl *is* old growth: an owl in the zoo is not an owl—as anyone who (who-who) knows owls knows. Human survival will depend on our being conscious of this biological metaphor that runs counter to our eyes' inherited tendency to separate organism from habitat; a fish's survival may depend on seeing that egrets are *not* reeds, an egret's survival may depend upon a fish seeing egrets as reeds; and so on. *Biology is metaphor.*

The mind grows out of the earth,	*(The mind grows in of the earth,*
And the dichotomous tree	*And the rhizome embodies a*
* embodies a logic*	* logic*
Of deep-rooted faith,	*Of unrooted rootedness,*
proud stem, delicate spray,	*no sides (no out or in), a net,*
And leaves of tender	*And no be(leave)ing in (or out)*
* thinking.*	* as yet.*
The great stone libraries	*The ancient forests*
Are alive inside:	*Are a hive inside.*
Ancient forests are folded on	*Great libraries are folded on*
* circuits*	* circuits*
To form deep pools;	*To pool deep forms.*
We come to drink freely as	*We come to think freely at*
* fawns,*	* dawn*
And run into the green city	*And run into the green city*
* pulsing*	* pulsing*
deer-like	*(de-light.)*

How does one enter a coral reef? Head first? One approaches the bank-barrier reef as does the barracuda—by way of the reef's precipitous walls and sometimes its perceptual pratfalls. Postmodern ecology can only begin in perceptual aporia—an impasse or difficulty—and so how to account for a fish with two heads or rather one head that is indistinguishable from its tail? Here the foureye butterfly fish (*Chaetodon capistratus*) re-presents itself as a deferment of itself. (I approach it and it darts unexpectedly backward?) The effect on me is disorientation—until I discover that its real eye is being held under erasure by a black Nike-like bar running through it. A false eye (a black, circular representation of an eyespot encircled itself in white) is located at the tail end of the fish. The tail, a dead give away of posteriority, is therefore enveloped by the long dorsal and ventral fins that wrap themselves almost entirely around the tail—masking the presence of the tail in an arc that mimics a facial ridge. And so my disorientation or aporia, I discover, is the barracuda's too; my experience is contiguous with its: and through this window, this portal of aporia the foureye butterfly fish escapes. (Of course, the name "foureye butterfly fish" is an after-the-fact name; "foureye" equals the two real eyes plus the two false eyes—an act of addition made possible only by solving the two-headed puzzle. And so names, the "foureye," the "rock beauty," all names, represent conquest. Alas, so much of naming, so much of science, is precisely after the (conquered) fact, is a stripping away of the teeth of experience from the jaws of representation.) But at that moment, the moment before naming, the moment of confrontation and contiguity with the reef, face to face is always face to faith—in ecology as in religion (How so? *The* *neighbor throws his house and window through a small child's ball, and the earth falls to land on me so softly that I am hardly broken off a tree.)* **How does one enter a coral reef? Perhaps backwards.**

4   *The mind grows out of the earth.* The body of the tropical marine fish called the rock beauty (*Holocanthus tricolor*), in conjunction with the mind of its predator, say the barracuda, consists of three figures of sight, one of which is iconic (i.e., it resembles something), one of which is indexical (i.e., it points to something), and one of which is constructed out of the relationship between the iconic sign and the indexical sign. The head and tail of the rock beauty are bright yellow; as indices generally do, the yellow head and tail call attention to (point to) themselves and also orient themselves (and any observer) spatially with respect to some object with which it is connected. In this case, the object is the rock beauty's own large, black midsection that breaks its body in two so as to appear to be in front of a yellow fish. This midsection is itself iconic of the spherical surface of a rock or a coral head. The boundary between the yellow indexical head of the rock beauty and its black iconic body roughly describes an arc of some 90%; the arc itself is an icon of both the long-term effects of erosion, effects which produce spherically shaped rocks, and the sphericality of coral heads, which heads often form on round boulders anyway, providing a natural base for their spherical growth. Thus the yellow indexical head and tail and the circular arc described by the boundary between head and body are part of a single indexical and iconic sign complex called the rock beauty—by some human beings. To the barracuda, though, there is no rock beauty (to Ptolemy there was no *solar* system; to Thomson, no nucleus). To the barracuda there is only a yellow fish behind a dark rock or coral head. In formal terms, then, the indexical head and iconic body of the rock beauty are signs that determine the interpretant, i.e., the mind of the barracuda, to refer to the (imagined) all-yellow fish as if it were behind an (imagined) rock; that is, the interpretant or predator is determined to refer to objects to which the indexical head and iconic body of the rock beauty (a fish that is both sign and in part its own object) themselves refer. *The ghost within the fish, the yellow fish within the rock beauty emerges to cast its spell over the whole reef.* Given the apparent inaccessibility of the yellow fish (within the fish), the barracuda may move on to more accessible prey, of which there are many in a reef. Other predatory fish may follow the barracuda's lead and move on as well. Their moving on is itself a sign in a greater web of signification that is a reef community. (And maximizing both protection and mobility, the rock beauty effortlessly carries its round rock or coral head with it where it wanders.)

> *The grammar of life and death in the reef.* When tropical marine fish of the family Scaridae or Libridae (parrotfish) wish to have parasites removed from their gills and mouths, they line up at "cleaning stations," i.e., coral heads around which live small, neon-colored fish

known as cleaning gobies. The neon colors of the gobies, like neon signs in human storefronts, advertise the cleaning stations. The gobies swim unmolested in and around the gills and mouths of the parrotfish, eating from the eater. The parrotfish, while in line, will swim at oblique angles, a sign that their intentions are not in line with their regular habits: they are presenting their oblique case that they are ready to be cleaned and have no intention of eating the very small gobies, fish that the parrotfish might very well eat in the case of regular predator-prey relations.

The predator-prey relation in nature is much like the subject-object relation in grammar. Subject equals predator, and objects equal prey. These relations of subject to object and predator to prey are direct, linear, in line: this eats that; subject does something to object. In grammar, any grammatical case that is not the subjective or objective case, that is, any case that is not in line with this straight-line, subject-object backbone of a sentence, is called an oblique case (e.g., the possessive case, the dative case, the instrumental case). Is it merely a coincidence that parrotfish, when hoping to avoid being the *subject* to the goby *object* (that is, when desiring not simply to attack in a straight line and to eat the goby but rather desiring to enter into a new kind of relationship with gobies), I ask, is it merely a coincidence that parrotfish in this special case swim at *oblique* angles to their usual place of orientation—one parallel to the water's surface? *No. Case in grammar is a biological structure; language is built up upon the life of the coral reef.* GRAMMAR PARROTS PARROTFISH.

The barracuda, however, might solve the complex visual puzzle presented by the rock beauty, effectively detaching from their objects the rock beauty's iconic and indexical signs (its "hey, look at me" yellow color and its rock-like or coral-head-like midsection) and thereby changing the status of those signs from motivated icons and indices (effective biological mimicry) to unmotivated symbols (pure decoration). The yellow fish behind the rock becomes the unprotected rock beauty—a dainty dish to set before a king or queen barracuda. Not all poetry lives. (*And we learn that this detachment proceeds at many levels, that endangered species are themselves like icons and indices that are in the process of being detached from their objects. We are the barracuda to the rock beauty of the earth, the earth's predator.*)

Whether it lives or dies, the lyric beauty of the rock beauty is its ecological modesty, its giving itself up to another (an other)—to a yellow "fish that never was." In such modesty the rock beauty may hope to escape the judgment of the barracuda. A thing of beauty is a joy (for a while anyway). And so we live and die by the metaphors we live by. (*And we learn that human language is primarily symbolic—its iconic and indexical body stripped away like an egret from reeds. The body of our language is a lie: "There is no* "away" in "Throw it away," says Garrett Hardin. "Away" is merely vanity—not the rock beauty's modesty; "away" is merely a symbol of our own detachment from those parts of the cycle that must ultimately take in what we throw out.)

Language is an ambivalent biological category:

Each sentence is a sentence; clause is claws;
His words are hiss words and the loss of laws.

The mind grows out of (and away from) the Earth. And like some species, some metaphors survive and some don't. In Shakespeare, for example, there are figures of speech that no longer mean the same thing to us that they did to the Elizabethans but which continue to work as metaphors today though with new meanings. Shakespeare's "salad days," which for Elizabethans meant those "days of youthful inexperience," is a metaphor that has a new vitality for contemporary readers in the context of our culture's concern with personal health, diet, and ecology. This new vitality is only obliquely related to the original meaning of "salad." Its meaning, however, is in the process of being re-figured (*as the meaning of oxygen was re-figured by respiration: oxygen, once deadly, was contextually re-figured so as to make ecological sense in terms of respiration (evolution's new "reader")*). However, some figures of speech seem to lack the potential for reinvention and become, in essence, extinct (as may the people who use them if the figures of speech are serious enough—see "throw it away" again). Take, for example, the rather common expression from Shakespeare, "Take me with you," which, to Elizabethans, meant "Make yourself clear." This figure, unlike "salad days," is not being re-figured by readers; rather it is producing only confusion (which itself when used in a controlled fashion can be useful—pity the confused barracuda who lets a perfectly accessible lunch get literally away by getting figuratively away). Some metaphors (be they reeds into egrets or salad days) are more adaptive than others and tend to survive.

Science too lives and dies by metaphor. (Little Robert races out into the field and like an ecological crier cries,

Calling all butterflies of every race
From source unknown but from no special place.)

There is a paradox here that runs deep into the tissue of science: in science, an unknown source is a special place, since science explores and seeks to articulate the unknown. Robert Frost, however, asserts that a source (here a biological one) is both unknown and not special. Frost's conception of modern physics informs this paradox. The key may lie in his understanding that an observer tends to influence or alter that which he or she attempts to observe. (*Reeds wrinkle into egrets for Oliver; a yellow fish swims out behind the rock of itself in the bright blaze of the barracuda's brain.*) Because of observer interference, population biologists can only make statistical claims about natural populations. The necessity of this may not at first be apparent: we might assume that given enough time each organism in an area might be enumerated. But there are theoretical, not merely practical, limitations to a population biologist's certainty. For population biologists, any attempt to trace the individuals of a given population back to their sources (or "homes" or home ranges) is likely to alter the population count. For example, some organisms have developed behaviors that mask their homes or presence. (*Seventeen yellow fish live within the rocks and coral heads of this reef; seventeen yellow fish live within the rock beauties of this reef: seventeen yellow-headed-and-tailed rock beauties live within this reef.*) Not only may the presence of a biologist cause these organisms to hide; some organisms have evolved deceptive behaviors that serve to lead predators (or biologists) away from their actual homes. Thus the very act of observation influences the outcome of the population biologist's measurement, and the source of butterflies in Frost's lines remains paradoxically both unknown and no special place. And this is the end of science, when everywhere is unknown again. To defamiliarize the familiar, the poet said. *The very structure of the process of science is poetic.*

8   How many of science's butterflies or fish may like Ptolemy's sun and moon for Copernicus turn out to be yellow fish behind the black rock of themselves? Indeed, how many individuals are not entities at all but merely parts of a much larger and as yet unrecognized entity? How many false eyes are there on the tail that wags the dog of the foureye butterfly fish of science? Oh reed and egret, how can we tell the dancer from the dance? *Nature is figurative (and hard to figure) and the scientist must sing her science like a bard to her.*

Personal Response

If you have had an experience similar to Coletta's with the barracuda, describe that experience. Otherwise, free-write for a few minutes on your response to this essay.

Questions for Class or Small Group Discussion

1. How does Coletta's experiences with the barracuda reflect the point he makes about the natural world? Do you agree with him? Why or why not?

2. Discuss what you think the following statements mean: "*Science . . . is literature . . . but better organized*" and "*The natural world is just as figurative as a poem, literally*" (paragraph 1). How do you think the egret–reed example illustrates what Coletta means by those sentences?

3. Discuss this statement: "*biology is metaphor*" (paragraph 3). What do you understand it to mean? Can you give examples to illustrate the statement?

4. What point does Coletta make with the examples of the foureye butterfly fish and the rock beauty (paragraphs 4–5)? Do you agree with
him? Explain why or why not.

5. Respond to this statement: "The body of our language is a lie" (paragraph 5).

THE CHEMIST

Roald Hoffmann

*Roald Hoffmann is professor of chemistry at Cornell University. He was
responsible for a twenty-six part PBS television series designed to explain chemistry to high school and junior college students and has been
active in writing to popularize chemistry. He is author, with Vivian Torrence as artistic collaborator, of* Chemistry Imagined: Reflections on
Science *(1993), from which this essay is taken.*

In describing what they do, scientists have by and large bought the
metaphor of discovery and artists that of creation. The cliché "uncovering
the secrets of nature" has set, like good cement, in our minds. But I think
that the metaphor of discovery is effective in describing only part of the activity of scientists, and a smaller piece still of the work of chemists. The
historical, psychological, philosophical, and sociological reasons for the
ready acceptance of the metaphor deserve a closer look.

History and Psychology

The rise of modern science in Europe coincided with the age of geographical exploration. Men set foot on distant shores, explored *terra incognita.*
Even in our century, a man I was named after first sailed the Northwest
passage and reached the South Pole. Voyages of discovery, maps filled in—
those are powerful images indeed. So is penetration into a royal tomb full
of glistening gold vessels. It's no surprise that these metaphors were and
are accepted by (predominantly male) scientists as appropriate descriptors
of their generally laboratory-bound activity. Is there some vicarious sharing of imagined adventures at work here?

Philosophy

The French rationalist tradition, and the systematization of astronomy and
physics before the other sciences, have left science with a reductionist philosophy at its core. There is supposed to exist a logical hierarchy of the
sciences, and understanding is to be defined solely in vertical terms as reduction to the more basic science. The more mathematical, the better.
So biological phenomena are to be explained by chemistry, chemistry by

physics, and so on. The logic of a reductionist philosophy fits the discovery metaphor—one digs deeper and discovers the truth.

4   But reductionism is only one face of understanding. We have been made not only to disassemble, disconnect, and analyze but also to build. There is no more stringent test of passive understanding than active creation. Perhaps "test" is not the word here, for building or creation differ inherently from reductionist analysis. I want to claim a greater role in science for the forward, constructive mode.

Sociology

Those philosophers of science who started out as practicing scientists have generally, I believe, come from physics and mathematics. The education of professional philosophers is likely to favor the same fields; quite understandably, there is a special role for logic in philosophy. No wonder that the prevailing ideology of reasoning in the underlying scientific areas of expertise of philosophers of science has been extended by them, unrealistically I believe, to all science.

What is strange is that chemists should accept the metaphor of discovery. Chemistry is the science of molecules (up to a hundred years ago one would have said "substances" or "compounds") and their transformations. Some of the molecules are indeed *there,* just waiting to be "known" by us, their static properties—what atoms are in them, how the atoms are connected, the shapes of molecules, their splendid colors—and in their dynamic characteristics—the molecules' internal motions, their reactivity. The molecules are those of the earth—for instance, simple water and complex malachite. Or of life—relatively simple cholesterol and more complicated hemoglobin. The discovery paradigm certainly applies to the study of these molecules.

But so many more molecules of chemistry are made by us, in the laboratory. We're awfully prolific. A registry of known, well-characterized compounds now numbers nearly ten million. These were not on earth before. It is true that their constitution follows underlying rules, and if chemist A had not made such-and-such a molecule on a certain day, then it is likely to have been synthesized a few days or decades later by chemist B. But it is a human being, a chemist, who chooses the molecule to be made and a distinct way to make it. This work is not so different from that of the artist who, constrained by the physics of pigment and canvas, shaped by his or her training, nevertheless creates the new.

8   Even when one is clearly operating in the discovery mode in chemistry, elucidating the structure or dynamics of a known, naturally occurring molecule, one usually has to intervene with created molecules. I recently heard a beautiful lecture by Alan Battersby, an outstanding British organic chemist, on the biosynthesis of uroporphyrinogen-III. (Even in the trade, the name of this molecule is abbreviated as uro'gen-III.) It's not a glamorous molecule, but it should be: for from this precursor plants make

chlorophyll, the basis of all photosynthetic activity. All cells use another uro'gen-III derivative in cytochromes for electron transport. And the crucial iron-containing, oxygen-carrier piece of hemoglobin derives from this small disk-shaped molecule.

Uro'gen-III, pictured below, is made from four rings, called pyrroles, themselves tied into a larger ring. Note the markers A and P in each ring. They're in the same order as one goes around the ring (from about 10 o'clock), except for the last set, which are "reverse." So the markers read A, P, A, P, A, P, P, A.

How this natural molecule is assembled, within us, is clearly a discovery question. In fact, the four pyrrole rings are connected up, with the aid of an enzyme, into a chain, then cyclized. But the last ring is first put in "incorrectly," that is, with the same order of the A, P labels as in the other rings: A, P, A, P, A, P, A, P. Then, in a fantastic separate reaction sequence, just that last ring, with its attached labels, is flipped into position.

This incredible but true story was deduced by Battersby and his coworkers using a sequence of synthetic molecules, not natural ones, which were made slightly different from the natural ones. Each was designed to test some critical part of the natural process in the living system. Each was then treated under the physiological conditions to allow the sequence of the natural events to be traced out. Using molecules we've made, we've learned how nature builds a molecule that makes life possible.

12   The synthesis of molecules puts chemistry very close to the arts. We create the objects that we or others then study or appreciate. That's exactly what writers, composers, visual artists, all working within their areas, working perhaps closer to the soul, do. I believe that, in fact, this creative capacity is exceptionally strong in chemistry. Mathematicians also study the objects of their own creation, but those objects, not to take anything away from their uniqueness, are mental concepts rather than real structures. Some branches of engineering are actually close to chemistry in this matter of synthesis. Perhaps this is a factor in the kinship the chemist-narrator feels for the builder Faussone, who is the main character in Primo Levi's novel *The Monkey's Wrench*.

In the building of theories and hypotheses, even more than in synthesis, the act is a creative one. One has to imagine, to conjure up a model

A = CH$_2$COOH

P = CH$_2$CH$_2$COOH

that fits often irregular observations. There are rules; the model should be consistent with previously received reliable knowledge. There are hints of what to do; one sees what was done in related problems. But what one seeks is an explanation that was not there before, a connection between two worlds. Often, actually, it's a metaphor that serves as the clue: "Two interacting systems, hmm . . . , let's model them with a resonating pair of harmonic oscillators, or . . . a barrier penetration problem." The world out there is moderately chaotic, frightening so, in the parts we do not understand. We want to see a pattern in it. We're clever, we "connoisseurs of chaos," so we find/create one. Had more philosophers of science been trained in chemistry, I'm sure we would have a very different paradigm of science before us.

Is art all creation? I don't think so. In substantial measure it is discovery, of the deep truths of what is also around us, often overlapping, but more often reaching outside the set of problems that science has set for itself to try to understand. Art aspires to discover, explore, unravel—whatever metaphor you please—the non-unique, chanced, irreducible world within us.

Personal Response

How much do you know about chemistry? Was chemistry required in your high school? If so, describe your experience with the class. Did you like it or not? Why?

Questions for Class or Small Group Discussion

1. Discuss this statement: "There is no more stringent test of passive understanding than active creation" (paragraph 4). Give an example from your own experiences to illustrate the statement.

2. What connections do you see between what chemists do and what artists do? Do you think the metaphors of discovery and of creation are appropriate for both, as Hoffmann suggests? Why or why not?

3. In class, list all of the things you can think of that are in some way touched by chemistry. After you have written for a few minutes, stop and compare your list with that of a classmate before writing for a few more minutes. Then volunteer to read your list aloud, having classmates check off identical items.

4. Despite the widespread influence of chemistry in almost every aspect of our lives, most people know very little about it. Discuss what difference it makes that few of us have any serious understanding of chemistry. Do you think it ought to be a required subject in high school? Why or why not?

Perspectives on Natural Sciences

Suggestions for Synthesis

1. Explore the connections between two essays in this chapter by comparing and contrasting them. Consider what ideas their authors have in common, how they differ, and what their observations have taught you about the natural sciences.

2. The writers in this chapter all share a firm belief in the importance of science and its connection to the imagination. Argue either in support of or against the position these writers take on the value of science by first summarizing the position of each one and then explaining why you do or do not support their viewpoints.

3. Write an essay exploring the connections between what scientists do and what artists do. In what ways are they similar? How do they differ? In your essay, draw on at least two essays from this chapter, and consider drawing on one or two of the essays in Chapter 5 ("Art and Artists").

Additional Writing Topics

1. Define the abstract term *imagination* by using examples from both science and the humanities to illustrate what you mean.

2. Support or argue against Roald Hoffmann's assertion that art is not all creation but "in substantial measure it is discovery" ("The Chemist," paragraph 14).

3. Write a personal essay in which you explore your own interest in and involvement with science.

4. Write a reflective essay explaining ways in which you are particularly imaginative. (See Jacob Bronowski's "The Reach of the Imagination.")

5. Write an essay explaining how just one scientific discipline has an impact on your everyday life and reasons why you believe it has that impact.

Research Topics

1. Read about research into how the brain works or the results of neurological damage, and write a paper that not only reports your findings but that also takes a position on some aspect of the subject. For example, Oliver Sacks's *The Man Who Mistook His Wife for a Hat* is a fascinating account of Sacks's work with people who have suffered damage to parts of their brains. One possible approach to making this subject suitable for a research paper is to find out what controversies surround treatment for neurological damage and then read opposing opinions on the controversy. Once you have read enough opposing viewpoints to form your own opinion, take a side and explain why you have chosen that position.

2. Scientists know much more about how the brain works now than they did when Jacob Bronowski wrote "The Reach of the Imagination." Research the latest thinking about the way the brain works, for example in relation to Bronowski's conjecture about the importance of the frontal lobe in imaginative thinking. Explore differing theories, take a position, and explain why you have taken that position.

3. Carl Sagan, Jacob Bronowski, and Roald Hoffmann all were involved in television series whose goals were to popularize science for laypeople. Research the life and efforts of one of these men, or do a comparative analysis of two or all three of them. In addition to reading about what they did on television, locate contemporary reviews of the programs. Then draw your own conclusions about the success or failure of their work.

4. Read about the efforts of schools to encourage students to take more math and sciences. Find out what their rationale is and what steps they have taken to increase interest in those subjects. Then draw your own conclusions about the relative importance of increasing enrollment in math and science courses and improving test scores in those subjects.

CHAPTER 17

BIOETHICS

Research into the complex structure of the human body since the discovery in 1964 of deoxyribonucleic acid (DNA) by James Watson and Francis Crick has made enormous advances. The Human Genome Project, a major undertaking by scientists around the world, promises to provide medical doctors with the tools to predict the development of human diseases. A genome is the complete set of instructions for making a human being. Each nucleus of the 100 trillion cells that make up the human body contains this set of instructions, which are written in the language of DNA. In the Human Genome Project, scientists are working to map the entire human genetic code. When the project began in 1988, scientists thought that it would take fifteen years to complete, but the project has gone faster than at first predicted and may be finished well ahead of schedule.

Once the human code is deciphered, scientists will better understand how humans grow, what causes human diseases, and what new drugs would combat those diseases by either preventing or curing them. Scientists will be able to determine what variations or defects in the genetic sequence in individual human bodies may result in diseases that are genetic in origin. They will also be able to develop tests that will detect whether an individual is likely to develop one of thousands of inherited diseases like sickle-cell anemia, cystic fibrosis, or muscular dystrophy, and even heart disease or cancer.

The Human Genome Project is fraught with difficult ethical questions, however, as the essays in this chapter indicate. For Dorothy Nelkin and M. Susan Lindee, the ethical implications of genetic research are an integral component of their discussion of the image of the gene in popular culture. In "The Powers of the Gene," Nelkin and Lindee give examples of representations of the gene in various media and other forms of popular culture as they discuss the implications of those images for laypeople's understanding of genetics. Before you read their essay, think about references to genetic research you have seen or heard in popular culture. As you read, consider how your understanding of genetic research has been influenced by mass media's representation of the gene.

Following this discussion of popular images of the gene are two companion pieces originally published together in a special UNESCO Courier feature on the bioethical implications of human genetic research. In "Scientific Knowledge and Human Dignity," Jean Dausset, a French medical doctor who founded and runs a medical research center active in the Human Genome Project, asks how

*far scientists should go in their research and how their findings should be ap-
plied. George B. Kutukdjian, in "UNESCO and Bioethics," elaborates on the
questions raised in Dausset's article and explains the role of the UNESCO
Bioethics Unit. These essays raise a number of questions about the Human
Genome Project that you will want to think about for class discussion and possible writing projects.*

*Finally, in "Facing Up to Bioethical Decisions," three professors of biomedi-
cal ethics call for a national forum to study and discuss difficult questions engendered by genetic research. John C. Fletcher, Franklin G. Miller, and Arthur L.
Caplan raise a number of questions as they argue for a national bioethics commission. As you read the points they raise, consider your own questions about
genetic research and your own position on the tough questions associated with
that research. Consider, too, the implications such research might have for you
personally or for your family and other loved ones.*

THE POWERS OF THE GENE

Dorothy Nelkin and M. Susan Lindee

*Dorothy Nelkin teaches at New York University and M. Susan Lindee
teaches at the University of Pennsylvania. Their work on the history of
human genetics, on biological testing, and on the relationship between
media images and public policy led to their book,* The DNA Mystique:
The Gene as a Cultural Icon *(1995). This excerpt comes from the introductory chapter of* The DNA Mystique, *in which they explain the
basic premise of the entire book.*

A full-color advertisement boasts that a new BMW sedan has a "genetic
advantage"—a "heritage" that comes from its "genealogy."[1] A *U.S. News
and World Report* article on the Baby M custody dispute states that it will
not make much difference which family brings up the child since her personality is already determined by her genes.[2] A cartoonist lists genetically
linked traits: "excessive use of hair spray, bottomless appetite for country-
western music, right wing politics."[3] A critic reviewing a play about the
persistence of racism says, "It's as if it has a DNA of its own."[4] The term
"gene pool" appears as the name of a comedy group, the title of a TV
show, and in the captions of comic books and the lyrics of rock music.

---

[1] Advertisement, BMW of North America Inc., 1983.

[2] John S. Long, "How Genes Shape Personality," *U.S. News and World Report,* 13 April 1987,
60–66.

[3] Cartoon by R. Chast, *Health,* July/August 1991, 29.

[4] Mervyn Rothstein, "From Cartoons to a Play about Racists in the 60s," *New York Times,* 14 August 1991.

Indeed, in the 1990s "gene talk" has entered the vernacular as a subject for drama, a source of humor, and an explanation of human behavior.[5]

In supermarket tabloids and soap operas, in television sitcoms and talk shows, in women's magazines and parenting advice books, genes appear to explain obesity, criminality, shyness, directional ability, intelligence, political leanings, and preferred styles of dressing. There are selfish genes, pleasure-seeking genes, violence genes, celebrity genes, gay genes, couch-potato genes, depression genes, genes for genius, genes for saving, and even genes for sinning. These popular images convey a striking picture of the gene as powerful, deterministic, and central to an understanding of both everyday behavior and the "secret of life."[6]

What is this crucial entity? In one sense, the gene is a biological structure, the unit of heredity, a sequence of deoxyribonucleic acid (DNA) that, by specifying the composition of a protein, carries information that helps to form living cells and tissues.[7] But it has also become a cultural icon, a symbol, almost a magical force. The biological gene—a nuclear structure shaped like a twisted ladder—has a cultural meaning independent of its precise biological properties. Both a scientific concept and a powerful social symbol, the gene has many powers.

4   In this book we explore those powers, showing how the images and narratives of the gene in popular culture reflect and convey a message we will call genetic essentialism.[8] Genetic essentialism reduces the self to a molecular entity, equating human beings, in all their social, historical, and moral complexity, with their genes.

DNA in popular culture functions, in many respects, as a secular equivalent of the Christian soul. Independent of the body, DNA appears to be immortal. Fundamental to identity, DNA seems to explain individual differences, moral order, and human fate. Incapable of deceiving, DNA seems to be the locus of the true self, therefore relevant to the problems of personal authenticity posed by a culture in which the "fashioned self" is

---

[5] Henry Howe and John Lynn, "Gene talk in sociobiology," in Stephen Fuller and James Collier, eds., *Social Epistemology* 6:2 (April-June 1992), 109–164.

[6] "The Secret of Life" is the name of an eight-hour "NOVA" series, directed by Graham Chedd and aired on public television on 26–30 September 1993. The phrase is widely used in descriptions of DNA.

[7] The gene is the fundamental unit of heredity. Each gene is arranged in tandem along a particular chromosome. A chromosome, the microscopic nuclear structure that contains the linear array of genes, is composed of proteins and deoxyribonucleic acid (DNA), the "double helix" molecule that encodes genetic information. Each gene generates, as the "readout" of its specific DNA sequence, a particular protein—its functional product in building the cell or organism. The 24 chromosomes in the human genome contain about 100,000 genes.

[8] This term is used by Sarah Franklin in "Essentialism, Which Essentialism? Some Implications of Reproductive and Genetic Technoscience," in John Dececco and John Elia, eds., *Issues in Biological Essentialism versus Social Construction in Gay and Lesbian Identities* (London: Harrington Park Press, 1993), 27–39. She defines genetic essentialism as "a scientific discourse . . . with the potential to establish social categories based on an essential truth about the body" (34).

the body manipulated and adorned with the intent to mislead.[9] In many popular narratives, individual characteristics and the social order both seem to be direct transcriptions of a powerful, magical, and even sacred entity, DNA.

Increasing popular acceptance of genetic explanations and the proliferation of genetic images reflects, in part, highly publicized research in the science of genetics. Such research, however, occurs in a specific cultural context, one in which heredity and natural ability have often seemed important to formulations of social policy and social practice.[10] Old ideas have been given new life at a time when individual identity, family connections, and social cohesion seem threatened and the social contract appears in disarray.

Changing technologies for the manipulation and assessment of DNA have, moreover, dramatically changed the social implications of these revived ideas. It seems imperative, therefore, to examine these trends critically at a time when diagnosis and prediction based on DNA analysis have so many new applications. In the laboratory, DNA can be used to detect unseen conditions of risk and predict future conditions of disability or disease. Within the family, DNA can be used to define meaningful relationships and make reproductive decisions. In the larger culture, DNA can be used to locate responsibility and culpability, as well as to justify social and institutional policies. Those on all sides of the political spectrum can proclaim that specific biological properties of DNA lend support to their policies or goals. And their claims all build on the DNA mystique.

8   Yet in the history of biology there are few concepts more problematic than that of the gene. It began as a linguistic fiction, coined by Danish geneticist Wilhelm Johannsen in 1909 to describe a presumed cellular entity capable of producing a particular trait. He drew the term from German physiologist and geneticist Hugo DeVries's "pangenes," a term derived from Charles Darwin's "pangenesis," a theory of the origins of biological variation. For the first generation of experimental geneticists (in the early twentieth century), a "gene" was, in practice, a physical trait—the wing shape or eye color of the fruit fly *Drosophila,* for example—which seemed to derive from a substrate of hereditary material, the actual constitution and functioning of which were unknown at the time.[11]

---

[9] Joanne Finkelstein, *The Fashioned Self* (Philadelphia: Temple University Press, 1991). See particularly 177–193.

[10] Anthropologists describe cultural differences in bodily skills that have far less to do with inherent biological limits than with social expectations. They find that bodily and mental capacities are shaped by social organization. They depend in great measure on and vary with social beliefs, practices, and techniques. Paul Hirst and Penny Woolley, *Social Relations and Human Attributes* (London: Tavistock, 1982), Chapter 2.

[11] On the gene and its changing meaning, see Elof Axel Carlson, *The Gene: A Critical History* (Ames: Iowa State University Press, 1989), 23–38, 124–130, 166–173, and 259–271. To quote

In the post–World War II era, the increasing elucidation of the gene as a molecular entity has both clarified its physical form—a double helix of deoxyribonucleic acid (DNA)—and complicated its biological meaning.[12] As contemporary genomics science has demonstrated, DNA does not produce bodily traits in a simple, linear way. It interacts with itself and with its larger environment: Identical sequences of DNA in different locations on the genome (the entire complement of DNA in any given organism's cells) can have different biological meanings. And different genes can have identical effects in different people. Genomes also have large regions, so-called "junk DNA," that seem to have no function at all.

For contemporary molecular geneticists, "gene" is convenient shorthand, referring generally to a stretch of DNA that codes for a protein. In the sense that some sections of DNA produce specific biological events, genes are real entities, but their workings are not simple. While increasing scientific knowledge of molecular processes has clarified some questions, it has also raised new and unexpected ones. Why is so much of the genome without obvious function? Why do many genetic diseases become more severe from generation to generation as a consequence of reduplication of short coding sections? And what does the ambiguity of the genome—its biological indeterminism—mean for our understanding of evolution and evolutionary processes? Much of this complexity disappears when the gene serves its public roles as a resource for scientists seeking

---

Carlson, "The gene has been considered to be an undefined unit, a unit-character, a unit factor, a factor, an abstract point on a recombination map, a three-dimensional segment of an anaphase chromosome, a linear segment of an interphase chromosome, a sac of genomeres, a series of linear subgenes, a spherical unit defined by a target theory, a dynamic functional quantity of one specific unit, a pseudoallele, a specific chromosome segment subject to position effect, a rearrangement within a continuous chromosome molecule, a cistron within which fine structure can be demonstrated, and a linear segment of nucleic acid specifying a structural or regulatory product. Are these concepts identical? . . . For some of these problems, the findings from different organisms are contradictory; for others, the agreements [between organisms] may be analogous rather than a reflection of identical genetic organization" (259). See also L. C. Dunn, *A Short History of Genetics: The Development of Some Main Lines of Thought 1864–1939* (1965; reprint, Ames: Iowa State University Press, 1991), 33–49 and 175–191; also, James D. Watson's treatment of the complexities surrounding the concept of the gene in his *Molecular Biology of the Gene,* 2nd ed. (Menlo Park, CA: W. A. Benjamin, Inc., 1970), 230–254 and 435–466. Watson notes that "even now it is often hard to identify the protein product of a given gene" (240) and "now . . . we realize that the rate of synthesis of a protein is itself partially under internal genetic control and partially determined by the external chemical environment" (435). Our point is that this is a complicated concept with a long, contentious history.

[12] The corn geneticist and Nobelist Barbara McClintock once began a presentation at Cold Spring Harbor that captured the complexities of the gene in the molecular age. She proclaimed that "with the tools and knowledge, I could turn a developing snail's egg into an elephant. It is not so much a matter of chemicals, because snails and elephants do not differ that much; it is matter of timing the action of genes." Cited in Bruce Wallace's colorful reconstruction of the history of the gene *The Search for the Gene* (Ithaca and London: Cornell University Press, 1992), 176.

public support and as a popular explanation for social problems and human behavior, and a justification for policy agendas.

The point of our analysis is not to identify popular distortions of science or to debunk scientific myths. The interesting question is not the contrast between scientific and popular culture; it is how they intersect to shape the cultural meaning of the gene. Some of the images we explore draw on well-established scientific ideas, some on findings that geneticists continue to question, while others seem to be independent of biological research. The precise scientific legitimacy of any image, however, is less important than the cultural use that is made of it. How do scientific concepts serve social ideologies and institutional agendas? Why do certain concepts gain social power to become the focus of significant popular and scientific attention? And what role do scientists play in shaping the appropriation of such concepts?

Science and Culture

12   It is not a coincidence that the popular appropriation of genetics has intensified just as scientists around the world have begun an effort to map and sequence the entire human genome, for in presenting their research to the public, scientists have been active players in constructing the powers of the gene. The cutting edge of this scientific exploration is the Human Genome Project, an international scientific program to map and sequence not only the genes but also the noncoding regions of all the DNA contained in the 24 human chromosomes.

Although gene mapping began in the 1910s with studies of the common fruit fly, *Drosophila,* large-scale mapping of human genes was not technically feasible until the development of greater computer capacity and a variety of new laboratory techniques in the 1980s. Building on these techniques, the human gene mapping program began in 1989 in the United States, where it is funded through the National Institutes of Health (NIH) and the United States Department of Energy (DOE) at a total anticipated cost of more than $3 billion over 15 years. Similar projects are underway in Great Britain, Japan, Russia, the European Community, and other industrialized nations.

Genome researchers hope to locate and determine the exact order of the base pairs in the estimated 100,000 human genes, as well as in the many sections of DNA with no known function. As of the summer of 1994 geneticists had identified over 2500 of the 3000 genetic markers (sections of DNA that can be used as signposts along the genome) needed to create a genetic map. Many single gene disorders—diseases caused by a known form of a particular gene—are already located on the map, either directly or through the identification of genetic markers that "follow" the disease through large, well-characterized family groups. These included cystic fibrosis, retinitis pigmentosa, one form of Alzheimer disease, and more rare conditions such as Huntington's disease, Gaucher disease, malignant hyperthermia, and epidermolysis bullosa.[13]

Geneticists are also exploring the patterns of inheritance of conditions with apparent multiple gene involvement, suggesting familial predispositions to some forms of cancer and Alzheimer's, emphysema, juvenile diabetes, cleft palate, heart disease, and mental illness. Researchers have identified the genetic markers for certain kinds of breast and ovarian cancer and have located the gene causing the mutation responsible for some colon cancers. One goal of such research is to identify susceptible individuals before their symptoms appear.[14]

16 Seeking to assure continued public funding of a long-term, costly project, genome researchers have been writing for popular magazines, giving public talks, and promoting their research in media interviews. They contribute to popular imagery as they popularize their work in ways that resonate with larger social concerns. Indeed, many of the values and assumptions expressed in popular representations of genes and DNA draw support from the rhetorical strategies of scientists—the promises they generate and the language they use to enhance their public image.[15]

Three related themes underlie the metaphors geneticists and other biologists use to describe work on the human genome. These are a characterization of the gene as the essence of identity, a promise that genetic research will enhance prediction of human behavior and health, and an image of the genome as a text that will define a natural order.

Some scientists borrow their images from the computer sciences: The body is less a conscious being than a set of "instructions," a "program" transmitted from one generation to the next. People are "readouts" of their genes. If scientists can decipher and decode the text, classify the markers on the map, and read the instructions, so the argument goes, they will be able to reconstruct the essence of human beings, unlocking the key to human ailments and even to human nature—providing ultimate

[13] The status of genetic disease and genetic therapy is reviewed in *Science,* 8 May 1992. In that issue, see Daniel E. Koshland, "Molecular Advances in Disease," 717; F. S. Collins, "Cystic Fibrosis: Molecular Biology and Therapeutic Implications," 774–779; K. S. Kosik, "Alzheimer's Disease: A Cell Biological Perspective," 780–783; C. T. Caskey et al., "Triplet Repeat Mutations in Human Disease," 784–788; D. H. MacLennan and M. S. Phillips, "Malignant Hyperthermia," 789–793; E. Beutler, "Gaucher Disease: New Molecular Approaches to Diagnosis and Treatment," 794–798; E. H. Epstein, Jr., "Molecular Genetics of Epidermolysis Bullosa," 799–803; P. Humphries et al., "On the Molecular Genetics of Retinitis Pigmentosa," 804–807; and W. F. Anderson, "Human Gene Therapy," 808–813.

[14] Neil Holtzman, *Proceed with Caution* (Baltimore: Johns Hopkins University Press, 1989), 88–105.

[15] See the discussion of rhetorical strategies by Jeremy Green, "Media Sensationalism and Science: The Case of the Criminal Chromosome," in Terry Shinn and Richard Whitley, eds., *Expository Science,* Sociology of the Sciences Yearbook 9 (1985), 139–161.

answers to the injunction "know thyself." Geneticist Walter Gilbert introduces his public lectures on gene sequencing by pulling a compact disk from his pocket and announcing to his audience: "This is you."[16]

Other metaphors used by scientists imply the possibilities of prediction, encouraging the use of their science for social policy. They call the genome a "Delphic oracle," a "time machine," a "trip into the future," a "medical crystal ball." Nobelist and first director of the U.S. Human Genome Project James Watson says in public interviews that "our fate is in our genes."[17] Futuristic scenarios promise that genetic prediction will enhance control over behavior and disease. Thus, a geneticist promises that "present methods of treating depression will seem as crude as former pneumonia treatments seem now."[18] A food scientist writes that food companies will sell specialized breakfast cereals to consumer targets who are genetically predisposed to particular diseases. "Computer models in the home will provide consumers with a diet customized to fit their genetic individuality, which will have been predetermined by simple diagnostic tests."[19] And a biologist and science editor, describing acts of violence, editorializes that "when we can accurately predict future behavior, we may be able to prevent the damage."[20]

20   Scientific illustrations, too, glamorize DNA and promote the notion of genetic essentialism. The log for the joint NIH-DOE publication, *Human Genome News,* portrays a human figure in silhouette, standing inside two swirling ribbons of DNA, contained within a circle. Inscribed around him are the names of scientific disciplines: "Chemistry, Biology, Physics, Mathematics, Engineering." The twisted double helix of DNA surrounding the figure suggests the imprisonment of the human being, who will be released through scientific knowledge. This logo conveys the power of science and its promise for the future.

Geneticists also refer to the genome as the Bible, the Holy Grail, and the Book of Man. Explicit religious metaphors suggest that the genome—when mapped and sequenced—will be a powerful guide to moral order. Other common references to the genome as a dictionary, a library, a recipe, a map, or a blueprint construct DNA as a comprehensive and unbiased resource, an orderly reference work. The population geneticist Bruce Wallace has compared the human genome to "the torn pages of a giant novel, written in an unknown language, blowing about helter-skelter

---

[16] See e.g. Walter Gilbert, "Current State of the H.G.I.," Harvard University Dibner Center Lecture, 15 June 1990.

[17] Leon Jaroff, "The Gene Hunt," *Time,* 20 March 1989, 62–67.

[18] Lois Wingerson, "Searching for Depression Genes," *Discover,* February 1982, 60–64.

[19] Fergus M. Clydesdale, "Present and Future of Food Science and Technology in Industrialized Countries," *Food Technology,* September 1989, 134–146.

[20] Daniel Koshland, "Elephants, Monstrosities and the Law," *Science* 255 (4 February 1992), 777.

in an air-conditioned, enclosed space such as Houston's Astrodome."[21] Wallace's chaotic image of the genome implies the promise that scientists engaged in mapping the human genome will (eventually) capture all the pages, put them in proper order, translate the language, and analyze the meaning of the resulting text.

The apparent precision of a map may make invisible the priorities and interests that shaped it. As forms of knowledge, all maps reflect social perspectives on the world at the time of their making; they are the products of cultural choices. Maps select and link features of the world, in effect transforming those features by making them part of a coherent, single landscape. The selectivity of maps is a part of their visual power, of course, for they are also instruments of persuasion. As one curator put it, "Every map is someone's way of getting you to look at the world in his or her way."[22] Map imagery suggests that once a gene is located, its interpretation will be objective and independent of context. But as molecular biologist Christopher Wills has observed, "simply determining the sequence of all this DNA will not mean we have learned everything there is to know about human beings, any more than looking up the sequence of notes in a Beethoven sonata gives us the capacity to play it."[23] A mapped gene may appear to be a straightforward detail, to be extracted and understood without reference to culture and experience. Yet the language of the genome, like the language of a dictionary, must be contextualized to be understood. Genes are, like words, products of (evolutionary) history, dependent on context, and often ambiguous, open to more than one interpretation.[24]

Meanwhile, the successes of molecular genetics and the high profile of the Human Genome Project are shaping the assumptions underlying research in other scientific fields. Behavioral geneticists and psychologists, working with human twins and extrapolating from animal models, have attributed shyness, intelligence, criminality, even religiosity and other complex human traits to heredity. The Minnesota Center for Twin and Adoption Research has provided percentage estimates of the extent to which certain personality traits are determined by heredity: extroversion,

---

[21] Bruce Wallace, *The Search for the Gene* (Ithaca: Cornell University Press, 1992), 199.

[22] Lucy Fellows, cited in John Noble Wilford, "Discovering the Old World of Maps," *New York Times,* 9 October 1992. See also Dennis Wood, *The Power of Maps* (New York: Guilford Press, 1992). The geographer Mark Monmonier has observed that "a good map tells a multitude of little white lies. It suppresses truth to help the user see what needs to be seen": *How to Lie with Maps* (Chicago: University of Chicago Press, 1991), 199.

[23] Christopher Wills, *Exons, Introns and Talking Genes: The Science Behind the Human Genome Project* (New York: Basic Books, 1991), 10.

[24] See discussion in Marga Vicedo, "The Human Genome Project," *Biology and Philosophy* 7 (1992), 255–278.

61 percent; conformity, 60 percent; tendency to worry, 55 percent; creativity, 55 percent; aggressiveness, 48 percent.[25] While human genome research has been promoted as a way to find disease genes, many within the scientific community believe that a map of the genome will also document the inheritance of these complex, socially important human traits. Indeed, some scientists believe this is a major goal. Nobelist David Baltimore has commented that the genome project "will allow us to examine human variability, for example, variations in mathematical ability, or what we call intelligence. . . . The rationale is not to find human disease genes, because we're doing moderately well at finding them right now. But the only way to study the genetics of the higher perceptual, higher integrative human functions is by actually studying human beings. . . . The genetic and physical maps are designed for that."[26]

24   The emphasis on genes for specific behaviors, however, is controversial. Some scientists argue that efforts to measure the relative effects of heredity and environment on behavior systematically misconstrue the two as independent rather than interactive forces, underestimating the influence of environmental forces on gene expression.[27] Critics point out that the heritability of any trait is simply a statistical construct that may suggest variations between populations but may have no simple meaning for the individual.[28] Stephen Jay Gould has observed that efforts to distinguish the relative effects of nature and nurture propose a false dichotomy by confusing correlation with causation: "Genes influence many aspects of human behavior, but we cannot say that such behavior is caused by genes in any direct way. We cannot even claim that a given behavior is, say, 40% genetic and 60% environmental. . . . Genes and environment interact in a nonadditive way."[29]

Some critics question the motivation behind efforts to measure the relative effects of nature and nurture on behavior. Psychologist Douglas Wahlsten, for example, believes that "the only practical application of the heritability coefficient is to predict the results of a program of selective

[25] See Thomas J. Bouchard, Jr., David T. Lykken, Matthew McGue, Nancy Segal, and Auke Tellegen, "Sources of Human Psychological Differences: The Minnesota Study of Twins Reared Apart," *Science* 250 (12 October 1990), 223. Also Val Dusek, "Bewitching Science," *Science for the People,* November/December 1987, 19.

[26] "Mapping the Genome: The Vision, the Science, the Implementation: A Roundtable Discussion," 18 February 1992, published in *Los Alamos Science* 20 (1992), 68–85.

[27] Douglas Wahlsten, "Insensitivity of the Analysis of Variance to Heredity-Environment Interaction," *Behavioral and Brain Sciences* 13 (1990), 109–161.

[28] Peter McGuffin and Randy Katz, "Who Believes in Estimating Heritability as an End in Itself?" 141–142, in Douglas Wahlsten, op. cit.

[29] Stephen Jay Gould, "The Confusion Over Evolution," *New York Review of Books,* 19 November 1992, 48. See also Richard Lewontin, *Biology as Ideology* (New York: Harper, 1992) and Ruth Hubbard and Elijah Wald, *Exploding the Gene Myth* (Boston: Beacon Press, 1993).

breeding."[30] And African American organizations, sensitive to the racist implications of deterministic explanations of deviance, attacked plans for a scholarly conference on "genetic factors in crime."[31]

Despite continued controversy over methods and motives, efforts to determine the genetic basis of human behaviors such as alcoholism and crime draw legitimacy from the rising fortunes of molecular biology. These efforts have captured public attention, for such research addresses critical social questions—about the basis of human identity and individual differences, the nature of deviance, and the location of responsibility for social problems.

Scientists often dismiss as oversimplified and distorted the way their work is appropriated. But the relationship between scientific and public culture is far more complex. As historian Robert Young put it, it is often "impossible to distinguish hard science from its economic and political context and from the generalizations which serve both as motives for the research and which are fed back into social and political debate."[32]

28   The history of science is the story of the selective analysis of reality, and many of the most interesting problems raised by historians and sociologists focus on this selectivity; that is, on how science, as a human and cultural process, can both depict nature and create culturally specific knowledge. As recent social and historical studies of science have suggested, an observation becomes a fact through social negotiation of critical questions. What does an experiment mean? What can it prove? What counts as a demonstration of a particular phenomenon? And what counts as a satisfying explanation? A different explanation, equally consistent with the phenomena observed, may not be accepted if it violates the researcher's expectations.[33] These expectations, often unarticulated, can be difficult to recognize, so integral are they to the culture of science.[34] And scientific culture itself reflects larger cultural concerns and assumptions— a point that seems obvious when we look back to the seventeenth century, but less evident when we consider contemporary science.

---

[30] Douglas Wahlsten, op. cit.

[31] In 1992 African American groups attacked plans for a University of Maryland conference on "Genetic Factors in Crime," perceiving this as racially motivated. The controversy resulted in the withdrawal of NIH funds. See David Wheeler, "University of Maryland Conference That Critics Charge Might Foster Racism Loses NIH Support," *Chronicle of Higher Education,* 2 September 1992, A6–A8.

[32] Robert Young, "Evolutionary Biology and Ideology," *Science Studies,* 1 (1971), 177–206.

[33] There is a very large literature on the social negotiation of scientific knowledge, but a good starting point is Steven Shapin and Simon Shaffer, *Leviathan and the Air-Pump: Hobbes, Boyle and the Experimental Life* (Princeton, NJ: Princeton University Press, 1985). See also Bruno Latour and S. Woolgar, *Laboratory Life* (Princeton, NJ: Princeton University Press, 1986).

[34] One of the clearest explications of this difficulty is Evelyn Fox Keller's essay on the pacemaker cell in the slime mold. The slime mold is a unicellular organism that can, when necessary, aggregate with other slime mold cells to form a slug and thereby crawl away to find a better place to

Popular imagery is far more transparent than scientific discourse. It provides a way to gain access to the social concerns and common understandings that are shaping contemporary concepts in both the science of molecular genetics and the culture at large.[35]

The Gene as an Icon

The "First Interstate Sperm Bank" was the setting for a 1991 episode of the popular prime-time television comedy series, "In Living Color."[36] As the scene opened, a doctor at the sperm bank handed a customer a small plastic container and thanked her for her patronage. Suddenly an armed woman barged in demanding to be given the sperm of Denzel Washington. The bank officer explained that the popular actor's sperm was not available, but offered instead that of athletes Mike Tyson or James Worthy. The agitated "bank robber" shouted that both had the "wrong genetics." Desperate to have a baby because her "biological clock is ticking," she accepted a stranger's offer to solve her dilemma the old-fashioned way. As she left, however, she shot a container of sperm labeled "The New Kids," announcing "I just saved everyone from another generation of 'New Kids.'"

The humor in this television episode drew on ideas about genes, heredity, and reproduction familiar to a prime-time television audience. The violent confrontation over sperm—presented as a sitcom satire—mocks the idea that personality and behavior are inherited and caricatures the desperation of those whose "biological clocks" inspire a sudden desire to become mothers. It also parodies concerns about the threat of future genetic decline through the reproduction of the unfit—in this case, the "unfit" being the (all white) members of the highly promoted singing group "New Kids on the Block," viewed by some in the African American community as rap music rip-off artists with degenerate musical taste.

32   This narrative of the genetic origins of behavior and the threat of future genetic decline conveys a cluster of expectations and fears that have significant historical resonance. Long before heredity could be biologically explained, notions of "blood" and kinship were used to account for social inequalities. The superiority of "blue bloods," the basic evil of "bad seeds," and the idea that "blood is thicker than water" were important historical

---

live. In their efforts to explain this phenomenon, biologists have consistently postulated a "pacemaker" cell that tells the other cells what to do. Keller argues that biological models featuring relationships of control and domination (rather than, for example, cooperation) may be especially compelling to those who expect the world to act that way. See Keller, "The Force of the Pacemaker Concept in Theories of Aggregation in Cellular Slime Mold" in her *Reflections on Gender and Science* (New Haven and London: Yale University Press, 1985), 150–157.

[35] See Stephen Hilgartner for an exploration of the issue of popularization and its utility to scientists, "The Dominant View of Popularization: Conceptual Problems, Political Uses," *Social Studies of Science* 20 (1990), 519–539.

[36] "In Living Color," 23 February 1991.

themes, reflecting social interest in family relationships.[37] Legends of baby
switching, the Oliver Twist story, and the folk tale of the "incognito
prince" suggested the overwhelming power of "blood ties" to determine a
child's fate.[38] Heredity has long been interpreted as socially powerful,
though the relative importance of heredity and environment has been the
focus of a continuing debate.

Renewed interest in genetic explanations reflects the high status of
the science of molecular genetics. But it is also a response to the stresses
and strains of an increasingly secularized, complex, and seemingly chaotic
society. Biological explanations often appear to be more objective and less
ambiguous than environmental or social ones. They also promise biomedical control of social problems. At a time of concern with ethnic and class
differences, genetics as a science of differences seems to provide reliable,
clear-cut ways to justify social policies on the basis of "natural" or predetermined characteristics, to differentiate "them" from "us." At a time of
significant public concern about alcoholism and crime, genetics as an explanation of good and evil seems to provide hard and certain ways to cod-
ify what is normal or deviant.

DNA, to borrow from Sherry Turkle's analysis of Freudian and computer concepts, has become "an object to think with," a malleable idea by
means of which different interpretive communities can express diverse,
even contradictory, concerns.[39] Genetic metaphors are used to buttress
class differences (the result of "good breeding") and to reinforce social
stereotypes ("differences lie in the genes"). They serve to explain human
exceptionalism on the basis of different DNA ("the genes of genius"), but
also to claim the rights of animals on the basis of shared DNA ("A rat is a
pig is a dog is a boy"[40]). Genetics can justify social harmony (based on
common ancestry) or social divisions (based on race). Genetic explanations can absolve an individual from responsibility for action, but the individual's genes can also become the focus of blame. Recourse to genetics
can express a sense of fatalism—"the luck of the draw"—or a moral judgment—there are "good" and "bad" genes.

---

[37] Daniel Kevles, "Out of Eugenics: The Historical Politics of the Human Genome," in Kevles and Lee Hood, eds., *The Code of Codes: Scientific and Social Issues in the Human Genome Project* (Cambridge: Harvard University Press, 1992), 3–37.

[38] On the cultural meaning of abandoned and switched babies there is some historical literature, including John Boswell, *The Kindness of Strangers: The Abandonment of Children in Western Europe from Late Antiquity to the Renaissance* (New York: Pantheon, 1988); Everett M. Ressler, *Unaccompanied Children: Care and Protection in Wars, Natural Disasters and Refugee Movements* (New York: Oxford University Press, 1988); and Barbara L. Estrin, *The Raven and the Lark: Lost Children in the Litera- ture of the English Renaissance* (Lewisburg, PA: Bucknell University Press, 1984).

[39] Sherry Turkle, *The Second Self: Computers and the Human Spirit* (New York: Simon & Schuster, 1991), 173.

[40] Statement by Ingrid Newkirk, frequently cited by animal rights activists. See James Jasper and Dorothy Nelkin, *The Animal Rights Crusade* (New York: Free Press, 1992), 46.

Clearly, the gene of popular culture is not a biological entity. Though it *refers* to a biological construct and derives its cultural power from science, its symbolic meaning is independent of biological definitions. The gene is, rather, a symbol, a metaphor, a convenient way to define personhood, identity, and relationships in socially meaningful ways. The gene is used, of course, to explain health and disease. But it is also a way to talk about guilt and responsibility, power and privilege, intellectual or emotional status. It has become a supergene, used to judge the morality or rightness of social systems and to explore the forces that will shape the human future.

Personal Response

Discuss your own understanding of the function of genes. Where did you get your information? Do you think, as Nelkin and Lindee suggest, that much of it comes from popular culture?

Questions for Class or Small Group Discussion

1. Nelkin and Lindee write: "The interesting question is not the contrast between scientific and popular culture; it is how they intersect to shape the cultural meaning of the gene" (paragraph 11). What do the examples of representations of the gene in popular culture that Nelkin and Lindee cite in their opening paragraphs and in paragraph 30 tell you about the cultural meaning of the gene? Can you give other examples of references to genes in any aspect of popular culture?

2. Discuss possible reasons why "the emphasis on genes for specific behaviors . . . is controversial" (paragraph 24).

3. What do you think the critics who "question the motivation behind efforts to measure the relative effects of nature and nurture on behavior" are worried about (paragraph 25)?

4. According to Nelkin and Lindee, geneticists involved in locating genetic markers that suggest familial predisposition to some hereditary diseases hope to "identify susceptible individuals before their symptoms appear" (paragraph 15). What do you think are the implications of such research? In what circumstances might people have mixed emotions about learning that they were susceptible to certain diseases?

5. Comment on these statements: "As forms of knowledge, all maps reflect social perspectives on the world at the time of their making; they are the products of cultural choices" (paragraph 22), and "The history of science is the story of the selective analysis of reality" (paragraph 28). Do you agree that maps and science are not "objective and independent of context" (paragraph 22)? Explain your answer.

SCIENTIFIC KNOWLEDGE AND HUMAN DIGNITY

Jean Dausset

Jean Dausset is a French medical doctor whose work on tissue groups has been instrumental in the progress made in organ transplants and grafts. His work earned him a share of the 1980 Nobel Prize for physiology or medicine. He is professor of immuno-haematology at the Larisboisière-Saint Louis Medical Faculty in Paris and of experimental medicine at the Collège de France. In 1984, he set up the Human Poly-morphism Study Center, which plays an active part in the Human Genome Project. He is a former member of France's National Advisory Council on Ethics and since 1982 has been president of the Universal Movement for Scientific Responsibility. This essay was first published in the September 1994 issue of UNESCO Courier.

Molecular biology has invaded all or very nearly all areas of medical re-search, investing scientists engaged in research in human genetics with heavy responsibilities.

Perhaps for the first time, these researchers are now faced with two agonizing questions: how far should they go in their research and how should their findings be applied?

The answer to the first question is quite unequivocal. There are no limits to knowledge, which is the pride and honour of humanity. We are the only creatures capable of understanding and influencing our environ-ment. Under no circumstances should research be halted or even slowed down. It must be pursued on condition that studies made on human beings respect human dignity.

4   In theory, the answer to the second question is also unequivocal but it nevertheless raises some serious problems. It is unequivocal because new knowledge should be used for the good of humanity and not be diverted to serve the interests of individuals or communities which do not respect human rights. In the case of human genetics, unwise use of new techniques could have disastrous consequences.

There can be no doubt that the powers now vested in research scien-tists impose new obligations on them and raise crucial ethical issues. We are only too aware that all technical progress has its positive and negative sides. It is up to society to reap the benefits from it, while as far as possible averting potential risks and deviations, so that the balance is tilted in favour of the advantages. There can be no denying that, in the long run, the ad-vantages accruing from genetics will be considerable.

An End to Hereditary Diseases

Thanks in particular to the work being done by the Human Polymorphism Study Centre, in Paris, in conjunction with Professor Daniel Cohen and the Généthon laboratory, the genetic map and the physical map of the human genome have been plotted more quickly than might have been hoped, and it is now possible to locate on the long DNA strand the genes responsible for the most common genetic diseases. For instance, it has proved possible not only to pinpoint the genes responsible for cystic fibrosis and Duchenne muscular dystrophy but actually to isolate, describe and sequence them. The same is true of many other genetic diseases, and hardly a week goes by without the genes responsible for one or another of them being identified.

These discoveries have given rise to a great wave of hope. Now that we know which genes are defective, we can start thinking about developing specific therapies either to correct the gene itself or the protein coding it.

8   This is how the idea of gene therapy came about. A distinction must be made between two types of such therapy. One is somatic therapy, which deals only with the cells of the body (or soma). This has absolutely no effect on heredity and is therefore perfectly ethical, since it can be likened to a simple graft. The other is germ-line therapy, which is concerned with reproductive cells, male or female, or with the embryos of certain cells. In this case, any change is handed down from generation to generation and, in some individuals, the human genetic heritage will be altered accordingly. Thus, as things stand at present, germ-line therapy must be strictly banned.

In addition to these hereditary diseases caused by a single flawed gene, we are now studying such widespread pathological conditions as diabetes, cardiovascular or neuropsychiatric diseases and cancer. These diseases may have a variety of causes, due to the action not only of certain genes but of environmental factors.

They are now thought to be due to the simultaneous existence in one and the same individual of a relatively limited number of defective genes, say five or six in the case of non-insulin dependent diabetes, for example. If, through bad luck, these five or six genes exist together in the same person, it is to some degree probable, though by no means certain, that he or she may contract the disease. We therefore now have a means of quantifying the risk.

Prevention Is Better Than Cure

This, in turn, is how the concept of predictive medicine came about. Prevention is better than cure. And preventing means predicting.

12   The concept of predictive medicine came to me when it was found that many diseases are connected with the antigens of the HLA system (human leucocyte antigen system).[1] For instance, somebody with the

---

[1] The antigens of the HLA system are present in virtually all the nuclear cells of the body, which is why they are called "cell antigens." They are genetic markers that are particularly useful for

HLA-B27 antigen is 600 times more liable to suffer from ankylosing spon-dylitis than somebody without it. It is now possible to identify in the genome the genes predisposing people to certain illnesses.

This gives an idea of the prospects being opened up by the application of genetics to medicine. With predictive medicine, we shall certainly be able to avoid much pain and suffering and perhaps even live in perfect health to a ripe old age. In short, medicine will be tailored to the individual and will prove less costly and more effective.

But these discoveries also have negative aspects. It seems pointless, indeed heartless, to tell people that they are predisposed to a disease when we still cannot offer any preventive treatment, not to mention the unnecessary anxiety and the host of psychological side-effects this may cause.

What is more, such information obviously has to be kept strictly confidential. The results of genetic testing should be divulged only with the authorization of the patient, since there is a risk that they may be used by insurance companies or employers to make unacceptable discriminations. If such abuses are to be avoided, it will be necessary to lay down strict rules. There must be a public debate on this issue. Universal answers will have to be found. UNESCO is actively engaged in this search.

16   In conclusion, I should like to dispel the myth that genetics creates in the public mind. It is only natural that current developments in this field should make people afraid. But are their fears justified? Or, rather, to what extent are they justified? People are often afraid of the seemingly all-powerful scientist. It is not the scientist they should be afraid of, but indi-viduals or groups of individuals driven by a lust for power that is often tainted by a totalitarian ideology.

And so we must regard with serenity the revolution that is taking place today. It is a revolution that must be harnessed in the service of hu-manity and lead to the long life, happy and free of ailments, which we all hope for.

This is the dream I invite you to share—a dream in which genes spell hope.

The only priority we have set ourselves is to relieve suffering. As Paracelsus[2] put it, "medicine is love."

Personal Response

If your doctor were able to predict that you had a chance of developing a debilitating disease, would you want to know? Under what conditions

---

studying the biological make-up of individuals or population groups and evaluating their suscep-tibility to certain diseases.

[2] Swiss doctor and alchemist (1493–1541).

would you absolutely want to know? What might make you hesitate about asking for that information?

Questions for Class or Small Group Discussion

1. Discuss your answers to the questions Dausset raises in paragraph 2: How far do you think researchers should go in their research, and how should their findings be applied?

2. Given Dausset's direct involvement in the Human Genome Project, it is not surprising he would say that "under no circumstances should research be halted or even slowed down" (paragraph 3). Who or what groups of people might not endorse the project so enthusiastically? What objections to carrying on at full speed might some people have?

3. In paragraph 15, Dausset writes that "there must be a public debate on this issue." Conduct your own class debate on the issue of how to handle the results of genetic testing of individuals.

4. In his conclusion, Dausset says he wants to "dispel the myth that genetics creates in the public mind" and acknowledges that people's fear of recent developments in this field are natural. What myth about genetics do you think Dausset is referring to? What fears do you suppose people have?

UNESCO AND BIOETHICS

Georges B. Kutukdjian

Georges B. Kutukdjian is the head of UNESCO's Bioethics Unit. (UNESCO is an acronym for the United Nations Educational, Scientific, and Cultural Organization.) A philosopher and anthropologist, Kutukdjian has published a number of papers on kinship systems and proverbs, and literary essays on Marguerite Duras, Kafka, and Proust. He was the coeditor, with Antonio Papisca, of a collective work on the rights of peoples, published in 1991. This article follows and elaborates on Jean Dausset's "Scientific Knowledge and Human Dignity" in the September 1994 UNESCO Courier.

Scientific research on the human genome, and especially on gene therapy and the diagnosis of genetic diseases, has far-reaching implications for the lives of all of us—children, men and women alike. It is a field holding out immense prospects for man's self-transformation and it will, in the long run, require societies to make certain choices. As a result, it is giving rise to anxieties that may in some cases be justified but are more often irrational.

These anxieties lie behind the effort many countries are now making to look into the ethical framework of such research. Legislation is starting to be adopted to define limits for medical practice and some types of research, in order to ensure that human dignity will be respected. Two points must be stressed, however. In the first place, the type of legislation differs significantly from one country to another and we do not have any common yardstick to judge it by. Secondly, it does not exist everywhere in the world, but only in some of the industrial countries. Elsewhere, there are still a number of grey areas surrounding research and experimentation.

It is for all these reasons that the Director-General of UNESCO decided to set up an International Bioethics Committee and invited Ms. Noëlle Lenoir, a member of the Constitutional Council of the French Republic, to preside over its deliberations.

4   The Committee met for the first time in September 1993 and commenced its work by identifying three priority themes. These are genetic screening and testing, the therapeutic applications of genetics research, and population genetics.

Genetic Testing

Should genetic screening be made compulsory for so-called "risk" populations or should it simply be made available to them? Should it be introduced into premarital examinations or be included in prenatal diagnosis? Should it be carried out before gamete donation or the implantation of embryos fertilized in vitro?

At the outset, a distinction must be made between two kinds of genetic tests. Tests in the first category are used to identify a particular gene which is virtually certain to bring on a hereditary disease. Those in the second category show whether or not a person has a predisposition to certain diseases and thus reveal situations involving varying degrees of probability. Depending on the environment and sundry other factors, about some of which little is known, the outward symptoms of a disease may appear in its early stages or may emerge only later, and the disease itself may vary in severity. A genetic mutation may become more dominant and grow worse from generation to generation. On the other hand, the tendency for genetic damage to occur may be reversed. In short, the same defect in a person's genotype (genetic constitution) may take different forms in his or her phenotype (the physical constitution as it interacts with the environment).

This influence of the environment on the form a genetic mutation may take brings into play the concept of the responsibility of individuals towards themselves and their families and the responsibility of citizens towards the community. Preventive medicine could therefore be said to go hand-in-hand with predictive medicine.

8   Should people be told that there is a probability that they will eventually develop Huntington's chorea, for example, and transmit it to their offspring? Should their close or distant relatives be warned? What about employers and insurance companies? Can a company's medical service insist on being given the results of genetic testing?

Since genetic testing may extend over several generations and involve varying numbers of individuals, questions about the storage and confidentiality of the data are bound to arise sooner or later. How long should genetic data be kept and how can its confidentiality be guaranteed? Who should be empowered to divulge or withhold information which often involves whole families?

Similarly, if people can choose to know what their genetic future will be, can they also choose not to know? Should they or should they not be compelled to take account of the results of genetic testing?

In this regard, it is important that people should be freely able to exercise their discretion. Information that is liable to change their whole lives and force added responsibilities on them should not expose them to any form of discrimination. Genetic testing should not prompt the authorities to adopt repressive policies leading to a restriction of individual freedoms.

12   Another ethical issue connected with genetic testing is bound up with the need to ensure that all countries, including the least advanced ones, reap benefit from them, so that they too can join the fight against hereditary diseases.

Therapeutic Applications

The first question that has to be raised relates to the pre-implantation diagnosis performed on artificially fertilized embryos which, in view of its greater simplicity and lower cost, is likely to replace gene therapy in cases of rare genetic diseases. This involves a choice that is already framed in ethical terms.

The second question is whether the work currently being done is not liable to become narrowly focused on looking for the genes that account for people's behaviour—their sexuality, for example—their talents and abilities, or even their "deviances." This could lead to a kind of genetic reductionism whereby people would be defined exclusively in terms of their genome, or to a situation in which some individuals or groups of individuals might be stigmatized by society, ostracized or even eliminated. This would be tantamount to adopting eugenic policies.

There are other problems. We know, for example, that through agriculture, gene therapy could bring about radical changes in public health. A diet of genetically modified plants could become a regular form of treatment, a sort of oral "vaccine" given in repeated doses. However, the in vivo reproduction of these plant species would be liable to give rise to new recombined organisms that could become vectors for diseases. In such an eventuality, what kind of preventive measures and legislation should be instituted?

16   The same applies, *mutatis mutandis,* to the use of human genes for the development of transgenic goals. What limits should be set on the supply of human genetic material? Should it be reserved solely for therapeutic purposes, say for xenografts, and its use for any other purpose, such as for improving livestock, be ruled out?

We have to accept that the issue of transgenesis applied to the human species now has to be faced. Reports of germ-line therapy experiments on embryonic cells or spermatozoa have recently been published in scientific journals.

As a result of the rapid strides being made by genetic engineering, it is now possible to store gametes and germ cells in "banks" for possible future use, such as for autografts. This practice is now regarded as acceptable, under certain conditions, for young cancer patients who have to undergo X-ray treatment or chemotherapy and who wish to preserve their chances of later conceiving children by in vitro fertilization techniques. With the exception of these medical cases, the storage of gametes and germ cells poses the problem of the storage of human products generally, as well as that of storage methods and the criteria governing access to such "banks."

Lastly, careful thought has to be given to the best ways of protecting the intellectual property of researchers whose inventions have industrial or commercial applications. Should such protection be regarded as akin to copyright? How is it possible to regulate access to genetic data banks and their possible industrial or commercial uses?

20   First, steps must be taken to secure the free and informed consent of population groups participating in major surveys on population genetics. The scientific aims and objectives of the surveys should be clearly explained to them.

The results of these surveys should not be detrimental to those who participate, nor should they lead to discrimination against them. Nor should they be allowed to lead to the establishment of a genetic pseudo-classification of the population groups involved.

These results should also be communicated to the individuals and population groups concerned. Access to genetic data banks where the information is stored, the processing of this information and its use should be rigorously defined.

The Human Genome Project

Deciphering the totality of genetic information on the human race is an ambitious project which calls for international co-operation. The ensuing progress will help to prevent and treat genetic diseases which are incurable today. It will also make a significant contribution to understanding the structure and the functions of the genetic system and individual development, as well as the "natural history" of DNA.

24   Such fundamental knowledge of human beings clearly raises ethical, social and legal problems, and consequently it is not surprising that UNESCO attaches very great importance to it. The human genome project has a place among UNESCO's activities because of UNESCO's ethical mission and its competence in the fields of education, science and culture. UNESCO offers an ideal environment for multidisciplinary debates on the different aspects of study of the human genome.

UNESCO is thus fully involved in this project. By organizing or encouraging meetings, holding workshops, helping to finance training programmes and awarding short-term scholarships, UNESCO is seeking to do three things: to encourage international co-operation and co-ordination, to stimulate debate on the many repercussions of the human genome project, and to promote the participation of countries of the South and East. The sharing of knowledge between North and South, East and West is, after all, an ethical imperative in itself.

Personal Response

How do you feel about genetics research? Do you think the potential good of such research outweighs the potential for devastating misuse? Explore your feelings on this issue.

Questions for Class or Small Group Discussion

1. Do you think genetic screening should be made compulsory in certain "risk" populations or as part of premarital examinations? Should it be part of prenatal diagnosis or required of donees for in vitro embryo fertilization (paragraph 5)?

2. Do you think people should be told of their probability for developing diseases? Do employees and insurance companies have a right to know of such predisposition? Do you think people should have the right to refuse information about their genetic future (paragraphs 8–11)?

3. What are the "eugenics policies" Kutukdjian refers to in paragraph 14? Where have eugenics policies been applied before in this century?

4. If you were a member of UNESCO's bioethics committee, what other questions besides the ones Kutukdjian mentions would you raise?

FACING UP TO BIOETHICAL DECISIONS

John C. Fletcher, Franklin G. Miller, and Arthur L. Caplan

John C. Fletcher is the Kornfeld Professor of Biomedical Ethics in the School of Medicine at the University of Virginia. Franklin G. Miller is assistant professor of biomedical ethics and medical education in the School of Medicine at the University of Virginia. Arthur L. Caplan is Trustee Professor of Bioethics at the University of Pennsylvania. Their article, which appeared in the Fall 1994 issue of Issues in Science and Technology, *calls for a national forum on the subject of genetic research.*

Bioethical controversies have become routine items in the daily news as society struggles with a host of complex moral problems posed by issues such as genetic testing, health care reform, and the spread of AIDS. The federal government once had an effective mechanism in place—a national commission—to address public bioethics, but the Reagan and Bush administrations allowed the mechanism to languish. As a result, lingering bioethical questions have festered and important research has been blocked. In addition, troubling new questions of public policy have emerged.

A brief survey of some of the critical unanswered questions reveals the breadth and depth of the impasse:

Are existing federal regulations and guidelines adequate to protect human subjects of research? Biomedical research drives medical progress; however, past efforts to develop beneficial knowledge by human experimentation have harmed or violated the rights of some research subjects. For example, the government conducted a syphilis study in Tuskegee, Alabama, from 1932 until 1972, in which poor black men were systematically deceived about the study to gain their cooperation, and researchers withheld treatment while merely monitoring the natural course of the disease. And during the 1950s and 1960s the government conducted surreptitious studies, only recently revealed by the Department of Energy, on the effects of radiation on humans, without the informed consent of the patients or parents involved. This issue pertains especially to research with "vulnerable" groups of people, such as those with severe mental illness and the growing population of elderly patients with severe cognitive impairment caused by Alzheimer's disease or stroke. Research involving such subjects holds out great promise for future benefits but also raises troubling questions when the individuals have diminished or fluctuating capacity to understand and consent to research. Federal regulations do not provide specific criteria for acceptable types of research involving mentally disabled patients, nor do they spell out specially designated safeguards for the conduct of research with such subjects.

4   *How should society use the exponential growth in knowledge of genetics to benefit human health and restrain possible abuses to individuals and their privacy?* The Human Genome Project—a 15-year, $3-billion federally funded program to "map" the location of all genes on the human chromosomes—is propelling this growth in knowledge and technology. Genetic information helps researchers devise new tests for diseases, including Huntington's disease and various types of cancer. However, this new knowledge about the probability of future diseases in particular persons will often occur in advance of effective preventive or therapeutic interventions. How should genetic testing be done? Should children be tested for incurable diseases? How do we prevent insurer or employer discrimination against persons whose genes set them up for higher risks of life-threatening or disabling diseases? When the Human Genome Project began, its founders persuaded Congress to permit 3 percent to 5 percent

of its annual budget to be spent on studies of the ethical, social, and legal implications of the new genetics. This effort has produced dozens of studies that may be sources of guidance, but there is no effective mechanism to ensure that these findings influence public policy.

Should federal funds be used for embryo research? Techniques of the new genetics and use of *in vitro* fertilization make possible valuable, but ethically troubling, research with human embryos. New knowledge can be gained about how genetic diseases—including some cancers—begin in the embryo, about the causes of infertility, and about contraception. How can embryos be legally and ethically obtained for research? What limitations, if any, should be placed on donations of sperm and eggs for research? Should embryos be fertilized solely for the sake of research, or should only those be used that are donated by infertile couples trying to have a baby using *in vitro* fertilization?

What actions are necessary and appropriate in dealing with the ever-widening global HIV disease and AIDS epidemic? Two broad issues deserve careful examination and public debate. The first concerns the design and timing of large-scale vaccine trials. The urgent need for prevention must be carefully balanced with the risks of vaccine research and potentially routine immunization, bearing in mind the state of scientific uncertainty. Second, the ethics of public policy with respect to HIV testing needs to be investigated. Respect for the autonomy and privacy of persons infected with HIV vies with the public health goal of preventing transmission. Should HIV testing be strictly voluntary? Or should it be mandatory for some groups, such as pregnant women (in light of data showing the effectiveness of the AIDS drug AZT in reducing the incidence of perinatal transmission), health care workers, prisoners, and adolescents?

What can and should be done to overcome the current scarcity of human organs for transplantation? As a partial solution, the American Medical Association's Council on Ethical and Judicial Affairs recently recommended legal changes permitting parents of infants with anencephaly (congenital lack of cerebral hemispheres) to donate the infant's organs without waiting for brain death. This proposal would require a new review of federal laws on the definition and determination of death, about which there has been continuing debate. Another potential solution involves the use of organs from higher animals for humans, but much research and many ethical questions remain to be addressed.

8   *What is the best way to manage and finance the provision of health care with the aim of providing universal access and cost control?* The vexing, but inescapable, issue of rationing, which has been a taboo topic in today's political debates, underlies this question. Since society is not prepared to pay for all potentially beneficial treatments or procedures for every patient, how ought decisions be made in allocating health care services? A related issue is the ethical relevance of "personal responsibility" in health care. Is it ethically acceptable to limit access to expensive treatments for

self-induced health problems in persons who continue to smoke cigarettes or abuse drugs?

How should society and government come to grips with the plight of dying patients? This question is being magnified by continued advances in medical treatment and life-sustaining technologies. Popular support for the deeply controversial practice of physician-assisted death, by providing lethal treatment to suffering, terminally ill patients, testifies to widespread concern about the circumstances of dying. It is doubtful that a consensus about the ethics and legal status of physician-assisted death will emerge in the near future. However, it is time for a full review of the ethical issues in caring for terminally ill persons, including standards of pain management, treatment of depression, and access to hospice care.

The Withering of Public Bioethics

The quality of public policy responses to these and other bioethical issues depends on careful analysis and study, expert advice, and public debate. The nation, however, has lacked an adequate mechanism to do this work of public bioethics for more than a decade. The routine modes of government inquiry—hearings, reports in the news media, and public opinion polls—are inadequate to assess the policy implications of complex bioethical problems. Fruitful interaction, sustained over time, between the bioethics community and policymakers requires an institutional linkage—a forum that functions to consolidate and augment existing knowledge concerning bioethical issues, to formulate or endorse consensus standards, and to make specific recommendations for reform of public policy. Such a forum can be provided by a national bioethics commission.

Establishing a national commission will build upon the government's earlier success in addressing bioethical issues. Its first concerted action came in 1966, in response to outcries about a number of biomedical studies in which researchers were found to have abused their power. The Public Health Service ordered that all federally funded research involving human beings be reviewed before start-up by an Institutional Review Board in the researcher's own institution. Although this certainly helped curb abuses, inappropriate research projects continued to come to light, and in 1973 the government took stronger steps to become an advocate and user of public bioethics. Between 1973 and 1978, Congress, the White House, and the Department of Health, Education, and Welfare (HEW)—now the Department of Health and Human Services (HHS)—cooperated to create three public bioethics bodies: the National Commission for the Protection of Human Subjects of Biomedical and Behavioral Research, an Ethics Advisory Board for the Secretary of HEW, and the President's Commission for the Study of Ethical Problems in Medicine and Biomedical and Behavioral Research.

12 These organizations had a major impact. The President's Commission, for example, issued 11 reports. The most notable supplied the ethical

premises and moral framework to reform the determination of death to include whole brain death, to formulate the evolving consensus on criteria for decisions to forgo life-supports (including artificial feeding and hydration) in incapacitated patients, and to lead the way to national policy on recombinant DNA research and the ethical aspects of human gene therapy. The commission's work was widely regarded as timely and valuable in setting public policy, and its reports are frequently used in the literature of bioethics and cited by federal and state courts.

The commission's term expired in 1983, however, and it disbanded. (The National Commission and the Ethics Advisory Board had disbanded earlier.) The commission recommended that a similar body be its successor, but political dynamics, largely due to controversy around the abortion issue, prevented it. The Reagan and Bush administrations could have continued to support a forum to debate public bioethics while maintaining a strong moral stance against abortion, embryo research, and other issues of sexuality. But rather than sponsor contentious public discussion, they chose to simply discourage or prevent those activities under federal control that were not perceived as compatible with their administrations' moral agenda. Consequently, public bioethics withered. At most, the government turned to appointing ad hoc committees for fact-finding and to make recommendations on specific issues, but this approach has proved woefully inadequate. Congress made an attempt to create a new national commission in 1990, but this also fell victim to the political power struggle surrounding abortion and related issues.

Absent an official forum for discussion of bioethics, federal officials have repeatedly and inappropriately intervened in bioethics controversies, particularly those involving human reproductive issues and sexuality. A striking example involves fetal tissue transplantation research. In 1986, neurosurgeons in the National Institutes of Health's Clinical Center proposed a project using fetal tissue transplantation in patients with Parkinson's disease. But the assistant secretary of HHS blocked the project and in 1987 imposed a moratorium on such research, maintaining that it could provide an incentive to promote elective abortions. The agency established an ad hoc committee to provide ethical guidance on the issue. The panel voted 18 to 3 in favor of supporting the research, subject to suitable guidelines. But the agency rejected the decision and continued the moratorium "indefinitely," with no public hearings or prior notice in the *Federal Register,* as required by the Administrative Procedures Act. This moratorium was lifted by President Clinton on his second day in office.

Apart from this cautionary tale about ad hoc panels, several general reasons support the creation of one standing national bioethics commission rather than relying on various ad hoc committees. In view of the large and complex bioethical agenda facing the nation, it would demand an unreasonable amount of time and effort to select, staff, and deploy enough ad hoc committees, as compared with implementing a single standing commission. More significantly, ad hoc committees must adhere to their problem-specific mandate, which may narrow the scope of ethical inquiry. A standing commission can identify principles and policy considerations that arise in a number of bioethical issues and weave them together in a larger framework. By considering several issues over time, a standing commission will enhance the quality and efficiency of its work. A crucial quality in public bioethics is appreciation for complex and diverse ethical perspectives. Commission members are more likely to develop and deploy such ethical insight by considering several issues in succession rather than only one. The ethical inquiry conducted by a standing commission is likely to be deeper and more inclusive and the final reports more wise and valuable as a result. Finally, as compared with short-lived ad hoc panels, a standing commission will enjoy more prestige in the eyes of the public and public participation could be more focused and sustained.

16   Some researchers, however, see either ad hoc committees or public bioethics commissions, which typically suggest new or revised regulations of biomedical research and health care, as needless obstructions to potentially beneficial innovations. But carefully designed regulations that limit unchecked professional autonomy constitute an acceptable and necessary price to pay to protect research subjects and patients and to ensure public accountability. It also is important to note that regulations are not, on balance, necessarily restrictive. Ethically controversial research and clinical practice may be barred entirely or exempted from government funding in the absence of acceptable regulations. It is probable that the long-standing federal ban on funding for embryo research, which has considerable potential for improving the success of fertility treatment and contributing to therapeutic developments for a variety of diseases, will not be lifted until regulations that can command a broad consensus are promulgated. Consequently, the work of a bioethics commission, by recommending regulations that gain public acceptance, can promote research and therapeutic innovations that otherwise would be obstructed by government.

Toward a National Bioethics Commission

The creation of a new national bioethics commission requires careful planning to maximize the chance that the work of public bioethics can proceed with success. Two goals should govern the commission's operation. First, it should serve the needs of government for intelligence and counsel on bioethical problems aimed at assuring public accountability and protecting the rights and welfare of individuals in research, health care, and public health. Second, it should operate as a process for examining and negotiating the different interests of medical and scientific professionals, the government, and individual patients and research subjects concerning bioethical controversies in service of the common good. Success in achieving these goals depends on the prestige of the commission, the leadership of the commission chair, the competence and integrity of commission members, the quality of the intellectual work and reports facilitated by the commission, and the readiness of government to translate recommendations, subject to appropriate modifications, into public policy.

We envision a national bioethics commission as composed of between 10 and 15 members, including representatives from law, medicine, biomedical and behavioral research, religion, the humanities, bioethics, and the public. The commission will have a set life span (as required for all government advisory bodies), but it can be renewed if deemed necessary. The commission would be assisted in fact-finding, deliberations, and report preparation by a professional staff. It would be mandated to address certain issues and would have the discretion to choose others for inquiry and recommendations. On some issues, such as research involving cognitively impaired subjects, the commission might develop detailed guidelines, with the aim of reforming operative federal regulations. These might include criteria for ethically acceptable studies with cognitively impaired subjects and procedures governing selection and informed consent of proxy decisionmakers. The commission, however, would not take on the role of review and approval of specific ethically problematic research protocols. On other issues, such as rationing health care, the commission might aim at public education by summarizing the results of relevant research, formulating standards based on ethical principles, and analyzing the competing policy options.

Fortunately, there has been significant change in the political climate, and conditions seem favorable for renewing public bioethics. Indeed, action has begun. The Clinton administration, through its Office of Science and Technology Policy, has proposed to create a National Bioethics Advisory Commission by executive order. The commission's charter was published in the *Federal Register* on Aug. 12, 1994. Following a mandatory 60-day comment period, the administration can implement the order at its discretion. HHS could fund the commission by redirecting funds, thus avoiding the congressional appropriation process.

20   In Congress, Sen. Mark Hatfield (R-Ore.) introduced a bill in 1993 to establish and define the mandate of a national bioethics commission. It would consist of 15 members, with the president, the House, and the Senate each appointing five. Another version of the bill is under discussion by Hatfield and Sen. Edward Kennedy (D-Mass.), but it has not been introduced for consideration.

Executive order is clearly the fastest way to create a new commission. Nevertheless, we believe that congressional authorization is preferable in order to create a commission with sufficient public stature and assurance of longevity. A precedent exists for taking this route in that both the National Commission and the President's Commission were established by Congress.

Congressional enactment of the commission would provide more systematic review and greater opportunity for public debate. It might gain greater bipartisan political support, and if the president is allowed to appoint some or all of the members, with the advice and consent of the Senate in selecting the chairperson and vice-chair, both branches of government could be involved. Presidential politics also might limit the longevity of a commission created by executive order. As administrations change, the commission could be dismantled by executive action as quickly as it was established. President Clinton's proposed commission would be chartered for two years, as required by law. By contrast, a congressionally mandated commission could be designed to have a longer life, perhaps to the end of the decade. If the commission's term was set by law, a new administration would replace members when their terms expired. This situation occurred with the President's Commission after the 1980 election, when members appointed by President Carter whose terms expired were replaced by members appointed by President Reagan. The commission continued to function well, with continuity of staff support, and completed its work.

If, in the current political climate, the only way to establish a commission is by executive order, then that is what should be done. In this event, we make two recommendations. The commission's charter should recommend that Congress reauthorize the commission after its initial two-year term, according to the details of whichever Senate bill gains final approval. Second, we suggest one change in the White House's proposal. The charter states that the commission's "decision to deliberate on a specific topic shall be made in consultation with the National Science and Technology Council," which is appointed by the president. A commission created by the president without the authorization of Congress and required to consult with another presidential body, would clearly be a mistake. It would compromise the commission's independence by providing too little insulation from the political process. This requirement should be dropped.

Providing a Helping Hand

24   A new national bioethics commission will, of course, confront the fiscal realities of downsizing in government today. It is unlikely to be adequately funded or staffed. For example, the White House proposal calls for a staff of six—less than one-third the size of the original President's Commission staff. For this and other reasons, we believe that the commission's work could be greatly enhanced by a new Institute for Bioethics and Public Policy, created outside government by a coalition of bioethics organizations and scholars. In fact, such an institute is needed even if a national commission does not soon materialize, given the compelling need to transfer bioethical scholarship into the public policy arena.

Assuming that a national commission is forthcoming, the institute's primary purpose would be to provide an organized intellectual resource to serve the commission and the public with ethical analysis and argument concerning issues on the commission's agenda. The institute's particular strength would be in marshaling a broad-based and diverse group of scholars to produce scholarly work in bioethics and public policy. The commission would be free to ask individual scholars to contribute papers and reports, but we believe this route alone will restrict the breadth of input vital for the commission's deliberations.

The institute also would participate, from as broad a base as possible, in the process of selecting and defining new issues for the commission's study. It could be one sounding board, among others, in deliberations about the timing and suitability of particular issues. In addition, the institute would serve as a clearinghouse for bioethics and public policy issues, collecting and disseminating documents and information relevant to the commission's tasks. The institute's staff could function as a liaison with the many and diverse bioethics organizations and scholars who will want to make their research and positions on the issues available to the commission, thus freeing a small commission staff from an important but time-consuming task.

To insure its independence, this institute should seek its funding from private foundations, whose initial support could help ensure that this initiative begins on solid footing. The institute—or a similar shared and unified forum—is critically needed by the profession of bioethics, by government policymakers, and by society as it grapples with a large and growing agenda of bioethical issues.

Personal Response

Explain whether you are persuaded by the arguments of Fletcher, Miller, and Caplan that we need a national bioethics commission.

Questions for Class or Small Group Discussion

1. Discuss your views on embryo research by addressing the questions posed in paragraph 5.

2. Discuss your views on the issues of HIV disease and AIDS by addressing the questions posed in paragraph 6.

3. Discuss your views on providing universal access to health care in light of shortages of donor organs and the high cost of health care (paragraphs 7–8).

4. What is your position on the issue of physician-assisted suicide (paragraph 9)?

5. Although Fletcher, Miller, and Caplan raise many important questions, what additional questions do you think need to be asked about this subject?

Perspectives on Bioethics

Suggestions for Synthesis

1. Drawing on at least two of the essays in this chapter, explain where you stand on one of the questions raised in them about the implications and dangers of genetics research.

2. Conduct a class forum on the ethical, social, and legal problems of the Human Genome Project and other genetics research. For a writing project, summarize the views of your classmates and state your own position on the project.

3. Invite professionals to speak to your class on the ethical, social, and legal problems of the Human Genome Project. For instance, you might invite a molecular biologist, an ethics professor, or other persons familiar with genetics research on the Human Genome Project to speak about such research. An alternative is to interview such persons. For a writing project, draw on the views of the professionals who visit your class or whom you interview as you explain your own position on the subject.

Additional Writing Topics

1. Explore the ethical questions surrounding the Human Genome Project, stating your own position on the subject.

2. Write a response to Georges B. Kutukdjian ("UNESCO and Bioethics") or Jean Dausset ("Scientific Knowledge and Human Dignity") in which you point out where you agree with him, where you disagree with him, or where you have real concerns about what he says. Be sure to state your reasons for agreeing or disagreeing.

3. Explain your views on the questions raised in "UNESCO and Bioethics" about making the results of genetic research available to everyone while protecting the rights of both researchers who make the discoveries and industries that want to profit from them.

4. Argue your position on one of these or any of the other topics raised by the essays in this chapter: physician-assisted suicide, universal health care, providing access to expensive treatments for self-induced health problems, embryo research, mandatory testing for HIV diseases, or compulsory genetic screening for certain risk groups or in premarital examinations.

Research Topics

1. Select a topic for research from "The Powers of the Gene" by Dorothy Nelkin and M. Susan Lindee. The notes to their article are an excellent starting point for sources. They list additional sources for such topics as the gene and its changing meaning, the status of genetic disease and genetic therapy, the social negotiation

of scientific knowledge, and the cultural meaning of abandoned and switched babies. Make sure that you state clearly your position on the topic you choose, explaining why you believe as you do.

2. Research the Human Genome Project, and write a paper in which you elaborate on its main objectives, provide representative views on the controversy surrounding the project, and explain your own position and why you believe as you do.

CHAPTER 18

PUBLIC HEALTH

Epidemics, pandemics, and plagues have been much dreaded realities from the very beginning of human existence. Consider such major outbreaks of disease as the bubonic plague in thirteenth- and fourteenth-century Europe, cholera epidemics in various parts of the world from time to time, including the present, the smallpox epidemic that swept Sweden in 1764, the typhus epidemic that killed more than 3 million Russians in World War I, or the influenza plague of 1918–19 that killed more than 20 million people around the world. More recently, untreatable, deadly viruses have infected certain areas of the world, worrying health officials that they may spread elsewhere. The Ebola virus in Africa, for instance, produces acute suffering in its victims, most of whom die within days of being infected. Viruses are particularly difficult to contain because they live inside our body cells, where antibiotics cannot reach them. Worse, once a person is infected with a virus, it can continue to live in the body's cells, waiting to strike again many years later.

Even such previously treatable diseases as herpes, hepatitis, and chicken pox are becoming resistant to treatment and causing deaths in increasingly higher numbers. Cases of deaths caused by herpes simplex 1 (HSV1) and related members of the herpes family, such as cytomegalovirus (CVM), chicken pox, and genital herpes (HSV2), have been reported. While certain groups such as pregnant women are particularly vulnerable to these diseases, they and other viruses pose a considerable threat to the general population. More than 3 million Americans are believed to harbor the mysterious and deadly hepatitis C virus, for instance, with even more people harboring the less mysterious but potentially life-threatening hepatitis A and hepatitis B viruses.

In "Outbreak of Fear," Geoffrey Cowley explains why viral diseases are difficult to contain and addresses the possibility of other worldwide viral epidemics. As you read the essay, consider what issues related to public health it raises and what your opinion of how they should be handled is. On a related topic, Bernard A. Weisberger, in "The Persistence of the Serpent," reviews the history of the American Social Hygiene Society (later renamed the American Social Health Association) and discusses the American public's changing attitudes toward matters associated with sex, particularly its attitude toward warning about and working to prevent sexually transmitted diseases. Before you read, think about what you already know about sexually transmitted diseases, where you learned about them, and what role you believe schools and other public institutions ought to play in disseminating such information.

The other two essays in this chapter debate two sides of the same subject: how much federal money should be allocated to AIDS research. In the first, Michael Fumento writes of his belief that too much money is dedicated to such research. In "The AIDS Lobby: Are We Giving It Too Much Money?" Fumento explains why he thinks both the general public and federal legislators are making too much of the AIDS epidemic. In sharp opposition, Naomi Freundlich in "No, Spending More on AIDS Isn't Unfair" addresses the criticisms raised by opponents of increased spending on AIDS research and offers her own counterarguments. Their strongly differing opinions on the subject may prompt you and your classmates to research the subject further and conduct your own debate on the issue.

OUTBREAK OF FEAR

Geoffrey Cowley

Geoffrey Cowley is a writer for Newsweek *magazine. In this article, written with the assistance of staff reporters in Kinshasa, Zaire, New York, Paris, and Johannesburg, Cowley reports on the deadly Ebola outbreak in central Africa. His report indicates just how serious and potentially devastating such epidemics are.*

When a 36-year-old lab technician known as Kinfumu checked into the general hospital in Kikwit, Zaire, last month, complaining of diarrhea and a fever, anyone could have mistaken his illness for the dysentery that was plaguing the city. Nurses, doctors, and nuns did what they could to help the young man. They soon saw that his disease wasn't just dysentery. Blood began oozing from every orifice in his body. Within four days he was dead. By then the illness had all but liquefied his internal organs.

That was just the beginning. The day Kinfumu died, a nurse and a nun who had cared for him fell ill. The nun was evacuated to another town 70 miles to the west where she died—but not until the contagion had spread to at least three of her fellow nuns. Two have since died. In Kikwit, the disease raged through the ranks of the hospital's staff. Inhabitants of the city began fleeing to neighboring villages. Some of the fugitives carried the deadly illness with them. Terrified health officials in Kikwit sent an urgent message to the World Health Organization. The Geneva-based group summoned expert help from around the globe: a team of experienced virus hunters composed of tropical-medicine specialists, microbiologists and other researchers. They grabbed their lab equipment and their bubble suits and clambered aboard transport planes headed for Kikwit.

Except for a handful of patients too sick to run away, the hospital was almost abandoned when the experts arrived. While the team went to work, the Zairean government tried to cordon off the city to prevent more inhabitants from spreading the contagion across the countryside—

possibly even to the sprawling slums of Kinshasa, the capital, where most of its 4.5 million people live in squalor and destitution. The quarantine was mostly a hollow announcement; it's been years since there was a functioning government in Zaire. The international doctors sent people with bullhorns through the streets pleading with residents to stay home. And they managed to get a preliminary death toll—at least 58 of 76 confirmed sufferers have now died—and rush 16 blood samples to the Atlanta-based Centers for Disease Control and Prevention for analysis. Last week the CDC announced it had linked the outbreak to a virus. It wasn't just any virus. As many experts had feared all along, it was Ebola.

4   If the word doesn't make your hair stand on end, it should. Discovered just 19 years ago, when similar outbreaks killed more than 400 people in Zaire and neighboring Sudan, the Ebola virus remains a gruesome mystery. No one knows where the virus resides in nature, how human epidemics get started or why they're so rare. We know only that the virus can spread from person to person through body secretions, and that 50 to 90 percent of the victims die in a matter of days. The first flulike symptoms typically appear within three days of infection. Then, as the virus starts replicating in earnest, the victim's capillaries clog with dead blood cells, causing the skin to bruise, blister and eventually dissolve like wet paper. By the sixth day, blood flows freely from the eyes, ears and nose, and the sufferer starts vomiting the black sludge of his disintegrating internal tissues. Death usually follows by day nine.

Ebola is a potent emblem of the microbial world's undiminished power over us. But it's not the only one. New viruses have emerged with terrifying regularity in recent decades. Most are still obscure tropical menaces with names like Machupo and Oropouche. But because they are *viral* menaces, they're largely untreatable. And the AIDS epidemic has shown us what an obscure tropical menace can make of itself when the circumstances are right. Fifteen years ago, it was unimaginable. By the end of this decade, the global number of HIV infections should reach 40 million. And despite billions of dollars spent on years of intense research, AIDS is still a death sentence.

Critical Mass

Scientists agree that AIDS won't be the last viral scourge, and that message has finally registered with the masses. Moviemakers have already churned out thrillers like "Robin Cook's Virus" (a made-for-TV movie) and "Outbreak," in which an airborne Ebola variant strikes a California town and threatens to wipe out the nation in 48 hours. And bookstores were already well stocked with nonfiction titles like Laurie Garrett's "The Coming Plague" and Richard Preston's "The Hot Zone," a novelistic account of earlier Ebola outbreaks that's been out less than a year and is already in its 21st printing. Obviously there is more at work here than concern for people in Kikwit or Kinshasa. We want to know whether Ebola is headed *our* way. Could it reach critical mass in a Third World capital, then engulf the globe? And what if Ebola somehow mutated into an airborne form? Could coughs and sneezes become the agents of mass death?

Not likely. Viruses are the ultimate parasites. Unlike bacteria, they have no life of their own. Bacteria absorb nutrients, excrete waste and reproduce by dividing; viruses are simply shreds of genetic information, encoded as DNA or RNA, that can integrate themselves into a living cell and use its machinery to run off copies of themselves. Their purpose is not to cause harm, just to replicate and spread. When a virus is more abundant in a person's saliva, for example, it stands a better chance of infecting the next person who comes into contact with that secretion, in a kiss or on a shared glass. But as Amherst College evolutionary biologist Paul Ewald has shown, microbial life involves trade-offs. If the virus multiplies too aggressively, immobilizing or killing the person carrying it (the host), it takes itself out of circulation. Viruses that can survive outside the host's body don't have to be so considerate. Once sneezed onto a tabletop, for example, they can sit and wait for another host to come along. Similarly, a virus that can travel from host to host by way of a "vector," such as a mosquito or rodent, has no stake in a particular host's well-being.

8   Man isn't Ebola's natural host. The virus occasionally infects people, but the adventure is ultimately suicidal—the victims die too quickly to infect many others. Within the walls of a Zairean hospital, an Ebola victim may be close enough to others to spread the infection. But if the hospital can employ strict infection-control measures—such as wearing gloves, gowns and masks—transmission can be thwarted. And contrary to the terrifying twist in "Outbreak," there's no reason to think that a virus normally transmitted only through body fluids would suddenly mutate and start traveling by air. In any case, even if it did become airborne, Ebola wouldn't survive more than a few minutes in the atmosphere: ultraviolet light destroys it. As deadly as it is, Ebola is ill equipped to go global, and humanity is well equipped to stop it.

Until recently, most experts thought of new viral diseases as accidents of genetic mutation. But of late, they have become less fearful of random genetic change—and more terrified by the effects of human social change. Consider the emergence of HIV-1 from sub-Saharan Africa. Many experts now assume the virus was present for decades or even centuries before it swept the globe in the 1970s and '80s. Until the 1960s, it would have had a hard time escaping the continent's isolated rural villages. But trucking and tourism brought the outside world to the countryside during that decade, while war and commerce drew villagers out into the world. Prostitution thrived along truck routes and in newly teeming cities, and for a sexually transmitted virus, the supply of hosts was suddenly limitless.

Sometimes it takes nothing more than a change in the weather to unleash a killer. In 1993, an exceptionally mild winter in the American Southwest caused an explosion of the region's native field mice population.

More people were exposed to the rodents. And consequently, some were stricken by a mouse-borne hanta virus that had never before been noticed on this continent. Fifty-five have since died, but the hanta-virus story is an exception. More often, says Stephen Morse, a virologist at Rockefeller University, human activities—from farming to urbanization and jet travel—are what speed the movement of viruses. "The primary problem," he says, "is no longer virological but social."

One way to stir up trouble is simply to encroach on a microbe's habitat. As more families have moved into rural areas of Wisconsin, for example, encephalitis from the once obscure La Crosse virus has become increasingly common among children. It's not just that the new exurbanites have placed their kids in the paths of the virus-carrying mosquitoes, says University of Wisconsin pathobiologist Thomas Yuill. They've done more than that. By sawing off hardwood trees—and letting new trunks sprout from the stumps—the newcomers have created countless small basins for the mosquitoes to breed in. Larger ecological disruptions can have more dramatic effects. Argentina's *campesinos* started plowing under grasslands and replacing them with cornfields after World War II. As a result, a field mouse known as *Calomys musculinus* thrived. And so did a virus called Junín, which survives in the rodents' urine and droppings and is easily inhaled on dust particles. By 1953, thousands of farmers were stricken with Junín each year, developing hemorrhagic fevers that kill one victim in five.

12 Urbanization has placed unprecedented numbers of people in close contact, making way for ever larger outbreaks. Without cities, we wouldn't even have diseases like measles. (To sustain a chain of transmission, the common measles virus requires access to at least 250,000 potential hosts.) And the trend toward urbanization continues unabated. At the beginning of this century, only 10 percent of the world's population lived in cities. By 2000, 50 percent will be city dwellers. "Since most of the megacities are in the developing world, where sanitation and health care are primitive," virus tracker Gerald Myers of Los Alamos National Laboratory warns, "we can expect a lot more trouble."

The cities of Zaire are a case in point. Some 44 percent of the country's estimated 43 million people live in towns and cities. Yet only 14 percent have access to clean water. The nation's urban hospitals remain breeding grounds for infection. New syringes are in short supply; sanitation is often inadequate. At the university hospital in Kinshasa, several patients share a single bed. And corpses have piled up for months in the morgue of the city's larger Mama Yemo Hospital; administrators lacked the funds to dispose of them. It's no coincidence that two of central Africa's three Ebola outbreaks have occurred in hospitals.

But who's to stop the factors contributing to viral emergence? When building a dam is the only way to grow crops, is the prospect of a new mosquito-borne illness more daunting than of famine? What experts agree on is this: by paying more attention to the openings we create for new viruses—and by keeping closer track of unusual disease outbreaks—we can wrest some control over our fate.

A first step would be to create a network of surveillance posts to monitor local health problems. If local health workers could quickly report anomalous illnesses to an international agency—and the agency had the means to respond swiftly—the next AIDS might be detected and contained before it went global. Unfortunately, local health systems are a shambles in many of the regions where surveillance is needed most. And developed countries are making little effort to pick up the slack. The U.S. military, as part of its effort to keep soldiers alive, maintains a small worldwide network of laboratories. But no U.S. agency is directly responsible for monitoring public health beyond U.S. borders.

16   To fill this perilous gap, Donald Henderson of the Johns Hopkins School of Public Health proposes that the United States and other developed countries spend $150 million a year to fund 15 surveillance clinics, located near rain forests and on the outskirts of large tropical cities, along with 10 state-of-the-art virology labs. That may sound expensive, but it is no more than the world spent to eradicate smallpox, and it's a small fraction of what a new global epidemic could cost. "We just haven't learned our lessons very well," says Dr. Joe McCormick, one of the CDC physicians who investigated the 1976 Ebola outbreaks in Zaire and Sudan. "We're going to pay now or pay later."

Personal Response

What is your view of reports such as this one that describe deadly infections or diseases over which health officials have little control? That is, do they alarm you, or do you consider yourself too far removed from where the diseases are to be affected? Explore for five to ten minutes your thoughts on this subject.

Questions for Class or Small Group Discussion

1. Cowley reports that, regarding new viral diseases, most experts now are "less fearful of random genetic change—and more terrified of the effects of human social change" (paragraph 9). Discuss your understanding of that statement. What human social changes does Cowley suggest might account for outbreaks of deadly viral infections?

2. The essay reports that some viruses are stirred into action when people "encroach on a microbe's habitat," as when they move into remote areas or saw off hardwood trees, or when "larger ecological disruptions" occur (paragraph 11). Discuss to what extent you think such activities should be curtailed or even prohibited in the face of an epidemic. In what circumstances would the health of a society in general

take precedence over individuals' rights to move where they wish and do what they want?

3. Discuss your own answers to the questions raised in paragraph 14 and your response to the suggestions for action in paragraphs 15 and 16.

4. Role-play the part of health officials on your campus responding to an outbreak of a highly contagious, deadly viral infection. What precautions would you warn college students to take? Would you close the campus and tell people to leave? Explore a number of possible responses to such an epidemic.

THE PERSISTENCE OF THE SERPENT

Bernard A. Weisberger

Bernard A. Weisberger began writing for American Heritage *in 1955, its first year of publication. A permanent contributing editor at that magazine, he is the only first-year contributor now writing a regular column for it. In his column, "In the News," Weisberger comments on a topical subject from his perspective as a historian. This essay, occasioned by the eightieth birthday of what was originally called the American Social Hygiene Association, first appeared in the November 1994 issue of* American Heritage.

It is not exactly a historical secret that sex is here to stay. But it is only in relatively recent times in this country that sexual behavior has been so openly described, depicted, and debated in the public forum. It has also become a fit subject for scholarly research; and these new studies are downright painful when they involve life-and-death matters like sexually transmitted disease, or STD, the abbreviation of current choice. When I was in my twenties, the term in use was VD—venereal disease—more euphemistic and not quite so terrifying, since the killer AIDS had yet to stalk its victims. Syphilis and gonorrhea were treatable—although if neglected, they could do extremely unpleasant things to your mind and body, as the United States Army kept reminding me and my buddies almost obsessively during World War II.

I am reminded of this topic by the arrival of a brochure noting that 1994 marks the eightieth birthday of the American Social Hygiene Association (now the American Social Health Association). I supplemented its information with Allan Brandt's *No Magic Bullet: A Social History of Venereal Disease in the United States Since 1880* (Oxford University Press, 1985). The tale they tell is important.

One of the peak years for the progressive spirit in America was 1914, and I was not surprised to learn that among ASHA's founders were many distinguished progressives from business, social work, law, education, and medicine. Participating were Jane Addams, John D. Rockefeller, Jr., David Starr Jordan, chancellor of Stanford, and Charles W. Eliot, president emeritus of Harvard, Henry James, Jr., the nephew of the novelist, Dr. Thomas Hepburn, the father of the actress, and Dr. William F. Snow (ASHA's first executive director and the grandfather of the editor of this magazine).

4   The problem that brought them together was the ravaging effect of venereal disease on "individuals, families and communities." Unknown numbers of men picked up infections from houses of prostitution, which were then an open and flourishing industry, and many of them brought syphilis and gonorrhea home to their unsuspecting wives, with disastrous medical results, including sterility in some cases and infection of their unborn children in others. Counterattack on these tragedies could take two forms: either the suppression of the "vice" that fed VD or vigorous programs of prophylaxis, prevention, and treatment. Most progressives in 1914 supported both, and few medical men then would have taken the stand of a Massachusetts physician who wanted simply to treat syphilis like any communicable disease, "leaving the academic discussion of its moral and social aspect to others."

Yet both the medical and moral approaches required breaking powerful taboos against even mentioning the subject in polite society. Solutions required enlightenment, and that was where progressives came into the picture, for it was their conviction that scientific research and publicity would conquer any hindrance to human advancement. "No evil ever flourished long in the world's history," said one, "after the limelight of knowledge had uncovered it." And so ASHA set out on a combined track: to encourage research and treatment (including chemotherapy with a brand-new drug, Neosalvarsan, an arsenic compound so effective that it was called a magic bullet) and to fight prostitution and "immoral" behavior by warning of VD's dire consequences.

What happened thereafter is an intriguing study in the interplay of the two strategies. ASHA's publicizing efforts got an early boost when the United States became involved in the war, which made it a patriotic duty to fight diseases that kept men off the firing line. The War Department initiated in 1917–18 the practical programs that reduced VD rates in France and that remained part of military life thereafter. Meanwhile, ASHA and allied organizations worked on other fronts, helping provide "wholesome" recreation for "the boys" and telling the home front, too, that VD was "the Invisible Enemy . . . the epitome of all that is unclean, malignant and menacing." A film, *Fit to Fight,* was produced, about some doughboys who fell to temptation and languished in hospitals while others kept clean for the girls back home and went on to manly triumphs. By 1919 VD seemed decidedly out of the closet, and an ASHA spokesman happily predicted that the soldiers "marching home" would "know more of the scientific and practical facts of sex hygiene than any similar group of men in the world" and pass on to their children "wholesome and sane information regarding healthful living."

Alas, it was not to be. The Roaring Twenties brought well-advertised increases in overt sexual activities but the twenties of Republican "normalcy" also brought cuts in funding for public health activities, and between the two developments VD rates rose anew. A censorious reaction blamed it all on the "revolution" in morals and manners, and anti-VD programs languished in the face of attitudes like that of the lawmaker who attacked the idea of a division of syphilis control in his state's health department because he hated its name. "I say this word is not decent," he argued, "and should not be spread among . . . the youths."

8   A defining moment in the retreat from openness came in 1934, when the New York State commissioner of public health, Dr. Thomas Parran, was told that he could not use the word *syphilis* in a radio address—and promptly refused to go on the air. But then the tide turned once more. The family breakups, vagrancy, and general poverty of the Depression years increased the number of VD infections and forced a public response in the New Deal, if only on the ground that war on economic stagnation required healthy workers. Parran himself was named U.S. Surgeon General, and ASHA continued its research, legal, and educational work, supporting such activities as community and industry drives to identify and treat gonorrhea and syphilis carriers, plus state legislation mandating blood tests before obtaining a marriage license. In 1938 Congress passed a Venereal Disease Control Act that provided federal assistance to states in carrying out anti-VD programs.

Conversion to ASHA's viewpoint was not unanimous—Roman Catholic officials, for instance, objected to the advocacy of condoms (actually avoided by ASHA); but despite pockets of resistance, government involvement in VD control continued to grow and ballooned after 1941 in the huge new campaigns to subdue vice and VD in the name of the war effort.

The 1940s brought a breakthrough when penicillin seemed to hold out the prospect of ending VD altogether—a prospect not cheering to some physicians like Dr. John Stokes, who worried that if science eliminated those diseases "without commensurate attention to the development of . . . self-control," it might be "bringing mankind to its fall instead of fulfillment." These precise sentiments had been voiced some thirty years earlier by one medical man who thought that if we could "eradicate the [venereal] diseases, we would . . . in one short generation, fall wholly under the domination of the animal passions."

Conservatives, however, had no need to fear the elimination of what we shall henceforth call STDs. By the 1960s and 1970s, after the Kinsey Report and the Pill had wrought yet another sexual revolution, new or resurgent forms of them were appearing—genital herpes, chlamydia, chancroid, human papillomavirus (HPV), or genital warts—stoutly resistant to existing antibiotics. By then ASHA, rechristened in 1960, had moved toward a more "holistic" approach consistent with the switch from "social hygiene" to "social health." It was investing more energy in collaboration with government programs to attack disorders broadly associated with STDs: drug use, promiscuity, teen-age pregnancy. But in light of the alarming increase in new infections, ASHA undertook to co-sponsor increased medical research, while it continued its tradition of spreading public information via the media as well as through a device undreamed of in 1914—the confidential STD information hot line founded in 1979, which fielded nearly two hundred thousand calls a year. Then came HIV (human immunodeficiency virus) and AIDS. An AIDS twenty-four-hour hot line was set up in 1986; it now answers about 1.5 million calls a year.

12   The AIDS epidemic itself defies a closing generalization, though the attentive reader will find that many of today's arguments about dealing with it (medically, morally, or in any other fashion) echo controversial positions struck throughout the years of ASHA's existence. The organization's birthday history, however, concludes with the game statement that its mission remains unchanged: "to bring the message about STDs home to Americans for as long as it takes, *until the problem is solved* [authors' italics].

There speaks the progressive voice, to which I listen as a historian with mixed pleasure and sadness. I cherish the survival of the spirit that insists that all problems have some reasonable solution. Without it, societies can become paralyzed by cynicism or gloom. But idealists who read history carefully can't deny that human emotions and instincts too often override reason—especially in contested areas like sex. Periods of "repression" and "liberation" may alternate, but STDs and debate over their proper treatment will go on a long time, keeping step with ASHA's hopeful endeavors.

Personal Response

Many public schools give students information about sexually transmitted diseases. What is your view of the way in which your school handled the issue? Do you feel you learned enough about the subject? Do you think your school paid enough or too much attention to the problem?

Questions for Class or Small Group Discussion

1. As Weisberger notes, the history of the American Social Health Association in part reflects the general public's attitude toward matters associated with sex. Do you think we are presently in a period of "liberation" or "repression" (paragraph 13) in attitudes toward sex and sexually transmitted diseases? How do you account for that attitude?

2. Weisberger points out that any discussion of how to handle research, education, and treatment of sexually transmitted diseases always

involves both moral and medical concerns and that both require "break-ing powerful taboos" (paragraph 5). What taboos is Weisberger refer-ring to? Does it surprise you that some doctors have believed that eradicating sexually transmitted diseases would lead to widespread promiscuity?

3. Weisberger points out in his concluding paragraph that if societies do not hold on to reasonable hope for solutions to their problems, they "can become paralyzed by cynicism or gloom." How do you and your classmates view the prospects for finding solutions for the problem of sexually transmitted diseases? Are you optimistic or pessimistic? Con-sider the attitudes of your friends and acquaintances toward sex and AIDS, for instance.

4. Discuss the AIDS epidemic in terms of the importance you think ought to be placed on moral issues as opposed to medical issues. Which do you think has priority, or are they equally important?

THE AIDS LOBBY: ARE WE GIVING IT TOO MUCH MONEY?

Michael Fumento

Michael Fumento holds degrees in political science and law and is a for-mer AIDS analyst for the U.S. Commission on Civil Rights. Forced to re-sign from the commission after he wrote an essay for the August 1988 issue of New Republic *on what he saw as alarmist views held by con-servatives, Fumento subsequently wrote* The Myth of Heterosexual AIDS: How a Tragedy Has Been Distorted by the Media and Par-tisan Politics *(1990), from which this chapter is taken.*

The evidence continues to come in that the scope of the epidemic—including its effect on homosexuals, its effect on sexually active hetero-sexuals, its effect on persons in neither category, and its effect on the economy—have been grossly overplayed. The time has come to ask whether spiraling increases in AIDS funding are justified.

It would be nice to live in a world where one could simply assign more money, more personnel, more resources in general to any given problem without worrying about any other problem being short-changed. But we live in a world of scarce resources. Money and attention devoted to one cause means resources pulled off another. And there's the rub. Clearly, there is a connection between the perception of AIDS as a world catastro-phe and the willingness to fund the campaign against it. It is not the pres-ent caseload; there are still fourteen causes of death in America that are ahead of AIDS. It was the predictions of millions or tens of millions or hun-dreds of millions of future cases that had many of us rating AIDS as the number-one health priority. As AIDS activists are well aware, to challenge those predictions could be tantamount to challenging the pouring of massive amounts of resources into the anti-AIDS fight.

Indeed, rumblings are being heard. Dr. Vincent T. DeVita, Jr., just before stepping down from his position as director of the National Cancer Institute (NCI), bemoaned the loss of resources to the AIDS industry: "[AIDS] has been an extraordinary drain on the energy of the scientific establishment. . . . It's been a big stress. It's taken a lot of intellectual energy away from the cancer program."[1] The American Heart Association, for its part, in order to trigger more donations for heart research, began running advertisements in early 1989 showing the risk of getting AIDS versus that of getting heart disease.

4   Despite the far greater health threat posed by cancer, federal AIDS funding allocated to the Public Health Service at $1,300,000,000 (of which about $400,000,000 goes to education, not research) now nearly matches cancer funding. In President Bush's budget proposal for fiscal year 1990, this figure rises to $1,600,000,000. Cancer funding, by contrast, with the AIDS portion pulled out, comes to about $1,450,000,000. Even if the AIDS epidemic kept up with the CDC projection and did not peak until 1993, AIDS cases diagnosed that year would be but a fourth of all 1993 cancer deaths. Each year a million cases of cancer are diagnosed, almost half of which end in death. This will be the case the next year and the year after that, with no peaking or decline anticipated until scientists bring one about. Heart disease kills more people than even cancer, over 750,000 Americans a year; yet funding to fight it is two thirds that of AIDS.[2]

AIDS research has now drained cancer research to a point where the NCI's ability to fund promising new research proposals is less than at any time in the past two decades. During fiscal year 1989, only 25 percent of cancer grant applications approved by review committees will receive funding. During the 1970s, between 43 percent and 60 percent of such approved grants were funded. Two top NCI doctors left the agency in 1988, partly in frustration over this. "They bled cancer to feed AIDS in terms of people's time," complained one.[3]

Perhaps we could just trade funds earmarked for F-16s or MX missiles for AIDS research, as some have suggested, but even this would not alleviate the problem that when it comes to researchers, this is pretty much

---

[1] Susan Okie, "Assessing the War on Cancer," *Washington Post,* 22 August 1988, p. A13.

[2] Spending figures are for fiscal year 1989, were allocated in the Labor, Health and Human Services and Education Appropriations Act of 1989, and were relayed to me by the Health and Human Services and Education Subcommittee. Cancer and heart disease death rates are from the Bureau of the Census.

[3] Susan Okie, "Cutbacks, AIDS Emphasis Seen Slowing Cancer Fight," *Washington Post,* 28 December 1988, p. A9.

a zero-sum game. It takes up to a decade to put a high school graduate through medical school. Thus, in the short run, AIDS researchers must come from and have come from other research areas, primarily but not exclusively cancer. In a medical newspaper editorial asking "Are We Spending Too Much Money on AIDS?" two young psychiatric researchers spoke of having to resist the "seduction" of AIDS research money. "Unfortunately," wrote the researchers, "many other young scientists may have no choice but to go into the field that offers the most easily obtained funding. If this happens, other areas of research important to the welfare of the U.S. public will be neglected for years to come."[4] One of the two retiring top NCI officials exclaimed that NCI "is withering away."[5] Further, the 1989 appropriations bill signed into law by President Reagan expressly called for hiring an additional 780 AIDS researchers. Where will they come from? They'll come from where they've *been* coming from. For non-AIDS work, the National Institutes of Health has lost almost 1,100 employees since 1984. At the same time, the number of employees engaged in AIDS work has increased by more than 400 to 580 workers or their full-time equivalents, according to *Science* magazine.[6]

Terrible as it sounds, there will never be enough researchers or money to go around. Hard decisions have to be made about what programs should be emphasized and what ones de-emphasized. AIDS has prompted a general de-emphasis of other medical problems. The blunt fact is that people will die of these other diseases because of the overemphasis on AIDS. We will never know their names, and those names will never be sewn into a giant quilt. We will never know their exact numbers. But they will die nonetheless.

8   Of course, a comparison of death counts is not the only appropriate factor in allocating funding and researchers. Another argument used to advocate massive AIDS spending is to look at federal spending for patient care; in other words, "pay me now or pay me later." But when the preceding two researchers did just that, they found that in terms of both persons affected and patient costs, direct and indirect, the toll caused by psychiatric disorders swamps that of AIDS. The ratio of AIDS research and development spending to federal patient costs is vastly out of proportion to other deadly diseases. For example, cancer research expenditures will equal about 4.5 percent of cancer patient costs. For heart disease, it is about 2.9 percent; and for Alzheimer's disease, federal research expenditures will equal less than 1 percent of federal patient costs. But with AIDS,

---

[4] Stephen Dilsaver and Jeffrey Coffman, "Are We Spending Too Much Money on AIDS?" *The Scientist* 2 (11 July 1988): 11.

[5] Okie, "Cutbacks," p. A9.

[6] William Booth, "No Longer Ignored, AIDS Funds Just Keep Growing," *Science* 242 (4880 [11 November 1988]): 859.

using a conservatively high estimate for federal patient costs, federal research expenditures will be an astounding 230 percent greater than federal patient costs for AIDS patients this year.[7]

Aside from death rates and patient costs, there may be some justification to spend more for AIDS. Perhaps AIDS research will lead to new discoveries in other areas. However, direct research is generally more efficient than spinoff research. As it happens, of the only five drugs approved for treatment of AIDS or its conditions, two (AZT and alpha interferon) are spinoffs of *cancer* research. Dr. Robert Gallo, co-discoverer of the AIDS virus, began his research as a cancer specialist. So the "overlap" argument really comes to something of a wash. Further, only about a fourth of the PHS AIDS budget goes for the kind of hard research that could even have the possibility of aiding other research. About $385 million out of the fiscal year 1989 budget of $1.3 billion. Nevertheless, perhaps a breakthrough for AIDS is closer than for other diseases. Perhaps AIDS deserves more money because it is a more horrible way to die. Perhaps it deserves more money because its victims tend to be younger than those of heart disease and cancer. Perhaps. But if the case for disproportionate AIDS spending is to be made, it must be done with realistic numbers, not projections driven by ignorance or political concerns.

Finally, such a massive increase in one area is begging for boondoggles. And while the media, undoubtedly out of a sense of national purpose, has circumspectly avoided reporting on these, they exist nonetheless. In December 1988, the National Institute of Allergies and Infectious Diseases announced two grants totaling $22,800,000 to, as the Associated Press put it, study non-IVDA heterosexuals in order to "prevent a huge new epidemic."[8] Speaking on condition of anonymity, one prominent federal epidemiologist said of the study, "I think it's complete bullshit." He said, "That amount of money is ridiculous. You can do a good study for a tenth of that amount; in fact, PHS already is. Plus, it's an area that's being studied intensively and my sense is they're not asking very good questions." He told me, "My sense was that a huge amount of money got dumped on NIAID and that by the time they got around to awarding the money a lot of good institutions had already been funded and all that was left was schlock." Alas, this "schlock" adds up to one third of the entire yearly federal allocation for Alzheimer's disease, a cruel, debilitating malady that wipes away memory and that, because people are living longer, will continue to take an ever-higher yearly toll unless medical intervention becomes possible. Indeed, if scientists do not find a way to treat Alzheimer's by the middle of the next century, there will be five times as many victims of this disease in the United States as there are now. Up to 6,000,000 older Americans will

---

[7] Figures for federal patient costs are from a personal communication with Hay.

[8] "Major AIDS Study on Drug-free Heterosexuals," AP, 16 December 1988.

be living in nursing homes, instead of the 1,000,000 there today.[9] The increased costs, of course, will be tremendous.

While writers like Randy Shilts have made an excellent case that too little was spent on the AIDS epidemic early on because its scope was understated, does that justify too much now being spent because it was subsequently overstated? Should there be an affirmative action program for AIDS spending? Put another way, while it's a tragedy that in the first two years of AIDS appropriations the federal government allocated only $34,000,000 to be spent on the disease, are we going to make amends for that by wasting $22,000,000 on a single project at this much later date?

12   Homosexuals have learned to use their victim status as a powerful lobbying tool. Their pink triangles are ubiquitous in major cities, slapped on everything from newspaper boxes to telephone booths to stoplights, with superadhesive that will probably keep some of the stickers stuck for longer than the AIDS epidemic will last. In the 1940s, the pink triangle was used to send homosexuals to German concentration camps, and often to their deaths. In the 1970s, the pink triangle became a symbol of Gay Liberation, of a demand to be treated with the same rights and respect given to heterosexuals. By the late 1980s, the pink triangle was used like an American Express Platinum Card, as a means of getting special privileges available only to the bearer. AIDS victims began the 1980s by asking to be treated no worse than victims of other fatal diseases. But within a few years they were demanding funding and other treatment far superior to that received by sufferers of any other disease.

Likewise, the problems AIDS victims had with the Food and Drug Administration were no different from the problems other disease sufferers have had for decades. The FDA has established testing procedures for all food additives and drugs. These procedures, which have been developed to ensure that these products are both safe and effective, are controversial because they can substantially delay the marketing of an important product. Nobody has established that the FDA slowed AIDS drug development any more than it had slowed up everything from life-saving beta blockers for heart disease to fat substitutes for food to a formula for growing hair. AIDS victims demanded preferential treatment. Like all special interests, the AIDS victims and their fellows wanted us to believe theirs was especially special. Yet why did the government have "blood on its hands" for AIDS, as some of the stickers claim, but for no other cause of death? It might have been because AIDS did not receive as much funding early on as it is now agreed it should have gotten. This was a strong theme in Randy Shilts's book. In hindsight, it is easy to see that much more money should have been spent much more quickly on AIDS than was the case. For that

---

[9] Daniel Perry and Robert N. Butler, "Aim Not Just for Longer Life, But Extended 'Health Span,'" *Washington Post,* 20 December 1988, p. H20.

matter, though, hindsight also tells us that those same public health authorities strongly overreacted to the swine-flu scare in the mid-1970s. But would funding have been substantially different if the afflicted had been, to use one congressman's comparison, tennis players instead of homosexuals?[10] This is something that Shilts's exhaustive research and his memos obtained under the Freedom of Information Act did not reveal. The conclusion is left more to conjecture and occasional conversational tidbits than anything else. If early funding had been made available, how greatly would this have affected the course of the epidemic? Again, this is a matter of conjecture.

AIDS advocates have said it is wrong to treat victims of this disease differently from victims of other diseases. After all, heart disease and cancer, especially lung cancer, are often behaviorally-linked as well. Nobody lectures the dying cigarette smoker, we are reminded. Fair enough. But nobody exalts him, either. If AIDS victims want to be treated as well as victims of other diseases, that is their right. But they have no right to be treated any better, either. There is no national guilt for AIDS, and there is no excuse for condescending to AIDS activists as if there were.

AIDS is a terrible disease that, even though the worst will soon be over, is not going to go away on its own. But there are many other terrible diseases that will not go away. All deserve our attention, and all their victims deserve our compassion. But compassion begins with allocating resources on the basis of where they can do the most good, not on the basis of oiling the wheel that squeaks the loudest. It is not fair to penalize victims of cancer and other life-threatening illnesses because they do not knit quilts or blockade the Golden Gate Bridge or picket magazines that say things they don't believe should be allowed in print. And lest they forget, homosexuals get cancer, too.

16   Dennis Altman, chronicler of the Gay Liberation movement, wrote in *AIDS in the Mind of America,*

> The real test posed by AIDS was expressed by Jesse Jackson in a speech to the Human Rights Campaign Fund dinner in New York in 1983 when he said: "Gay health issues, such as a cure for AIDS, *are* important. But I suggest to you this night that when you give life you gain life. If there is a commitment to health care for *whatever* the disease, based upon need and not based upon wealth or class—then within health care is encompassed the issue of AIDS. AIDS is not the only disease in the nation tonight. Be concerned about AIDS but also sickle cell. Never let it be said that you are a one-agenda, self-centered, narcissistic movement."[11]

[10] "Kaposi's Sarcoma and Related Opportunistic Infection," hearings before House of Representatives Subcommittee on Health and the Environment, 13 April 1982, p. 2, as cited in Dennis Altman, *AIDS in the Mind of America* (New York: Anchor/Doubleday, 1986), p. 113.

[11] Altman, *AIDS in the Mind of America,* p. 190.

If that was the test of AIDS, then clearly the test was failed. AIDS activists, homosexual and otherwise, have become exactly what the Reverend Jackson warned against.

Personal Response

What is your answer to the question Fumento poses in his title? Explain your reasons.

Questions for Class or Small Group Discussion

1. Summarize Fumento's argument and analyze its logic. Do you find his evidence convincing? Do you find any weaknesses in his reasoning?

2. What questions do you still have about funding the AIDS lobby after reading this essay? Do you think Fumento has taken into account all perspectives on this issue? If not, whose perspective is missing?

3. In small groups, create a scenario involving the following people and role-play their parts: an AIDS victim, a terminally ill cancer patient, a scientist seeking funds for AIDS research, a scientist seeking funds for cancer research, and the chair of the government agency that has just enough money to fund one or the other of the scientists, but not both.

NO, SPENDING MORE ON AIDS ISN'T UNFAIR

Naomi Freundlich

Naomi Freundlich is the science and technology editor for Business Week *magazine. She writes frequently on controversial topics, as in this September 1990 essay. Here, she argues strongly against the positions of people like Michael Fumento in "The AIDS Lobby: Are We Giving It Too Much Money?"*

Just a year or so ago, it would have been political suicide for a scientist, politician, or journalist to speak out against increased spending for AIDS research. After a regrettably slow start, the federal government took up the campaign in 1983 and has steadily increased research funding in an effort to curb the deadly epidemic. By the end of fiscal 1989, AIDS had garnered nearly $2.5 billion in government funds. And this year, the National Institutes of Health will kick in $740 million more. Last month, Congress allocated an additional $875 million for states to use for AIDS treatment.

Now, as activists stage protests demanding even more money for AIDS, a backlash is forming. For a few critics, the attack is a value judgment on the lifestyles of AIDS sufferers. Other critics just question whether AIDS research should be such a high priority. Politicians from rural states, for instance, complain that the funds Congress is allocating for AIDS can't be used to fight other diseases. And there is growing resentment among some cancer and other non-AIDS researchers.

They charge that a project without a mention of AIDS in the title runs an unfair risk of getting turned down. An Office of Technology Assessment report released last April [1990] shows how pervasive that feeling is. Of some 148 scientists who answered a poll on AIDS research, nearly half complained that too much funding has been diverted to AIDS. This year, some 1 million people will die of heart disease, and an additional 500,000 or so of cancer. So why, the argument goes, spend so much on a disease that has killed just 83,000 Americans in nine years?

4   It doesn't take much digging to come up with the answer. Heart disease and cancer occur at a fairly stable rate. AIDS, by contrast, is an infectious disease and can spread rapidly through a population. In fact, the number of cases is expected to triple in the U.S. by 1993. And in the next decade alone, doctors will be treating a million or more people who are already infected with HIV, the virus that leads to AIDS.

Beyond that, the most recent figures from the Centers for Disease Control in Atlanta show that the malady is no longer confined to gays and drug users. Countrywide, the ratio of men to women who carry the HIV virus has dropped from 11 to 1 early in the epidemic to close to 3 to 1 today. In some rural areas, says Dr. June E. Osborn, dean of the University of Michigan's School of Public Health and chairwoman of the National Commission on AIDS, the ratio is closer to 1 to 1. Because the number of people infected with HIV in these rural areas is growing faster than in urban centers, that raises the specter of a heterosexual epidemic such as is now sweeping parts of Africa. And unlike cancer and heart disease, which usually strike older people, AIDS is a disease of the young. Some 82% of its victims are below the age of 44—in the most productive years of their lives.

If all this isn't reason enough to fund AIDS work, there is one more factor. According to Osborn, AIDS research is yielding a wealth of knowledge about viruses, cancer, the brain, and, most important, the immune system. "We have already learned many broadly important facts about how the body works, and there have been more spin-offs for cancer and other disease than for AIDS directly," she says. For example, she adds, before AIDS, there was only speculation that the immune system helps fight off cancer. Now, boosting the body's defenses has become a key part of cancer research. The [Office of Technology Assessment] OTA report came to the same conclusion, citing benefits in public health, epidemiology, and basic science from AIDS research.

If there is a problem of scarce resources, moreover, it's not that money used for AIDS is being taken away from cancer and heart disease. It's true that the AIDS share of the NIH budget is rising rapidly. Funding for AIDS is growing 23% this fiscal year, while support for non-AIDS research is rising by only 4.4%. But William F. Raub, acting director of the NIH, says there is no guarantee that AIDS money would have gone to other diseases. More likely, it would have been used elsewhere in the federal budget, he says.

8   The problem he and others see is too little funding for biomedical research in general. The U.S. spent $600 billion last year on health care—but just 2% of it went to research on disease. Only one-quarter of the research grants submitted to NIH are now approved, compared with 60% in 1975. That's because the funding pie is growing slower than both the cost of research and the number of scientists clamoring for a slice. As a result, young investigators are less able to get research funds, and even established researchers are leaving basic science to work in industry or to practice medicine.

For many researchers and other critics, AIDS funding is a convenient target. But ultimately, the real issue is how much should be spent on biomedical research. Giving AIDS short shrift while that question is hashed out would be a tragic mistake.

Personal Response

Discussions of AIDS and its victims are often emotionally charged. Describe your own views on the disease and its victims.

Questions for Class or Small Group Discussion

1. Summarize Freundlich's argument and analyze its logic. Do you find her evidence convincing? Do you find any weaknesses in her reasoning?

2. Compare Freundlich's essay with Michael Fumento's "The AIDS Lobby: Are We Giving It Too Much Money?" Which do you think the stronger, more convincing argument? Does each make valid points? How would you resolve the conflict?

3. Comment on the various perspectives from which people view the AIDS epidemic, as Freundlich summarizes them in paragraphs 2 and 3, by stating your own feeling about each perspective and explaining the degree to which you think each is valid.

Perspectives on Public Health Issues
Suggestions for Synthesis

1. Invite a public health official or a health officer from your campus to speak to your class about epidemics such as AIDS, Ebola, and the like, as well as other issues raised by the readings in this chapter. For a writing assignment, narrow your focus to one aspect of public health and then synthesize the comments of the speaker and the opinions of the writers represented in this chapter as you explain your own view on the topic.

2. On the basis of two or more essays in this chapter, take a position on the AIDS controversy and defend it in a position paper.

3. Conduct a class debate on the issue of government spending for AIDS research. For a writing assignment, explain your own position on the subject of government spending for AIDS research, using Michael Fumento's "The AIDS Lobby: Are We Giving It Too Much Money?" and Naomi Freundlich's "No, Spending More on AIDS Isn't Unfair" as source materials.

Additional Topics for Writing or Discussion

1. Read either Randy Shilts's book *And the Band Played On: Politics, People, and the AIDS Epidemic* (1987) or Michael Fumento's book *The Myth of Heterosexual AIDS: How a Tragedy Has Been Distorted by the Media and Partisan Politics* (1990) and write a critique of it.

2. Write a letter to Michael Fumento or Naomi Freundlich in which you outline the points on which you agree or disagree with what he or she has to say about funding for AIDS research. Or, do the same thing in a formal argument.

3. If you know someone with AIDS or another grave illness, describe that person's condition, the problems it poses for the person's family, and the concerns you have about the person and the illness.

4. Read either Laurie Garrett's *The Coming Plague* or Richard Preston's *The Hot Zone* ("Outbreak of Fear," paragraph 6) and then write a summary of and thoughtful response to the book.

Research Topics

1. Research and assess the importance or success of the work of either a national health agency, such as the United States' Centers for Disease Control (CDC), or an international health agency, such as the World Health Organization (WHO).

2. Geoffrey Cowley's "Outbreak of Fear" was published in 1995. Research the Ebola epidemic to find out what the state of the epidemic is now, what measures were taken to prevent its spread, and related issues.

3. Research a major plague from the past, such as the bubonic plague in thirteenth- and fourteenth-century Europe, cholera epidemics, the smallpox epidemic that swept Sweden in 1764, the typhus epidemic that killed more than 3 million Russians in World War I, or the influenza plague of 1918–19 that killed more than 20 million people around the world. Determine the consequences for the country (countries) affected by the plague as well as possible origins of the plague and how it was finally conquered.

4. Research the AIDS epidemic and ways in which public health officials have responded to the disease. You will discover many controversies on this subject, so identify one major controversy, explore the issues involved, and arrive at your

own position on the subject. You may want to take a historical approach, for instance, by exploring various theories on the origins of AIDS; or you may want to focus on controversial treatments for the disease.

5. Do a literature search in the library on articles about AIDS published in the last year or two, select those that you feel represent conflicting viewpoints on the subject, and create an annotated bibliography in which you list the author, title, and source of each article with a brief one-paragraph synopsis or summary of it.

CHAPTER 19

ENVIRONMENTAL SCIENCES

Environmental issues such as depletion of the ozone layer, global warming, deforestation, and air and water pollution are just a few of the many causes for concern when considering the health of animal and vegetable life on Earth. Closely connected to environmental problems is the rapid rate of increase in the world population. As the number of people grows, more and more pressure is put on all of our natural resources. Will there be enough food for everyone? How can our water supplies be kept safe for drinking? How does pollution produced by so many humans affect the quality of the air we breathe? How do we stop the ever-widening hole in the ozone layer that protects us from the harmful rays of the sun? How are future generations going to sustain the rapidly increasing numbers of people worldwide? These are just some of the questions confronting scientists, civic leaders, and ordinary humans everywhere.

While most people recognize that humans must keep their environments safe, not everyone agrees on either the nature of the problems nor the severity of their consequences. For instance, resource depletion and global warming are the subjects of much debate. Researchers and scientists differ in their beliefs on such things as the earth's ability to sustain life indefinitely and whether the earth is experiencing global warming and, if so, whether such a warming is cause for alarm. Sandra Postel is one person who believes we have much cause for concern. In "Carrying Capacity: Earth's Bottom Line," she warns that Earth's resources are being depleted so rapidly that humans will soon be unable to survive on this planet. Postel cites three trends she believes have placed excessive pressures on the earth's resources and offers suggestions for reversing those trends. As you read her argument, consider the weight of her evidence and whether you find her reasoning compelling.

Wallace S. Broecker is also worried about the rapidly increasing world population, but his primary focus is on the global warming issue. In "Global Warming on Trial," Broecker reviews the development of theories about global warming and imagines a mock trial between opposing sides of the greenhouse effect debate. Consider both positions on the issue as you read his essay, and see if you agree with the conclusion he arrives at.

In the next essay, Aaron Sachs profiles the nineteenth-century scientist Baron Alexander von Humboldt in "Humboldt's Legacy and the Restoration of Science." Sachs maintains that modern science would do well to adopt Humboldt's integrated vision of nature. He laments the relatively low federal allocation for furthering our understanding of the environment, and he believes that ecologists and environmentalists should adopt a broader, interdisciplinary approach to environmental problems. The chapter ends with some practical guides to conservation in a number of areas. In Paul Hawken's "A Declaration of Sustainability," he makes suggestions of things both individuals and groups can do to help the environment. According to his subtitle, Hawken offers "twelve steps society can take to save the whole enchilada." As you read both Sachs's and Hawken's essays, think about what you already to do conserve the resources and help curb environmental problems and whether these writers persuade you to do even more.

CARRYING CAPACITY: EARTH'S BOTTOM LINE

Sandra Postel

Sandra Postel is vice president for research at the Worldwatch Institute, an independent nonprofit organization in Washington, D.C., that monitors and reports on worldwide environmental trends. Before joining Worldwatch, Postel was a consultant for a private firm on water conservation and groundwater issues. She serves as associate project director for Worldwatch Institute's annual State of the World *reports. "Carrying Capacity: Earth's Bottom Line" is excerpted from her chapter by that name in the 1994 edition of* State of the World.

It takes no stretch of the imagination to see that the human species is now an agent of change of geologic proportions. We literally move mountains to mine the earth's minerals, redirect rivers to build cities in the desert, torch forests to make way for crops and cattle, and alter the chemistry of the atmosphere in disposing of our wastes. At humanity's hand, the earth is undergoing a profound transformation—one with consequences we cannot fully grasp.

It may be the ultimate irony that in our efforts to make the earth yield more for ourselves, we are diminishing its ability to sustain life of all kinds, humans included. Signs of environmental constraints are now pervasive. Cropland is scarcely expanding any more, and a good portion of existing agricultural land is losing fertility. Grasslands have been overgrazed and fisheries overharvested, limiting the amount of additional food from these sources. Water bodies have suffered extensive depletion and pollution, severely restricting future food production and urban expansion. And natural forests—which help stabilize the climate, moderate water supplies, and harbor a majority of the planet's terrestrial biodiversity—continue to recede.

These trends are not new. Human societies have been altering the earth since they began. But the pace and scale of degradation that started about mid-century—and continues today—is historically new. The central conundrum of sustainable development is now all too apparent: population and economies grow exponentially, but the natural resources that support them do not.

4   Biologists often apply the concept of "carrying capacity" to questions of population pressures on an environment. Carrying capacity is the largest number of any given species that a habitat can support indefinitely. When that maximum sustainable population level is surpassed, the resource base begins to decline—and sometime thereafter, so does the population.

A simple but telling example of a breach of carrying capacity involved the introduction of twenty-nine reindeer to St. Matthew Island in the Bering Sea in 1944. Under favorable conditions, the herd expanded to six thousand by the summer of 1963. The following winter, however, the population crashed, leaving fewer than fifty reindeer. According to a 1968 study by biologist David R. Klein of the University of Alaska, the large herd had overgrazed the island's lichens, its main source of winter forage, and the animals faced extreme competition for limited supplies during a particularly severe winter. Klein concluded that "food supply, through its interaction with climatic factors, was the dominant population regulating mechanism for reindeer on St. Matthew Island."[1]

Of course, human interactions with the environment are far more complicated than those of reindeer on an island. The earth's capacity to support humans is determined not just by our most basic food requirements but also by our levels of consumption of a whole range of resources, by the amount of waste we generate, by the technologies we choose for our varied activities, and by our success at mobilizing to deal with major threats. In recent years, the global problems of ozone depletion and greenhouse warming have underscored the danger of overstepping the earth's ability to absorb our waste products. Less well recognized, however, are the consequences of exceeding the sustainable supply of essential resources—and how far along that course we may already be.

As a result of our population size, consumption patterns, and technology choices, we have surpassed the planet's carrying capacity. This is plainly evident by the extent to which we are damaging and depleting natural capital. The earth's environmental assets are now insufficient to sustain both our present patterns of economic activity and the life-support systems we depend on. If current trends in resource use continue and if world population grows as projected, by 2010 per capita availability of rangeland will drop by 22 percent and the fish catch by 10 percent. Together, these provide much of the world's animal protein. The per capita area of irrigated land, which now yields about a third of the global food

---

[1] David R. Klein, "The Introduction, Increase, and Crash of Reindeer on St. Matthew Island," *Journal of Wildlife Management,* April 1968.

harvest, will drop by 12 percent. And cropland area and forestland per person will shrink by 21 and 30 percent, respectively.[2]

8   The days of the frontier economy—in which abundant resources were available to propel economic growth and living standards—are over. We have entered an era in which global prosperity increasingly depends on using resources more efficiently, distributing them more equitably, and reducing consumption levels overall. Unless we accelerate this transition, powerful social tensions are likely to arise from increased competition for the scarce resources that remain. The human population will not crash wholesale as the St. Matthew Island reindeer did, but there will likely be a surge in hunger, crossborder migration, and conflict—trends already painfully evident in parts of the world.[3]

Wiser and more discriminating use of technology offers the possibility of tremendous gains in resource efficiency and productivity, helping us get more out of each hectare [2.47 acres] of land, ton of wood, or cubic meter of water. In this way, technology can help stretch the earth's capacity to support humans sustainably. Trade also has an important, though more limited role. Besides helping spread beneficial technologies, it enables one country to import ecological capital from another. Trade can thus help surmount local or regional scarcities of land, water, wood, or other resources.

In these ways, technology and trade can buy time to tackle the larger challenges of stabilizing population, reducing excessive consumption, and redistributing wealth. Unfortunately, past gains in these two areas have deluded us into thinking that any constraint can be overcome, and that we can therefore avoid the more fundamental tasks. And rather than directing technology and trade toward sustainable development, we have more often used them in ways that hasten resource depletion and degradation.

The roots of environmental damage run deep. Unless they are unearthed soon, we risk exceeding the planet's carrying capacity to such a degree that a future of economic and social decline will be impossible to avoid.

Driving Forces

12   Since mid-century, three trends have contributed most directly to the excessive pressures now being placed on the earth's natural systems—the doubling of world population, the quintupling of global economic output, and the widening gap in the distribution of income. The environmental

---

[2] The resource projections for 2010 are not predictions but extrapolations based largely on recent trends—primarily those observed from 1980 to 1990—and current knowledge of the resource base.

[3] Thomas F. Homer-Dixon et al., "Environmental Change and Violent Conflict," *Scientific American,* February 1993; Norman Myers, *Ultimate Security: The Environmental Basis of Political Security* (New York; W.W. Norton & Company, 1993).

impact of our population, now numbering 5.5 billion, has been vastly multiplied by economic and social systems that strongly favor growth and ever-rising consumption over equity and poverty alleviation; that fail to give women equal rights, education, and economic opportunity—and thereby perpetuate the conditions under which poverty and rapid population growth persist; and that do not discriminate between means of production that are environmentally sound and those that are not.

Of the three principal driving forces, the growing inequality in income between rich and poor stands out in sharpest relief. In 1960, the richest 20 percent of the world's people absorbed 70 percent of global income; by 1989 (the latest year for which comparable figures are available), the wealthy's share had climbed to nearly 83 percent. The poorest 20 percent, meanwhile, saw their share of global income drop from an already meager 2.3 percent to just 1.4 percent. The ratio of the richest fifth's share to the poorest's thus grew from 30 to 1 in 1960 to 59 to 1 in 1989. . . .

This chasm of inequity is a major cause of environmental decline: it fosters overconsumption at the top of the income ladder and persistent poverty at the bottom. By now, ample evidence shows that people at either end of the income spectrum are far more likely than those in the middle to damage the earth's ecological health—the rich because of their high consumption of energy, raw materials, and manufactured goods, and the poor because they must often cut trees, grow crops, or graze cattle in ways harmful to the earth merely to survive from one day to the next.[4]

Families in the western United States, for instance, often use as much as 3,000 liters [800 gallons] of water a day—enough to fill a bathtub twenty times. Overdevelopment of water there has contributed to the depletion of rivers and aquifers, destroyed wetlands and fisheries, and, by creating an illusion of abundance, led to excessive consumption. Meanwhile, nearly one out of every three people in the developing world—some 1.2 billion in all—lack access to a safe supply of drinking water. This contributes to the spread of debilitating disease and death, and forces women and children to trek many hours a day to collect a few jugs of water to meet their family's most basic needs.[5]

16   Disparities in food consumption are revealing as well. . . . As many as 700 million people do not eat enough to live and work at their full potential. The average African, for instance, consumes only 87 percent of the calories needed for a healthy and productive life. Meanwhile, diets in many rich countries are so laden with animal fat as to cause increased rates

---

[4] Alan Thein Durning, *How Much Is Enough? The Consumer Society and the Future of the Earth* (New York: W.W. Norton & Company, 1992); Alan Durning, *Poverty and the Environment: Reversing the Downward Spiral,* Worldwatch Paper 92 (Washington, D.C.; Worldwatch Institute, November 1989).

[5] Sandra Postel, *Last Oasis: Facing Water Scarcity* (New York: W.W. Norton & Company, 1992); 1.2 billion figure from Joseph Christmas and Carel de Rooy, "The Decade and Beyond: At a Glance," *Water International,* September 1991.

of heart disease and cancers. Moreover, the meat-intensive diets of the wealthy usurp a disproportionately large share of the earth's agricultural carrying capacity since producing one kilogram of meat takes several kilograms of grain. If everyone in the world required as much grain for their diet as the average American does, the global harvest would need to be 2.6 times greater than it is today—a highly improbable scenario.[6]

Economic growth—the second driving force—has been fueled in part by the introduction of oil onto the energy scene. Since mid-century, the global economy has expanded fivefold. As much was produced in two-and-a-half months of 1990 as in the entire year of 1950. World trade, moreover, grew even faster: exports of primary commodities and manufactured products rose elevenfold.[7]

The extent to which the overall scale of economic activity damages the earth depends largely on the technologies used and the amount of resources consumed in the process. Electricity generated by burning coal may contribute as much to economic output as an equal amount generated by wind turbines, for example, but burning coal causes far more environmental harm. A similar comparison holds for a ton of paper made from newly cut trees and a ton produced from recycled paper.

Unfortunately, economic growth has most often been of the damaging variety—powered by the extraction and consumption of fossil fuels, water, timber, minerals, and other resources. Between 1950 and 1990, the industrial roundwood harvest doubled, water use tripled, and oil production rose nearly sixfold. Environmental damage increased proportionately.[8]

20   Compounding the rises in both poverty and resource consumption related to the worsening of inequality and rapid economic expansion, population growth has added greatly to pressures on the earth's carrying capacity. The doubling of world population since 1950 has meant more or less steady increases in the number of people added to the planet each

---

[6] Number of people without enough food and percentage of necessary calories consumed by the average African from Kevin Cleaver and Gotz Schreiber, *The Population, Agriculture, and Environment Nexus in Sub-Sarahan Africa* (Washington, D.C.: World Bank, 1992); fat-laden diets in rich countries from Alan Durning and Holly Brough, *Taking Stock: Animal Farming and the Environment*. Worldwatch Paper 203 (Washington, D.C.: Worldwatch Institute, July 1991); increase in global harvest is a Worldwatch Institute estimate, based on U.S. Department of Agriculture (USDA), *World Grain Database* (unpublished printout) (Washington, D.C.: 1992), and on Population Reference Bureau (PRB), *1990 World Population Data Sheet* (Washington, D.C.: 1990).

[7] Gross world product in 1950 from Herbert R. Block. *The Planetary Product in 1980: A Creative Pause?* (Washington, D.C.: U.S. Department of State, 1981); gross world product in 1990 from International Monetary Fund (IMF), *World Economic Outlook: Interim Assessment* (Washington, D.C.: 1993); increase in value of internationally traded goods from $308 million in 1950 to $3.58 trillion in 1992 (in 1990 dollars) is a Worldwatch Institute estimate, based on IMF, Washington, D.C., unpublished data base; World Bank, Washington, D.C., unpublished data base.

[8] Industrial roundwood from United Nations, *Statistical Yearbook, 1953* (New York: 1954), and from U.N. Food and Agriculture Organization (FAO), *1991 Forest Products Yearbook* (Rome: 1993); water from Postel, op. cit. note 5; oil from American Petroleum Institute, *Basic Petroleum Data Book* (Washington, D.C.: 1992).

year. Whereas births exceeded deaths by 37 million in 1950, the net population gain in 1993 was 87 million—roughly equal to the population of Mexico. . . .

Rarely do the driving forces of environmental decline operate in isolation; more often they entangle, like a spider's web. Where people's livelihoods depend directly on the renewable resource base around them, for example, poverty, social inequity, and population growth fuel a vicious cycle in which environmental decline and worsening poverty reduce options for escaping these traps. This is plainly evident in the African Sahel, where traditional agricultural systems that depended on leaving land fallow for a time to restore its productivity have broken down under population pressures.[9]

On Burkina Faso's Mossi Plateau, for instance, some 60 percent of the arable land is under cultivation in a given year, which means it is not lying idle long enough to rejuvenate. The reduced organic content and moisture-storage capacity of the soil lowers crop productivity and makes farmers more vulnerable to drought. In addition, with firewood in scarce supply in many Sahelian countries, families often use livestock dung for fuel, which also robs the land of nutrients. The result is a lowering of the land's carrying capacity, reduced food security, greater poverty, and continued high population growth.[10]

To take another example, the U.S. government protects domestic sugar producers by keeping sugar prices at three to five times world market levels. Because of the lost market opportunity, low-cost sugarcane growers in the Philippines produce less, putting cane-cutters out of work. The inequitable distribution of cropland in the Philippines combines with rapid population growth to leave the cutters little choice but to migrate into the hills to find land to grow subsistence crops. They clear plots by deforesting the upper watershed, causing increased flooding and soil erosion, which in turn silts up reservoirs and irrigation canals downstream. Poverty deepens, the gap between the rich and poor widens, and the environment deteriorates further.[11]

The Resource Base

24   The outer limit of the planet's carrying capacity is determined by the total amount of solar energy converted into biochemical energy through plant photosynthesis minus the energy those plants use for their own life processes. This is called the earth's net primary productivity (NPP), and it is the basic food source for all life.

---

[9] IUCN-The World Conservation Union, *The IUCN Sahel Studies 1991* (Gland, Switzerland: 1992).

[10] Ibid.

[11] Maria Concepcion Cruz et al., *Population Growth, Poverty, and Environmental Stress: Frontier Migration in the Philippines and Costa Rica* (Washington, D.C.: World Resources Institute, 1992).

Prior to human impacts, the earth's forests, grasslands, and other terrestrial ecosystems had the potential to produce a net total of some 150 billion tons of organic matter per year. Stanford University biologist Peter Vitousek and his colleagues estimate, however, that humans have destroyed outright about 12 percent of the terrestrial NPP and now directly use or co-opt an additional 27 percent. Thus, one species—*Homo sapiens*—has appropriated nearly 40 percent of the terrestrial food supply, leaving only 60 percent for the millions of other land-based plants and animals.[12]

It may be tempting to infer that, at 40 percent of NPP, we are still comfortably below the ultimate limit. But this is not the case. We have appropriated the 40 percent that was easiest to acquire. It may be impossible to double our share, yet theoretically that would happen in just sixty years if our share rose in tandem with population growth. And if average resource consumption per person continues to increase, that doubling would occur much sooner.

Perhaps more important, human survival hinges on a host of environmental services provided by natural systems—from forests' regulation of the hydrological cycle to wetlands' filtering of pollutants. As we destroy, alter, or appropriate more of these natural systems for ourselves, these environmental services are compromised. At some point, the likely result is a chain reaction of environmental decline—widespread flooding and erosion brought on by deforestation, for example, or worsened drought and crop losses from desertification, or pervasive aquatic pollution and fisheries losses from wetlands destruction. The simultaneous unfolding of several such scenarios could cause unprecedented human hardship, famine, and disease. Precisely when vital thresholds will be crossed, no one can say. But as Vitousek and his colleagues note, those "who believe that limits to growth are so distant as to be of no consequence for today's decision makers appear unaware of these biological realities."[13]

28   How have we come to usurp so much of the earth's productive capacity? In our efforts to feed, clothe, house, and otherwise satisfy our ever-growing material desires, we have steadily converted diverse and complex biological systems to more uniform and simple ones that are managed for human benefit. Timber companies cleared primary forests and replaced them with monoculture pine plantations to make pulp and paper. Migrant peasants torched tropical forests in order to plant crops merely to survive. And farmers plowed the prairie grasslands of the U.S. Midwest to plant corn, creating one of the most productive agricultural regions in the world. Although these transformations have allowed more humans to be supported at a higher standard of living, they have come at

---

[12] Peter M. Vitousek et al., "Human Appropriation of the Products of Photosynthesis," *BioScience,* June 1986.

[13] Ibid.

the expense of natural systems, other plant and animal species, and ecological stability.

Continuing along this course is risky. But the flip side of the problem
is equally sobering. What do we do when we have claimed virtually all that
we can, yet our population and demands are still growing?

This is precisely the predicament we now face. Opportunities to expand our use of certain essential resources—including cropland, rangeland, fisheries, water, and forests—are severely limited, and a good share
of the resources we have already appropriated, and depend on, are losing
productivity. And unlike energy systems, where we can envisage a technically feasible shift from fossil fuels to solar-based sources, there are
no identifiable substitutes for these essential biological and water resources. . . .

Redirecting Technology

Advances in technology—which is used broadly here to mean the application of knowledge to an activity—offer at least a partial way out of our
predicament. The challenge of finding ways to meet the legitimate needs of
our growing population without further destroying the natural resource
base certainly ranks among the greatest missions humanity has ever faced.
In most cases, "appropriate" technologies will no longer be engineering
schemes, techniques, or methods that enable us to claim more of nature's
resources, but instead systems that allow us to benefit more from the resources we already have. As long as the resulting gains are directed toward bettering the environment and the lives of the less fortunate instead
of toward increased consumption by the rich, such efforts will reduce human impacts on the earth.

32   The power of technology to help meet human needs was a critical
missing piece of the world view of Thomas Malthus, the English curate
whose famous 1798 essay postulated that the growth of human population would outstrip the earth's food-producing capabilities. His prediction
was a dire one—massive famine, disease, and death. But a stream of agricultural advances combined with the productivity leaps of the Industrial
Revolution made the Malthusian nightmare fade for much of the world.

Without question, technological advances have steadily enhanced our
capacity to raise living standards. They not only helped boost food production, the main concern of Malthus, they also increased our access to
sources of water, energy, timber, and minerals. In many ways, however,
technology has proved to be a double-edged sword. Take, for example,
the chlorofluorocarbons that at first appeared to be ideal chemicals for so
many different uses. It turned out that once they reached the upper atmosphere they began destroying the ozone layer, and thus threatened life
on the planet.

Likewise, the irrigation, agricultural chemicals, and high-yielding crop
varieties that made the Green Revolution possible also depleted and

contaminated water supplies, poisoned wildlife and people, and encouraged monoculture cropping that reduced agricultural diversity. Huge driftnets boosted fish harvests but contributed to overfishing and the depletion of stocks. And manufacturing processes that rapidly turn timber into pulp and paper have fueled the loss of forests and created mountains of waste paper.

As a society, we have failed to discriminate between technologies that meet our needs in a sustainable way and those that harm the earth. We have let the market largely dictate which technologies move forward, without adjusting for its failure to take proper account of environmental damages. Now that we have exceeded the planet's carrying capacity and are rapidly running down its natural capital, such a correction is urgently needed.

36   Meeting future food needs, for instance, now depends almost entirely on raising the productivity of land and water resources. Over the last several decades, remarkable gains have been made in boosting cropland productivity. Between 1950 and 1991, world grain production rose 169 percent despite only a 17 percent increase in the area of grain harvested. An impressive 131 percent increase in average grain yield—brought about largely by Green Revolution technologies—allowed production to expand so greatly. If today's grain harvest were being produced at 1950s average yield, we would need at least twice as much land in crops as today—and pressure to turn forests and grasslands into cropland would have increased proportionately.[14]

Whether technological advances continue to raise crop yields fast enough to meet rising demand is, at the moment, an open question. Given the extent of cropland and rangeland degradation and the slowdown in irrigation expansion, it may be difficult to sustain the past pace of yield increases. Indeed, per capita grain production in 1992 was 7 percent lower than the historic peak in 1984. Whether this is a short-term phenomenon or the onset of a longer-term trend will depend on what new crop varieties and technologies reach farmers' fields and if they can overcome the yield-suppressing effects of environmental degradation. Another factor is whether agricultural policies and prices encourage farmers to invest in raising land productivity further.[15]

Currently, yields of the major grain crops are still significantly below their genetic potential, so it is possible that scientists will develop new crop varieties that can boost land productivity. They are working, for

---

[14] USDA, op. cit. note 6.

[15] 1992 grain production figure from Francis Urban, section leader, Markets and Competition, Economic Research Service, USDA, Washington, D.C., private communication, October 20, 1993; 1984 grain figure from USDA, op. cit. note 6; population figures from U.S. Bureau of the Census, in Francis Urban and Ray Nightingale, *World Population by Country and Region, 1950–1990 and Projections to 2050* (Washington, D.C.: USDA, Economic Research Service, 1993).

example, on a new strain of rice that may offer yield gains within a decade. And they have developed a wheat variety that is resistant to leaf rust disease, which could both increase yields and allow wheat to be grown in more humid regions.[16]

Gains from biotechnology may be forthcoming soon as well. According to Gabrielle Persley of the World Bank, rice varieties bioengineered for virus resistance are likely to be in farmers' fields by 1995. Wheat varieties with built-in disease and insect resistance, which could reduce crop losses to pests, are under development. And scientists are genetically engineering maize varieties for insect resistance, although no commercial field applications are expected until sometime after 2000. It remains to be seen whether these and other potential gains materialize and whether they collectively increase yields at the rates needed. The recent cutback in funding for international agricultural research centers, where much of the work on grain crops takes place, is troubling.[17]

40   Paralleling the need to raise yields, however, is the less recognized challenge of making both existing and future food production systems sustainable. A portion of our current food output is being produced by using land and water unsustainably. Unless this is corrected, food production from these areas will decline at some point.

For instance, in parts of India's Punjab, the nation's breadbasket, the high-yielding rice paddy–wheat rotation that is common requires heavy doses of agricultural chemicals and substantial amounts of irrigation water. A recent study by researchers from the University of Delhi and the World Resources Institute in Washington, D.C., found that in one Punjab district, Ludhiana, groundwater pumping exceeds recharge by one third and water tables are dropping nearly 1 meter per year. Even if water use were reduced to 80 percent of the recommended level, which would cause yields to drop an estimated 8 percent, groundwater levels would still decline by a half-meter per year. Given the importance of the Punjab to India's food production, the authors' conclusion is sobering, to say the least: "Unless production practices are developed that dramatically reduce water use, any paddy production system may be unsustainable in this region."[18]

Indeed, in many agricultural regions—including northern China, southern India (as well as the Punjab), Mexico, the western United States, parts

---

[16] Genetic yield potential from Lloyd T. Evans, *Crop Evolution, Adaptation, and Yield* (Cambridge: Cambridge University Press, 1993); new crop strains from Donald O. Mitchell and Merlinda D. Ingco, International Economics Department, *The World Food Outlook: Malthus Must Wait* (Washington, D.C.: World Bank, July 1993 [draft].

[17] Engineering of maize from Gabrielle J. Persley, *Beyond Mendel's Garden: Biotechnology in the Service of World Agriculture* (Wallingford, U.K.: CAB International, 1990); Gabrielle J. Persley, World Bank, Washington, D.C., private communications, July 1993.

[18] R.P.S. Malik and Paul Faeth, "Rice-Wheat Production in Northwest India," in Paul Faeth, ed., *Agricultural Policy and Sustainability: Case Studies from India, Chile, the Philippines, and the United States* (Washington, D.C.; World Resources Institute, 1993).

of the Middle East, and elsewhere—water may be much more of a constraint to future food production than land, crop yield potential, or most other factors. Developing and distributing technologies and practices that improve water management is critical to sustaining the food production capability we now have, much less increasing it for the future.

Water-short Israel is a front-runner in making its agricultural economy more water-efficient. Its current agricultural output could probably not have been achieved without steady advances in water management—including highly efficient drip irrigation, automated systems that apply water only when crops need it, and the setting of water allocations based on predetermined optimum water applications for each crop. The nation's success is notable: between 1951 and 1990, Israeli farmers reduced the amount of water applied to each hectare of cropland by 36 percent. This allowed the irrigated area to more than triple with only a doubling of irrigation water use.[19]

44   Whether high-tech, like the Israeli systems, or more traditional, like the vast canal schemes in much of Asia, improvements in irrigation management are critical. At the same time, technologies and methods to raise the productivity of rainfed lands are urgently needed. Particularly in dry regions, where land degradation and drought make soil and water conservation a matter of survival, improvements on many traditional methods could simultaneously raise local food production, reduce hunger, and slow environmental decline.[20]

In the Burkina Faso province of Yatenga, for example, farmers have revived a traditional technique of building simple stone lines across the slopes of their fields to reduce erosion and help store moisture in the soil. With the aid of Oxfam, a U.K.-based development organization, they improved on the earlier technique by constructing the stone walls along contour lines, using a simple water-tube device to help them determine a series of level points. The technique has raised yields by up to 50 percent, and is now being used on more than 8,000 hectares in the province.[21]

Matching the need for sustainable gains in land and water productivity is the need for improvements in the efficiency of wood use and reductions in wood and paper waste in order to reduce pressures on forests and woodlands. A beneficial timber technology is no longer one that improves logging efficiency—the number of trees cut per hour—but rather one that makes each log harvested go further. Raising the efficiency of

---

[19] Willem Van Tuijl, *Improving Water Use in Agriculture: Experiences in the Middle East and North Africa* (Washington, D.C.: World Bank, 1993).

[20] Postel, op. cit. note 5.

[21] For an overview of some traditional methods and their use, see Chris Reij, *Indigenous Soil and Water Conservation in Africa* (London: International Institute for Environment and Development, 1991); Will Critchley, *Looking after Our Land; Soil and Water Conservation in Dryland Africa* (Oxford: Oxfam, 1991).

forest product manufacturing in the United States, the world's largest wood consumer, roughly to Japanese levels would reduce U.S. timber needs by about a fourth, for instance. Together, available methods of reducing waste, increasing manufacturing efficiency, and recycling more paper could cut U.S. wood consumption in half; a serious effort to produce new wood-saving techniques would reduce it even more.[22]

With the world's paper demand projected to double by the year 2010, there may be good reason to shift production toward "treeless paper"— that made from nonwood pulp. Hemp, bamboo, jute, and kenaf are among the alternative sources of pulp. The fast-growing kenaf plant, for example, produces two to four times more pulp per hectare than southern pine, and the pulp has all of the main qualities needed for making most grades of paper. In China, more than 80 percent of all paper pulp is made from nonwood sources. Treeless paper was manufactured in forty-five countries in 1992, and accounted for 9 percent of the world's paper supply. With proper economic incentives and support for technology and market development, the use of treeless paper could expand greatly.[23]

48   These are but a few examples of the refocusing of technology that is needed. A key policy instrument for encouraging more sustainable and efficient means of production is the institution of environmental taxes, which would help correct the market's failure to include environmental harm in the pricing of products and activities. In addition, stronger criteria are needed within development institutions and aid agencies to ensure that the projects they fund are ecologically sound and sustainable.

The many past gains from technological advances might make concerns about resource constraints seem anachronistic. But as Dartmouth College professor Donella Meadows and her coauthors caution in their 1992 study *Beyond the Limits,* "the more successfully society puts off its limits through economic and technical adaptations, the more likely it is in the future to run into several of them at the same time." The wiser use of technology can only buy time—and precious time it is—to bring consumption and population growth down to sustainable levels and to distribute resources more equitably.[24]

Lightening the Load

Ship captains pay careful attention to a marking on their vessels called the Plimsoll line. If the water level rises above the Plimsoll line, the boat is too heavy and is in danger of sinking. When that happens, rearranging items on

---

[22] Sandra Postel and John C. Ryan, "Reforming Forestry," in Lester R. Brown, et al., *State of the World 1991* (New York: W. W. Norton & Company, 1991).

[23] Ed Ayres, "Making Paper without Trees," *World Watch,* September/October 1993; 9 percent figure from FAO, *Pulp and Paper Capacities 1992–1997* (Rome; 1993).

[24] Quotation from Donella H. Meadows, Dennis L. Meadows, and Jørgen Randers, *Beyond the Limits* (Post Mills, Vt.; Chelsea Green Publishing Company, 1992).

the ship will not help much. The problem is the total weight, which has surpassed the carrying capacity of the ship.[25]

Economist Herman Daly sometimes uses this analogy to underscore that the scale of human activity can reach a level that the earth's natural systems can no longer support. The ecological equivalent of the Plimsoll line may be the maximum share of the earth's biological resource base that humans can appropriate before a rapid and cascading deterioration in the planet's life-support systems is set in motion. Given the degree of resource destruction already evident, we may be close to this critical mark. The challenge, then, is to lighten our burden on the planet before "the ship" sinks.

52   More than 1,600 scientists, including the 102 Nobel laureates, underscored this point in collectively signing a "Warning to Humanity" in late 1992. It states that "No more than one or a few decades remain before the chance to avert the threats we now confront will be lost and the prospects for humanity immeasurably diminished. . . . A new ethic is required—a new attitude towards discharging our responsibility for caring for ourselves and for the earth. . . . This ethic must motivate a great movement, convincing reluctant leaders and reluctant governments and reluctant peoples themselves to effect the needed changes."[26]

A successful global effort to lighten humanity's load on the earth would directly address the three major driving forces of environmental decline—the grossly inequitable distribution of income, resource-consumptive economic growth, and rapid population growth—and would redirect technology and trade to buy time for this great movement. Although there is far too much to say about each of these challenges to be comprehensive here, some key points bear noting.

Wealth inequality may be the most intractable problem, since it has existed for millennia. The difference today, however, is that the future of both rich and poor alike hinges on reducing poverty and thereby eliminating this driving force of global environmental decline. In this way, self-interest joins ethics as a motive for redistributing wealth, and raises the chances that it might be done.

Important actions to narrow the income gap include greatly reducing Third World debt, much talked about in the eighties but still not accomplished, and focusing foreign aid, trade, and international lending policies more directly on improving the living standards of the poor. If decision makers consistently asked themselves whether a choice they were about to make would help the poorest of the poor—that 20 percent of the

---

[25] This analogy is borrowed from Herman Daly, senior economist, World Bank; Herman E. Daly, "Allocation, Distribution, and Scale: Towards an Economics That is Efficient, Just, and Sustainable," *Ecological Economics,* December 1992.

[26] Union of Concerned Scientists, "World's Leading Scientists Issue Urgent Warning to Humanity," Washington, D.C., press release, November 18, 1992.

world's people who share only 1.4 percent of the world's income—and acted only if the answer were yes, more people might break out of the poverty trap and have the opportunity to live sustainably.[27]

56   Especially in poorer countries, much could be gained from greater support for the myriad grass-roots organizations working for a better future. These groups constitute a powerful force for achieving sustainable development in its truest form—through bottom-up action by local people. In an October 1993 address at the World Bank, Kenyan environmentalist Wangari Maathai noted that among the great benefits of the Green Belt Movement, the tree planting campaign she founded, was the understanding it gave people that "no progress can be made when the environment is neglected, polluted, degraded, and overexploited. Many people have also come to appreciate that taking care of the environment is not the responsibility of only the government but of the citizens as well. This awareness is empowering and brings the environment close to the people. Only when this happens do people feel and care for the environment."[28]

A key prescription for reducing the kinds of economic growth that harm the environment is the same as that for making technology and trade more sustainable—internalizing environmental costs. If this is done through the adoption of environmental taxes, governments can avoid imposing heavier taxes overall by lowering income taxes accordingly. In addition, establishing better measures of economic accounting is critical. Since the calculations used to produce the gross national product do not account for the destruction or depletion of natural resources, this popular economic measure is extremely misleading. It tells us we are making progress even as our ecological foundations are crumbling. A better beacon to guide us toward a sustainable path is essential. The United Nations and several individual governments have been working to develop such a measure, but progress has been slow.[29]

Besides calling on political leaders to effect these changes, individuals in wealthier countries can help lighten humanity's load by voluntarily reducing their personal levels of consumption. By purchasing "greener products" for necessities and reducing discretionary consumption, the top one billion can help create ecological space for the bottom one billion to consume enough for a decent and secure life.

---

[27] External debt in developing countries from IMF, *Annual Report of the Executive Board for the Fiscal Year Ended April 30, 1993* (Washington, D.C.; 1993).

[28] Wangari Maathai, "The Green Belt Movement for Environment & Development," presented at the International Conference on Environmentally Sustainable Development, World Bank, Washington, D.C., October 1, 1993.

[29] United Nations, Statistical Division, *Integrated Environment and Economic Accounting: Handbook of National Accounting,* Studies in Methods (New York; forthcoming); Peter Bartelmus, Officer in Charge of the Environment and Energy Statistics Branch, Statistical Division of the United Nations, New York, private communication, October 21, 1993.

Personal Response

Explain whether you are persuaded that we are at the point of exceeding the earth's carrying capacity and that action must be taken immediately to reverse the damage.

Questions for Class or Small Group Discussion

1. In your own words, summarize the three trends Postel sees as having been responsible for placing excessive pressures on the earth's resources.

2. Respond to Postel's suggestions for easing the strain on the earth's resources and reversing or stemming the three trends responsible for the crisis. Can you suggest other solutions to the problem? What can individuals do?

3. Respond to this statement: "As a society, we have failed to discriminate between technologies that meet our needs in a sustainable way and those that harm the earth" (paragraph 35). Do you agree with Postel? Can you offer examples to prove her wrong?

4. Not everyone agrees that we are heading for environmental disaster. What do you think people who regard Postel and others like her as alarmists would offer to counter her arguments?

GLOBAL WARMING ON TRIAL

Wallace S. Broecker

Wallace S. Broecker is an atmospheric scientist. In this essay, which first appeared in the April 1992 issue of Natural History, *Broecker conducts a mock trial in which he presents two opposing positions on the issue of global warming.*

Jim Hansen, a climatologist at NASA's Goddard Space Institute, is convinced that the earth's temperature is rising and places the blame on the buildup of greenhouse gases in the atmosphere. Unconvinced, John Sununu, former White House chief of staff, doubts that the warming will be great enough to produce a serious threat and fears that measures to reduce the emissions would throw a wrench into the gears that drive the United States' troubled economy. During his three years at the White House, Sununu's view prevailed, and although his role in the debate has diminished, others continue to cast doubt on the reality of global warming. A new lobbying group called the Climate Council has been created to do just this.

The stakes in this debate are extremely high, for it pits society's short-term well-being against the future of all the planet's inhabitants. Our past transgressions have altered major portions of the earth's surface, but the effects have been limited. Now we can foresee the possibility that to satisfy the energy needs of an expanding human population, we will rapidly change the climate of the entire planet, with consequences for even the most remote and unspoiled regions of the globe.

The notion that certain gases could warm the planet is not new. In 1896 Svante Arrhenius, a Swedish chemist, resolved the longstanding question of how the earth's atmosphere could maintain the planet's relatively warm temperature when the oxygen and nitrogen that make up 99 percent of the atmosphere do not absorb any of the heat escaping as infrared radiation from the earth's surface into space. He discovered that even the small amounts of carbon dioxide in the atmosphere could absorb large amounts of heat. Furthermore, he reasoned that the burning of coal, oil, and natural gas could eventually release enough carbon dioxide to warm the earth.

4   Hansen and most other climatologists agree that enough greenhouse gases have accumulated in the atmosphere to make Arrhenius's prediction come true. Burning fossil fuels is not the only problem; a fifth of our emissions of carbon dioxide now come from clearing and burning forests. Scientists are also tracking a host of other greenhouse gases that emanate from a variety of human activities; the warming effect of methane, chlorofluorocarbons, and nitrous oxide combined equals that of carbon dioxide. Although the current warming from these gases may be difficult to detect against the background noise of natural climate variation, most climatologists are certain that as the gases continue to accumulate, increases in the earth's temperature will become evident even to skeptics.

The issue under debate has implications for our political and social behavior. It raises the question of whether we should renew efforts to curb population growth and reliance on fossil fuels. In other words, should the age of exponential growth initiated by the Industrial Revolution be brought to a close?

The battle lines for this particular skirmish are surprisingly well balanced. Those with concerns about global warming point to the recent report from the United Nations' Intergovernmental Plan on Climate Change, which suggests that with "business as usual," emissions of carbon dioxide by the year 2025 will be 25 percent greater than previously estimated. On the other side, the George C. Marshall Institute, a conservative think tank, published a report warning that without greenhouse gases to warm things up, the world would become cool in the next century. Stephen Schneider, a leading computer modeler of future climate change, accused Sununu of "brandishing the [Marshall] report as if he were holding a crucifix to repel a vampire."

If the reality of global warming were put on trial, each side would have trouble making its case. Jim Hansen's side could not prove beyond a reasonable doubt that carbon dioxide and the other greenhouse gases have warmed the planet. But neither could John Sununu's side prove beyond a reasonable doubt that the warming expected from greenhouse gases has not occurred.

8   To see why each side would have difficulty proving its case, let us review the arguments that might be presented at such a hearing. The primary evidence would be the temperature records that have been kept by meteorologists since the 1850s. A number of independent analyses of these measurements have reached the same basic conclusions. Over the last century the planet has warmed about one degree. This warming was especially pronounced during the last decade, which had eight of the warmest years on record, with 1990 being the hottest. While Sununu's group might question the adequacy of the geographic coverage of weather stations during the early part of the record and bicker a bit about whether the local warming produced by the growth of cities has biased some of the records, in the end they would concede that this record provides a reasonably good picture of the trend in the earth's temperature. Sununu's advocate would then counter by asking, "Isn't it strange that between about 1940 and 1975 no warming occurred?" The Hansen group would have to admit that there is no widely accepted explanation for this leveling. Sununu's advocate would continue, "Isn't it true that roughly half the warming occurred before 1940, even though almost all the emissions of carbon dioxide and other greenhouse gases have taken place after this date?" Again the Hansen group would have to admit this to be the case.

At this point, a wise judge might pose the following question to both sides: "What do we know about the temperature fluctuations that occurred prior to the Industrial Revolution?" The aim of this question would be to determine what course the earth's temperature might have taken if the atmosphere had not been polluted with greenhouse gases. The answer by both sides would have to be that instead of remaining the same as it was in 1850, the planet's temperature would have undergone natural fluctuations, which could have been as large as the changes measured over the last one hundred years. Neither side, however, would be able to supply the judge with an acceptable estimate of what would have happened to the earth's temperature without the release of greenhouse gases.

Perhaps a longer record of the earth's climate would shed light on its natural variability. The climate prior to 1850 can be reconstructed from historical records of changing ice cover on mountaintops and on the sea. The earliest evidence of this type dates from the end of the tenth century A.D., when Eric the Red first sailed from Iceland to Greenland. Ship logs written between that time and 1190 indicate that sea ice was rarely seen along the Viking sailing routes. The temperature was warm enough that grain could be grown in Iceland. At the end of the twelfth century, however, conditions deteriorated, and sea ice appeared along the Viking sailing routes during the winters. By the mid-fourteenth century, these routes were forced far to the south because of the ice, and sometime in the late fifteenth century, ships were cut off altogether from Greenland and Iceland because of severe ice conditions. As temperatures dropped, people could no longer grow grain in Iceland. The Medieval Warm had given way to the Little Ice Age.

After 1600, records of sea-ice coverage around Iceland and of the extent of mountain glaciers in the Alps improved, giving us an even better idea of recent climate change. The glaciers attracted the attention of seventeenth-century tourists, including artists whose drawings and paintings document the position of a number of major Alpine glaciers. Modern measurements show that the leading edges of these glaciers fluctuated with temperature changes over the last century. Assuming that this correlation held true throughout the Little Ice Age, the historical evidence shows a long interval of glacier expansion, and thus cold climate, lasting until 1860. During the late 1800s, a widespread recession of Alpine glaciers heralded the end of the Little Ice Age. Ridges of rock and earth bulldozed into position by the advancing ice still mark the point of maximum glacial progress into the valleys. (The glaciers are still shrinking; less than half of their 1860 volume remains.) The mild conditions that prevailed during the Medieval Warm did not return until this century.

12   The problem with all this evidence is that it represents only one region of the earth and is, in a sense, anecdotal. An informed judge might also challenge this evidence by pointing out that the northern Atlantic Ocean and its surrounding lands are warmed by powerful ocean currents, collectively known as the Great Conveyor, that transport heat away from the equator (see "The Biggest Chill," *Natural History,* October 1987). A temporary shutdown of this circulation 11,000 years ago brought about an 800-year cold period called the Younger Dryas, during which northern Europe was chilled by a whopping 12°F. Could the Little Ice Age have been brought about by a similar weakening of the Great Conveyor? If heat release from the northern Atlantic was the key factor, the Little Ice Age would have been restricted to the surrounding region, and the historical evidence from Iceland and the Alps could not be taken as an index of global temperatures.

Although records of similar duration and quality are not available from other parts of the world, we do have firm evidence that by 1850, mountain glaciers in some regions, such as New Zealand and the Andes, reached down into valleys as far as they had at any time during the last 8,000 years. Furthermore, by 1870 these glaciers had also begun their retreat. This suggests that the Little Ice Age was indeed global in extent.

The global warming that caused the demise of the Little Ice Age confuses attempts to estimate how much of the last century's warming is natural and how much has been caused by pumping greenhouse gases into the atmosphere. The Sununu side would pin as much of the blame as possible on the natural warming trend that ended the Little Ice Age, while Hansen's side would emphasize the role of the greenhouse gases. What is needed to resolve this dispute is a detailed, continuous temperature record that extends back beyond the Medieval Warm to see if cycles could be identified.

By extending these cycles into the present century, scientists could estimate the course the earth's temperature would have taken in the absence of the Industrial Revolution.

I made such an attempt in 1975, at a time when the earth' temperature seemed to have remained almost constant since the mid-1940s. Puzzled scientists were asking, "Where's the expected greenhouse warming?" I looked for the answer in the only detailed long-term record then available, which came from a deep hole bored into northern Greenland's icecap at a place called Camp Century. In the 1950s, Willi Dansgaard, a Danish geochemist, had demonstrated that the ratio of heavy to light oxygen isotopes (18 neutrons to 16 neutrons per atom, respectively) in the snow falling in polar regions reflected the air temperature. Dansgaard made measurements of oxygen isotopes in different layers of the ice core; each represented the compressed snowfall of an arctic year. His results served as a proxy for the changes in the mean annual temperature. Dansgaard and his colleagues analyzed the record to see if the temperature fluctuations were cyclic. They found indications of two cycles, one operating on an 80-year time scale and a weaker one operating on a 180-year time scale. (The Milankovitch cycles, caused by changes in the earth's orbit around the sun, operate on a much longer time scale. Ranging from 20,000 years upward, these cycles are thought to control the large swings between glacial and interglacial climates.)

16   I took Dansgaard's analysis a step further by extending his cyclic pattern into the future. When combined with the expected greenhouse warming, a most interesting result appeared. Temperatures leveled off during the 1940s and 1950s and dropped somewhat during the 1960s and 1970s. Then, in the 1980s, they began to rise sharply. If there is a natural eighty-year cycle and it was acting in conjunction with a greenhouse effect, I would explain the leveling of temperature after 1940 as follows: Dansgaard's eighty-year cycle would have produced a natural warming between 1895 and 1935 and a natural cooling from 1935 to 1975. The cooling in the second half of the cycle might have counterbalanced the fledgling greenhouse warming. After 1975, when the natural cycle turned once again, its warming effect would have been augmented by the ever stronger greenhouse phenomenon, producing a sharp upturn in temperature in the 1980s.

My exercise showed that the lack of warming between 1940 and 1975 could not be used to discount the possibility that the pollution we are pumping into the atmosphere will ultimately warm the globe. We cannot rule out this possibility until that time in the future when the predicted warming is so great that it can no longer be masked by natural temperature fluctuations. My projection suggested that a firm answer will not be available until the first decade of the next century.

While the Camp Century record seemed to provide a good method of determining how natural variations and increasing greenhouse gases were working in concert to produce the measured global temperatures, additional ice core data only created confusion. Oxygen isotope records from ice cores extracted from the Antarctica icecap and mountain glaciers in China and Peru do not follow the Camp Century ice core pattern. Even worse, oxygen isotope records from three additional Greenland ice cores differ significantly from one another and from the original Camp Century record. Perhaps the most disconcerting feature of these ice core records is that the Medieval Warm and Little Ice Age do not even stand out as major features. Local temperature variations could account for these discrepancies, but oxygen isotope ratios also depend on the season the snow falls and the source of the moisture. For these reasons, ice cores may provide good records of large changes, but the smaller ones we are looking for over the last several hundred years are obscured.

At this point, the judge would likely lose his patience and call a halt to this line of argument, saying, "while regional climate changes certainly occurred during the centuries preceding the Industrial Revolution, firm evidence for a coherent global pattern in these natural fluctuations is lacking." The judge might then suggest a different approach to settle the question of whether we are causing the earth to warm. What drives the natural changes? If we could pin down the villain, then perhaps we could say more about how temperature would have changed in the absence of the Industrial Revolution. Witnesses would point to three such mechanisms. First, the sun's energy output may have changed. Second, large volcanic eruptions may have injected enough material into the stratosphere to reflect a substantial amount of solar radiation back into space, cooling the planet. Third, the operation of the ocean-atmosphere system may have changed internally, causing the earth's temperature to wander.

20   For several centuries astronomers have been observing the cycles of the sun and trying to link them with climate patterns on earth. Sunspots, caused by knots in the sun's magnetic field, undergo cyclic change, alternating between a maximum of spots in the Northern Hemisphere and then a maximum in the Southern Hemisphere. Between these peaks, the number of sunspots drops almost to zero. A complete solar cycle takes twenty-two years. With satellites, astronomers have been able to directly monitor the sun's energy output over the last cycles. Although the energy seems to dip slightly when sunspots disappear, the change seems too small to greatly alter the earth's temperature.

An intriguing proposal was recently made in this regard. Two Danish meteorologists, Eigil Friss-Christensen and Knud Lassen, point out that over the last 130 years for which observations are available, the sunspot cycle has lengthened and shortened with a periodicity of about 80 years, and that these changes closely parallel the earth's temperature. The Danes suggest that during intervals when the sunspot cycle is longer than average, the sun's energy output is a bit lower, and that when the cycle is shorter, the energy output is higher. Could it be that Dansgaard was correct in thinking that the earth's temperature changes on an eighty-year time scale and that these changes are driven by the sun? Most scientists remain skeptical because no physical mechanism has been proposed tying solar output to the length of the sunspot cycle. Others say that the strong similarity between the length of the sunspot cycle and the earth's temperature could be a coincidence.

In addition to the twenty-two-year solar cycle, however, change on a longer time scale has been documented. Between 1660 and 1720, sunspots disappeared altogether. Auroras, which are created when charged particles driven out from the sunspots enter the earth's upper atmosphere, were also absent from the skies during this period. Further, we know from measurements of carbon 14 in tree rings that this radioactive element, produced by cosmic rays bombarding the atmosphere, increased substantially during this time. Normally, charged particles streaming outward from sunspots create a magnetic shield that deflects cosmic rays away from the earth and the inner planets. From 1660 to 1720, this magnetic shield failed, permitting a larger number of cosmic rays to strike our atmosphere and form an unusually large number of radioactive carbon atoms.

From the record of radiocarbon locked up in tree rings, we can identify two even earlier periods of reduced sunspot activity: the Wolf sunspot minimum, from about 1260 to about 1320, and the Spörer sunspot minimum, from about 1400 to 1540. These three periods span a major portion of the Little Ice Age, but the last ended more than a hundred years before the Little Ice Age did—too long a time lag. This mismatch in timing and the small change in the sun's energy output (as measured by satellites over the last solar cycle) make a link between the Little Ice Age and the absence of sunspots unlikely. But the partial match prevents a firm rejection of the sun as a cause of the earth's natural temperature changes.

24   What about volcanic eruptions? Major volcanic eruptions occur roughly once per decade. Most have little effect on the climate, but occasionally an eruption blasts a large volume of sulfur dioxide high into the stratosphere. Within a month or two, the sulfur dioxide is transformed into droplets of sulfuric acid, which remain aloft in the stratosphere for a year or more. These tiny spheres reflect sunlight away from the earth, cooling the planet. Hansen and his colleagues predict that the recent eruption of Mount Pinatubo in the Philippines (which shot more sulfur dioxide into the upper atmosphere than any other eruption this century) will cool the planet about one degree Fahrenheit over the next two years.

Could the Little Ice Age have been caused by 500 years of intense volcanism releasing copious amounts of sulfur dioxide? This seems implausible, as the world's 100 or so major volcanoes erupt independently of one another and no mechanism exists that could cause them all to erupt with great frequency. Therefore, the chance is slim that one long interval would be followed by a similar period of lesser activity.

Fortunately, a record is available in ice cores to check this assumption. When the droplets of sulfuric acid from a volcanic eruption drift down from the stratosphere, they are quickly incorporated into raindrops and snowflakes and carried to the earth's surface. So, in the years immediately following a major volcanic eruption, snow layers rich in sulfuric acid are deposited on all the world's icecaps. An ice core taken from the Dye 3 site in southern Greenland reveals that at about the time of the transition from the Medieval Warm to the Little Ice Age the acid content in the ice doubled. On the other hand, low acidity from 1750 to 1780 (during a time of cold weather) and the relatively high acidity from 1870 to 1920 (when the climate was warming) do not fit the pattern of climate change. Therefore, no strong correlation exists between the trends in volcanic sulfur dioxide and the trend in the earth's temperature.

The last of the three mechanisms that might account for the natural variations in the earth's temperature is a dramatic shift in the way the planet's ocean and wind currents operate. Of the three mechanisms, this one is the hardest to build a case around because we have only a rudimentary understanding of how the interacting elements of the earth's climate system might cause natural fluctuations in temperature. The only well-documented example of such a mechanism is the El Niño cycle, in which winds and ocean currents cause the temperatures of the surface waters of the eastern equatorial Pacific to alternate between warm and cold. The cycle was first noticed because of the severe drops in fish production along the west coast of South America during the warm episodes. Since the timing between these disruptive events ranges from three to seven years, scientists became interested in predicting their arrival. What emerged from these studies is that El Niño cycles are the product of a complex interaction between winds and ocean currents. The importance of this discovery to the global warming debate is that it raises the possibility that cycles involving larger-scale interactions between the atmosphere and oceans—over longer periods—may play an important role. If the earth's temperature is being pushed up and down by such an internal cycle, our chances of determining what would have happened in the absence of the extra greenhouse gases are indeed slim.

28   Again the judge would become restive and call a halt to this line of evidence as well. At this point he would likely dismiss the case and suggest that the litigants return a decade from now when additional evidence regarding the warming trend has accumulated.

Sununu would deem this decision a victory, for it would provide an excuse to delay actions directed toward reductions in carbon dioxide emissions. On the other hand, Hansen could surely maintain that in the absence of proof that the world is not warming at the rate predicted by computer simulations, we should follow the standard applied to other environmental threats and rule on the side of caution. Instead of placing the burden of proof on the environmentalists, the proponents of "business as usual" should be obliged to prove that the unfettered release of greenhouse gases will *not* significantly warm the planet. And such proof does not exist; the balance of scientific opinion is that business as usual will alter the climate.

The debate over global warming is merely a small skirmish that marks the beginning of a far broader war. Many of the things that we could do to curb the buildup of greenhouse gases—such as conserving energy, switching to renewable energy sources, or increasing our use of nuclear power—will be stopgap measures if the underlying problem of population growth is not addressed. World population is now 5.5 billion and growing by about 1.8 percent every year. If this rate is not substantially reduced, world population will double by the year 2030. If by that time the rate of population growth has not been greatly reduced, we run the risk that the population will skyrocket to 20 billion or more before it finally levels off. Each additional person adds to the pressure to increase the use of fossil fuels, pumping ever larger amounts of carbon dioxide into the atmosphere. In countries such as the United States and Canada, where per capita energy consumption is the highest in the world, each person, on average, adds twenty tons of carbon dioxide a year to the atmosphere. In developing countries, where most of the population growth will occur, per capita energy consumption is much smaller, with less than three tons of carbon dioxide emitted per person. But as these countries strive to better the lot of their citizens through industrialization, their energy demands will climb. Most of the increase will be met by burning fossil fuels, particularly coal, which releases more carbon dioxide per unit of energy produced than oil or gas. Therefore, annual emissions of greenhouse gases are likely to increase.

We are rapidly approaching a limit beyond which we cannot maintain our numbers without long-term damage to our planet's environment and its remaining wildlife and to the quality of life of its human populations. While Sununu may be particularly shortsighted with regard to the effects of greenhouse gases on the climate, most of the world's leaders are shortsighted with regard to the population problem. They seem to ignore it completely. I hope the concern about global warming will force us to develop a broader perspective of our planet's future—one that will include the reality of the population bomb. Only then will we be able to begin the extraordinarily difficult task of defusing it.

Personal Response

If you were the judge in this hypothetical trial, what additional questions would you ask? Do you agree that the evidence for either side is not compelling enough to make a decision at this time?

Questions for Class or Small Group Discussion

1. Broecker remarks that the debate on the global warming issue "pits society's short-term well-being against the future of all the planet's inhabitants" (paragraph 2). Do you think that is a fair assessment of the debate?

2. To what extent do you think pressure from lobbyists should influence the thinking of legislators considering measures that would tighten regulations on environmental issues?

3. Summarize in your own words the arguments on both sides in this hypothetical trial.

4. In light of the lack of clear evidence supporting either side in the debate on global warming, do you agree with Sununu that there is reason to delay action on reducing carbon dioxide emissions, or do you side with Hansen, who believes we must proceed as if such emissions were responsible for global warming (paragraph 29)?

5. Conduct your own mock trial on the global warming issue. Divide your class into thirds with one group taking the side of Sununu and his supporters, another the side of Hansen and his supporters, and the third the position of the judge.

6. Broecker ends with the hope that we pay attention to the ultimately larger burden on the earth's resources, the rapidly increasing global population. Discuss ways to curb the world's population, especially in countries where poverty and women's unequal status result in high population growth rates.

HUMBOLDT'S LEGACY AND THE RESTORATION OF SCIENCE

Aaron Sachs

Aaron Sachs is a research associate at Worldwatch Institute. He is coauthor of State of the World 1995. *In this essay from the March/April 1995 issue of* World Watch *magazine, Sachs profiles early-nineteenth-century scientist Baron Alexander von Humboldt and suggests that modern science would do well to adopt his integrated vision of nature.*

On September 15, 1869, the *New York Times* ran a one-word headline: "HUMBOLDT." Every literate American knew the name. "The One Hundredth Birthday of the Philosopher," explained the subtitle. "Celebration Generally Throughout the Country." The story took up the entire front page.

It is unthinkable today that Americans would celebrate the birthday of any dead philosopher, let alone a foreign one. Yet from San Francisco to Peoria to New York, on that Tuesday afternoon, people read speeches, unrolled banners, and unveiled statues in honor of the late Baron Alexander von Humboldt. Of course, Humboldt was much more than a philosopher: he was also an explorer, a geographer, a writer, a naturalist—and the man most responsible for bringing the practice of science into mainstream western culture.

The word "scientist" first entered the English language in the 1830's, specifically in reference to Humboldt and his disciples—Charles Darwin among them. Originally, then, the term meant "natural scientist." The new profession Humboldt had carved out and popularized took as its goal the transformation of natural history studies, to cover not just the detailed cataloging of the phenomena of the physical world but also the formulation of a grand, unifying theory that would link all those phenomena together. Humboldt wanted to know what tied the rivers to the trees, how climate influenced vegetation, why particular animals thrived only in particular habitats; he also wanted to reveal humanity's place within these interdependent relationships. And in an early 19th-century culture of amateur naturalists obsessed with the romance of the wilderness, his quest struck many chords.

4   Initially, Humboldt earned his fame by exploring the New World between 1799 and 1804, when he surveyed the headwaters of the Orinoco in the jungles of Venezuela and scaled the Andes to heights never before attained in any of the world's mountain ranges. On that trip, between the ages of 30 and 35, the "Rediscoverer of America" witnessed the immense diversity of humanity and nature. He saw just how different life was among the natives of the Venezuelan rainforest and the politicians of the newly formed U.S. Congress—among the insects swarming in marshlands along the Colombian coast and the birds floating above Ecuadorean volcanoes and the wildflowers lining fertile Cuban valleys. Yet he never wavered in his belief that there existed a "chain of connection," that all elements of earthly life, including humans, were "mutually dependent"—and that a knowledge of that interdependence was the "noblest and most important result" of all scientific inquiry. For the last 55 years of his life—he lived to age 90—he struggled to "recognize unity in the vast diversity of physical phenomena." While acknowledging the world's chaos, he saw within it what the ancient Greeks called a *kosmos,* a beautifully ordered and harmonious system, and he coined the modern word "cosmos" to use as the title of his final, multivolume work—a book Walt Whitman kept on his desk as he was writing *Leaves of Grass.*

Today, most environmentalists would be shocked to learn that nature's interrelationships were once in the mainstream of scientific thought. The dominant theme in science over the past century has been *fission,* the breaking down of life and matter and ideas into their smaller components: life science and its organic theories have given way to specialization, to microbiology and nuclear physics. In our rush to gain in-depth knowledge about particular elements of a complicated, seemingly chaotic world, we have tacitly decided that it would be futile to try to tie those elements together. Science has lost its delicate balance between chaos and cosmos, between diversity and unity.

It now seems clear that this century-old imbalance is inextricably linked to our global ecological crisis. If we assume that the world on which we depend is utterly chaotic, there is no reason to do anything but try to control and conquer it—which has become science's new goal. And though specialization has proved itself invaluable in the pursuit of knowledge, its narrow, short-range focus, in the absence of a complementary organic approach, is extremely dangerous. We have directed society's accumulated scientific knowledge toward constantly improving our exploitation of each individual natural resource, without recognizing the threat we are posing to the basic ecosystems that create those resources. As Rachel Carson observed in her classic *Silent Spring,* we failed to predict the environmental impacts of extensive pesticide use because chemical companies paid researchers simply to kill pests—and not to worry about the pesticides' effects on other plants and animals, or groundwater supplies, or farmworkers' lungs. Perhaps the highest goal of the environmental movement, then, is to reclaim science, to ensure that we use it not for the domination of nature but for the appreciation of our connectedness to it—to restore, in other words, the legacy that Humboldt tried to leave us.

In the 19th century, Humboldt's appeal was wide-ranging. Many people saw him as the world's historian, the man who would explain where we came from and how we fit into the universe. He provided an enthralled public with glimpses of exotic natural worlds they would never see for themselves. Scholars flocked to his study in Germany to soak up his wisdom, to examine his field notes and sprawling maps and native artifacts. And laypeople gathered at the newly opened natural history museums to which Humboldt had donated his famous collections of intricate jungle plants and multi-colored birds. By organizing lectures and workshops all over the world, he made huge numbers of people feel involved in the progress of science. Moreover, his theories themselves were attractive for their inclusiveness, their ambitious attempts at painting a unified picture of all the world's complexities.

8   Just as every lowly plant and minute insect had a crucial role in Humboldt's vision of the world, so too did every type of human being, no matter how powerless or marginalized. Humboldt was a hero to Simon Bolivar, who used the scientist's writings in his campaigns for Latin American independence, to help prove that colonialism was wreaking havoc on both the people and the environment of the New World. And Humboldt was especially popular among Americans, by the time of the 1869 centennial, because he had been one of the world's most outspoken opponents of slavery. "In maintaining the unity of the human race," he had written, "we also reject the disagreeable assumption of superior and inferior peoples." Four years after the end of the Civil War, Americans found in Humboldt's scientific work a parallel to the political heroism of President Lincoln. Both men had staked everything on the concept of Union.

In 1869, Humboldt was as well known and respected, globally, as Lincoln and Bolivar; he had been as influential in 19th-century science as Beethoven had been in music, as Napoleon had been in politics. Darwin once wrote that "my whole career is due to having read and reread" Humboldt's *Personal Narrative to the Equinoctial Regions of America,* and he often sent his manuscripts to the older scientist for comment. When the great theoretician of evolution set off on his voyage aboard *The Beagle,* he brought with him only three books: the Bible, a copy of Milton, and Humboldt's *Narrative.* Humboldt's magnum opus, *Cosmos,* bore the daunting subtitle, "A Sketch of a Physical Description of the Universe," and it had an index that ran to more than 1,000 pages. But it was translated into all the major languages and sold hundreds of thousands of copies. "The demand is epoch-making," Humboldt's publisher claimed. "Book parcels destined for London and St. Petersburg were torn out of our hands by agents who wanted their orders filled for the bookstores in Vienna and Hamburg." Science, it seems, could easily have gone in the direction Humboldt was taking it.

Today, Humboldt's name is woven tightly into our geographical fabric: the index of a good atlas might list it some 25 times, referring not only to towns like Humboldt, Iowa, and Humboldt, South Dakota, but also to the Humboldt Mountains in China, Venezuela, and Nevada; the Humboldt Current off the coast of Peru; and even a Humboldt Glacier in Greenland. But almost no one today has any idea who Humboldt was.

Science, and Western society in general, underwent a huge transformation toward the end of the 19th century. In 1859, Humboldt died, Darwin published *On the Origin of Species,* and the modern age was born— though the full implications of evolution did not become clear until 1871, when Darwin delivered the ultimate comeuppance of his own species in *The Descent of Man.* The theory of evolution was revolutionary both because it directly undermined the centuries-old assumption that there was a divine plan separating human beings from the lowly animals, and because it posed a significant threat to the dearly held Humboldtian notion that nature was fundamentally a harmonious, unified entity. To most educated Westerners, the Darwinian concept of "the struggle for existence" meant that humanity's origins were steeped in animal violence and conflict—that the different facets of nature were not working together to form an organic whole but were competing with each other, fighting over ecological niches, fighting just to survive.

12   The one redeeming element of Darwinism, for many shocked Victorians, was that their civilization had at least seemed to come out of the competition victorious. In the hands of so-called Social Darwinists, "the struggle for existence" became "the survival of the fittest," and theorizers were quick to assert that Darwin's explanation of biological fitness proved the superiority of white, Christian Europeans. After all, they argued, a

careful reading of *On the Origin of Species* revealed that the successful animals were those that had bodies perfectly designed to perform a particular function or adapt to a particular environment. The key to a species' success, in other words, was *specialization*—a word Darwin probably coined in the 1840s. And Europeans were without question becoming the world's experts in specialization.

By the second half of the 19th century, specialization was beginning to seep into almost every aspect of Western culture and thought. Graduate schools were offering highly specialized training in narrow professions. Huge new businesses were dividing their production processes into the smallest possible components, with the aim of improving efficiency and becoming more fit competitors in the capitalist economy. Laborers no longer saw products through from start to finish, but rather performed their one limited function, over and over again. By the turn of the century, someone had to coin the term "Renaissance man" to refer to that rare person who hearkened back to the era before intense specialization was the norm, back when most people cultivated a variety of linked interests and skills.

Gradually, Humboldt's bigger picture came to seem neither appealing nor important, since specialization was paying off so well by making labor and the exploitation of nature so much more efficient. Now, Darwinists reasoned, man might be on his way to breaking his connections with animal savagery and freeing himself from all the other harsh forces of nature. Evolutionary progress came to mean the conquest of the natural world by science and technology, and distancing oneself from nature became a cultural imperative. Survival depended on winning an all-out competition with other living things—including other members of our own species. And knowledge depended on the ability to observe nature purely as object, as something unrelated to us and best understood when broken down mechanistically into its smallest components.

The embrace of Darwinism and the transformation of science, then, went hand in hand with rapid industrialization, the rise of free-market capitalism, and the expansion of colonialism. Social Darwinists defended empire-building on the grounds that vigorous self-aggrandizement was only natural. And they used similar arguments to validate their racism: the affluence and technological prowess of the Western world, they argued, proved that the races and nations of the "Third World" really were "less developed." As C. S. Lewis, the British writer and critic, once pointed out, the ironies of this new world order ran deep: "At the moment, then, of man's victory over nature, we find the whole human race subjected to some individual men, and individuals subjected to that in themselves which is purely 'natural'—to their irrational impulses." The leaders of a culture that worshipped civilization and science were calmly calling for the massacre or repression of several indigenous nations in the Americas, the methodical deforestation of the United States, and the military invasion of most of Africa.

16   Of course, given Humboldt's direct influence on Darwin, there had to be elements of the theory of evolution that hearkened back to the elder scientist's approach. Indeed, the most significant implication of the *Origin* may have been its assertion that man, on the most fundamental level, was but a part of nature—as Humboldt had argued for decades. Some 19th-century thinkers, accordingly, managed to find in evolutionary theory a spirit of cooperation and union. To the author and naturalist W. H. Hudson, for instance, Darwin's work mean that "we are no longer isolated, standing like starry visitors on a mountain-top, surveying life from the outside; but are on a level with and part and parcel of it."

Darwin was fascinated with the idea of nature as a "web"—"we may all be netted together," he mused in the late 1830s—and strong ecological currents run through many of his early writings. The world "oecologie" was in fact coined in 1866 by Germany's foremost Darwinian scientist, Ernst Haeckel. And when Haeckel defined his new scientific discipline, he invoked his mentor by name: ecology, he explained, was "the body of knowledge concerning the economy of nature . . . , the study of all those complex interrelations referred to by Darwin."

In the end, however, Darwin chose to focus on the violent, competitive aspects of his theory. He was explicitly lending his support to the colonialist ethic when he asserted the evolutionary doctrine that an "endless number of lower races" had to be "beaten and supplanted" by "the higher civilized races." Such competitive replacement was inevitable, Darwin argued, because niches in the economy of nature were only so big—as he had learned from the work of the Reverend Thomas Malthus. To Darwin, Malthus's 1798 *Essay on Population* proved that no species could rely on the myth of nature's abundance. Since our population seems to grow at a much faster rate than our food supply, Malthus argued, human society is destined to face starvation on a massive scale. Darwin made this doomsday theme the engine of his theory of evolution: crises caused by environmental constraints brutally forced out the species that could not compete. He considered it part of his mission to convince naive Romantics that, in the words of the evolutionary biologist Stephen Jay Gould, "we should never have sought solace or moral instruction in Nature."

Humboldt, conversely, held up the natural world as a model, as something worthy of our ultimate respect. In his writings, he sought "to depict the contemplation of natural objects as a means of exciting a pure love of nature." Yet he was no naive Romantic. Just as Darwin recognized the organicist ecological perspective, so too did Humboldt recognize the elements of violence, competition, and disunity in nature. After all, he had cut his way through the swarming, dripping jungles of South America, had witnessed such bizarre events as the mass electrocution of several horses by a colony of eels—and he had seen men enslaving other men. While Darwin focused on the disunity, though, and the specialized adaptations of species to local environments, Humboldt focused on the unity, and the global forces that link different environments and their inhabitants together. Both perspectives reveal important truths. Humboldt's ideas were marginalized simply because Darwin's were more fit in the late 19th century—because Darwinism in effect captured the essence of the modernizing Western world.

20   In general, Humboldt's work is still marginalized, but where it is known, experts accept it as good, hard science. One representative contribution he made to the development of ecology was his theory relating the geographical distribution of plants to the effects of climate—a radical idea that remains a cornerstone of our understanding of plant ecosystems. At the base of peaks like Mount Chimborazo in the Ecuadorean Andes, he found the vines and bright orchids and tall hardwoods of the rainforest, while on the snowclad summit he found only the hardiest mosses and lichens. On mountain after mountain, vegetation got sparser at higher altitudes, as if during his ascent he were walking from the equator to one of the poles: vertical geography mirrored horizontal geography. Humboldt was the first to classify forests as tropical, temperate, or boreal. Climate, he realized, seemed to govern the development of life everywhere; all plants and animals were "subject to the same laws" of temperature.

Humboldt had traveled to a continent less touched by human influence in order to look into the past and discover the forces that had shaped nature into its present form. "In the New World," he wrote, "man and his productions almost disappear amidst the stupendous display of wild, and gigantic nature. . . . On no other part of the globe is [the naturalist] called upon more powerfully to raise himself to general ideas on the cause of phenomena and their mutual connection." This historical technique and his "habit of viewing the Globe as a great whole" allowed Humboldt to identify climate as a unifying global force, proving, in a sense, that we all live under the same roof. Changes in one locale, he pointed out, might cause, or at least signal, changes somewhere else. And by drawing lines on the map connecting points with the same mean temperature—he coined the word "isotherm"—he established permanent scientific structures that would enable future generations to think globally. Humboldt's innovations in the field of comparative climatology underlie current attempts to understand the threat of global warming.

Long before any suspicion of change in the atmosphere, Humboldt was worrying about the effect of humanity's actions on terra firma; his knowledge of ecology translated into a nascent environmentalism. Again, the New World taught him an important lesson. European systems of commerce insulated the wealthy from the ecological consequences of their consumption, but the less developed economies of the Americas could not hide their dependence on surrounding natural systems. A year in Mexico, for instance, showed Humboldt that "the produce of the earth is in fact the sole basis of permanent opulence"—and that we could not afford to use that produce wastefully.

Studying a lake in Venezuela, Humboldt used his ecological perspective to relate the lake's decline to the deforestation of the surrounding watershed. Once deprived of the trees' root systems, he explained, the surrounding soils had a greatly diminished capacity for water retention, so they could no longer recharge the springs that fed the lake. And, meanwhile, because the area was deforested, "the waters falling in rain are no longer impeded in their course; and instead of slowly augmenting the level of the rivers by progressive filtrations, they furrow [the hillsides with] sudden inundations," causing widespread soil erosion. "Hence it results that the destruction of the forests, the want of permanent springs, and the existence of torrents are three phenomena closely connected together." Humboldt saw the social consequences as well: "by felling trees . . . , men in every climate prepare at once two calamities for future generations: the want of fuel and a scarcity of water."

24   Humboldt's fear of resource scarcity reflects his own reading of Malthus's essay, which he called "one of the most profound works of political economy ever written." Yet Humboldt's analysis of environmental limits was far more sophisticated than Malthus's: to Humboldt, increases in resource consumption reflected not inevitable demographic pressures but simple, conscious decisions. If our population increased to several billion, then perhaps our basic needs might become too much for the earth to handle, but Humboldt realized that the resource scarcities of his own day were caused by overconsumption and mismanagement. Those trees in Venezuela didn't have to be chopped down.

Even more radical was Humboldt's interest in linking such problems to the injustices of colonialism. In his analysis of the resource base of Mexico, which he published as *A Political Essay on the Kingdom of New Spain*—and which ventured into the fields of demography, medicine, anthropology, sociology, political science, economics, agriculture, biology, geology, and geography—Humboldt took great pains to show that it was not necessary for so many Mexicans to go without land and food. His multi-faceted approach helped him to see that such outrages were being driven not by population pressures but by basic socio-economic structures. Many peasants were landless, he explained, because "the property in New Spain . . . is in a great measure in the hands of a few powerful families who have gradually absorbed the smaller estates." And impoverished Mexicans were starving because wealthy landlords grew cash crops for export instead of food crops for domestic consumption. "Whenever the soil can produce both indigo and maize," Humboldt noted indignantly, "the former prevails over the latter, although the general interest requires that a preference be given to those vegetables which supply nourishment to man over those which are merely objects of exchange with strangers."

Humboldt was still a man of his time: in general, he approved of the development of the New World, and he never openly demanded that the Spanish American colonies receive full independence. But his interdisplinary research did lead him to a scathing critique of colonialism. With the conviction of one who knows his subject thoroughly, Humboldt asserted that "the restless and suspicious colonial policies of the nations of Europe . . . have thrown insurmountable obstacles in the way of the . . . prosperity of their distant possessions. . . . A colony has for ages been considered useful to the parent state only in so far as it supplied a great number of raw materials." Because Humboldt was so aware of the interpendent relationships that governed the world, his science could never have been used to validate dominance over other people or the environment; he knew the Europeans' abuse of other lands would come back to haunt them. Later in the 19th century, politicians would repeatedly refer to Darwinism in claiming that certain human and natural resources were expendable for the sake of the evolutionary progress of "the higher civilized races." But according to Humboldt, nothing was expendable.

Today, the destruction of the developing world's environment—the burning of the rainforest, the strip-mining of mountain ranges, the appropriation of valuable croplands for the raising of tradable commodities—is still largely driven by the demands of the world's wealthiest countries. The structure of the global economy dictates that developing nations put all their efforts into raising cash—usually by exporting whatever virgin resources the industrial world might desire. They need the cash to pay off their "debt."

28 Even Humboldt accepted Darwinian conflict and chaos as basic facts of life. The whole time he was working on *Cosmos*—during the last 30 years of his life—he knew that the grand, unifying theory he sought was unattainable, because the world was too complicated and chaotic and contingent. "Experimental sciences," he wrote, "based on the observation of the external world, cannot aspire to completeness; the nature of things, and the imperfection of our organs, are alike opposed to it. . . . The attempt perfectly to represent unity in diversity must therefore necessarily prove unsuccessful."

The existence of chaos, however, does not invalidate the search for a cosmos. "Even a partial solution," Humboldt wrote, "—the tendency toward a comprehension of the phenomena of the universe—will not the less remain the eternal and sublime aim of every investigation of nature." And modern chaos theory has in fact demonstrated that beneath almost every manifestation of disorder lurks some sort of pattern or equilibrium. As Daniel Botkin, author of *Discordant Harmonies: A New Ecology for the 21st Century,* has noted, it is important for us to realize, with Darwin, that nature is not calm and balanced but rather constantly changing; but we must also understand that "certain rates of change are natural, desirable, and acceptable, while others are not." It is possible to differentiate between natural and unnatural rates of change and to seek to uphold nature's dynamic equilibrium.

Up to now, unfortunately, scientists and policy-makers have put far too much emphasis on bracing for disorder—on exploiting and stockpiling natural resources in ever greater quantities, and on stockpiling weapons to defend those resources. The United States, for instance, spends $50 billion annually on the development of defense and space technologies, but less than $2 billion in furthering our understanding of the environment. There is a perfectly straightforward reason why we have more sophisticated techniques for planting land mines in the desert than for planting corn on an erodible hillside.

Restoring the balance of modern science, then, would entail devoting more time and money to the search for order in nature, to the mapping of the world's interconnections. A more prominent, better-funded environmental science could help stop over-exploitation by forcing people to realize that each part of the living world is equally valuable. And a major redistribution of research dollars could produce creative, long-term solutions to the problems inherent in resource extraction. New studies could help us, for instance, to pinpoint sustainable yields from fisheries and water supplies; to harvest crops, including trees, without losing so much soil to erosion; and to harness renewable, efficient forms of energy instead of going to war to ensure a steady supply of oil.

32   In lobbying for the research dollars they deserve, ecologists and environmentalists should begin by spreading an ethic of interdisciplinary cooperation. Their unique perspective, which emphasizes holistic, synthetic thinking, is crucial to scientists and developers alike, who need to understand the full impacts of their work over the long term. Even more important, though, ecologists and environmentalists should extend their interdisciplinary approach to include the public at large. People everywhere need to realize that they have a stake in the direction science is taking. All over the world, people concerned about their environments are already clamoring for more information, so that they can hold developers, corporations, and governments accountable for their actions. But they need more help from the scientists themselves, who too often come across as aloof experts with little interest in the public sphere. Only by bridging the gap between "laypeople" and "specialists," only by building connections among ourselves, will we be able to alter the scientific research agenda and rebuild our connections with the natural world.

So far, what limited success environmentalists have had in broadening their coalitions and garnering more research grants has been due to their eloquent public warnings about the dangers of ignoring the ecological perspective. Over the last few years, for instance, by pointing out that most rainforests are probably nurturing valuable medicines, food crops, fibers, soil-restoring vegetation, or petroleum substitutes, environmentalists have convinced major drug companies and agribusiness firms to join with indigenous peoples in conserving tropical ecosystems. As the wilderness philosopher Aldo Leopold once noted, "To keep every cog and wheel is the first precaution of intelligent tinkering."

Unfortunately, though, ecological warnings sometimes deteriorate into scare tactics, and a public that already has too much to worry about is quickly becoming disdainful of doomsday scenarios. Well-meaning environmentalists too often claim that if we don't do the right thing immediately, we'll end up fighting each other for whatever resources remain—in other words, we'll be stuck in a world of Malthusian scarcity and Darwinian conflict. Yet the goal of ecological thinking should be to offer an alternative to conflict. If environmentalists truly want to restore science's balance, they will have to go beyond warnings and give us a positive reason to take an interest in scientific research priorities. They will have to popularize science the way Humboldt did—by conveying to people the exhilaration of understanding one's place in the world, the "intellectual delight and sense of freedom" that comes of "insight into universal nature."

Humboldt considered himself above all an educator, and his ultimate goal was to teach people a basic love of nature, something today's environmental movement rarely seems to do. All his life, he encouraged people simply to leave their houses and escape their specialized lifestyles, to experience the wide-open land. Once we were surrounded by nature, Humboldt felt sure, an awareness of our dependence on it would arise in us "intuitively . . . , from the contrast we draw between the narrow limits of our own existence and the image of infinity revealed on every side—whether we look upward to the starry vault of heaven, scan the far-stretching plain before us, or seek to trace the dim horizon across the vast expanse of ocean." That intuition of our indebtedness to the natural world, that recognition of our own smallness, should be the force driving scientific research.

Personal Response

What did you know about Humboldt before you read this essay? What is your impression of him now that you have read about his work and importance?

Questions for Class or Small Group Discussion

1. Identify a passage or a particular point in this essay that you consider especially significant or intriguing and explain why you find it so.

2. Sachs writes in paragraph 19 that the perspectives of both Darwin and Humboldt "reveal important truths." Summarize the different perspectives of those two and then discuss what truths their differing perspectives reveal.

3. Discuss the fact that the United States "spends $50 billion annually on the development of defense and space technologies, but less than $2 billion on furthering our understanding of the environment" (paragraph 30). Are you comfortable with that ordering of priorities? Explain whether you would make any changes in allocations if you had the authority to do so.

4. Sachs maintains that ecologists and environmentalists should spread "an ethic of interdisciplinary cooperation" (paragraph 32). How do you think that might be done?

A DECLARATION OF SUSTAINABILITY

Paul Hawken

Paul Hawken writes frequently of the need for businesses to take social and environmental responsibility. The ideas in this essay, which first appeared in the September/October 1993 issue of Utne Reader, *are from his book* The Ecology of Commerce *(1993) and from* Our Future and the Making of Things *(1994), which he wrote with William McDonough. Here Hawken lists twelve steps he believes we need to take to conserve resources and ensure that Earth will continue to sustain life.*

I recently performed a social audit for Ben & Jerry's Homemade Inc., America's premier socially responsible company. After poking and prodding around, asking tough questions, trying to provoke debate, and generally making a nuisance of myself, I can attest that their status as the leading social pioneer in commerce is safe for at least another year. They are an outstanding company. Are there flaws? Of course. Welcome to planet Earth. But the people at Ben & Jerry's are relaxed and unflinching in their willingness to look at, discuss, and deal with problems.

In the meantime, the company continues to put ice cream shops in Harlem, pay outstanding benefits, keep a compensation ratio of seven to one from the top of the organization to the bottom, seek out vendors from disadvantaged groups, and donate generous scoops of their profit to others. And they are about to overtake their historic rival Häagen-Dazs, the ersatz Scandinavian originator of super-premium ice cream, as the market leader in their category. At present rates of growth, Ben & Jerry's will be a $1 billion company by the end of the century. They are publicly held, nationally recognized, and rapidly growing, in part because Ben wanted to show that a socially responsible company could make it in the normal world of business.

Ben & Jerry's is just one of a growing vanguard of companies attempting to redefine their social and ethical responsibilities. These companies no longer accept the maxim that the business of business is business. Their premise is simple: Corporations, because they are the dominant institution on the planet, must squarely face the social and environmental problems that afflict humankind. Organizations such as Business for Social Responsibility and the Social Venture Network, corporate "ethics" consultants, magazines such as *In Business* and *Business Ethics,* non-profits including the Council on Economic Priorities, investment funds such as Calvert and Covenant, newsletters like *Greenmoney,* and thousands of unaffiliated companies are drawing up new codes of conduct for corporate life that integrate social, ethical, and environmental principles.

4   Ben & Jerry's and the roughly 2,000 other committed companies in the social responsibility movement here and abroad have combined annual sales of approximately $2 billion, or one-hundredth of 1 percent of the $20 trillion sales garnered by the estimated 80 million to 100 million enterprises worldwide. The problems they are trying to address are vast and unremittingly complex: 5.5 billion people are breeding exponentially, and fulfilling their wants and needs is stripping the earth of its biotic capacity to produce life; a climactic burst of consumption by a single species is overwhelming the skies, earth, waters, and fauna.

As the Worldwatch Institute's Lester Brown patiently explains in his annual survey, *State of the World,* every living system on earth is in decline. Making matters worse, we are having a once-in-a-billion-year blowout sale of hydrocarbons, which are being combusted into the atmosphere, effectively double glazing the planet within the next 50 years with unknown climatic results. The cornucopia of resources that are being extracted, mined, and harvested is so poorly distributed that 20 percent of the earth's people are chronically hungry or starving, while the top 20 percent of the population, largely in the north, control and consume 80 percent of the world's wealth. Since business in its myriad forms is primarily responsible for this "taking," it is appropriate that a growing number of companies ask the question, How does one honorably conduct business in the latter days of industrialism and the beginning of an ecological age? The ethical dilemma that confronts business begins with the acknowledgment that a commercial system that functions well by its own definitions unavoidably defies the greater and more profound ethic of biology. Specifically, how does business face the prospect that creating a profitable, growing company requires an intolerable abuse of the natural world?

Despite their dedicated good work, if we examine all or any of the businesses that deservedly earn high marks for social and environmental responsibility, we are faced with a sobering irony: If every company on the planet were to adopt the environmental and social practices of the best companies—of, say, the Body Shop, Patagonia, and Ben & Jerry's—the world would still be moving toward environmental degradation and collapse. In other words, if we analyze environmental effects and create an input-output model of resources and energy, the results do not even approximate a tolerable or sustainable future. If a tiny fraction of the world's most intelligent companies cannot model a sustainable world, then that tells us that being socially responsible is only one part of an overall solution, and that what we have is not a management problem but a design problem.

At present, there is a contradiction inherent in the premise of a socially responsible corporation: to wit, that a company can make the world

better, can grow, and can increase profits by meeting social and environmental needs. It is a have-your-cake-and-eat-it fantasy that cannot come
true if the primary cause of environmental degradation is overconsumption. Although proponents of socially responsible business are making an
outstanding effort at reforming the tired old ethics of commerce, they are
unintentionally creating a new rationale for companies to produce, advertise, expand, grow, capitalize, and use up resources: the rationale that they
are doing good. A jet flying across the country, a car rented at an airport,
an air-conditioned hotel room, a truck full of goods, a worker commuting
to his or her job—all cause the same amount of environmental degradation whether they're associated with the Body Shop, the Environmental
Defense Fund, or R. J. Reynolds.

8   In order to approximate a sustainable society, we need to describe a
system of commerce and production in which each and every act is inherently sustainable and restorative. Because of the way our system of commerce is designed, businesses will not be able to fulfill their social contract
with the environment or society until the system in which they operate
undergoes a fundamental change, a change that brings commerce and government into alignment with the natural world from which we receive our
life. There must be an integration of economic, biologic, and human systems in order to create a sustainable and interdependent method of commerce that supports and furthers our existence. As hard as we may strive
to create sustainability on a company level, we cannot fully succeed until
the institutions surrounding commerce are redesigned. Just as every act of
production and consumption in an industrial society leads to further environmental degradation, regardless of intention or ethos, we need to imagine—and then design—a system of commerce where the opposite is true,
where doing good is like falling off a log, where the natural, everyday acts
of work and life accumulate into a better world as a matter of course, not
a matter of altruism. A system of sustainable commerce would involve
these objectives:

1. It would reduce absolute consumption of energy and natural
   resources among developed nations by 80 percent within 40
   to 60 years.
2. It would provide secure, stable, and meaningful employment
   for people everywhere.
3. It would be self-actuating as opposed to regulated, controlled,
   mandated, or moralistic.
4. It would honor human nature and market principles.
5. It would be perceived as more desirable than our present way
   of life.
6. It would exceed sustainability by restoring degraded habitats
   and ecosystems to their fullest biological capacity.
7. It would rely on current solar income.

8. It should be fun and engaging, and strive for an aesthetic outcome.

Strategies for Sustainability

At present, the environmental and social responsibility movements consist of many different initiatives, connected primarily by values and beliefs rather than by design. What is needed is a conscious plan to create a sustainable future, including a set of design strategies for people to follow. For the record, I will suggest 12.

1. Take back the charter.   Although corporate charters may seem to have little to do with sustainability, they are critical to any long-term movement toward restoration of the planet. Read *Taking Care of Business: Citizenship and the Charter of Incorporation,* a 1992 pamphlet by Richard Grossman and Frank T. Adams (Charter Ink, Box 806, Cambridge, MA 02140). In it you find a lost history of corporate power and citizen involvement that addresses a basic and crucial point: Corporations are chartered by, and exist at the behest of, citizens. Incorporation is not a right but a privilege granted by the state that includes certain considerations such as limited liability. Corporations are supposed to be under our ultimate authority, not the other way around. The charter of incorporation is a revocable dispensation that was supposed to ensure accountability of the corporation to society as a whole. When Rockwell criminally despoils a weapons facility at Rocky Flats, Colorado, with plutonium waste, or when any corporation continually harms, abuses, or violates the public trust, citizens should have the right to revoke its charter, causing the company to disband, sell off its enterprises to other companies, and effectively go out of business. The workers would have jobs with the new owners, but the executives, directors, and management would be out of jobs, with a permanent notice on their résumés that they mismanaged a corporation into a charter revocation. This is not merely a deterrent to corporate abuse but a critical element of an ecological society because it creates feedback loops that prompt accountability, citizen involvement, and learning. We should remember that the citizens of this country originally envisioned corporations to be part of a public-private partnership, which is why the relationship between the chartering authority of state legislatures and the corporation was kept alive and active. They had it right.

2. Adjust price to reflect cost.   The economy is environmentally and commercially dysfunctional because the market does not provide consumers with proper information. The "free market" economies that we love so much are excellent at setting prices but lousy when it comes to recognizing costs. In order for a sustainable society to exist, every purchase must reflect or at least approximate its actual costs, not only the direct cost of production but also the costs to the air, water, and soil; the cost to future generations; the cost to worker health; the cost of waste, pollution, and toxicity. Simply stated, the marketplace gives us the wrong information. It tells us that flying across the country on a discount airline ticket is cheap when it is not. It tells us that our food is inexpensive when its method of production destroys aquifers and soil, the viability of eco-systems, and workers' lives. Whenever an organism gets wrong infor-mation, it is a form of toxicity. In fact, that is how pesticides work. A herbicide kills because it is a hormone that tells the plant to grow faster than its capacity to absorb nutrients allows. It literally grows itself to death. Sound familiar? Our daily doses of toxicity are the prices in the market-place. They are telling us to do the wrong thing for our own survival. They are lulling us into cutting down old-growth forests on the Olympic Penin-sula for apple crates, into patterns of production and consumption that are not just unsustainable but profoundly short-sighted and destructive. It is surprising that "conservative" economists do not support or understand this idea, because it is they who insist that we pay as we go, have no debts, and take care of business. Let's do it.

12   **3. Throw out and replace the entire tax system.**   The present tax system sends the wrong messages to virtually everyone, encourages waste, discourages conservation, and rewards consumption. It taxes what we want to encourage—jobs, creativity, payrolls, and real income—and ignores the things we want to discourage—degradation, pollution, and depletion. The present U.S. tax system costs citizens $500 billion a year in record-keeping, filing, administrative, legal, and governmental costs—more than the actual amount we pay in personal income taxes. The only incentive in the present system is to cheat or hire a lawyer to cheat for us. The entire tax system must be incrementally replaced over a 20-year pe-riod by "Green fees," taxes that are added onto existing products, energy, services, and materials so that prices in the marketplace more closely ap-proximate true costs. These taxes are not a means to raise revenue or bring down deficits, but must be absolutely revenue neutral so that people in the lower and middle classes experience no real change of income, only a shift in expenditures. Eventually, the cost of non-renewable resources, extractive energy, and industrial modes of production will be more expen-sive than renewable resources, such as solar energy, sustainable forestry, and biological methods of agriculture. Why should the upper middle class be able to afford to conserve while the lower income classes cannot? So far the environmental movement has only made the world better for up-per middle class white people. The only kind of environmental movement that can succeed has to start from the bottom up. Under a Green fee sys-tem the incentives to save on taxes will create positive, constructive acts that are affordable for everyone. As energy prices go up to three to four times their existing levels (with commensurate tax reductions to offset the increase), the natural inclination to save money will result in carpooling, bi-cycling, telecommuting, public transport, and more efficient houses. As taxes on artificial fertilizers, pesticides, and fuel go up, again with offsetting reductions in income and payroll taxes, organic farmers will find that their

produce and methods are the cheapest means of production (because they truly are), and customers will find that organically grown food is less expensive than its commercial cousin. Eventually, with the probable exception of taxes on the rich, we will find ourselves in a position where we pay no taxes, but spend our money with a practiced and constructive discernment. Under an enlightened and redesigned tax system, the cheapest product in the marketplace would be best for the customer, the worker, the environment, and the company. That is rarely the case today.

4. Allow resource companies to be utilities.   An energy utility is an interesting hybrid of public-private interests. A utility gains a market monopoly in exchange for public control of rates, open books, and a guaranteed rate of return. Because of this relationship and the pioneering work of Amory Lovins, we now have markets for "negawatts." It is the first time in the history of industrialism that a corporation has figured out how to make money by selling the absence of something. Negawatts are the opposite of energy: They represent the collaborative ability of a utility to harness efficiency instead of hydrocarbons. This conservation-based alternative saves ratepayers, shareholders, and the company money— savings that are passed along to everyone. All resources systems, including oil, gas, forests, and water, should be run by some form of utility. There should be markets in negabarrels, negatrees, and negacoal. Oil companies, for example, have no alternative at present other than to lobby for the absurd, like drilling in the Arctic National Wildlife Refuge. That project, a $40 billion to $60 billion investment for a hoped-for supply of oil that would meet U.S. consumption needs for only six months, is the only way an oil company can make money under our current system of commerce. But what if the oil companies formed an oil utility and cut a deal with citizens and taxpayers that allowed them to "invest" in insulation, super-glazed windows, conservation rebates on new automobiles, and the scrapping of old cars? Through Green fees, we would pay them back a return on their conservation investment equal to what utilities receive, a rate of return that would be in accord with how many barrels of oil they save, rather than how many barrels they produce. Why should they care? Why should we? A $60 billion investment in conservation will yield, conservatively, four to ten times as much energy as drilling for oil. Given Lovins' principle of efficiency extraction, try to imagine a forest utility, a salmon utility, a copper utility, a Mississippi River utility, a grasslands utility. Imagine a system where the resource utility benefits from conservation, makes money from efficiency, thrives through restoration, and profits from sustainability. It is possible today.

5. Change linear systems to cyclical ones.   Our economy has many design flaws, but the most glaring one is that nature is cyclical and industrialism is linear. In nature, no linear systems exist, or they don't exist for long because they exhaust themselves into extinction. Linear industrial systems take resources, transform them into products or services, discard waste, and sell to consumers, who discard more waste when they have consumed the product. But of course we don't consume TVs, cars, or most of the other stuff we buy. Instead, Americans produce six times their body weight every week in hazardous and toxic waste water, incinerator fly ash, agricultural wastes, heavy metals, and waste chemicals, paper, wood, etc. This does not include CO_2 which if it were included would double the amount of waste. Cyclical means of production are designed to imitate natural systems in which waste equals food for other forms of life, nothing is thrown away, and symbiosis replaces competition. Bill McDonough, a New York architect who has pioneered environmental design principles, has designed a system to retrofit every window in a major American city. Although it still awaits final approval, the project is planned to go like this: The city and a major window manufacturer form a joint venture to produce energy-saving super-glazed windows in the town. This partnership company will come to your house or business, measure all windows and glass doors, and then replace them with windows with an R-8 to R-12 energy-efficiency rating within 72 hours. The windows will have the same casements, molding, and general appearance as the old ones. You will receive a $500 check on installation, and you will pay for the new windows over a 10- to 15-year period in your utility or tax bill. The total bill is less than the cost of the energy the windows will save. In other words, the windows will cost the home or business owner nothing. The city will pay for them initially with industrial development bonds. The factory will train and employ 300 disadvantaged people. The old windows will be completely recycled and reused, the glass melted into glass, the wooden frames ground up and mixed with recycled resins that are extruded to make the casements. When the city is reglazed, the residents and businesses will pocket an extra $20 million to $30 million every year in money saved on utility bills. After the windows are paid for, the figure will go even higher. The factory, designed to be transportable, will move to another city; the first city will retain an equity interest in the venture. McDonough has designed a win-win-win-win-win system that optimizes a number of agendas. The ratepayers, the homeowners, the renters, the city, the environment, and the employed all thrive because they are "making" money from efficiency rather than exploitation. It's a little like running the industrial economy backwards.

   6. Transform the making of things.   We have to institute the Intelligent Product System created by Michael Braungart of the EPEA (Environmental Protection Encouragement Agency) in Hamburg, Germany. The system recognizes three types of products. The first are consumables, products that are either eaten, or, when they're placed on the ground, turn into dirt without any bio-accumulative effects. In other words, they are products whose waste equals food for other living systems. At present, many of the products that should be "consumable," like clothing and shoes, are not. Cotton cloth contains hundreds of different chemicals, plasticizers, defoliants, pesticides, and dyes; shoes are tanned with chromium and their soles contain lead; neckties and silk blouses contain zinc, tin, and toxic dye. Much of what we recycle today turns into toxic by-products, consuming more energy in the recycling process than is saved by recycling. We should be designing more things so that they can be thrown away—into the compost heap. Toothpaste tubes and other non-degradable packaging can be made out of natural polymers so that they break down and become fertilizer for plants. A package that turns into dirt is infinitely more useful, biologically speaking, than a package that turns into a plastic park bench. Heretical as it sounds, designing for decomposition, not recycling, is the way of the world around us.

16   The second category is *durables,* but in this case, they would not be sold, only licensed. Cars, TVs, VCRs, and refrigerators would always belong to the original manufacturer, so they would be made, used, and returned within a closed-loop system. This is already being instituted in Germany and to a lesser extent in Japan, where companies are beginning to design for disassembly. If a company knows that its products will come back someday, and that it cannot throw anything away when they do, it creates a very different approach to design and materials.

Last, there are *unsalables*—toxins, radiation, heavy metals, and chemicals. There is no living system for which these are food and thus they can never be thrown away. In Braungart's Intelligent Product System, unsalables must always belong to the original maker, safeguarded by public utilities called "parking lots" that store the toxins in glass-lined barrels indefinitely, charging the original manufacturers rent for the service. The rent ceases when an independent scientific panel can confirm that there is a safe method to detoxify the substances in question. All toxic chemicals would have molecular markers identifying them as belonging to their originator, so that if they are found in wells, rivers, soil, or fish, it is the responsibility of the company to retrieve them and clean up. This places the problem of toxicity with the makers, where it belongs, making them responsible for full-life-cycle effects.

7. Vote, don't buy.   Democracy has been effectively eliminated in America by the influence of money, lawyers, and a political system that is the outgrowth of the first two. While we can dream of restoring our democratic system, the fact remains that we live in a plutocracy—government by the wealthy. One way out is to vote with your dollars, to withhold purchases from companies that act or respond inappropriately. Don't just avoid buying a Mitsubishi automobile because of the company's participation in the destruction of primary forests in Malaysia, Indonesia, Ecuador, Brazil, Bolivia, Canada, Chile, Canada, Siberia, and Papua New Guinea. Write and tell them why you won't. Engage in dialogue, send one postcard a week, talk, organize, meet, publish newsletters, boycott, patronize, and communicate with companies like General Electric. Educate non-profits, organizations, municipalities, and pension funds to act affirmatively, to support the ecological CERES (formerly *Valdez*)

Principles for business, to invest intelligently, and to *think* with their money, not merely spend it. Demand the best from the companies you work for and buy from. You deserve it and your actions will help them change.

8. Restore the "guardian."   There can be no healthy business sector unless there is a healthy governing sector. In her book *Systems of Survival,* author Jane Jacobs describes two overarching moral syndromes that permeate our society: the commercial syndrome, which arose from trading cultures, and the governing, or guardian, syndrome that arose from territorial cultures. The guardian system is hierarchical, adheres to tradition, values loyalty, and shuns trading and inventiveness. The commercial system, on the other hand, is based on trading, so it values trust of outsiders, innovation, and future thinking. Each has qualities the other lacks. Whenever the guardian tries to be in business, as in Eastern Europe, business doesn't work. What is also true, but not so obvious to us, is that when business plays government, governance fails as well. Our guardian system has almost completely broken down because of the money, power, influence, and control exercised by business and, to a lesser degree, other institutions. Business and unions have to get out of government. We need more than campaign reform. We need a vision that allows us all to see that when Speaker of the House Tom Foley exempts the aluminum industry in his district from the proposed Btu tax, or when Philip Morris donates $200,000 to the Jesse Helms Citizenship Center, citizenship is mocked and democracy is left gagging and twitching on the Capitol steps. The irony is that business thinks that its involvement in governance is good corporate citizenship or at least is advancing its own interests. The reality is that business is preventing the economy from evolving. Business loses, workers lose, the environment loses.

20   **9. Shift from electronic literacy to biologic literacy.**   That an average adult can recognize one thousand brand names and logos but fewer than ten local plants is not a good sign. We are moving not to an information age but to a biologic age, and unfortunately our technological education is equipping us for corporate markets, not the future. Sitting at home with virtual reality gloves, 3D video games, and interactive cable TV shopping is a barren and impoverished vision of the future. The computer revolution is not the totem of our future, only a tool. Don't get me wrong. Computers are great. But they are not an uplifting or compelling vision for culture or society. They do not move us toward a sustainable future any more than our obsession with cars and televisions provided us with newer definitions or richer meaning. We are moving into the age of living machines, not, as Corbusier noted, "machines for living in." The Thomas Edison of the future is not Bill Gates of Microsoft, but John and Nancy Todd, founders of the New Alchemy Institute, a Massachusetts design lab and think tank for sustainability. If the Todds' work seems less commercial, less successful, and less glamorous, it is because they are working on the real problem—how to live—and it is infinitely more complex than a

microprocessor. Understanding biological processes is how we are going to create a new symbiosis with living systems (or perish). What we can learn on-line is how to model complex systems. It is computers that have allowed us to realize how the synapses in the common sea slug are more powerful than all of our parallel processors put together.

10. Take inventory.   We do not know how many species live on the planet within a factor of ten. We do not know how many are being extirpated. We do not know what is contained in the biological library inherited from the Cenozoic age. (Sociobiologist E. O. Wilson estimates that it would take 25,000 person-years to catalog most of the species, putting aside the fact that there are only 1,500 people with the taxonomic ability to undertake the task.) We do not know how complex systems interact—how the transpiration of the giant lily, *Victoria amazonica,* of Brazil's rainforests affects European rainfall and agriculture, for example. We do not know what happens to 20 percent of the CO_2 that is off-gassed every year (it disappears without a trace). We do not know how to calculate sustainable yields in fisheries and forest systems. We do not know why certain species, such as frogs, are dying out even in pristine habitats. We do not know the long-term effects of chlorinated hydrocarbons on human health, behavior, sexuality and fertility. We do not know what a sustainable life is for existing inhabitants of the planet, and certainly not for future populations. (A Dutch study calculated that your fair share of air travel is one trip across the Atlantic in a lifetime.) We do not know how many people we can feed on a sustainable basis, or what our diet would look like. In short, we need to find out what's here, who has it, and what we can or can't do with it.

11. Take care of human health.   The environmental and socially responsible movements would gain additional credibility if they recognized that the greatest amount of human suffering and mortality is caused by environmental problems that are not being addressed by environmental organizations or companies. Contaminated water is killing a hundred times more people than all other forms of pollution combined. Millions of children are dying from preventable diseases and malnutrition.

The movement toward sustainability must address the clear and present dangers that people face worldwide, dangers that ironically increase population levels because of their perceived threat. People produce more children when they're afraid they'll lose them. Not until the majority of people in the world, all of whom suffer in myriad preventable yet intolerable ways, understand that environmentalism means improving their lives directly will the ecology movement walk its talk. Americans will spend more money in the next 12 months on the movie and tchotchkes of *Jurassic Park* than on foreign aid to prevent malnutrition or provide safe water.

24   **12. Respect the human spirit.**   If hope is to pass the sobriety test, then it has to walk a pretty straight line to reality. Nothing written, suggested, or proposed here is possible unless business is willing to integrate itself into the natural world. It is time for business to take the

initiative in a genuinely, open process of dialogue, collaboration, reflection, and redesign. "It is not enough," writes Jeremy Seabrook of the British Green party, "to declare, as many do, that we are living in an unsustainable way, using up resources, squandering the substance of the next generation however true this may be. People must feel subjectively the injustice and unsustainability before they will make a more sober assessment as to whether it is worth maintaining what is, or whether there might not be more equitable and satisfying ways that will not be won at the expense either of the necessities of the poor or of the wasting fabric of the planet."

Poet and naturalist W.S. Merwin (citing Robert Graves) reminds us that we have one story, and one story only, to tell in our lives. We are made to believe by our parents and businesses, by our culture and televisions, by our politicians and movie stars that it is the story of money, of finance, of wealth, of the stock portfolio, the partnership, the country house. These are small, impoverished tales and whispers that have made us restless and craven; they are not stories at all. As author and garlic grower Stanley Crawford puts it, "The financial statement must finally give way to the narrative, with all its exceptions, special cases, imponderables. It must finally give way to the story, which is perhaps the way we arm ourselves against the next and always unpredictable turn of the cycle in the quixotic dare that is life; across the rock and cold of lifelines, it is our seed, our clove, our filament cast toward the future." It is something deeper than anything commercial culture can plumb, and it is waiting for each of us.

Business must yield to the longings of the human spirit. The most important contribution of the socially responsible business movement has little to do with recycling nuts from the rainforest, or employing the homeless. Their gift to us is that they are leading by trying to do something, to risk, take a chance, make a change—change. They are not waiting for "the solution," but are acting without guarantees of success or proof of purchase. That is what all of us must do. Being visionary has always been given a bad rap by commerce. But without a positive vision for humankind we can have no meaning, no work, and no purpose.

Personal Response

In what way(s) has this essay changed or influenced your views about your personal consumption habits and about steps our society must take to make businesses socially responsible? If you are not persuaded by the essay that changes must be made, explain why.

Questions for Class or Small Group Discussion

1. Discuss your understanding of the phrase "socially responsible" (paragraph 2). Can you give examples, other than those Hawken names, of businesses that are not "socially responsible"?

2. In paragraph 8, Hawken lists the objectives involved in his proposed "system of sustainable commerce." Discuss those objectives and the likelihood that the majority of commercial enterprises worldwide would adopt them and work toward such a system.

3. Discuss the twelve steps Hawken lists. Include in your discussion an assessment of how effective you believe the steps to be as reasonable conservation measures, what their adoption would entail, and how likely you think it is that Hawken's recommendations will be adopted.

4. Respond to this statement: "Democracy has been effectively eliminated in America by the influence of money, lawyers, and a political system that is the outgrowth of the first two" (paragraph 18).

5. Respond to this statement: "Computers are great. But they are not an uplifting or compelling vision for culture or society" (paragraph 20).

6. Brainstorm ways in which you personally can make changes or take action that will contribute to improving the environment.

Perspectives on Environmental Sciences
Suggestions for Synthesis

1. Several of the writers in this chapter maintain that basic socioeconomic structures are responsible for the depletion of the world's natural resources. Draw on two or more of the essays in this chapter as you argue your own position on the implications of socioeconomic inequities for a specific environmental issue.

2. Incorporating the comments of at least two of the writers in this chapter, explain your own position on the controversy over the seriousness of global warming.

3. Taking into account the opinions of Wallace S. Broecker in "Global Warming on Trial" and Paul Hawken in "A Declaration of Sustainability," argue the extent to which you think pressure from lobbyists should influence the thinking of legislators considering measures that would tighten regulations on environmental issues.

4. Incorporate the remarks of at least two of the writers in this chapter in an essay that offers possible solutions to one of the major environmental issues confronting people today.

Additional Writing Topics

1. Argue for or against Sandra Postel's position in "Carrying Capacity: Earth's Bottom Line" that the earth is in such serious danger of depleting its resources that soon humans will not be able to survive on the planet.

2. Sandra Postel in "Carrying Capacity: Earth's Bottom Line" maintains that "as a society, we have failed to discriminate between technologies that meet our needs in a sustainable way and those that harm the earth" (paragraph 35). Explain whether you agree or disagree with her on that point, providing examples wherever possible to illustrate general statements.

3. Write a letter to the editor of your campus or community newspaper in which you urge students on your campus and citizens in the community to take actions to reverse the current abuse of natural resources.

4. Propose practical conservation steps students on your campus can take.

5. Write a letter to the president of a corporation that you know abuses the environment in which you urge him or her to make changes in the way the company produces its product. If you refuse to buy the product because of its production methods, say so.

6. While the writers in this chapter address a wide range of environmental issues, their coverage is not exhaustive. Select an environmental issue that is not addressed in these essays. Then explain the problem in detail, and, if possible, offer solutions.

7. Read any of the books mentioned in the articles in this chapter and write a critique of it.

Research Topics

1. Research the work of Baron Alexander von Humboldt, Charles Darwin, or Thomas Malthus, and write a paper arguing the relevance of their ideas to today's environmental issues.

2. Conduct library research on the impact of socioeconomic inequities on environmental issues and argue your position on the subject. Consider including interviews of environmentalists, sociologists, and/or economists from your campus in your research.

3. Expand on "Additional Writing Topics" 1 or 2 by adding library research to bolster your argument. Make sure, however, that you fairly present both sides of the issue as you explain your own position on the topic.

PART FIVE

BUSINESS AND ECONOMICS

CHAPTER 20

MARKETING AND THE AMERICAN CONSUMER

On the matter of consumption and materialism, Americans are both the envy of people in other nations and the object of criticism. America has long been regarded as the "land of plenty," with a plethora of products to buy and a standard of living that allows the majority of its citizens to buy them. Yet such plenitude can lead to overconsumption, creating a need to buy for the sake of buying that can become a kind of obsession. Some people seek psychological counseling for this compulsion, while others seek financial counseling to find out how to manage the debts they have built up as a result of their need to buy things.

Indeed, so central to the lives of Americans is shopping that malls have become more than places to find virtually any product people want and need; they have become social centers, where people gather to meet friends, eat, hang out, exercise, and be entertained. Some regard this penchant for spending money and acquiring goods as a symptom of some inner emptiness, with malls, shopping strips, and discount stores replacing the spiritual centers that once held primary importance in people's lives. Others, especially manufacturers of products and the people who sell them, regard consumerism as a hearty indicator of the nation's economic health.

The selections in this chapter begin with "America's Changing Face," an excerpt from Marlene L. Rossman's 1994 book Multicultural Marketing, *written for an audience of business owners and marketing specialists. In it, Rossman urges marketers to invest in marketing campaigns that target ethnic or minority segments of the American population. As you read the essay, think about the products you buy and the way in which they are marketed. If you are a member of a minority group, how well do you think manufacturers appeal to your particular group? Consider, too, the perspective from which the essay is written. How does the perspective of marketers differ from your own as a consumer?*

The other essays in the chapter provide fairly critical commentaries on American consumerism. In "Work and Spend," Juliet B. Schor argues that Americans are not naturally materialistic but, rather, conditioned by capitalism to buy in excess. William Severini Kowinski examines the reasons teenagers hang out in shopping malls and the effects that doing so has on them in "Kids in the Mall: Growing Up Controlled." Finally, Phyllis Rose takes an amused look at consumerism in America in "Shopping and Other Spiritual Adventures in America Today." As you read each of these essays, think of your own spending habits. Are you "addicted" to shopping? Do you like to buy for the sake of buy-ing, whether you need a product or not? Did you hang out in malls when you were in high school? Do you visit them frequently now? Consider the ways in which those behaviors help portray a particular image of America and whether you think that image is necessarily negative, as these writers suggest.

AMERICA'S CHANGING FACE

Marlene L. Rossman

Marlene L. Rossman works in the field of marketing and market re-search and has designed and delivered sales training seminars on sell-ing to women and on selling to ethnic markets. She is the author of The International Businesswoman of the 1990s *(1990) and* Multi-cultural Marketing *(1994), from which this piece is excerpted.*

America has always been a consumer's—and a marketer's—paradise. The United States is a vast market of more than 255 million people who, de-spite their cultural diversity, have all been influenced in one way or an-other by the American dream. It has always been a country of immigrants, most coming to the United States to improve their lives, some coming not at all by choice. But everyone who has come to this, the greatest of all consumerist societies, has been caught up in the goal of "getting and spending."

Compared to the ancient states of Europe, Asia, and Africa, the United States is a young country. In almost 220 years of existence, we have been looked at by others as the powerful upstart, "big (but young) brother." We have been called naive and unsophisticated, as well as by any number of unpublishable epithets. Often, one group or another in our het-erogeneous society has been reviled or ignored by "pure" racial and ethnic groups, not only outside the United States but inside, as well. But the true spirit of America is the dynamism that different groups have brought here and that has become integrated into mainstream American culture.

Call Americans wasteful, materialistic, concerned only with consum-ing, yet we are the envy and the dream of millions of people worldwide who are hoping or fighting to get into this country.

4   Many come for purposes other than consuming for its own sake; many would like to avoid starving to death or being put into jail for op-posing their country's politician of the moment. Ultimately, however, all are caught up in the rows of shining goods and tantalizing services that make up the trappings of the mythical American dream. Our job as mar-keters is getting a lot tougher these days. Although the United States has never had a homogeneous culture or population, until recently it was safe for companies to pretend that it did. But no longer. Because of the new groups of immigrants coming to our shores and their different patterns of assimilation, and because of the growing number of ethnic and racial

minorities living in the United States, we need to track the changing trends in our population. We need to develop goods and services targeted to different groups and their individual needs.

That's not enough, however. In addition to developing new goods and services, we need to find ways to appeal to and reach many segments of our diverse population.

Some marketers are already riding this wave. Levi Strauss's Dockers slacks for men ran an ad on prime-time television that covered all the ethnic bases; it featured three handsome young men, an African-American, an Asian, and a Caucasian. Some observers thought the camaraderie among these three could also suggest that they were gay.

It might not seem surprising that Budweiser beer would run a TV ad in which a young fellow's girlfriend helps him train for a race that he then wins, after which they flirt outrageously (and suggestively) over cold beers. What is surprising about the ad, which appeared on prime-time TV in 1992, is that the woman is able-bodied and the man is in a wheelchair. Brewers have always used sex to sell beer, but never before has the idea of a sexually active athlete with disabilities been seen as attractive to middle America.

8   If you have any doubt about the massive changes taking place in American society, just turn on the television. You'll see that over the last forty years we have moved from Ozzie and Harriet to the Cosbys, from scotch and soda to margaritas, from Walter Cronkite to Connie Chung, and from Chevrolet to Honda. Today, Jesse Jackson is an elder statesman; McDonald's sells burritos along with cheeseburgers; and Azucar Moreno, a Hispanic female pop group (whose name means brown sugar), does prime-time national television ads for Diet Coke.

During the late 1950s Campbell's Soup Company could reach half of all American households just by sponsoring "Lassie" on television. That may have been the last time things were so simple. Such a uniform market no longer exists as a result of the many changes reshaping American society.

By 1993 the networks' share of the prime-time television audience had dropped to about 70 percent from 92 percent in 1979. And even if marketers could reach everyone with one commercial, that commercial would no longer appeal to every segment of the market. Even good old Campbell's has regionalized its products and marketing mix to appeal to wildly divergent segments, such as yuppies, ethnics, the elderly, and sodium and fat watchers. When you eat an "all-American" diet of a bagel for breakfast, a slice of pizza for lunch, and a hamburger for dinner, you may not realize that all of these foods were introduced into the United States by immigrants. The impact of immigrants may be even clearer to you if you have a breakfast burrito at McDonald's, sushi for lunch, and Szechuan chicken for dinner. And if you still aren't sure about "immigrant power," you should know that in 1991, salsa outsold ketchup by $40 million in U.S. retail sales.

In 1992, total salsa sales hit $500 million—up almost 12 percent from 1991. Elizabeth Rozin, a cookbook author, explains that the mainstream palate is changing, because the mainstream itself is changing—it no longer consists exclusively of white American Protestants. And in the salty snack category, the penetration rate of tortilla chips has hit close to 60 percent of all U.S. households.

12   Taquerias, little taco stands selling Mexican specialties, once could only be found in the Southwest and the West. Today, Mexican food has become so popular in New York that one *taqueria* is owned and staffed by a Chinese family. Packaged tortillas can be found in practically every U.S. supermarket. Similarly, producers of packaged soul food are finding tremendous interest nationally in their meals, even in upscale neighborhoods.

The trend in every aspect of American life is toward greater cultural, ethnic, and linguistic diversity. Hispanics, Asians, African-Americans, and other culturally distinct segments can't all be successfully targeted with the same goods and services via the same marketing and advertising strategies that succeeded when the United States was (or thought it was) a monolithic, Anglo-dominated market.

In these difficult economic times, businesses have learned that money is just as green when it is spent by people of color. Jack Kraft, vice chairman and CEO of Leo Burnett Company, a Chicago-based ad agency, explains that recessionary times make companies look at every market segment a little more deeply.

No longer does it suffice to dub English commercials into Spanish with lip movements out of synch or to translate print ads word for word, which can result in unintentional obscenities, as the Perdue poultry company found in 1987. (The popular ad in which company owner Frank Perdue explains that "it takes a tough man to make a tender chicken" was translated into Spanish for the East Coast market by someone not familiar with regional slang. The translation came out something like "it takes a sexually aroused man to make a chick affectionate.")

16   No longer do African-American women have to make do with "suntan" shades of foundation cosmetics intended for Caucasian skin. First small and then large companies have developed cosmetics that enhance the vast range of black skin tones and that don't make black women look ashen.

Flori Roberts, an entrepreneur, was a pioneer in cosmetics for African-Americans; big companies have also jumped on the money wagon. In 1991 Prescriptives, Estee Lauder's slickly packaged cosmetic brand aimed at urban working women, launched All Skins—makeup formulated for all skin colors—in a direct appeal to ethnic women and attracted almost four thousand new customers a month.

Although the often self-sufficient Chinatowns and Koreatowns still serve their communities, marketers are targeting these and other groups with goods and services designed and promoted with Asians' unique requirements and preferences in mind.

These previously untargeted minority markets spend billions of dollars annually. The total annual spending power of African- and Asian-American and Hispanic consumers is estimated at more than $500 billion dollars!

20   Just as U.S. business learned in the 1970s and 1980s that a deep understanding of different cultures is necessary to sell overseas, in the 1990s companies are having to develop the same kind of multicultural awareness to compete successfully in the U.S. domestic market.

The mainstream market is wildly overtapped. While many companies have fought over slices of the tiny yuppie market, the mature market, the senior market, the women's market, and other slow-growth markets, they have ignored the ethnic market, the fastest-growing and the most profitable market of all.

Some say that these markets are made up primarily of poor people who are not worth targeting; others respond that this attitude smacks of conscious or unconscious racism. But those marketers who have targeted and captured a slice of the very sweet ethnic pie have profited enormously.

Look at Binney & Smith, the company that has enchanted generations of kids with Crayola crayons. Their "flesh" color had traditionally been a sort of beigy-pink. Many Americans, however, have darker shades of flesh. Although the company had other "fleshlike" tones of crayons, ranging from apricot to mahogany, in their sixty-four-pack, those colors weren't called "flesh." In the early 1990s, Binney & Smith came out with a pack of skin-tone crayons in their own box.

24   I have always wondered why manufacturers of bandages spent so many years selling pink bandages to Americans of all colors before discovering that clear bandages look good on all skin tones. Late in 1992 one small company also came out with brown-toned bandages.

A brand of panty hose called Afrotique is sold in Pueblo supermarkets in the U.S. Virgin Islands, where the population is predominantly African-American. The panty hose are sold in all the traditional shades of beige, brown, and black. The stores also sell the beigy-pink called nude by many mainstream marketers of panty hose, but Afrotique simply calls it light beige.

Major companies such as Procter & Gamble, Anheuser-Busch, and Campbell's spent $734 million in 1991 for ad campaigns that targeted only Hispanics. And companies such as J. C. Penney, Mattel, Pillsbury, and Quaker Oats spent more than $750 million advertising to African-Americans in 1992.

Mainstream companies such as Revlon, Maybelline, and Estee Lauder, with their cosmetics for black, Hispanic, and Asian women, see the strong advantages of marketing to ethnic and minority customers. Although sales of standard cosmetic products in the $4 billion cosmetics industry are barely growing at 3 percent a year, some new smaller lines aimed at minorities have increased sales by as much as 25 percent annually.

28   Developing cosmetics for ethnic and minority women is an especially good idea when we realize that the median age for Caucasians is almost thirty-three, while the median age for black and Hispanics is far younger. And younger customers are more likely to try new products, according to Lafayette Jones, president of Segmented Marketing Services, Inc., a marketing company in Winston-Salem, North Carolina.

U.S. companies that learn about the tastes and preferences of the ethnic markets within this country are also finding an extra benefit; they can use their new knowledge to enter overseas markets in the Pacific Rim and in Latin America, where there is great pent-up consumer demand for U.S. goods.

For some companies, it works the other way. Greg Walker, marketing communications manager at Eastman Kodak in Rochester, New York, says, "Like many companies, we had a global focus before we had an ethnic focus. That experience provided valuable insights for reaching different segments of the domestic market."

Even if a company doesn't export, its domestic market is increasingly made up of foreign-born consumers. The U.S. population will continue to be reshaped by millions of immigrants and their children through the rest of the 1990s and into the twenty-first century. Many workers will be immigrants, and many immigrants will open their own businesses. The strongest impact of immigration will continue to be on the East and West Coasts, but the changes will be felt nationwide.

32   Our cultural model is becoming the mosaic, not the melting pot. Since the civil rights struggles of the 1960s, many groups are choosing ethnic pride, separatism, and even militance. Some recent arrivals aren't willing to join the mainstream but prefer the old language and ways. If you are considering selling to them, you must be aware of these issues and design your marketing mix to reflect it.

The issue of assimilation is a very complex one and affects different ethnic groups differently. "You won't find Hispanics at Taco Bell," according to George Rosenbaum, CEO of Leo J. Shapiro & Associates, a market research company in Chicago. "You'll find Hispanics and other second-generation ethnics eating cheeseburgers at McDonald's."

Some African-Americans have chosen not to push the assimilation and integration process and prefer to associate mostly with other African-Americans. Radamase Cabrera, an urban planner for Washington, D.C., chooses to live in the nearby affluent black suburb of Prince George's County, Maryland. Quoted in *The New York Times Magazine,* Cabrera says, "Why should I beg some cracker to integrate me into his society when he doesn't want to? Why keep beating my head up against a wall?"

Similarly, there are communities in New York, San Francisco, and other cities where Chinese-Americans go to school, marry, and live almost their entire lives without speaking to a non-Chinese. On the other hand, there are large numbers of Chinese-Americans who integrate into mainstream communities and assimilate almost completely in accordance with the standard rule of thumb that assimilation takes place by the third generation.

36   Assimilation is not an either/or. It's a continuum, and marketers must deal with varying degrees of assimilation within any ethnic market. Companies need to be aware of each subgroup's pattern of assimilation and then determine whether it's cost-effective to target these segments with specific marketing campaigns.

The most successful businesses in the coming years will be the ones that make the effort to understand that ethnic and other segmentation—appealing to the tastes and preferences of different groups—is the key to profitability. Those marketers with the vision to develop product and market strategies to appeal to the coming "new majority" will be the ones that prosper.

Personal Response

What insights into the perspective of marketers did you get from reading this essay?

Questions for Class or Small Group Discussion

1. What characteristics of American culture do you think make it "the greatest of all consumerist societies" (paragraph 1)? Do you agree that Americans are "wasteful, materialistic, concerned only with consuming" (paragraph 3)? Explain your answer.

2. Rossman writes, "Our job as marketers is getting a lot tougher these days" (paragraph 4). What evidence does she supply to prove that point? If you were a marketer or a business owner, would you be persuaded to spend advertising money to target minority populations?

3. How do you think businesses can reach targeted audiences that do not speak English, such as immigrant populations?

4. Bring to class copies of print advertisements that target specific groups and discuss the marketing techniques they employ. What products do you typically buy that are marketed for or associated with ethnic groups other than your own?

WORK AND SPEND

Juliet B. Schor

Juliet B. Schor is a professor of economics at Harvard University. This reading is from her book The Overworked American: The Unexpected Decline of Leisure *(1992). Schor contends in the book that Americans are working longer hours than they were twenty years ago*

*and have fewer hours for leisure time, resulting in a lowered standard
of living. In this excerpt from her book, Schor argues that Americans
are conditioned to be materialistic by a capitalist system that leaves
them discontented and stuck in a cycle of work and spend.*

[M]aterialism (and its attendant discontent) is taken for granted. It is
widely believed that our unceasing quest for material goods is part of the
basic makeup of human beings. According to the folklore, we may not like
it, but there's little we can do about it.

Despite its popularity, this view of human nature is wrong. While
human beings may have innate desires to strive toward something, there
is nothing preordained about material goods. There are numerous examples of societies in which *things* have played a highly circumscribed role.
In medieval Europe, there was relatively little acquisitiveness. The common people, whose lives were surely precarious by contemporary standards, showed strong preferences for leisure rather than money. In
the nineteenth- and early twentieth-century United States, there is also
considerable evidence that many working people exhibited a restricted
appetite for material goods. Numerous examples of societies where consumption is relatively unimportant can be found in the anthropological and
historical literature.[1]

Consumerism is not an ahistorical trait of human nature, but a specific
product of capitalism. With the development of the market system, consumerism "spilled over," for the first time, beyond the charmed circles of
the rich. The growth of the middle class created a large group of potential
buyers and the possibility that mass culture could be oriented around material goods. This process can be seen not only in historical experiences
but is now going on in places such as Brazil and India, where the growth of
large middle classes have contributed to rampant consumerism and the
breakdown of longstanding values.[2]

4   In the United States, the watershed was the 1920s—the point at
which the "psychology of scarcity" gave way to the "psychology of abundance." This was a crucial period for the development of modern materi-
alist culture. Thrift and sobriety were out; waste and excess were in. The

---

[1] On the United States, see Herbert Gutman, *Work, Culture and Society in Industrializing America*
(New York: Vintage, 1977). See also the discussion of the 1925 Consumer League of New York
study in Benjamin Hunnicutt, *Work Without End: Abandoning Shorter Hours for the Right to Work*
(Philadelphia: Temple University Press, 1988), 68–69, where respondents displayed strong preferences for leisure.

On the anthropological evidence, see Marshall Sahlins, *Stone Age Economics* (New York: Aldine,
1972).

[2] See Neil McKendrick, John Brewer, and J. H. Plumb, *The Birth of a Consumer Society: The
Commercialization of Eighteenth-Century England* (London: Europa Publications, 1982); and Arjun
Appadurai, "Technology and the Reproduction of Values in Rural Western India," in Frédérique
Apffel-Marglin and Stephen A. Marglin, eds., *Dominating Knowledge: Development, Culture, and Re-
sistance* (Oxford: Clarendon Press, 1990), 185–216.

nation grew giddy with its exploding wealth. Consumerism blossomed—both as a social ideology and in terms of high rates of real spending. In the midst of all this buying, we can discern the origins of modern consumer discontent.

This was the decade during which the American dream, or what was then called "the American standard of living," captured the nation's imagination. But it was always something of a mirage. The historian Winifred Wandersee explains:

> It is doubtful that the average American could have described the precise meaning of the term "American standard of living," but nearly everyone agreed that it was attainable, highly desirable, and far superior to that of any other nation. Its nature varied according to social class and regional differences, but no matter where a family stood socially and financially, it was certain to have aspirations set beyond that stance. This was the great paradox posed by the material prosperity of the twentieth century: prosperity was conspicuously present, but it was always just out of reach, for nearly every family defined its standard of living in terms of an income that it hoped to achieve rather than the reality of the paycheck.[3]

The phenomenon of yearning for more is evident in studies of household consumption. In a 1928 study of Yale University faculty members, the bottom category (childless couples with incomes of $2,000) reported that their situation was "life at the cheapest and barest with nothing left over for the emergencies of sickness and childbirth." Yet an income of $2,000 a year put them above 60 percent of all American families. Those at the $5,000 level (the top 10 percent of the income distribution) reported that they "achieve nothing better than 'hand to mouth living.'" At $6,000, "the family containing young children can barely break even." Yet these were the top few percent of all Americans. Even those making $12,000—a fantastic sum in 1928—complained about items they could not afford. A 1922 Berkeley study revealed similar sentiments of discontent—despite the facts that all the families studied had telephones, virtually all had purchased life insurance, two-thirds owned their own homes and took vacations, over half had motor cars, and nearly every family spent at least a little money on servants or housecleaning help.[4]

The discontent expressed by many Americans was fostered—and to certain extent even created—by manufacturers. Business embarked on the path of the "hard sell." The explosion of consumer credit made

---

[3] Winifred D. Wandersee, *Women's Work and Family Values, 1920–1940* (Cambridge, Mass.: Harvard University Press, 1981), 7–8.

[4] On the Yale study, see ibid., 10, table 1.1, and 21–22. On the Berkeley study, see Jessica Peixotto, *Getting and Spending at the Professional Standard of Living* (New York: Macmillan, 1927). Data from chapter 6.

the task easier, as automobiles, radios, electric refrigerators, washing machines—even jewelry and foreign travel—were bought on the install- ment plan. By the end of the 1920s, 60 percent of cars, radios, and furni- ture were being purchased on "time."[5] The ability to buy without actually having money helped foster a climate of instant gratification, expanding ex- pectations, and, ultimately, materialism.

8   The 1920s was also the decade of advertising. The admen went wild: everything from walnuts to household coal was being individually branded and nationally advertised. Of course, ads had been around for a long time. But something new was afoot, in terms of both scale and strategy. For the first time, business began to use advertising as a psychological weapon against consumers. "Scare copy" was invented. Without Listerine, Postum, or a Buick, the consumer would be left a spinster, fall victim to a crippling disease, or be passed over for a promotion. Ads developed an association between the product and one's very identity. Eventually they came to promise everything and anything—from self-esteem, to status, friendship, and love.[6]

The psychological approach responded to the economic dilemma business faced. Americans in the middle classes and above (to whom virtu- ally all advertising was targeted) were no longer buying to satisfy basic needs—such as food, clothing and shelter. These had been met. Advertis- ers had to persuade consumers to acquire things they most certainly did not need. In the words of John Kenneth Galbraith, production would have to "create the wants it seeks to satisfy." This is exactly what manufactur- ers tried to do. The normally staid AT&T attempted to transform the utili- tarian telephone into a luxury, urging families to buy "all the telephone facilities that they can conveniently use, rather than the smallest amount they can get along with." One ad campaign targeted fifteen phones as the style for an affluent home. In product after product, companies introduced designer colors, styles, even scents. The maid's uniform had to match the room decor, flatware was color-coordinated, and Kodak cameras came in five bird-inspired tints—Sea Gull, Cockatoo, Redbreast, Bluebird, and Jenny Wren.[7]

Business clearly understood the nature of the problem. It even had a name—"needs saturation." Would-be sellers complained of a buyer's strike and organized a "Prosperity Bureau," urging people to "Buy Now." According to historian Frederick Lewis Allen: "Business had learned as never before the importance of the ultimate consumer. Unless he could be persuaded to buy and buy lavishly, the whole stream of six-cylinder cars,

---

[5] Roland Marchand, *Advertising the American Dream: Making Way for Modernity* (Berkeley: Univer- sity of California Press, 1985), 4, 5.

[6] Ibid.

[7] John Kenneth Galbraith, *The Affluent Society,* 4th ed. (Boston: Houghton Mifflin, 1984), 127. Marchand, *Advertising the American Dream,* chap. 5.

super helerodynes, cigarettes, rouge compacts, and electric ice boxes would be dammed up at its outlets."[8]

But would the consumer be equal to her task as "the savior of private enterprise"? The general director of General Motors' Research Labs, Charles Kettering, stated the matter baldly: business needs to create a "dissatisfied consumer"; its mission is "the organized creation of dissatisfaction." Kettering led the way by introducing annual model changes for GM cars—planned obsolescence designed to make the consumer discontented with what he or she already had. Other companies followed GM's lead. In the words of advertising historian Roland Marchand, success now depended on "the nurture of qualities like wastefulness, self-indulgence, and artificial obsolescence." The admen and the businessmen had to instill what Marchand has called the "consumption ethic," or what Benjamin Hunnicutt termed "the new economic gospel of consumption."[9]

12   The campaign to create new and unlimited wants did not go unchallenged. Trade unionists and social reformers understood the long-term consequences of consumerism for most Americans: it would keep them imprisoned in capitalism's "squirrel cage." The consumption of luxuries necessitated long hours. Materialism would provide no relief from the tedium, the stultification, the alienation, and the health hazards of modern work; its rewards came outside the workplace. There was no mystery about these choices: business was explicit in its hostility to increases in free time, preferring consumption as the *alternative* to taking economic progress in the form of leisure. In effect, business offered up the cycle of work-and-spend. In response, many trade unionists rejected what they regarded as a Faustian bargain of time for money: "Workers have declared that their lives are not to be bartered at any price, that no wage, no matter how high can induce them to sell their birthright. [The worker] is not the slave of fifty years ago. . . . he [*sic*] reads . . . goes to the theater . . . [*and*] has established his own libraries, his own educational institutions. . . . And he wants time, time, time, for all these things."[10]

Progressive reformers raised ethical and religious objections to the cycle of work-and-spend. Monsignor John A. Ryan, a prominent Catholic spokesman, articulated a common view:

> One of the most baneful assumptions of our materialistic industrial society is that all men should spend at least one-third of the twenty-four hour day in some productive occupation. . . . If men still have leisure [after needs are satisfied], new luxuries must be invented to

---

[8] Hunnicutt, *Work Without End,* 38. Allen quoted in ibid., 45.

[9] The savior" phrase is Thomas Cochran's, cited in Hunnicutt, *Work Without End,* 44. Charles F. Kettering, "Keep the Consumer Dissatisfied," *Nation's Business,* January 1929; "organized creation," Marchand, *Advertising the American Dream,* 156. Marchand, *Advertising the American Dream,* 158, and Hunnicutt, *Work Without End,* chap. 2.

[10] From an ILGWU pamphlet cited in Hunnicutt, *Work Without End,* 75.

keep them busy and new wants must be stimulated . . . to take the luxuries off the market and keep the industries going. Of course, the true and rational doctrine is that when men have produced sufficient necessaries and reasonable comforts and conveniences to supply all the population, they should spend what time is left in the cultivation of their intellects and wills, in the pursuit of the higher life.[11]

The debates of the 1920s clearly laid out the options available to the nation. On the one hand, the path advocated by labor and social reformers: take productivity growth in the form of increases in free time, rather than the expansion of output; limit private consumption, discourage luxuries, and emphasize public goods such as education and culture. On the other hand, the plan of business: maintain current working hours and aim for maximal economic growth. This implied the encouragement of "discretionary" consumption, the expansion of new industries, and a culture of unlimited desires. Production would come to "fill a void that it has itself created."[12]

It is not difficult to see which alternative was adopted. Between 1920 and the present, the bulk of productivity advance has been channeled into the growth of consumption. Economist John Owen has found that between 1920 and 1977, the amount of labor supplied over the average American's lifetime fell by only 10 percent; and since 1950, there has even been a slight increase.[13] The attitude of businessmen was crucial to this outcome. As employers, they had strong reasons for preferring long hours. As sellers, they craved vigorous consumption to create markets for their products. Labor proved to be no match for the economic and political power of business.

16   Finally, we should not underestimate the appeal of consumption itself. The working classes and the poor, particularly those migrating from Europe or the rural United States, grew up in conditions of material deprivation. The array of products available in urban America was profoundly alluring, at times mesmerizing. For the middle classes, consumption held its own satisfactions. Designer towels or the latest GM model created a sense of privilege, superiority, and well-being. A Steinway "made life worth living." Once the Depression hit, it reinforced these tendencies. One of its legacies was a long-lasting emphasis on finding security in the form of material success.[14]

---

[11] Ibid., 94.

[12] Galbraith, *Affluent Society,* 127.

[13] This conclusion is from John Owen, *Working Lives: The American Work Force Since 1920* (Lexington, Mass.: Lexington Books, 1986), 23.

[14] On "mesmerization," see Stuart Ewen and Elizabeth Ewen, *Channels of Desire: Mass Images and the Shaping of American Consciousness* (New York: McGraw-Hill, 1982). From a Steinway ad cited in Marchand, *Advertising the American Dream,* 142.

The Pitfalls of Consumerism

The consumerism that took root in the 1920s was premised on the idea of *dissatisfaction*. As much as one has, it is never enough. The implicit mentality is that the next purchase will yield happiness, and then the next. In the words of the baby-boom writer, Katy Butler, it was the new couch, the quieter street, and the vacation cottage. Yet happiness turned out to be elusive. Today's luxuries became tomorrow's necessities, no longer appreciated. When the Joneses also got a new couch or a second home, these acquisitions were no longer quite as satisfying. Consumerism turned out to be full of pitfalls—a vicious pattern of wanting and spending which failed to deliver on its promises.

The inability of the consumerist life style to create durable satisfaction can be seen in the syndrome of "keeping up with the Joneses." This competition is based on the fact that it is not the absolute level of consumption that matters, but how much one consumes relative to one's peers. The great English economist John Maynard Keynes made this distinction over fifty years ago: "[Needs] fall into two classes—those which are absolute in the sense that we feel them whatever the situation of our fellow human beings may be, and those which are relative only in that their satisfaction lifts us above, makes us feel superior to, our fellows." Since then, economists have invented a variety of terms for "keeping up with the Joneses": "relative income or consumption," "positional goods," or "local status." A brand-new Toyota Corolla may be a luxury and a status symbol in a lower-middle-class town, but it appears paltry next to the BMWs and Mercedes that fill the driveways of the fancy suburb. A 10-percent raise sounds great until you find that your co-workers all got 12 percent. The cellular phone, fur coat, or _____ (fill in the blank) gives a lot of satisfaction only before everyone else has one. In the words of one 1980s investment banker: "You tend to live up to your income level. You see it in relation to the people of your category. They're living in a certain way and you want to live in that way. You keep up with other people of your situation who have also leveraged themselves."[15]

Over time, keeping up with the Joneses becomes a real trap—because the Joneses also keep up with you. If everyone's income goes up by 10 percent, then relative positions don't change at all. No satisfaction is gained. The more of our happiness we derive from comparisons with others, the less additional welfare we get from general increases in

---

[15] John Maynard Keynes, "Economic Possibilities for Our Grandchildren," in *Essays in Persuasion* (New York: Harcourt, Brace, 1932), 365. The classic statement of the importance of relative consumption was made in 1949 by Harvard economist James Duesenberry in *Income, Saving and the Theory of Consumer Behavior* (Cambridge, Mass.: Harvard University Press, 1949). Unfortunately, the ideas put forward in this pioneering work have not been adequately tested and pursued. For further discussion of these issues, in addition to Duesenberry, see the works of Tibor Scitovsky, Richard Easterlin, Fred Hirsch, and Robert Frank. Investment banker from Brooke Kroeger, "Feeling Poor," p. 8.

income—which is probably why happiness has failed to keep pace with economic growth. This dynamic may be only partly conscious. We may not even be aware that we are competing with the Joneses, or experience it as a competition. It may be as simple as the fact that exposure to their latest "life-style upgrade" plants the seed in our own mind that we must have it, too—whether it be a European vacation, this year's fashion statement, or piano lessons for the children.

20   In the choice between income and leisure, the quest for relative standing has biased us toward income. That's because status comparisons have been mostly around commodities—cars, clothing, houses, even second houses. If Mrs. Jones works long hours, she will be able to buy the second home, the designer dresses, or the fancier car. If her neighbor Mrs. Smith opts for more free time instead, her two-car garage and walk-in closet will be half empty. As long as the competition is more oriented to visible commodities, the tendency will be for both women to prefer income to time off. But once they both spend the income, they're back to where they started. Neither is *relatively* better off. If free time is less of a "relative" good than other commodities, then true welfare could be gained by having more of it, and worrying less about what the Joneses are buying.

It's not easy to get off the income treadmill and into a new, more leisured life style. Mrs. Smith won't do it on her own, because it'll set her back in comparison to Mrs. Jones. And Mrs. Jones is just like Mrs. Smith. They are trapped in a classic Prisoner's Dilemma: both would be better off with more free time; but without cooperation, they will stick to the long hours, high consumption choice.[16] We also know their employers won't initiate a shift to more leisure, because they prefer employees to work long hours.

A second vicious cycle arises from the fact that the satisfactions gained from consumption are often short-lived. For many, consumption can be habit forming. Like drug addicts who develop a tolerance, consumers need additional hits to maintain any given level of satisfaction.[17] The switch from black and white to color television was a real improvement when it occurred. But soon viewers became habituated to color. Going back to black and white would have reduced well-being, but having color may not have yielded a permanently higher level of satisfaction. Telephones are another example. Rotary dialing was a major improvement. Then came touch-tone, which made us impatient with rotaries. Now numbers are preprogrammed and some people begin to find any dialing a chore.

---

[16] In a Prisoner's Dilemma, both partners would be made better off if they cooperated, but failure to do so leads both to be worse off. This point has been made by Robert H. Frank in *Choosing the Right Pond* (New York: Oxford University Press, 1985), 133–35.

[17] Galbraith calls this "the dependence effect"; Scitovsky, the difference between "pleasure" (what one gets at first) and "comfort" (the sensation after habituation).

Our lives are filled with goods to which we have become so habituated that we take them for granted. Indoor plumbing was once a great luxury—and still is in much of the world. Now it is so ingrained in our life style that we don't give it a second thought. The same holds true for all but the newest household appliances—stoves, refrigerators, and vacuum cleaners are just part of the landscape. We may pay great attention to the kind of automobile we drive, but the fact of having a car is something adults grew accustomed to long ago.

24   The process of habituation can be seen as people pass through life stages—for example, in the transition from student life to a first job. The graduate student makes $15,000 a year. He has hand-me-down furniture, eats at cheap restaurants, and, when traveling long distances, finds a place in someone else's car. After graduation, he gets a job and makes twice as much money. At first, everything seems luxurious. He rents a bigger apartment (with no roommates), buys his own car, and steps up a notch in restaurant quality. His former restaurant haunts now seem unappetizing. Hitching a ride becomes too inconvenient. As he accumulates possessions, the large apartment starts to shrink. In not too many years, he has become habituated to twice as much income and is spending the entire $30,000. It was once a princely sum, which made him feel rich. Now he feels it just covers a basic standard of living, without much left over for luxuries. He may not even feel any better off. Yet to go back to $15,000 would be painful.

Over time, further increases in income set in motion another round of the same. He becomes dissatisfied with renting and "needs" to buy a home. Travel by car takes too long, so he switches to airplanes. His tastes become more discriminating, and the average price of a restaurant meal slowly creeps upward. Something like this process is why Americans making $70,000 a year end up feeling stretched and discontented.[18]

Of course, part of this is a life-cycle process. As our young man grows older, possessions like cars and houses become more important. But there's more to it than aging. Like millions of other American consumers, he is becoming addicted to the accoutrements of affluence. This may well be why the doubling of per-capita income has not made us twice as well

---

[18] This passage from Jonathan Freedman, the author of a book on happiness, describes the syndrome: "As a student, I lived on what now seems no money at all, but I lived in a style which seemed perfectly fine . . . As my income has grown since then, I have spent more . . . but it has always seemed to be just about the same amount of money and bought just about the same things. The major change is that I have spent more on everything, and I consider buying more expensive items. None of this has had an appreciable effect on my life or on my feelings of happiness or satisfaction. I imagine that if I earned five times as much, the same would be true—at least it would once I got used to the extra money. This is not to say that I would turn down a raise—quite the contrary. But after a while everything would settle down, the extra money would no longer be 'extra,' and my life would be the same as before." From *Happy People* (New York: Harcourt, Brace, Jovanovich, 1978), 140.

off. In the words of psychologist Paul Wachtel, we have become an "asymptote culture . . . in which the contribution of material goods to life satisfaction has reached a point of diminishing returns. . . . Each individual item seems to us to bring an increase in happiness or satisfaction. But the individual increments melt like cotton candy when you try to add them up."[19]

These are not new ideas. Economists such as James Duesenberry, Edward Schumacher, Fred Hirsch, Tibor Scitovsky, Robert Frank, and Richard Easterlin have explored these themes. Psychologists have also addressed them, providing strong support for the kinds of conclusions I have drawn. My purpose is to add a dimension to this analysis of consumption which has heretofore been neglected—its connection to the incentive structures operating in labor markets. The consumption traps I have described are just the flip side of the bias toward long hours embedded in the production system. We are not merely caught in a pattern of spend-and-spend—the problem identified by many critics of consumer culture. The whole story is that we work, and spend, and work and spend some more.

Personal Response

Do you consider yourself a compulsive consumer, addicted to buying for the sake of buying? Explain your answer.

Questions for Class or Small Group Discussion

1. Discuss those characteristics of consumerism in the 1920s, as Schor describes them, that you believe accurately apply to many Americans today.

2. Do you agree with Schor that materialism fosters discontent? If so, can you give examples of such discontent from your own personal experience or from knowledge of other people's spending habits?

3. In paragraph 5, Schor quotes the historian Winifred Wandersee, who doubts that most Americans in the 1920s could define "American standard of living" even though everyone agreed that it was attainable and highly desirable. Try defining the "American standard of living" today and discuss your goals in terms of that standard.

4. Discuss whether you agree with Schor's analysis of the process of habituation (paragraphs 21–24). Do you agree that the young man she uses in her example "is becoming addicted to the accoutrements of affluence"? Is there any other perspective from which to consider this young man's spending habits?

---

[19] Paul Wachtel, *The Poverty of Affluence: A Psychological Portrait of the American Way of Life* (Philadelphia: New Society Publishers, 1989), 39.

KIDS IN THE MALL: GROWING UP CONTROLLED

William Severini Kowinski

William Severini Kowinski has published articles in the New York Times Magazine, American Film, Esquire, *and* West, *among others. This essay is reprinted from his first book,* The Malling of America: An Inside Look at the Great Consumer Paradise *(1985). In the book, Kowinski examines why teenagers hang out in shopping malls and the effects that doing so has on them.*

Butch heaved himself up and loomed over the group. "Like it was different for me," he piped. "My folks used to drop me off at the shopping mall every morning and leave me all day. It was like a big free baby-sitter, you know? One night they never came back for me. Maybe they moved away. Maybe there's some kind of a Bureau of Missing Parents I could check with."

—Richard Peck
Secrets of the Shopping Mall,
a novel for teenagers

From his sister at Swarthmore, I'd heard about a kid in Florida whose mother picked him up after school every day, drove him straight to the mall, and left him there until it closed—all at his insistence. I'd heard about a boy in Washington who, when his family moved from one suburb to another, pedaled his bicycle five miles every day to get back to his old mall, where he once belonged.

These stories aren't unusual. The mall is a common experience for the majority of American youth; they have probably been going there all their lives. Some ran within their first large open space, saw their first fountain, bought their first toy, and read their first book in a mall. They may have smoked their first cigarette or first joint or turned them down, had their first kiss or lost their virginity in the mall parking lot. Teenagers in America now spend more time in the mall than anywhere else but home and school. Mostly it is their choice, but some of that mall time is put in as the result of two-paycheck and single-parent households, and the lack of other viable alternatives. But are these kids being harmed by the mall?

I wondered first of all what difference it makes for adolescents to experience so many important moments in the mall. They are, after all, at play in the fields of its little world and they learn its ways; they adapt to it and make it adapt to them. It's here that these kids get their street sense, only it's mall sense. They are learning the ways of a large-scale artificial environment: its subtleties and flexibilities, its particular pleasures and resonances, and the attitudes it fosters.

4   The presence of so many teenagers for so much time was not something mall developers planned on. In fact, it came as a big surprise. But kids became a fact of mall life very early, and the International Council of Shopping Centers found it necessary to commission a study, which they published along with a guide to mall managers on how to handle the teenage incursion.

The study found that "teenagers in suburban centers are bored and come to the shopping centers mainly as a place to go. Teenagers in suburban centers spent more time fighting, drinking, littering, and walking than did their urban counterparts, but presented fewer overall problems." The report observed that "adolescents congregated in groups of two to four and predominantly at locations selected by them rather than management." This probably had something to do with the decision to install game arcades, which allow management to channel these restless adolescents into naturally contained areas away from major traffic points of adult shoppers.

The guide concluded that mall management should tolerate and even encourage the teenage presence because, in the words of the report, "The vast majority support the same set of values as does shopping center management." *The same set of values* means simply that mall kids are already preprogrammed to be consumers and that the mall can put the finishing touches to them as hardcore, lifelong shoppers just like everybody else. That, after all, is what the mall is about. So it shouldn't be surprising that in spending a lot of time there, adolescents find little that challenges the assumption that the goal of life is to make money and buy products, or that just about everything else in life is to be used to serve those ends.

Growing up in a high-consumption society already adds inestimable pressure to kids' lives. Clothes consciousness has invaded the grade schools, and popularity is linked with having the best, newest clothes in the currently acceptable styles. Even what they read has been affected. "Miss [Nancy] Drew wasn't obsessed with her wardrobe," noted *The Wall Street Journal*. "But today the mystery in teen fiction for girls is what outfit the heroine will wear next." Shopping has become a survival skill and there is certainly no better place to learn it than the mall, where its importance is powerfully reinforced and certainly never questioned.

8   The mall as a university of suburban materialism, where Valley Girls and Boys from coast to coast are educated in consumption, has its other lessons in this era of change in family life and sexual mores and their economic and social ramifications. The plethora of products in the mall, plus the pressure on teens to buy them, may contribute to the phenomenon that psychologist David Elkind calls "the hurried child": kids who are exposed to too much of the adult world too quickly, and must respond with a sophistication that belies their still-tender emotional development. Certainly the adult products marketed for children—formfitting designer jeans, sexy tops for preteen girls—add to the social pressure to look like

an adult, along with the home-grown need to understand adult finances (why mothers must work) and adult emotions (when parents divorce).

Kids spend so much time at the mall partly because their parents allow it and even encourage it. The mall is safe, it doesn't seem to harbor any unsavory activities, and there is adult supervision; it is, after all, a controlled environment. So the temptation, especially for working parents, is to let the mall be their babysitter. At least the kids aren't watching TV. But the mall's role as a surrogate mother may be more extensive and more profound.

Karen Lansky, a writer living in Los Angeles, has looked into the subject and she told me some of her conclusions about the effects on its teenaged denizens of the mall's controlled and controlling environment. "Structure is the dominant idea, since true 'mall rats' lack just that in their home lives," she said, "and adolescents about to make the big leap into growing up crave more structure than our modern society cares to acknowledge." Karen pointed out some of the elements malls supply that kids used to get from their families, like warmth (Strawberry Shortcake dolls and similar cute and cuddly merchandise), old-fashioned mothering ("We do it all for you," the fast-food slogan), and even home cooking (the "homemade" treats at the food court).

The problem in all this, as Karen Lansky sees it, is that while families nurture children by encouraging growth through the assumption of responsibility and then by letting them rest in the bosom of the family from the rigors of growing up, the mall as a structural mother encourages passivity and consumption, as long as the kid doesn't make trouble. Therefore all they learn about becoming adults is how to act and how to consume.

12   Kids are in the mall not only in the passive role of shoppers—they also work there, especially as fast-food outlets infiltrate the mall's enclosure. There they learn how to hold a job and take responsibility, but still within the same value context. When *CBS Reports* went to Oak Park Mall in suburban Kansas City, Kansas, to tape part of their hour-long consideration of malls, "After the Dream Comes True," they interviewed a teenaged girl who worked in a fast-food outlet there. In a sequence that didn't make the final program, she described the major goal of her present life, which was to perfect the curl on top of the ice-cream cones that were her store's specialty. If she could do that, she would be moved from the lowly soft-drink dispenser to the more prestigious ice-cream division, the curl on top of the status ladder at her restaurant. These are the achievements that are important at the mall.

Other benefits of such jobs may also be overrated, according to Laurence D. Steinberg of the University of California at Irvine's social ecology department, who did a study on teenage employment. Their jobs, he found, are generally simple, mindlessly repetitive, and boring. They don't really learn anything, and the jobs don't lead anywhere. Teenagers also work primarily with other teenagers; even their supervisors are often just a little older than they are. "Kids need to spend time with adults," Steinberg told me. "Although they get benefits from peer relationships, without parents and other adults it's one-sided socialization. They hang out with each other, have age-segregated jobs, and watch TV."

Perhaps much of this is not so terrible or even so terribly different. Now that they have so much more to contend with in their lives, adolescents probably need more time to spend with other adolescents without adult impositions, just to sort things out. Though it is more concentrated in the mall (and therefore perhaps a clearer target), the value system there is really the dominant one of the whole society. Attitudes about curiosity, initiative, self-expression, empathy, and disinterested learning aren't necessarily made in the mall; they are mirrored there, perhaps a bit more intensely—as through a glass brightly.

Besides, the mall is not without its educational opportunities. There are bookstores, where there is at least a short shelf of classics at great prices, and other books from which it is possible to learn more than how to do sit-ups. There are tools, from hammers to VCRs, and products, from clothes to records, that can help the young find and express themselves. There are older people with stories, and places to be alone or to talk one-on-one with a kindred spirit. And there is always the passing show.

6   The mall itself may very well be an education about the future. I was struck with the realization, as early as my first forays into Greengate [Mall], that the mall is only one of a number of enclosed and controlled environments that are part of the lives of today's young. The mall is just an extension, say of those large suburban schools—only there's Karmelkorn instead of chem lab, the ice rink instead of the gym: It's high school without the impertinence of classes.

Growing up, moving from home to school to the mall—from enclosure to enclosure, transported in cars—is a curiously continuous process, without much in the way of contrast or contact with unenclosed reality. Places must tend to blur into one another. But whatever differences and dangers there are in this, the skills these adolescents are learning may turn out to be useful in their later lives. For we seem to be moving inexorably into an age of preplanned and regulated environments, and this is the world they will inherit.

Still, it might be better if they had more of a choice. One teenaged girl confessed to *CBS Reports* that she sometimes felt she was missing something by hanging out at the mall so much. "But I'm here," she said, "and this is what I have."

Personal Response

Describe your favorite places for hanging out when you were growing up.

Questions for Class or Small Group Discussion

1. Discuss the positive and negative effects that Kowinski claims spending so much time at the mall has on kids. Do you agree him?

2. How would you answer the question Kowinski poses in paragraph 2: Are kids being harmed by the mall?

3. Comment on this statement: "Growing up in a high-consumption society already adds inestimable pressure to kids' lives" (paragraph 7). Do you agree with Kowinski on this point? If so, what pressures do you think America's high-consumption society puts on young people?

4. Discuss this statement: "[T]he goal of life is to make money and buy products" (paragraph 6). Do you agree or disagree with it?

SHOPPING AND OTHER SPIRITUAL ADVENTURES IN AMERICA TODAY

Phyllis Rose

Phyllis Rose is the author of Woman of Letters: A Life of Virginia Woolf *(1978),* Parallel Lives: Five Victorian Marriages *(1983),* Jazz Cleopatra: Josephine Baker in Her Time *(1989), and* Never Say Good-bye *(1991), from which this essay is taken. Here, Rose takes an amused look at Americans' penchant for shopping.*

Last year a new Waldbaum's Food Mart opened in the shopping mall on Route 66. It belongs to the new generation of superduper-markets open twenty-four hours that have computerized checkout. I went to see the place as soon as it opened and I was impressed. There was trail mix in Lucite bins. There was freshly made pasta. There were coffee beans, four kinds of tahini, ten kinds of herb teas, raw shrimp in shells and cooked shelled shrimp, fresh-squeezed orange juice. Every sophistication known to the big city, even goat's cheese covered with ash, was now available in Middletown, Conn. People raced from the warehouse aisle to the bagel bin to the coffee beans to the fresh fish market, exclaiming at all the new things. Many of us felt elevated, graced, complimented by the presence of this food palace in our town.

This is the wonderful egalitarianism of American business. Was it Andy Warhol who said that the nice thing about Coke is, no can is any better or worse than any other? Some people may find it dull to cross the country and find the same chain stores with the same merchandise from coast to coast, but it means that my town is as good as yours, my shopping mall as important as yours, equally filled with wonders.

Imagine what people ate during the winter as little as seventy-five years ago. They ate food that was local, long-lasting, and dull, like acorn squash, turnips, and cabbage. Walk into an American supermarket in February and the world lies before you: grapes, melons, artichokes, fennel, lettuce, peppers, pistachios, dates, even strawberries, to say nothing of ice cream. Have you ever considered what a triumph of civilization it is to be able to buy a pound of chicken livers? If you lived on a farm and had to kill a chicken when you wanted to eat one, you wouldn't ever accumulate a pound of chicken livers.

4   Another wonder of Middletown is Caldor, the discount department store. Here is man's plenty: tennis racquets, panty hose, luggage, glassware, records, toothpaste. Timex watches, Cadbury's chocolate, corn poppers, hair dryers, warm-up suits, car wax, light bulbs, television sets. All good quality at low prices with exchanges cheerfully made on defective goods. There are worse rules to live by. I feel good about America whenever I walk into this store, which is almost every midwinter Sunday afternoon, when life elsewhere has closed down. I go to Caldor the way English people go to pubs: out of sociability. To get away from my house. To widen my horizons. For culture's sake. Caldor provides me too with a welcome sense of seasonal change. When the first outdoor grills and lawn furniture appear there, it's as exciting a sign of spring as the first crocus or robin.

Someone told me about a Soviet emigré who practices English by declaiming, at random, sentences that catch his fancy. One of his favorites is, "Fifty percent off all items today only." Refugees from Communist countries appreciate our supermarkets and discount department stores for the wonders they are. An Eastern European scientist visiting Middletown wept when she first saw the meat counter at Waldbaum's. On the other hand, before her year in America was up, her pleasure turned sour. She wanted everything she saw. Her approach to consumer goods was insufficiently abstract, too materialistic. We Americans are beyond a simple, possessive materialism. We're used to abundance and the possibility of possessing things. The things, and the possibility of possessing them, will still be there next week, next year. So today we can walk the aisles calmly.

It is a misunderstanding of the American retail store to think we go there necessarily to buy. Some of us shop. There's a difference. Shopping has many purposes, the least interesting of which is to acquire new articles. We shop to cheer ourselves up. We shop to practice decision-making. We shop to be useful and productive members of our class and society. We shop to remind ourselves how much is available to us. We shop to remind ourselves how much is to be striven for. We shop to assert our superiority to the material objects that spread themselves before us.

Shopping's function as a form of therapy is widely appreciated. You don't really need, let's say, another sweater. You need the feeling of power that comes with buying or not buying it. You need the feeling that some-one wants something you have—even if it's just your money. To get the benefit of shopping, you needn't actually purchase the sweater, any more than you have to marry every man you flirt with. In fact, window-shopping, like flirting, can be more rewarding, the same high without the distressing commitment, the material encumbrance. The purest form of shopping is provided by garage sales. A connoisseur goes out with no goal in mind, open to whatever may come his or her way, secure that it will cost very little. Minimum expense, maximum experience. Perfect shopping.

8   I try to think of the opposite, a kind of shopping in which the object is all-important, the pleasure of shopping at a minimum. For example, the purchase of blue jeans. I buy new blue jeans as seldom as possible because the experience is so humiliating. For every pair that looks good on me, fifteen look grotesque. But even shopping for blue jeans at Bob's Surplus on Main Street—no frills, bare-bones shopping—is an event in the life of the spirit. Once again I have to come to terms with the fact that I will never look good in Levi's. Much as I want to be mainstream, I never will be.

In fact, I'm doubly an oddball, neither Misses nor Junior, but Misses Pe-tite. I look in the mirror, I acknowledge the disparity between myself and the ideal, I resign myself to making the best of it: I will buy the Lee's Misses Petite. Shopping is a time of reflection, assessment, spiritual self-discipline.

It is appropriate, I think, that Bob's Surplus has a communal dressing room. I used to shop only in places where I could count on a private dress-ing room with a mirror inside. My impulse then was to hide my weak-nesses. Now I believe in sharing them. There are other women in the dressing room at Bob's Surplus trying on blue jeans who look as bad as I do. We take comfort from one another. Sometimes a woman will ask me which of two items looks better. I always give a definite answer. It's the least I can do. I figure we are all in this together, and I emerge from the dressing room not only with a new pair of jeans but with a renewed sense of belonging to a human community.

When a Solzhenitsyn rants about American materialism, I have to look at my digital Timex and check what year this is. Materialism? Like con-formism, a hot moral issue of the fifties, but not now. How to spread the goods, maybe. Whether the goods are the Good, no. Solzhenitsyn, like the visiting scientist who wept at the beauty of Waldbaum's meat counter but came to covet everything she saw, takes American materialism too mate-rialistically. He doesn't see its spiritual side. Caldor, Waldbaum's, Bob's Surplus—these, perhaps, are our cathedrals.

Personal Response

Explain your attitude toward shopping. Do you go to discount stores or malls to shop or to buy? Does shopping give you the pleasure Rose says it gives most Americans?

Questions for Class or Small Group Discussion

1. Discuss whether you get the pleasure from shopping in American discount stores and supermarkets that Rose describes in her essay. Consider, for instance, Rose's comment in paragraph 9 that "shopping is a time of reflection, assessment, spiritual self-discipline."

2. What criticisms of American consumerism does Rose imply in her ironic descriptions of shopping as a spiritual adventure and department stores as America's cathedrals?

3. In paragraph 10, Rose describes trying on jeans in a communal dressing room and of taking comfort from other women there. Do men experience the same kind of camaraderie when shopping that women often do? To what extent do you think there are differences between the way men and women view shopping in general?

4. What do you think America's multitude of malls, discount stores, and supermarkets and its avalanche of advertisements urging people to buy, suggest about American values?

Perspectives on Marketing and the American Consumer

Suggestions for Synthesis

1. Drawing on at least two of the readings in this chapter, explain the pressures you think America's high-consumption society puts on young people and the effects of those pressures.

2. Drawing on the comments of at least two writers in this chapter, write an essay on the image you think foreigners have of Americans as consumers and whether you think that image is good or bad.

Additional Writing Topics

1. Imagine that you are marketing a product that has traditionally been sold to white, middle-class males. Now you want to increase your sales by targeting other groups. Select a particular group and create a sales campaign aimed at that group.

2. Elaborate on William Severini Kowinski's observation in "Kids in the Mall: Growing Up Controlled" that the mall is "a university of suburban materialism" (paragraph 8).

3. Using examples of people you know, support or refute Juliet Schor's contention in "Work and Spend" that consumerism breeds dissatisfaction.

4. Explain the effects that a change in your income, suddenly coming into money, or acquiring some coveted material possession has had on you or someone you know.

5. In a reflective essay, consider whether you think that being rich enough to buy everything you wanted would make you content.

6. Phyllis Rose in "Shopping and Other Spiritual Adventures in America Today" refers to the "wonderful egalitarianism of American business" (paragraph 2). Using that comment as a starting point, write an essay on American consumerism as a social equalizer.

7. Analyze the positive and negative effects of America's emphasis on consumerism on one particular group of people, such as young people, the elderly, working class people, the wealthy, or those living in poverty.

8. Explain what you think shopping malls, discount stores, and overstocked supermarkets suggest about American values. For instance, what impression of America do you think foreigners visiting this country get when they see the size and quantity of those marketplaces?

Research Topics

1. Research the marketing strategies of one of the major businesses mentioned in Marlene L. Rossman's "America's Changing Face" and assess what you see as its successes and/or failures in promoting its products.

2. Select a particular product (such as automobiles, cosmetics, or beer) or a particular target population (such as children, African-American women, or the elderly) and research the market strategies used by major companies for that particular product or group. You will be able to narrow your focus and give direction to your paper once you begin your research and discover what resources are available on your subject.

3. Research the subject of American consumerism and arrive at your own conclusion about its effects on Americans and American values. This is a broad subject, so look for ways to narrow your focus once you locate books and articles on the general subject.

CHAPTER 21

THE WORKPLACE

The workplace can have enormous influence on people's lives. A majority of the American population work outside the home, either full or part-time, spending a significant portion of their time on the job. The physical atmosphere of the workplace, the friendliness of coworkers, and the attitude of supervisors or bosses play pivotal roles not only in the way workers perform but also in the way they feel about themselves. Tension, anxiety, and stress in the workplace can lower production for the company and produce actual illness in workers, while a pleasant atmosphere, good benefits, and relatively low levels of stress can boost production and make employees look forward to going to work. The quality of life in the workplace has a direct effect on the quality of work employees do and on their general well-being.

The essays in this chapter examine some of the major issues related to the subject of the workplace. In "For Love or Money," Jay Matthews explains the debate over what motivates employees to do their best. Some research suggests that extrinsic rewards such as financial or other material bonuses do not necessarily result in better work or increased productivity. Rather, intrinsic rewards such as a sense of accomplishment or a feeling of contributing to the good of the company may prove more powerful incentives in the long run. What motivates you to do well at something? Is it the promise of something tangible or material, such as a high grade, a gift, or money? Or is it the inner reward of knowing you have done your best work and that you are satisfied with your performance? Think about these questions as you read Matthews' review of the complex and multifaceted subject of what motivates human behavior.

Reinforcing an aspect of Matthews' piece, Ellen Goodman in "A Working Community" elaborates on her observation that the workplace has replaced the neighborhood as a center of community. In that case, workers' identities are closely connected with what they do for a living rather than where they live, and their sense of self-worth is linked closely with how well they perform their job. If, like most college students, you have had a job or are currently working, think about your coworkers and the atmosphere at your workplace. Do you feel a sense of community there?

The last two essays in this chapter explore gender issues in the workplace. In "The Rite of Work: The Economic Man," an excerpt from his book Fire in the Belly, *Sam Keen argues that "masculinity" as defined by corporate America is devastating to men, while in "Women at Risk," Suzanne Gordon argues that to succeed in the corporate world, women have adopted male values, much to their detriment. As you read their discussions of the effects of corporate America on men and women, think about the people you know who already work in corporations and consider whether their experiences confirm or refute Keen's and Gordon's arguments. Consider, too, whether your college education is training you for the kind of life these authors say men and women must conform to if they want to be successful.*

FOR LOVE OR MONEY
Jay Matthews

Jay Matthews is a journalist who wrote this article for the December 1993 issue of The Washington Post National Weekly Edition. *In it, Matthews reviews some theories of behaviorists on what makes employees do their best work.*

In the early 1960s, two graduate students working independently on the ancient problem of coaxing the best from human beings stumbled across results they did not understand. Louise Brightwell Miller at the University of Kentucky discovered that 9-year-old boys were less likely to solve a simple identification test when they were paid for right answers than when they worked for free. Sam Glucksberg at New York University found the same result for adults given a household engineering problem.

Among the behaviorists who have dominated much of American psychology and motivational research since World War II, the notion that people would do better without a material incentive was, as Miller and her adviser said in their report, "an unexpected result, unaccountable for by theory and/or previous empirical evidence."

Thirty years later, the Miller and Glucksberg experiments have become intriguing parts of an intense academic debate over the roots of human motivation and have raised doubts about the methods that American businesses have used for decades to improve employee performance.

In books such as "Punished by Rewards: The Trouble with Gold Stars, Incentive Plans, A's, Praise and Other Bribes" by Alfie Kohn, who cites Miller and Glucksberg, and "Second to None: How Our Smartest Companies Put People First" by Charles Garfield, anti-behaviorist psychologists are arguing that money not only does not buy happiness, it can also, if misapplied, kill a worker's desire to do his or her best.

"When you do something for a reward you tend to become less interested in what you're doing," says Kohn, a writer and lecturer on human behavior who cites the work of dozens of social scientists. "It comes to seem like a chore, something you have to get through in order to pick up the dollar or the A or the extra dessert. What this means is that millions of well-meaning teachers and parents and managers are killing off creativity and curiosity in their attempt to bribe people to do a good job."

To a certain extent, Kohn and Garfield and several other thinkers who take this stand are reviving an old and much-ignored argument just as the anti-reward school is having its greatest impact on Corporate America.

"We are involved in a major change in our culture," says Jim Schmitt, corporate communications director for Westinghouse Electric Corp., speaking of the redesign of jobs and work structures going on in many industries. "We have seen a culture emerging where people are more involved in the decision making regardless of their position in the organization."

8   But to those who want to encourage this trend, the day is still far off when everyone will leap out of bed eager for a day of intrinsically motivated work at the office.

"There are companies that are attempting to understand what truly motivates human beings and then there are others, and I am afraid they are the majority, that have this peculiar affection for pop psychology," including the latest ideas on how to create desire with cash, says Garfield, an associate clinical professor at the University of California at San Francisco.

Raises, promotions, stock options, performance bonuses, merit increases, trips to Disney World and even new cars are still the prime motivators in American business. Many psychologists see nothing wrong with that. "I have worked with many people for whom a kind word doesn't mean a thing," says E. Scott Geller, professor of psychology at Virginia Polytechnic Institute and State University, "but money can mean many things to many people."

Critics of monetary rewards begin by making sure everyone understands they are not advocating a return to slavery. They say people should be paid well enough so that they are no longer distracted by worries that they are underpaid. "Managers need to divorce the task from the compensation as best they can by paying people well and then doing everything possible to help them put money out of their minds," Kohn says.

12   A material reward might work in the short term, the anti-behaviorists argue. Who wouldn't get excited about a trip to Paris for the sales agent who unloads the most Pismo Beach condominiums? But over time, the theory says, the most successful salespeople will grow tired of trips to Paris and require a motive closer to their sense of themselves or lose their spark altogether.

Kohn even cites studies by his behaviorist critics to buttress his point. In 1987 Geller and several associates reviewed the effects of 28 seat-belt use programs at nine different companies. The results, Geller and his group admitted in their research paper, were "inconsistent with basic reinforcement theory." Programs that did not offer cash or prizes for buckling up reported an average 152 percent increase in seat-belt use over periods up to a year, while the long-term gain for programs with rewards was no higher than 62 percent.

Several business surveys add to the impression of money as a comfort rather than a goal. A 1978 survey of more than 50,000 utility company applicants found pay ranked sixth out of 10 job factors. (The same applicants thought others would put money first.) A 1991 poll showed that even among allegedly money-fixated salespeople, increased compensation was the least commonly cited reason for changing jobs.

But the core of Kohn's book, and its most controversial aspect, is a long appreciation of the research of Edward Deci at the University of Rochester and Mark Lepper at Stanford. The two men insist material rewards do not motivate well, and actually poison natural motivators such as curiosity and self-esteem.

16   Lepper watched children in Head Start classrooms react to an experiment with Magic Markers. Some were told that if they used the markers they would be given a special certificate. Some were given the markers with no anticipated reward. After a week, the children who were told they would get a certificate were using the markers not only less frequently than the unrewarded children, but also less frequently than they themselves had used the markers before they were told of the reward.

Deci put college students in a room and asked each to work a puzzle. Half were promised money; half were not. He then announced a pause before "the next phase of the study began" and watched what they did in those idle moments. Those who had been promised money spent less time playing with the puzzle than those who had not anticipated reward.

Deci concluded that "money may work to 'buy off' one's intrinsic motivation for an activity." Deci and Lepper speculated that people thought they were being manipulated when offered a reward. Although they might do what was necessary to receive their prize, it left a bad taste that tainted what had once been an enjoyable activity for them.

Geller says the Deci-Lepper research is flawed. "People say, 'Well, yeah, once I started playing cards for money, I didn't enjoy playing just for fun any more,'" Geller says. "It has an intuitive feel." But the experiment overlooks what Geller calls "the contrast effect"—the sudden disappointment when the reward is no longer available. If the experimenter continued to watch a card player for several months after he swore off gambling, "you might find he would again eventually want to play cards for free."

20   Kohn says studies show that the harm to intrinsic motivation is enduring.

Some psychologists complain that human motivation and its impact on productivity is just too complex a subject to reduce to debates over extrinsic or intrinsic rewards. J. William Townsend, an industrial organizational psychologist and consultant in Memphis, says he accepts much of the anti-reward research but also knows that some employees will always be motivated by money and little else.

Another factor often overlooked in the debate is talent. "People cannot outperform their abilities," Townsend says. "I don't care how much you motivate me, I'm not going to play basketball better than Michael Jordan."

The anti-behaviorists nod at this and say, fine, what we are doing is giving each person the chance to do his best with the greatest joy in the effort, and without being distracted by money. Kohn offers three ways to stimulate workers' natural desire to do well: Find ways for them to work in teams; give them variety and a sense of worthwhile work; and give them as much choice as possible of what they do and how they do it.

24   "Choice is very important," says Marion Gindes, a psychologist and president of Marion Gindes & Associates in Larchmont, N.Y. "In one very old experiment with monkeys, some were able to control to some extent when they received an electric shock and some were not. Those that had some choice ended up in better shape." Many human studies have reached the same conclusion.

Once a worker has a comfortable salary, Garfield says, "you are looking at other motivators like autonomy, the opportunity to be creative in one's work."

Human resources executives began to play with different motivational formulas in the 1970s, says Neil Lewis, management psychologist in Atlanta, "but then we got into the '80s and everybody lost sight of these things. A monkey could have made money in the '80s. We didn't have to worry about all this employee motivation stuff."

Now that corporate downsizing and restructuring have revived the interest in such research, experts warn that there is still little verifiable data to guide executives who have to decide how to get better results from fewer people. Edward Lazear, a Stanford Business School economist and senior fellow at the Hoover Institution, says some initial studies—admittedly in factories with many complicating problems—are disappointing. Even when the new techniques seem to work, he says, they appear to be tied to other motivators that include money.

28   The motives of the critics of motivational methods are often as complex as those of the workers they study. Graef S. Crystal, editor of the Crystal Report and a passionate advocate of tying executive pay to corporate financial performance, admits that more or less money probably would not motivate million-dollar executives very much. So why argue so hard for linking their compensation to the stock price?

"Because," Crystal says, indulging his love for exaggerated metaphor, "even if none of this motivates the person, it still gives the shareholders the pleasure of sitting in the stands when the stock is plummeting and seeing the executives ripped to shreds by wild animals."

The long history of the debate between behaviorists, devotees of psychologists such as B. F. Skinner, and anti-behaviorists, who prefer the work of thinkers such as Frederick Herzberg, has made many business executives skeptical of both sides.

University of Chicago psychologist Mihaly Csikszentmihalyi says it is useful to remember that different situations produce different motivational needs. "Under the right conditions, material incentives can add to the intrinsic reward," he says, "but sometimes they don't make a difference and sometimes they detract from the intrinsic rewards."

32   Crystal says that although he accepts that money can be a poor motivator, he could not resist a chance years ago to tease Herzberg when the famous anti-behaviorist haggled with him over a fee for a lecture Herzberg was to give on why money doesn't motivate.

"Money in fact doesn't motivate me," Herzberg told Crystal without embarrassment, "but it sure as hell helps me sort out my priorities."

Personal Response

Do you find that rewards—grades, money, prizes—motivate you to try harder or do better work than a sense of satisfaction for having done a good job does?

Questions for Class or Small Group Discussion

1. What do you think of the idea that people should be paid so well that they are not distracted by money worries (paragraph 11)? Would such a plan be possible in all workplaces? Might employers see the proposal differently from the way employees see it?

2. Alfie Kohn, author of *Punished by Rewards: The Trouble with Gold Stars, Incentive Plans, A's, Praise and Other Bribes,* says that "'millions of well-meaning teachers and parents and managers are killing off creativity and curiosity in their attempt to bribe people to do a good job'" (paragraph 5). Now that you have read a little about the debate over incentives, do you agree with him? In what ways have teachers you have had "bribed" you to do well? Do you think you would have done just as well or better without the extra incentives?

3. Discuss the three ways to stimulate workers' natural desire to do well that Kohn suggests in paragraph 23. Do you think they would motivate workers more than the incentive of money, trips, or prizes?

4. Discuss the work experiences you have had. To what extent did self-satisfaction or self-motivation play a part in how you performed your work?

A WORKING COMMUNITY

Ellen Goodman

Ellen Goodman has been a columnist for the Boston Globe *since 1967. Her column, "At Large," has been syndicated by the Washington Post Writers Group since 1976. In 1980 she won a Pulitzer Prize for distinguished commentary. In addition to her study of human change,*

Turning Points *(1979), she has collected many of her columns in* Close to Home *(1979),* At Large *(1981),* Keeping in Touch *(1985), and* Making Sense *(1989). This essay is excerpted from* Keeping in Touch.

I have a friend who is a member of the medical community. It does not say that, of course, on the stationery that bears her home address. This membership comes from her hospital work.

I have another friend who is a member of the computer community. This is a fairly new subdivision of our economy, and yet he finds his sense of place in it.

Other friends and acquaintances of mine are members of the academic community, or the business community, or the journalistic community. Though you cannot find these on any map, we know where we belong.

4   None of us, mind you, was born into these communities. Nor did we move into them, U-Hauling our possessions along with us. None has papers to prove we are card-carrying members of one such group or another. Yet it seems that more and more of us are identified by work these days, rather than by street.

In the past, most Americans lived in neighborhoods. We were members of precincts or parishes or school districts. My dictionary still defines community, first of all in geographic terms, as "a body of people who live in one place."

But today fewer of us do our living in that one place; more of us just use it for sleeping. Now we call our towns "bedroom suburbs," and many of us, without small children as icebreakers, would have trouble naming all the people on our street.

It's not that we are more isolated today. It's that many of us have transferred a chunk of our friendships, a major portion of our everyday social lives, from home to office. As more of our neighborhoods work away from home, the workplace becomes our neighborhood.

8   The kaffeeklatsch of the fifties is the coffee break of the eighties. The water cooler, the hall, the elevator, and the parking lot are the back fences of these neighborhoods. The people we have lunch with day after day are those who know the running saga of our mother's operations, our child's math grades, our frozen pipes, and faulty transmissions.

We may be strangers at the supermarket that replaced the corner grocer, but we are known at the coffee shop in the lobby. We share with each other a cast of characters from the boss in the corner office to the crazy lady in Shipping, to the lovers in Marketing. It's not surprising that when researchers ask Americans what they like best about work, they say it is "the shmoose [chatter] factor." When they ask young mothers at home what they miss most about work, it is the people.

Not all the neighborhoods are empty, nor is every workplace a friendly playground. Most of us have had mixed experiences in these environments. Yet as one woman told me recently, she knows more about the people she passes on the way to her desk than on her way around the block.

Our new sense of community hasn't just moved from house to office building. The labels that we wear connect us with members from distant companies, cities, and states. We assume that we have something "in common" with other teachers, nurses, city planners.

12   It's not unlike the experience of our immigrant grandparents. Many who came to this country still identified themselves as members of the Italian community, the Irish community, the Polish community. They sought out and assumed connections with people from the old country. Many of us have updated that experience. We have replaced ethnic identity with professional identity, the way we replaced neighborhoods with the workplace.

This whole realignment of community is surely most obvious among the mobile professions. People who move from city to city seem to put roots down into their professions. In an age of specialists, they may have to search harder to find people who speak the same language.

I don't think that there is anything massively disruptive about this shifting sense of community. The continuing search for connection and shared enterprise is very human. But I do feel uncomfortable with our shifting identity. The balance has tipped and we seem increasingly dependent on work for our sense of self.

If our offices are our new neighborhoods, if our professional titles are our new ethnic tags, then how do we separate our selves from our jobs? Self-worth isn't just something to measure in the marketplace. But in these new communities, it becomes harder and harder to tell who we are without saying what we do.

Personal Response

Do you have a strong sense of belonging to your neighborhood? Do you know all of your neighbors' names? Explain your attitude toward your neighborhood.

Questions for Class or Small Group Discussion

1. Discuss Goodman's statement that "the balance has tipped and we seem increasingly dependent on work for our sense of self" (paragraph 14). Do you agree with her that such a dependency means that people cannot separate themselves from their jobs? Do you think it is necessarily a negative thing if people cannot "tell who we are without saying what we do" (paragraph 15)?

2. Goodman says that the workplace has replaced the neighborhood in a variety of ways (paragraph 8). Do your own experiences support or

refute Goodman? In what ways do you think neighborhoods can never replace workplaces?

3. Discuss the community you feel most connected to. Is it your school, your work, your hometown, your neighborhood, your family, or your religious or ethnic group?

4. Discuss your own job experiences and whether you have felt a strong sense of connection to the people you work with.

THE RITE OF WORK: THE ECONOMIC MAN

Sam Keen

Sam Keen is a contributing editor of Psychology Today. *He is the author of several books,* The Passionate Life *(1983),* Faces of the Enemy: Reflections of the Hostile Imagination *(1988), and* Fire in the Belly: On Being a Man *(1991), from which this piece is excerpted. Keen was nominated for an Emmy Award for his PBS series* The Enemy Within.

> *One does not work to live; one lives to work.*
> —Max Weber,
> *The Protestant Ethic and the Spirit of Capitalism*
>
> *Have leisure and know that I am God.*
> —Psalm 65

Preparations for the male ritual of work begin even before the age of schooling. Long before a boy child has a concept of the day after tomorrow, he will be asked by well-meaning but unconscious adults, "What do you want to be when you grow up?" It will not take him long to discover that "I want to be a horse" is not an answer that satisfies adults. They want to know what men plan to do, what job, profession, occupation we have decided to follow at five years of age! Boys are taught early that they are what they do. Later, as men, when we meet as strangers on the plane or at a cocktail party we break the ice by asking, "What do you do?"

Formal preparation for the rites of manhood in a secular society takes place first through the institution of schooling. Our indoctrination into the dominant myths, value system, and repertoire of heroic stories is homogenized into the educational process. My fifteen-year-old nephew put the matter more accurately than any social scientist. "Schools," he said, "are designed to teach you to take life sitting down. They prepare you to work in office buildings, to sit in rows or cubicles, to be on time, not to talk back, and to let somebody else grade you." From the first grade onward, schools teach us to define and measure ourselves against others. We learn that the world is composed of winners and losers, pass or fail.

The games that make up what we call physical education—football, basketball, and baseball—are minibattles that teach boys to compete in the game of life. Pregame pep talks, like salesmen's meetings, begin with the Vince Lombardi prayer: "Winning isn't the most important thing. It's the only thing." For many boys making the team, from Little League to college, provides the ritual form of combat that is central to male identity.

4 The first full-time job, like the first fight or first sex, is a rite of passage for men in our time. Boys have paper routes, but men have regular paychecks. Like primitive rites, work requires certain sacrifices and offers certain insignia of manhood. In return for agreeing to put aside childish dalliance and assume the responsibility for showing up from nine to five at some place of work, the initiate receives the power object—money—that allows him to participate in the adult life of the community.

Getting a credit card is a more advanced rite of passage. The credit card is for the modern male what killing prey was to a hunter. To earn a credit rating a man must certify that he has voluntarily cut himself off from childhood, that he has foregone the pleasure of languid mornings at the swimming hole, and has assumed the discipline of a regular job, a fixed address, and a predictable character. The Visa card (passport to the good life) is an insignia of membership, a sign that the system trusts you to spend what you have not yet earned because you have shown good faith by being regularly employed. In modern America going into debt is an important part of assuming the responsibilities of manhood. Debt, the willingness to live beyond our means, binds us to the economic system that requires both surplus work and surplus consumption. The popular bumper sticker, "I owe, I owe, so off to work I go" might well be the litany to express the commitment of the working man.

After accepting the disciplines of work and credit, a whole hierarchy of graduated symbolic initiations follows, from first to thirty-second degree. Mere employment entitles one to display the insignia of the Chevette. Acquiring the executive washroom key qualifies one for a Buick or Cadillac. Only those initiated into the inner sanctum of the boardroom may be borne in the regal Rolls-Royce. To the victors belong the marks of status and the repair bills. The right to wear eagle feathers or to sing certain sacred songs was recognized in American Indian tribes to signify the possession of a high degree of power and status, just as in contemporary society certain brand names and logos are tokens of class and rank. A man wears a Rolex not because it tells time more accurately than a $14.95 Timex but because, like a penis shield, it signifies an advanced degree of manhood. In a society where the marks of virtue are created by advertising, possession of stylish objects signifies power. For economic man a Ralph Lauren polo shirt says something very different than its Fruit of the

Loom equivalent. The implicit message is that manhood can be purchased. And the expense of the luxury items we own marks our progress along the path of the good life as it is defined by a consumer society.

Within the last decade someone upped the ante on the tokens required for manhood. A generation ago providing for one's family was the only economic requirement. Nowadays, supplying the necessities entitles a man only to marginal respect. If your work allows you only to survive you are judged to be not much of a man. To be poor in a consumer society is to have failed the manhood test, or at least to have gotten a D−. The advertising industry reminds us at every turn that real men, successful men, powerful men, are big spenders. They have enough cash or credit to consume the best. Buying is status. "It's the cost of the toys that separates the men from the boys." The sort of man who reads *Playboy* or *The New Yorker* is dedicated to a life of voluntary complexity, conspicuous consumption, and adherence to the demanding discipline of style.

8   The rites of manhood in any society are those that are appropriate and congruent with the dominant myth. The horizon within which we live, the source of our value system, and the way we define "reality" are economic. The bottom line is the almighty dollar. Time is money, money is power, and power makes the world go round. In the same sense that the cathedral was the sacred center of the medieval city, the bank and other commercial buildings are the centers of the modern city.

Once upon a time work was considered a curse. As the result of Adam and Eve's sin we were driven from the Garden of Eden and forced to earn our bread by the sweat of our brows. Men labored because of necessity, but found the meaning and sweetness of life in free time. According to the Greeks, only slaves and women were bound to the life of work. Free men discovered the joys and dignity of manhood in contemplation and in the cultivation of leisure. Until the time of the Protestant Reformation the world was divided between the realm of the secular, to which work and the common life belonged, and the realm of the sacred, which was the monopoly of the Church. Martin Luther changed all of this by declaring that every man and woman had a sacred vocation. The plowman and the housewife no less than the priest were called by God to express their piety in the common life of the community. Gradually the notion of the priesthood of all believers came to mean that every man and woman had a calling to meaningful secular work.

In the feudal era manhood involved being the lord of a manor, the head of a household, or at least a husbandman of the land. As the industrial revolution progressed men were increasingly pulled out of the context of nature, family, church, and community to find the meaning of their lives in trading, industry, the arts, and the professions, while women practiced their vocations by ministering to the needs of the home and practicing charity within the community. Gradually, getting and spending assumed the place of greatest importance, virtually replacing all of the old activities that previously defined manhood—hunting, growing, tending, celebrating, protesting, investigating. As "the bottom line" became our ultimate concern, and the Dow Jones the index of reality, man's world shrank. Men no longer found their place beneath the dome of stars, within the brotherhood of animals, by the fire of the hearth, or in the company of citizens. Economic man spends his days with colleagues, fellow workers, bosses, employees, suppliers, lawyers, customers, and other strangers. At night he returns to an apartment or house that has been empty throughout the day. More likely than not, if he is married with children, his wife has also been away at work throughout the day and his children have been tended and educated by another cadre of professionals. If he is successful his security (*securus*—"free from care") rests in his investments (from "vestment"—a religious garment) in stocks, bonds, and other commodities whose future value depends upon the whims of the market.

Nowadays only a fortunate minority are able to find harmony between vocation and occupation. Some artists, professionals, businessmen, and tradesmen find in their work a calling, a lifework, an arena within which they may express their creativity and care. But most men are shackled to the mercantile society in much the same way medieval serfs were imprisoned in the feudal system. All too often we work because we must, and we make the best of a bad job.

12   "In the secular theology of economic man Work has replaced God as the source from whom all blessings flow. The escalating gross national product, or at least the rising Dow Jones index, is the outward and visible sign that we are progressing toward the kingdom of God; full employment is grace; unemployment is sin. The industrious, especially entrepreneurs with capital, are God's chosen people, but even laborers are sanctified because they participate in the productive economy.

As a form of secular piety Work now satisfies many of the functions once served by religion. In the words of Ayn Rand, whose popular philosophy romanticized capitalism and sanctified selfishness, "Your work is the process of achieving your values. Your body is a machine but your mind is its driver. Your work is the purpose of your life, and you must speed past any killer who assumes the right to stop you. . . . Any value you might find outside your work, any other loyalty or love, can only be travelers going on their own power in the same direction."

We don't work just to make a living. Increasingly, the world of work provides the meaning of our lives. It becomes an end in itself rather than a means. A decade ago, only twenty-eight percent of us enjoyed the work we did. And yet, according to a Yankelovich survey, eighty percent of us reported that we would go right on working even if we didn't need the money. By the 1980s this profile changed. We are just as attached to our work, but now we are demanding that the workplace provide an outlet for our creativity. Yankelovich reports in 1988 that fifty-two percent of Americans respond "I have an inner need to do the very best job I can, regardless of the pay" and sixty-one percent when asked what makes for the good life say "a job that is interesting."[1]

Something very strange has happened to work and leisure in the last generation. The great promise of emerging technology was that it would finally set men free from slavery and we could flower. As late as the 1960s philosophers, such as Herbert Marcuse, sociologists, and futurists were predicting a coming leisure revolution. We were just around the corner from a twenty-hour work week. Soon we would be preoccupied by arts, games, and erotic dalliance on leisurely afternoons. At worst we would have to learn to cope with "pleasure anxiety" and the threat of leisure.

16   Exactly the opposite happened. Work is swallowing leisure. The fast lane has become a way of life for young professionals who are giving their all to career. In the 1990s Americans may come more and more to resemble the Japanese—workaholics all, living to work rather than working to live, finding their identity as members of corporate tribes. . . .

Part of the problem is that work, community, and family are getting mixed up and lumped together. Increasingly, Americans live in places where they are anonymous, and seek to find their community at work. Companies, with the help of organizational development consultants, are trying to make the workplace the new home, the new family. The new motto is: humanize the workplace, make it a community; let communication flourish on all levels. The best (or is it the worst?) of companies have become paternalistic or maternalistic, providing their employees with all the comforts and securities of home. . . .

In short, the workplace is rapidly becoming its own culture that defines who we are. Like minisocieties, professions and corporations create their own ritual and mythology. Doctors share a common story, a history of disease and cure, a consensus about the means of healing with other doctors. Businessmen share the language of profit and loss with other businessmen and acknowledge the same tokens of success. As economic organizations have grown larger than governments, employees render them a type of loyalty previously reserved for God, country, or family.

To determine what happens to men within the economic world we need to look critically at its climate, its ruling mood, its ethos, its aims, and its method. We should no more accept a profession's or a corporation's self-evaluation, its idealistic view of itself (we are a family, a "service" organization, dedicated to the highest ideals of quality, etc.) than we would accept the propaganda of any tribe or nation.

20   A recent critical study of the climate of corporate culture suggests it may be more like a tyrannical government than a kindly family. Earl Shorris, in a neglected and very important book, suggests that the modern corporation represents a historically new form of tyranny in which we are

---

[1] *American Health* (September 1988).

controlled by accepting the definitions of happiness that keep us in harness for a lifetime. Herewith, in short, his argument:

> The most insidious of the many kinds of power is the power to define happiness. . . .
>
> The manager, like the nobleman of earlier times, serves as the exemplary merchant: since happiness cannot be defined, he approximates his definition through the display of symbols, such as expense account meals, an expensive house, stylish clothing, travel to desirable places, job security, interesting friends, membership in circles of powerful people, advantages for his children, and social position for his entire family. . . .
>
> In the modern world, a delusion about work and happiness enables people not only to endure oppression but to seek it and to believe that they are happier because of the very work that oppresses them. At the heart of the delusion lies the manager's definition of happiness: sweat and dirty hands signify oppression and a coat and tie signify happiness, freedom, and a good life.
>
> Blue-collar workers . . . resist symbolic oppression. One need only visit an assembly line and observe the styles of dress, speech, and action of the workers to realize the symbolic freedom they enjoy. . . . They live where they please, socialize with whomever they please, and generally enjoy complete freedom outside the relatively few hours they spend at their jobs. . . . No matter how much money a blue-collar worker earns, he is considered poor; no matter how much he enjoys his work, he is thought to be suffering. In that way, blue-collar wages are kept low and blue-collar workers suffer the indignity of low status.
>
> The corporation or the bureaucracy . . . becomes a place, the cultural authority, the moral home of a man. The rules of the corporation become the rules of society, the future replaces history, and the organization becomes the family of the floating man. . . . By detaching him from the real world of place, the corporation becomes the world for him.
>
> Men abandoned the power to define happiness for themselves, and having once abandoned that power, do not attempt to regain it. . . . [2]

The new rhetoric about the workplace as home and family needs to be balanced by an honest evaluation of the more destructive implications of the iron law of profit. Home and family are ends in themselves. They are, or should be, about sharing of love to no purpose. They file no

---

[2] Earl Shorris, *The Oppressed Middle: Politics of Middle Management* (Garden City, NY: Doubleday, 1989). Now in print under a different title: *Scenes from Corporate Life* (NY: Penguin, 1990).

quarterly reports. Business is an activity organized to make a profit. And any activity is shaped by the end it seeks. Certainly business these days wears a velvet glove, comporting itself with a new facade of politeness and enlightened personnel policies, but beneath the glove is the iron fist of competition and warfare.

The recent spate of best-selling books about business that make use of military metaphors tell an important story about economic life and therefore about the climate within which most men spend their days. Listen to the metaphors, the poetry of business as set forth in David Rogers's *Waging Business Warfare* from the jacket copy:

> Become a master of strategy on today's corporate killing fields—and win the war for success. . . . How to succeed in battle: believe it: if you're in business, you're at war. Your enemies—your competitors—intend to annihilate you. Just keeping your company alive on the battlefield is going to be a struggle. Winning may be impossible—unless you're a master of military strategy. . . . You can be—if you'll follow the examples of the great tacticians of history. Because the same techniques that made Genghis Khan, Hannibal, and Napoleon the incomparable conquerors they were are still working for Chrysler's Lee Iacocca, Procter & Gamble's John Smale, Remington's Victor Kiam, and other super-strategists on today's corporate killing-fields. . . . Join them at the command post! Mastermind the battle! Clobber the enemy! Win the war![3]

Or, maybe to succeed you need to know *The Leadership Secrets of Attila the Hun?* Or listen to the language of Wall Street: corporate raiders, hostile takeovers, white knights, wolf packs, industrial spies, the underground economy, head-hunting, shark-repellent, golden parachutes, poison pills, making a killing, etc.

24   When we organize our economic life around military metaphors and words such as *war, battle, strategy, tactics, struggle, contest, competition, winning, enemies, opponents, defenses, security, maneuver, objective, power, command, control, willpower, assault* we have gone a long way toward falling into a paranoid worldview. And when men live within a context where their major function is to do battle—economic or literal—they will be shaped by the logic of the warrior psyche.

The High Price of Success

At the moment the world seems to be divided between those countries that are suffering from failed economies and those that are suffering from successful economies. After a half century of communism the USSR,

---

[3] David J. Rogers, *Waging Business Warfare: Lessons from the Military Masters in Achieving Corporate Superiority* (New York: Scribner, 1987).

Eastern Europe, and China are all looking to be saved from the results of stagnation by a change to market economies. Meanwhile, in the U.S., Germany, and Japan we are beginning to realize that our success has created an underclass of homeless and unemployed, and massive pollution of the environment. As the Dow rises to new heights everyone seems to have forgotten the one prophetic insight of Karl Marx: where the economy creates a class of winners it will also create a class of losers, where wealth gravitates easily into the hands of the haves, the fortunes of the have-nots become more desperate.

On the psychological level, the shadow of our success, the flip side of our affluence, is the increasing problem of stress and burnout. Lately, dealing with stress and burnout has become a growth industry. Corporations are losing many of their best men to the "disease" of stress. Every profession seems to have its crisis: physician burnout, teacher burnout, lawyer burnout. Experts in relaxation, nutrition, exercise, and meditation are doing a brisk business.

But finally, stress cannot be dealt with by psychological tricks, because for the most part it is a philosophical rather than a physiological problem, a matter of the wrong worldview. Perhaps the most common variety of stress can best be described as "rustout" rather than burnout. It is a product, not of an excess of fire but of a deficiency of passion. We, human beings, can survive so long as we "make a living," but we do not thrive without a sense of significance that we gain only by creating something we feel is of lasting value—a child, a better mousetrap, a computer, a space shuttle, a book, a farm. When we spend the majority of our time doing work that gives us a paycheck but no sense of meaning we inevitably get bored and depressed. When the requirements of our work do not match our creative potential we rust out. The second kind of burnout is really a type of combat fatigue that is the inevitable result of living for an extended period within an environment that is experienced as a battle zone. If the competition is always pressing you to produce more and faster, if life is a battle, if winning is the only thing, sooner or later you are going to come down with battle fatigue. Like combat veterans returning from Vietnam, businessmen who live for years within an atmosphere of low-intensity warfare begin to exhibit the personality traits of the warrior. They become disillusioned and numb to ethical issues, they think only of survival and grow insensitive to pain. You may relax, breathe deeply, take time for R and R, and remain a warrior. But ultimately the only cure for stress is to leave the battlefield.

28   The feminist revolution made us aware of how the economic order has discriminated against women, but not of how it cripples the male psyche. In ancient China the feet of upperclass women were broken, bent backwards, and bound to make them more "beautiful." Have the best and brightest men of our time had their souls broken and bent to make them "successful"?

Let's think about the relation between the wounds men suffer, our overidentification with work, and our captivity within the horizons of the economic myth.

Recently, a lament has gone out through the land that men are becoming too tame, if not limp. The poet Robert Bly, who is as near as we have these days to a traveling bard and shaman for men, says we have raised a whole generation of soft men—oh-so-sensitive, but lacking in thunder and lightning. He tells men they must sever the ties with mother, stop looking at themselves through the eyes of women, and recover the "wild man" within themselves.

I suspect that if men lack the lusty pride of self-affirmation, if we say "yes" too often but without passion, if we are burned out without ever having been on fire, it is mostly because we have allowed ourselves to be engulfed by a metabody, a masculine womb—The Corporation. . . .

32   At what cost to the life of our body and spirit do we purchase corporate and professional success? What sacrifices are we required to make to these upstart economic gods?

Here are some of the secrets they didn't tell you at the Harvard Business School, some of the hidden, largely unconscious, tyrannical, unwritten rules that govern success in professional and corporate life:

> *Cleanliness is next to prosperity.* Sweat is lower class, lower status. Those who shower before work and use deodorant make more than those who shower after work and smell human throughout the day. As a nation we are proud that only three percent of the population has to work on the land—get soiled, be earthy—to feed the other ninety-seven percent.
>
> *Look but don't touch.* The less contact you have with real stuff—raw material, fertilizer, wood, steel, chemicals, making things that have moving parts—the more money you will make. Lately, as we have lost our edge in manufacturing and production, we have comforted ourselves with the promise that we can prosper by specializing in service and information industries. Oh, so clean.
>
> 36   *Prefer abstractions.* The further you move up toward the catbird seat, the penthouse, the office with the view of all Manhattan, the more you live among abstractions. In the brave new world of the market you may speculate in hog futures without ever having seen a pig, buy out an airline without knowing how to fly a plane, grow wealthy without having produced anything.
>
> *Specialize.* The modern economy rewards experts, men and women who are willing to become focused, concentrated, tightly bound, efficient. Or to put the matter more poignantly, we succeed in our professions to the degree that we sacrifice wide-ranging curiosity and fascination with the world at large, and become departmental in our thinking. The professions, like medieval castles, are

small kingdoms sealed off from the outer world by walls of jargon. Once initiated by the ritual of graduate school, MBAs, economists, lawyers, and physicians speak only to themselves and theologians speak only to God.

Sit still and stay indoors. The world is run largely by urban, sedentary males. The symbol of power is the chair. The chairman of the board sits and manages. As a general rule those who stay indoors and move the least make the most money. Muscle doesn't pay. Worse yet, anybody who has to work in the sun and rain is likely to make the minimum wage. With the exception of quarterbacks, boxers, and race car drivers, whose bodies are broken for our entertainment, men don't get ahead by moving their bodies.

Live by the clock. Ignore your intimate body time, body rhythms, and conform to the demands of corporate time, work time, professional time. When "time is money," we bend our bodies and minds to the demands of EST (economic standard time). We interrupt our dreams when the alarm rings, report to work at nine, eat when the clock strikes twelve, return to our private lives at five, and retire at sixty-five—ready or not. As a reward we are allowed weekends and holidays for recreation. Conformity to the sacred routine, showing up on time, is more important than creativity. Instead of "taking our time" we respond to deadlines. Most successful men, and lately women, become Type A personalities, speed freaks, addicted to the rush of adrenaline, filled with a sense of urgency, hard driven, goal oriented, and stressed out. The most brutal example of this rule is the hundred-hour week required of physicians in their year of residency. This hazing ritual, like circumcision, drives home the deep mythic message that your body is no longer your own.

40　　*Wear the uniform.* It wouldn't be so bad if those who earned success and power were proud enough in their manhood to peacock their colors. But no. Success makes drab. The higher you rise in the establishment the more colorless you become, the more you dress like an undertaker or a priest. Bankers, politicians, CEOs wear black, gray, or dark blue, with maybe a bold pinstripe or a daring "power tie." And the necktie? That ultimate symbol of the respectable man has obviously been demonically designed to exile the head from the body and restrain all deep and passionate breath. The more a corporation, institution, or profession requires the sacrifice of the individuality of its members, the more it requires uniform wear. The corp isn't really looking for a few good men. It's looking for a few dedicated Marines, and it knows exactly how to transform boys into uniform men. As monks and military men have known for centuries, once you get into the habit you follow the orders of the superior.

Keep your distance, stay in your place. The hierarchy of power and prestige that governs every profession and corporation establishes the proper distance between people. There are people above you, people below you, and people on your level, and you don't get too close to any of them. Nobody hugs the boss. What is lacking is friendship. I know of no more radical critique of economic life than the observation by Earl Shorris that nowhere in the vast literature of management is there a single chapter on friendship.

Desensitize yourself. Touch, taste, smell—the realm of the senses— receive little homage. What pays off is reason, will-power, planning, discipline, control. There has, of course, recently been a move afoot to bring in potted plants and tasteful art to make corporate environments more humane. But the point of these exercises in aesthetics, like the development of communication skills by practitioners of organizational development, is to increase production. The bottom line is still profit, not pleasure or persons.

Don't trouble yourself with large moral issues. The more the world is governed by experts, specialists, and professionals, the less anybody takes responsibility for the most troubling consequences of our success-failure. Television producers crank out endless cop and killing tales, but refuse to consider their contribution to the climate of violence. Lawyers concern themselves with what is legal, not what is just. Physicians devote themselves to kidneys or hearts of individual patients while the health delivery system leaves masses with medicine. Physicists invent new generations of genocidal weapons which they place in the eager arms of the military. The military hands the responsibility for their use over to politicians. Politicians plead that they have no choice—the enemy makes them do it. Professors publish esoterica while students perish from poor teaching. Foresters, in cahoots with timber companies, clear-cut or manage the forest for sustained yield, but nobody is in charge of oxygen regeneration. Psychologists heal psyches while communities fall apart. Codes of professional ethics are for the most part, like corporate advertisements, high sounding but self-serving.

44   When we live within the horizons of the economic myth, we begin to consider it honorable for a man to do whatever he must to make a living. Gradually we adopt what Erich Fromm called "a marketing orientation" toward our selves. We put aside our dreams, forget the green promise of our young selves, and begin to tailor our personalities to what the market requires. When we mold ourselves into commodities, practice smiling and charm so we will have "winning personalities," learn to sell ourselves, and practice the silly art of power dressing, we are certain to be haunted by a sense of emptiness.

Men, in our culture, have carried a special burden of unconsciousness, of ignorance of the self. The unexamined life has been worth quite a lot in economic terms. It has enabled us to increase the gross national product yearly. It may not be necessary to be a compulsive extrovert to be financially successful, but it helps. Especially for men, ours is an outer-directed culture that rewards us for remaining strangers to ourselves, unacquainted with feeling, intuition, or the subtleties of sensation and dreams.

Many of the personality characteristics that have traditionally been considered "masculine"—aggression, rationality—are not innate or biological components of maleness but are products of a historical era in which men have been socially assigned the chief roles in warfare and the economic order. As women increasingly enter the quasimilitary world of the economic system they are likely to find themselves governed by the logic of the system. Some feminists, who harbor a secret belief in the innate moral superiority of women, believe that women will change the rules of business and bring the balm of communication and human kindness into the boardroom. To date this has been a vain hope. Women executives have proven themselves the equal of men in every way—including callousness. The difference between the sexes is being eroded as both sexes become defined by work. It is often said that the public world of work is a man's place and that as women enter it they will become increasingly "masculine" and lose their "femininity." To think this way is to miss the most important factor of the economic world. Economic man, the creature who defines itself within the horizons of work and consumption, is not man in any full sense of the word, but a being who has been neutralized, degendered, rendered subservient to the laws of the market. The danger of economics is not that it turns women into men but that it destroys the fullness of both manhood and womanhood.

Personal Response

What is your reaction to Keen's criticism of the corporate world? Is your college education training you for the kind of life Keen says successful adult males—and increasingly females—must conform to in order to succeed?

Questions for Class or Small Group Discussion

1. Discuss whether you agree with Keen's analysis of the rites of passage that define manhood in America.

2. Discuss Keen's analysis of the "unwritten rules that govern success in professional and corporate life" (paragraph 33). Do you think he is exaggerating, or do you think he is accurate in his assessment?

3. Discuss Keen's closing comment that corporate and professional life "destroys the fullness of both manhood and womanhood."

4. To what degree does Keen's argument about economic man apply to women as well? Which observations about how corporate and professional success wound men apply only to men and which also apply to women? Try substituting female words for male-specific words to test your answer.

5. Discuss this statement: "The world of work provides the meaning of our lives" (paragraph 14). Do you agree with Keen?

WOMEN AT RISK

Suzanne Gordon

Suzanne Gordon is a freelance reporter whose articles have appeared in such publications as The Nation, The Atlantic Monthly, *the* Washington Post, *and the* Boston Globe. *She is the author of several books, including* Prisoners of Men's Dreams *(1991), from which this excerpt is taken. Here, Gordon argues that the corporate world has changed women for the worse and that a host of social services have suffered as a result.*

Women and their vision of a more humane world are at risk.

Only a few short years ago, women's liberation promised to change our world. Our emphasis on the value of relationships, interdependence, and collaboration sought to balance work with love, hierarchy with healing, individualism with community. Through our profound commitment to caring, we hoped finally to teach American society that care was neither a reward for hard work nor an indulgence meted out to the infirm and vulnerable, but rather a fundamental human need. Many women who participated in our movement demanded that equality make a difference—not only for our sisters and ourselves, but for men and for generations to come.

Now, two decades after the great social upheavals of the 1960s, women are in danger of becoming prisoners of men's dreams.

4   It has required centuries of excruciating struggle, but we have finally arrived on the shores of the masculine world. And yet, as we have moved inland, slowly, almost imperceptibly, too many of us seem to have been wooed away from our original animating goal of changing this landscape.

We have not attained as much power and influence as we'd hoped. Although millions of us live in poverty that has been increasingly feminized, we have nonetheless been assimilated into the American marketplace. Millions of us now participate in an economic, social, and political system that is highly competitive, aggressive, and individualistic; a system that values workplace success and the accumulation of wealth, power, and privilege above all else.

Many of us are now doctors and lawyers, bankers and stockbrokers, scientists and engineers, legislators and congressional representatives, mayors and even governors. We are telephone workers and underground miners, carpenters and house painters, auto mechanics, mailpersons, and cab drivers. A few of us sit on the boards of the nation's major corporations. We have started our own magazines and secured positions of influence in the media—editing newspapers, producing network news

shows, writing and directing for television, running major motion picture studios and determining the content of at least some of the films
they make.

Some of us supervise not only other women but men. We boss
secretaries, give orders to nursers, hire nannies, and are served by flight
attendants as we fly the nation's skies. Not all of us, but some of us, participate in making the decisions that govern other women's lives.

8   We are lobbyists, political consultants, and politicians. We advise
women—and sometimes men—how to run campaigns and shepherd bills
through state legislatures and Congress. We may not have all the votes,
and we certainly do not have the final veto—but to our constituents we
interpret reality, define the possible, and help create the probable.

We have entered the male kingdom—and yet, we have been forced
to play by the king's rules.

That is not what an important segment of the feminist movement
promised.

Feminism was, and remains, one of the most powerful social movements of the twentieth century. When women marched and protested
and united to recast the contours of our world, many of us carried a very
different transformative vision in our hearts and minds. Twenty years ago,
a significant group of feminists believed in women, in the potential of
femininity and the transformative power of feminism. It was clear, these
transformative feminists'[1] argued, that our masculine socialization—our
ingrained insecurity about our competence and talents outside of the domestic sphere—was a wound. But our feminine socialization, so many
sensed, was a source of strength to be mobilized not only for the private
but for the public good.

12   Socialized in the home, the community, and the helping professions,
women devoted themselves to nurturing, empowering, and caring for others. In a society little dedicated to sustaining relationships, encouraging
cooperation and community, recognizing the value of collaboration, or rewarding altruism rather than greed, women have historically defined, defended, and sustained a set of insights, values, and activities which, if never
dominant, at least provided a counterweight and an alternative ideal to the
anomie, disconnectedness, fragmentation, and commercialization of our
culture.

Many of us saw women's experiences and concerns as the source of
a sorely needed transformative vision. And our dream of liberation was

---

[1] There are many different ways to refer to the feminisms and feminists that I am describing. In
her work, Nancy Cott distinguishes between those who focused on equal rights and those who
were concerned with using the insights of feminine socialization to show that women could make
a difference in the world. Some feminists refer to "liberal" and "radical" feminists. Nel Noddings
distinguishes between first, second, and third generations of feminists and Jane Mansbridge
talks about "nurturant" feminism. . . . I will refer to "transformative" and "adaptive," or "equal-
opportunity," feminism.

fueled by the hope that we could carry this vision with us into the marketplace and encourage a new ethic of caring even as we demonstrated our own competence. Our vision of a more humane society was based on a profound commitment to caring—to the emotional and physical activities, attitudes, and ethical comportment that help people grow and develop, that nurture and empower them, affirming their strengths and helping them cope with their weaknesses, vulnerabilities, and life crises.

Thus we hoped to create a less hierarchical workplace, one in which people could help others grow and develop; in which knowledge, experience, power, and wealth could be shared more equitably. We wanted both the private and public sector to allow and even help us fulfill our caring responsibilities by implementing the kinds of social policies that are essential to any real integration of work and personal relationships. And we wanted to infuse our society with a greater respect for the caring work that women have so long performed and refined both inside and outside the home. Most importantly, we wanted men to value and share that caring with us in the home and the workplace.

American society has made it enormously difficult for women—or men—to hold to such an alternative ideal. Many men have sabotaged women's struggle for equality and difference from its inception, and they continue to resist our every effort to improve our lives. When America's masculine-dominated, marketplace culture has not openly thwarted women's hopes and dreams, it has often tried to co-opt women's liberation. Thus while many women have remained faithful to this transformative vision and still struggle valiantly to make it a reality, it has been difficult for millions of others to resist a barrage of messages from corporate America and the media that define mastery and liberation in competitive, marketplace terms. Corporate America and the media have declared that feminism triumphs when women gain the opportunity to compete in what Abraham Lincoln once called the great "race of life." Following a classic pattern in which the victims of aggression identify with their aggressors, many prominent advocates of women's liberation within the highly competitive capitalist marketplace have themselves embraced this masculinized corruption of feminist ideals.

16   Placing competition above caring, work above love, power above empowerment, and personal wealth above human worth, corporate America has created a late-twentieth-century hybrid—a refashioned feminism that takes traditional American ideas about success and repackages them for the new female contestants in the masculine marketplace. This hybrid is equal-opportunity feminism—an ideology that abandons transformation to adaptation, promoting male-female equality without questioning the values that define the very identity it seeks.

Betty Friedan, whose important work launched the liberal branch of the feminist movement, was one of the first to give voice to this ideology, in 1963 in *The Feminine Mystique*. For her, feminism and competition seemed to be synonymous. "When women take their education and abilities seriously and put them to use, ultimately they have to compete with men," she wrote. "It is better for a woman to compete impersonally in society, as men do, than to compete for dominance in her own home with her husband, compete with her neighbors for empty status, and so smother her son that he cannot compete at all."[2]

From the equal-opportunity feminism first envisaged in *The Feminine Mystique* to that promoted today by *Working Woman* and *Savvy* magazines, and the dozens of primers that promote the dress-for-success philosophy that often pretends to speak for all of feminism, progress and liberation have been defined in male, market terms. While some equal-opportunity feminists pay lip service to the work of their more care-oriented sisters, claiming that they would support a broad agenda that addresses our caring needs, the overarching mission of many is to help women adapt to the realities of the masculine marketplace. This brand of feminism often appeals to women's understandable fears that to discuss human beings' mutual need to care for one another is to argue that only women—not men—shoulder the duty to care. Rather than reaffirming our caring commitments so that we can all—male and female alike—share them, equal-opportunity feminism often seems to define caring as a masculine attempt to imprison women in the home and caring professions.

In this environment, the goal of liberation is to be treated as a man's equal *in a man's world,* competing for oneself against a very particular kind of man—the artists, scientists, politicians, and professionals that Friedan speaks of throughout her book. Or, as a recent *New York Times* series about the progress of women and feminism stated, "The basic goal of the women's movement was to eliminate the barriers that kept women from achieving as much as men and which did not allow them to *compete* with men on an equal basis"[3] (my italics).

20   For equal-opportunity feminism, then, the ultimate goal is traditional American success—making money; relentlessly accumulating possessions; capturing and hoarding power, knowledge, access, and information; grasping and clinging to fame, status, and privilege; proving that you are good enough, smart enough, driven enough to get to the top, and tough enough to stay there. In America—particularly the America of the Reagan and post-Reagan years—this is, after all, the meaning of "having it all."

In a world where allegiance to family, community, and politics has eroded, the American marketplace, with its glittering prize of success, has co-opted many of us, undermining our hopes and expectations. Others among us had a different vision. We had hoped that by going into the marketplace and taking our posts there as individuals, we would somehow

---

[2] Betty Friedan, *The Feminine Mystique* (New York: Dell Publishing Company, 1963), 369.

[3] Lisa Belkin, "Bars to Equality of Sexes Seen as Eroding, Slowly," *New York Times,* August 20, 1989.

subvert it. Many believed that our femininity would protect us, that the force of our feminism would make us invulnerable to the seductive logic of either patriarchy or capitalism.

In fact, we were remarkably naive about this foreign land into which we had journeyed. Yes, we were quick to admit that American society is too ruthless, too violent, too aggressive and uncaring. But many of us believed that the market's ills were a direct result of the sex of those who ruled and served it—men. As Betty Friedan, among so many others, has said over and over again, "Society was created by and for men."[4]

It seemed logical, therefore, to argue that the aggressive, elitist, hierarchical attitudes, values, and behaviors that kept women oppressed served the needs of and benefited all men, and that the natural solution was simply to change the sex of the players. It seemed natural to believe that putting women in power—without radically changing the system of power—would improve things for *all*. After all, like so many oppressed groups who believe oppression is a shield against the temptations of tyranny, women, who had been oppressed and subordinate for so long themselves, would never turn around and oppress and dominate others.

24   What we had not counted on was the strength of the marketplace, its ability to seduce and beguile the best and brightest, and its capacity to entrap us in its rules and entangle us in its imperatives. A few women have won great wealth and privilege. But, not unlike men in similar positions, many of them are unwilling to jeopardize what they've acquired in order to work for change. Some are so caught up in their own personal sagas of success that they have forgotten the women who have been left behind. . . .

Today, many women have . . . joined men in denigrating the care-giving activities that they used to protect, preserve, and defend. It has become all too common for professional women to look down on those who have continued to do caring work in traditional women's professions like nursing, social work, teaching, and mothering. Nurses and others are constantly asked, "Why didn't someone as intelligent as you become a doctor?" or "Why didn't you become a psychologist rather than a social worker?" Teachers who leave the profession to become entrepreneurs are promoted as examples of "career courage," as if maintaining one's commitment to educating the young were an act of cowardice.[5]

Even our child-rearing practices have been affected. Today more and more mothers—particularly those among high-powered two-career couples—are told that good parenting equals pushing their young children to learn competitive, cognitive skills that will supposedly pave the way for future career advancement. In the process, they are producing families in which both parents now subscribe to the kind of performance-oriented,

[4] Betty Friedan, *The Second Stage* (New York: Summit Books, 1986), 70, 80.

[5] Beverly Kempton, "Great Transformations," *Working Woman,* January 1989.

competitive child rearing so often associated with masculine parenting styles. And we, as a culture, risk dissolving the positive bonds of love and nurturing and losing the irretrievable freedom of childhood.

The fact that women are now encouraged to devalue caring work has exacerbated a widespread societal crisis in caring that has deep political and social roots. As a society we cannot seem to muster the will or political courage to care for the most precious things we produce—other human beings.

28   By devaluing care we have, for example, abandoned our moral responsibility to the children who represent our future. The United States has risen to twenty-first in its infant mortality rate. Twenty percent of America's children are destitute, and American poverty is increasingly feminized. Over thirty-seven million people have no employer-paid health insurance coverage, and twenty to thirty million more are underinsured. Even those who can produce an insurance card when they arrive at the hospital may receive inadequate care. Moreover, older Americans are denied even catastrophic health care coverage and must pauperize themselves before they are eligible for government assistance with long-term nursing home care.

America's public education system—once the cornerstone of our democracy—is in a shambles. Millions of Americans today are homeless. Childcare is unobtainable for many, substandard for most, and frequently unaffordable for women who work in the home and also need support and respite. The only kind of parental and medical leaves that Congress seems willing to legislate are unpaid ones that will never be utilized by the majority of Americans because they cannot afford the loss of income involved. And presidential vetoes are threatened even for those.

Our need is greater than ever for more people to care for our children and teach them the cognitive, moral, and social skills they will need to grow and develop; to tend the sick; to nurture the emotionally vulnerable and physically handicapped; and to help an aging population deal with infirmity, chronic illness, and death. And yet our society's widespread devaluation of care is discouraging potential recruits—whether male or female—from entering the caring professions and making it more difficult to induce those already in those professions to remain. These negative attitudes toward care pose a severe threat to existing political programs and policies that support and sustain caring activities. And if women retreat from caring, how can we possibly expect men to enter the caregiving professions or to be more caring in their personal and professional relationships?

The crisis in caring that women—and society—face today is more serious than many of us could have imagined. Yet, too many acknowledge the problem by essentially denying it. Like male CEO's rationalizing their failures to promote more women to positions of corporate power, they insist that the enemy is not their own values and beliefs, but rather time. It takes years, men often say, to produce women who have the skills and knowledge required to follow the commands, execute the orders, and play the game to win. Change, they insist, is forthcoming—dozens of women are in the pipeline; just wait and you will see them.

32   Some contemporary defenders of feminism echo these same rationalizations. Understandably concerned about providing antifeminist ammunition for the right, they insist that the problem is time, not values; quantity, not quality. Women have not been liberated long enough, there are not yet enough of us in positions of power. If the ratio of women to men were just greater—then things would definitely change for the better.

Of course, all this is true. But it is only a partial explanation. A cold, clear look at reality reveals that these, if not amplified, are but empty assurances. Yes, we do need more time. Of course, it takes years, perhaps even decades, to change human behavior. But change is a *process,* not an *event.* If the women waiting in the wings for their moment on stage have been trained in the male method, if they behave like men, abide by the rules of the male marketplace, and merely join men in administering the status quo rather than taking risks to change it, then only the names and shapes of the players will have altered. The substance of our lives will stay the same. Indeed, things may be even worse. If women abandon caring for competition, rather than working to encourage *all of us* to share in the real work of the human community, then *who will* care? What kind of liberation will we have purchased?

Personal Response

Are you sympathetic to Gordon's views, or do you disagree with what she says? Explain your answer.

Questions for Class or Small Group Discussion

1. Discuss the difference between "transformative" feminists and "adaptive" feminists, as Gordon sees it. Do you agree with Gordon's analysis of the way in which adaptive feminists have adopted male values and behaviors in the professions and corporate world?

2. How do you think an organization would be run were it to adopt the visions of transformative feminists? Discuss whether such a change would be beneficial. Do you foresee any problems with a corporation's adopting the values and beliefs of transformative feminists?

3. Gordon makes a connection between the way adaptive feminists have abandoned caring as they took on positions of power and a host of social problems, ranging from the high infant mortality rate to homelessness and poverty. Review paragraphs 25–29 and discuss whether you agree with her argument about the effects of women joining men "in denigrating the care-giving activities that they used to protect, preserve, and defend" (paragraph 25).

4. Do you have evidence from your own experiences or observations to support Gordon's assertion that our society devalues caretakers and caretaking professions? What professions is she talking about? Do you think there is a decline in the quality and quantity of good care in our country?

Perspectives on the Workplace

Suggestions for Synthesis

1. Both Sam Keen ("The Rite of Work: The Economic Man") and Suzanne Gordon ("Women at Risk") argue that men and women are socialized to conform to gender roles with specific sex-related characteristics and behaviors. They insist that conforming to those roles "wounds" both men and women and that breaking away from stereotypical gender roles is a struggle. Using the comments of both of these writers, explore the degree to which you agree that boys and girls are brought up with entirely different sets of expectations for their behavior and the extent to which you believe such socialization prevents men and women from being fully human.

2. Interview people who work in corporations for their views on how they perceive their workplace. Is it their "community," as Ellen Gordon describes it in "A Working Community"? Is it a place that devalues caring human relationships, as Suzanne Gordon maintains in "Women at Risk"? Is it a place that "wounds" men and women, as both Gordon and Sam Keen in "The Rite of Work" argue? You might even want to excerpt passages from each of these articles and ask the people you interview for their responses. Then report on the results of your interview, either to the class as a whole or in a formal essay, explaining what conclusions you have drawn on the importance of the workplace.

3. Compare Suzanne Gordon's "Women at Risk" with Sam Keen's "The Rite of Work: Economic Man." To what extent do you think that both Keen and Gordon are making the same argument? How do they differ? Explain your own conclusions about the effect of corporate America on women and men.

Additional Writing Topics

1. Explain your career goal and what you think will motivate you to do well at it.

2. Describe what you see as the ideal job and ideal working conditions.

3. Using Sam Keen's "The Rite of Work: The Economic Man" as a starting point for your thinking, describe the attitudes, values, and behavior of "economic woman."

4. In Chapter 20, Phyllis Rose, in "Shopping and Other Spiritual Adventures in America Today," suggests that malls, discount stores, and supermarkets are America's cathedrals, while in this chapter, Sam Keen in "The Rite of Work: The

Economic Man" suggests that "the bank and other commercial buildings are the [sacred] centers of the modern city" (paragraph 8). Explain the extent to which you agree with one or both of these writers. Can you name other structures that would be more appropriate symbols of America's spiritual center?

5. Support or refute Suzanne Gordon's contention in "Women at Risk" that American society devalues caretakers and caretaking professions, using personal experience or personal observation as examples to illustrate your position.

6. Alfie Kohn, author of *Punished by Rewards: The Trouble with Gold Stars, Incentive Plans, A's, Praise and Other Bribes,* says that "'millions of well-meaning teachers and parents and managers are killing off creativity and curiosity in their attempt to bribe people to do a good job'" (paragraph 5, Jay Matthews' "For Love or Money"). Argue in support of or against this statement.

Research Topics

1. Combine library research and personal interviews with area employers for a paper on ways to motivate employees to perform well. As Jay Matthews points out in "For Love or Money," the subject is open for debate, so you will need to take a position on which you think works better, extrinsic or intrinsic incentives.

2. Suzanne Gordon in "Women at Risk" asserts that American society devalues caretakers and caretaking professions. Conduct library research into that subject to either support or refute Gordon's contention. Is there a decline in the quality and quantity of good care in our country?

3. Using the essays in this chapter as starting points for your thinking, conduct library research on the subject of the effects of corporate America on male and/or female employees. You may want to expand your research to include interviews as well. Make sure you arrive at some conclusion of your own, which you support with appropriate and relevant materials from your research.

CHAPTER 22

THE AMERICAN IMAGE ABROAD

The term global village *has been used for decades to describe the way in which the world's countries are linked in many ways. But given the speed of communication and travel between countries today, it seems a more apt phrase than ever to describe the close interrelationship of all the world's nations. Satellites link people around the globe, for instance, making it possible for millions worldwide to watch a single event on television simultaneously. The various media of popular culture—television, magazines, and newspapers— play crucial roles in conveying certain images of America and Americans to other nations.*

The image of America that is projected to people abroad creates certain stereotypes, or fixed images, of what America represents—materialism, consumerism, opportunity, power, and freedom, to name a few of the qualities foreigners associate with America. Given the place of the United States in the world market, these images can play important roles in trade and other business relations. Thus, as you read the essays in this chapter, keep in mind the general focus of the unit on business and economics and consider the implications of the American image abroad for the U.S. economy and for conducting international business.

In the first essay, Pico Iyer in "Selling Our Innocence Abroad" examines the image of America abroad as represented by American popular culture. Iyer points out that the projects of America's popular culture—its movies, songs, magazines, T-shirts, and the like—make up "the largest single source of America's export earnings." The images these products of American pop culture convey help perpetuate certain notions about America as a land of glamour, wealth, excitement, and even a kind of innocence. Hollywood, Broadway, and Nashville have particular influence in conveying this image, according to Iyer. Before you read, think about what Hollywood suggests to you. Do you think of glamour, of classic films and famous stars? Or do you think of cheap sensationalism, escapism, and money-hungry exploiters out to make money in any way they can? What picture of America do you think today's Hollywood stars, pop recording artists, and famous Broadway actors project?

In "Unsuitable Reading," Mark Salzman recounts some of his experiences living in China, especially his acquaintance with a Chinese man who wished to translate American books and stories into Chinese but who could not find any "suitable" reading for the Chinese. For the translator, American authors' frankness about sex and violence, among other things, were simply too outspoken and graphic to pass the Chinese censors. As you read the responses of the Chinese man to the American short stories and novels he read, think of the literature you have read in and out of school. What images would they project of American culture?

Next, Raymonde Carroll in "Money and Seduction" writes of the French view of Americans as preoccupied with money and the cost of things. Suggesting that, for the French, the dollar sign could easily replace the face of an American, Carroll contends that, for Americans, money represents a whole range of opposite abstractions: good and bad, power and weakness, love and hate, and a host of others. Above all, and despite these seemingly contradictory representations, Carroll says, Americans use their wealth as a measure of success. You may be surprised, angered, or amused to read this assessment of what money means to Americans from a foreign perspective, but try to remain objective. As you read, think of your own values and what money means within that system and whether the French may be at least partially right.

Finally, writing from his perspective as a British immigrant to the United States, Michael Elliott in "Here to Stay" celebrates America as a "land of plenty." Taking a position that conflicts a bit with Raymonde Carroll's, Elliott thinks native-born Americans are not appreciative enough of the material goods they have. He urges Americans to show more gratitude for that plenitude and not to take for granted the many things they have that people in other countries do not. If you are a native-born American, do you take for granted the riches and opportunities available to you? If you are foreign born, how do you regard America?

SELLING OUR INNOCENCE ABROAD

Pico Iyer

Pico Iyer was born in England to Indian parents and studied at Oxford and Harvard universities. His books include Video Night in Kathmandu: And Other Reports from the Not-So-Far-East *(1988),* The Lady and the Monk: A Season in Kyoto *(1991),* Falling Off the Map: Some Lovely Places of the World *(1994), and* The Contagion of Innocence *(1991), from which the following piece is excerpted. Iyer lives in the United States and writes for* Time *magazine.*

There is a genuine sense in many parts of the world that America is being left behind by the rise of a unified Europe and the new East Asian powers. The largest debtor nation in the world, where ten million blacks live in poverty and whose capital, run by a cocaine addict, had a murder rate during the Eighties higher than that of Sri Lanka or Beirut, seems an unlikely model for emulation. And yet America maintains a powerful hold on the world's imagination.

A visitor today in Vietnam, one of the last of America's official enemies, will find crowds in Hue, in waterside cafes, desperate to get a glimpse of Meryl Streep on video; at night, in Dalat, he will hear every last word of "Hotel California" floating across Sighing Lake. In Bhutan, where all the citizens must wear traditional medieval dress and all the buildings must be constructed in thirteenth-century style—in Bhutan, perhaps the most tightly closed country in the world, which has never seen more than 3,000 tourists in a single year—the pirated version of Eddie Murphy's *Coming to America* went on sale well before the video had ever come to America.

All this, of course, is hardly surprising and hardly new. Pop culture makes the world go round, and America makes the best pop culture. By now, indeed, such products represent the largest single source of America's export earnings, even as America remains the single most popular destination for immigrants. The more straitened or shut off a culture, the more urgent its hunger for the qualities it associates with America: freedom, wealth, and modernity. The Japanese may be the leaders in technology, the Europeans may have a stronger and more self-conscious sense of their aesthetic heritage, yet in the world of movies and songs and images America is still, and long will continue to be, the Great Communicator. The capital of the world, as Gore Vidal has said, is not Washington but Hollywood. And however much America suffers an internal loss of faith, it will continue to enjoy, abroad, some of the immunity that attaches to all things in the realm of myth. As much as we—and everyone else—assume that the French make the best perfumes and the Swiss the finest watches, the suspicion will continue that Americans make the best dreams.

4   As borders crumble and cultures mingle, more and more of us are becoming hyphenated. I, perhaps, am an increasingly typical example: entirely Indian by blood, yet unable to speak a word of any Indian language; a British citizen, born and educated in England, yet never having really worked or lived in the country of my birth; an American permanent resident who has made his home for two thirds of his life in America, in part because it feels so little like home; and a would-be resident of Japan. As people like me proliferate, and Filipinos in San Francisco marry Salvadorans, and Germans in Japan take home women from Kyoto, the global village becomes internalized, until more and more of us are products of everywhere and citizens of nowhere.

And though Paris, Tokyo, and Sydney are all in their way natural meeting points for this multi-polar culture, America, as the traditional land of immigrants, is still the spiritual home of the very notion of integration. Everyone feels at home in only two places, Milos Forman has said: at home and in America. That is one reason why America's domination of pop culture is unlikely to subside, even if the reality of American power increasingly seems a thing of the past. The notion of America itself attracts more and more people to come and revive or refresh the notion of America. And the more international a culture is, the more, very often, it draws from the center of internationalism—the United States. The French may rail against cultural imperialism and try to enforce a kind of aesthetic protectionism by striving to keep out *le burger* and *le video*. But as soon as Madonna shows up in Cannes—so efficient is her command of all the media and so self-perpetuating her allure—she sets off the biggest stir in thirty years.

Madonna's global appeal is not unlike that of the Kentucky Fried Chicken parlor in Tiananmen Square: Both provide a way for people to align themselves, however fleetingly, with a world that is—in imagination at least—quick and flashy and rich. The lure of the foreign is quickened by the lure of the forbidden.

I got my own best sense of this in a friend's apartment in Havana some years ago. My friend was an intellectual dissident, fluent in several languages, eager to talk about Spinoza and Saroyan, and able to make a living by reading people's futures from their photographs and translating the latest Top 40 hits—recorded from radio stations in Miami—into Spanish. One night, trying to convey his desperation to escape, he pulled out what was clearly his most precious possession: a copy of Michael Jackson's album *Bad*, on which he had scrawled some heartfelt appeals to Jackson to rescue him. He did not, I suspect, know that Jackson was reclusive, eccentric, and about as likely to respond to political appeals as Donald Duck. What he did know was that Jackson was black, rich, and sexually ambiguous—all things that it is not good to be in Castro's Cuba. What he also knew was that Jackson had succeeded on his own terms, an individual who had proved himself stronger than the system. The less my friend knew about Jackson the man, the closer he could feel to Jackson the symbol. And so it is with America: Since the America that he coveted does not quite exist, it is immutable, a talisman that will fail him only if he comes here.

8   People everywhere, whatever their circumstances, will always have a hunger for innocence, and America seems to have a limitless supply of that resource. Somehow the moguls of Hollywood and Broadway and Nashville—perhaps because they were immigrants themselves, with half a heart on the streets they left—have never lost their common touch: *E.T.* and *Back to the Future* strike universal chords as surely as *Gone With the Wind* and *Casablanca* did half a century ago. These stories continue to affect us because they speak to our most innocent dreams. To renounce them would be to renounce our own innocence.

Personal Response

What does the term *global village* mean to you (paragraph 4)?

Questions for Class or Small Group Discussion

1. Why do you think everyone feels "at home" in America (paragraph 5)?

2. In what way is America "the center of internationalism" (paragraph 5) and Hollywood "the capital of the world" (paragraph 3)?

3. What dreams and myths do you think America represents to people around the world (paragraph 3)?

4. In what way(s) do you think the films Iyer mentions in the last paragraph "speak to our most innocent dreams"? Can you name more recent films as examples of the kind of innocence Iyer is referring to?

5. How does the innocent image of America that some movies portray fit with the "quick and flashy and rich" image of Madonna and Kentucky Fried Chicken (paragraph 6)? That is, how can America be both "innocent" and "forbidden"?

UNSUITABLE READING

Mark Salzman

Mark Salzman is a sinologist and a master of Chinese martial arts. He holds a degree in Chinese language and literature from Yale University. Salzman is the author of Iron and Silk *(1986), which was made into a film of the same name in 1990, and* The Laughing Sutra *(1991). "Unsuitable Reading," an excerpt from* Iron and Silk, *recounts Salzman's experiences with long meetings in China and the Chinese view of American literature as unsuitable reading.*

On October 1, China's National Day, the Provincial Foreign Affairs Bureau arranged a banquet for all the foreigners living and working in Hunan. Prior to the banquet our host, a high official within the Provincial Government, held a meeting at which he gave us a "brief review of current political, economic and social issues affecting the province." This brief review, translated a sentence at a time into English, turned out to be a very lengthy recitation of statistics, all showing remarkable growth, interspersed with firm declarations of purpose, goals for the year 2000 and conclusive evidence that these goals would be met. The official sat completely still as he delivered this speech, moving his lips only as much as he had to except at the end of paragraphs, when he pulled them open to smile, shaking his head from side to side so that the smile fell upon all members of the audience equally.

After two hours the translator showed signs of fatigue. Something about striving from victory to victory was translated as "And the broad collective masses, by means of the leadership of the Chinese Communist Party, and under the protection of the new Constitution approved during the Twelfth Party Congress, shall—shall strike from factory to factory in order to realize the goals of the Four Modernizations by the year 2000."

By the third hour, the poor translator had become delirious, stumbling over nearly every sentence.

No one experienced fatigue more than the audience, however, for of the fifty foreigners there, about ten spoke both English and Chinese, whereas the rest, from Japan and Romania, understood neither English nor Chinese.

4   In the room sat an almost equal number of Chinese, mostly Foreign Affairs representatives, some local government bureaucrats and translators from the institutions with foreign expert programs. Watching them, I could understand why they do not appreciate the Westerner's irritation with long, boring meetings. The Chinese have, by necessity, increased their endurance manyfold by making listening optional. During meetings they talk with one another, doze, get up to stretch or walk around, and in general do not pretend to pay attention. This does not seem to offend the speaker, who, in general, does not pretend to be interested in what he or she is saying.

A Chinese man sitting next to me had been dozing quite freely since the first hour of the speech. He opened his eyes during the third hour to reach for his teacup, and noticed me looking at him. He had extremely thick glasses, a bloated face and a few beads of sweat on his forehead that he wiped at with a dirty handkerchief. He stared at me with no expression on his face for a long time, then suddenly asked me what I thought of the meeting. I said I thought it was very boring, too long and repetitious. His face did not change at all and he continued to stare at me. "That is because you are listening," he said, and went back to sleep.

I happened to see this man again on several occasions, and each time talked with him at greater length. Though extremely shy at first, he eventually loosened up and spoke freely about his interests and ambitions. In time I found him to be a very warm person, and despite his stiff, expressionless manner, he had a sense of humor as well. No matter how funny something was, however, he always told or heard it with that deadpan face, wiping at his forehead and staring at me from behind his colossal lenses.

Some time later he came to my house to talk about a project that he wanted help with. He translated Western novels into Chinese in his spare time and hoped one day to publish. The problem was that, like most Chinese, he had no access to recent works—meaning nearly everything published since 1930. He wondered if I could lend him some contemporary American novels that might be suitable for translation. I said that he could borrow as many as he liked from my bookcase, and that if he had anything specific in mind, I would try to get it for him. He didn't seem to have anything specific in mind, so I let him take a few books at random and asked that he return them by the end of the year.

8   To my surprise he returned a few weeks later, having read all of them. He put them carefully back into the bookcase, exactly where they had

been before, and stared at me. "How did you like them?" I asked. Without blinking he replied, "Thank you very much, but I'm afraid these books would be unsuitable for publication in China. They contain scenes and language that would be considered decadent, or even pornographic." I said that I was sorry to hear that, and tried to think of books I had that might be more suitable. I chose a few short story collections and told him to read through them. "Even though these aren't novels, they are examples of recent American literature, and since this is a high school English textbook, I doubt they contain much pornography." He thanked me again and left.

A month or so later he returned, and once again put the books very carefully back into the bookcase. He wiped his forehead and apologized for keeping the books so long. "I'm afraid that these stories are also unsuitable for publication in China. They have heroes who represent pessimism, alienation and individualism, all of which, as you know, are considered detrimental to the cause of Socialism. Do you have anything else?" I had to admit, with some irritation, that I could think of no books in my possession that would be considered beneficial to the cause of Socialism. "I understand," he said, and began to leave. Passing by the bookshelf he noticed a large book that had not been there before. It was *The World According to Garp*. He asked what it was about, and I laughed and said he should read it and find out. He took it down, put it in his bag and said he would.

Several months passed. One day I found him sitting stiffly on a chair in my room; Old Sheep had seen him waiting and put him in my room while I taught class. After saying hello he took the book from his bag and apologized for keeping it so long. "It contained many words not found in most dictionaries," he said, "and was long to begin with." I asked him what he thought of it, noticing that he was not putting it back in the bookcase as he usually did. He looked at it, seemed to think for a few moments, then stared at me. "This book," he began, "is very, very unsuitable." He paused, then went on. "In fact, in my whole life, I have never read or even imagined something so unsuitable." Here he stopped, still staring at me. He held the book up slightly and pointed at it with his chin. "May I keep it?"

Personal Response

What books or stories have you read that you think the Chinese man Salzman writes about would reject as unsuitable? What would make them unsuitable for him? Name books you think *would* be suitable.

Questions for Class or Small Group Discussion

1. What do their different attitudes toward long, boring meetings suggest about the different natures of Chinese and Americans?

2. Discuss the Chinese man's criteria for suitable reading. What do you think of those criteria? What do they suggest about the Chinese? What image do you think the Chinese man has of Americans who read the books and stories he rejects?

3. If you have read *The World According to Garp,* discuss those aspects of it that you think made the Chinese man regard it as extremely unsuitable. Why do you think he wanted to keep the book despite its unsuitability?

4. What is the image of America and Americans portrayed in the most recent American book or short story you have read? That is, what impression do you think a foreigner reading the same book or story would get of America?

MONEY AND SEDUCTION

Raymonde Carroll

Raymonde Carroll is an anthropologist who was born in Tunisia and educated in France and the United States. She lived for three years on the Pacific atoll of Nukuoro and published Nukuoro Stories *(1980). As a result of interviews with many people in France and the United States, she wrote* Évidences Invisible *(1987). The book was translated by Carol Volk and published in America as* Cultural Misunderstanding: The French-American Experience *(1988), from which this excerpt is taken.*

Money. For a French person, the face of an American could easily be replaced by a dollar sign. A sign of "incurable materialism," of arrogance, of power, of "vulgar," unrefined pleasure . . . the list goes on. I have never read a book about Americans, including those written with sympathy, which did not speak of the "almighty dollar"; I have never had or heard a conversation about Americans which did not mention money.

Foreigners often discover with "horror" or "repulsion" that "everything in the United States is a matter of money." Indeed, one need only read the newspapers to find constant references to the price of things. Thus, a fire is not a news item but an entity (natural or criminal), the dimensions of which are calculated by what it has destroyed—for example, ". . . a house worth two hundred *thousand* dollars . . ." In fact, if it is at all possible to attach a price to something, as approximate as it may be, that price will surely be mentioned. Thus, a French woman became indignant toward her American brother-in-law: "He showed us the engagement ring he had just bought, and he just had to give us all the details about the deal he got in buying the diamond. . . . Talk about romantic!" I cannot even count the number of informants who had similar stories to tell ("I was admiring the magnificent antique pieces in his living room, and do you know what he did? He gave me the price of each piece, with all kinds of details I hadn't asked for. I felt truly uncomfortable . . . really . . ."). Many French informants claimed to be shocked by the "constant showing off," the "lack of taste typical of nouveaux riches" and added, some not in so many words, "As for me, you know, I am truly repulsed by money."

On the other side, many Americans expressed surprise at the frequency with which French people spoke about money, only to say that "they weren't interested in it" ("so why talk about it?"), or at the frequency with which they say "it's too expensive" about all types of things. Some find the French to be "cheap" ("They always let you pay") or "hypocritical" ("Why, then, do the French sell arms to just anyone?"), too respectful of money to trifle with it, or too petty to take risks. The list of adjectives hurled from either side on this topic seems particularly long.

4   Yet a brief examination of certain ethnographic details left me puzzled. For instance, what is the American article, about the forest fire that destroyed the row of two-hundred-thousand-dollar homes in California, really saying? Living in the United States, I know that a house worth two-hundred-thousand dollars in California is far from a palace; on the contrary. Thus, if I took the price quoted literally, I would misinterpret the article as meaning that the fire had destroyed a row of quite ordinary houses—in which case the mention of the "price" is uninformative, uninteresting, and useless. Therefore, what this article conveys, by talking about hundreds of thousands of dollars, is the fact that the fire destroyed very valuable homes. This meaning is also conveyed by the use of the word "homes," which connotes individuality and uniqueness, rather than "houses," which suggests plain buildings. The mention of the price, therefore, carries meaning of a different nature: I think that this "price" serves only as a common point of reference; it does not represent the true monetary values but a symbolic value which can be grasped immediately by anyone reading this article. A French equivalent would be a reference to the period ("from the seventeenth century") with no mention of the state of the building.

Similarly, it is difficult to take the example of the engagement ring literally ("I'm a tightwad"; "I'm not romantic"); it is more comprehensible if we interpret it as a message with a different meaning. For the American in question, having obtained a discount in no way altered the true value of the diamond or the symbolic value of the gesture; this "feat" probably made the gesture even more significant because of the time and attention devoted to it (the worst gift is the one that demands no effort) and probably earned him the admiration and appreciation of his fiancée.

The study of cases in which money is mentioned would require an entire book. . . . I will content myself merely with raising the question here and will indicate the general orientation of my interpretation.

The striking thing is that money is charged with a multiplicity of meanings in American culture, that it has attained a level of abstraction difficult to imagine elsewhere. Money represents both good and bad, dependence and independence, idealism and materialism, and the list of opposites can go on indefinitely, depending on whom one speaks to. It is power, it is weakness, seduction, oppression, liberation, a pure gamble, a high-risk sport; a sign of intelligence, a sign of love, a sign of scorn; able to be tamed, more dangerous than fire; it brings people together, it separates them, it is constructive, it is destructive; it is reassuring, it is anxiety-producing; it is enchanting, dazzling, frightening; it accumulates slowly or comes in a windfall; it is displayed, it is invisible; it is solid, it evaporates. It is everything and nothing, it is sheer magic, it exists and does not exist at the same time; it is a mystery. The subject provokes hatred, scorn, or impassioned defense from Americans themselves, who are constantly questioning themselves on the topic.

8   I believe that one association remains incontestable, no matter how much resentment it provokes. Money symbolizes success. It is not enough to have money to be admired, but quite the contrary; there is no excuse for the playboy who squanders an inherited fortune. To earn money, a lot of money, and to spend it, is to give the most concrete, the most visible sign that one has been able to realize one's potential, that one has not wasted the "opportunities" offered by one's parents or by society, and that one always seeks to move on, not to stagnate, to take up the challenge presented in the premises shaping the education of children. . . .

As a result, money has become a common denominator. It is supposed to be accessible to all, independent of one's origins. And if it creates classes, it also allows free access to those classes to whoever wants to enter. (Let's not forget that we are talking here about "local verities," about cultural premises, and not about social realities.) Money is therefore the great equalizer, in the sense that the highest social class is, in principle, open to everyone, and that while those who are born into this social class have definite advantages, they must nonetheless deserve to remain there, must "prove themselves." And the newspapers are filled with enough stories of poor people turned millionaires to reinforce this conviction.

From this perspective, it is understandable that one does not hide one's success but displays it, shows it off. By making my humble origins known, by displaying my success, I am not trying to humiliate others (although it is possible that I, personally, am a real "stinker"), but I am showing others that it is possible, I am encouraging emulation through example, I am reaffirming a cultural truth: "if I can do it, you can do it." Hence the constant copresence of dreams and success, that is to say, the constant reaffirmation that the impossible is possible, and that attaining the dream depends solely on me. The logical, and ironic, conclusion to all this is the essentially idealistic significance of money in American culture, which does not exclude its "materialistic" utilization.

I do not believe that the misunderstanding between the French and Americans concerning money can be resolved by performing a parallel analysis of the meaning of money in French culture, not because money is not a concern for the French, but because I believe that what Americans express through money is expressed by the French in another domain.

12   From this brief analysis, I will reiterate three points. The first is that money in America serves as a common point of reference, a shortcut for communication, a means of defining a context that is recognizable by all and comprehensible no matter what one's financial situation may be. The second is that it is not in bad taste to recount one's triumphs, one's success in this domain, whether it is a matter of having obtained a half-price diamond or of having accumulated a veritable fortune, insofar as this in no way implies that I wish to put down others, that I am conceited, and so on, characteristics which depend not on money but on my personality. And the third is that money is accessible to all, makes possible upward mobility, that is to say, access to any class.

To the extent that these three points I just made are not "true" for French culture—and that they might in fact provoke "real repulsion"— one must look in a realm other than that of money for what carries the same message. . . .

The repulsion with which many French people react to the "bad taste" of Americans who "brag about their wealth," "show off their money," and so on closely resembles the disgust with which many Americans speak of the "bad taste," the "vulgarity" of French people who "brag about their sexual exploits," "are proud of their sexual successes," which is a subject reserved by Americans for the "uncivilized" world of locker rooms, for the special and forced intimacy of these dressing rooms for athletes. (Although the expression "locker-room talk" traditionally evokes male conversation, it is just as applicable today to female locker-room talk.) The repugnance on the part of "tasteful" Americans to speak in public about their successes with men or women or their sexual "conquests" is interpreted, among the French, as additional proof of American "puritanism," whereas the French "modesty" concerning public conversations about money would tend to be interpreted by Americans as a type of French "puritanism."

This reciprocal accusation of "bad taste" led me to wonder if what was true for financial successes and conquests in American culture was not true for seduction, for amorous conquests, for sexual successes in French culture.

16   While it is not looked on favorably, in France, to show off one's money or titles, one may speak of one's amorous conquests without shocking anyone (unless one does it to belittle others with one's superiority, to insult them, etc., in which case it is not the subject that is important but the manner in which a particular person makes use of it). We have, in France, a great deal of indulgence and admiration for the "irresistible" man or woman, for "charmers" large and small of both cases. Seduction is an art which is learned and perfected.

Like money for Americans, amorous seduction is charged with a multiplicity of contradictory meanings for the French, depending on the person to whom one is speaking and the moment one raises the topic. Nonetheless, if a (French) newspaper article defines a particular person as *séduisante,* the term does not refer to indisputable characteristics but to a category recognizable by all, to a common point of reference, to a comprehensible descriptive shortcut. (It is interesting to note that the American translation of *séduisante* would be "attractive," a word which, as opposed to the French, evokes identifiable and predictable characteristics. The word *seductive*—not an adequate translation—evokes manipulation and the negative connotations attached to taking advantage of naïveté.)

Seduction, as I have said, is an art for the French. It is not enough to be handsome or beautiful to seduce; a certain intelligence and expertise are necessary, which can only be acquired through a long apprenticeship, even if this apprenticeship begins in the most tender infancy. (Thus, an ad for baby clothing, a double spread in the French version of the magazine *Parents,* shows the perfect outfit for the "heartbreak girl" and for the "playboy"; this is an indication of the extent to which this quality is desirable, since I assume the ad is geared toward the parents who provide for and teach these babies, and not toward the babies themselves.) It is therefore "normal" for me to be proud of my successes, for me to continually take up the challenge of new conquests, for me never to rest on my laurels, for me not to waste my talent. It is therefore not in "bad taste" to talk about it (bad taste and seduction are, in a sense, mutually exclusive in French). What is more, I can "freely" share my secrets and my "reflections" on the subject of men or women—a topic I have thoroughly mastered.

Like money for Americans, seduction for the French may be the only true class equalizer. In fact, one of the greatest powers of amorous seduction is precisely the fact that it permits the transgression of class divisions. The French myths of the "kept woman," of the attractiveness of the *midinette* (a big-city shopgirl or office clerk, who is supposed to be very sentimental), of the seductive powers of "P'tit Louis" (a "hunk," a good dancer, from the working class), and the innumerable seducers of both sexes in French novels, songs, and films are sufficient proof.

20   The interest of a parallel such as the one I have just established is that it shows how astonishingly similar meanings can be expressed in areas which seem to be completely unrelated. Yet the greatest attraction of cultural analysis, for me, is the possibility of replacing a dull exchange of invectives with an exploration that is, at the very least, fascinating—a true feast to which I hereby invite you.

Personal Response

How do you feel about the negative comments that the French people Carroll interviewed made about Americans?

Questions for Class or Small Group Discussion

1. To what extent do you agree with the French interviewees that Americans are preoccupied with money and the cost of things and use wealth as a measure of success?

2. To what extent do you agree with the American interviewees who think that the French are preoccupied with sex and use sexuality as a measure of success?

3. Do you agree with Carroll's analysis of the article about the forest fire and the young man talking about the engagement ring (paragraphs 4–5)? Do you think she is right on all three points she makes about money in America in paragraph 12?

4. Look at the list of what Carroll says money represents to Americans (paragraph 7). Discuss how accurate you think she is. Do you have evidence from your own experience or observations that would support her claims?

5. How does Carroll use the differing stereotypes that French and Americans have about each other to suggest the way in which they are more similar than different? What "true feast" does Carroll invite the reader to take part in (paragraph 20)?

HERE TO STAY
Michael Elliott

Michael Elliott wrote this essay for a special feature on defining an American in the July 10, 1995, issue of Newsweek. *Elliott immigrated to the United States from Great Britain in 1974 and has recently become a permanent resident.*

Last month I got my green card, which is neither green, nor a card. It's a smudgy orange stamp in my passport that reads, confusingly, "Temporary evidence of lawful admission for permanent residence." In six months, if I'm lucky, the real card will arrive, though my lawyer tells me that half of them get lost in the mail. Still, "permanent residence" has a nice ring to it. I no longer have to stew in the alphabet soup of Visas A–Z. If my daughters decide to settle in the United States—and this is their home—I can, too. But that's not the whole story. I fell in love with the United States long before I had two suburban kids whose idea of joy is a sidewalk lemonade stand, and I trust I'll be in love with it long after they've left home.

I first arrived in America from Britain in the middle of a hot August night in 1974. There was nobody to meet me—arrangements had gone awry—but a student returning from a year in Paris invited me home. We were soon in Great Neck, on New York's Long Island. I was shown to my room, slept, and then went downstairs for breakfast with my hosts (whose name was Cohen, and whose address I promptly lost: if you read this, thanks). It was a classic August day, dripping with humidity. We were on a patio, beyond which a perfect lawn swooped down to a pool, and then to a dock, and then to a blue-gray slab of water, shimmering in a heat haze: Long Island Sound. I was almost precisely on the spot which, in "The Great Gatsby," Scott Fitzgerald described as a "fresh, green breast of the world," which is just how it felt. Then came breakfast: huge jugs of coffee; bagels (bagels?); gallons of orange juice. I felt like a horn of plenty had been emptied into my lap, and I've never lost the feeling.

"Plenty" is a dangerous quality on which to base one's love for somewhere. It can sound grasping, as if the only true measure of a place is what it can give you: the more the better. Yet the idea of plenty captures America's enduring appeal better than anything else. "Whatever it is," Bill Bennett once said to me, "America has more of it: more good, more bad, more beauty, more ugliness, more everything." Crucially, more space: the magical emptiness of the intermountain West still fills me with awe.

4   Paradoxically, that endowment of "more" has proved tricky. Perhaps the problem lies in the fact that Americans thank divine providence for their good fortune, rather than hard work or, as the Australians do, dumb luck. In "People of Plenty," a brilliantly prophetic book written in 1954, David Potter warned that America's success bore within it the seeds of its own destruction. Americans, Potter argued, had grown up to expect that life would keep on getting better—which would leave them at a loss when, as was bound to happen, their luck ran out. And, of course, luck *did* run out. In the awful five years between 1963 and 1968, political stability and social cohesion both collapsed, and then the economy stopped growing at its post-1945 rate. My arrival in the United States coincided with the end of the long postwar boom, and in large measure American opinion has never come to terms with that truth.

This inability to cope with something less than unbounded plenty has left America a place strangely unable to see its own strengths, with a mood which runs from dyspepsia to anger and then paranoia. In 12 years, nothing has so upset me as the aftermath of the Oklahoma City bombing, as the television screens filled with first, those who had grown to hate their government, and then with their sharp-suited apologists. Yet—and perhaps immigrants understand this better than natives—there is no government on earth so hemmed in by constitutive rules which limit its power to do harm. The stability of American institutions should be the wonder of the world.

And, to a large extent, is. Immigration is the acid test of a society's character; people do not immigrate to lands where they will be less free, less able to realize their dreams. By that measure, modern America is a startling success. The success, to be sure, has come at a price; America is a more messy, Babel of a place than it was in the 1950s. My children have friends whose parents were born in India, Turkey, Guatemala, France,

Ireland and other countries too numerous to list. This delights me. In the next century, *everywhere* is going to be multiethnic—it's just that in this respect (as in so many others) America has got there first. My kids are learning, better than they would anywhere else, what it means to grow up in an ethnic mosaic with shared values.

Shared values? Aren't we supposed to be "Balkanizing," or something? Oh, tosh. America has a remarkable unity on the things that really matter: In May I asked my 89-year-old aunt, visiting America for the first time, what had most impressed her. "They love their country," she said (as I knew she would).

8   This Independence Day, I'll be on Long Island Sound once more, on the "most domesticated body of saltwater in the western hemisphere" (Fitzgerald again, inevitably). There'll be barbecues and flags and fireworks and ice cream (how sensible to have a national day in high summer). I will think no great, solemn thoughts; Independence Day is too much fun for that. But at some point I will allow myself an old wish: that native-born Americans could have as much confidence in their nation as those of us who willingly came here from elsewhere. We are indeed a people of plenty: why can't we enjoy it?

Personal Response

Describe your feelings about your country. Do you have a strong sense of commitment to and belief in it? Are you critical of any aspects of it?

Questions for Class or Small Group Discussion

1. For Elliott, the "idea of plenty captures America's enduring appeal better than anything else" (paragraph 3). Do you feel that way about America as well? If not, what do you find most appealing about America?

2. Elliott suggests that Americans grew so used to expecting things to get better that they were unable to cope when "the economy stopped growing at its post-1945 rate" (paragraph 4) and that this inability to cope is responsible for "a mood which runs from dyspepsia to anger and then paranoia" (paragraph 5). Where do you see evidence of this unhappiness with America?

3. Elaborate on Elliott's comment about what immigrants to America "understand . . . better [perhaps] than natives" (paragraph 5).

4. Do you agree with Elliott that Americans do not enjoy their position of being "a people of plenty" (paragraph 8)?

5. Why do you think Elliott quotes from *The Great Gatsby* (paragraphs 2 and 8)? What relevance does it have to the central idea of his essay?

Perspectives on the American Image Abroad
Suggestions for Synthesis

1. Interview foreign students on your campus for their impressions of American people and culture and write an essay in which you summarize your findings and analyze reasons to account for those impressions. Incorporate into your paper the views of one or more of the writers in this chapter.

2. Interview people who have immigrated to America for their reasons for coming to this country. Find out what image they had of America before they came and whether their impression has changed now that they are living here. Include Michael Elliott's viewpoints in "Here to Stay" in your paper.

3. Using two or more of the essays in this chapter in combination with your own thoughts on the subject, write a paper on some aspect of the American image abroad.

Additional Writing Topics

1. Write an essay explaining what you think is the appeal of America's popular culture to people in other countries.

2. Select a recent popular film and analyze the image of America it projects.

3. Do a close analysis of a person or thing from popular culture that you think represents an aspect of American culture.

4. Define *global village* by using specific examples from your own experiences or observations.

5. Write an essay in which you analyze an American book or story for the image it projects of America. Try to view the book or story objectively, as if you were a foreigner looking for information about America.

6. Explore the subject of cultural stereotypes by looking at the way in which Americans stereotype people in a particular foreign country. What accounts for the stereotype? How does it prevent full understanding of the culture? What can you do to help dispel the stereotype?

7. If you have ever traveled abroad, describe the experience from the perspective of how you were treated by natives of the country you visited.

8. Write an essay explaining what it means to you to be an American. If you are not American, write about your own nationality.

Research Topics

1. Pico Iyer in "Selling Our Innocence Abroad" says that America is "the center of internationalism" (paragraph 5). Conduct library research on this subject with a view to either supporting or refuting Iyer's assertion.

2. Conduct library research to expand on the views of writers in this chapter on the American image abroad. From your research, draw some conclusions about that image. Is there a particular image or are there many images? What aspects of America are responsible for the image(s)? Does the image of America differ from country to country or even continent to continent? You should be able to narrow your focus and determine a central idea for your paper after your preliminary search for sources and early review of the materials.

CHAPTER 23

THE U.S. IN THE GLOBAL MARKETPLACE

If we live in a "global village," we also buy and sell in a "global marketplace." Manufacturers that used to export goods to other nations now build their plants and sell their goods directly in those countries. American businesses that once limited themselves to the domestic market are now expanding operations beyond the United States as they compete in foreign markets. Indeed, most trade analysts predict that the twenty-first century will see enormous growth in global prosperity as businesses compete for foreign trade and increase their expansion in the global marketplace. Certainly the ease of international travel makes conducting business with other countries not much more difficult than travel from state to state used to be for salespeople, and the fax machine and Internet capabilities have had enormous impact on business communication. Combine those factors with the rise in market economies in previously communist countries, and you have some compelling reasons to account for the optimism forecasters have for the global economy as we enter the twenty-first century.

The essays in this chapter focus on America's relationship with other countries and its place in the global market. The first two take a general look at worldwide business prospects. In "The Triple Revolution," Christopher Farrell discusses the upheavals in politics, technology, and economics that may usher in an age of global prosperity. And in their analysis of what lies ahead for businesses in the next decade, Ian Morrison and Greg Schmid, in "The Global Market: Here, There, Everywhere," examine the new set of market conditions for U.S. firms as competitors in the global marketplace. These essays raise some questions for you to think about in terms of your own future: What are the implications of these predictions about the economy and America's place in the global market for you personally? Do they make you feel more secure about finding employment after you graduate from college? Do they possibly even suggest a particular direction you might take now as you plan for your future?

The other two essays in this chapter offer some very practical guidelines for doing business abroad, specifically with Asians. In "Some Basic Cultural Differences," Scott D. Seligman provides some concrete tips on important cultural differences between Chinese and Americans when doing business, based on his experiences living with and doing business with the Chinese. James Fallows in "A Few Pointers" writes from personal experience as well. In contrast to those who see a connection between economic progress and political freedom,

Fallows draws "a darker conclusion from the rise of the Asian economies" and explains why he believes that the repressive natures of many Asian countries actually contribute to their economic success. Thus, these concluding essays invite you to think about America in contrast to the ways in which the world's most populated country, China, and one of the world's biggest players in the world economy, Japan, conduct business with other countries and run their businesses at home.

THE TRIPLE REVOLUTION

Christopher Farrell

Christopher Farrell is an economics editor for BusinessWeek. "The Triple Revolution" is one of the articles in "21st Century Capitalism," a special 1994 issue of BusinessWeek that looks at how nations and industries will compete in the emerging global economy. The result of a six-month process that involved three editors and more than eighty correspondents, editors, designers and photo editors, this special edition projects a spectacular future for the global economy.

Every once in a great while, the established order is overthrown. Within a span of decades, technological advances, organizational innovations, and new ways of thinking transform economies. From the 1760s to the 1830s, steam engines, textile mills, and the Enlightenment produced the Industrial Revolution. The years 1880 to 1930 were shaped by the spread of electric power, mass production, and democracy.

On the eve of the 21st century, the signs of monumental change are all around us. Chinese capitalists. Russian entrepreneurs. Nelson Mandela President of South Africa. Inflation at 7% in Argentina. Internet connections expanding by 15% a month. Fiber optics transmitting 40 billion bits of data per second. From government dictators to assembly-line workers, everyone seems aware that unfamiliar and unusually powerful forces are at work. Says Shimon Peres, Israel's Foreign Minister: "We are not entering a new century. We are entering a new era."

A great transformation in world history is creating a new economic, social, and political order. Communism's collapse and the embrace of freer markets by much of the developing world are driving huge increases in global commerce and international investment. The Information Revolution is forging strong links between nations, companies, and peoples. Improving education levels are creating a global middle class that shares "similar concepts of citizenship, similar ideas about economic progress, and a similar picture of human rights," says John Meyer, professor of sociology at Stanford University. Almost 150 years following the publication of the *Communist Manifesto,* and more than half a century after the rise of totalitarianism, the bourgeoisie has won.

Plunging Poverty

4   Indeed, behind these simultaneous revolutions lies one powerful idea: openness. Governments everywhere are pursuing liberal economic policies. Multinational corporations are accelerating the exchange of innovations across open borders. Global investors are pressuring companies everywhere to open their books. Populations are demanding stronger political and civil rights.

Already, signs of a payoff are apparent. The growth rate for developing Asia averaged a heady 7.8% a year from 1985 to 1990, and by the end of the decade, one-tenth of everything produced in the world will hail from developing Asia, according to DRI/McGraw-Hill, the economic consulting firm. In China, the percentage of people living below the poverty line has plunged from 33% in 1970 to 10% in 1990. Latin America, stagnant for much of the 1970s and 1980s, has been expanding at a 3% pace since 1991. The traumatized economies of Eastern Europe appear ready to generate growth rates of 4% to 6% over the next several years. Even in sub-Saharan Africa, a region of the world experiencing severe economic problems, the global investment community has been taking a keen look at the new South Africa.

A growing number of governments in developing countries and emerging markets are struggling to get the fundamentals right: keep inflation low and fiscal policies prudent; maintain high savings and investment rates; improve the education level of the population; trade with the outside world and encourage foreign direct investment. In the 1990s, the 16 largest developing economies have all sharply reduced tariff, tax, and other barriers to foreign direct investment. And any country that runs the currency printing presses or walls out private foreign capital pays a steep price in economic welfare these days. "Most developing nations have turned away from self-sufficiency and hostility to the outside world, and see it is in their interests to connect [to it] as rapidly as they can," says Paul Romer, economist at the University of California at Berkeley.

What's more, the usual yardsticks may underestimate prospects for global prosperity. In the decades following the Bolshevik Revolution of 1917 and colonialism's end in the 1950s and 1960s, economic-development efforts largely focused on central planning and government-led investment. And the best and brightest people from Brazil to the Soviet Union joined the government bureaucracy, the military, or other economically unproductive institutions. When P. T. Bauer, the late development economist, lectured at a dozen or so Indian universities and research centers in 1970, teachers and students alike believed that central planning was indispensable for raising living standards. The only question was whether the Soviet or the Chinese model was the superior approach for development.

8   Today, the balance of power has decisively shifted away from government planners and toward markets. When markets are large and laws

allow people to build companies and keep their profits, more and more talented citizens become entrepreneurs and wealth-creators. One study, covering many of the world's economies, by economists Andrei Schliefer, Kevin Murphy, and Robert Vishny, estimated that if an extra 10% of university students went into engineering, the growth rate of an economy would rise by 0.5% a year. "What were once called Third World countries are developing much faster than you would suppose if constrained by the traditional models of economic growth," says Donald N. McCloskey, economist at the University of Iowa.

And over long periods of time, small differences loom large. For example, from 1870 to 1990, real per capita gross domestic product in the U.S. rose by 1.75% a year, to the world's highest level—from $2,224 to $18,258. Had the American growth rate been only one percentage point less a year—0.75%—then real per capita GDP in 1990 would have been $5,519, or about that of Mexico and Hungary, according to Robert J. Barro, economist at Harvard University.

Ethnic Conflict

On a global scale, freer trade will spur growth by providing entrepreneurs from major economies access to bigger markets. Trade also encourages the spread of new technologies and manufacturing techniques. General Electric Co. is sinking tens of millions of dollars into building factories and power plants in Mexico and India. Microsoft Corp. gets more than 50% of its revenue from international sales. Toyota Motor Corp. is powering its way into Southeast Asia as is Volkswagen into China.

To be sure, revolutions are tumultuous. From the vast lands of the former Soviet Union to the Amazon forest in Brazil, frontier capitalism is brutal and very often criminal. In many developing countries, sweatshops and slums are commonplace, a bleak, Dickensian world of worker misery and raw social and political tensions. Fast growth in China and elsewhere creates dismaying environmental destruction. Corruption and sclerotic bureaucracies are deeply entrenched. Ethnic conflicts are flaring.

12   Still, the impact of global integration on growth could be staggering. Over the past two centuries, as national boundaries have shrunk in importance, the pace of economic development has quickened. Britain needed nearly 60 years to double its output per person beginning in 1780. It took Japan 34 years starting in the 1880s and South Korea only 11 years after 1966. "At the turn of the century, stellar growth meant 4% a year. Now, it means 10% plus," says Jeffrey D. Sachs, economist at Harvard University. Adds Henry S. Rowan, a professor at Stanford University's business school: "A process is under way that promises within a generation to make most of the world's population rich or much richer than it is today."

Take the three regions of the world where private enterprise is being unleashed: most of Asia, including India and China; Mexico and parts of Latin America; and several East European countries. These areas make up

50% of the world's population and about 20% of the GDP of the industrial nations. If these three regions achieve annual growth rates of 8% over the next 10 years—somewhat less than the sizzling performance of Asia's Four Tigers in the 1980s—then they would contribute almost as much to world growth as the industrial nations. Within several decades, a number of developing nations including Taiwan and Korea will join the club of wealthy nations. "Because the emerging markets' growth rates are much higher than those in the developed world, we are definitely seeing convergence," says Giles Keating, economist at CS First Boston in London.

Another benefit of global interdependence is lower inflation rates. True, industrial commodity prices will go up, especially with the new demand from the emerging economies. But heated international competition will keep wage demands moderate and put a lid on the ability of domestic producers to hike prices, especially in the developed countries. Perhaps even more important, the policy actions of central bankers, the most powerful economic actors on the world stage, all share a similar anti-inflation ideology.

Hotbeds of Talent

It's ironic, then, that at a time when prospects for global prosperity seem better than ever, gloom envelops much of the industrial world. Japan's economic juggernaut is stalled. Unemployment is at 11% in Europe. Companies are still slashing payrolls in the relatively vibrant U.S. economy. At the same time, U.S., European, and Japanese multinationals have stepped up their investment spending in developing and former communist countries. It's no surprise that "ordinary citizens in most advanced industrial countries are confused and scared by what is happening to them," says Richard Lipsey, economist at the Canadian Institute for Advanced Research.

16   And there's much more to come. From Eastern Europe to Asia to Latin America, many countries are eager to compete with bountiful low-wage labor. Heightened international competition, along with rapid technological change, largely accounts for the 22.5% plunge in real hourly wages for high school dropouts from 1973 to 1993 in the U.S. And in a sharp break with the past, German manufacturers are looking elsewhere when building new plants. After all, hourly wages of German manufacturing workers are 4.5 times higher than in Taiwan, 9 times greater than for Mexican workers, and 54 times the wages of Russian labor.

It isn't just cheap brawn, however. The competition is heating up for producing the kind of high-quality goods and sophisticated services in which the industrial nations have traditionally dominated. Cities such as Singapore, Penang in Malaysia, and Taipei in Taiwan are hotbeds of engineering talent. India has millions of computer-literate workers. Central Europe is peppered with brilliant scientists. And when Hewlett-Packard Co.

opened a research and development center in Guadalajara three years ago, it signaled Mexico's coming of high-tech age.

In the industrial world, protests against the new competition are starting to get louder and take on a nasty edge. Keep immigrants out. Bar low-wage imports from China and Hungary. Preserve our native culture. Frets André Lévy-Lang, chairman of the management board at Compagnie Finacière de Paribas, the big French investment bank: "The great temptation is going to be to say: 'Let's close the borders, and let's live happily ever after by ourselves.'"

Yet if policymakers succumb, it could lead to political and economic devastation. That, at least, seems to be the lesson of history. The period from 1870 to 1913, like this one, was a time of vast international capital flows. In 1913, the shares of foreign securities traded in London was 59% of all traded securities; and by 1914, the stock value of foreign direct investment had reached an estimated $14 billion, or one-third of world investment. Some 36 million people left Europe; two-thirds of them emigrated to the U.S. and an even larger number of Chinese and Indians went to Burma, Indonesia, and elsewhere. Trade soared, technological innovation flourished, and economic growth surged. Yet beggar-thy-neighbor protectionist policies ended up contributing to two global wars and the Great Depression.

20   Today, international economic interdependence is once again generating a lot of discord. Nations are engaged in bitter international negotiations over cross-border pollution, intellectual-property rights, and differing workplace standards. Worse are the savage wars in Kuwait, the Balkans, Angola, and other hot spots. Military buildups and the spread of nuclear weapons in Asia and elsewhere offer the potential of even larger conflagrations.

Still, there's no gainsaying the geopolitical progress in the Middle East and in relations between the U.S. and Russia. And global economic integration isn't a zero-sum game. Worldwide trade has expanded by more than 6% a year since 1950, more than 50% faster than the growth in world GDP. The growing numbers of working-class and middle-class citizens in the emerging capitalist nations are demanding better housing, roads, water, and phones, as well as more consumer goods. Rising demands will create bigger markets and new opportunities for profits for everyone including the industrial nations. "The forces of integration are so much more powerful than at the end of the 19th century," says David Hale, economist at Kemper Financial Cos.

Thanks largely to the Information Revolution, companies headquartered in the industrial nations will still have a formidable edge in the global growth stakes. "Information technologies are the most powerful forces ever generated to make things cost-effective," says John S. Mayo, president of AT&T Bell Laboratories. It is the industrial nations, especially the U.S., that are behind the Internet boom and that are building the vast fiber-optic networks and web of new services of the Information Superhighway. The industrial world is setting high standards for quality and manufacturing flexibility to produce low-cost goods, and its rich capital markets offer ample resources for financing new ventures or rejuvenating old ones.

Wealthy Elite

Of course, it's a market axiom that big returns come attached with greater risks—some fortunes will suffer spectacular declines even as others leap forward. It's a world where IBM can show a net income of $6.5 billion in 1984 and a loss of nearly $9 billion in 1993. And emerging-country stock markets are up an average of 20% in 1994 in dollar terms. But that spectacular return masks some huge setbacks, including a drop of 50% in the Turkish market, 48% in China, and more than 30% in Israel.

24   Such nerve-racking volatility is encouraging a lot of U.S., Japanese, and European multinationals to link up with foreign partners. It expands their presence in the world economy and hedges their investment risks at the same time. AT&T is forging broad alliances with a host of European telecommunications companies, and Mitsubishi has a cooperative relationship with Daimler Benz. Alliances are common in such knowledge-based and capital-intensive industries as information technologies and biotechnology. Says Paul A. Allaire, chief executive of Xerox Corp.: "You will see people working more closely than ever before."

There will be no shortage of consumers to buy products and services. Global capitalism is creating a wealthy international elite of cosmopolitan professionals comfortable working for companies headquartered in New York, Tokyo, or Buenos Aires. Millions more are joining the middle class in Asia, Latin America, and elsewhere. As in the U.S. or Japan, the middle class in the emerging capitalist nations is boosting its living standards by buying material goods. In Ho Chi Minh City, Vietnam, three Toyota dealerships are within a few miles of one another, and a Mercedes dealership is being built.

Consumers are demanding better services, too. Poorer countries will spend trillions of dollars on new roads, sewers, telephone systems, education, and health-care facilities in coming decades. Over the past 15 years, the share of households with access to clean water has increased by half, and power production and telephone lines per capita have doubled in developing nations. Still, 1 billion people lack clean water, electric power has yet to reach 2 billion people, and the demand for modern telecommunications networks far outstrips supply, according to the World Bank. To boost efficiency, many countries are privatizing their infrastructure. From 1988 to 1992, the value of developing-country privatizations in 25 countries totaled $61.6 billion. And infrastructure investment can propel giant leaps in economic activity.

Clearly, global integration comes with enormous benefits. At the same time, pessimists proclaiming the decline of the industrial world often argue that global convergence is closer at hand than is the case. Even if all went smoothly, the inequalities between rich and poor nations are so vast that it will take decades for them to disappear. Much of the wage gap between manufacturing workers in rich and poor nations reflects large skill differences and exchange rates. According to Harvard economist Richard B. Freeman, some 43% of Mexican manufacturing laborers have less than six years of schooling, vs. 3% of American manufacturing workers.

28   Nor do economies grow in a straight line. At capitalism's frontier, including many of the Soviet Union's successor states and China, vicious cycles of reform and regression are probable in coming decades. Environmental problems and population pressures will worsen in many developing nations. Policymakers worldwide also worry that rising social and economic pressures in a competitive global economy will spark "culture wars." Hinduism vs. Islam. Confucian values vs. Western values. "The fault lines between civilizations will be the battle lines of the future," wrote Harvard University professor Samuel P. Huntington in an influential 1993 *Foreign Affairs* article.

Similar Logic

Cultural differences between economies are deep-rooted. Modern Japanese capitalism has been extremely successful in building large organizations, while American capitalism does better creating whole new industries, says Peter Berger, director of the Institute for the Study of Economic Culture at Boston University. Chinese capitalism is very different from French *dirigisme*. Yet the remarkable aspect of capitalism is the ability of citizens from around the world to strike deals with one another. Japanese, American, French, Chinese, and Russian capitalists can compete, negotiate alliances, and trade securities with the same goals and similar logic, according to economist Robert Heilbroner.

Indeed, capitalism is triumphant because it is multicultural. Unlike communism, it is open-ended and adaptive, and in the 21st century a range of capitalisms will evolve.

Ever since the Industrial Revolution began, the reality has been how much material wealth has grown in the modern nations of the industrial world. Given time, the triumph of the liberal ideas of the bourgeoisie, from free trade to democracy, coupled with the spread of technological innovations, should improve living standards throughout the world—bringing most people an opportunity for a better, richer life.

Personal Response

How do you see changes in the global economy affecting you personally, both as a consumer and as a (perhaps future) member of the workforce?

Questions for Class or Small Group Discussion

1. Analyze the connections between the Information Revolution and the spread of market economies globally. How do they affect or influence one another?

2. Farrell writes that it is ironic "that at a time when prospects for global prosperity seem better than ever, gloom envelops much of the industrial world" (paragraph 15). Discuss reasons why the industrial world has cause for concern in spite of prospects for global prosperity.

3. Discuss the positive and negative implications of "the triple revolution," that is, of the enormous changes globally in politics, technology, and economics. How do you think these changes will affect the American economy in the next decade?

4. Role-play the position of a market researcher for a new corporation looking for rapid growth through global marketing. Make up a product and a corporation name; then prepare a report for the board of directors of your company in which you recommend expanding efforts in one of the world's newest market areas.

THE GLOBAL MARKET: HERE, THERE, EVERYWHERE

Ian Morrison and Greg Schmid

Ian Morrison and Greg Schmid are researchers who have spent nearly twenty years producing ten-year forecasts of the business environment for the Institute for the Future (IFTF), a research organization dedicated to looking at the strategic issues of the future. The reading reprinted here is from Chapter 3 of their book, Future Tense: The Business Realities of the Next Ten Years *(1994).*

Along with a sophisticated, demanding customer and insecure workers, business must contend with fundamental changes in the way markets are operating. Competition from both global and domestic forces has never been as fierce as it is today.

In the past, we have been able to separate the marketplace into local, regional, and national markets. Today there is just one market—the global market. There is such a wide penetration of foreign products into daily life that virtually every American consumer has access to the global market in one way or another. On the other hand, every American firm now has to compete in the global marketplace with products and services from every other country. This means that new products and services are entering the marketplace every day, that new competitors are looking for shelf space at every store, that new brand names are striving to reach new customers, that daily marketing conferences are trading off placements of products in Peoria and Beijing.

This new global marketplace has created a completely new set of market conditions for U.S. firms. Understanding these conditions and how they will change in the next decade is essential for business planners in the 1990s.

The World Consumer

4   The new U.S. consumer is richer, more educated, and more demanding than ever. But the United States is not alone. The average consumer in every industrial country fits nearly the same bill—more households have substantial discretionary spending power, more young adults have high levels of education, and more consumers are showing increasing discrimination in their spending patterns.

Growing Numbers of Affluent Consumers.   In the new global market, information about products and services travels as fast as TV signals or the latest MTV video. Households with spending power will pick and select the products they purchase from the range of choices that surrounds them. Let's define the potential pool of middle-class consumers as any household, located anywhere in the world, with an income of more than twenty-five thousand dollars per year.

But not every high-earning household can have equal access to markets. Some are geographically isolated from the concentrations of purchasers that create an effective market. Let's look only at middle-class households in countries that have potential groupings of more than 1 million of these consumers in regions where there are significant concentrations of such countries or where the potential for such concentrations will be high over the next couple of decades. By these definitions, virtually every major industrial country qualifies as a middle-class center. But a number of other countries qualify as well, in particular, countries in three regions: Asia, Latin America, and Eastern Europe.

Taken together, these areas currently have nearly 181 million households earning more than $25,000 (Table 23–1). Of these, 80 percent are in the industrial countries, with 36 percent of the total in North America, 32 percent in Western Europe, and 10 percent in Japan.

8   The rich industrial countries' middle-class population is growing fairly steadily over the long run. At the current growth rate, it is expanding at about 2 percent per year; by 2010, the total number of middle-income households in the industrial world will rise from 143 million to 211 million.

But the real growth will be elsewhere. Each year, the emerging market areas of the world will have an increasing portion of the world's

TABLE 23–1
SPENDING POWER BY REGION*

	Millions of Middle-Class Households with incomes averaging over $25,000	Share of the World Market (in percent)
Industrial Countries		
North America	66	36
Western Europe	57	32
Asia/Pacific	20	11
Emerging areas		
Asia	19	10
Eastern Europe	5	3
Latin America	14	8
Total	181	100

*Based on current purchasing power parities
SOURCE: IFTF; data derived from the World Bank, *World Development Indicators*

middle-income households. Today, the emerging countries have 21 percent of such households, but the numbers are growing by close to 5 percent per year. By the year 2010, if current growth rates continue, the emerging areas of the world will have 37 percent of all middle-income households, totaling 122 million—almost as many as the industrial countries have to-day (Figure 23–1).

As a result, the newly emerging middle class in the countries of Asia, Latin America, and Eastern Europe will play an increasing role in the global market in years to come. The most rapid growth will take place in the countries moving away from Socialist restrictions. In China, Russia, and Eastern Europe, fewer restrictions on property ownership, more rewards for entrepreneurial skills, and greater encouragement for wider discrepancies in incomes will open opportunities for the revival of the old middle class and the emergence of a new one.

Already investment patterns are showing a tremendous movement of consumer goods companies into Eastern Europe, the former Soviet Union, and China. The list of companies that have made substantial investments or commitments in those areas just over the last six months reads like a roll call of the international *Fortune* 500: Ford, GM, Suzuki, Nissan, Isuzu, Volkswagen, Renault, and Mitsubishi in automobiles; Philip Morris, Pepsi-Cola, Coca-Cola, Unilever, Grand Met, Procter & Gamble, Parmalat, and Foster's in food and consumer products; Corning and Continental Can in packaging; Daewoo, Mitsui, and Tandem in electronics; AT&T, Sprint, and Alcatel in communications.

FIGURE 23–1
THE EMERGENCE OF NEW MARKETS

(SHARE OF WORLD MIDDLE-CLASS MARKET)

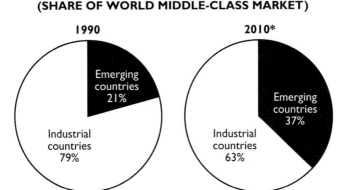

1990

2010*

Emerging
countries
21%

Industrial
countries
79%

Emerging
countries
37%

Industrial
countries
63%

*Projection
SOURCE: IFTF; data derived from the World Bank, *World Development Indicators*

12   These firms are anticipating the future. By the year 2010, China will have as many middle-class households as Germany has today; India and Brazil as many as France; Korea, Indonesia, Taiwan, Argentina, and Mexico as many as Canada and Spain (Table 23–2). We are quickly reaching a time where middle-class consumers, with their appetites for the whole range of consumer goods, will be found shopping en masse, in all parts of the globe.

Education Blossoms Around the Globe.   Not only will there be more middle-class consumers, but, as we have noted in the United States, tomorrow's middle-class consumers will have a very different set of needs and expectations from yesterday's. The key driver will be education. Higher levels of education mean greater discrimination in the marketplace, a demand for better services, skepticism, declining brand loyalty, and a greater focus on value.

The increase in the general level of education is dramatic in the countries associated with the emergence of the middle-class market. In the industrial countries of the world, secondary school attendance is virtually universal. In the emerging middle-class countries, it can range from 50 percent of a particular age group (India, China, Colombia, and Mexico) to more than 80 percent (Poland, the Czech Republic, Taiwan, and Korea).

Even more striking is the increasing share of young adults going on to college. While no other country reaches the level of the United States and Canada, where 60 percent of college-age students go on to college, the industrial countries have doubled the share of young adults going to college over the past twenty-five years (Figure 23–2). While the expansion will

TABLE 23–2
THE KEY EMERGING MARKETS

	(MILLIONS OF HOUSEHOLDS EARNING MORE THAN $25,000 IN 1990 DOLLARS)	
	1990	2010*
Asia		
China	2	24
Korea	3	7
Indonesia	3	6
India	5	12
Taiwan	3	7
Thailand	1	3
Latin America		
Argentina	4	8
Brazil	4	11
Colombia, Venezuela	2	4
Mexico	3	6
Eastern Europe		
Poland, Hungary, Czechoslovakia	1	7
Russia	3	12

*Projection
SOURCE: IFTF; historical data derived from the World Bank, *World Development Indicators*

FIGURE 23–2
EDUCATIONAL ATTAINMENT TAKES OFF IN THE INDUSTRIAL WORLD

(SHARE OF 20–24-YEAR-OLDS ENROLLED IN POSTSECONDARY EDUCATION IN INDUSTRIAL COUNTRIES)

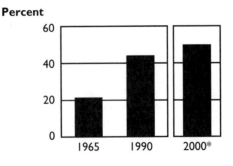

*Projection
SOURCE: IFTF; historical data derived from the World Bank, *World Development Indicators*

not be as rapid in the future, the gradual growth of the middle class and the upgrading of the work force in the industrial countries will increase the share of young adults who feel that postsecondary training is essential to their future.

16   While postsecondary education in the emerging countries lags behind that of the industrial countries, the rate of growth over the past twenty-five years has been astounding, with the share of young adults in college more than tripling in this time. This combination of education and rising income creates the context for the same phenomenon that fills the suburban malls of the United States—shoppers with money in their purses and pockets, looking for products or services that offer value and style. For the emerging markets, there has been a critical change. No longer is the enormous purchasing power in the hands of the few who could be seen in their chauffeur-driven Mercedeses and on the monthly flights to Miami or Paris. Now the spending power is spreading to the growing middle class. The share of young adults going to college in these emerging countries will continue to grow at a rapid pace, which in turn will fuel the continuing growth of the middle class (Figure 23–3).

As the world middle class continues to grow rapidly with the rising levels of affluence and education, a sense of their identification with a world group will grow, too. All members will know that they have equal access to the new ideas, products, and fashions that flow from just about anywhere on the globe.

FIGURE 23–3
THE EMERGING COUNTRIES ARE NOT FAR BEHIND

(SHARE OF 20–24-YEAR-OLDS ENROLLED IN POSTSECONDARY EDUCATION IN EMERGING COUNTRIES)

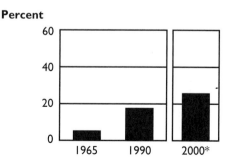

*Projection

SOURCE: IFTF; historical data derived from the World Bank, *World Development Indicators*

Meeting the Demands of the New Middle Class

The emerging middle class wants a world of easy access to products and services unhindered by geographical boundaries. How can we ensure that Coke and Pepsi are available in Kyrgyzstan, Fords in São Paulo, Macintoshes in Bangkok, and Chinese pajamas in Waco? This is the challenge that the world economy is responding to; the key movers are international firms. Today we see these international firms struggling to meet the challenge in a variety of ways that include moving goods, setting up operations abroad, looking for partners, investing money, and transferring ideas. Where the international firm fails, people will take things in their own hands and move to where the action is—international immigration will reach new heights in the 1990s.

Trade: The Building Block of Globalism.   Trade has always been the standard measure of the internationalization of the world economy. The ability to walk into a local store and purchase goods from foreign countries lies at the heart of the global market.

20   Since the end of World War II, a series of internationally negotiated accords under the auspices of the General Agreement on Tariffs and Trade (GATT) have successively lowered the average level of tariffs restricting trade. Today, tariff barriers among the industrial countries average less than 10 percent of the value of goods traded. Compared to tariffs of 50 percent or more in the 1930s and 1940s, current tariffs are no longer a significant barrier to trade.

Under the impetus of these multilaterally negotiated accords, international trade has been growing faster than world production. In the early 1950s, trade accounted for about 6.5 percent of world production; by the early 1990s, 15 percent (Figure 23–4). Trade across borders now accounts for about one out of every six dollars of the world's total final sales. This is the simplest and most forceful measure of the importance of trade and the gradual internationalization of the world economy.

Let's look at the impact of trade in the United States, the world's biggest market. Traditionally, the U.S. economy has been relatively self-contained. Independent since the eighteenth century and outside any imperial system, separated by oceans from Europe and Asia, and rich in its own resources with plentiful supplies of people and capital, the United States economy grew on its own. For a hundred years, from 1870 to 1970, only about 5 percent of final consumption in the United States was provided by other countries. But as the other industrial countries recovered from the devastation of World War II and barriers to trade fell, the big, rich, and open U.S. consumer market became a global honeypot for vendors worldwide.

Every country with dreams of building its own productive capacity by way of exports sees the U.S. market as an opportunity. With trade barriers falling, transport costs dropping, and marketing and distribution systems getting more sophisticated, the share of total U.S. product accounted for by foreign imports grew enormously, jumping from 4 percent of our GDP to almost 11 percent between 1960 and 1990. Excluding the petroleum market, where wild price changes have masked the movement of goods, the growth in import penetration has been a steady and long-term phenomenon affecting U.S. markets (Figure 23–5). In years to come,

FIGURE 23–4
THE WORLD'S DEPENDENCE ON TRADE IS GROWING

(EXPORTS AS A SHARE OF WORLD PRODUCTION)

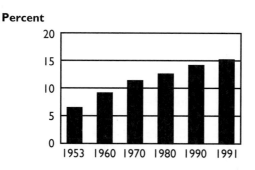

SOURCE: IFTF; data derived from GATT, *International Trade,* and World Bank, *World Development Indicators*

FIGURE 23–5
FOREIGN IMPORTS GROW

(NONPETROLEUM IMPORTS AS A SHARE OF U.S. GDP)

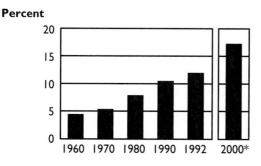

*Projection
SOURCE: IFTF; historical data from U.S. Department of Commerce, Bureau of Economic Analysis, *National Income Accounts*

imports will continue to grow. The development of new consumer electronic products, the more competitive world markets in communications and medical supplies, and the emergence of new competitors for consumer products like Mexico will all contribute to higher levels of traded goods. By the year 2000, look for some 12.5 percent of the economy to be accounted for by imports.

24   Imports cover a wide range of products and services: cars from Japan, wines from France, machine tools from Germany, assembled PCs from Singapore, clothes from Malaysia, and flowers from Colombia. Imports have had an uneven impact in the United States, dominating a number of specific product markets and leaving others untouched. Imports cover about one third of all domestic market supply for industries such as petroleum, machine tools, computers, motor vehicles, and apparel. Whole product categories such as VCRs are dominated by imports. This focused penetration of particular markets has been well publicized. But what is even more striking is that the import share has been increasing dramatically across a wide range of industries, even those in which imports have traditionally been low. Figure 23–6 shows a sampling of some of the product markets where imports during the 1970s accounted for between 2 percent and 5 percent of the market. In some of these categories over the past two decades, the import share has doubled, tripled, or even quadrupled.

FIGURE 23–6
IMPORT PENETRATION JUMPS OVER THE PAST DECADE

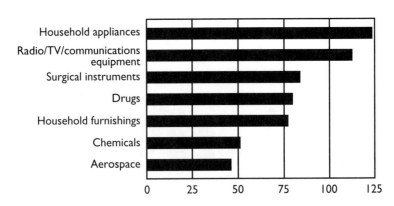

(PERCENT INCREASE IN IMPORTS BY INDUSTRY
AS A SHARE OF DOMESTIC SUPPLY)

SOURCE: U.S. Department of Commerce, *U.S. Industrial Outlook*

The consumer has welcomed the growth of imports. In each one of these markets, the American consumer is getting a clear benefit, either in price, quality, design, or selection. In addition, trade is a two-way street—as more imports enter the United States, U.S. firms send more exports abroad. But the bottom line remains the same—to be competitive in the new American market means that virtually the whole spectrum of American businesses must compete with products that were not in their markets ten or twenty years ago or they must find ways of penetrating foreign markets to keep sales up or both.

The Engines of Trade: Multinational Firms.   Trade does not move by itself, and products don't automatically go from a port of entry to the shelf of the store in the mall. Products move when they can reach customers who are willing to buy them. This means that to trade goods a company needs people in the host country who can provide a diverse set of skills: marketing, advertising, distribution, servicing, legal services, and so on. The boom in world trade has taken place because an efficient mechanism—the multinational firm—arose to move goods across borders and deal with the cultural issues of national distribution. Multinational firms are firms that have operating offices in more than one country. They now account for the overwhelming share of the international movement of goods, services, and technology.

By providing efficient vehicles for transferring goods and conduits for selling those goods in foreign countries, multinational firms currently account for a sizable share of total trade. In the United States, for example, 80 percent of international trade is accounted for by multinational firms, either as intrafirm trade, as trade from one multinational to another, or as purchases by a multinational firm. In fact, about 35 percent of U.S. trade is accounted for by intrafirm trade, including large oil and petroleum exploration firms like Chevron and ARCO, consumer goods companies like Philip Morris and Procter & Gamble, basic manufacturing firms like GM and Ford, and high-tech firms like Hewlett-Packard and Microsoft. U.S. multinationals are not unique. In both Japan and the United Kingdom, intrafirm trade was one third of total trade. In the words of the United Nations, multinational firms are "increasingly the driving force of international economic transactions."

28   The number of multinational firms is large. There are currently well over 35,000 multinational firms with 150,000 affiliates around the world. The growth in the number and size of these enterprises has been especially large since the mid-1980s. The best measure of growth of multinational firms is the increase in dollars of direct investment. Direct investment is the outlay of dollars in one country for building plant and equipment or purchasing a controlling stake in a company in a foreign country. The amount of money spent on multinationals' direct investment tripled between the late 1970s and the late 1980s (Figure 23–7).

FIGURE 23–7
INTERNATIONAL DIRECT INVESTMENT IS UP SUBSTANTIALLY

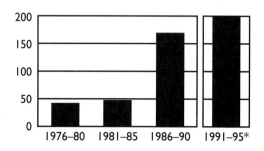

(ANNUAL AVERAGE IN BILLIONS OF DOLLARS)

*Projection
SOURCE: United Nations, Programme on Transnational Corporations, *World Investment Report*

Even during the current international recession, the growth of multi-national enterprises through direct investment continues to be well above the levels of a decade ago. This implies that the multinationals will expand further during the 1990s and that these firms will continue to play the critical role in fostering trade and international exchange.

Personal Response

Where do you see evidence of the influence of the global market in your own life?

Questions for Class or Small Group Discussion

1. Morrison and Schmid comment that "there is such a wide penetration of foreign products into daily life that virtually every American consumer has access to the global market" (paragraph 2). Name some products you own that come from foreign manufacturers.

2. Summarize the factors that, according to Morrison and Schmid, contribute to the rise in the number of middle-class households in emerging nations.

3. Discuss the implications for both American consumers and American businesses of the rapid expansion of the global marketplace.

4. Why do you think that "multinational firms are 'increasingly the driving force of international economic transactions'" (paragraph 27)?

Do you think that all firms that want to do well in the global market-place will need to become multinational?

SOME BASIC CULTURAL DIFFERENCES
Scott D. Seligman

Scott D. Seligman has worked as a trade representative to China and is author of Chinese at a Glance: A Phrase Book and Dictionary for Travelers *(1986) and* Dealing with the Chinese: A Practical Guide to Business Etiquette in the People's Republic Today *(1989). This chapter from* Dealing with the Chinese *offers some very concrete tips for those who want to conduct business with China.*

The single most important and fundamental difference between Chinese and Occidental peoples is undoubtedly the role played by the individual in the society. In the West, we place a strong emphasis on personal achievement, creativity, and initiative. We glory in our individual differences, nurture them, and value them as the essential features that make us unique. Indeed, uniqueness is a goal unto itself in the West; it's vitally important to us that we *not* be exactly like other people.

Who in the West hasn't been admonished to be your own person, or to look out for yourself because no one else can be counted on to look out for you? Who has never been praised for standing up for what you personally believe in, especially when the tide of opinion is flowing in the opposite direction? Among Western peoples, the premium is not on conformity, it is on individual expression and rugged independence.

In China, on the other hand—and no matter which side of the Taiwan strait—children are given an entirely different set of messages. Don't question the world around you or try to change it; accept it. Submit willingly and unquestioningly to authority. Your importance as an individual is not nearly as great as that of the role you play in a larger group.

4   That "larger group" may have appeared different in ancient China from what it looks like today. In Imperial China it would have been one's extended family—grandparents, father, mother, siblings, uncles, aunts, and cousins of all descriptions, all of whom might well have lived together in the same compound. In modern-day China the group might be one's nuclear family, one's class at school, one's military unit, fellow members of a delegation, or one's *danwei* or work unit (see below). The situation varies; the dynamics, however, are much the same no matter what the group is.

Group process in China is not merely based on the authority of the leaders; there is a real premium on consensus. Matters are often debated at great length until agreement is reached on a course of action. And once a decision has been made, individual group members are expected to embrace it and act on it. This is one reason you will seldom hear a Chinese make an irreverent comment, or openly express a view at odds with that of his or her unit. Toeing the mark is important, and it is enforced.

In essence, Chinese enter into a sort of compact with their groups; in exchange for obedience and loyalty, they can expect protection and support and be confident that their well-being will be a matter of concern to the group as a whole. Group membership requires that they subordinate their own wills to that of the whole and make decisions based on the best interests of the larger group, not personal selfishness. Chinese people must listen to those in authority and do as they say. And their actions, for good or ill, reflect not only on themselves but also on all of their compatriots.

Consider that fate of former Korean President Chun Doo Hwan, who in spring of 1988 was forced to resign the few government and party posts he had retained after he stepped down from the presidency. Chun's action was necessary not because he had personally done anything wrong, but rather because his *brother* was charged with embezzling money. "Although I exerted myself to the utmost to promote the welfare of the people during my presidential term," Chun was quoted as saying, "I failed to control my brother. It is because of my lack of virtue." He continued: "I feel very sorry for causing trouble to the people with various scandalous actions brought about by my brother's ineptitude."

8   Though this example comes from Korea—another Confucian society (see below)—rather than China, it might have taken place in Taipei nearly as easily as in Seoul. The principle is the same: you bear responsibility for the actions of members of your family—or your group. Chun's own words contain an apology for "causing trouble" even though it was clearly not he personally who was at fault.

It would be difficult to imagine a similar situation in the West. It would hardly have occurred to former U.S. president Jimmy Carter, for example, to resign because of any of his brother Billy's transgressions. On the other hand, the case should not be overstated. The ideal is one thing; actual practice is another. In truth, many Chinese cadres try desperately to remain in office even after members of their family are caught trading on their positions and engaging in very questionable activities.

For another example, take the case of Chinese tennis star Hu Na, who defected to the United States from the PRC in the early 1980s. The American government, in reaching a decision on whether to grant her political asylum, cited, among other things, the fact that Ms. Hu did not wish to return to the PRC. But the Chinese position was that the young woman's wishes were only one consideration, and a minor one at that; it was also important to take into account the interests and desires of her parents, her work unit, and the government of the society that had given her so much.

The discussion of telephone etiquette [in an earlier chapter] provides still another illustration of the preeminence of the group in Chinese society. You'll recall that you generally do not identify yourself personally when answering the telephone; what is deemed important is your work unit. The fact that common practice is to answer "I am the Ministry of Foreign Trade" rather than "I am Mr. Wang" speaks volumes about the relative importance of the individual and the group. So does the fact that it is units, and not individuals, that invite foreign guests, arrange activities for them, and sign contracts with them. None of this should be interpreted to mean that the Chinese do not possess unique personalities, however. They most certainly do. The distinction lies in the issue of when and under what circumstances it is permissible for people to express their individual differences.

12   Although Chinese people must be ever vigilant in fulfilling obligations to fellow group members, it's important to note that as a rule they feel no comparable responsibility toward outsiders. Courtesy and hospitality are frequently not forthcoming when Chinese deal with people with whom they have no connections. Indeed, they are capable of treating one another with indifference that can border on cruelty. The "us-them" dichotomy often surfaces in the work of the government in the form of intractable bureaucratic rivalries that impede progress and innovation. It has sometimes been pointed out that one of Chinese culture's major failings is that its people just don't know how to treat outsiders. Ironically but luckily, foreigners are generally exempt from this kind of treatment, their very foreignness earning them favorable treatment as honored guests.

The *Danwei* or "Work Unit"

It is the work unit or *danwei* that tends to wield the most power over an individual's life in China today. Employers in Taiwan and Hong Kong probably hold more sway over the lives of their employees than those in the West, but they do not have nearly as much influence as the *danwei* in the PRC. In China, the work unit has a say in just about any major decision in one's life, and in a great number of minor ones as well.

Chinese typically do not choose their work units the way an individual may shop for an employer in the capitalist economies of the West, except in the case of foreign joint ventures. Typically, once a young person has graduated from school, the local government's labor bureau will *fenpei* or assign him or her to a job in the community. This bureau's responsibility is to coordinate with all the other government units in the area to identify available jobs and establish relevant qualifications and then to attempt to match people with slots.

It is an impersonal and inefficient system. While it can sometimes be manipulated through the use of *guanxi* (see below), the system mostly manages to assign individuals to positions they do not want. Indeed, individual preferences are largely irrelevant to the process. To compound the problem, there has traditionally been almost no job mobility in the PRC—someone assigned to be a factory worker, for example, can for all practical purposes expect to work in the same unit for the rest of his or her working life, though promotions and job changes within the unit are possible.

16   Switching to another *danwei* is also difficult because it requires that both the old and new unit sign off on the transfer. Someone who is talented may thus find it relatively easy to get a job offer elsewhere, but next to impossible to persuade his or her work unit to grant a discharge. This system is becoming more liberal, however, and switching *danwei* is becoming more commonplace. Job swapping, accomplished through *guanxi* and even through advertising, is on the increase. But organizational change in China is always a painfully slow process.

The influence of a typical Chinese unit extends far beyond employees' working lives and well into their personal lives. Not only does the unit decide what job you do, how much you are paid, and when promotions come; it also may control where you live; how much space you are allocated; whether and when you may travel within China or to other countries, study abroad, or take a vacation. Through your work unit—and only through your work unit—you obtain coupons that permit you to purchase certain scarce commodities: at various times in the last twenty years pork, sugar, eggs, salt, grain, cooking oil, cotton cloth, gas, coal, bicycles, and wooden furniture have all been rationed in the PRC. The unit also controls your access to health care and child care, and pays you your pension after you retire.

Workers must also obtain permission from the unit before they may marry, a decision that has obvious implications for where they live, single people being assigned to dormitories with roommates. Apartments, when available at all, are reserved for those who are married and need the additional space. The *danwei* also has a role in enforcing the one-child-per-couple policy. A good relationship with the decision makers in the unit can pave the way for many comforts and privileges; similarly, the unit can make your life a living hell if you buck the system, and it may discipline you if you break a rule.

The exception to most of these rules is the joint-venture unit. An enterprise that is a joint venture between a Chinese organization and a foreign company operates quite a bit differently from the typical Chinese unit. Here there is a great deal of mobility; jobs are advertised and filled by applicants in a more or less supply-and-demand fashion. Employers find it far easier to hire and fire staff. Subsidies have been reduced to bare bones and are generally limited to housing, medical care, and unemployment compensation. And there are far fewer intrusions into individuals' personal affairs. Though joint-venture employees constitute only a small fraction of China's workers today, the government has said that such enterprises are to be treated as models for future development of state-owned enterprises. Thus the tremendous social control exerted by the *danwei* is quite likely to diminish considerably in the future.

20   Though there is little direct insubordination in a Chinese work unit, this is not to say that there isn't a good deal of passive resistance on the part of the workers. When decisions come down from above, one is obligated to obey, but one doesn't have to like it. Since socialism traditionally offered workers nothing in the way of material incentives to perform, the work of people in the PRC has historically been uninspired and their performance lackluster. Raising productivity has thus become a key goal of the Chinese regime, and in recent years they have proven themselves willing to experiment with a system of material incentives that owes a good deal to capitalism.

The best example I know of the pervasive control exercised by the work unit is the story of a young American woman who went to Beijing to teach English at a small language institute. After she arrived in China, it became clear to her that the meager salary to which she had naïvely agreed before her arrival was going to be insufficient to meet her expenses. She complained to the school's authorities, who immediately convened a committee to look into the problem. The teacher was asked to appear before the committee and to submit to them a detailed listing of her monthly expenses. The matter was ostensibly resolved—to their satisfaction if not to hers—when the committee members offered her "helpful" suggestions as to ways in which she might economize to stretch the salary she was already receiving.

Confucianism

The position of the individual in Chinese society cannot be fully understood without a discussion of the teachings of the sage Confucius (551–479 B.C.) and his disciples, which has exerted a potent influence on Chinese culture through the centuries. Confucianism is actually more a system of ethics and morals than a religion per se, and it stresses the obligations of people to one another as a function of the relationships among them.

It would be hard to overstate the contribution of Confucius, who delineated the five important human relationships—those between ruler and subject, husband and wife, father and son, brother and brother, and friend and friend. He taught of a social order that emphasized duty, loyalty, filial piety, respect for age and seniority, and sincerity. Such traits remain valued among Chinese the world over even to this day, despite a brief period toward the end of the Cultural Revolution when Confucius's teachings were severely criticized on the mainland as feudalistic and counterrevolutionary.

24   Confucius's philosophy can be seen at work in myriad ways in China today. Deference to people in authority and to elders is an obvious one. Chinese are seldom guilty of outright insubordination and are taught to know their places in any given hierarchy. Characteristic Chinese unwillingness to depart from the straight and narrow path set by the leaders—

as evidenced in the reluctance to offer an irreverent opinion discussed above—is also traceable to Confucius; to do otherwise would mean to fail in your duty and to be disloyal.

None of the above should be construed to mean that Chinese are not capable of sabotage, subversion, or revenge—their capacity for these things is as great as anyone's. It's just that expressing them directly or overtly would be un-Confucian. Passive resistance can be every bit as effective as the active kind, and it goes it one better in that it needn't involve any disturbance of the surface harmony.

China's bureaucracy probably owes as much to the Confucian heritage as it does to the Soviet Union, on which the government structure of the PRC is largely modeled. Far from the "classless" organization of communist mythology, it is in fact strictly hierarchical, with rank and its privileges defined extremely clearly. People relate to one another not as individuals, but rather according to their relative ranks. Decision making is strictly from the top down, and nothing much is accomplished without support from the higher echelons. Personal loyalty is highly valued, and it is common for high-ranking cadres to install cronies in important positions under their control.

Confucianism is an inherently conservative belief system. It suffers innovation rather badly, and does nothing whatever to encourage it. On the contrary; a hierarchical, vertical system of government where decisions of even minor import must be referred upward is no crucible for revolutionary change. No one is willing to stick his or her neck out, and so new ground is seldom broken, except by those at the very top. Characteristically, the Chinese bureaucracy is notorious for long delays and nearly imperceptible progress.

28   In Confucius's ideal society, each individual occupies his or her proper place—rank is critical and there is no real equality. In his writings, Confucius speaks frequently of the "superior man," who embodies a number of virtues, most of which are as highly valued among Chinese today as they have ever been. Traditionally, there are eight such virtues: *zhong* (loyalty); *xiao* (filial piety), *ren* (benevolence); *ai* (love); *xin* (trust); *yi* (justice); *he* (harmony), and *ping* (peace). The superior man embodies all of them in some measure.

The superior man is modest, even self-deprecating; he is moderate in habits, generous, and given to compromise and conciliation rather than direct confrontation. He has no need to parade his belongings or his accomplishments before others. He is driven by a well-developed sense of duty. He endeavors to make others comfortable, and is solicitous of guests. He never loses his temper, and remains poised no matter what the situation. A man of integrity, he overlooks deficiencies in others and demonstrates honesty and propriety in all of his dealings.

Confucius and all he stood for took a major drubbing in China during the tumultuous Cultural Revolution period from the mid-1960s to the mid-1970s, when his teachings were widely and vehemently criticized as bourgeois and counterrevolutionary. But more recently there has been a pronounced return to Confucian values. Even the government stepped in with a manufactured propaganda campaign that began in the early 1980s urging people to learn to follow the *wu jiang si mei* or the "five stresses and the four beauties." These are admonitions to stress culture, etiquette, hygiene, order, and morals and to strive for beauty in spirit, language, environment, and behavior.

Mianzi or "Face"

Another important cultural concept is that of *mianzi,* which is Chinese for "face." Interestingly, the Chinese term is the exact equivalent of the English word, no matter whether one means by it the area between one's forehead and one's chin, the surface of an object, or the less tangible commodity that is related to a person's dignity and prestige.

32   The Chinese are acutely sensitive to the regard in which they are held by others or the light in which they appear, and it is very important to be aware of the concept of *mianzi* if only to head off situations in which you cause someone to lose it. The consequences can be severe; at the very least you will cease to receive cooperation from the person; you are quite likely as well to open yourself up to some form of retaliation.

Face is a fragile commodity in China, and there are many ways in which one can cause someone to lose it. One sure way is to dress someone down or insult someone in front of his or her peers. Another is to treat someone as if his or her feelings do not matter, or to deliberately patronize someone. Failing to treat someone with proper respect is a real sin with the Chinese, and it almost always comes back to haunt you. For if you cause someone to lose face you will not only lose the respect of the person you have wronged; you will also lose that of others who are aware of your transgression.

The story in the last chapter of the Chinese minster who was insulted after being met at the airport by a deputy assistant secretary is an excellent case study in *mianzi*. The reason the Chinese were so furious at the treatment the minister received was that it appeared to them for all the world as if the U.S. government was delivering a deliberate slap in the face. Only after it was made clear that the offense had been inadvertent rather than deliberate could the Chinese forgive; forgetting was out of the question.

I can offer another, more personal "losing face" story. I once wrote a business letter to a Chinese minister in an attempt to set up a meeting with him for my boss, who was coming to China the following month. In the letter I mentioned that he would be visiting China at the personal invitation of a vice premier. In point of fact, although the vice premier had indeed suggested to my boss that he lead a delegation to China, the actual invitation had been issued by our host organization, which considered itself the official host and thus interpreted my letter as patronizing.

36   I was summoned in the very next day by the host unit and summarily dressed down for my perceived offense. I explained that I had certainly not intended a slight and to this day believe that my hosts overreacted to the situation. But offense exists in the eye of the beholder and my intentions were seen as somewhat less important than my crime. The matter was not to end to their satisfaction until I wrote a formal retraction, which of course was a blow to my *own* prestige. The fact that *I* was caused to lose face in the process was of little concern because I was seen as responsible for the whole situation. Having delivered the first blow, I apparently had no right to expect any magnanimity in my host unit's posture toward me. And I got none.

The vehemence of my host unit's reaction surprised me, but it really just underscores how important face is to the Chinese. When you cause someone to lose it, you can just about count on retribution of one type or another. The Chinese do not usually show anger; to do so would fly in the face of the Confucian virtues. They do, however, get even. And while active confrontation would also be viewed as unacceptable behavior on the part of the superior man, passive aggression is always fair game. The Chinese, in fact, are masters of the art. It can take different forms, but often appears as "inability" to accomplish something they know you wish to get done, or failure to show up at an appointed time with an obviously fabricated excuse. All the while, however, etiquette will never be breached.

One of my favorite examples of "saving face" is a volleyball game in which I once participated at the Chinese Embassy in Washington. The Embassy team played volleyball nearly every day; it was their chief form of recreation and exercise. The American challengers, on the other hand, were a pick-up team that had never really practiced together and whose members varied tremendously in skill. From the beginning it was clear that this was not to be a serious match; it had been billed as more of a social occasion than anything else. But from the start the Chinese played to win, and win they did—the first game was, as I recall, a shutout.

The second game turned out to be quite the opposite. Without so much as a word being spoken among them, the Chinese team members suddenly started to miss shots they had had no trouble making during the previous game. In the end they tallied up a respectable score, but it was the Americans who won—or, as I quickly realized, had been *permitted* to win—the second game. Had it been a legitimate test of skill, the Chinese would no doubt have played mercilessly and the second game would have ended up very much like the first. But it was a social gathering and it would have been unsociable in the extreme to cause guests to lose self-respect—face—in such a situation. Far better to even out the score and let everyone go away feeling like a winner.

40   The concept of "face" certainly exists in the West as well, but perhaps not to the same degree as it does in the Orient. In the West people tend to be more willing to forgive slights that cause them to lose face. Friendly hazing is, after all, somewhat acceptable in the West. Name-calling, playful dressing down, and sarcastic commentary may occur, but all is seen as good, clean fun. Such behavior, however, seldom occurs among Asians, for whom face is always very serious business.

The Chinese concept of face is also broader and better defined than it is in the West. In English you can *lose* face and you can *save* face; in Chinese, however, you can also *give* face. Giving face means doing something to enhance someone else's reputation or prestige. Complimenting a worker to his or her superior and publicly recognizing someone's contribution are good ways of giving face. Thanking someone who has worked hard on a particular project, even someone of very low rank, is also an excellent example of this. Such actions carry a great deal of weight among Chinese when they come from foreign guests.

My host organization once placed me in the seat of honor next to its chairman during a reception held in Beijing. Though I was flattered by the attention, I did not think much of it until a representative of that organization approached me for a favor a few months later. To ensure my compliance, he was careful to remind me of how much face the unit had accorded to me through that action.

Guanxi or "Connections"

It's often the case that you can't even get to first base in China without *guanxi,* and you can do just about anything—even things you probably ought not to do—when you have it. *Guanxi* literally means "relationships," but "connections" is a far better translation in this sense of the word. It has everything to do with who you know and what these people are willing—or obligated—to do for you.

44   To the Chinese, *guanxi* is a sort of "tit-for-tat," "you-scratch-my-back-I'll-scratch-yours" kind of arrangement. Someone with whom you have *guanxi* can be counted on to do you favors, bend the rules, and even break them sometimes on your behalf. It is a cultural phenomenon common to Chinese all over the world, and by no means the exclusive province of the PRC. In an economy of scarcity such as that of China, however, the use of *guanxi* can gain you access to goods and services that are otherwise difficult or impossible to come by.

Guanxi is, of course, a reciprocal obligation. You are expected to behave in similar fashion and to deliver favors to those with whom you have *guanxi.* Most often the currency of *guanxi* is not cash. You might be asked to procure airplane or train tickets, admission to a movie or a play, or even a hospital. Or the request might be for foreign electronic equipment, hard-to-get foodstuffs such as fresh fish or fruit, or even an introduction to someone you know who has the bureaucratic power to do an important favor. It may, however, also be a loan of money. In its more advanced form, *guanxi* becomes *houmen*—literally, the "back door." . . . "Going through the back door" is often the only real way to get some things accomplished in the PRC.

The Chinese tend to extrapolate from their own system and they generally expect foreigners to understand *guanxi* and behave according to its rules. A woman I knew in Beijing once explained to me that she had worked hard to develop *guanxi* within her work unit, and she had established a relationship with someone who had access to the chop—the official seal—of the unit. This person could be counted on to stamp her application to the Public Security Bureau for a passport. Luckily, a former colleague of her father's was well-placed at the Bureau and she was reasonably certain that her father's relationship with this man would guarantee that the application would be approved after it was submitted.

She lacked only *guanxi* at the U.S. Embassy, which would have to issue her a visa before she could leave China and travel to the U.S.—her fondest wish. That was where I was to come in; although she knew I was not a diplomat, she figured that as an American I was very likely to know someone at the Embassy I could pressure on her behalf. When I attempted to explain to her that the U.S. system didn't really work the same way and that I had no particular sway with the U.S. consular officers, it was like talking to a brick wall. I had a dreadfully difficult time convincing her that I wasn't simply shirking what she perceived as my responsibility as her friend and refusing to help.

48   This same woman once asked a colleague of mine who was leaving for a week in Hong Kong to make a purchase on her behalf. She asked for a Japanese cassette deck, which my associate generously agreed to bring back for her. This was no small favor, for it involved laundering some local Chinese currency and exchanging it for hard, Hong Kong dollars, and it also involved evading Chinese Customs, which assessed excessive duties on such articles.

It turned out that the tape player wasn't even intended for her—it was really for a friend of hers. She was using her *guanxi* with my colleague to do a favor for a friend to whom she herself had an obligation. When the deed was done, my coworker and I were invited to a dinner hosted by the recipient of the cassette deck as a way of expressing her own appreciation. But since *her* parents' apartment was too small to accommodate all the people, the home of *another* friend was borrowed for the purpose. Again, *guanxi* at work.

Reciprocity

Closely related to the concept of *guanxi* is that of reciprocity. It is as applicable to interpersonal relationships as it is to business dealings, and what it means is that the economy of favors between two individuals or units is expected to remain in rough balance over a period of time. Reciprocity is the reason that Chinese people feel comfortable presuming on those with whom they have *guanxi*—if they have done a favor for a friend, they feel they are owed a favor in return.

A corollary to this is that you should proceed with extreme caution before putting a Chinese in a position in which he or she is totally unable to return a favor. Giving an extremely expensive gift can place the recipient in an uncomfortable situation. If there is no possibility of the person ever repaying the gift with something of approximately equal value, he or she will always be beholden to the giver.

52   Sometimes someone seeking a favor will approach even a relative stranger with a gift. Though it is seldom expressed overtly, the obvious implication is that accepting the gift means accepting an obligation to perform the favor. If you do not wish to be beholden to such a supplicant, you should decline the present.

The Chinese New Year—called Spring Festival on the mainland—is a common time chosen to settle accounts, and many gifts change hands at this time of the year. People visit friends, colleagues, bosses, and business associates bearing fruit, meat, and other presents that may be very expensive. Sometimes they are repaying specific favors done for them in the course of the previous year; other times it is more like positioning themselves for favors they may need to ask in the future.

Guanxi is not an inexhaustible commodity. A former colleague of mine once treated his organization's relationship with a Chinese official as if it were, and the strategy backfired badly. Because his company had once hosted the official's delegation trip to the United States, my friend constantly asked this person for favors. He was successful up to a point—the point, presumably, at which the Chinese official figured that the obligation had pretty much been repaid. After that, when the requests did not cease, the Chinese official became more remote and less and less available. The relationship ultimately deteriorated to the point that my friend's telephone calls to the unit were no longer returned.

Privacy

I count views of privacy as a basic cultural difference not because the Chinese would consider it a particularly important concept in their society, but because Westerners find it to be conspicuously absent. There is no direct translation in Chinese for the English word "privacy"; the notion simply doesn't exist in the same way among Chinese people.

56   Perhaps the difference is that the idea of being alone-and-unobserved never had much meaning in a land that has always been overpopulated and overcrowded, where a half-dozen people may live in one room, and where there has never been much mobility. Prying eyes are everywhere in China,

aimed not only in the direction of foreigners, but also at the Chinese themselves. Neighbors are *encouraged* to know one another's business and people are generally very much aware of the comings and goings of those around them.

This can be seen as a form of social control, and indeed, it is; suspicious goings-on are noted and reported to the authorities. One of the many unfortunate consequences of the Cultural Revolution, during which people were encouraged to inform on one another if any bourgeois activities were suspected, is that many people in China harbor suspicion of other Chinese they do not know well. Only close friends may be completely trusted.

When foreigners encounter the issue of privacy, it is generally in their apartments or hotels, and then primarily in the Chinese-style hotels where service personnel are everywhere. Until recently it was standard practice in the PRC for hotel staff to enter guest rooms at will, often without knocking first. Many old Chinese hotels did not even have locks on guest room doors, and there was simply no awareness of the fact that a guest might be indisposed to entertaining visitors, or engaged in any sort of private activity. This is not so much of a problem in the joint-venture hotels, and in fact it is much less of an issue than before in Chinese-run hotels in the major cities catering to foreigners. Enough embarrassing incidents occurred that most Chinese service personnel have learned to knock before entering.

PRC guesthouses typically have a service desk on each floor that commands a view of all of the guest rooms. The desk is strategically placed so that all guests and visitors must pass it on their way to the rooms, and it provides an excellent means of keeping tabs on the guests. Similarly, elevators in high-rise buildings in which diplomats and other long-term foreign residents reside are generally operated by service personnel. The fact that an occasional foreign male has been "busted" for inviting a local female into his room for ostensibly nefarious purposes supports the notion that these people are expected to spy on foreign guests and report any suspicious goings-on to the Public Security Bureau.

60   When Chinese need to be alone, they generally go outside for a walk. There is enough anonymity in the larger cities, especially after dusk, to allow people to be apart with their own thoughts. Where the real problem comes in is when couples wish some privacy to court or to make love. So few single people have access to private quarters that if they can't persuade a roommate to make him or herself scarce for a period of time, they, too, will take to the streets. Public parks in Beijing, Shanghai, Tianjin, Guangzhou, and indeed, in nearly any large city in China are jammed after dark with young couples locked in passionate embrace who literally have nowhere else to go. The irony is that it is only in the most public of situations that many Chinese are able to find privacy.

Personal Response

Have you ever visited China—or any Asian country—or do you personally know any people from that part of the world? If not, do you have an interest in visiting China or meeting Chinese people in your own country? Explain your answer.

Questions for Class or Small Group Discussion

1. Discuss the points of cultural differences explained here. Which strike you as particularly alien to or different from practices in your own culture? Which seem to you to have advantages over the way things are done in your own country? Explain your answer.

2. Discuss the Chinese concepts of "face" and "connections." How are they similar to and different from those concepts in the West?

3. Discuss what you see as advantages and disadvantages of the *danwei,* or "work unit," in China.

4. If you have particular knowledge about China or the Chinese, share what you know with the rest of your class.

A FEW POINTERS

James Fallows

James Fallows is the Washington editor of The Atlantic Monthly *and a contributing editor for the* Washington Monthly. *He has written two books,* The Water Lords *(1971) and* More Like Us: Making America Great Again *(1989). Fallows graduated from Harvard and was a Rhodes Scholar, earning a degree in economic development from Queen's College, Oxford. He wrote this essay, first published in the November 1989 issue of* The Atlantic Monthly, *near the end of one of his many stays in Asia.*

Living in a foreign culture is, most of the time, exhilarating and liberating. You don't have to feel responsible for the foibles of your temporary home; you can forget about the foibles of your real home for a while. Your life seems longer, because each day is dense with new and surprising experiences. I can remember distinctly almost every week of the past three and a half years. The preceding half dozen years more or less run together in a blur.

But there is also distress in foreign living, particularly in living in Asia at this time in its history. It comes not from daily exasperations, which after all build character, but from the unsettling thoughts that living in Asia introduces. As I head for home, let me mention the thought that disturbs me most.

It concerns the nature of freedom: whether free societies are fit to compete, in a Darwinian sense. Until the repression in China last summer [1989], many Westerners assumed that the world had entered an era of overall progress. True, environmental problems were getting worse rather than better, and many African and Latin American societies were still in bad shape. But in Asia it seemed possible to believe that people had learned how to make their societies both richer and freer year by year. As countries in Asia became more advanced and prosperous, they loosened their political controls—and as the controls came off, economic progress speeded up. This was the moral of the Korean and Taiwanese success stories, as those countries evolved toward the ideal set by stable, prosperous Japan. Even China, before the summer [of 1989], seemed to be loosening up, both economically and politically. China's crackdown made the spread of democracy and capitalism seem less certain than it had seemed before, but even this step backward confirmed the idea that political freedoms and economic progress were naturally connected. Everyone assumes that as China makes its political system more repressive, its economy will stagnate.

4   I draw a darker conclusion from the rise of the Asian economies. The economic success stories of Asia do not prove that political freedom and material progress go hand in hand. On the contrary: the Asian societies are, in different ways, fundamentally more repressive than America is, and their repression is a key to their economic success. Japan, Korea, Taiwan, and Singapore allow their citizens much less latitude than America does, and in so doing they make the whole society, including the business sector, function more efficiently than ours does. The lesson of the Soviet economic collapse would seem to be that a completely controlled economy cannot survive. The lesson of the rising Asian system is that economies with some degree of control can not only survive but prevail.

The crucial concepts here are "excessive" choice and "destructive" competition. Classical free-market economic theory says that these are impossibilities; a person can never have too much choice, and there can never be too much competition in a market. Asian societies approach this issue from a fundamentally different perspective. They were built on neither an Enlightenment concept of individual rights nor a capitalist concept of free and open markets, and they demonstrate in countless ways that less choice for individuals can mean more freedom and success for the social whole.

The examples of economic efficiency are the most familiar. Japanese businessmen have almost no freedom to move to another company, even if they're dissatisfied with conditions where they're working. (Of course, they're technically free to quit, but very few reputable big companies will hire someone who has left another big firm.) This may be frustrating for the businessmen, but so far it has been efficient for the companies. For instance, they can invest in employee training programs without fear that newly skilled workers will use their skills somewhere else. Singaporeans have been forced to put much of their income into a national retirement fund; Koreans have been discouraged from squandering their money overseas on tourism (until this year, only people planning business trips and those in a few other narrow categories were granted passports); Japanese consumers are forced to pay inflated prices for everything they buy. All these measures have been bad for individuals but efficient for the collective. In different ways they have transferred money from people to large institutions, which then invest it for future productivity. To illustrate the point the opposite way: Korea has in the past two years become a more successful democracy and a less successful export economy. Precisely because workers have been going on strike and consumers demanding a higher standard of living, Korean companies have temporarily lost their edge against competitors in Taiwan and Japan.

Yu-Shan Wu, of The Brookings Institution, has suggested a useful way to think about this combination of economic freedom and political control. In communist economies, he says, property is owned by the state, and investment decisions are made by the state. The result is a disaster. The style of capitalism practiced in the United States takes the opposite approach: Private owners control most property, and private groups make most investment decisions. The result over the past century has been a big success, but now some inefficiencies are showing up. Japan, Wu says, has pioneered a new approach: private ownership of property, plus public guidance of investment decisions. The big industrial combines of Japan are as private and profit-oriented as those of the United States, and therefore at least as efficiency-minded (unlike state enterprises in Russia or China). But in Japan's brand of capitalism some of the largest decisions are made by the state, not the "invisible hand." This private-public approach, Wu concludes, reduces the freedom of people and single companies, but it has certain long-term advantages over the private-private system.

8   Last year two U.S. companies made supercomputers, the Cray corporation and a subsidiary of Control Data. This year only one does. Control Data abandoned the business, finding it unprofitable. The same circumstances have applied in Japan—difficult but important technology, lean or nonexistent profits for the foreseeable future—but the results have been different, because the state occasionally overrules the invisible hand. It is inconceivable that the Japanese government would have let one of only two participants abandon an area of obvious future technical importance. If Japan left decisions to the invisible hand, there would be no aircraft engineers at work in the country, because Mitsubishi and Kawasaki cannot hope to earn a profit competing against Boeing. But the big Japanese companies keep their aerospace-engineering departments active, in part because of government-directed incentives to do so. (These range from

explicit subsidies, like the FSX fighter-plane contracts, to a system of industrial organization that makes it possible for companies to subsidize unprofitable divisions for years.) Eventually, Japanese planners believe, the aerospace expertise will pay off.

Americans should not be surprised by what the private-public system can accomplish. It's essentially the way our economy worked during the Second World War. People were forced to save, through Liberty Bonds, and forced not to consume, through rationing. Big companies were privately owned and run, but overall goals were set by the state. Under this system the output of the U.S. economy rose faster than ever before or since. (Part of the reason for the rapid rise, of course, was that wartime production finally brought America out of the Great Depression.) For the United States this managed economy was a wartime exception. For the Japanese-style economic systems of Asia it has been the postwar rule. This is not to say that we need a wartime mentality again but, rather, to show that the connection between individual freedom and collective prosperity is more complicated than we usually think. We may not like the way the Japanese-style economic system operates, but we'd be foolish not to recognize that it does work, and in many ways works better than ours.

Here's an even harder truth to face: The most successful Asian economies employ a division of labor between men and women that we may find retrograde but that has big practical advantages for them. Despite some signs of change—for instance, the rising influence of Takako Doi at the head of the Socialist Party in Japan—the difference between a man's role and a woman's is much more cut and dried in Asia than in the United States. It is tempting to conclude that a time lag is all that separates Asian practices from American, and that Japanese and Korean women will soon be demanding the rights that American women have won during the past generation. But from everything I've seen, such an assumption is as naive as imagining that Japan is about to be swept by an American-style consumer-rights movement.

There is a lot to dislike in this strict assignment of sex roles. It's unfair in an obvious way to women, because 99 percent of them can never really compete for business, political, academic, or other opportunities and success. I think it's ultimately just as bad for men, because most of them are cut off from the very idea of dealing with women as equals, and have what we would consider emotionally barren family lives. The average Japanese salaryman takes more emotional satisfaction in his workplace life than the average American does, but less in his relations with wife and children. Nonetheless, this system has one tremendous practical advantage. By making it difficult for women to do anything except care for their families, the traditional Asian system concentrates a larger share of social energy on the preparation of the young.

12   The best-educated American children are a match for the best in Asia, but the average student in Japan, Korea, Singapore, or Taiwan does better

in school than the average American. The fundamental reason, I think, is that average students in these countries come from families with two parents, one of whom concentrates most of her time and effort on helping her children through school. Limits on individual satisfaction undergird this educational achievement in two ways: The mother is discouraged from pursing a career outside the house, and she and the father are discouraged from even thinking about divorce. The typical Asian marriage is not very romantic. In most countries arranged marriages are still common, and while extramarital affairs are at least as frequent as they are in the United States, they seem to cause less guilt. But because most husbands and wives expect less emotional fulfillment from marriage, very few marriages end in divorce. Individual satisfaction from marriage may be lower, but the society enjoys the advantages of having families that are intact.

The Asian approach to the division of labor is not one that Americans want to emulate, or can. Except in emergencies we have believed in satisfying individual desires rather than suppressing them. But, to come back to the central point, we shouldn't fool ourselves about the sheer effectiveness of the system that the Asian societies have devised. Their approach to child-rearing, as to economic development, is worse for many individuals but better for the collective welfare than ours seems to be. The Asian model is not going to collapse of its own weight, unlike the Soviet communist system. So the puzzle for us is to find ways to evoke similar behavior—moderation of individual greed, adequate attention to society's long-term interests, commitment to raising children—within our own values of individualism and free choice.

I hope somebody has figured out the answer to this while I've been away.

Personal Response

Do you think American society would benefit by adopting the Japanese view that devotion to one's work supersedes personal desires and that women belong in the home?

Questions for Class or Small Group Discussion

1. Discuss Fallows's theory that the "repression [of Asian societies] is a key to their economic success" (paragraph 4). Are you persuaded by his analysis? What do you see as its strengths and weaknesses?

2. Discuss the relationship Fallows sees between the way in which Asian societies maintain a strict division of labor for men and women and the quality of preparation in their young people. Do you agree that "the average student in Japan, Korea, Singapore, or Taiwan does better in school than the average American" because Asian mothers stay at home and devote themselves to their children (paragraph 12)?

3. Discuss this statement: "Individual satisfaction from marriage may be lower, but the society enjoys the advantages of having families that are intact" (paragraph 12).

4. Discuss possible solutions to the puzzle of how to "moderat[e] individual greed," provide "adequate attention to society's long-term interests," and commit "to raising children—within our own values of individualism and free choice" (paragraph 13).

5. If you are familiar with the terms "classical free-market economic theory" (paragraph 5) and "invisible hand" (paragraph 7), explain what they mean to your classmates. If no one in the class is familiar with the terms, volunteer to find out what they mean, either by consulting economics textbooks or asking an economics professor for brief definitions.

Perspectives on the U.S. in the Global Marketplace

Suggestions for Synthesis

1. Invite Chinese—or other Asian—students from your campus to speak to your class on the cultural differences they have experienced in America. Or, interview Asian students for their perspectives on the cultural differences between their country and yours. Then incorporate both the students' comments and those of at least one of the writers represented in this chapter as you do a comparative analysis of selected aspects of both American and Asian cultures.

2. Invite a specialist in international marketing or economics to speak to your class about the global market and its importance for the American economy in the twenty-first century (or interview such a person). Then write an essay on America's future in the global economy in which you include both the specialist's remarks and those of Christopher Farrell in "The Triple Revolution" and Ian Morrison and Greg Schmid in "The Global Market: Here, There, Everywhere."

Additional Writing Topics

1. Explain what you see as the implications for America of the prospects for a global economy that Christopher Farrell writes about in "The Triple Revolution."

2. Assess the impact of foreign products on a typical day in your life.

3. If you have firsthand experience with a business or businesses in a foreign country, describe that experience.

4. Discuss possible solutions to the puzzle of how to "moderat[e] individual greed," provide "adequate attention to society's long-term interests," and commit "to raising children—within our own values of individualism and free choice" (paragraph 13, James Fallows's "A Few Pointers").

5. Argue in support of or against James Fallows's theory that "repression [of Asian societies] is a key to their economic success" ("A Few Pointers").

6. Read one of the following by writers in this chapter: Ian Morrison's and Greg Schmid's *Future Tense: The Business Realities of the Next Ten Years*, Scott D. Seligman's *Dealing with the Chinese: A Practical Guide to Business Etiquette in the People's Republic Today*, or James Fallows's *More Like Us: Making America Great Again*. (Or read the entire special 1994 *BusinessWeek* issue entitled "21st Century Capitalism.") Then write a critique of the book in which you summarize key points and identify its strengths and weaknesses.

Research Topics

1. Research economic changes in the last decade in any of these geographic areas: Asia, Latin America, Eastern Europe, or sub-Saharan Africa. Read about developments in the area and projections for the future and then report your findings and conclusions.

2. Research the global investment strategies of any major American corporation, such as those mentioned in paragraph 9 of "The Triple Revolution" and paragraph 11 of "The Global Market: Here, There, Everywhere." Draw some conclusions about the effectiveness of such strategies in your paper on this topic.

3. Select one of the three subjects discussed in Christopher Farrell's "The Triple Revolution," that is, either politics, technology, or economics. Then conduct library research to determine both the positive and negative implications of the enormous changes globally in that area, including a prediction of how you think these changes will affect the American economy in the next decade.

4. Use the works listed in topic number 6 of "Additional Writing Topics" as starting points for a research project on the subject of America's place in the global economy.

APPENDIX

DEFINITIONS OF TERMS USED IN DISCUSSION QUESTIONS AND WRITING TOPICS

Abstract. A summary of the essential points of a text. It is usually quite short, no more than a paragraph.

Analysis. A dividing of a subject into its separate parts for individual study.

Argument/Persuasion. An argument is an attempt to prove the validity of a position by offering supporting proof. Persuasion takes argument one step further by convincing an audience to adopt a viewpoint or to take action.

Book review. A report that summarizes only the main ideas of a book and provides critical commentary on it. Usually in a book review, you will also be asked to give your personal response to the book, including both your opinion of the ideas presented in it and an evaluation of the worth or credibility of the book.

Case study. A situation or profile of a person or persons, for which you provide a context and background.

Citation. A reference that provides supporting illustrations or examples for your own ideas; the authority or source of that information is identified.

Comparison. A likeness or strong similarity between two things.

Contrast. A difference or strong dissimilarity between two things.

Debate. A discussion involving opposing points in an argument. In formal debate, opposing teams defend and attack a specific proposition.

Description. A conveyance through words of the essential nature of a thing.

Evaluation. A judgment about the worth, quality, or credibility of a thing.

Forum. An open discussion or exchange of ideas among many people. (See the *Time* magazine forum "Tough Talk on Entertainment" in Chapter 7.)

Freewriting. The act of writing down everything that occurs to you about your topic without stopping to examine what you are saying.

Hypothesis. A tentative explanation to account for some phenomenon or set of facts. It is in essence a theory or an assumption that can be tested by further investigation and is assumed to be true for the purpose of argument or investigation.

Illustration. An explanation or clarification, usually using example or comparison.

Journal. A personal record of experiences, thoughts, or responses to something, usually kept separate from other writings, as in a diary or notebook.

Literature search. A locating of titles of articles, books, and other material on a specific subject.

Narration. A telling of a story.

Panel Discussion. A small group of people (usually between three and six) gathered to discuss a topic. Often each member of a panel is prepared to represent a certain position or point of view on the subject of discussion, with time left after the presentations for questions from audience members.

Paraphrase. A restatement of a passage, using your own words. A paraphrase is somewhat shorter than the original but retains its essential meaning.

Position paper. A detailed report that explains, justifies, or recommends a particular course of action.

Proposition. A statement of a position on a subject, a course of action, or a topic for discussion or debate.

Reflective writing. A drawing on personal experience that requires your own response to something. For this kind of writing, you will use the first person.

Report. A detailed account of something.

Subject. A general or broad area of interest.

Summary. A shortened version of a passage, put in your own words. A summary is like a paraphrase, in that you are conveying the essence of the original, but it is shorter than a paraphrase.

Synthesis. A combining of the ideas of two or more authors and the integration of those ideas into your own discussion.

Thesis. A statement of the specific purpose of a paper. A thesis is essentially a one-sentence summary of what you will argue, explain, illustrate, define, describe, or otherwise develop in the rest of the paper. It usually comes very early in a paper.

Topic. A specific, focused, and clearly defined area of interest. A topic is a narrow aspect of a subject.

Workshop. Similar in intent to a forum, a workshop is characterized by the exchange of information, ideas, and opinions, usually among a small group of people. Both workshops and forums involve interaction and exchanges of ideas more than panel discussions, which typically allot more time to panel members than to audience participants.

PERMISSIONS AND ACKNOWLEDGMENTS

Aring, Charles. "In Defense of Orphanages." Reprinted from *The American Scholar,* volume 60, number 4, Autumn 1991. Copyright © 1991 by the author. By permission of the publisher.

Baldwin, Deborah. "If This is the Information Highway, Where are the Rest Stops?" Reprinted with permission from *Common Cause Magazine,* 2030 M Street, NW, Washington, D.C. 10036.

Barrett, Wayne M., and Bernard Rowe. "What's Wrong With America and Can Anything Be Done About It?" Reprinted from *USA Today Magazine,* November 1994, Copyright © 1994 by the Society for the Advancement of Education.

Bassuk, Ellen L. "Homeless Families." *Scientific American,* December 1991. Reprinted by permission of *Scientific American.*

Beers, David, and Catherine Capellaro. "Greenwash." Reprinted with permission from *Mother Jones* magazine, 1991, Foundation for National Progress.

Bernikow, Louise. "Cinderella at the Movies," pp. 17–37 of *Among Women* by Louise Bernikow. Reprinted by permission of the author.

Bly, Robert. *Iron John: A Book About Men,* © 1990 by Robert Bly. Reprinted by permission of Addison-Wesley Publishing Company, Inc.

Broecker, Wallace S. "Global Warming on Trial." With permission from *Natural History,* April 1992, copyright © The American Museum of Natural History, 1992.

Bronowski, Jacob. "The Reach of the Imagination." Delivered as the Blashfield Address, May 1966. Reprinted by permission from the *Proceedings* of the American Academy of Arts and Letters and the National Institute of Arts and Letters, second series, no. 17, 1967.

Buckley, Jr., William F. "Don't Blame Violence on the Tube." Copyright © 1994 by William F. Buckley, Jr. Originally appeared in *TV Guide,* March 19, 1994. Reprinted by permission of the Wallace Literary Agency, Inc.

Buczynski, Alan. "Iron Bonding," from *The New York Times Magazine,* July 19, 1992. Copyright © 1992 by the New York Times Company. Reprinted by permission.

Carroll, Raymonde. "Money and Seduction," reprinted by permission of author and The University of Chicago Press from pages 128–133 of *Cultural Misunderstanding: The French-American Experience,* trans. Carol Volk. Copyright © 1988, The University of Chicago Press, 5801 South Ellis Avenue, Chicago, IL 60637.

Coletta, John. "Minding the Reef." Reprinted by permission of the author.

Copland, Aaron. "How We Listen to Music," from *What to Listen for in Music* by Aaron Copland. Reprinted by permission of The Aaron Copland Fund for Music, Inc.

Cousins, Norman. "The Poet and the Computer," from *Beyond Literacy: The Second Gutenburg Revolution,* published by Saybrook Publishers. This book won the Benjamin Franklin Award for Non-fiction.

Cowley, Geoffrey, with Contreras, Rogers, Lach, Dickey and Raghavan. "Outbreak of Fear," from *Newsweek,* May 22, 1995. Copyright © 1995, Newsweek, Inc. All rights reserved. Reprinted by permission.

Dausset, Jean. "Scientific Knowledge and Human Dignity," reprinted from *The UNESCO Courier,* September 1994.

Ehrenreich, Barbara. "Hers: Cultural Baggage," from *The New York Times Magazine,* April 5, 1992. Copyright © 1992 by the New York Times Company. Reprinted by permission.

Elliott, Michael. "Here to Stay," from *Newsweek,* July 10, 1995. Copyright © 1995, Newsweek, Inc. All rights reserved. Reprinted by permission.

Fallows, James. "A Few Pointers." Copyright © 1989 by James Fallows, as first published in *The Atlantic Monthly.* Reprinted by permission of the author.

Farrell, Christopher. "The Triple Revolution." Reprinted from November 19, 1994, issue of *Business Week* by special permission. Copyright © 1994 by The McGraw-Hill Companies.

Fjermedal, Grant. "Artificial Intelligence." Reprinted by permission of *Omni,* © 1986. OMNI Publications International, Ltd.

Fletcher et al., "Facing Up to Bioethical Decisions," *Issues in Science and Technology,* Fall 1994, pp. 75–80. Reprinted with permission from *Issues in Science and Technology.* Copyright © 1994 by the University of Texas at Dallas, Richardson, TX.

Freundlich, Naomi. "No, Spending More on AIDS Isn't Unfair." Reprinted from September 17, 1990, issue of *Business Week* by special permission. Copyright © 1990 by McGraw-Hill, Inc.

Fumento, Michael. "The AIDS Lobby: Are We Giving It Too Much Money?" from *The Myth of Heterosexual AIDS* by Michael Fumento. Copyright © 1990 by Michael Fumento. Reprinted by permission of BasicBooks, a division of HarperCollins Publishers, Inc.

Goodman, Ellen. "Working Community." Reprinted with the permission of Simon & Schuster from *Keeping in Touch* by Ellen Goodman. Copyright © 1985 by The Washington Post Company.

Gordon, Suzanne. "Women at Risk," from *Prisoners of Men's Dreams* by Suzanne Gordon. Copyright © 1991 by Suzanne Gordon. By permission of Little, Brown and Company.

Gould, Lois. "X: A Fabulous Child's Story." Copyright © 1978 by Lois Gould. Reprinted with permission from the Charlotte Sheedy Literary Agency, Inc.

Gowing, Nik. "Instant TV and Foreign Policy," *The World Today,* October 1994, pp. 187–190. Reprinted by permission.

Graff, Gerald. "Ships in the Night," from *Beyond the Culture Wars: How Teaching Can Revitalize American Education* by Gerald Graff, with the permission of W. W. Norton & Company, Inc. Copyright © 1992 by Gerald Graff.

Hamill, Pete. "Crack and the Box." First published in *Esquire,* 1990. Reprinted by permission of International Creative Management, Inc. Copyright © 1990 by Pete Hamill.

Hawken, Paul. "A Declaration of Sustainability," from *The Utne Reader,* September/October 1993. Reprinted by permission of the author.

Heiman, Melissa. "The Banning of Smoking in Public Places." Excerpts reprinted by permission of author.

Hoffmann, Roald. "The Chemist." Reprinted from *Chemistry Imagined: Reflections on Science* by Hoffmann and Torrence (Washington, DC: Smithsonian Institution Press), pages 67–72, by permission of the publisher. Copyright © 1993.

Hughes, Robert. "Behold the Stone Age," from *Time,* February 13, 1995. Copyright © 1995 Time Inc. Reprinted by permission.

Isasi-Diaz, Ada María. "Hispanic in America: Starting Points," pages 22–27 of *Perspectives,* edited by Deck, Torango and Motavina. Reprinted by permission of Sheed & Ward, 115 E. Armour Blvd., Kansas City, MO 64111. To order, call (800) 333–7373.

Iyer, Pico. "Selling Our Innocence Abroad," which first appeared in *New Perspectives Quarterly,* Fall 1991, pp. 34–39. Reprinted by permission of Blackwell Publishers.

Johnson, Paul. "Colonialism's Back—And Not A Moment Too Soon." Copyright © 1993 by The New York Times Company. Reprinted by permission.

Keen, Sam. "The Rite of Work: The Economic Man." From *Fire in the Belly* by Sam Keen. Copyright © 1991 by Sam Keen. Used by permission of Bantam Books, a division of Bantam Doubleday Dell Publishing Group, Inc.

Kilbourn, Jean. "Beauty and the Beast of Advertising." Reprinted with permission from the Winter, 1989, issue of *Media&Values* magazine: *Redesigning Women,* published by the Center for Media Literacy, Los Angeles.

Kowinski, William Severini. "Kids in the Mall: Growing Up Controlled," from *The Malling of America* by William Severini Kowinski. Copyright © 1985 by William Severini Kowinski. Reprinted by permission of William Morrow and Company, Inc.

Krauthammer, Charles. "Must America Slay All the Dragons?" Copyright © 1991 Time Inc. Reprinted by permission.

Kutukdjian, Georges B. "UNESCO and Bioethics," reprinted from *The UNESCO Courier,* September 1994.

Matthews, Jay. "For Love or Money." Copyright © 1993, The Washington Post. Reprinted with permission.

Minow, Newton N. "Making Television Safe for Kids." Introduction from *Abandoned in the Wasteland: Children, Television, and the First Amendment* by Newton N. Minow and Craig L. LaMay. Copyright © 1995 by Newton N. Minow and Craig L. LaMay. Reprinted by permission of Hill & Wang, a division of Farrar, Straus & Giroux, Inc.

Lacayo, Richard. "Violent Reaction," *Time,* June 12, 1995. Copyright © 1995 by Time, Inc. Reprinted by permission.

Lamson, Susan R. "TV Violence: Does It Cause Real-Life Mayhem?" First published on pages 34, 35, 64 and 65 of the July 1993 issue of *American Hunter.* Reprinted with permission from the National Rifle Association of America.

Leland, John, with Rhodes, Katel, Kalb, Peyser, Joseph, and Brant. "Bisexuality Emerges as a New Sexual Identity," from *Newsweek,* July 17, 1995. Copyright © 1995, Newsweek, Inc. All rights reserved. Reprinted by permission.

Levine, Arthur. "The Making of a Generation," from *Change,* September/October 1993. Reprinted with permission of the Helen Dwight Reid Educational Foundation. Published by Heldref Publications, 1319 Eighteenth St., N. W., Washington, D.C. 20036–1802. Copyright © 1993.

Levy, Steven. "The Luddites Are Back," from *Newsweek,* June 12, 1995. Copyright © 1995, Newsweek, Inc. All rights reserved. Reprinted by permission.

Leymarie, Isabelle. "Rock 'n' Revolt," reprinted from *The UNESCO Courier,* February 1993.

Lukacs, John. "Revising the Twentieth Century," from *American Heritage,* September 1994. Reprinted by permission of *American Heritage.*

Lutz, William. "With These Words I Can Sell You Anything," from *Doublespeak* by William Lutz. Copyright © 1989 by Blonde Bear, Inc. Reprinted by permission of HarperCollins Publishers, Inc.

McCall, Nathan. "Native Son," from *Makes Me Wanna Holler: A Young Black Man in America* by Nathan McCall. Copyright © 1994 by Nathan McCall. Reprinted by permission of Random House, Inc.

McCrary, Teresa. "Getting Off the Welfare Carousel," from *Newsweek,* December 6, 1993. Copyright © 1993, Newsweek, Inc. All rights reserved. Reprinted by permission.

Medved, Michael. "Hollywood Poison Factory," from the November 1992 issue of *Imprimis.* Reprinted by permission from *Imprimis,* the monthly journal of Hillsdale College.

Morrison, Ian, and Greg Schmid. "The Global Market: Here, There, Everywhere," from *Future Tense: The Business Realities of the Next Ten Years* by Ian Morrison and Greg Schmid. Copyright © 1994 by Ian Morrison and Greg Schmid. Reprinted by permission of William Morrow and Company, Inc.

Nelkin, Dorothy, and M. Susan Lindee. "The Power of the Gene," from *The DNA Mystique* by Nelkin and Lindee. Copyright © 1995 by W. H. Freeman and Company. Used with permission.

Niedermair, Steph. "Nature vs. Nurture." Excerpts reprinted by permission of author.

Overbye, Dennis. "Born to Raise Hell?", *Time,* February 21, 1994. Copyright © 1994 by Time, Inc. Reprinted by permission.

Noda, Kesaya E. "Growing Up Asian in America." Reprinted by permission of author, from *Making Waves,* by Asian Women United. Copyright © 1989 by Asian Women United.

O'Toole, John. "What Advertising Isn't," from *The Trouble with Advertising* by John O'Toole. Copyright © 1985. Reprinted by permission of Chelsea House Publishers.

"Tough Talk on Entertainment," *Time,* June 12, 1995. Copyright © 1995 by Time, Inc. Reprinted by permission.

Parenti, Michael. "Class and Virtue." Copyright © 1992. From *Make Believe Media* by Michael Parenti. Reprinted with permission of St. Martin's Press, Incorporated.

Postal, Sandra. "Carrying Capacity: Earth's Bottom Line," from *State of the World 1994: A Worldwatch Institute Report on Progress Toward a Sustainable Society* by Lester R. Brown, et al., eds. by Worldwatch Institute. Reprinted by permission of W. W. Norton & Company, Inc.

Rose, Mike. "I Just Wanna Be Average." Reprinted with the permission of The Free Press, an imprint of Simon & Schuster from *Lives on the Boundary: The Struggles and Achievements of America's Underprepared* by Mike Rose. Copyright © by Mike Rose.

Rose, Phyllis. "Shopping and Other Spiritual Adventures in America Today," from *Never Say Goodbye* by Phyllis Rose. Copyright © 1984, 1987, 1989, 1990 by Phyllis Rose. Reprinted by permission of Georges Borchardt, Inc., for the author.

Ross, Alex. "Generation Exit." Reprinted by permission. Copyright © 1994 Alex Ross. Originally in *The New Yorker.* All rights reserved.

Rossman, Marlene L. "America's Changing Face." Reprinted with permission of the publisher, from *Multicultural Marketing: Selling to a Diverse America* by Marlene L. Rossman © 1994. Published by AMACOM, a division of American Management Association. All rights reserved.

Sachs, Aaron. "Humboldt's Legacy." Published by permission of Worldwatch Institute.

Sagan, Carl. "Can We Know the Universe?: Reflections on a Grain of Sand," from *Broca's Brain: Reflections on the Romance of Science* by Carl Sagan. Copyright © 1974, 1975, 1976, 1977, 1978, 1979 by Carl Sagan. Reprinted by permission of the author.

Salzman, Mark. "Unsuitable Reading," from *Iron and Silk* by Mark Salzman. Copyright © 1986 by Mark Salzman. Reprinted by permission of Random House, Inc.

Santino, Jack. "Rock and Roll as Music; Rock and Roll as Culture," which appeared in the July 1990 issue and is reprinted with permission from *The World & I,* a publication of The Washington Times Corporation, Copyright © 1990.

Schemo, Diana Jean. "Between the Art and the Artist Lies the Shadow." Copyright © 1995 by the New York Times Company. Reprinted by permission.

Schor, Juliet B. "Work and Spend," from *The Overworked American: The Unexpected Decline of Leisure* by Juliet B. Schor. Copyright © 1991 by BasicBooks, a division of Harper-Collins Publishers, Inc. Reprinted by permission of BasicBooks, a division of Harper-Collins Publishers, Inc.

Seligman, Scott D. "Some Basic Cultural Differences." Reprinted by permission of Warner Books/New York from *Dealing with the Chinese: A Practical Guide to Business Etiquette in the People's Republic Today,* copyright © 1989 by Scott D. Seligman.

Sollod, Robert. "The Hollow Curriculum," from *The Chronicle of Higher Education,* 1992. Reprinted by permission of the author.

Tisdale, Sally. "It's Been Real," *Esquire,* 1991. Reprinted by permission of author.

Vandertie, Cory. "The Phonics Controversy." Excerpts reprinted by permission of the author.

Weisberger, Bernard A. "The Persistence of the Serpent," from *American Heritage,* November 1994. Reprinted by permission of American Heritage.

Yanaka, Hisako. "Building Bridges Between Young Japanese and African Americans." Reprinted by permission of the author.

Zimring, Franklin E. "Firearms, Violence and Public Policy." *Scientific American,* November 1991. Reprinted by permission of *Scientific American.*

INDEX